Prescott's Histories

The Essence of
FERDINAND AND ISABELLA
THE CONQUEST OF MEXICO
THE CONQUEST OF PERU
PHILIP II

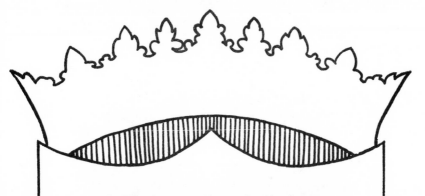

PRESCOTT'S HISTORIES:

The Rise and Decline of the Spanish Empire

Selected and Edited and with
a Biographical Introduction by
IRWIN R. BLACKER

DORSET PRESS
NEW YORK

To Harry and Irma Rosen

This edition published by Dorset Press
a division of Marboro Books Corporation,
by arrangement with Viking Penguin Inc.
1990 Dorset Press

ISBN 0-88029-476-0

Printed in the United States of America

M 9 8 7 6 5 4 3 2 1

Contents

History of the Reign of Ferdinand and Isabella

History of the Conquest of Mexico

History of the Conquest of Peru

History of Philip the Second

Chronology of Prescott's Life and Work

Introduction

"Much of my historical reading, all before, & much since I began to write has been with the eyes of another. The discouragements under which I have labour'd have nearly determined me more than once to abandon the enterprise. I met with a remark by Dr Johnson on Milton, at an early period, stating that the poet gave up his history of Britain, on becoming blind, since no one could pursue such investigations under such disadvantages. This remark of the great doctor confirmed me in the resolution to attempt the contrary."

Once he had made the resolution recorded in his journal, William Hickling Prescott stood by it. Ten years before this he had jotted down another note in the journal—"I subscribe to the Hist. of the reign of Ferd. & Isabella," and now he was bringing that book to an end. It had been a most difficult ten years. He had had to learn the Spanish language, had had to learn his sources, had had to learn a *modus operandi* by which a man blinded in one eye and losing the sight of the other might write history.

Born of a wealthy and proper New England family, Prescott had every reason to believe life would not be difficult. He entered Harvard as a sophomore, from a private school, and was doing well until his second year, when he was struck in the left eye by a crust of bread thrown playfully by a classmate. The result was permanent blindness in that eye, and, though Prescott was able to graduate, he had to give up the idea of reading for the law in his father's office.

Two years after he graduated from college, Prescott fell ill. A rheumatic infection temporarily cost him the sight of his right eye and left him for weeks in total darkness. When he recovered his sight, he sailed to visit his grandfather, who was a consul in the Azores. While he was there, blindness struck a second time, and for the next several months Prescott lived in a dark room in his grandfather's house. When his sight finally returned, he sought help in England. There the doctors could give him no assurance of a complete recovery. In despair, he cut his stay short and visited France and Italy before sailing for Boston.

When he returned home, Prescott was twenty-one and without any plans. For the next several years he was a man-about-town. He was popular and accepted in the best circles. He married and brought his bride to his father's home, where he lived until his parents died. Four uncertain years passed. He founded a literary club, edited a small literary magazine, wrote brief articles for the then prominent *North American Review*. This much was expected of him. He was educated in the classics and European literature, and the writing of articles was part of being a gentleman. He was fortunate in that there was no need for him to earn a living. Neither his family nor his neighbors expected anything of the handicapped youth. However, Prescott was a descendant of Puritans. His grandfather was the Colonel William Prescott who had commanded at Bunker Hill. And the concept of idle hands as tools of the devil tarried long in New England.

The pretenses and idleness were insufficient for Prescott's conscience, and he set himself a program of scholarship. He planned an intensive study of European literature, the accession of Italian, French, and German. He already knew Greek and Latin, and he intended to translate from these. It was an ambitious program for a man who did not need to do anything. It was also the first of many which Prescott laid out with care and drove himself to complete.

After three years he shifted his plan from the study of German and began to study Spanish instead. His old friend and classmate, George Ticknor, was the new professor of French and Spanish languages at Harvard, and Ticknor—"to amuse" his handicapped friend—began to read his lectures on Spanish literature to him. Ticknor himself had already made the traditional scholarly tour expected of the younger Harvard faculty members. He had visited Europe and studied in Germany, and, as important as anything else, he had brought back with him a library of Spanish materials.

Sometime during his years of study, Prescott determined to write one significant book. For a time he contemplated a history of literature. He was not certain whether it should be Italian or

English. He believed that he was a literary man, and both histories intrigued him. However, in 1825 he began to think about a history of Spain from the time of the Arab invasion to the consolidation of the empire under Charles V. For months he wrestled with the ideas and directions his history might take.

An American history was added to the list of possible projects, as well as a history of Roman literature or of Rome itself during the last days of the Republic. On January 15, 1826, he was "still doubting" his course and arguing pro and con in his journal— "The Italian subject has advantages over the Spanish," he wrote. He weighed the availability of sources: the American envoy to Spain could obtain materials for him. The fact that the "subject was a new one" seemed important. His thinking on the Spanish theme had already shifted to a more manageable period, one that would not require him to use a thousand years of "barbaric records."

Finally, his ideas came into focus. "I believe the Spanish subject will be more new than the Italian, more interesting to the majority of readers, more useful to me by opening more & more practical departments of study, & not more laborious, in relation to authorities to be consulted . . . the advantages of the Spanish topic, on the whole, overbalance the inconvenience of the requisite preliminary year [of study]. For these reasons I subscribe to the Hist. of the reign of Ferd. & Isabella.—Jany 19. 1826."

Twenty-one years later, he opened that same journal and added the comment: *"A fortunate choice. May 1847."*

THE HISTORY OF THE REIGN OF FERDINAND AND ISABELLA

In deciding to write a history of Spain in transition, Prescott was following a tradition—that of the literary man turned historian.

Such a writer is usually an amateur without academic standing. His histories are generally of epic proportions—the decline and fall of an empire, the rise of civilization, the history of a nation, etc. Rarely does the literary man turned historian deal in minutiae. Such details are left for the academic historian to ferret out and make available to the amateur. For the past two centuries it has been the amateur, rather than the academic historian, who has been able to build the available facts into a form acceptable to the general public.

Gibbon, Voltaire, Macaulay, Carlyle, Parkman, Motley, and in more recent times Will Durant and Bernard De Voto were all literary men turned historians. And they brought with them skills different from those of the research scholar. They wrote well, they told history as story, and they made it exciting and interesting. Not all of them were profound thinkers. Not all of them were able to develop and write history from any particular philosophical point of view. But all of them knew how to write history so that it could be read and enjoyed.

Prescott had studied his predecessors with great care. He admired Voltaire's genius and respected his contribution to historical writing, but the Frenchman's cynicism disturbed the Puritan in Prescott. Equally disturbing was Gibbon's "sneer of philosophical indifference." Prescott cut to the heart of what he thought were the weaknesses of both Voltaire and Gibbon when he wrote that their "writings are nowhere warmed with generous moral sentiment"—a judgment as revealing of Prescott as of his predecessors.

More to his taste and equally revealing of his developing attitude toward the history he was himself undertaking were his views concerning the historian-novelist Sir Walter Scott. For Prescott, Scott "had a natural relish for gunpowder and his mettle roused, like that of a war horse at the sound of the trumpet." Scott was the "master of the picturesque," and Prescott was convinced that there were advantages in this approach for the writer in search of an audience.

Scott, the novelist turned historian, had brought "new charms to history by embellishing it with the graces of romance," and it was upon the quality of romance that Prescott intended to build.

From the very beginning of his plans to write history, Prescott set out to find what would interest an audience. Time and again he jotted down in his journal his belief that the subject on which he was working had to be "novel." He did not plan to write a history for the specialist, but he believed that his scholarship had to be exact. He wanted to write history to be read by a large audience and at the same time to have a purpose. Where

Voltaire and Gibbon had neglected the moral aspects of history, Prescott determined to illustrate those aspects. His mentor became the Abbé Mably, whose *Etude de l'Histoire* he said he had read at least ten times. For Prescott, Mably was "a perspicuous, severe, shrewd & sensible writer." And the New Englander liked "particularly his notion of the necessity of giving an interest as well as a utility to history by letting events tend to some obvious point or moral—in short in paying some attention to the development of events tending to this leading result as one would in the construction of a romance or drama."

In pursuit of accuracy and sound scholarship, Prescott sought materials which had not previously been utilized by historians. He asked friends abroad to search out books and manuscripts for him. And though he agreed in part with Macaulay's thesis that facts were dross, he was aware that he had to be accurate, and he was prepared to go to whatever lengths he had to to obtain the information which he needed, upon which to build his history. It was his good fortune that the Spanish archives had recently been opened to scholars for the first time and that the finest scholars in Spain were not themselves writing histories but were rather collecting and editing documents which would in time be used by other historians. Washington Irving had only a short time before fallen heir to these labors and had rewritten the documents collected by Fernandez de Navarrete into his account of the Columbian voyages as well as his fictionalized *Conquest of Granada.*

The interest in things Spanish was part of the climate of opinion. The campaigns of Wellington had brought public attention to the otherwise neglected peninsula. The Romantic poets of England were writing about it. Southey had translated several of the ancient Spanish tales, and, in Ticknor, Harvard had the foremost scholar of Spanish literature. All these things helped in the decision Prescott made and remade to stay with his Spanish project.

He had made his decision to write the book on January 19, 1826. He started to write the first chapter in October 1829. The three volumes were finished in June 1836. Ten years had elapsed—ten years of listening six hours a day to his secretary reading aloud to him while he took notes on a board lined with wires to guide his hand; ten years in which he kept his efforts to himself. There were few in Boston who knew that he was writing a book. Once he was finished with his work, he hesitated to publish. He may have been uncertain of the merits of his history, or he may have been self-conscious. In any case, as he did with all the major decisions of his life, he discussed the problem with his father. The elder Prescott, a lawyer and businessman, was blunt: "The man who writes a book he is afraid to publish is a coward."

The *History of the Reign of Ferdinand and Isabella* was published on Christmas Day, 1837. The sales were phenomenal, considering that the author had no particular literary reputation and that his three volumes were on a remote subject.

Though Prescott claimed a thoroughness for his work, this was not altogether true. His essays on the literature of the times were ordinary and far from all-inclusive. His treatment of manners and customs was cursory. He neglected completely the day-to-day life of the ordinary citizen of Spain, making no attempt to understand the problems of those persons below the level of the court—an odd omission for an avowed democrat and a Yankee Federalist.

What Prescott did capture for all time were the personalities who governed and fought for Spain. He traced with care the development of the splintered peninsula into a single great nation. He followed the internal conflicts, the wars with the Moors, the wars with France, the wars in Italy, as well as the beginnings of the overseas empire which was to help thrust the newly formed country into the first rank of nations. In his ten years of labor Prescott learned how to relate history as an engrossing story, and whenever he paused to fill in the details—as in the essays on literature and culture—he lost the onward impetus. If he wrote well of battles and diplomacy, he wrote biography equally well. For a time he had considered writing a collection of biographies of geniuses, and he had apparently studied the art of biography. His portraits of the two Catholic monarchs, of Cardinal Ximenes and Captain General Gonsalvo were among the best portions of his three volumes and have not been surpassed. These running stories of his heroes and heroine helped bring a unity to the structure of his history. He also developed the practice in this history which he was to use again and again in the books which followed: a detailed summary of each personality of importance. Here he set down his own opinions, admittedly dropping all pretense at objectivity.

Just before releasing the book to the public, Prescott asked himself, "What do I expect from it, now it is done? And may it not be all in vain and labour lost after all?" At the same time he expressed his hopes for the book: "As a plain veracious record of facts, the work, therefore, till someone else shall be found to make a better one, I should hope would give it a permanent value—a value founded on its utility, though bringing no great fame or gain to its author."

Prescott need not have been so modest. Though the reviews were published slowly, they were favorable. The historian George Bancroft approved, as did Prescott's old friend William Gardiner. Ticknor, of course, had words of praise. Then the reviews began to arrive from Europe, and they matched those in the American press. The lengthiest and most impressive was that of the brilliant French scholar Count Adolphe de Circourt, who in five articles covering a hundred and eighty pages analyzed and evaluated every facet of the history. As Ticknor was later to write of the review, ". . . it sounds more like the voice of posterity than the American and English reviews that were contemporary with it."

For Prescott, however, the most important review was to be that of a young Spanish scholar who had the special knowledge to do the history justice. The comments of Don Pascual de Gayangos appeared in the *Edinburgh Review* in January 1839, over a year after the book was first published in the United States. In reviewing the book, Gayangos unwittingly took the first step in establishing a relationship that was to last as long as Prescott lived. The young Spaniard, who had married an English girl and moved from his native country to London, was the first person to catalogue the Spanish materials in the British Museum. And as a scholar and researcher he was to become in time Prescott's alter ego on the continent, searching out those rare volumes and miscellaneous manuscripts that the American wanted. Gayangos gave years of his life to helping Prescott, and the American came to appreciate the fact that his histories would have been quite different had it not been for the help given him by Gayangos, who in time became a great historian in his own right.

THE CONQUEST OF MEXICO

With the assured success of his first history, Prescott began to search for the subject of his second, one that would be "a natural continuation of the last." In June 1837, with the help of the Spanish Minister, Don A. Calderon de la Barca, he began to collect "such curious original and authentic documents as might throw light on the discovery of and the conquest of Mexico and Peru. . . . Without such documents, however, it will hardly be worthwhile to prosecute the plan, as the general story is too familiar to readers. . . ."

With the help of de la Barca and the Secretary of the American Legation in Madrid, and, eventually, Gayangos, he began to gather his special materials. However, before he could begin this new project he had to assure himself that he would have the field clear. The popular storyteller Washington Irving—"the Devil may take him"—had twice tilled the Spanish fields, once in his biography of Columbus and once in his account of the conquest of Granada. Whatever the failings of Irving's works, and they were many, Prescott did not want to find himself beaten in the race to public attention by Irving. The New Yorker, writing rapidly as a professional writer living on the proceeds of his works, could be expected to publish before Prescott unless the Bostonian took some action. And so, though he did not know Irving, he wrote to him and asked if Irving would relinquish the field in his favor.

Irving admitted that he had always intended to write an account of the conquest of Mexico as a companion to his Columbus biography. But he did not feel he had the time or the research materials at hand and, for these reasons, he wrote, "had felt more and more doubtful whether he would be able to treat it conscientiously—that is with the extensive research and thorough investigation which it merited." He was convinced, after reading the "noble history of Ferdinand and Isabella," that Prescott was "the man to undertake the subject."

This serious matter settled, Prescott made his decision, because "the daring achievements of these bold adventurers is a striking subject to the imagination." In spite of his enthusiasm, there were aspects of the subject to which Prescott did not thrill in anticipation. "I do not relish," he wrote in his journal, "the annals or conquests of barbarians, so much as those of civilized people, nor do I think they will bear expatiating on to any great length." However, as he debated the subject with himself as he always did before undertaking a book, he wrote, "The overturning of their old empires by a handful of warriors is a brilliant subject, full of important results, and connected with our own history." In a final judgment in favor of the conquests he abandoned the biography of Molière he had been contemplating— "The conquests will hit the popular tastes here much more than disquisitions on French players and comedies. . . ."

Three years and ten months were to pass before Prescott completed his *History of the Conquest of Mexico*. During those years his good eye served him better than it had for his previous book, and he was able to write as many as nine pages a day for print. With the help of Gayangos and friends at the American embassy in Madrid, materials flowed in to meet his needs. Navarrete opened the archives in Spain and arranged for a research assistant, who set a team of copyists at work to gather manuscripts never previously used in writing the history of the conquests. At the same time, Prescott's friends began collecting materials for the book which would follow *Mexico* and for the volume which would follow that. For Prescott was finally thinking in terms of his total subject.

Very early in his Spanish studies he had written into his journal that perhaps he could find those seeds sown in the time of Ferdinand and Isabella which would, when fully grown, choke the empire they created. In short, he had begun to think in terms of a series of books which would reveal the rise and decay of the Spanish empire. He appears to have committed himself to this project *in toto* while working on the Cortes materials. It is difficult to estimate how deeply concerned he was with his overall plan, because he did not refer to it often in his letters or his journal. One thing is certain: each history was intended to be an entity in itself.

From the very beginning of the *Conquest of Mexico*, he was faced with one of the knottiest problems a historian could imagine—the explanation and interpretation of the Aztecs. As he wrote Irving, he felt his hands were not suited to untying this knot. The disciplines of archaeology and anthropology were in their infancy, and a great deal of useless information had been gathered. One of the fullest sources available to him—and one Irving had recommended—was the collection of papers on ancient Mexico gathered by Lord William Kingsborough for the purpose of proving that the Aztecs were one of the lost tribes of Israel. Other materials were rarely more logically conceived. Prescott was wise enough to draw on sources closest to the period, such as Sahagun's *Historia Antiqua Mexicana,* the letters of Cortes to the Emperor Charles, and the *True History of the Conquest of New Spain* by Bernal Diaz del Castillo. Sahagun, who came to Mexico after the conquest, had gathered such materials as he could on the Aztec civilization, with a determination to salvage the information for posterity. Cortes and Diaz recorded what they themselves had seen on their initial incursions into the country. In the second half of the nineteenth century Prescott was roundly criticized for having accepted the Spanish accounts at face value. Lewis Morgan, the pioneer anthropologist, and his followers were convinced that the Aztec civilization could have been no higher than that of the Iroquois and other American Indian tribes above the Rio Grande. Contemporary anthropologists have declared in favor of Prescott, some even stating that his is the best single statement on the Aztecs to the time it was written.

However, as that great authority George C. Vaillant wrote in 1944, "new finds, new conclusions, new dates appear every year . . . and much of the modern Mexican work has yet to reach print." Though Prescott's descriptions of Aztec customs were based upon contemporary accounts compiled by the conquistadores and the priests who could have observed them, the subject of Aztec culture remains to this day "a highly speculative" and "confusing subject."

In the writing of the *Conquest of Mexico,* Prescott found the materials which best suited his skills. He had a simple theme, a great hero pitted against a vacillating monarch, and the destruction of a morally corrupt and barbaric empire. He had religious pageantry and political intrigue and—as important as anything else—he had the tableaux of great battles. He recognized that he was dealing with the stuff of epics and rose to the occasion.

In the first of five books he set out to describe the Aztec civilization, showing the tragic flaw of moral corruption at its core. Then he introduced his hero, a man of destiny. He sharpened the picture by creating a slothful and wasteful young Cortes who must change his entire personality to cope with the history into which he is thrust. Then Prescott recounted the trials and tribulations faced by his hero until he reached Mexico. There the hero met face to face his principal antagonist—Montezuma, a weak-willed man incapable of decision. For Cortes the future was bright, and then, in a series of rapid defeats, he was thrust down. His political opponents in Cuba sent an army against him, which he had to defeat. His lieutenant, who had been left behind as his caretaker in Mexico, committed a political blunder of epic proportions, and the Aztecs rose against the Spaniards. Hurrying to relieve his garrison, Cortes found himself trapped inside Mexico. A bloody retreat followed. Prescott told the story of *la noche triste*—the sad night—in which Cortes was at the bottom of his fortunes. Following this with the pageantry of the retreat and the battle of Otumba, Prescott revealed the energies and discipline of his hero, his cunning and ingenuity in the preparations for and the final reconquest of the city in the lake. Here Prescott set his opponents against each other with the religious fervor that marked both the age and his subject.

Trying always to see the Spaniard through Spanish eyes, trying not to judge except as the Spaniard himself might judge, Prescott wrote to a friend, "The immorality of the act and of the actor seem to me two very different things; and while we judge the one by immutable principles of right and wrong, we must try the other by the fluctuating standards of the age. The real question is whether a man was sincere, and acted according to the lights of his age. We cannot fairly demand of a man to be in advance of a generation, and where a generation goes wrong, we may be sure it is an error of the head, not the heart. For a whole community, including the best and wisest, will not deliberately sanction the habitual perpetuation of a crime."

With this as a point of view and his belief in the superiority of Christianity in any form over a barbarian religion, Prescott was able to sanction in part the destruction which resulted from the conquest.

In writing the *Conquest of Mexico,* Prescott assumed the additional task of writing a biography. He might have ended his history at the close of the conquest, but instead he took it to the death of Cortes, through the ill fortune that followed the later years of his hero, and he attempted to show the hero as builder, agriculturalist, administrator, and explorer. The final and seventh book of the *Conquest* covers much too briefly the last part of his hero's life and becomes merely a sketch of events. Here the heroic epic failed, and Prescott himself was aware that he had slighted this part of his materials. Like an unskilled playwright, he had let his denouement last too long after the climax.

However, while the seventh book weakened, it did not destroy the epic pattern of the romance, and for many the *Conquest of Mexico* is the best book that Prescott ever wrote.

In December 1843, the *History of the Conquest of Mexico* was published. It represented five years of work, and in many ways these were the most fortunate five years in Prescott's career, in that he had a greater use of his good eye during this time than he had had before or was to have again. Though his eye was always to remain a handicap, Prescott devised the *modus operandi* which permitted him to work regardless of its condition at any given moment. He took notes from the materials read to him by his secretaries. If his eye was capable of the strain, he read the notes himself; if not, he had them read to him, rarely fewer than six times; some, he says, "a dozen times." In this way they were impressed on his memory, which had become prodigious. Then he began to turn the material over in his head until he felt it was organized. He began to compose only after he felt that the materials were digested. "My way has lately been," he wrote, "to go over a large mass—over and over until ready to throw it on paper." A chapter of concentrated work took as brief a time as three days. As the years passed, he was able to keep as many as two chapters—which filled fifty-six pages of printed text—in his memory. Before he died he was able to retain the contents of seventy-two pages, which he worked over and revised many times in a sixty-two-day period before he finally committed them to paper.

Once the material was committed to paper, Prescott himself was less interested. He would do the "fine" work if he had time, or would allow his old friend William Gardiner to do it for him. There is no doubt that this was in part necessitated by his handicap. Also, he honored and respected the opinions of Gardiner.

With the publication of the *Conquest of Mexico,* Prescott

did not sit back and wait for reviews. He moved directly ahead toward his next volume, the long-contemplated *Conquest of Peru*. He started his work in February of 1844. However, as the reviews of the first *Conquest* began to arrive, he took time out to evaluate them with care. He had, with the reception of *Ferdinand and Isabella*, already lost some of his eagerness and respect for reviews, but, as he wrote in his journal, "Yet I shall be sorry if the work does not receive the approbation of my friends here and abroad—and of the few." Again, he need not have concerned himself. The reviews were favorable, though they did contain a strange point of view. The *Spectator* praised him for discovering the information which had not been available to the historian Robertson years before. In fact, as Prescott was to comment, "I think the tone is friendly enough though the idea that what is granted me detracts from Robertson is a very silly and narrow one. . . ." The *Edinburgh Review* followed the *Quarterly* with high praise, and Prescott laughingly commented, "I begin to have a high opinion of reviews!" But not all critics were in his corner. *The United States Magazine and Democratic Review* condemned his position regarding Cortes and felt he should have been more critical of the man and his actions. Considering that Prescott was writing in a country essentially Protestant, and that the elements of the Black Legend were basic to all interpretations of the Spanish conquests, it is astonishing that he was not more severely criticized for his attempt to see things Spanish from a Spanish point of view. He decided to answer the criticism, but he avoided what might lead to a quarrel. He pointed out that H. H. Milman's review in the *Quarterly* had approved of his stand regarding Cortes—"this from the great organ of Orthodoxy." He defended his position further by pointing out that the attack upon him had been made on the basis of a reading of Bernal Diaz and that "Truth cannot be drawn from one source, but from complicated and often contradictory sources."

THE CONQUEST OF PERU

The reviews continued to come in as he plunged ahead with the *Conquest of Peru*. In many ways this was to prove one of the most difficult volumes he ever undertook. He saw from the beginning that he had a problem of structure. The story wandered beyond its natural limits, and the heroes were numerous and not wholly related. The conquest of Peru was accomplished long before his story was to be finished.

Beginning as he had with *Mexico,* he told the story of the native peoples—this time Incas instead of Aztecs. The problems were similar insofar as his sources were concerned. Then he was faced with his hero or heroes. He found little to admire in Pizarro and threw his own favor to the older partner, the ill-starred Almagro. The five years in which the partners suffered through the discovery of the Inca empire, Prescott presents in meticulous detail. The approach to the Inca, the massacre which marked his capture, the room of treasure, and the final betrayal are all described and were all part of a simple pattern —the quest and conquest.

However, after this point Prescott had difficulties. The wars between the Pizarrists and the Almagrists had to be described, as well as the final wars between the *conquistadores.* And because of the shifting patterns, Prescott lost focus in his history and was committed to tying together in a loose chronology many diverse elements.

The writing of *Peru* took three trying years, during which time Prescott's father died. The historian had been greatly attached to his father and was deeply disturbed. For a long period of time he was unable to work. He commented in his journal, "A long interval since my last entry, and one pregnant with important and most melancholy results for me, for in it I have lost my father, my counsellor, companion and friend from boyhood to the hour of his death."

Before resuming work on *Peru,* Prescott prepared the *Miscellanies,* a collection of his articles and reviews. They ranged from a commentary on Italian literature to a literary biography of the early American novelist Charles Brockden Brown and an article on an "Asylum for the Blind." He also included his review of Madame Calderón's *Life in Mexico,* a book to which he had written a prefatory note and to which he had gone for part of the physical background in his own *Conquest of Mexico.* He revised the *Miscellanies* in later years, and in 1850 he added his review of Ticknor's *History of Spanish Literature.*

For almost a year after his father's death Prescott did very little work on *Peru,* and then he began "in earnest" to push it to a conclusion. However, as soon as he made this decision his eye went bad, and he was reduced to half an hour a day of vision, and then, for a time, only ten minutes. In spite of these problems he wrote five hundred and twenty-five pages, text and notes, in the eleven-month period between April 1845 and March 1846. His final chapter was completed on November 7; a thousand pages had been written in the two years and nine months since the day he started writing.

When he finally published in 1847, he had great fears that he might have written too rapidly. He was worried about his style, for though he had achieved great success and was to achieve even greater, he doubted his ability to write well, to write simply and dramatically. However, as far as the *Conquest of Peru* was concerned, he need not have been afraid, for the critics again acclaimed his achievement. He himself had known from the beginning what the book lacked: "Its great defect is want of unity." And he had known, too, that there was something to be desired in the subject itself. "Second rate," he commented, "the quarrels of banditti over the spoils." But he had done as much as was possible within the limitations.

THE HISTORY OF PHILIP II

With the conclusion of the two *Conquests,* Prescott moved without hesitation to his next project, the history of the period of Philip II. It was 1847, but he had had this task in mind since 1839—"a fruitful theme if discussed under all its relations, civil and literary as well as military." This was to be like his first history, a study of a period and the personality who dominated it. When he first conceived the idea in 1839, he felt the task impossible without ready access to the archives of Spain. And most especially he believed he had to have opened to him the archives at the small town of Simancas. Here, at the suggestion of Cardinal Ximenes, the royal Spanish papers of state had been placed in 1536. There were said to be fifty rooms containing eighty thousand packages of documents—perhaps as many as thirty million different documents, letters, private reports, etcetera. Prescott, using his excellent connections in the American embassy, inquired into the availability of this scholars' treasure trove, only to be informed that all the documents of his period of interest were thrown together with those of the following century "without order or index." The problem presented was insurmountable, and Prescott temporarily backed away from his study of Philip II. But the over-all plan to write of the rise and decay of the Spanish empire continued to hold his imagination. In 1848 he was finally prepared to proceed without the Simancas archives. By this time he had collected many papers on the subject, and there was no reason for not attempting the history in spite of its massive scope.

No sooner had he begun than he was approached by a younger literary man turned historian, in the same manner that he himself had years before approached Irving. J. Lothrop Motley, a member of the diplomatic corps and later United States Minister to Austria and Great Britain, wrote to ask if Prescott would mind if he, Motley, were to undertake the history of the rise of the Dutch Republics. For Prescott this might have been a blow, as Motley's obvious central figure could be none other than the same Philip II about whom he himself was planning to write. And at the same time the subject of Dutch independence from Spain and the lengthy wars that followed would certainly have to be part of his own study. With the same kind of generosity which Irving had shown him, Prescott not only told Motley that he felt the subject was large enough to take both of their studies, but offered the use of the books he had collected on the period. Now he knew for the first time that he was facing competition. Motley and he did both write of the same conflict, but Motley viewed it through Dutch eyes and Prescott through Spanish. As Prescott worked on his history, it became apparent that the entire Netherlands affair was somehow on the periphery of his work.

He perused the subject for almost two years without pause. The history had many problems. In large part it was an unnatural subject for the writer of epics. The activities in most instances took place outside of Spain itself, his central character was Philip, always lurking in the background and almost never center stage. This weakness of structure caused Prescott to make several diversions. He drew too large a picture of the siege of Malta and the Netherlands uprising, compared to their actual

significance to the history of Spain or Philip. And Philip as a
central character disturbed Prescott's own sense of morality.
"With all my good nature," he wrote, "I can't wash him even
into the darkest French grey. He is black and all black."

By 1850 Prescott was weary and he decided to rest. On a trip
to Washington he was entertained by both the President and
Daniel Webster. This pleased him, though he had little political
interest in his life. He had been approached by publishers during
the war with Mexico and asked to write a history of the event,
but it smelled too much of politics and was too contemporary to
capture his imagination. The Washington journey was followed
by one to Europe. In England he was treated as no unofficial
personality had ever been previously. He and a Napalese prince
were the social lions of the season. Though he was a Unitarian,
Oxford bestowed a doctorate on him. Macaulay, Wellington,
Peel, Disraeli, and the Queen all met and praised him. This was
a very different visit to London from that first one in his youth,
when he had gone to hear that there was no hope for his failing
eyesight. From London, Prescott toured the Continent, visiting
Paris, Belgium, and Holland. For reasons which may have been
romantic, he, the greatest Spanish historian, avoided Spain. Nor,
during the many months that he was abroad, did he write to his
old friend Gayangos or make any attempt to meet the man with
whom he had worked more closely than any other in his lifetime.

On his return home he picked up once again his work on
Philip II. For the next five years he held to this task, and in
1855 he published the first two volumes of what was planned as
a six-volume study. The hand was sure, the materials, as always,
were accurate, the battles impressive, and the personalities sharp,
but somehow the spirit was missing. The two volumes lack the
inspiration of Prescott's earlier work. The critics were, however,
as enthusiastic as they had been in the past, though most of
them waited to see the completed work before committing themselves.

The following year, instead of publishing a third volume of his
Philip II, Prescott published a continuation of the *History of the
Reign of Emperor Charles V* by the Scottish historian William
Robertson. Prescott had fallen onto documents covering the
period of Charles's life after his abdication, which rounded out

the Robertson history and which he felt would somehow complete his own studies. Much of this same material he used again in *Philip II.*

In 1858, while working on the third volume of his history, he suffered an attack of apoplexy and his health began to fail. The third and last volume to be completed was published in that year. And in it the old fire is again visible, for the lengthy description of the Battle of Lepanto is as fine a piece of writing as any he had ever done. When he finished writing it, he hoped "it will smell of the sea." Washington Irving thought it the best thing in the book.

After the publication of the third volume in April, Prescott did little work on his history. He edited a new edition of the *Conquest of Mexico,* and though he tried to do more, somehow he could not bring himself to work. Then on January 28, 1859, he collapsed of an apoplectic stroke while at home in Boston, and he died several hours later.

The final volumes of his last and largest study were never completed. The grand design of Spanish history which he once envisioned was only partly structured. The decay under Philip that would lead to the final decline of the Spain created by Ferdinand and Isabella was only partly revealed.

At the time of his death, Prescott had written only four histories—*Ferdinand and Isabella,* the *Conquest of Mexico,* the *Conquest of Peru,* and the incomplete *Philip II.* Yet these titles established him as the most frequently published and widely sold historian in America. While never slighting accuracy and integrity, he wrote history as dramatic narration. These two qualities—scholarship and storytelling—were so well wedded in Prescott that after more than a century his writings about the Spanish have not been superseded.

History of the Reign

of

Ferdinand and Isabella

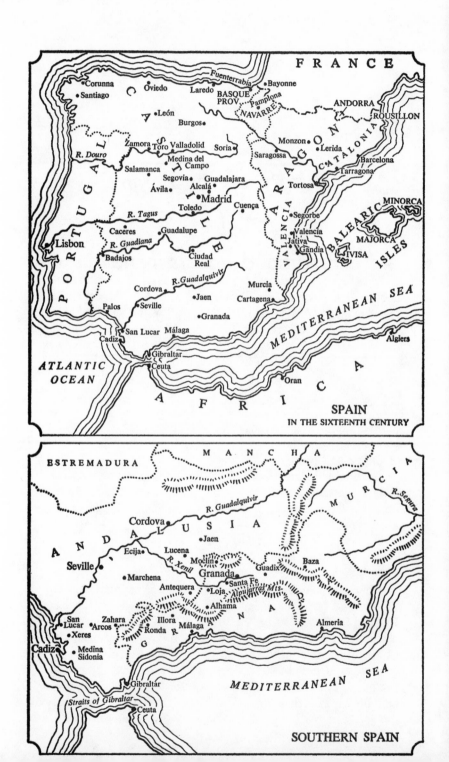

SPAIN
IN THE SIXTEENTH CENTURY

SOUTHERN SPAIN

PART FIRST

Marriage of Ferdinand and Isabella

1468–1469

AN INTERVIEW took place between Henry and Isabella, each attended by a brilliant cortège of cavaliers and nobles, at a place called Toros de Guisando, in New Castile. (September 9, 1468.) The monarch embraced his sister with the tenderest marks of affection, and then proceeded solemnly to recognize her as his future and rightful heir. An oath of allegiance was repeated by the attendant nobles, who concluded the ceremony by kissing the hand of the princess in token of their homage. In due time the representatives of the nation, convened in cortes at Ocaña, unanimously concurred in their approbation of these preliminary proceedings, and thus Isabella was announced to the world as the lawful successor to the crowns of Castile and Leon. . . .

The new and legitimate basis on which the pretensions of Isabella to the throne now rested drew the attention of neighboring princes, who contended with each other for the honor of her hand. Among these suitors was a brother of Edward the Fourth of England, not improbably Richard, duke of Gloucester, since Clarence was then engaged in his intrigues with the earl of Warwick, which led a few months later to his marriage with the daughter of that nobleman. Had she listened to his proposals, the duke would in all likelihood have exchanged his residence in England for Castile, where his ambition, satisfied with the certain reversion of a crown, might have been spared the commission of the catalogue of crimes which blackens his memory.

Another suitor was the duke of Guienne, the unfortunate brother of Louis the Eleventh, and at that time the presumptive heir of the French monarchy. Although the ancient intimacy which subsisted between the royal families of France and Castile in some measure favored his pretensions, the disadvantages resulting from such a union were too obvious to escape attention. The two countries were too remote from each other, and their inhabitants too dissimilar in character and institutions, to permit the idea of their ever cordially coalescing as one people under a common sovereign. Should the duke of Guienne fail in the inheritance of the crown, it was argued, he would be every way an unequal match for the heiress of Castile; should he succeed to it, it might be feared that, in case of a union, the smaller kingdom would be considered only as an appendage, and sacrificed to the interests of the larger.

The person on whom Isabella turned the most favorable eye was her kinsman Ferdinand of Aragon. The superior advantages of a connection which should be the means of uniting the people of Aragon and Castile into one nation were indeed manifest. They were the descendants of one common stock, speaking one language, and living under the influence of similar institutions, which had molded them into a common resemblance of character and manners. From their geographical position, too, they seemed destined by nature to be one nation; and, while separately they were condemned to the rank of petty and subordinate states, they might hope, when consolidated into one monarchy, to rise at once to the first class of European powers. While arguments of this public nature pressed on the mind of Isabella, she was not insensible to those which most powerfully affect the female heart. Ferdinand was then in the bloom of life, and distinguished for the comeliness of his person. In the busy scenes in which he had been engaged from his boyhood, he had displayed a chivalrous valor, combined with maturity of judgment far above his years. Indeed, he was decidedly superior to his rivals in personal merit and attractions. But, while private inclinations thus happily coincided with considerations of expediency for inclining her to prefer the Aragonese match, a scheme was devised in another quarter for the express purpose of defeating it.

A fraction of the royal party, with the family of Mendoza at their head, had retired in disgust with the convention of Toros de Guisando, and openly espoused the cause of the princess Joanna. They even instructed her to institute an appeal before the tribunal of the supreme pontiff, and caused a placard, exhibiting a protest against the validity of the late proceedings, to be nailed secretly in the night to the gate of Isabella's mansion. Thus were sown the seeds of new dissensions, before the old were completely eradicated. With this disaffected party the marquis of Villena, who, since his reconciliation, had resumed his ancient ascendancy over Henry, now associated himself. Nothing, in the opinion of this nobleman, could be more repugnant to his interests than the projected union between the houses of Castile and Aragon; to the latter of which, as already noticed, once belonged the ample domains of his own marquisate, which he imagined would be held by a very precarious tenure should any of this family obtain a footing in Castile.

In the hope of counteracting this project, he endeavored to revive the obsolete pretensions of Alfonso, king of Portugal; and, the more effectually to secure the cooperation of Henry, he connected with his scheme a proposition for marrying his daughter Joanna with the son and heir of the Portuguese monarch; and thus this unfortunate princess might be enabled to assume at once a station suitable to her birth, and at some future opportunity assert with success her claim to the Castilian crown. In furtherance of this complicated intrigue, Alfonso was invited to renew his addresses to Isabella in a more public manner than he had hitherto done; and a pompous embassy, with the archbishop of Lisbon at its head, appeared at Ocaña, where Isabella was then residing, bearing the proposals of their master. The princess returned, as before, a decided though temperate refusal. Henry, or rather the marquis of Villena, piqued at this opposition to his wishes, resolved to intimidate her into compliance, and menaced her with imprisonment in the royal fortress at Madrid. Neither her tears nor entreaties would have availed against this tyrannical proceeding; and the marquis was only deterred from putting it in execution by his fear of the inhabitants of Ocaña, who openly espoused the cause of Isabella. Indeed, the common people of Castile very generally supported her in her preference of the Aragonese match. Boys paraded the streets, bearing banners emblazoned with the arms of Aragon, and singing verses prophetic of the glories of the auspicious union. They even assembled round the palace gates, and insulted the ears of Henry and his minister by the repetition of satirical stanzas which contrasted Alfonso's years with the youthful graces of Ferdinand.

Notwithstanding this popular expression of opinion, however, the constancy of Isabella might at length have yielded to the importunity of her persecutors, had she not been encouraged by her friend the archbishop of Toledo, who had warmly entered into the interests of Aragon, and who promised, should matters come to extremity, to march in person to her relief at the head of a sufficient force to insure it. (1469.)

Isabella, indignant at the oppressive treatment which she experienced from her brother, as well as at his notorious infraction of almost every article in the treaty of Toros de Guisando, felt herself released from her corresponding engagements, and determined to conclude the negotiations relative to her marriage without any further deference to his opinion. Before taking any decisive step, however, she was desirous of obtaining the concurrence of the leading nobles of her party. This was affected without difficulty, through the intervention of the archbishop of Toledo, and of Don Frederick Henriquez, admiral of Castile, and the maternal grandfather of Ferdinand; a person of high consideration, both from his rank and character, and connected by blood with the principal families in the kingdom. Fortified by their approbation, Isabella dismissed the Aragonese envoy with a favorable answer to his master's suit.

Her reply was received with almost as much satisfaction by the old King of Aragon, John the Second, as by his son. This monarch, who was one of the shrewdest princes of his time, had always been deeply sensible of the importance of consolidating the scattered monarchies of Spain under one head. He had solicited the hand of Isabella for his son when she possessed only a contingent reversion of the crown. But, when her succession had been settled on a more secure basis, he lost no time in effecting this favorite object of his policy. With the consent of the states, he had transferred to his son the title of king of Sicily, and associated him with himself in the government at home, in order to give him greater consequence in the eyes of his mistress. He then despatched a confidential agent into Castile, with instructions to gain over to his interests all who exercised any influence on the mind of the princess; furnishing him for this purpose with *cartes blanches,* signed by himself and Ferdinand, which he was empowered to fill at his discretion.

Between parties thus favorably disposed there was no unnecessary delay. The marriage articles were signed, and sworn to by Ferdinand at Cervera on the 7th of January, 1469. He promised faithfully to respect the laws and usages of Castile; to fix his residence in that kingdom, and not to quit it without the consent of Isabella; to alienate no property belonging to the crown; to prefer no foreigners to municipal offices, and indeed to make no appointments of a civil or military nature, without her consent and approbation; and to resign to her exclusively the right of nomination to ecclesiastical benefices. All ordinances of a public nature were to be subscribed equally by both. Ferdinand engaged, moreover, to prosecute the war against the Moors; to respect King Henry; to suffer every noble to remain unmolested in the possession of his dignities; and not to demand restitution of the domains formerly owned by his father in Castile. The treaty concluded with a specification of a magnificent dower to be settled on Isabella, far more ample than that usually assigned to the queens of Aragon. The circumspection of the framers of this instrument is apparent from the various provisions introduced into it solely to calm the apprehensions and to conciliate the good will of the party disaffected to the marriage; while the national partialities of the Castilians in general were gratified by the jealous restrictions imposed on Ferdinand, and the relinquishment of all the essential rights of sovereignty to his consort.

While these affairs were in progress, Isabella's situation was becoming extremely critical. She had availed herself of the absence of her brother and the marquis of Villena in the south, whither they had gone for the purpose of suppressing the still lingering spark of insurrection, to transfer her residence from Ocaña to Madrigal, where, under the protection of her mother, she intended to abide the issue of the pending negotiations with Aragon. Far, however, from escaping the vigilant eye of the marquis of Villena by this movement, she laid herself more open to it. She found the bishop of Burgos, the nephew of the marquis, stationed at Madrigal, where he served as an effectual spy upon her actions. Her most confidential servants were corrupted, and conveyed intelligence of her proceedings to her enemy. Alarmed at the actual progress made in the negotiations for her marriage, the marquis was now convinced that he could only hope to defeat them by resorting to the coercive system which he had before abandoned. He accordingly instructed the archbishop of Seville to march at once to Madrigal with a sufficient force to secure Isabella's person; and letters were at the same time addressed by Henry to the citizens of that place, menacing them with his resentment if they should presume to interpose in her behalf. The timid inhabitants disclosed the purport of the mandate to Isabella, and besought her to provide for her own safety. This was perhaps the most critical period in her life. Betrayed by her own domestics, deserted even by those friends of her own sex who might have afforded her sympathy and counsel, but who fled affrighted from the scene of danger, and on the eve of falling into the snares of her enemies, she beheld the sudden extinction of those hopes which she had so long and so fondly cherished.

In this exigency, she contrived to convey a knowledge of her situation to Admiral Henriquez and the archbishop of Toledo. The active prelate, on receiving the summons, collected a body of horse, and, reinforced by the admiral's troops, advanced with such expedition to Madrigal that he succeeded in anticipating the arrival of the enemy. Isabella received her friends with unfeigned satisfaction; and bidding adieu to her dismayed guardian, the bishop of Burgos, and his attendants, she was borne off by her little army in a sort of military triumph to the friendly city of Valladolid, where she was welcomed by the citizens with a general burst of enthusiasm.

In the meantime, Gutierre de Cardenas, one of the household of the princess, and Alonso de Palencia, the faithful chronicler of these events, were despatched into Aragon in order to quicken Ferdinand's operations during the auspicious interval afforded by the absence of Henry in Andalusia. On arriving at the frontier town of Osma, they were dismayed to find that the bishop of that place, together with the duke of Medina Celi, on whose active cooperation they had relied for the safe introduction of Ferdinand into Castile, had been gained over to the interests of the marquis of Villena. The envoys, however, adroitly concealing the real object of their mission, were permitted to pass unmolested to Saragossa, where Ferdinand was then residing. They could not have arrived at a more inopportune season. The old king of Aragon was in the very heat of the war against the insurgent Catalans, headed by the victorious John of Anjou. Although so sorely pressed, his forces were on the eve of disbanding, for want of the requisite funds to maintain them. His exhausted treasury did not contain more than three hundred *enriques*. In this exigency he was agitated by the most distressing doubts. As he could spare neither the funds nor the force necessary for covering his son's entrance into Castile, he must either send him unprotected into a hostile country already aware of his intended enterprise and in arms to defeat it, or abandon the long-cherished object of his policy at the moment when his plans were ripe for execution. Unable to extricate himself from this dilemma, he referred the whole matter to Ferdinand and his council.

It was at length determined that the prince should undertake the journey, accompanied by half a dozen attendants only, in the disguise of merchants, by the direct route from Saragossa; while another party, in order to divert the attention of the Castilians, should proceed in a different direction, with all the ostentation of a public embassy from the king of Aragon to Henry the Fourth. The distance was not great which Ferdinand and his suite were to travel before reaching a place of safety; but this intervening country was patrolled by squadrons of cavalry for the purpose of intercepting their progress; and the whole extent of the frontier, from Almazan to Guadalajara, was defended by a line of fortified castles in the hands of the family of Mendoza. The greatest circumspection, therefore, was necessary. The party journeyed chiefly in the night; Ferdinand assumed the disguise of a servant, and, when they halted on the road, took care of the mules, and served his companions at table. In this guise, with no other disaster except that of leaving at an inn the purse which contained the funds for the expedition, they arrived, late on the second night, at a little place called the Burgo, or Borough, of Osma, which the count of Treviño, one of the partisans of Isabella, had occupied with a considerable body of men-at-arms. On knocking at the gate, cold and faint with traveling, during which the prince had allowed himself to take no repose, they were saluted by a large stone discharged by a sentinel from the battlements, which, glancing near Ferdinand's head, had wellnigh brought his romantic enterprise to a tragical conclusion; when his voice was recognized by his friends within, and, the trumpets proclaiming his arrival, he was received with great joy and festivity by the count and his followers. The remainder of his journey, which he commenced before dawn, was performed under the convoy of a numerous and well-armed escort; and on the 9th of October he reached Dueñas in the kingdom of Leon, where the Castilian nobles and cavaliers of his party eagerly thronged to render him the homage due to his rank.

The intelligence of Ferdinand's arrival diffused universal joy in the little court of Isabella at Valladolid. Her first step was to transmit a letter to her brother Henry, in which she informed him of the presence of the prince in his dominions, and of their intended marriage. She excused the course she had taken by the embarrassments in which she had been involved by the malice of her enemies. She represented the political advantages of the connection, and the sanction it had received from the Castilian nobles; and she concluded with soliciting his approbation of it, giving him at the same time affectionate assurances of the most dutiful submission on the part both of Ferdinand and of herself. Arrangements were then made for an interview between the royal pair, in which some courtly parasites would fain have persuaded their mistress to require some act of homage from Ferdinand, in token of the inferiority of the crown of Aragon to that of Castile; a proposition which she rejected with her usual discretion.

Agreeably to these arrangements, Ferdinand, on the evening of the 15th of October, passed privately from Dueñas, accompanied by only four attendants, to the neighboring city of Valladolid, where he was received by the archbishop of Toledo and conducted to the apartment of his mistress. Ferdinand was at this time in the eighteenth year of his age. His complexion was fair, though somewhat bronzed by constant exposure to the sun; his eye quick and cheerful; his forehead ample, and approaching to baldness. His muscular and well-proportioned frame was invigorated by the toils of war, and by the chivalrous exercises in which he delighted. He was one of the best horsemen in his court, and excelled in field sports of every kind. His voice was somewhat sharp, but he possessed a fluent eloquence; and, when he had a point to carry, his address was courteous and even insinuating. He secured his health by extreme temperance in his diet, and by such habits of activity that it was said he seemed to find repose in business. Isabella was a year older than her lover. In stature she was somewhat above the middle size. Her complexion was fair; her hair of a bright chestnut color, inclining to red; and her mild blue eye beamed with intelligence and sensibility. She was exceedingly beautiful; "the handsomest lady," says one of her household, "whom I ever beheld, and the most gracious in her manners." The portrait still existing of her in the royal palace is conspicuous for an open symmetry of features, indicative of the natural serenity of temper, and that beautiful harmony of intellectual and moral qualities, which most distinguished her. She was dignified in her demeanor, and modest even to a degree of reserve. She spoke the Castilian language with more than usual elegance, and early imbibed a relish for letters, in which she was superior to Ferdinand, whose education in this particular seems to have been neglected. It is not easy to obtain a dispassionate portrait of Isabella. The Spaniards who revert to her glorious reign are so smitten with her moral perfections that, even in depicting her personality, they borrow somewhat of the exaggerated coloring of romance.

The interview lasted more than two hours, when Ferdinand retired to his quarters at Dueñas as privately as he came. The preliminaries of the marriage, however, were first adjusted; but so great was the poverty of the parties that it was found necessary to borrow money to defray the expenses of the ceremony. Such were the humiliating circumstances attending the commencement of a union destined to open the way to the highest prosperity and grandeur of the Spanish monarchy!

The marriage between Ferdinand and Isabella was publicly celebrated, on the morning of the 19th of October, 1469, in the palace of John de Vivero, the temporary residence of the princess, and subsequently appropriated to the chancery of Valladolid. The nuptials were solemnized in the presence of Ferdinand's grandfather, the admiral of Castile, of the archbishop of Toledo, and a multitude of persons of rank, as well as of inferior condition, amounting in all to no less than two thousand. A papal bull of dispensation was produced by the archbishop, relieving the parties from the impediment incurred by their falling within the prohibited degrees of consanguinity. This spurious document was afterwards discovered to have been devised by the old king of Aragon, Ferdinand, and the archbishop, who were deterred from applying to the court of Rome by the zeal with which it openly espoused the interests of Henry, and who knew that Isabella would never consent to a union repugnant to the canons of the established Church, and one which involved such heavy ecclesiastical censures. A genuine bull of dispensation was obtained, some years later, from Sixtus the Fourth; but Isabella, whose honest mind abhorred everything like artifice, was filled with no little uneasiness and mortification at the discovery of the imposition. The ensuing week was consumed in the usual festivities of this joyous season; at the expiration of which the new-married pair attended publicly the celebration of mass, agreeably to the usage of the time, in the collegiate church of Santa Maria.

An embassy was despatched by Ferdinand and Isabella to Henry, to acquaint him with their proceedings, and again request his approbation of them. They repeated their assurances of loyal submission, and accompanied the message with a copious extract from such of the articles of marriage as, by their import, would be most likely to conciliate his favorite disposition. Henry coldly replied that "he must advise with his ministers."

CHAPTER V

Accession of Ferdinand and Isabella

1474–1476

Most of the contemporary writers are content to derive Isabella's title to the crown of Castile from the illegitimacy of her rival Joanna. But as this fact, whatever probability it may receive from the avowed licentiousness of the queen, and some other collateral circumstances, was never established by legal evidence, or even made the subject of legal inquiry, it cannot reasonably be adduced as affording in itself a satisfactory basis for the pretensions of Isabella.

These are to be derived from the will of the nation as expressed by its representatives in cortes. The power of this body to interpret the laws regulating the succession, and to determine the succession itself, in the most absolute manner, is incontrovertible, having been established by repeated precedents from a very ancient period. In the present instance, the legislature, soon after the birth of Joanna, tendered the usual oaths of allegiance to her as heir apparent to the monarchy. On a subsequent occasion, however, the cortes, for reasons deemed sufficient by itself, and under a conviction that its consent to the preceding measure had been obtained through an undue influence on the part of the crown, reversed its former acts, and did homage to Isabella as the only true and lawful successor. In this disposition the legislature continued so resolute that, notwithstanding Henry twice convoked the states for the express purpose of renewing their allegiance to Joanna, they refused to comply with the summons; and thus Isabella, at the time of her brother's death, possessed a title to the crown unimpaired, and derived from the sole authority which could give it a constitutional validity. It may be added that the princess was so well aware of the real basis of her pretensions that in her several manifestoes, although she adverts to the popular notion of her rival's illegitimacy, she rests the strength of her cause on the sanction of the cortes.

On learning Henry's death, Isabella signified to the inhabitants of Segovia, where she then resided, her desire of being proclaimed queen in that city, with the solemnities usual on such occasions. Accordingly, on the following morning, being the 13th of December, 1474, a numerous assembly, consisting of the nobles, clergy, and public magistrates in their robes of office, waited on her at the alcazar, or castle, and, receiving her under a canopy of rich brocade, escorted her in solemn procession to the principal square of the city, where a broad platform or scaffold had been erected for the performance of the ceremony. Isabella, royally attired, rode on a Spanish jennet, whose bridle was held by two of the civic functionaries, while an officer of her court preceded her on horseback, bearing aloft a naked sword, the symbol of sovereignty. On arriving at the square, she alighted from her palfrey, and, ascending the platform, seated herself on a throne which had been prepared for her. A herald with a loud voice proclaimed, "Castile, Castile for the king Don Ferdinand and his consort Doña Isabella, queen proprietor (*reina proprietaria*) of these kingdoms!" The royal standards were then unfurled, while the peal of bells and the discharge of ordnance from the castle publicly announced the accession of the new sovereign. Isabella, after receiving the homage of her subjects, and swearing to maintain inviolate the liberties of the realm, descended from the platform, and, attended by the same cortège, moved slowly towards the cathedral church; where, after Te Deum had been chanted, she prostrated herself before the principal altar, and, returning thanks to the Almighty for the protection hitherto vouchsafed her, implored him to enlighten her future counsels, so that she might discharge the high trust reposed in her with equity and wisdom. Such were the simple forms that attended the coronation of the monarchs of Castile, previously to the sixteenth century.

The cities favorable to Isabella's cause, comprehending far the most populous and wealthy throughout the kingdom, followed the example of Segovia, and raised the royal standard for their new sovereign. The principal grandees, as well as most of the inferior nobility, soon presented themselves from all quarters, in order to tender the customary oaths of allegiance; and an assembly of the estates, convened for the ensuing month of February at Segovia, imparted, by a similar ceremony, a constitutional sanction to these proceedings.

On Ferdinand's arrival from Aragon, where he was staying at the time of Henry's death, occupied with the war of Roussillon, a disagreeable discussion took place in regard to the respective authority to be enjoyed by the husband and wife in the administration of the government. Ferdinand's relatives, with the admiral Henriquez at their head, contended that the crown of Castile, and of course the exclusive sovereignty, was limited to him, as the nearest male representative of the house of Trastamara. Isabella's friends, on the other hand, insisted that these rights devolved solely on her, as the lawful heir and proprietor of the kingdom. The affair was finally referred to the arbitration of the cardinal of Spain and the archbishop of Toledo, who, after careful examination, established by undoubted precedent that the exclusion of females from the succession did not obtain in Castile and Leon, as was the case in Aragon, that Isabella was consequently sole heir of these dominions; and that whatever authority Ferdinand might possess could only be derived through her. A settlement was then made on the basis of the original marriage contract. All municipal appointments, and collation to ecclesiastical benefices, were to be made in the name of both with the advice and consent of the queen. All fiscal nominations, and issues from the treasury, were to be subject to her order. The commanders of the fortified places were to render homage to her alone. Justice was to be administered by both conjointly when residing in the same place, and by each independently when separate. Proclamations and letters patent were to be subscribed with the signatures of both; their images were to be stamped on the public coin, and the united arms of Castile and Aragon emblazoned on a common seal.

Ferdinand, it is said, was so much dissatisfied with an arrangement which vested the essential rights of sovereignty in his consort, that he threatened to return to Aragon; but Isabella reminded him that this distribution of power was rather nominal than real; that their interests were indivisible; that his will would be hers; and that the principle of the exclusion of females from the succession, if now established, would operate to the disqualification of their only child, who was a daughter. By these and similar arguments the queen succeeded in soothing her offended husband, without compromising the prerogatives of her crown.

Although the principal body of the nobility, as has been stated, supported Isabella's cause, there were a few families, and some of them the most potent in Castile, who seemed determined to abide the fortunes of her rival. Among these was the marquis of Villena, who, inferior to his father in talent for intrigue, was of an intrepid spirit, and is commended by one of the Spanish historians as "the best lance in the kingdom." His immense estates, stretching from Toledo to Murcia, gave him an extensive influence over the southern regions of New Castile. The duke of Arevalo possessed a similar interest in the frontier province of Estremadura. With these were combined the grand master of Calatrava and his brother, together with the young marquis of Cadiz, and, as it soon appeared, the archbishop of Toledo. This latter dignitary, whose heart had long swelled with secret jealousy at the rising fortunes of the cardinal Mendoza, could no longer brook the ascendency which that prelate's consummate sagacity and insinuating address had given him over the counsels of his young sovereigns. After some awkward excuses, he abruptly withdrew to his own estates; nor could the most conciliatory advances on the part of the queen, nor the deprecatory letters of the old king of Aragon, soften his inflexible temper, or induce him to resume his station at the court; until it soon became apparent, from his correspondence with Isabella's enemies, that he was busy in undermining the fortunes of the very individual whom he had so zealously labored to elevate.

Under the auspices of this coalition, propositions were made to Alfonso the Fifth, king of Portugal, to vindicate the title of his niece Joanna to the throne of Castile, and, by espousing her, to secure to himself the same rich inheritance. An exaggerated estimate was at the same time exhibited of the resources of the confederates, which, when combined with those of Portugal, would readily enable them to crush the usurpers, unsupported as the latter must be by the cooperation of Aragon, whose arms already found sufficient occupation with the French.

Alfonso, whose victories over the Barbary Moors had given him the cognomen of "the African," was precisely of a character to be dazzled by the nature of this enterprise. The protection of an injured princess, his near relative, was congenial with the spirit of chivalry; while the conquest of an opulent territory, adjacent to his own, would not only satisfy his dreams of glory, but the more solid cravings of avarice. In this disposition he was confirmed by his son, Prince John, whose hot and enterprising temper found a nobler scope for ambition in such a war than in the conquest of a horde of African savages.

Still there were a few among Alfonso's counselors possessed of sufficient coolness to discern the difficulties of the undertaking. They reminded him that the Castilian nobles on whom he principally relied were the very persons who had formerly been most instrumental in defeating the claims of Joanna and securing the succession to her rival; that Ferdinand was connected by blood with the most powerful families of Castile; that the great body of the people, the middle as well as the lower classes, were fully penetrated not only with a conviction of the legality of Isabella's title, but with a deep attachment to her person; while, on the other hand, their proverbial hatred of Portugal would make them too impatient of interference from that quarter to admit the prospect of permanent success.

These objections, sound as they were, were overruled by John's impetuosity and the ambition or avarice of his father. War was accordingly resolved on; and Alfonso, after a vaunting and, as may be supposed, ineffectual summons to the Castilian sovereigns to resign their crown in favor of Joanna, prepared for the immediate invasion of the kingdom at the head of an army amounting, according to the Portuguese historians, to five thousand six hundred horse and fourteen thousand foot. This force, though numerically not so formidable as might have been expected, comprised the flower of the Portuguese chivalry, burning with the hope of reaping similar laurels to those won of old by their fathers on the plains of Aljubarrotta; while its deficiency in numbers was to be amply compensated by recruits from the disaffected party in Castile, who would eagerly flock to its banners on its advance across the borders. At the same time negotiations were entered into with the king of France, who was invited to make a descent upon Biscay, by a promise, somewhat premature, of a cession of the conquered territory.

Early in May (1475), the king of Portugal put his army in motion, and, entering Castile by the way of Estremadura, held a northerly course towards Placencia, where he was met by the duke of Arevalo and the marquis of Villena, and by the latter nobleman presented to the princess Joanna, his destined bride. On the 12th of the month he was affianced with all becoming pomp to this lady, then scarcely thirteen years of age; and a messenger was despatched to the court of Rome, to solicit a dispensation for their marriage, rendered necessary by the consanguinity of the parties. The royal pair were then proclaimed, with the usual solemnities, sovereigns of Castile; and circulars were transmitted to the different cities, setting forth Joanna's title and requiring their allegiance.

After some days given to festivity, the army resumed its march, still in a northerly direction, upon Arevalo, where Alfonso determined to await the arrival of the reinforcements which he expected from his Castilian allies. Had he struck at once into the southern districts of Castile, where most of those friendly to his cause were to be found, and immediately commenced active operations with the aid of the marquis of Cadiz, who it was understood was prepared to support him in that quarter, it is difficult to say what might have been the result. Ferdinand and Isabella were so wholly unprepared at the time of Alfonso's invasion, that it is said they could scarcely bring five hundred horse to oppose it. By this opportune delay at Arevalo they obtained space for preparation. Both of them were indefatigable in their efforts. Isabella, we are told, was frequently engaged through the whole night in dictating despatches to her secretaries. She visited in person such of the garrisoned towns as required to be confirmed in their allegiance, performing long and painful journeys on horseback with surprising celerity, and enduring fatigues which, as she was at that time in delicate health, wellnigh proved fatal to her constitution. [The queen, who was at that time in a state of pregnancy, brought on a miscarriage by her incessant personal exposure.] On an excursion to Toledo, she determined to make one effort more to regain the confidence of her ancient minister, the archbishop. She accordingly sent an envoy to inform him of her intention to wait on him in person at his residence in Alcala de Henares. But as the surly prelate, far from being moved by this condescension, returned for answer that, "if the queen entered by one door, he would go out at the other," she did not choose to compromise her dignity by any further advances.

By Isabella's extraordinary exertions, as well as those of her husband, the latter found himself, in the beginning of July, at the head of a force amounting in all to four thousand men-at-arms, eight thousand light horse, and thirty thousand foot, an ill-disciplined militia, chiefly drawn from the mountainous districts of the north, which manifested peculiar devotion to his cause; his partisans in the south being preoccupied with suppressing domestic revolt, and with incursions on the frontiers of Portugal.

Meanwhile Alfonso, after an unprofitable detention of nearly two months at Arevalo, marched on Toro, which, by a preconcerted agreement, was delivered into his hands by the governor of the city, although the fortress, under the conduct of a woman, continued to maintain a gallant defense. While occupied with its reduction, Alfonso was invited to receive the submission of the adjacent city and castle of Zamora. The defection of these places, two of the most considerable in the province of Leon, and peculiarly important to the king of Portugal from their vicinity to his dominions, was severely felt by Ferdinand, who determined to advance at once against his rival and bring their quarrel to the issue of a battle; in this, acting in opposition to the more cautious counsel of his father, who recommended the policy, usually judged most prudent for an invaded country, of acting on the defensive, instead of risking all on the chances of a single action.

Ferdinand arrived before Toro on the 19th of July, and immediately drew up his army before its walls in order of battle. As the king of Portugal, however, still kept within his defenses, Ferdinand sent a herald into his camp, to defy him to a fair field of fight with his whole army, or, if he declined this, to invite him to decide their differences by personal combat. Alfonso accepted the latter alternative; but, a dispute arising respecting the guaranty for the performance of the engagements on either side, the whole affair evaporated, as usual, in an empty vaunt of chivalry.

The Castilian army, from the haste with which it had been mustered, was wholly deficient in battering artillery, and in other means for annoying a fortified city; and, as its communications were cut off in consequence of the neighboring fortresses being in possession of the enemy, it soon became straitened for provisions. It was accordingly decided in a council of war to retreat without further delay. No sooner was this determination known than it excited general dissatisfaction throughout the camp. The soldiers loudly complained that the king was betrayed by his nobles; and a party of over-loyal Biscayans, inflamed by the suspicions of a conspiracy against his person, actually broke into the church where Ferdinand was conferring with his officers, and bore him off in their arms to his own tent, notwithstanding his reiterated explanations and remonstrances. The ensuing retreat was conducted in so disorderly a manner by the mutinous soldiery that Alfonso, says a contemporary, had he but sallied with two thousand horse, might have routed and perhaps annihilated the whole army. Some of the troops were detached to reinforce the garrisons of the loyal cities, but most of them dispersed again among their native mountains. The citadel of Toro soon afterwards capitulated. The archbishop of Toledo, considering these events as decisive of the fortunes of the war, now openly joined the king of Portugal at the head of five hundred lances, boasting at the same time that he "had raised Isabella from the distaff, and would soon send her back to it again."

So disastrous an introduction to the campaign might indeed well fill Isabella's bosom with anxiety. The revolutionary movements which had so long agitated Castile had so far unsettled every man's political principles, and the allegiance of even the most loyal hung so loosely about them, that it was difficult to estimate how far it might be shaken by such a blow occurring at this crisis. Fortunately, Alfonso was in no condition to profit by his success. His Castilian allies had experienced the greatest difficulty in enlisting their vassals in the Portuguese cause, and, far from furnishing him with the contingents which he had expected, found sufficient occupation in the defense of their own territories against the loyal partisans of Isabella. At the same time, numerous squadrons of light cavalry from Estremadura and Andalusia, penetrating into Portugal, carried the most terrible desolation over the whole extent of its unprotected borders. The Portuguese knights loudly murmured at being cooped up in Toro while their own country was made the theater of war; and Alfonso saw himself under the necessity of detaching so considerable a portion of his army for the defense of his frontier as entirely to cripple his future operations. So deeply, indeed, was he impressed by these circumstances with the difficulty of his enterprise, that, in a negotiation with the Castilian sovereigns at this time, he expressed a willingness to resign his claims to their crown in consideration of the cession of Galicia, together with the cities of Toro and Zamora, and a considerable sum of money. Ferdinand and his ministers, it is reported, would have accepted the proposal; but Isabella, although acquiescing in the stipulated money payment, would not consent to the dismemberment of a single inch of the Castilian territory.

In the meantime both the queen and her husband, undismayed by past reverses, were making every exertion for the reorganization of an army on a more efficient footing. To accomplish this object, an additional supply of funds became necessary, since the treasure of King Henry, delivered into their hands by Andres de Cabrera at Segovia, had been exhausted by the preceding operations. The old king of Aragon advised them to imitate their ancestor Henry the Second, of glorious memory, by making liberal grants and alienations in favor of their subjects, which they might, when more firmly seated on the throne, resume at pleasure. Isabella, however, chose rather to trust to the patriotism of her people than have recourse to so unworthy a stratagem. She accordingly convened an assembly of the states, in the month of August, 1475, at Medina del Campo. As the nation had been too far impoverished under the late reign to admit of fresh exactions, a most extraordinary expedient was devised for meeting the stipulated requisitions. It was proposed to deliver into the royal treasury half the amount of plate belonging to the churches throughout the kingdom, to be redeemed in the term of three years, for the sum of thirty *cuentos,* or millions, of maravedis. The clergy, who were very generally attached to Isabella's interests, far from discouraging this startling proposal, endeavored to vanquish the queen's repugnance to it by arguments and pertinent illustrations drawn from Scripture. This transaction certainly exhibits a degree of disinterestedness, on the part of this body, most unusual in that age and country, as well as a generous confidence in the good faith of Isabella, of which she proved herself worthy by the punctuality with which she redeemed it.

Thus provided with the necessary funds, the sovereigns set about enforcing new levies and bringing them under better discipline, as well as providing for their equipment in a manner more suitable to the exigencies of the service than was done for the preceding army. The remainder of the summer and the ensuing autumn were consumed in these preparations, as well as in placing their fortified towns in a proper posture of defense, and in the reduction of such places as held out against them. The king of Portugal, all this while, lay with his diminished forces in Toro, making a sally on one occasion only, for the relief of his friends, which was frustrated by the sleepless vigilance of Isabella.

Early in December, Ferdinand passed from the siege of Burgos, in Old Castile, to Zamora, whose inhabitants expressed a desire to return to their ancient allegiance; and, with the cooperation of the citizens, supported by a large detachment from his main army, he prepared to invest its citadel. As the possession of this post would effectually intercept Alfonso's communications with his own country, he determined to relieve it at every hazard, and for this purpose despatched a messenger into Portugal, requiring his son, Prince John, to reinforce him with such levies as he could speedily raise. All parties now looked forward with eagerness to a general battle, as to a termination of the evils of this long-protracted war.

The Portuguese prince, having with difficulty assembled a

corps amounting to two thousand lances and eight thousand infantry, took a northerly circuit round Galicia, and effected a junction with his father in Toro, on the 14th of February, 1476. Alfonso, thus reinforced, transmitted a pompous circular to the pope, the king of France, his own dominions, and those well affected to him in Castile, proclaiming his immediate intention of taking the usurper, or of driving him from the kingdom. On the night of the 17th, having first provided for the security of the city by leaving in it a powerful reserve, Alfonso drew off the residue of his army, probably not much exceeding three thousand five hundred horse and five thousand foot, well provided with artillery and with arquebuses, which latter engine was still of so clumsy and unwieldy construction as not to have entirely superseded the ancient weapons of European warfare. The Portuguese army, traversing the bridge of Toro, pursued their march along the southern side of the Douro, and reached Zamora, distant only a few leagues, before the dawn.

At break of day, the Castilians were surprised by the array of floating banners, and martial panoply glittering in the sun, from the opposite side of the river, while the discharges of artillery still more unequivocally announced the presence of the enemy. Ferdinand could scarcely believe that the Portuguese monarch, whose avowed object had been the relief of the castle of Zamora, should have selected a position so obviously unsuitable for this purpose. The intervention of the river, between him and the fortress situated at the northern extremity of the town, prevented him from relieving it, either by throwing succors into it, or by annoying the Castilian troops, who, intrenched in comparative security within the walls and houses of the city, were enabled by means of certain elevated positions, well garnished with artillery, to inflict much heavier injury on their opponents than they could possibly receive from them. Still Ferdinand's men, exposed to the double fire of the fortress and the besiegers, would willingly have come to an engagement with the latter; but the river, swollen by winter torrents, was not fordable, and the bridge, the only direct avenue to the city, was enfiladed by the enemy's cannon, so as to render a sally in that direction altogether impracticable. During this time, Isabella's squadrons of light cavalry, hovering on the skirts of the Portuguese camp, effectually cut off its supplies, and soon reduced it to great straits for subsistence. This circumstance, together with the tidings of the rapid advance of additional forces to the support of Ferdinand, determined Alfonso, contrary to all expectation, on an immediate retreat; and accordingly, on the morning of the 1st of March, being little less than a fortnight from the time in which he commenced this empty gasconade, the Portuguese army quitted its position before Zamora, with the same silence and celerity with which it had occupied it.

Ferdinand's troops would instantly have pushed after the fugitives, but the latter had demolished the southern extremity of the bridge before their departure; so that, although some few affected an immediate passage in boats, the great body of the army was necessarily detained until the repairs were completed, which occupied more than three hours. With all the expedition they could use, therefore, and leaving their artillery behind them, they did not succeed in coming up with the enemy until nearly four o'clock in the afternoon, as the latter was defiling through a narrow pass formed by a crest of precipitous hills on the one side, and the Douro on the other, at the distance of about five miles from the city of Toro.

A council of war was then called, to decide on the expediency of an immediate assault. It was objected, that the strong position of Toro would effectually cover the retreat of the Portuguese in case of their discomfiture; that they would speedily be reinforced by fresh recruits from that city, which would make them more than a match for Ferdinand's army, exhausted by a toilsome march, as well as by its long fast, which it had not broken since the morning; and that the celerity with which it had moved had compelled it not only to abandon its artillery, but to leave a considerable portion of the heavy-armed infantry in the rear. Notwithstanding the weight of these objections, such were the high spirit of the troops and their eagerness to come to action, sharpened by the view of the quarry, which after a wearisome chase seemed ready to fall into their hands, that they were thought more than sufficient to counterbalance every physical disadvantage; and the question of battle was decided in the affirmative.

As the Castilian army emerged from the defile into a wide and open plain, they found that the enemy had halted, and was already forming in order of battle. The king of Portugal led the center, with the archbishop of Toledo on his right wing, its extremity resting on the Douro; while the left, comprehending the arquebusiers and the strength of the cavalry, was placed under the command of his son, Prince John. The numerical force of the two armies, although in favor of the Portuguese, was nearly equal, amounting pobably in each to less than ten thousand men, about one-third being cavalry. Ferdinand took his station in the center, opposite his rival, having the admiral and the duke of Alva on his left; while his right wing, distributed into six battles or divisions, under their several commanders, was supported by a detachment of men-at-arms from the provinces of Leon and Galicia.

The action commenced in this quarter. The Castilians, raising the war-cry of "St. James and St. Lazarus," advanced on the enemy's left under Prince John, but were saluted with such a brisk and well-directed fire from his arquebusiers, that their ranks were disconcerted. The Portuguese men-at-arms, charging them at the same time, augmented their confusion, and compelled them to fall back precipitately on the narrow pass in their rear, where, being supported by some fresh detachments from the reserve, they were with difficulty rallied by their officers, and again brought into the field. In the meanwhile, Ferdinand closed with the enemy's center, and the action soon became general along the whole line. The battle raged with redoubled fierceness in the quarter where the presence of the two monarchs infused new ardor into their soldiers, who fought as if conscious that this struggle was to decide the fate of their masters. The lances were shivered at the first encounter, and, as the ranks of the two armies mingled with each other, the men fought hand to hand with their swords, with a fury sharpened by the ancient rivalry of the two nations, making the whole a contest of physical strength rather than skill.

The royal standard of Portugal was torn to shreds in the attempt to seize it on the one side and to preserve it on the other; while its gallant bearer, Edward de Almeyda, after losing first his right arm, and then his left, in its defense, held it firmly with his teeth until he was cut down by the assailants. The armor of this knight was to be seen as late as Mariana's time, in the cathedral church of Toledo, where it was preserved as a trophy of this desperate act of heroism, which brings to mind a similar feat recorded in Grecian story.

The old archbishop of Toledo, and the cardinal Mendoza, who, like his reverend rival, had exchanged the crosier for the corselet, were to be seen on that day in the thickest of the *mêlée*. The holy wars with the infidel perpetuated the unbecoming spectacle of militant ecclesiastics among the Spaniards, to a still later period, and long after it had disappeared from the rest of civilized Europe.

At length, after an obstinate struggle of more than three hours, the valor of the Castilian troops prevailed, and the Portuguese were seen to give way in all directions. The duke of Alva, by succeeding in turning their flank while they were thus vigorously pressed in front, completed their disorder, and soon converted their retreat into a rout. Some, attempting to cross the Douro, were drowned; and many, who endeavored to effect an entrance into Toro, were entangled in the narrow defile of the bridge, and fell by the sword of their pursuers, or miserably perished in the river, which, bearing along their mutilated corpses, brought tidings of the fatal victory to Zamora. Such were the heat and fury of the pursuit, that the intervening night, rendered darker than usual by a driving rain-storm, alone saved the scattered remains of the army from destruction. Several Portuguese companies, under favor of this obscurity, contrived to elude their foes by shouting the Castilian battle-cry. Prince John, retiring with a fragment of his broken squadrons to a neighboring eminence, succeeded, by lighting fires and sounding his trumpets, in rallying round him a number of fugitives; and, as the position he occupied was too strong to be readily forced, and the Castilian troops were too weary, and well satisfied with their victory, to attempt it, he retained possession of it till morning, when he made good his retreat into Toro. The king of Portugal, who was missing, was supposed to have perished in the battle, until, by advices received from him late on the following day, it was ascertained that he had escaped without personal injury, and with three or four attendants only, to the fortified castle of Castro Nuño, some leagues distant from the field of action. Numbers of his troops, attempting to escape across the neighboring frontiers into their own country, were maimed or massacred by the Spanish peasants, in retaliation of the excesses wantonly committed by them in their invasion of Castile. Ferdinand, shocked at this barbarity, issued orders for the protection of their persons, and freely gave safe-conducts to such as desired to return into Portugal. He even, with a degree of humanity more honorable, as well as more rare, than military success, distributed clothes and money to several prisoners brought into Zamora in a state of utter destitution, and enabled them to return in safety to their own country.

The Castilian monarch remained on the field of battle till after midnight, when he returned to Zamora, being followed in the morning by the cardinal of Spain and the admiral Henriquez, at the head of the victorious legions. Eight standards, with the greater part of the baggage, were taken in the engagement, and more than two thousand of the enemy slain or made prisoners. Queen Isabella, on receiving tidings of the event at Tordesillas, where she then was, ordered a procession to the church of St. Paul in the suburbs, in which she herself joined, walking barefoot with all humility, and offered up a devout thanksgiving to the God of battles for the victory with which he had crowned her arms.

It was indeed a most auspicious victory, not so much from the immediate loss inflicted on the enemy, as from its moral influence on the Castilian nation. Such as had before vacillated in their faith, and, in the expressive language of Bernaldez, "estaban aviva quien vence"—were prepared to take sides with the strongest—now openly proclaimed their allegiance to Ferdinand and Isabella; while most of those who had been arrayed in arms, or had manifested by any other overt act their hostility to the government, vied with each other in demonstrations of the most loyal submission, and sought to make the best terms for themselves which they could. Among these latter, the duke of Arevalo, who indeed had made overtures to this effect some time previous through the agency of his son, together with the grand master of Calatrava, and his brother, the count of Urueña, experienced the lenity of government, and were confirmed in the entire possession of their estates. The two principal delinquents, the marquis of Villena and the archbishop of Toledo, made a show of resistance for some time longer, but, after witnessing the demolition of their castles, the capture of their towns, the desertion of their vassals, and the sequestration of their revenues, were fain to purchase a pardon at the price of the most humble concessions, and the forfeiture of an ample portion of their domains.

The castle of Zamora, expecting no further succors from Portugal, speedily surrendered, and this event was soon followed by the reduction of Madrid, Baeza, Toro, and other principal cities; so that, in little more than six months from the date of the battle, the whole kingdom, with the exception of a few insignificant posts still garrisoned by the enemy, had acknowledged the supremacy of Ferdinand and Isabella.

Soon after the victory of Toro, Ferdinand was enabled to concentrate a force amounting to fifty thousand men, for the purpose of repelling the French from Guipuscoa, from which they had already twice been driven by the intrepid natives, and whence they again retired with precipitation on receiving news of the king's approach.

Alfonso, finding his authority in Castile thus rapidly melting away before the rising influence of Ferdinand and Isabella, withdrew with his virgin bride into Portugal, where he formed the resolution of visiting France in person, and soliciting succor from his ancient ally, Louis the Eleventh. In spite of every remonstrance, he put this extraordinary scheme into execution. He reached France, with a retinue of two hundred followers, in the month of September. He experienced everywhere the honors due to his exalted rank, and to the signal mark of confidence which he thus exhibited towards the French king. The keys of the cities were delivered into his hands, the prisoners were released from their dungeons, and his progress was attended by a general jubilee. His brother monarch, however, excused himself from affording more substantial proofs of his regard, until he should have closed the war then pending between him and Burgundy, and until Alfonso should have fortified his title to the Castilian crown by obtaining from the pope a dispensation for his marriage with Joanna.

The defeat and death of the duke of Burgundy, whose camp before Nancy Alfonso visited in the depth of winter, with the chimerical purpose of effecting a reconciliation between him and Louis, removed the former of these impediments; as, in good time, the compliance of the pope did the latter. But the king of

Portugal found himself no nearer the object of his negotiations; and, after waiting a whole year a needy suppliant at the court of Louis, he at length ascertained that his insidious host was concerting an arrangement with his mortal foes, Ferdinand and Isabella. Alfonso, whose character always had a spice of Quixotism in it, seems to have completely lost his wits at this last reverse of fortune. Overwhelmed with shame at his own credulity, he felt himself unable to encounter the ridicule which awaited his return to Portugal, and secretly withdrew, with two or three domestics only, to an obscure village in Normandy, whence he transmitted an epistle to Prince John, his son, declaring "that, as all earthly vanities were dead within his bosom, he resolved to lay up an imperishable crown by performing a pilgrimage to the Holy Land, and devoting himself to the service of God in some retired monastery"; and he concluded with requesting his son "to assume the sovereignty at once, in the same manner as if he had heard of his father's death."

Fortunately Alfonso's retreat was detected before he had time to put his extravagant project in execution, and his trusty followers succeeded, though with considerable difficulty, in diverting him from it; while the king of France, willing to be rid of his importunate guest, and unwilling perhaps to incur the odium of having driven him to so desperate an extremity as that of his projected pilgrimage, provided a fleet of ships to transport him back to his own dominions, where, to complete the farce, he arrived just five days after the ceremony of his son's coronation as king of Portugal (November 15, 1478). Nor was it destined that the luckless monarch should solace himself, as he had hoped, in the arms of his youthful bride; since the pliant pontiff, Sixtus the Fourth, was ultimately persuaded by the court of Castile to issue a new bull overruling the dispensation formerly conceded, on the ground that it had been obtained by a misrepresentation of facts.

Prince John, whether influenced by filial piety or prudence, resigned the crown of Portugal to his father, soon after his return; and the old monarch was no sooner reinstated in his authority than, burning with a thirst for vengeance, which made him insensible to every remonstrance, he again prepared to throw his country into combustion by reviving his enterprise against Castile.

While these hostile movements were in progress (1478), Ferdinand, leaving his consort in possession of a sufficient force for the protection of the frontiers, made a journey into Biscay for the purpose of an interview with his father, the king of Aragon, to concert measures for the pacification of Navarre, which still continued to be rent with those sanguinary feuds that were bequeathed like a precious legacy from one generation to another. In the autumn of the same year a treaty of peace was definitively adjusted between the plenipotentiaries of Castile and France, at St. Jean de Luz, in which it was stipulated, as a principal article, that Louis the Eleventh should disconnect himself from his alliance with Portugal, and give no further support to the pretensions of Joanna.

Thus released from apprehension in this quarter, the sovereigns were enabled to give their undivided attention to the defense of the western borders. Isabella, accordingly, early in the ensuing winter, passed into Estremadura for the purpose of repelling the Portuguese, and still more of suppressing the insurrectionary movements of certain of her own subjects, who, encouraged by the vicinity of Portugal, carried on from their private fortresses a most desolating and predatory warfare over the circumjacent territory. Private mansions and farmhouses were pillaged and burnt to the ground, the cattle and crops swept away in their forays, the highways beset, so that all traveling was at an end, all communication cut off, and a rich and populous district converted at once into a desert. Isabella, supported by a body of regular troops and a detachment of the Holy Brotherhood, took her station at Truxillo, as a central position, whence she might operate on the various points with greatest facility. Her counselors remonstrated against this exposure of her person in the very heart of the disaffected country; but she replied that "it was not for her to calculate perils or fatigues in her own cause, nor by an unseasonable timidity to dishearten her friends, with whom she was now resolved to remain until she had brought the war to a conclusion." She then gave immediate orders for laying siege at the same time to the fortified towns of Medellin, Merida, and Deleytosa.

At this juncture the infanta Doña Beatriz of Portugal, sister-in-law of King Alfonso, and maternal aunt of Isabella, touched with grief at the calamities in which she saw her country involved by the chimerical ambition of her brother, offered herself as the mediator of peace between the belligerent nations. Agreeably to her proposal, an interview took place between her and Queen Isabella at the frontier town of Alcantara. As the conferences of the fair negotiators experienced none of the embarrassments usually incident to such deliberations, growing out of jealousy, distrust, and a mutual design to overreach, but were conducted in perfect good faith, and a sincere desire, on both sides, of establishing a cordial reconciliation, they resulted, after eight days' discussion, in a treaty of peace, with which the Portuguese infanta returned into her own country, in order to obtain the sanction of her royal brother. The articles contained in it, however, were too unpalatable to receive an immediate assent; and it was not until the expiration of six months, during which Isabella, far from relaxing, persevered with increased energy in her original plan of operations, that the treaty was formally ratified by the court of Lisbon (September 24, 1479).

It was stipulated in this compact that Alfonso should relinquish the title and armorial bearings which he had assumed as king of Castile; that he should resign his claims to the hand of Joanna, and no longer maintain her pretensions to the Castilian throne; that that lady should make the election within six months, either to quit Portugal forever, or to remain there on the condition of wedding Don John, the infant son of Ferdinand and Isabella, so soon as he should attain a marriageable age, or to retire into a convent and take the veil; that a general amnesty should be granted to all such Castilians as had supported Joanna's cause; and, finally, that the concord between the two nations should be cemented by the union of Alonso, son of the prince of Portugal, with the infanta Isabella of Castile.

Thus terminated, after a duration of four years and a half, the War of the Succession. It had fallen with peculiar fury on the border provinces of Leon and Estremadura, which, from their local position, had necessarily been kept in constant collision with the enemy. Its baneful effects were long visible there, not only in the general devastation and distress of the country, but in the moral disorganization which the licentious and predatory habits of the soldiers necessarily introduced among a simple peasantry. In a personal view, however, the war had terminated most triumphantly for Isabella, whose wise and vigorous administration, seconded by her husband's vigilance, had dispelled the storm which threatened to overwhelm her from abroad, and established her in undisturbed possession of the throne of her ancestors.

Joanna's interests alone were compromised, or rather sacrificed, by the treaty. She readily discerned in the provision for her marriage with an infant still in the cradle, only a flimsy veil intended to disguise the king of Portugal's desertion of her cause. Disgusted with a world in which she had hitherto experienced nothing but misfortune herself, and been the innocent cause of so much to others, she determined to renounce it forever, and seek a shelter in the peaceful shades of the cloister. She accordingly entered the convent of Santa Clara at Coimbra, where, in the following year, she pronounced the irrevocable vows which divorce the unhappy subject of them forever from her species. Two envoys from Castile, Ferdinand de Talavera, Isabella's confessor, and Dr. Diaz de Madrigal, one of her council, assisted at this affecting ceremony; and the reverend father, in a copious exhortation addressed to the youthful novice, assured her "that she had chosen the better part approved in the Evangelists; that, as spouse of the Church, her chastity would be prolific of all spiritual delights; her subjection, liberty—the only true liberty, partaking more of Heaven than of earth. No kinsman," continued the disinterested preacher, "no true friend, or faithful counselor, would divert you from so holy a purpose."

Not long after this event, King Alfonso, penetrated with grief at the loss of his destined bride—the "excellent lady," as the Portuguese continue to call her—resolved to imitate her example, and exchange his royal robes for the humble habit of a Franciscan friar. He consequently made preparation for resigning his crown anew, and retiring to the monastery of Varatojo, on a bleak eminence near the Atlantic Ocean, when he suddenly fell ill, at Cintra, of a disorder which terminated his existence, on the 28th of August, 1481. Alfonso's fiery character, in which all the elements of love, chivalry, and religion were blended together, resembled that of some paladin of romance; as the chimerical enterprises in which he was perpetually engaged seem rather to belong to the age of knight-errantry than to the fifteenth century.

In the beginning of the same year in which the pacification with Portugal secured to the sovereigns the undisputed possession of Castile, another crown devolved on Ferdinand by the death of his father, the king of Aragon, who expired at Barcelona, on the 20th of January, 1479, in the eighty-third year of his age. Such was his admirable constitution, that he retained not only his intellectual but his bodily vigor unimpaired to the last. His long life was consumed in civil faction or foreign wars; and his restless spirit seemed to take delight in these tumultuous scenes, as best fitted to develop its various energies. He combined, however, with this intrepid and even ferocious temper, an address in the management of affairs, which led him to rely, for the accomplishment of his purposes, much more on negotiation than on positive force. He may be said to have been one of the first monarchs who brought into vogue that refined science of the cabinet, which was so profoundly studied by statesmen at the close of the fifteenth century, and on which his own son Ferdinand furnished the most practical commentary.

The crown of Navarre, which he had so shamelessly usurped, devolved, on his decease, on his guilty daughter Leonora, countess of Foix, who . . . survived to enjoy it only three short weeks. Aragon, with its extensive dependencies, descended to Ferdinand. Thus the two crowns of Aragon and Castile, after a separation of more than four centuries, became indissolubly united, and the foundations were laid of the magnificent empire which was destined to overshadow every other European monarchy.

FROM CHAPTER VI

Internal Adminstration of Castile

1475–1482

I have deferred to the present chapter a consideration of the important changes introduced into the interior administration of Castile, after the accession of Isabella, in order to present a connected and comprehensive view of them to the reader without interrupting the progress of the military narrative. The subject may afford an agreeable relief to the dreary details of blood and battle with which we have been so long occupied, and which were rapidly converting the garden of Europe into a wilderness. Such details, indeed, seem to have the deepest interest for contemporary writers; but the eye of posterity, unclouded by personal interest or passion, turns with satisfaction from them to those cultivated arts which can make the wilderness to blossom as the rose.

If there be any being on earth that may be permitted to remind us of the Deity himself, it is the ruler of a mighty empire, who employs the high powers intrusted to him exclusively for the benefit of his people; who, endowed with intellectual gifts corresponding with his station, in an age of comparative barbarism, endeavors to impart to his land the light of civilization which illumines his own bosom, and to create from the elements of discord the beautiful fabric of social order. Such was Isabella; and such the age in which she lived. And fortunate was it for Spain that her scepter, at this crisis, was swayed by a sovereign possessed of sufficient wisdom to devise, and energy to execute, the most salutary schemes of reform, and thus to infuse a new principle of vitality into a government fast sinking into premature decrepitude.

The whole plan of reform introduced into the government by Ferdinand and Isabella, or more properly by the latter, to whom the internal administration of Castile was principally referred, was not fully unfolded until the completion of her reign. But the most important modifications were adopted previously to the war of Granada in 1482. These may be embraced under the following heads. I. The efficient administration of justice. II. The codification of the laws. III. The depression of the nobles. IV. The vindication of ecclesiastical rights belonging to the crown from the usurpation of the papal see. V. The regulation of trade. VI. The pre-eminence of the royal authority.

I. The administration of justice. In the dismal anarchy which prevailed in Henry the Fourth's reign, the authority of the monarch and of the royal judges had fallen into such contempt that the law was entirely without force. The cities afforded no better protection than the open country. Every man's hand seemed to be lifted against his neighbor. Property was plundered; persons were violated; the most holy sanctuaries profaned; and the numerous fortresses scattered throughout the country, instead of sheltering the weak, converted into dens of robbers. Isabella saw no better way of checking this unbounded license than to direct against it that popular engine, the Santa Hermandad, or Holy Brotherhood, which had more than once shaken the Castilian monarchs on their throne.

The project for the reorganization of this institution was introduced into the cortes held, the year after Isabella's accession, at Madrigal, in 1476. It was carried into effect by the junta of deputies from the different cities of the kingdom, convened at Dueñas in the same year. The new institution differed essentially from the ancient hermandades, since, instead of being partial in its extent, it was designed to embrace the whole kingdom; and, instead of being directed, as had often been the case, against the crown itself, it was set in motion at the suggestion of the latter, and limited in its operation to the maintenance of public order. The cries reserved for its jurisdiction were all violence or theft committed on the highways or in the open country, and in cities by such offenders as escaped into the country; house-breaking; rape; and resistance of justice. The specification of these crimes shows their frequency; and the reason for designating the open country, as the particular theater for the operations of the hermandad, was the facility which criminals possessed there for eluding the pursuit of justice, especially under shelter of the strongholds or fortresses with which it was plentifully studded.

An annual contribution of eighteen thousand maravedis was assessed on every hundred vecinos or householders, for the equipment and maintenance of a horseman, whose duty it was to arrest offenders and enforce the sentence of the law. On the flight of a criminal, the tocsins of the villages through which he was supposed to have passed were sounded, and the quadrilleros or officers of the brotherhood, stationed on the different points, took up the pursuit with such promptness as left little chance of escape. A court of two alcaldes was established in every town containing thirty families, for the trial of all crimes within the jurisdiction of the hermandad; and an appeal lay from them in specified cases to a supreme council. A general junta, composed of deputies from the cities throughout the kingdom, was annually convened for the regulation of affairs, and their instructions were transmitted to provincial juntas, who superintended the execution of them. The laws enacted at different times in these assemblies were compiled into a code, under the sanction of the junta general, at Tordelaguna, in 1485. The penalties for theft, which are literally written in blood, are specified in this code with singular precision. The most petty larceny was punished with stripes, the loss of a member, or of life itself; and the law was administered with an unsparing rigor, which nothing but the extreme necessity of the case could justify. Capital executions were conducted by shooting the criminal with arrows. The enactment relating to this provides that "the convict shall receive the sacrament like a Catholic Christian, and after that be executed as speedily as possible, in order that his soul may pass the more securely."

Notwithstanding the popular constitution of the hermandad, and the obvious advantages attending its introduction at this juncture, it experienced so decided an opposition from the nobility, who discerned the check it was likely to impose on their authority, that it required all the queen's address and perseverance to effect its general adoption. The constable de Haro, however, a nobleman of great weight from his personal character, and the most extensive landed proprietor in the north, was at length prevailed on to introduce it among his vassals. His example was gradually followed by others of the same rank; and when the city of Seville and the great lords of Andalusia had consented to receive it, it speedily became established throughout the kingdom. Thus a standing body of troops, two thousand in number, thoroughly equipped and mounted, was placed at the disposal of the crown, to enforce the law and suppress domestic insurrection. The supreme junta, which regulated the counsels of the hermandad, constituted moreover a sort of inferior cortes, relieving the exigencies of government, as we shall see hereafter, on more than one occasion, by important supplies of men and money. By the activity of this new military police, the country was, in the course of a few years, cleared of its swarms of banditti, as well as of the robber chieftains, whose strength had enabled them to defy the law. The ministers of justice found a sure protection in the independent discharge of their duties; and the blessings of personal security and social order, so long estranged from the nation, were again restored to it.

The important benefits resulting from the institution of the hermandad secured its confirmation by successive cortes, for the period of twenty-two years, in spite of the repeated opposition of the aristocracy. At length, in 1498, the objects for which it was established having been completely obtained, it was deemed advisable to relieve the nation from the heavy charges which its maintenance imposed. The great salaried officers were dismissed; a few subordinate functionaries were retained for the administration of justice, over whom the regular courts of criminal law possessed appellate jurisdiction; and the magnificent apparatus of the Santa Hermandad, stripped of all but the terrors of its name, dwindled into an ordinary police, such as it has existed, with various modifications of form, down to the present century.

Isabella was so intent on the prosecution of her schemes of reform, that, even in the minuter details, she frequently superintended the execution of them herself. For this she was admirably fitted by her personal address, and presence of mind in danger, and by the influence which a conviction of her integrity gave her over the minds of the people. A remarkable exemplification of this occurred, the year but one after her coronation, at Segovia. The inhabitants, secretly instigated by the bishop of that place and some of the principal citizens, rose against Cabrera, marquis of Moya, to whom the government of the city had been intrusted, and who had made himself generally unpopular by his strict discipline. They even proceeded so far as to obtain possession of the outworks of the citadel, and to compel the deputy of the alcayde, who was himself absent, to take shelter, together with the princess Isabella, then the only daughter of the sovereigns, in the interior defenses, where they were rigorously blockaded.

The queen, on receiving tidings of the event at Tordesillas, mounted her horse and proceeded with all possible despatch towards Segovia, attended by Cardinal Mendoza, the count of Benavente, and a few others of her court. At some distance from the city, she was met by a deputation of the inhabitants, requesting her to leave behind the count of Benavente and the marchioness of Moya (the former of whom as the intimate friend, and the latter as the wife, of the alcayde, were peculiarly obnoxious to the citizens), or they could not answer for the consequences. Isabella haughtily replied that "she was queen

of Castile; that the city was hers, moreover, by right of inheritance; and that she was not used to receive conditions from rebellious subjects." Then, pressing forward with her little retinue
through one of the gates, which remained in the hands of her
friends, she effected her entrance into the citadel.

The populace, in the meanwhile, assembling in greater numbers than before, continued to show the most hostile dispositions, calling out, "Death to the alcayde! Attack the castle!" Isabella's attendants, terrified at the tumult, and at the preparations
which the people were making to put their menaces into execution, besought their mistress to cause the gates to be secured
more strongly, as the only mode of defense against the infuriated mob. But, instead of listening to their counsel, she bade
them remain quietly in the apartment, and descended herself into
the courtyard, where she ordered the portals to be thrown open
for the admission of the people. She stationed herself at the
further extremity of the area, and, as the populace poured in,
calmly demanded the cause of the insurrection. "Tell me," said
she, "what are your grievances, and I will do all in my power
to redress them; for I am sure that what is for your interest must
be also for mine, and for that of the whole city." The insurgents,
abashed by the unexpected presence of their sovereign, as well
as by her cool and dignified demeanor, replied that all they
desired was the removal of Cabrera from the government of the
city. "He is deposed already," answered the queen, "and you
have my authority to turn out such of his officers as are still in
the castle, which I shall intrust to one of my own servants, on
whom I can rely." The people, pacified by these assurances,
shouted, "Long live the queen!" and eagerly hastened to obey
her mandates.

After thus turning aside the edge of popular fury, Isabella
proceeded with her retinue to the royal residence in the city,
attended by the fickle multitude, whom she again addressed on
arriving there, admonishing them to return to their vocations, as
this was no time for calm inquiry, and promising that, if they
would send three or four of their number to her on the morrow
to report the extent of their grievances, she would examine into
the affair, and render justice to all parties. The mob accordingly
dispersed, and the queen, after a candid examination, having
ascertained the groundlessness or gross exaggeration of the

charges against Cabrera, and traced the source of the conspiracy
to the jealousy of the bishop of Segovia and his associates, reinstated the deposed alcayde in the full possession of his dignities,
which his enemies, either convinced of the altered dispositions
of the people, or believing that the favorable moment for resistance had escaped, made no further attempts to disturb. Thus
by a happy presence of mind, an affair which threatened, at its
outset, disastrous consequences, was settled without bloodshed,
or compromise of the royal dignity.

In the summer of the following year, 1477, Isabella resolved
to pay a visit to Estremadura and Andalusia, for the purpose of
composing the dissensions, and introducing a more efficient police, in these unhappy provinces; which, from their proximity to
the stormy frontier of Portugal, as well as from the feuds between the great houses of Guzman and Ponce de Leon, were
plunged in the most frightful anarchy. Cardinal Mendoza and
her other ministers remonstrated against this imprudent exposure of her person, where it was so little likely to be respected.
But she replied, "it was true there were dangers and incon-
veniences to be encountered; but her fate was in God's hands,
and she felt a confidence that he would guide to a prosperous
issue such designs as were righteous in themselves and resolutely
conducted."

Isabella experienced the most loyal and magnificent reception
from the inhabitants of Seville, where she established her headquarters. The first days of her residence there were consumed in
fêtes, tourneys, tilts of reeds, and other exercises of the Castilian
chivalry. After this she devoted her whole time to the great purpose of her visit, the reformation of abuses. She held her court
in the saloon of the alcazar, or royal castle, where she revived
the ancient practice of the Castilian sovereigns, of presiding in
person over the administration of justice. Every Friday, she
took her seat in her chair of state, on an elevated platform covered with cloth of gold, and surrounded by her council, together
with the subordinate functionaries, and the insignia of a court
of justice. The members of her privy council, and of the high
court of criminal law, sat in their official capacity every day in
the week, and the queen herself received such suits as were referred to her adjudication, saving the parties the usual expense
and procrastination of justice.

By the extraordinary despatch of the queen and her ministers, during the two months that she resided in the city, a vast number of civil and criminal causes were disposed of, a large amount of plundered property was restored to its lawful owners, and so many offenders were brought to condign punishment, that no less than four thousand suspected persons, it is computed, terrified by the prospect of speedy retribution for their crimes, escaped into the neighboring kingdoms of Portugal and Granada. The worthy burghers of Seville, alarmed at this rapid depopulation of the city, sent a deputation to the queen, to deprecate her anger, and to represent that faction had been so busy of late years in their unhappy town, that there was scarcely a family to be found in it some of whose members were not more or less involved in the guilt. Isabella, who was naturally of a benign disposition, considering that enough had probably been done to strike a salutary terror into the remaining delinquents, was willing to temper justice with mercy, and accordingly granted an amnesty for all past offenses, save heresy, on the condition, however, of a general restitution of such property as had been unlawfully seized and retained during the period of anarchy.

But Isabella became convinced that all arrangements for establishing permanent tranquillity in Seville would be ineffectual so long as the feud continued between the great families of Guzman and Ponce de Leon. The duke of Medina Sidonia and the marquis of Cadiz, the heads of these houses, had possessed themselves of the royal towns and fortresses, as well as of those which, belonging to the city, were scattered over its circumjacent territory, where, as has been previously stated, they carried on war against each other, like independent potentates. The former of these grandees had been the loyal supporter of Isabella in the War of the Succession. The marquis of Cadiz, on the other hand, connected by marriage with the house of Pacheco, had cautiously withheld his allegiance, although he had not testified his hostility by any overt act. While the queen was hesitating as to the course she should pursue in reference to the marquis, who still kept himself aloof in his fortified castle of Xerez, he suddenly presented himself by night at her residence in Seville, accompanied only by two or three attendants. He took this step, doubtless, from the conviction that the Portuguese faction had nothing further to hope in a kingdom where Isabella reigned not only by the fortune of war, but by the affections of the people; and he now eagerly proffered his allegiance to her, excusing his previous conduct as he best could. The queen was too well satisfied with the submission, however tardy, of this formidable vassal, to call him to severe account for past delinquencies. She exacted from him, however, the full restitution of such domains and fortresses as he had filched from the crown and from the city of Seville, on condition of similar concessions by his rival, the duke of Medina Sidonia. She next attempted to establish a reconciliation between these belligerent grandees; but, aware that, however pacific might be their demonstrations for the present, there could be little hope of permanently allaying the inherited feuds of a century whilst the neighborhood of the parties to each other must necessarily multiply fresh causes of disgust, she caused them to withdraw from Seville to their estates in the country, and by this expedient succeeded in extinguishing the flame of discord.

In the following year, 1478, Isabella accompanied her husband in a tour through Andalusia, for the immediate purpose of reconnoitering the coast. In the course of this progress, they were splendidly entertained by the duke and marquis at their patrimonial estates. They afterwards proceeded to Cordova, where they adopted a similar policy to that pursued at Seville, compelling the count de Cabra, connected with the blood royal, and Alonso de Aguilar, lord of Montilla, whose factions had long desolated this fair city, to withdraw into the country, and restore the immense possessions which they had usurped both from the municipality and the crown.

One example among others may be mentioned, of the rectitude and severe impartiality with which Isabella administered justice, that occurred in the case of a wealthy Galician knight, named Alvaro Yañez de Lugo. This person, being convicted of a capital offense, attended with the most aggravating circumstances, sought to obtain a commutation of his punishment by the payment of forty thousand doblas of gold to the queen, a sum exceeding at that time the annual rents of the crown. Some of Isabella's counselors would have persuaded her to accept the donative and appropriate it to the pious purposes of the Moorish war. But, far from being blinded by their sophistry, she suffered the law to take its course, and, in order to place her conduct above every suspicion of a mercenary motive, allowed his estates, which might legally have been confiscated to the crown, to descend to his natural heirs. Nothing contributed more to re-establish the supremacy of law in this reign than the certainty of its execution, without respect to wealth or rank; for the insubordination prevalent throughout Castile was chiefly imputable to persons of this description, who, if they failed to defeat justice by force, were sure of doing so by the corruption of its ministers.

Ferdinand and Isabella employed the same vigorous measures in the other parts of their dominions, which had proved so successful in Andalusia, for the extirpation of the hordes of banditti, and of the robber-knights, who differed in no respect from the former but in their superior power. In Galicia alone, fifty fortresses, the strongholds of tyranny, were razed to the ground, and fifteen hundred malefactors, it was computed, were compelled to fly the kingdom. "The wretched inhabitants of the mountains," says a writer of that age, "who had long since despaired of justice, blessed God for their deliverance, as it were, from a deplorable captivity."

While the sovereigns were thus personally occupied with the suppression of domestic discord, and the establishment of an efficient police, they were not inattentive to the higher tribunals, to whose keeping, chiefly, were intrusted the personal rights and property of the subject. They reorganized the royal or privy council, whose powers, although . . . principally of an administrative nature, had been gradually encroaching on those of the superior courts of law. During the last century, this body had consisted of prelates, knights, and lawyers, whose numbers and relative proportions had varied in different times. The right of the great ecclesiastics and nobles to a seat in it was, indeed, recognized, but the transaction of business was reserved for the counselors specially appointed. Much the larger proportion of these, by the new arrangement, was made up of jurists, whose professional education and experience eminently qualified them for the station. The specific duties and interior management of the council were prescribed with sufficient accuracy. Its authority as a court of justice was carefully limited; but, as it was charged with the principal executive duties of government, it was consulted in all important transactions by the sovereigns, who paid great deference to its opinions, and very frequently assisted at its deliberations.

No change was made in the high criminal court of alcaldes de corte, except in its forms of proceeding. But the royal audience, or chancery, the supreme and final court of appeal in civil causes, was entirely remodeled. The place of its sittings, before indeterminate, and consequently occasioning much trouble and cost to the litigants, was fixed at Valladolid. Laws were passed to protect the tribunal from the interference of the crown, and the queen was careful to fill the bench with magistrates whose wisdom and integrity would afford the best guarantee for a faithful interpretation of the law.

In the cortes of Madrigal (1476), and still more in the celebrated one of Toledo (1480), many excellent provisions were made for the equitable administration of justice, as well as for regulating the tribunals. The judges were to ascertain every week, either by personal inspection or report, the condition of the prisons, the number of the prisoners, and the nature of the offenses for which they were confined. They were required to bring them to a speedy trial, and afford every facility for their defense. An attorney was provided at the public expense, under the title of "advocate for the poor," whose duty it was to defend the suits of such as were unable to maintain them at their own cost. Severe penalties were enacted against venality in the judges, a gross evil under the preceding reigns, as well as against such counsel as took exorbitant fees, or even maintained actions that were manifestly unjust. Finally, commissioners were appointed to inspect and make report of the proceedings of municipal and other inferior courts throughout the kingdom.

The sovereigns testified their respect for the law by reviving the ancient but obsolete practice of presiding personally in the tribunals, at least once a week. "I well remember," says one of their court, "to have seen the queen, together with the Catholic king, her husband, sitting in judgment in the alcazar of Madrid, every Friday, dispensing justice to all such, great and small, as came to demand it. This was indeed the golden age of justice," continues the enthusiastic writer, "and since our sainted mistress has been taken from us, it has been more difficult, and far more costly, to transact business with a stripling of a secretary, than it was with the queen and all her ministers."

By the modifications then introduced, the basis was laid of the judiciary system, such as it has been perpetuated to the present age. The law acquired an authority which, in the language of a Spanish writer, "caused a decree, signed by two or three judges, to be more respected since that time than an army before." But perhaps the results of this improved administration cannot be better conveyed than in the words of an eyewitness. "Whereas," says Pulgar, "the kingdom was previously filled with banditti and malefactors of every description, who committed the most diabolical excesses, in open contempt of law, there was now such terror impressed on the hearts of all, that no one dared to lift his arm against another, or even to assail him with contumelious or discourteous language. The knight and the squire, who had before oppressed the laborer, were intimidated by the fear of that justice which was sure to be executed on them; the roads were swept of the banditti; the fortresses, the strongholds of violence, were thrown open, and the whole nation, restored to tranquillity and order, sought no other redress than that afforded by the operation of the law."

II. Codification of the laws. Whatever reforms might have been introduced into the Castilian judicatures, they would have been of little avail without a corresponding improvement in the system of jurisprudence by which their decisions were to be regulated. This was made up of the Visigothic code, as the basis, the fueros of the Castilian princes, as far back as the eleventh century, and the "Siete Partidas," the famous compilation of Alfonso the Tenth, digested chiefly from maxims of the civil law. The deficiencies of these ancient codes had been gradually supplied by such an accumulation of statutes and ordinances as rendered the legislation of Castile in the highest degree complex, and often contradictory. The embarrassment resulting from this occasioned, as may be imagined, much tardiness, as well as uncertainty, in the decisions of the courts, who, despairing of reconciling the discrepancies in their own law, governed themselves almost exclusively by the Roman, so much less accommodated, as it was, than their own, to the genius of the national institutions, as well as to the principles of freedom.

The nation had long felt the pressure of these evils, and made attempts to redress them in repeated cortes. But every effort proved unavailing during the stormy or imbecile reigns of the princes of Trastamara. At length, the subject having been resumed in the cortes of Toledo, in 1480, Dr. Alfonso Diaz de Montalvo, whose professional science had been matured under the reigns of three successive sovereigns, was charged with the commission of revising the laws of Castile, and of compiling a code which should be of general application throughout the kingdom.

This laborious undertaking was accomplished in little more than four years; and his work, which subsequently bore the title of *Ordenanças Reales,* was published, or, as the privilege expresses it, written with types, "excrito de letra de molde," at Huete, in the beginning of 1485. It was one of the first works, therefore, which received the honors of the press in Spain; and surely none could have been found, at that period, more deserving of them. It went through repeated editions in the course of that and the commencement of the following century. It was admitted as paramount authority throughout Castile; and, although the many innovations which were introduced in that age of reform required the addition of two subsidiary codes in the latter years of Isabella, the *Ordenanças* of Montalvo continued to be the guide of the tribunals down to the time of Philip the Second, and may be said to have suggested the idea, as indeed it was the basis, of the comprehensive compilation, *Nueva Recopilacion,* which has since formed the law of the Spanish monarchy.

III. Depression of the nobles. In the course of the preceding chapters, we have seen the extent of the privileges constitutionally enjoyed by the aristocracy, as well as the enormous height to which they had swollen under the profuse reigns of John the Second and Henry the Fourth. This was such, at the accession of Ferdinand and Isabella, as to disturb the balance of the constitution, and to give serious cause of apprehension both to the monarch and the people. The nobles had introduced themselves into every great post of profit or authority. They had ravished from the crown the estates on which it depended for its maintenance as well as dignity. They coined money in their own mints, like sovereign princes; and they covered the country with their fortified castles, whence they defied the law, and desolated the unhappy land with interminable feuds. It was obviously necessary for the new sovereigns to proceed with the greatest caution against this powerful and jealous body, and, above all, to attempt no measure of importance in which they would not be supported by the hearty cooperation of the nation.

The first measure which may be said to have clearly developed their policy was the organization of the hermandad, which, although ostensibly directed against offenders of a more humble description, was made to bear indirectly upon the nobility, whom it kept in awe by the number and discipline of its forces, and the promptness with which it could assemble them on the most remote points of the kingdom; while its rights of jurisdiction tended materially to abridge those of the seignorial tribunals. It was accordingly resisted with the greatest pertinacity by the aristocracy; although, as we have seen, the resolution of the queen, supported by the constancy of the commons, enabled her to triumph over all opposition, until the great objects of the institution were accomplished.

Another measure, which insensibly operated to the depression of the nobility, was making official preferment depend less exclusively on rank, and much more on personal merit, than before. "Since the hope of guerdon," says one of the statutes enacted at Toledo, "is the spur to just and honorable actions, when men perceive that offices of trust are not to descend by inheritance, but to be conferred on merit, they will strive to excel in virtue, that they may attain its reward." The sovereigns, instead of confining themselves to the grandees, frequently advanced persons of humble origin, and especially those learned in the law, to the most responsible stations, consulting them, and paying great deference to their opinions, on all matters of importance. The nobles, finding that rank was no longer the sole, or indeed the necessary, avenue to promotion, sought to secure it by attention to more liberal studies, in which they were greatly encouraged by Isabella, who admitted their children into her palace, where they were reared under her own eye.

But the boldest assaults on the power of the aristocracy were made in the famous cortes of Toledo, in 1480, which Carbajal enthusiastically styles "cosa divina para reformacion y remedio de las desordenes pasadas." The first object of its attention was the condition of the exchequer, which Henry the Fourth had so exhausted by his reckless prodigality that the clear annual revenue amounted to no more than thirty thousand ducats, a sum much inferior to that enjoyed by many private individuals; so that, stripped of his patrimony, it at last came to be said, he was "king only of the highways." Such had been the royal necessities that blank certificates of annuities assigned on the public rents were hawked about the market, and sold at such a depreciated rate that the price of an annuity did not exceed the amount of one year's income. The commons saw with alarm the weight of the burdens which must devolve on them for the maintenance of the crown thus impoverished in its resources; and they resolved to meet the difficulty by advising at once a resumption of the grants unconstitutionally made during the latter half of Henry the Fourth's reign, and the commencement of the present. This measure, however violent and repugnant to good faith it may appear at the present time, seems then to have admitted of justification, as far as the nation was concerned; since such alienation of the public revenue was in itself illegal, and contrary to the coronation oath of the sovereign; and those who accepted his obligations held them subject to the liability of their revocation, which had frequently occurred under the preceding reigns.

As the intended measure involved the interests of most of the considerable proprietors in the kingdom, who had thriven on the necessities of the crown, it was deemed proper to require the attendance of the nobility and great ecclesiastics in cortes by a special summons, which it seems had been previously omitted. Thus convened, the legislature appears, with great unanimity, and much to the credit of those most deeply affected by it, to have acquiesced in the proposed resumption of the grants, as a measure of absolute necessity. The only difficulty was to settle the principles on which the retrenchment might be most equitably made, with reference to creditors, whose claims rested on a great variety of grounds. The plan suggested by Cardinal Mendoza seems to have been partially adopted. It was decided that all whose pensions had been conferred without any corresponding services on their part should forfeit them entirely; that those who had purchased annuities should return their certificates on a reimbursement of the price paid for them; and that the remaining creditors, who composed the largest class, should retain such a proportion only of their pensions as might be judged commensurate with their services to the state.

By this important reduction, the final adjustment and execution of which were intrusted to Fernando de Talavera, the queen's confessor, a man of austere probity, the gross amount of thirty millions of maravedis, a sum equal to three-fourths of the whole revenue on Isabella's accession, was anually saved to the crown. The retrenchment was conducted with such strict impartiality that the most confidential servants of the queen, and the relatives of her husband, were among those who suffered the most severely. It is worthy of remark that no diminution whatever was made of the stipends settled on literary and charitable establishments. It may be also added that Isabella appropriated the first-fruits of this measure, by distributing the sum of twenty millions of maravedis among the widows and orphans of those loyalists who had fallen in the War of the Succession. This resumption of grants may be considered as the basis of those economical reforms which, without oppression to the subject, augmented the public revenue more than twelvefold during this auspicious reign.

Several other acts were passed by the same cortes, which had a more exclusive bearing on the nobility. They were prohibited from quartering the royal arms on their escutcheons, from being attended by a mace-bearer and a body-guard, from imitating the regal style of address in their written correspondence, and other insignia of royalty which they had arrogantly assumed. They were forbidden to erect new fortresses, and we have already seen the activity of the queen in procuring the demolition or restitution of the old. They were expressly restrained from duels, an inveterate source of mischief, for engaging in which the parties, both principals and seconds, were subjected to the penalties of treason. Isabella evinced her determination to enforce this law on the highest offenders, by imprisoning, soon after its enactment, the counts of Luna and Valencia for exchanging a cartel of defiance, until the point at issue should be settled by the regular course of justice.

It is true the haughty nobility of Castile winced more than once at finding themselves so tightly curbed by their new masters. On one occasion, a number of the principal grandees, with the duke of Infantado at their head, addressed a letter of remonstrance to the king and queen, requiring them to abolish the hermandad, as an institution burdensome to the nation, deprecating the slight degree of confidence which their highnesses reposed in their order, and requesting that four of their number might be selected to form a council for the general direction of affairs of state, by whose advice the king and queen should be governed in all matters of importance, as in the time of Henry the Fourth.

Ferdinand and Isabella received this unseasonable remonstrance with great indignation, and returned an answer couched in the haughtiest terms. "The hermandad," they said, "is an institution most salutary to the nation, and is approved by it as such. It is our province to determine who are best entitled to preferment, and to make merit the standard of it. You may follow the court, or retire to your estates, as you think best; but, so long as Heaven permits us to retain the rank with which we have been intrusted, we shall take care not to imitate the example of Henry the Fourth, in becoming a tool in the hands of our nobility." The discontented lords, who had carried so high a hand under the preceding imbecile reign, feeling the weight of an authority which rested on the affections of the people, were so disconcerted by the rebuke, that they made no attempt to rally, but condescended to make their peace separately as they could, by the most ample acknowledgments.

An example of the impartiality as well as spirit with which Isabella asserted the dignity of the crown is worth recording. During her husband's absence in Aragon in the spring of 1481, a quarrel occurred, in the antechamber of the palace at Valladolid, between two young noblemen, Ramiro Nuñez de Guzman, lord of Toral, and Frederick Henriquez, son of the admiral of Castile, King Ferdinand's uncle. The queen, on receiving intelligence of it, granted a safe-conduct to the lord of Toral, as the weaker party, until the affair should be adjusted between them. Don Frederick, however, disregarding this protection, caused his enemy to be waylaid by three of his followers, armed with bludgeons, and sorely beaten one evening in the streets of Valladolid.

Isabella was no sooner informed of this outrage on one whom she had taken under the royal protection, than, burning with indignation, she immediately mounted her horse, though in the midst of a heavy storm of rain, and proceeded alone towards the castle of Simancas, then in possession of the admiral, the father of the offender, where she supposed him to have taken refuge, traveling all the while with such rapidity that she was not over-taken by the officers of her guard until she had reached the for-tress. She instantly summoned the admiral to deliver up his son to justice; and, on his replying that "Don Frederick was not there, and that he was ignorant where he was," she commanded him to surrender the keys of the castle, and, after a fruitless search, again returned to Valladolid. The next day Isabella was confined to her bed by an illness occasioned as much by chagrin as by the excessive fatigue which she had undergone. "My body is lame," said she, "with the blows given by Don Frederick in contempt of my safe-conduct."

The admiral, perceiving how deeply he and his family had incurred the displeasure of the queen, took counsel with his friends, who were led by their knowledge of Isabella's character to believe that he would have more to hope from the surrender of his son than from further attempts at concealment. The young man was accordingly conducted to the palace by his uncle, the constable de Haro, who deprecated the queen's resentment by representing the age of his nephew, scarcely amounting to twenty years. Isabella, however, thought proper to punish the youthful delinquent, by ordering him to be publicly conducted as a pris-oner, by one of the alcaldes of her court, through the great square of Valladolid to the fortress of Arevalo, where he was detained in strict confinement, all privilege of access being denied to him; and when at length, moved by the consideration of his consan-guinity with the king, she consented to his release, she banished him to Sicily, until he should receive the royal permission to re-turn to his own country.

Notwithstanding the strict impartiality as well as vigor of the administration, it could never have maintained itself by its own resources alone, in its offensive operations against the high-spirited aristocracy of Castile. Its most direct approaches, how-ever, were made, as we have seen, under cover of the cortes. The sovereigns showed great deference, especially in this early period of their reign, to the popular branch of this body; and, far from pursuing the odious policy of preceding princes in diminishing the amount of represented cities, they never failed to direct their writs to all those which, at their accession, retained the right of representation, and subsequently enlarged the number by the conquest of Granada; while they exercised the anomalous privilege . . . of omitting altogether, or issuing only a partial summons to the nobility. By making merit the standard of preferment, they opened the path of honor to every class of the community. They uniformly manifested the greatest tenderness for the rights of the commons in reference to taxation; and, as their patriotic policy was obviously directed to secure the personal rights and general prosperity of the people, it insured the co-operation of an ally whose weight, combined with that of the crown, enabled them eventually to restore the equilibrium which had been disturbed by the undue preponderance of the aristocracy. . . .

IV. Vindication of ecclesiastical rights belonging to the crown from papal usurpation. In the earlier stages of the Castilian monarchy, the sovereigns appear to have held a supremacy in spiritual, very similar to that exercised by them in temporal matters. It was comparatively late that the nation submitted its neck to the papal yoke, so closely riveted at a subsequent period; and even the Romish ritual was not admitted into its churches till long after it had been adopted in the rest of Europe. But, when the code of the Partidas was promulgated in the thirteenth century, the maxims of the canon law came to be permanently established. The ecclesiastical encroached on the lay tribunals. Appeals were perpetually carried up to the Roman court; and the popes, pretending to regulate the minutest details of Church economy, not only disposed of inferior benefices, but gradually converted the right of confirming elections to the episcopal and higher ecclesiastical dignities, into that of appointment.

These usurpations of the Church had been repeatedly the subject of grave remonstrance in cortes. Several remedial enactments had passed that body during the present reign, especially in relation to the papal provision of foreigners to benefices; an evil of much greater magnitude in Spain than in other countries of Europe, since the episcopal demesnes, frequently covering the Moorish frontier, became an important line of national defense, obviously improper to be intrusted to the keeping of foreigners and absentees. Notwithstanding the efforts of cortes, no effectual remedy was devised for this latter grievance, until it became the subject of actual collision between the crown and the pontiff, in reference to the see of Taraçona, and afterwards of Cuenca.

Sixtus the Fourth had conferred the latter benefice, on its becoming vacant in 1482, on his nephew, Cardinal San Giorgio, a Genoese, in direct opposition to the wishes of the queen, who would have bestowed it on her chaplain, Alfonso de Burgos, in exchange for the bishopric of Cordova. An ambassador was accordingly despatched by the Castilian sovereigns to Rome, to remonstrate on the papal appointment; but without effect, as Sixtus replied, with a degree of presumption which might better have become his predecesors of the twelfth century, that "he was head of the Church, and, as such, possessed of unlimited power in the distribution of benefices, and that he was not bound to consult the inclination of any potentate on earth, any further than might subserve the interests of religion."

The sovereigns, highly dissatisfied with this response, ordered their subjects, ecclesiastical as well as lay, to quit the papal dominions; an injunction which the former, fearful of the sequestration of their temporalities in Castile, obeyed with as much promptness as the latter. At the same time, Ferdinand and Isabella proclaimed their intention of inviting the princes of Christendom to unite with them in convoking a general council for the reformation of the manifold abuses which dishonored the Church. No sound could have grated more unpleasantly on the pontifical ear than the menace of a general council, particularly at this period, when ecclesiastical corruptions had reached a height which could but ill endure its scrutiny. The pope became convinced that he had ventured too far, and that Henry the Fourth was no longer monarch of Castile. He accordingly despatched a legate to Spain, fully empowered to arrange the matter on an amicable basis.

The legate, who was a layman, by name Domingo Centurion, no sooner arrived in Castile than he caused the sovereigns to be informed of his presence there, and the purpose of his mission; but he received orders instantly to quit the kingdom, without attempting so much as to disclose the nature of his instructions, since they could not but be derogatory to the dignity of the crown. A safe-conduct was granted for himself and his suite; but, at the same time, great surprise was expressed that anyone should venture to appear, as envoy from his Holiness, at the court of Castile, after it had been treated by him with such unmerited indignity.

Far from resenting this ungracious reception, the legate affected the deepest humility, professing himself willing to waive whatever immunities he might claim as papal ambassador, and to submit to the jurisdiction of the sovereigns as one of their own subjects, so that he might obtain an audience. Cardinal Mendoza, whose influence in the cabinet had gained him the title of "third king of Spain," apprehensive of the consequences of a protracted rupture with the Church, interposed in behalf of the envoy, whose conciliatory deportment at length so far mitigated the resentment of the sovereigns that they consented to open negotiations with the court of Rome. The result was the publication of a bull by Sixtus the Fourth, in which his Holiness engaged to provide such natives to the higher dignities of the Church in Castile as should be nominated by the monarchs of that kingdom; and Alfonso de Burgos was accordingly translated to the see of Cuenca. Isabella, on whom the duties of ecclesiastical preferment devolved by the act of settlement, availed herself of the rights thus wrested from the grasp of Rome, to exalt to the vacant sees persons of exemplary piety and learning, holding light, in comparison with the faithful discharge of this duty, every minor consideration of interest, and even the solicitations of her husband. . . . And the chronicler of her reign dwells with complacency on those good old times, when churchmen were to be found of such singular modesty as to require to be urged to accept the dignities to which their merits entitled them.

V. The regulation of trade. It will be readily conceived that trade, agriculture, and every branch of industry must have languished under the misrule of preceding reigns. For what purpose, indeed, strive to accumulate wealth, when it would only serve to sharpen the appetite of the spoiler? For what purpose cultivate the earth, when the fruits were sure to be swept away, even before harvest time, in some ruthless foray? The frequent famines and pestilences, which occurred in the latter part of Henry's reign and the commencement of his successor's, show too plainly the squalid condition of the people, and their utter destitution of all useful arts. We are assured by the curate of Los Palacios that the plague broke out in the southern districts of the kingdom, carrying off eight, or nine, or even fifteen thousand inhabitants from the various cities; while the prices of the ordinary aliments of life rose to a height which put them above the reach of the poorer classes of the community. In addition to these physical evils, a fatal shock was given to commercial credit by the adulteration of the coin. Under Henry the Fourth, it is computed that there were no less than one hundred and fifty mints openly licensed by the crown, in addition to many others erected by individuals without any legal authority. The abuse came to such a height that people at length refused to receive in payment of their debts the debased coin, whose value depreciated more and more every day; and the little trade which remained in Castile was carried on by barter, as in the primitive stages of society.

The magnitude of the evil was such as to claim the earliest attention of the cortes under the new monarchs. Acts were passed fixing the standard and legal value of the different denominations of coin. A new coinage was subsequently made. Five royal mints were alone authorized, afterwards augmented to seven, and severe penalties denounced against the fabrication of money elsewhere. The reform of the currency gradually infused new life into commerce, as the return of the circulations, which have been interrupted for a while, quickens the animal body. This was furthered by salutary laws for the encouragement of domestic industry. Internal communication was facilitated by the construction of roads and bridges. Absurd restrictions on change of residence, as well as the onerous duties which had been imposed on commercial intercourse between Castile and Aragon, were repealed. Several judicious laws were enacted for the protection of foreign trade; and the flourishing condition of the mercantile marine may be inferred from that of the military, which enabled the sovereigns to fit out an armament of seventy sail in 1482, from the ports of Biscay and Andalusia, for the defense of Naples against the Turks. Some of their regulations, indeed, as those prohibiting the exportation of the precious metals, savor too strongly of the ignorance of the true principles of commercial legislation which has distinguished the Spaniards to the present day. But others, again, as that for relieving the importation of foreign books from all duties, "because," says the statute, "they bring both honor and profit to the kingdom, by the facilities which they afford for making men learned," are not only in advance of that age, but may sustain an advantageous comparison with provisions on corresponding subjects in Spain at the present time. Public credit was re-established by the punctuality with which the government redeemed the debt contracted during the Portuguese war; and, notwithstanding the repeal of various arbitrary imposts, which enriched the exchequer under Henry the Fourth, such was the advance of the country under the wise economy of the present reign, that the revenue was augmented nearly sixfold between the years 1477 and 1482.

Thus released from the heavy burdens imposed on it, the spring of enterprise recovered its former elasticity. The productive capital of the country was made to flow through the various channels of domestic industry. The hills and the valleys again rejoiced in the labor of the husbandman; and the cities were embellished with stately edifices, both public and private, which attracted the gaze and commendation of foreigners. The writers of that day are unbounded in their plaudits of Isabella, to whom they principally ascribe this auspicious revolution in the condition of the country and its inhabitants, which seems almost as magical as one of those transformations in romance wrought by the hands of some benevolent fairy.

VI. The pre-eminence of the royal authority. This, which, as we have seen, appears to have been the natural result of the policy of Ferdinand and Isabella, was derived quite as much from the influence of their private characters as from their public measures. Their acknowledged talents were supported by a dignified demeanor, which formed a striking contrast with the meanness in mind and manners that had distinguished their predecessor. They both exhibited a practical wisdom in their own personal relations, which always commands respect, and which, however it may have savored of worldly policy in Ferdinand, was, in his consort, founded on the purest and most exalted principle. Under such a sovereign, the court, which had been little better than a brothel under the preceding reign, became the nursery of virtue and generous ambition. Isabella watched assiduously over the nurture of the high-born damsels of her court, whom she received into the royal palace, causing them to be educated under her own eye, and endowing them with liberal portions on their marriage. By these and similar acts of affectionate solicitude, she endeared herself to the higher classes of her subjects, while the patriotic tendency of her public conduct established her in the hearts of the people. She possessed, in combination with the feminine qualities which beget love, a masculine energy of character, which struck terror into the guilty. She enforced the execution of her own plans, oftentimes even at great personal hazard, with a resolution surpassing that of her husband. Both were singularly temperate, indeed frugal, in their dress, equipage, and general style of living; seeking to affect others less by external pomp than by the silent though more potent influence of personal qualities. On all such occasions as demanded it, however, they displayed a princely magnificence, which dazzled the multitude, and is blazoned with great solemnity in the garrulous chronicles of the day.

The tendencies of the present administration were undoubtedly to strengthen the power of the crown. This was the point to which most of the feudal governments of Europe at this epoch were tending. But Isabella was far from being actuated by the selfish aim or unscrupulous policy of many contemporary princes, who, like Louis the Eleventh, sought to govern by the arts of dissimulation, and to establish their own authority by fomenting the divisions of their powerful vassals. On the contrary, she endeavored to bind together the disjointed fragments of the state, to assign to each of its great divisions its constitutional limits, and, by depressing the aristocracy to its proper level and elevating the commons, to consolidate the whole under the lawful supremacy of the crown. At least, such was the tendency of her administration up to the present period of our history. These laudable objects were gradually achieved, without fraud or violence, by a course of measures equally laudable; and the various orders of the monarchy, brought into harmonious action with each other, were enabled to turn the forces which had before been wasted in civil conflict to the glorious career of discovery and conquest which it was destined to run during the remainder of the century.

FROM CHAPTER IX

Capture of Alhama

1481–1482

No sooner had Ferdinand and Isabella restored internal tranquillity to their dominions, and made the strength effective which had been acquired by their union under one government, than they turned their eyes to those fair regions of the peninsula over which the Moslem crescent had reigned triumphant for nearly eight centuries. Fortunately, an act of aggression on the part of the Moors furnished a pretext for entering on their plan of conquest, at the moment when it was ripe for execution. Aben Ismail, who had ruled in Granada during the latter part of John the Second's reign and the commencement of Henry the Fourth's, had been partly indebted for his throne to the former monarch; and sentiments of gratitude, combined with a naturally amiable disposition, had led him to foster as amicable relations with the Christian princes as the jealousy of two nations, that might be considered the natural enemies of each other, would permit; so that, notwithstanding an occasional border foray, or the capture of a frontier fortress, such a correspondence was maintained between the two kingdoms that the nobles of Castile frequently resorted to the court of Granada, where, forgetting their ancient feuds, they mingled with the Moorish cavaliers in the generous pastimes of chivalry.

Muley Abul Hacen, who succeeded his father in 1466, was of a very different temperament. His fiery character prompted him, when very young, to violate the truce by an unprovoked inroad into Andalusia; and, although after his accession domestic troubles occupied him too closely to allow leisure for foreign war, he still cherished in secret the same feelings of animosity against the Christians. When, in 1476, the Spanish sovereigns required, as the condition of a renewal of the truce which he solicited, the payment of the annual tribute imposed on his pred-ecessors, he proudly replied that "the mints of Granada coined no longer gold, but steel." His subsequent conduct did not belie the spirit of this Spartan answer.

At length, towards the close of the year 1481, the storm which had been so long gathering burst upon Zahara, a small fortified town on the frontier of Andalusia, crowning a lofty eminence, washed at its base by the river Guadalete, which from its position seemed almost inaccessible. The garrison, trusting to these nat-ural defenses, suffered itself to be surprised, on the night of the 26th of December, by the Moorish monarch, who, scaling the walls under favor of a furious tempest, which prevented his ap-proach from being readily heard, put to the sword such of the guard as offered resistance, and swept away the whole popula-tion of the place, men, women, and children, into slavery in Granada.

The intelligence of this disaster caused deep mortification to the Spanish sovereigns, especially to Ferdinand, by whose grand-father Zahara had been recovered from the Moors. Measures were accordingly taken for strengthening the whole line of fron-tier, and the utmost vigilance was exerted to detect some vulner-able point of the enemy, on which retaliation might be success-fully inflicted. Neither were the tidings of their own successes welcomed by the people of Granada with the joy that might have been expected. The prognostics, it was said, afforded by the ap-pearance of the heavens, boded no good. More sure prognostics were afforded in the judgments of thinking men, who deprecated the temerity of awakening the wrath of a vindictive and power-ful enemy. "Woe is me!" exclaimed an ancient Alfaki, on quitting the hall of audience. "The ruins of Zahara will fall on our own heads; the days of the Moslem empire in Spain are now num-bered!"

It was not long before the desired opportunity for retalia-tion presented itself to the Spaniards. One Juan de Ortega, a captain of escaladores, or scalers, so denominated from the peculiar service in which they were employed in besieging cities, who had acquired some reputation under John the Second in the wars of Roussillon, reported to Diego de Merlo, assistant of Seville, that the fortress of Alhama, situated in the heart of the Moorish territories, was so negligently guarded that it might be easily carried by an enemy who had skill enough to approach it. The fortress, as well as the city of the same name, which it commanded, was built, like many others in that turbulent period, along the crest of a rocky eminence, encompassed by a river at its base, and, from its natural advantages, might be deemed impregnable. This strength of position, by rendering all other precautions apparently superfluous, lulled its defenders into a security like that which had proved so fatal to Zahara. Alhama, as this Arabic name implies, was famous for its baths, whose annual rents are said to have amounted to five hundred thousand ducats. The monarchs of Granada, indulging the taste common to the people of the East, used to frequent this place, with their court, to refresh themselves with its delicious waters, so that Alhama became embellished with all the magnificence of a royal residence. The place was still further enriched by its being the depot of the public taxes on land, which constituted a principal branch of the revenue, and by its various manufactures of cloth, for which its inhabitants were celebrated throughout the kingdom of Granada.

Diego de Merlo, although struck with the advantages of this conquest, was not insensible to the difficulties with which it would be attended; since Alhama was sheltered under the very wings of Granada, from which it lay scarcely eight leagues distant, and could be reached only by traversing the most populous portion of the Moorish territory, or by surmounting a precipitous *sierra,* or chain of mountains, which screened it on the north. Without delay, however, he communicated the information which he had received to Don Rodrigo Ponce de Leon, marquis of Cadiz, as the person best fitted by his capacity and courage for such an enterprise. This nobleman, who had succeeded his father, the count of Arcos, in 1469, as head of the great house of Ponce de Leon, was at this period about thirty-nine years of age. Although a younger and illegitimate son, he had been preferred to the succession in consequence of the extraordinary promise which his early youth exhibited. When scarcely seventeen years old, he achieved a victory over the Moors, accompanied with a signal display of personal prowess. Later in life, he formed a connection with the daughter of the marquis of Villena, the factious minister of Henry the Fourth, through whose influence he was raised to the dignity of marquis of Cadiz. This alliance attached him to the fortunes of Henry, in his disputes with his brother Alfonso, and subsequently with Isabella, on whose accession, of course, Don Rodrigo looked with no friendly eye. He did not, however, engage in any overt act of resistance, but occupied himself with prosecuting an hereditary feud which he had revived with the duke of Medina Sidonia, the head of the Guzmans, a family which from ancient times had divided with his own the great interests of Andalusia. The pertinacity with which this feud was conducted, and the desolation which it carried not only into Seville, but into every quarter of the province, have been noticed in the preceding pages. The vigorous administration of Isabella repressed these disorders, and, after abridging the overgrown power of the two nobles, effected an apparent (it was only apparent) reconciliation between them. The fiery spirit of the marquis of Cadiz, no longer allowed to escape in domestic broil, urged him to seek distinction in more honorable warfare; and at this moment he lay in his castle at Arcos, looking with a watchful eye over the borders, and waiting, like a lion in ambush, the moment when he could spring upon his victim.

Without hesitation, therefore, he assumed the enterprise proposed by Diego de Merlo, imparting his purpose to Don Pedro Henriquez, adelantado of Andalusia, a relative of Ferdinand, and to the alcaydes of two or three neighboring fortresses. With the assistance of these friends he assembled a force, which, including those who marched under the banner of Seville, amounted to two thousand five hundred horse and three thousand foot. His own town of Marchena was appointed as the place of rendezvous. The proposed route lay by the way of Antequera, across the wild sierras of Alzerifa. The mountain passes, sufficiently difficult at a season when their numerous ravines were choked up by the winter torrents, were rendered still more formidable by being traversed in the darkness of night; for the party, in order to conceal their movements, lay by during the day. Leaving their baggage on the banks of the Yeguas, that they might move forward with greater celerity, the whole body at length arrived, after a rapid and most painful march, on the third night from their departure, in a deep valley about half a league from Alhama. Here the marquis first revealed the real object of the expedition to his soldiers, who, little dreaming of anything beyond a mere border inroad, were transported with joy at the prospect of the rich booty so nearly within their grasp.

The next morning, being the 28th of February, a small party was detached, about two hours before dawn, under the command of John de Ortega, for the purpose of scaling the citadel, while the main body moved forward more leisurely under the marquis of Cadiz, in order to support them. The night was dark and tempestuous, a circumstance which favored their approach in the same manner as with the Moors at Zahara. After ascending the rocky heights which were crowned by the citadel, the ladders were silently placed against the walls, and Ortega, followed by about thirty others, succeeded in gaining the battlements unobserved. A sentinel, who was found sleeping on his post, they at once despatched, and, proceeding cautiously forward to the guard-room, put the whole of the little garrison to the sword, after the short and ineffectual resistance that could be opposed by men suddenly roused from slumber. The city in the meantime was alarmed, but it was too late; the citadel was taken; and the outer gates, which opened into the country, being thrown open, the marquis of Cadiz entered, with trumpet sounding and banner flying, at the head of his army, and took possession of the fortress.

After allowing the refreshment necessary to the exhausted spirits of his soldiers, the marquis resolved to sally forth at once upon the town, before its inhabitants could muster in sufficient force to oppose him. But the citizens of Alhama, showing a resolution rather to have been expected from men trained in a camp than from peaceful burghers of a manufacturing town, had sprung to arms at the first alarm, and, gathering in the narrow street on which the portal of the castle opened, so completely commanded it with their arquebuses and crossbows, that the Spaniards, after an ineffectual attempt to force a passage, were compelled to recoil upon their defenses, amid showers of bolts and balls, which occasioned the loss, among others, of two of their principal alcaydes.

A council of war was then called, in which it was even advised by some that the fortress, after having been dismantled, should be abandoned as incapable of defense against the citizens on the one hand, and the succors which might be expected speedily to arrive from Granada on the other. But this counsel was rejected with indignation by the marquis of Cadiz, whose fiery spirit rose with the occasion; indeed, it was not very palatable to most of his followers, whose cupidity was more than ever inflamed by the sight of the rich spoil which, after so many fatigues, now lay at their feet. It was accordingly resolved to demolish part of the fortifications which looked towards the town, and at all hazards to force a passage into it. This resolution was at once put into execution; and the marquis, throwing himself into the breach thus made, at the head of his men-at-arms, and shouting his war-cry of "St. James and the Virgin," precipitated himself into the thickest of the enemy. Others of the Spaniards, running along the outworks contiguous to the buildings of the city, leaped into the street, and joined their companions there, while others again sallied from the gates, now opened for the second time.

The Moors, unshaken by the fury of this assault, received the assailants with brisk and well-directed volleys of shot and arrows; while the women and children, thronging the roofs and balconies of the houses, discharged on their heads boiling oil, pitch, and missiles of every description. But the weapons of the Moors glanced comparatively harmless from the mailed armor of the Spaniards, while their own bodies, loosely arrayed in such habiliments as they could throw over them in the confusion of the night, presented a fatal mark to their enemies. Still they continued to maintain a stout resistance, checking the progress of the Spaniards by barricades of timber hastily thrown across the streets; and, as their intrenchments were forced one after another, they disputed every inch of ground with the desperation of men who fought for life, fortune, liberty—all that was most dear to them. The contest hardly slackened till the close of day, while the kennels literally ran with blood, and every avenue was choked up with the bodies of the slain. At length, however, Spanish valor proved triumphant in every quarter, except where a small and desperate remnant of the Moors, having gathered their wives and children around them, retreated as a last resort into a large mosque near the walls of the city, from which they kept up a galling fire on the close ranks of the Christians. The latter, after enduring some loss, succeeded in sheltering themselves so effectually under a roof or canopy constructed of their own shields, in the manner practised in war previous to the exclusive use of firearms, that they were enabled to approach so near the mosque as to set fire to its doors; when its tenants, menaced with suffocation, made a desperate sally, in which many perished, and the remainder surrendered at discretion. The prisoners thus made were all massacred on the spot, without distinction of sex or age, according to the Saracen accounts. But the Castilian writers make no mention of this; and, as the appetites of the Spaniards were not yet stimulated by that love of carnage which they afterwards displayed in their American wars, and which was repugnant to the chivalrous spirit with which their contests with the Moslems were usually conducted, we may be justified in regarding it as an invention of the enemy.

Alhama was now delivered up to the sack of the soldiery, and rich indeed was the booty which fell into their hands—gold and silver plate, pearls, jewels, fine silks and cloth, curious and costly furniture, and all the various appurtenances of a thriving, luxurious city. In addition to this, the magazines were found well stored with the more substantial, and at the present juncture more serviceable, supplies of grain, oil, and other provisions. Nearly a quarter of the population is said to have perished in the various conflicts of the day, and the remainder, according to the usage of the time, became the prize of the victors. A considerable number of Christian captives, who were found immured in the public prisons, were restored to freedom, and swelled the general jubilee with their grateful acclamations. The contemporary Castilian chroniclers record also, with no less satisfaction, the detection of a Christian renegade, notorious for his depredations on his countrymen, whose misdeeds the marquis of Cadiz requited by causing him to be hung up over the battlements of the castle, in the face of the whole city. Thus fell the ancient city of Alhama, the first conquest, and achieved with a gallantry and daring unsurpassed by any other during this memorable war.

The report of this disaster fell like the knell of their own doom in the ears of the inhabitants of Granada. . . .

FROM CHAPTER XV

Siege and Surrender of Granada

1490–1492

In the spring of 1490, ambassadors arrived from Lisbon for the purpose of carrying into effect the treaty of marriage which had been arranged between Alonso, heir of the Portuguese monarchy, and Isabella, infanta of Castile. An alliance with this kingdom, which from its contiguity possessed such ready means of annoyance to Castile, and which had shown such willingness to employ them in enforcing the pretensions of Joanna Beltraneja, was an object of importance to Ferdinand and Isabella. No inferior consideration could have reconciled the queen to a separation from this beloved daughter, her eldest child, whose gentle and uncommonly amiable disposition seems to have endeared her beyond their other children to her parents.

The ceremony of the affiancing took place at Seville, in the month of April, Don Fernando de Silveira appearing as the representative of the prince of Portugal; and it was followed by a succession of splendid fêtes and tourneys. Lists were enclosed, at some distance from the city, on the shores of the Guadalquivir, and surrounded with galleries hung with silk and cloth of gold, and protected from the noontide heat by canopies or awnings, richly embroidered with the armorial bearings of the ancient houses of Castile. The spectacle was graced by all the rank and beauty of the court, with the infanta Isabella in the midst, attended by seventy noble ladies, and a hundred pages of the royal household. The cavaliers of Spain, young and old, thronged to the tournament, as eager to win laurels on the mimic theater of war, in the presence of so brilliant an assemblage, as they had shown themselves in the sterner contests with the Moors. King Ferdinand, who broke several lances on the occasion, was among the most distinguished of the combatants for personal dexterity and horsemanship. The martial exercises of the day were relieved by the more effeminate recreations of dancing and music in the evening; and everyone seemed willing to welcome the season of hilarity, after the long-protracted fatigues of war.

In the following autumn, the infanta was escorted into Portugal by the cardinal of Spain, the grand master of St. James, and a numerous and magnificent retinue. Her dowry exceeded that usually assigned to the infantas of Castile, by five hundred marks of gold and a thousand of silver; and her wardrobe was estimated at one hundred and twenty thousand gold florins. The contemporary chroniclers dwell with much complacency on these evidences of the stateliness and splendor of the Castilian court. Unfortunately, these fair auspices were destined to be clouded too soon by the death of the prince, her husband.

No sooner had the campaign of the preceding year been brought to a close than Ferdinand and Isabella sent an embassy to the king of Granada, requiring a surrender of his capital, conformably to his stipulations at Loja, which guaranteed this on the capitulation of Baza, Almeria, and Guadix. That time had now arrived. King Abdallah, however, excused himself from obeying the summons of the Spanish sovereign, replying that he was no longer his own master, and that, although he had the strongest desire to keep his engagements, he was prevented by the inhabitants of the city, now swollen much beyond its natural population, who resolutely insisted on its defense.

It is not probable that the Moorish king did any great violence to his feelings in this evasion of a promise extorted from him in captivity. At least it would seem so from the hostile movements which immediately succeeded. The people of Granada resumed all at once their ancient activity, foraying into the Christian territories, surprising Alhendin and some other places of less importance, and stirring up the spirit of revolt in Guadix and other conquered cities. Granada, which had slept through the heat of the struggle, seemed to revive at the very moment when exertion became hopeless.

Ferdinand was not slow in retaliating these acts of aggression. In the spring of 1490, he marched with a strong force into the cultivated plain of Granada, sweeping off, as usual, the crops and cattle, and rolling the tide of devastation up to the very walls of the city. In this campaign he conferred the honor of knighthood on his son, Prince John, then only twelve years of age, whom he had brought with him, after the ancient usage of the Castilian nobles, of training up their children from very tender years in the Moorish wars. The ceremony was performed on the banks of the grand canal, under the battlements almost of the beleaguered city. The dukes of Cadiz and Medina Sidonia were Prince John's sponsors; and, after the completion of the ceremony, the new knight conferred the honors of chivalry in like manner on several of his young companions-in-arms.

In the following autumn, Ferdinand repeated his ravages in the vega, and, at the same time appearing before the disaffected city of Guadix with a force large enough to awe it into submission, proposed an immediate investigation of the conspiracy. He promised to inflict summary justice on all who had been in any degree concerned in it; at the same time offering permission to the inhabitants, in the abundance of his clemency, to depart with all their personal effects wherever they would, provided they should prefer this to a judicial investigation of their conduct. This politic proffer had its effect. There were few, if any, of the citizens who had not been either directly concerned in the conspiracy or privy to it. With one accord, therefore, they preferred exile to trusting to the tender mercies of their judges. In this way, says the Curate of Los Palacios, by the mystery of our Lord, was the ancient city of Guadix brought again within the Christian fold: the mosques were converted into Christian temples, filled with the harmonies of Catholic worship, and the pleasant places, which for nearly eight centuries had been trampled under the foot of the infidel, once more restored to the followers of the cross.

A similar policy produced similar results in the cities of Almeria and Baza, whose inhabitants, evacuating their ancient homes, transported themselves, with such personal effects as they could carry, to the city of Granada, or the coast of Africa. The space thus opened by the fugitive population was quickly filled by the rushing tide of Spaniards.

It is impossible at this day to contemplate these events with the triumphant swell of exultation with which they are recorded by contemporary chroniclers. That the Moors were guilty (though not so generally as pretended) of the alleged conspiracy, is not in itself improbable, and is corroborated indeed by the

Arabic statements. But the punishment was altogether dispro-
portionate to the offense. Justice might surely have been satisfied
by a selection of the authors and principal agents of the meditated insurrection; for no overt act appears to have occurred.
But avarice was too strong for justice; and this act, which is in
perfect conformity to the policy systematically pursued by the
Spanish crown for more than a century afterwards, may be considered as one of the first links in the long chain of persecution
which terminated in the expulsion of the Moriscoes.

During the following year, 1491, a circumstance occurred il-
lustrative of the policy of the present government in reference to
ecclesiastical matters. The chancery of Valladolid having appealed to the pope in a case coming within its own exclusive jurisdiction, the queen commanded Alonso de Valdivieso, bishop of
Leon, the president of the court, together with all the auditors,
to be removed from their respective offices, which she delivered
to a new board, having the bishop of Oviedo at its head. This is
one among many examples of the constancy with which Isabella,
notwithstanding her reverence for religion and respect for its
ministers, refused to compromise the national independence by
recognizing in any degree the usurpations of Rome. From this
dignified attitude, so often abandoned by her successors, she
never swerved for a moment during the course of her long reign.

The winter of 1490 was busily occupied with preparations for
the closing campaign against Granada. Ferdinand took command
of the army in the month of April, 1491, with the purpose of
sitting down before the Moorish capital, not to rise until its final
surrender. The troops, which mustered in the Val de Velillos,
are computed by most historians at fifty thousand horse and
foot, although Martyr, who served as a volunteer, swells the number to eighty thousand. They were drawn from the different cities,
chiefly, as usual, from Andalusia, which had been stimulated to
truly gigantic efforts throughout this protracted war, and from
the nobility of every quarter, many of whom, wearied out with
the contest, contented themselves with sending their quotas, while
many others, as the marquises of Cadiz and Villena, the counts
of Tendilla, Cabra, and Ureña, and Alonso de Aguilar, appeared
in person, eager, as they had borne the brunt of so many hard
campaigns, to share in the closing scene of triumph.

On the 26th of the month the army encamped near the fountain of Ojos de Huescar, in the vega, about two leagues distant from Granada. Ferdinand's first movement was to detach a considerable force, under the marquis of Villena, which he subsequently supported in person with the remainder of the army, for the purpose of scouring the fruitful regions of the Alpujarras, which served as the granary of the capital. This service was performed with such unsparing rigor that no less than twenty-four towns and hamlets in the mountains were ransacked and razed to the ground. After this, Ferdinand returned loaded with spoil to his former position on the banks of the Xenil, in full view of the Moorish metropolis, which seemed to stand alone, like some sturdy oak, the last of the forest, bidding defiance to the storm which had prostrated all its brethren.

Notwithstanding the failure of all external resources, Granada was still formidable from its local position and its defenses. On the east it was fenced in by a wild mountain barrier, the Sierra Nevada, whose snow-clad summits diffused a grateful coolness over the city through the sultry heats of summer. The side towards the vega, facing the Christian encampment, was encircled by walls and towers of massive strength and solidity. The population, swelled to two hundred thousand by the immigration from the surrounding country, was likely, indeed, to be a burden in a protracted siege; but among them were twenty thousand, the flower of the Moslem chivalry, who had escaped the edge of the Christian sword. In front of the city, for an extent of nearly ten leagues, lay unrolled the magnificent vega, . . . whose prolific beauties could scarcely be exaggerated in the most florid strains of the Arabian minstrel, and which still bloomed luxuriant, notwithstanding the repeated ravages of the preceding season.

The inhabitants of Granada were filled with indignation at the sight of their enemy, thus encamped under the shadow, as it were, of their battlements. They sallied forth in small bodies, or singly, challenging the Spaniards to equal encounter. Numerous were the combats which took place between the high-mettled cavaliers on both sides, who met on the level arena, as on a tilting-ground, where they might display their prowess in the presence of the assembled beauty and chivalry of their respective nations; for the Spanish camp was graced, as usual, by the presence of Queen Isabella and the infantas, with the courtly train of ladies who had accompanied their royal mistress from Alcala la Real. The Spanish ballads glow with picturesque details of these knightly tourneys, forming the most attractive portion of this romantic minstrelsy, which, celebrating the prowess of Moslem as well as Christian warriors, sheds a dying glory round the last hours of Granada.

The festivity which reigned throughout the camp on the arrival of Isabella did not divert her attention from the stern business of war. She superintended the military preparations, and personally inspected every part of the encampment. She appeared on the field superbly mounted, and dressed in complete armor; and, as she visited the different quarters and reviewed her troops, she administered words of commendation or sympathy, suited to the condition of the soldier.

On one occasion she expressed a desire to take a nearer survey of the city. For this purpose a house was selected, affording the best point of view, in the little village of Zubia, at no great distance from Granada. The king and queen stationed themselves before a window which commanded an unbroken prospect of the Alhambra and the most beautiful quarter of the town. In the meanwhile, a considerable force, under the marquis duke of Cadiz, had been ordered, for the protection of the royal persons, to take up a position between the village and the city of Granada, with strict injunctions on no account to engage the enemy, as Isabella was unwilling to stain the pleasures of the day with unnecessary effusion of blood.

The people of Granada, however, were too impatient long to endure the presence and, as they deemed it, the bravado of their enemy. They burst forth from the gates of the capital, dragging along with them several pieces of ordinance, and commenced a brisk assault on the Spanish lines. The latter sustained the shock with firmness, till the marquis of Cadiz, seeing them thrown into some disorder, found it necessary to assume the offensive, and, mustering his followers around him, made one of those desperate charges which had so often broken the enemy. The Moorish cavalry faltered, but might have disputed the ground, had it not been for the infantry, which, composed of the rabble population of the city, was easily thrown into confusion, and hurried the horse along with it. The rout now became general. The Spanish cavaliers, whose blood was up, pursued to the very gates of Granada; "and not a lance," says Bernaldez, "that day, but was dyed in the blood of the infidel." Two thousand of the enemy were slain and taken in the engagement, which lasted only a short time; and the slaughter was stopped only by the escape of the fugitives within the walls of the city.

About the middle of July, an accident occurred in the camp, which was like to have been attended with fatal consequences. The queen was lodged in a superb pavilion, belonging to the marquis of Cadiz, and always used by him in the Moorish war. By the carelessness of one of her attendants, a lamp was placed in such a situation that during the night, perhaps owing to a gust of wind, it set fire to the drapery or loose hangings of the pavilion, which was instantly in a blaze. The flame communicated with fearful rapidity to the neighboring tents, made of light, combustible materials, and the camp was menaced with general conflagration. This occurred at the dead of night, when all but the sentinels were buried in sleep. The queen, and her children, whose apartments were near hers, were in great peril, and escaped with difficulty, though fortunately without injury. The alarm soon spread. The trumpets sounded to arms, for it was supposed to be some night attack of the enemy. Ferdinand, snatching up his arms hastily, put himself at the head of his troops, but, soon ascertaining the nature of the disaster, contented himself with posting the marquis of Cadiz, with a strong body of horse, over against the city, in order to repel any sally from that quarter. None, however, was attempted, and the fire was at length extenguished without personal injury, though not without loss of much valuable property, in jewels, plate, brocade, and other costly decorations of the tents of the nobility.

In order to guard against a similar disaster, as well as to provide comfortable winter quarters for the army, should the siege be so long protracted as to require it, it was resolved to build a town of substantial edifices on the place of the present encampment. The plan was immediately put in execution. The work was distributed in due proportions among the troops of the several cities and of the great nobility; the soldier was on a sudden converted into an artisan, and, instead of war, the camp echoed with the sounds of peaceful labor.

In less than three months this stupendous task was accomplished. The spot so recently occupied by light, fluttering pavilions was thickly covered with solid structures of stone and mortar, comprehending, besides dwelling-houses, stables for a thousand horses. The town was thrown into a quadrangular form, traversed by two spacious avenues, intersecting each other at right angles in the center, in the form of a cross, with stately portals at each of the four extremities. Inscriptions on blocks of marble, in the various quarters, recorded the respective shares of the several cities in the execution of the work. When it was completed, the whole army was desirous that the new city should bear the name of their illustrious queen; but Isabella modestly declined this tribute, and bestowed on the place the title of Santa Fe, in token of the unshaken trust manifested by her people throughout this war in Divine Providence. With this name it still stands as it was erected in 1491, a monument of the constancy and enduring patience of the Spaniards, "the only city in Spain," in the words of a Castilian writer, "that has never been contaminated by the Moslem heresy."

The erection of Santa Fe by the Spaniards struck a greater damp into the people of Granada than the most successful military achievement could have done. They beheld the enemy setting foot on their soil with a resolution never more to resign it. They already began to suffer from the rigorous blockade, which effectually excluded supplies from their own territories, while all communication with Africa was jealously intercepted. Symptoms of insubordination had begun to show themselves among the overgrown population of the city, as it felt more and more the pressure of famine. In this crisis, the unfortunate Abdallah and his principal counselors became convinced that the place could not be maintained much longer; and at length, in the month of October, propositions were made, through the vizier Abul Cazim Abdelmalic, to open a negotiation for the surrender of the place. The affair was to be conducted with the utmost caution; since the people of Granada, notwithstanding their precarious condition and their disquietude, were buoyed up by indefinite expectations of relief from Africa or some other quarter.

The Spanish sovereigns intrusted the negotiation to their secretary, Fernando de Zafra, and to Gonsalvo de Cordova, the latter of whom was selected for this delicate business from his uncommon address and his familiarity with the Moorish habits and language. Thus the capitulation of Granada was referred to the man who acquired in her long wars the military science which enabled him, at a later period, to foil the most distinguished generals of Europe.

The conferences were conducted by night, with the utmost secrecy, sometimes within the walls of Granada, and at others in the little hamlet of Churriana, about a league distant from it. At length, after large discussion on both sides, the terms of capitulation were definitively settled, and ratified by the respective monarchs on the 25th of November, 1491.

The conditions were of similar though somewhat more liberal import than those granted to Baza. The inhabitants of Granada were to retain possession of their mosques, with the free exercise of their religion, with all its peculiar rites and ceremonies; they were to be judged by their own laws, under their own cadis or magistrates, subject to the general control of the Castilian governor; they were to be unmolested in their ancient usages, manners, language, and dress; to be protected in the full enjoyment of their property, with the right of disposing of it on their own account, and of migrating when and where they would; and to be furnished with vessels for the conveyance of such as chose within three years to pass into Africa. No heavier taxes were to be imposed than those customarily paid to their Arabic sovereigns, and none whatever before the expiration of three years. King Abdallah was to reign over a specified territory in the Alpujarras, for which he was to do homage to the Castilian crown. The artillery and the fortifications were to be delivered into the hands of the Christians, and the city was to be surrendered in sixty days from the date of the capitulation. Such were the principal terms of the surrender of Granada, as authenticated by the most accredited Castilian and Arabic authorities; which I have stated the more precisely, as affording the best data for estimating the extent of Spanish perfidy in later times.

The conferences could not be conducted so secretly but that some report of them got air among the populace of the city, who now regarded Abdallah with an evil eye for his connection with the Christians. When the fact of the capitulation became known, the agitation speedily mounted into an open insurrection, which menaced the safety of the city, as well as of Abdallah's person. In this alarming state of things, it was thought best by that monarch's counselors to anticipate the appointed day of surrender; and the 2d of January, 1492, was accordingly fixed on for that purpose.

Every preparation was made by the Spaniards for performing this last act of the drama with suitable pomp and effect. The mourning which the court had put on for the death of Prince Alonso of Portugal, occasioned by a fall from his horse a few months after his marriage with the infanta Isabella, was exchanged for gay and magnificent apparel. On the morning of the 2d, the whole Christian camp exhibited a scene of the most animating bustle. The grand cardinal Mendoza was sent forward at the head of a large detachment, comprehending his household troops, and the veteran infantry grown gray in the Moorish wars, to occupy the Alhambra preparatory to the entrance of the sovereigns. Ferdinand stationed himself at some distance in the rear, near an Arabian mosque, since consecrated as the hermitage of St. Sebastian. He was surrounded by his courtiers, with their stately retinues, glittering in gorgeous panoply, and proudly displaying the armorial bearings of their ancient houses. The queen halted still farther in the rear, at the village of Armilla.

As the column under the grand cardinal advanced up the Hill of Martyrs, over which a road had been constructed for the passage of the artillery, he was met by the Moorish prince Abdallah, attended by fifty cavaliers, who, descending the hill, rode up to the position occupied by Ferdinand on the banks of the Xenil. As the Moor approached the Spanish king, he would have thrown himself from his horse and saluted his hand in token of homage; but Ferdinand hastily prevented him, embracing him with every mark of sympathy and regard. Abdallah then delivered up the keys of the Alhambra to his conqueror, saying, "They are thine, O king, since Allah so decrees it: use thy success with clemency and moderation." Ferdinand would have uttered some words of consolation to the unfortunate prince, but he moved forward with a dejected air to the spot occupied by Isabella, and, after similar acts of obeisance, passed on to join his family, who had preceded him with his most valuable effects on the route to the Alpujarras.

The sovereigns during this time awaited with impatience the signal of the occupation of the city by the cardinal's troops, which, winding slowly along the outer circuit of the walls, as previously arranged, in order to spare the feelings of the citizens as far as possible, entered by what is now called the gate of Los Molinos. In a short time, the large silver cross, borne by Ferdinand throughout the crusade, was seen sparkling in the sunbeams, while the standards of Castile and St. Jago waved triumphantly from the red towers of the Alhambra. At this glorious spectacle the choir of the royal chapel broke forth into the solemn anthem of the Te Deum, and the whole army, penetrated with deep emotion, prostrated themselves on their knees in adoration of the Lord of hosts, who had at length granted the consummation of their wishes, in this last and glorious triumph of the cross. The grandees who surrounded Ferdinand then advanced towards the queen, and, kneeling down, saluted her hand in token of homage to her as sovereign of Granada. The procession took up its march towards the city, "the king and queen moving in the midst," says an historian, "emblazoned with royal magnificence; and, as they were in the prime of life, and had now achieved the completion of this glorious conquest, they seemed to represent even more than their wonted majesty. Equal with each other, they were raised far above the rest of the world. They appeared, indeed, more than mortal, and as if sent by Heaven for the salvation of Spain."

In the meanwhile the Moorish king, traversing the route of the Alpujarras, reached a rocky eminence which commanded a last view of Granada. He checked his horse, and, as his eye for the last time wandered over the scenes of his departed greatness, his heart swelled, and he burst into tears. "You do well," said his more masculine mother, "to weep like a woman for what you could not defend like a man!" "Alas!" exclaimed the unhappy exile, "when were woes ever equal to mine!" The scene of this event is still pointed out to the traveler by the people of the district; and the rocky height from which the Moorish chief took his sad farewell of the princely abodes of his youth is commemorated by the poetical title of El ultimo Sospiro del Moro, "The Last Sigh of the Moor."

The sequel of Abdallah's history is soon told. Like his uncle, El Zagal, he pined away in his barren domain of the Alpujarras, under the shadow, as it were, of his ancient palaces. In the following year he passed over to Fez with his family, having commuted his petty sovereignty for a considerable sum of money paid him by Ferdinand and Isabella, and soon after fell in battle in the service of an African prince, his kinsman. "Wretched man," exclaims a caustic chronicler of his nation, "who could lose his life in another's cause, though he did not dare to die in his own! Such," continues the Arabian, with characteristic resignation, "was the immutable decree of destiny. Blessed be Allah, who exalteth and debaseth the kings of the earth, according to his divine will, in whose fulfilment consists that eternal justice which regulates all human affairs." The portal through which King Abdallah for the last time issued from his capital was at his request walled up, that none other might again pass through it. In this condition it remains to this day, a memorial of the sad destiny of the last of the kings of Granada.

The fall of Granada excited a general sensation throughout Christendom, where it was received as counterbalancing, in a manner, the loss of Constantinople nearly half a century before. At Rome the event was commemorated by a solemn procession of the pope and cardinals to St. Peter's, where high mass was celebrated, and the public rejoicing continued for several days. The intelligence was welcomed with no less satisfaction in England, where Henry the Seventh was seated on the throne. The circumstances attending it, as related by Lord Bacon, will not be devoid of interest for the reader.

Thus ended the war of Granada, which is often compared by the Castilian chroniclers to that of Troy in its duration, and which certainly fully equaled the latter in variety of picturesque and romantic incidents, and in circumstances of poetical interest. With the surrender of its capital terminated the Arabian empire in the peninsula, after an existence of seven hundred and forty-one years from the date of the original conquest. The consequences of this closing war were of the highest moment to Spain. The most obvious was the recovery of an extensive territory, hitherto held by a people whose difference of religion, language, and general habits made them not only incapable of assimilating with their Christian neighbors, but almost their natural enemies; while their local position was a matter of just concern, as interposed between the great divisions of the Spanish monarchy, and opening an obvious avenue to invasion from Africa. By the new conquest, moreover, the Spaniards gained a large extent of country, possessing the highest capacities for production, in its natural fruitfulness of soil, the temperature of climate, and the state of cultivation to which it had been brought by its ancient occupants; while its shores were lined with commodious havens, that afforded every facility for commerce. The scattered fragments of the ancient Visigothic empire were now again, with the exception of the little state of Navarre, combined into one great monarchy, as originally destined by nature; and Christian Spain gradually rose, by means of her new acquisitions, from a subordinate situation to the level of a first-rate European power.

The moral influence of the Moorish war, its influence on the Spanish character, was highly important. The inhabitants of the great divisions of the country, as in most countries during the feudal ages, had been brought too frequently into collision with each other to allow the existence of a pervading national feeling. This was particularly the case in Spain, where independent states insensibly grew out of the detached fragments of territory recovered at different times from the Moorish monarchy. The war of Granada subjected all the various sections of the country to one common action, under the influence of common motives of the most exciting interest; while it brought them in conflict with a race the extreme repugnance of whose institutions and character to their own served greatly to nourish the nationality of sentiment. In this way the spark of patriotism was kindled throughout the whole nation, and the most distant provinces of the peninsula were knit together by a bond of union which has remained indissoluble.

The consequences of these wars in a military aspect are also worthy of notice. Up to this period, war had been carried on by irregular levies, extremely limited in numerical amount and in period of service, under little subordination, except to their own immediate chiefs, and wholly unprovided with the apparatus required for extended operations. The Spaniards were even lower than most of the European nations in military science, as is apparent from the infinite pains of Isabella to avail herself of all foreign resources for their improvement. In the war of Granada, masses of men were brought together far greater than had hitherto been known in modern warfare. They were kept in the field not only through long campaigns, but far into the winter; a thing altogether unprecedented. They were made to act in concert, and the numerous petty chiefs brought into complete sub-

jection to one common head, whose personal character enforced
the authority of station. Lastly, they were supplied with all the
requisite munitions, through the providence of Isabella, who
introduced into the service the most skillful engineers from other
countries, and kept in pay bodies of mercenaries—as the Swiss,
for example, reputed the best disciplined troops of that day. In
this admirable school the Spanish soldier was gradually trained
to patient endurance, fortitude, and thorough subordination; and
those celebrated captains were formed, with that invincible infantry, which in the beginning of the sixteenth century spread
the military fame of their country over all Christendom. . . .

FROM CHAPTER XVIII

The New World

1493-1494

The discoveries of Columbus excited a sensation, particularly
among men of science, in the most distant parts of Europe,
strongly contrasting with the apathy which had preceded them.
They congratulated one another on being reserved for an age
which had witnessed the consummation of so grand an event.
The learned Martyr, who, in his multifarious correspondence,
had not even deigned to notice the preparations for the voyage
of discovery, now lavished the most unbounded panegyric on its
results; which he contemplated with the eye of a philosopher,
having far less reference to considerations of profit or policy than
to the prospect which they unfolded of enlarging the boundaries
of knowledge. Most of the scholars of the day, however, adopted
the erroneous hypothesis of Columbus, who considered the lands
he had discovered as bordering on the eastern shores of Asia,
and lying adjacent to the vast and opulent regions depicted in
such golden colors by Mandeville and the Poli. This conjecture,
which was conformable to the admiral's opinions before undertaking the voyage, was corroborated by the apparent similarity
between various natural productions of these islands, and of the

East. From this misapprehension, the new dominions soon came to be distinguished as the West Indies, an appellation by which they are still recognized in the titles of the Spanish crown.

Columbus, during his residence at Barcelona, continued to receive from the Spanish sovereigns the most honorable distinctions which royal bounty could confer. When Ferdinand rode abroad, he was accompanied by the admiral at his side. The courtiers, in emulation of their master, made frequent entertainments, at which he was treated with the punctilious deference paid to a noble of the highest class. But the attentions most grateful to his lofty spirit were the preparations of the Spanish court for prosecuting his discoveries on a scale commensurate with their importance. A board was established for the direction of Indian affairs, consisting of a superintendent and two subordinate functionaries. The first of these officers was Juan de Fonseca, archdeacon of Seville, an active, ambitious prelate, subsequently raised to high episcopal preferment, whose shrewdness and capacity for business enabled him to retain the control of the Indian department during the whole of the present reign. An office for the transaction of business was instituted at Seville, and a custom-house placed under its direction at Cadiz. This was the origin of the important establishment of the Casa de la Contratacion de las Indias, or India House.

The commercial regulations adopted exhibit a narrow policy in some of their features, for which a justification may be found in the spirit of the age, and in the practice of the Portuguese particularly, but which entered still more largely into the colonial legislation of Spain under later princes. The new territories, far from being permitted free intercourse with foreign nations, were opened only under strict limitations to Spanish subjects, and were reserved, as forming, in some sort, part of the exclusive revenue of the crown. All persons of whatever description were interdicted, under the severest penalties, from trading with or even visiting the Indies without license from the constituted authorities. It was impossible to evade this, as a minute specification of the ships, cargoes, crews, with the property appertaining to each individual, was required to be taken at the office in Cadiz, and a corresponding registration in a similar office established at Hispaniola. A more sagacious spirit was manifested in the ample provision made of whatever could contribute to the support or permanent prosperity of the infant colony. Grain, plants, the seeds of numerous vegetable products, which in the genial climate of the Indies might be made valuable articles for domestic consumption or export, were liberally furnished. Commodities of every description for the supply of the fleet were exempted from duty. The owners of all vessels throughout the ports of Andalusia were required, by an ordinance somewhat arbitrary, to hold them in readiness for the expedition. Still further authority was given to impress both officers and men, if necessary, into the service. Artisans of every sort, provided with the implements of their various crafts, including a great number of miners for exploring the subterraneous treasures of the new regions, were enrolled in the expedition; in order to defray the heavy charges of which, the government, in addition to the regular resources, had recourse to a loan, and to the sequestrated property of the exiled Jews.

Amid their own temporal concerns, the Spanish sovereigns did not forget the spiritual interests of their new subjects. The Indians who accompanied Columbus to Barcelona had been all of them baptized, being offered up, in the language of a Castilian writer, as the first-fruits of the gentiles. King Ferdinand and his son, Prince John, stood as sponsors to two of them, who were permitted to take their names. One of the Indians remained attached to the prince's establishment; the residue were sent to Seville, whence, after suitable religious instruction, they were to be returned as missionaries for the propagation of the faith among their own countrymen. Twelve Spanish ecclesiastics were also destined to this service. . . . The most explicit directions were given to the admiral to use every effort for the illumination of the poor heathen, which was set forth as the primary object of the expedition. He was particularly enjoined "to abstain from all means of annoyance, and to treat them well and lovingly, maintaining a familiar intercourse with them, rendering them all the kind offices in his power, distributing presents of the merchandise and various commodities which their Highnesses had caused to be embarked on board the fleet for that purpose; and finally, to chastise, in the most exemplary manner, all who should offer the natives the slightest molestation." Such were the instructions emphatically urged on Columbus for the regulation of his intercourse with the savages; and their indulgent tenor sufficiently attests the benevolent and rational views of Isabella in religious matters, when not warped by any foreign influence.

Towards the last of May, Columbus quitted Barcelona for the purpose of superintending and expediting the preparations for departure on his second voyage. He was accompanied to the gates of the city by all the nobility and cavaliers of the court. Orders were issued to the different towns to provide him and his suite with lodgings free of expense. His former commission was not only confirmed in its full extent, but considerably enlarged. For the sake of despatch, he was authorized to nominate to all offices, without application to government; and ordinances and letters patent, bearing the royal seal, were to be issued by him, subscribed by himself or his deputy. He was intrusted, in fine, with such unlimited jurisdiction as showed that, however tardy the sovereigns may have been in granting him their confidence, they were not disposed to stint the measure of it when his deserts were once established.

Soon after Columbus's return to Spain, Ferdinand and Isabella applied to the court of Rome to confirm them in the possession of their recent discoveries and invest them with similar extent of jurisdiction with that formerly conferred on the kings of Portugal. It was an opinion, as ancient perhaps as the crusades, that the pope, as vicar of Christ, had competent authority to dispose of all countries inhabited by heathen nations, in favor of Christian potentates. Although Ferdinand and Isabella do not seem to have been fully satisfied of this right, yet they were willing to acquiesce in its assumption in the present instance, from the conviction that the papal sanction would most effectually exclude the pretensions of all others, and especially their Portuguese rivals. In their application to the Holy See they were careful to represent their own discoveries as in no way interfering with the rights formerly conceded by it to their neighbors. They enlarged on their services in the propagation of the faith, which they affirmed to be a principal motive of their present operations. They intimated, finally, that, although many competent persons deemed their application to the court of Rome for a title to territories already in their possession to be unnecessary, yet, as pious princes, and dutiful children of the Church, they were unwilling to proceed further without the sanction of him to whose keeping its highest interests were intrusted.

The pontifical throne was at that time filled by Alexander the Sixth; a man who, although degraded by unrestrained indulgence of the most sordid appetites, was endowed by nature with singular acuteness as well as energy of character. He lent a willing ear to the application of the Spanish government, and made no hesitation in granting what cost him nothing, while it recognized the assumption of powers which had already begun to totter in the opinion of mankind.

On the 3d of May, 1493, he published a bull, in which, taking into consideration the eminent services of the Spanish monarchs in the cause of the Church, especially in the subversion of the Mahometan empire in Spain, and willing to afford still wider scope for the prosecution of their pious labors, he, "out of his pure liberality, infallible knowledge, and plenitude of apostolic power," confirmed them in the possession of all lands discovered, or hereafter to be discovered, by them in the western ocean, comprehending the same extensive rights of jurisdiction with those formerly conceded to the kings of Portugal.

This bull he supported by another, dated on the following day, in which the pope, in order to obviate any misunderstanding with the Portuguese, and acting, no doubt, on the suggestion of the Spanish sovereigns, defined with greater precision the intention of his original grant to the latter, by bestowing on them all such lands as they should discover to the west and south of an imaginary line, to be drawn from pole to pole, at the distance of one hundred leagues to the west of the Azores and Cape de Verd Islands. It seems to have escaped his Holiness that the Spaniards, by pursuing a western route, might in time reach the eastern limits of countries previously granted to the Portuguese. At least this would appear from the import of a third bull, issued September 25th of the same year, which invested the sovereigns with plenary authority over all countries discovered by them, whether in the East, or within the boundaries of India, all previous concessions to the contrary notwithstanding. With the title derived from actual possession thus fortified by the highest ecclesiastical sanction, the Spaniards might have promised themselves an uninterrupted career of discovery, but for the jealousy of their rivals the Portuguese.

The court of Lisbon viewed with secret disquietude the increasing maritime enterprise of its neighbors. While the Portu-

guese were timidly creeping along the barren shores of Africa,
the Spaniards had boldly launched into the deep, and rescued unknown realms from its embraces, which teemed in their fancies
with treasures of inestimable wealth. Their mortification was
greatly enhanced by the reflection that all this might have been
achieved for themselves, had they but known how to profit by
the proposals of Columbus. From the first moment in which
the success of the admiral's enterprise was established, John the
Second, a politic and ambitious prince, had sought some pretense
to check the career of discovery, or at least to share in the spoils
of it.

In his interview with Columbus, at Lisbon, he suggested that
the discoveries of the Spaniards might interfere with the rights
secured to the Portuguese by repeated papal sanctions since the
beginning of the present century, and guaranteed by the treaty
with Spain in 1479. Columbus, without entering into the discussion, contented himself with declaring that he had been instructed
by his own government to steer clear of all Portuguese settlements on the African coast, and that his course indeed had led
him in an entirely different direction. Although John professed
himself satisfied with the explanation, he soon after despatched
an ambassador to Barcelona, who, after dwelling on some irrele-
vant topics, touched as it were incidentally on the real object of
his mission, the late voyage of discovery. He congratulated the
Spanish sovereigns on its success, expatiated on the civilities
shown by the court of Lisbon to Columbus on his late arrival
there, and acknowledged the satisfaction felt by his master at the
orders given to the admiral to hold a western course from the
Canaries, expressing a hope that the same course would be pursued in future, without interfering with the rights of Portugal by
deviation to the south. This was the first occasion on which the
existence of such claims had been intimated by the Portuguese.

In the meanwhile, Ferdinand and Isabella received intelligence
that King John was equipping a considerable armament in order
to anticipate or defeat their discoveries in the west. They instantly sent one of their household, Don Lope de Herrera, as
ambassador to Lisbon, with instructions to make their acknowledgments to the king for his hospitable reception of Columbus,
accompanied with a request that he would prohibit his subjects
from interference with the discoveries of the Spaniards in the

west, in the same manner as these latter had been excluded from the Portuguese possessions in Africa. The ambassador was furnished with orders of a different import, provided he should find the reports correct respecting the equipment and probable destination of a Portuguese armada. Instead of a conciliatory deportment, he was in that case to assume a tone of remonstrance, and to demand a full explanation from King John of his designs. The cautious prince, who had received, through his secret agents in Castile, intelligence of these latter instructions, managed matters so discreetly as to give no occasion for their exercise. He abandoned, or at least postponed, his meditated expedition, in the hope of adjusting the dispute by negotiation, in which he excelled. In order to quiet the apprehensions of the Spanish court, he engaged to fit out no fleet from his dominions within sixty days; at the same time he sent a fresh mission to Barcelona, with directions to propose an amicable adjustment of the conflicting claims of the two nations, by making the parallel of the Canaries a line of partition between them; the right of discovery to the north being reserved to the Spaniards, and that to the south to the Portuguese.

While this game of diplomacy was going on, the Castilian court availed itself of the interval afforded by its rival, to expedite preparations for the second voyage of discovery; which, through the personal activity of the admiral, and the facilities everywhere afforded him, were fully completed before the close of September. Instead of the reluctance, and indeed avowed disgust, which had been manifested by all classes to his former voyage, the only embarrassment now arose from the difficulty of selection among the multitude of competitors who pressed to be enrolled in the present expedition. The reports and sanguine speculations of the first adventurers had inflamed the cupidity of many, which was still further heightened by the exhibition of the rich and curious products which Columbus had brought back with him, and by the popular belief that the new discoveries formed part of that gorgeous East

> *whose caverns teem*
> *With diamond flaming, and with seeds of gold,*

and which tradition and romance had alike invested with the supernatural splendors of enchantment. Many others were stimu-

lated by the wild love of adventure which had been kindled in
the long Moorish war, but which now, excluded from that career,
sought other objects in the vast, untraveled regions of the New
World. The complement of the fleet was originally fixed at
twelve hundred souls, a number eventually swelled through importunity or various pretenses of the applicants to fifteen hundred. Among these were many who enlisted without compensation, including several persons of rank, hidalgos, and members
of the royal household. The whole squadron amounted to seventeen vessels, three of them of one hundred tons' burden each.
With this gallant navy, Columbus, dropping down the Guadalquivir, took his departure from the bay of Cadiz on the 25th of
September, 1493; presenting a striking contrast to the melancholy plight in which, but the year previous, he had sallied forth
like some forlorn knight-errant on a desperate and chimerical
enterprise.

No sooner had the fleet weighed anchor than Ferdinand and
Isabella despatched an embassy in solemn state to advise the
king of Portugal of it. This embassy was composed of two persons of distinguished rank, Don Pedro de Ayala and Don Garci
Lopez de Carbajal. Agreeably to their instructions, they represented to the Portuguese monarch the inadmissibility of his
propositions respecting the boundary-line of navigation; they
argued that the grants of the Holy See, and the treaty with Spain
in 1479, had reference merely to the actual possessions of Portugal, and the right of discovery by an eastern route along the
coasts of Africa to the Indies; that these rights had been invariably respected by Spain; that the late voyage of Columbus
struck into a directly opposite track; and that the several bulls
of Pope Alexander the Sixth, prescribing the line of partition,
not from east to west, but from the north to the south pole, were
intended to secure to the Spaniards the exclusive right of discovery in the western ocean. The ambassadors concluded with
offering, in the name of their sovereigns, to refer the whole
matter in dispute to the arbitration of the court of Rome, or of
any common umpire.

King John was deeply chagrined at learning the departure of
the Spanish expedition. He saw that his rivals had been acting,
while he had been amused with negotiation. He at first threw out
hints of an immediate rupture, and endeavored, it is said, to

intimidate the Castilian ambassadors by bringing them accidentally, as it were, in presence of a splendid array of cavalry,
mounted and ready for immediate service. He vented his spleen
on the embassy, by declaring that "it was a mere abortion, having neither head nor feet"; alluding to the personal infirmity of
Ayala, who was lame, and to the light, frivolous character of the
other envoy.

These symptoms of discontent were duly notified to the Spanish government, who commanded the superintendent, Fonseca,
to keep a vigilant eye on the movements of the Portuguese, and,
in case any hostile armament should quit their ports, to be in
readiness to act against it with one double its force. King John,
however, was too shrewd a prince to be drawn into so impolitic
a measure as war with a powerful adversary, quite as likely to
baffle him in the field as in the council. Neither did he relish the
suggestion of deciding the dispute by arbitration, since he well
knew that his claim rested on too unsound a basis to authorize
the expectation of a favorable award from any impartial umpire.
He had already failed in an application for redress to the court of
Rome, which answered him by reference to its bulls, recently
published. In this emergency, he came to the resolution at last,
which should have been at first adopted, of deciding the matter
by a fair and open conference. It was not until the following year,
however, that his discontent so far subsided as to allow his
acquiescence in this measure.

At length, commissioners named by the two crowns convened
at Tordesillas, and on the 7th of June, 1494, subscribed articles
of agreement, which were ratified in the course of the same
year by the respective powers. In this treaty the Spaniards were
secured in the exclusive right of navigation and discovery in the
western ocean. At the urgent remonstrance of the Portuguese,
however, who complained that the papal line of demarcation
cooped up their enterprises within too narrow limits, they consented that, instead of one hundred, it should be removed three
hundred and seventy leagues west of the Cape de Verd islands,
beyond which all discoveries should appertain to the Spanish
nations. It was agreed that one or two caravels should be provided by each nation, to meet at the Grand Canary and proceed
due west the appointed distance, with a number of scientific men
on board, for the purpose of accurately determining the longi-

tude; and, if any lands should fall under the meridian, the direction of the line should be ascertained by the erection of beacons at suitable distances. The proposed meeting never took place. But the removal of the partition-line was followed by important consequences to the Portuguese, who derived from it their pretensions to the noble empire of Brazil.

Thus the singular misunderstanding, which menaced an open rupture at one time, was happily adjusted. Fortunately, the accomplishment of the passage round the Cape of Good Hope, which occurred soon afterwards, led the Portuguese in an opposite direction to their Spanish rivals, their Brazilian possessions having too little attractions, at first, to turn them from the splendid path of discovery thrown open in the East. It was not many years, however, before the two nations, by pursuing opposite routes of circumnavigation, were brought into collision on the other side of the globe; a circumstance never contemplated, apparently, by the treaty of Tordesillas. Their mutual pretensions were founded, however, on the provisions of that treaty, which, as the reader is aware, was itself only supplementary to the original bull of demarcation of Alexander the Sixth. Thus this bold stretch of papal authority, as often ridiculed as chimerical and absurd, was in a measure justified by the event, since it did, in fact, determine the principles on which the vast extent of unappropriated empire in the eastern and western hemispheres was ultimately divided between two petty states of Europe.

PART SECOND

Italian Wars

1502–1503

The war now began to assume many of the romantic features of that of Granada. The knights on both sides, not content with the usual military rencontres, defied one another to jousts and tourneys, eager to establish their prowess in the noble exercises of chivalry. One of the most remarkable of these meetings took place between eleven Spanish and as many French knights, in consequence of some disparaging remarks of the latter on the cavalry of their enemies, which they affirmed inferior to their own. The Venetians gave the parties a fair field of combat in the neutral territory under their own walls of Trani. A gallant array of well-armed knights of both nations guarded the lists and maintained the order of the fight. On the appointed day (September 20th, 1502) the champions appeared in the field, armed at all points, with horses richly caparisoned, and barbed or covered with steel panoply like their masters. The roofs and battlements of Trani were covered with spectators, while the lists were thronged with the French and Spanish chivalry, each staking in some degree the national honor on the issue of the contest. Among the Castilians were Diego de Paredes and Diego de Vera, while the good knight Bayard was most conspicuous on the other side.

As the trumpets sounded the appointed signal, the hostile parties rushed to the encounter. Three Spaniards were borne from their saddles by the rudeness of the shock, and four of their antagonists' horses slain. The fight, which began at ten in the morning, was not to be protracted beyond sunset. Long before that hour, all the French save two, one of them the chevalier Bayard, had been dismounted, and their horses, at which

104

the Spaniards had aimed more than at the riders, disabled or slain. The Spaniards, seven of whom were still on horseback, pressed hard on their adversaries, leaving little doubt of the fortune of the day. The latter, however, intrenching themselves behind the carcasses of their dead horses, made good their defenses against the Spaniards, who in vain tried to spur their terrified steeds over the barrier. In this way the fight was protracted till sunset; and, as both parties continued to keep possession of the field, the palm of victory was adjudged to neither, while both were pronounced to have demeaned themselves like good and valiant knights.

The tourney being ended, the combatants met in the center of the lists, and embraced each other in the true companionship of chivalry, "making good cheer together," says an old chronicler, before they separated. The Great Captain was not satisfied with the issue of the fight. "We have, at least," said one of his champions, "disproved the taunt of the Frenchmen, and shown ourselves as good horsemen as they." "I sent you for better," coldly retorted Gonsalvo.

A more tragic termination befell a combat à l'outrance between the chevalier Bayard and a Spanish cavalier, named Alonso de Sotomayor, who had accused the former of uncourteous treatment of him while his prisoner. Bayard denied the charge, and defied the Spaniard to prove it in single fight, on horse or on foot, as he best liked. Sotomayor, aware of his antagonist's uncommon horsemanship, preferred the latter alternative.

At the day and hour appointed (February 2d, 1503) the two knights entered the lists, armed with sword and dagger, and sheathed in complete harness; although, with a degree of temerity unusual in these combats, they wore their visors up. Both combatants knelt down in silent prayer for a few moments, and then, rising and crossing themselves, advanced straight against each other; "the good knight Bayard," says Brantôme, "moving as light of step as if he were going to lead some fair lady down the dance."

The Spaniard was of a large and powerful frame, and endeavored to crush his enemy by weight of blows, or to close with him and bring him to the ground. The latter, naturally inferior in strength, was rendered still weaker by a fever, from which he had not entirely recovered. He was more light and agile than his adversary, however, and superior dexterity enabled him not only to parry his enemy's strokes, but to deal him occasionally one of his own, while he sorely distressed him by the rapidity of his movements. At length, as the Spaniard was somewhat thrown off his balance by an ill-directed blow, Bayard struck him so sharply on the gorget that it gave way, and the sword entered his throat. Furious with the agony of the wound, Sotomayor collected all his strength for a last struggle, and, grasping his antagonist in his arms, they both rolled in the dust together. Before either could extricate himself, the quick-eyed Bayard, who had retained his poniard in his left hand during the whole combat, while the Spaniard's had remained in his belt, drove the steel with such convulsive strength under his enemy's eye that it pierced quite through the brain. After the judges had awarded the honors of the day to Bayard, the minstrels as usual began to pour forth triumphant strains in praise of the victor; but the good knight commanded them to desist, and, having first prostrated himself on his knees in gratitude for his victory, walked slowly out of the lists, expressing a wish that the combat had had a different termination, so that his honor had been saved.

In these jousts and tourneys, described with sufficient prolixity, but in a truly heart-stirring tone, by the chroniclers of the day, we may discern the last gleams of the light of chivalry, which illumined the darkness of the Middle Ages; and, although rough in comparison with the pastimes of more polished times, they called forth such displays of magnificence, courtesy, and knightly honor as throw something like the grace of civilization over the ferocious features of the age. . . .

FROM CHAPTER XII

The Victory

1503

Before his departure for France, Philip, anxious to re-establish harmony between that country and Spain, offered his services

to his father-in-law in negotiating with Louis the Twelfth, if possible, a settlement of the differences respecting Naples. Ferdinand showed some reluctance at intrusting so delicate a commission to an envoy in whose discretion he placed small reliance,
which was not augmented by the known partiality which Philip
entertained for the French monarch. Before the archduke had
crossed the frontier, however, he was overtaken by a Spanish
ecclesiastic named Bernaldo Boyl, abbot of St. Miguel de Cuxa,
who brought full powers to Philip from the king for concluding a
treaty with France, accompanied at the same time with private
instructions of the most strict and limited nature. He was enjoined, moreover, to take no step without the advice of his reverend coadjutor, and to inform the Spanish court at once if different propositions were submitted from those contemplated by
his instructions.

Thus fortified, the archduke Philip made his appearance at the
French court in Lyons, where he was received by Louis with the
same lively expressions of regard as before. With these amiable
dispositions, the negotiations were not long in resulting in a
definitive treaty, arranged to the mutual satisfaction of the parties, though in violation of the private instructions of the archduke. In the progress of the discussions, Ferdinand, according
to the Spanish historians, received advices from his envoy, the
abate Boyl, that Philip was transcending his commission; in consequence of which the king sent an express to France, urging his
son-in-law to adhere to the strict letter of his instructions. Before
the messenger reached Lyons, however, the treaty was executed.
Such is the Spanish account of this blind transaction.

The treaty, which was signed at Lyons, April 5th, 1503, was
arranged on the basis of the marriage of Charles, the infant son
of Philip, and Claude, princess of France; a marriage which, settled by three several treaties, was destined never to take place.
The royal infants were immediately to assume the titles of King
and Queen of Naples, and Duke and Duchess of Calabria. Until
the consummation of the marriage, the French division of the
kingdom was to be placed under the administration of some
suitable person named by Louis the Twelfth, and the Spanish under that of the archduke Philip, or some other deputy appointed
by Ferdinand. All places unlawfully seized by either party were
to be restored; and, lastly, it was settled, with regard to the dis-

puted province of the Capitanate, that the portion held by the
French should be governed by an agent of King Louis, and the
Spanish by the archduke Philip on behalf of Ferdinand.

Such in substance was the treaty of Lyons; a treaty which,
while it seemed to consult the interests of Ferdinand, by securing
the throne of Naples eventually to his posterity, was in fact far
more accommodated to those of Louis, by placing the immediate
control of the Spanish moiety under a prince over whom that
monarch held entire influence. It is impossible that so shrewd a
statesman as Ferdinand could, from the mere consideration of
advantages so remote and dependent on so precarious a contingency as the marriage of two infants then in their cradles,
have seriously contemplated an arrangement which surrendered
all the actual power into the hands of his rival; and that, too, at
the moment when his large armament, so long preparing for
Calabria, had reached that country, and when the Great Captain,
on the other quarter, had received such accessions of strength
as enabled him to assume the offensive, on at least equal terms
with the enemy.

No misgivings on this head, however, appear to have entered
the minds of the signers of the treaty, which was celebrated by
the court at Lyons with every show of public rejoicing, and
particularly with tourneys and tilts of reeds, in imitation of the
Spanish chivalry. At the same time, the French king countermanded the embarkation of fresh troops on board a fleet equipping at the port of Genoa for Naples, and sent orders to his generals in Italy to desist from further operations. The archduke for-
warded similar instructions to Gonsalvo, accompanied with a
copy of the powers intrusted to him by Ferdinand. That prudent
officer, however, whether in obedience to previous directions
from the king, as Spanish writers affirm, or on his own responsibility, from a very natural sense of duty, refused to comply with
the ambassador's orders; declaring "he knew no authority but
that of his own sovereigns, and that he felt bound to prosecute
the war with all his ability, till he received their commands to the
contrary."

Indeed, the archduke's despatches arrived at the very time
when the Spanish general, having strengthened himself by a reinforcement from the neighboring garrison of Tarento under
Pedro Navarro, was prepared to sally forth and try his fortune in

battle with the enemy. Without further delay, he put his purpose into execution, and on Friday the 28th of April, 1503, marched out with his whole army from the ancient walls of Barleta; a spot ever memorable in history as the scene of the extraordinary sufferings and indomitable constancy of the Spanish soldier.

The road lay across the field of Cannae, where, seventeen centuries before, the pride of Rome had been humbled by the victorious arms of Hannibal, in a battle which, though fought with far greater numbers, was not so decisive in its consequences as that which the same scenes were to witness in a few hours. The coincidence is certainly singular; and one might almost fancy that the actors in these fearful tragedies, unwilling to deface the fair haunts of civilization, had purposely sought a more fitting theater in this obscure and sequestered region.

The weather, although only at the latter end of April, was extremely sultry; the troops, notwithstanding Gonsalvo's orders on crossing the river Ofanto, the ancient Aufidus, had failed to supply themselves with sufficient water for the march; parched with heat and dust, they were soon distressed by excessive thirst; and, as the burning rays of the noontide sun beat fiercely on their heads, many of them, especially those cased in heavy armor, sank down on the road, fainting with exhaustion and fatigue. Gonsalvo was seen in every quarter, administering to the necessities of his men, and striving to reanimate their drooping spirits. At length, to relieve them, he commanded that each trooper should take one of the infantry on his crupper, setting the example himself by mounting a German ensign behind him on his own horse.

In this way, the whole army arrived early in the afternoon before Cerignola, a small town on an eminence about sixteen miles from Barleta, where the nature of the ground afforded the Spanish general a favorable position for his camp. The sloping sides of the hill were covered with vineyards, and its base was protected by a ditch of considerable depth. Gonsalvo saw at once the advantages of the ground. His men were jaded by the march; but there was no time to lose, as the French, who, on his departure from Barleta, had been drawn up under the walls of Canosa, were now rapidly advancing. All hands were put in requisition, therefore, for widening the trench, in which they planted sharp-pointed stakes; while the earth which they excavated enabled them to throw up a parapet of considerable height on the side next the town. On this rampart he mounted his little train of artillery, consisting of thirteen guns, and behind it drew up his forces in order of battle.

Before these movements were completed in the Spanish camp, the bright arms and banners of the French were seen glistening in the distance amid the tall fennel and cane-brakes with which the country was thickly covered. As soon as they had come in view of the Spanish encampment, they were brought to a halt, while a council of war was called, to determine the expediency of giving battle that evening. The duke of Nemours would have deferred it till the following morning, as the day was already far spent and allowed no time for reconnoitring the position of his enemy. But Ives d'Alègre, Chandieu, the commander of the Swiss, and some other officers, were for immediate action, representing the importance of not balking the impatience of the soldiers, who were all hot for the assault. In the course of the debate, Alègre was so much heated as to throw out some rash taunts on the courage of the viceroy, which the latter would have avenged on the spot, had not his arm been arrested by Louis d'Ars. He had the weakness, however, to suffer them to change his cooler purpose, exclaiming, "We will fight tonight, then; and perhaps those who vaunt the loudest will be found to trust more to their spurs than their swords"; a prediction bitterly justified by the event.

While this dispute was going on, Gonsalvo gained time for making the necessary disposition of his troops. In the center he placed his German auxiliaries, armed with their long pikes, and on each wing the Spanish infantry under the command of Pedro Navarro, Diego de Paredes, Pizarro, and other illustrious captains. The defense of the artillery was committed to the left wing. A considerable body of men-at-arms, including those recently equipped from the spoils of Ruvo, was drawn up within the intrenchments, in a quarter affording a convenient opening for a sally, and placed under the orders of Mendoza and Fabrizio Colonna, whose brother Prospero and Pedro de la Paz took charge of the light cavalry, which was posted without the lines to annoy the advance of the enemy, and act on any point, as occasion might require. Having completed his preparations, the Spanish general coolly waited the assault of the French.

The duke of Nemours had marshaled his forces in a very different order. He distributed them into three battles or divisions, stationing his heavy horse, composing altogether, as Gonsalvo declared, "the finest body of cavalry seen for many years in Italy," under the command of Louis d'Ars, on the right. The second and center division, formed somewhat in the rear of the right, was made up of the Swiss and Gascon infantry, headed by the brave Chandieu; and his left, consisting chiefly of his light cavalry, and drawn up, like the last, somewhat in the rear of the preceding, was intrusted to Alègre.

It was within half an hour of sunset when the duke de Nemours gave orders for the attack, and, putting himself at the head of the gendarmerie on the right, spurred at full gallop against the Spanish left. The hostile armies were nearly equal, amounting to between six and seven thousand men each. The French were superior in the number and condition of their cavalry, rising to a third of their whole force; while Gonsalvo's strength lay chiefly in his infantry, which had acquired a lesson of tactics under him that raised it to a level with the best in Europe.

As the French advanced, the guns on the Spanish left poured a lively fire into their ranks, when, a spark accidentally communicating with the magazine of powder, the whole blew up with a tremendous explosion. The Spaniards were filled with consternation; but Gonsalvo, converting the misfortune into a lucky omen, called out, "Courage, soldiers! these are the beacon-lights of victory! We have no need of our guns at close quarters."

In the meantime, the French van under Nemours, advancing rapidly under the dark clouds of smoke which rolled heavily over the field, were unexpectedly brought up by the deep trench, of whose existence they were unapprised. Some of the horse were precipitated into it, and all received a sudden check, until Nemours, finding it impossible to force the works in this quarter, rode along their front in search of some practicable passage. In doing this, he necessarily exposed his flank to the fatal aim of the Spanish arquebusiers. A shot from one of them took effect on the unfortunate young nobleman, and he fell, mortally wounded, from his saddle.

At this juncture, the Swiss and Gascon infantry, briskly moving up to second the attack of the now disordered horse, arrived before the intrenchments. Undismayed by this formidable barrier, their commander, Chandieu, made the most desperate attempts to force a passage; but the loose earth freshly turned up afforded no hold to the feet, and his men were compelled to recoil from the dense array of German pikes which bristled over the summit of the breastwork. Chandieu, their leader, made every effort to rally and bring them back to the charge, but, in the act of doing this, was hit by a ball, which stretched him lifeless in the ditch; his burnished arms, and the snow-white plumes above his helmet, making him a conspicuous mark for the enemy.

All was now confusion. The Spanish arquebusiers, screened by their defenses, poured a galling fire into the dense masses of the enemy, who were mingled together indiscriminately, horse and foot, while, the leaders being down, no one seemed capable of bringing them to order. At this critical moment, Gonsalvo, whose eagle eye took in the operations of the whole field, ordered a general charge along the line; and the Spaniards, leaping their intrenchments, descended with the fury of an avalanche on their foes, whose wavering columns, completely broken by the violence of the shock, were seized with a panic, and fled, scarcely offering any resistance. Louis d'Ars, at the head of such of the men-at-arms as could follow him, went off in one direction, and Ives d'Alègre, with his light cavalry, which had hardly come into action, in another; thus fully verifying the ominous prediction of his commander. The slaughter fell most heavily on the Swiss and Gascon foot, whom the cavalry under Mendoza and Pedro de la Paz rode down and cut to pieces without sparing, till the shades of evening shielded them at length from their pitiless pursuers. . . .

The Great Captain passed the night on the field of battle, which on the following morning presented a ghastly spectacle of the dying and the dead. More than three thousand French are computed by the best accounts to have fallen. The loss of the Spaniards, covered as they were by their defenses, was inconsiderable. All the enemy's artillery, consisting of thirteen pieces, his baggage, and most of his colors fell into their hands. Never was there a more complete victory, achieved too within the space of little more than an hour. The body of the unfortunate Nemours, which was recognized by one of his pages from the rings on the fingers, was found under a heap of slain, much disfigured. It appeared that he had received three several wounds, disproving, if need were, by his honorable death the injurious taunts of Alègre. Gonsalvo was affected even to tears at beholding the mutilated remains of his young and gallant adversary, who, whatever judgment might be formed of his capacity as a leader, was allowed to have all the qualities which belong to a true knight. With him perished the last scion of the illustrious house of Armagnac. Gonsalvo ordered his remains to be conveyed to Barleta, where they were laid in the cemetery of the convent of St. Francis, with all the honors due to his high station. . . .

The day after the battle of Cerignola the Spaniards received tidings of another victory, scarcely less important, gained over the French in Calabria, the preceding week. The army sent out under Portocarrero had reached that coast early in March; but soon after its arrival its gallant commander fell ill and died. The dying general named Don Fernando de Andrada as his successor; and this officer, combining his forces with those before in the country under Cardona and Benavides, encountered the French commander D'Aubigny in a pitched battle, not far from Seminara, on Friday, the 21st of April. It was near the same spot on which the latter had twice beaten the Spaniards. But the star of France was on the wane; and the gallant old officer had the mortification to see his little corps of veterans completely routed after a sharp engagement of less than an hour, while he himself was retrieved with difficulty from the hands of the enemy by the valor of his Scottish guard.

The Great Captain and his army, highly elated with the news of this fortunate event, which annihilated the French power in Calabria, began their march on Naples; Fabrizio Colonna having been first detached into the Abruzzi to receive the submission of the people in that quarter. The tidings of the victory had spread far and wide; and, as Gonsalvo's army advanced, they beheld the ensigns of Aragon floating from the battlements of the towns upon their route, while the inhabitants came forth to greet the conqueror, eager to testify their devotion to the Spanish cause. The army halted at Benevento; and the general sent his summons to the city of Naples, inviting it in the most courteous terms to resume its ancient allegiance to the legitimate branch of Aragon. It was hardly to be expected that the allegiance of a people who had so long seen their country set up as a mere stake for political gamesters should sit very closely upon them, or that they should care to peril their lives on the transfer of a crown which had shifted on the heads of half a dozen proprietors in as many successive years. With the same ductile enthusiasm, therefore, with which they had greeted the accession of Charles the Eighth and of Louis the Twelfth, they now welcomed the restoration of the ancient dynasty of Aragon; and deputies from the principal nobility and citizens waited on the Great Captain at Acerra, where they tendered him the keys of the city and requested the confirmation of their rights and privileges.

Gonsalvo, having promised this in the name of his royal master, on the following morning, the 14th of May, 1503, made his entrance in great state into the capital, leaving his army without the walls. He was escorted by the military of the city under a royal canopy borne by the deputies. The streets were strewed with flowers, the edifices decorated with appropriate emblems and devices and wreathed with banners emblazoned with the united arms of Aragon and Naples. As he passed along, the city rang with the acclamations of countless multitudes who thronged the streets; while every window and housetop was filled with spectators, eager to behold the man who, with scarcely any other resources than those of his own genius, had so long defied, and at length completely foiled, the power of France.

On the following day a deputation of the nobility and people waited on the Great Captain at his quarters, and tendered him the usual oaths of allegiance for his master, King Ferdinand, whose accession finally closed the series of revolutions which had so long agitated this unhappy country.

The city of Naples was commanded by two strong fortresses still held by the French, which, being well victualled and supplied with ammunition, showed no disposition to surrender. The Great Captain determined, therefore, to reserve a small corps for their reduction, while he sent forward the main body of his army to besiege Gaeta. But the Spanish infantry refused to march until the heavy arrears, suffered to accumulate through the negligence of the government, were discharged; and Gonsalvo, afraid of awakening the mutinous spirit which he had once found it so difficult to quell, was obliged to content himself with sending forward his cavalry and German levies, and to permit the infantry to take up its quarters in the capital, under strict orders to respect the persons and property of the citizens.

He now lost no time in pressing the siege of the French fortresses, whose impregnable situation might have derided the efforts of the most formidable enemy in the ancient state of military science. But the reduction of these places was intrusted to Pedro Navarro, the celebrated engineer, whose improvements in the art of mining have gained him the popular reputation of being its inventor, and who displayed such unprecedented skill on this occasion as makes it a memorable epoch in the annals of war.

Under his directions, the small tower of St. Vincenzo having been first reduced by a furious cannonade, a mine was run under the outer defenses of the great fortress called Castel Nuovo. On the 21st of May, the mine was sprung; a passage was opened over the prostrate ramparts, and the assailants, rushing in with Gonsalvo and Navarro at their head, before the garrison had time to secure the drawbridge, applied their ladders to the walls of the castle and succeeded in carrying the place by escalade, after a desperate struggle, in which the greater part of the French were slaughtered. An immense booty was found in the castle. The Angevin party had made it a place of deposit for their most valuable effects, gold, jewels, plate, and other treasures, which, together with its well-stored magazines of grain and ammunition, became the indiscriminate spoil of the victors. As some of these, however, complained of not getting their share of the plunder, Gonsalvo, giving full scope in the exultation of the moment to military license, called out, gaily, "Make amends for it, then, by what you can find in my quarters!" The words were not uttered to deaf ears. The mob of soldiery rushed to the splendid palace of the Angevin prince of Salerno, then occupied by the Great Captain, and in a moment its sumptuous furniture, paintings, and other costly decorations, together with the contents of its generous cellar, were seized and appropriated without ceremony by the invaders, who thus indemnified themselves at their general's expense for the remissness of the government.

After some weeks of protracted operations, the remaining fortress, Castel d'Uovo, as it was called, opened its gates to Navarro; and a French fleet, coming into the harbor, had the mortification to find itself fired on from the walls of the place it was intended to relieve. Before this event, Gonsalvo, having obtained funds from Spain for paying off his men, quitted the capital and directed his march on Gaeta. The important results of his victories were now fully disclosed. D'Aubigny, with the wreck of the forces escaped from Seminara, had surrendered. The two Abruzzi, the Capitanate, all the Basilicate, except Venosa, still held by Louis d'Ars, and indeed every considerable place in the kingdom, had tendered its submission, with the exception of Gaeta. Summoning, therefore, to his aid Andrada, Navarro, and his other officers, the Great Captain resolved to concentrate all his strength on this point, designing to press the siege, and thus exterminate at a blow the feeble remains of the French power in Italy. . . .

CHAPTER XVI

Illness and Death of Isabella

1504

The acquisition of an important kingdom in the heart of Europe, and of the New World beyond the waters, which promised to pour into her lap all the fabled treasures of the Indies, was rapidly raising Spain to the first rank of European powers. But, in this noontide of her success, she was to experience a fatal shock in the loss of that illustrious personage who had so long and so gloriously presided over her destinies. We have had occasion to notice more than once the declining state of the queen's health during the last few years. Her constitution had been greatly impaired by incessant personal fatigue and exposure, and by the unremitting activity of her mind. It had suffered far more severely, however, from a series of heavy domestic calamities, which had fallen on her with little intermission since the death of her mother, in 1496. The next year, she followed to the grave the remains of her only son, the heir and hope of the monarchy, just entering on his prime; and, in the succeeding, was called on to render the same sad office to the best-beloved of her daughters, the amiable queen of Portugal.

The severe illness occasioned by this last blow terminated in a dejection of spirits, from which she never entirely recovered. Her surviving children were removed far from her into distant lands; with the occasional exception, indeed, of Joanna, who caused a still deeper pang to her mother's affectionate heart, by exhibiting infirmities which justified the most melancholy presages for the future.

Far from abandoning herself to weak and useless repining, however, Isabella sought consolation, where it was best to be found, in the exercises of piety, and in the earnest discharge of the duties attached to her exalted station. Accordingly, we find her attentive as ever to the minutest interests of her subjects; supporting her great minister Ximenes in his schemes of reform, quickening the zeal for discovery in the west, and, at the close of the year 1503, on the alarm of the French invasion, rousing her dying energies to kindle a spirit of resistance in her people. These strong mental exertions, however, only accelerated the decay of her bodily strength, which was gradually sinking under that sickness of the heart which admits of no cure, and scarcely of consolation.

In the beginning of that very year she had declined so visibly that the cortes of Castile, much alarmed, petitioned her to provide for the government of the kingdom after her decease, in case of the absence or incapacity of Joanna. She seems to have rallied in some measure after this; but it was only to relapse into a state of greater debility, as her spirits sunk under the conviction, which now forced itself on her, of her daughter's settled insanity.

Early in the spring of the following year (1504) that unfortunate lady embarked for Flanders, where, soon after her arrival, the inconstancy of her husband, and her own ungovernable sensibilities, occasioned the most scandalous scenes. Philip became openly enamored of one of the ladies of her suite; and his injured wife, in a paroxysm of jealousy, personally assaulted her fair rival in the palace, and caused the beautiful locks which had excited the admiration of her fickle husband to be shorn from her head. This outrage so affected Philip that he vented his indignation against Joanna in the coarsest and most unmanly terms, and finally refused to have any further intercourse with her.

The account of this disgraceful scene reached Castile in the month of June. It occasioned the deepest chagrin and mortification to the unhappy parents. Ferdinand soon after fell ill of a fever, and the queen was seized with the same disorder, accompanied by more alarming symptoms. Her illness was exasperated by anxiety for her husband, and she refused to credit the favorable reports of his physicians, while he was detained from her presence. His vigorous constitution, however, threw off the malady, while hers gradually failed under it. Her tender heart was more keenly sensible than his to the unhappy condition of their child, and to the gloomy prospects which awaited her beloved Castile.

Her faithful follower, Martyr, was with the court at this time in Medina del Campo. In a letter to the court of Tendilla, dated October 7th, he states that the most serious apprehensions were entertained by the physicians for the queen's fate. "Her whole system," he says, "is pervaded by a consuming fever. She loathes food of every kind, and is tormented with incessant thirst, while the disorder has all the appearance of terminating in a dropsy."

In the meanwhile, Isabella lost nothing of her solicitude for the welfare of her people and the great concerns of government. While reclining, as she was obliged to do a great part of the day, on her couch, she listened to the recital or reading of whatever occurred of interest, at home or abroad. She gave audience to distinguished foreigners, especially such Italians as could acquaint her with particulars of the late war, and above all in regard to Gonsalvo de Cordova, in whose fortunes she had always taken the liveliest concern. She received with pleasure, too, such intelligent travelers as her renown had attracted to the Castilian court. She drew forth their stores of various information, and dismissed them, says a writer of the age, penetrated with the deepest admiration of that masculine strength of mind which sustained her so nobly under the weight of a mortal malady.

This malady was now rapidly gaining ground. On the 15th of October we have another epistle of Martyr, of the following melancholy tenor. "You ask me respecting the state of the queen's health. We sit sorrowful in the palace all day long, tremblingly waiting the hour when religion and virtue shall quit the earth with her. Let us pray that we may be permitted to follow hereafter where she is soon to go. She so far transcends all human excellence, that there is scarcely anything of mortality about her. She can hardly be said to die, but to pass into a nobler existence, which should rather excite our envy than our sorrow. She leaves the world filled with her renown, and she goes to enjoy life eternal with her God in heaven. I write this," he concludes, "between hope and fear, while the breath is still fluttering within her."

The deepest gloom now overspread the nation. Even Isabella's long illness had failed to prepare the minds of her faithful people for the sad catastrophe. They recalled several ominous circumstances which had before escaped their attention. In the preceding spring, an earthquake, accompanied by a tremendous hurricane, such as the oldest men did not remember, had visited Andalusia, and especially Carmona, a place belonging to the queen, and occasioned frightful desolation there. The superstitious Spaniards now read in these portents the prophetic signs by which Heaven announces some great calamity. Prayers were put up in every temple, processions and pilgrimages made in every part of the country, for the recovery of their beloved sovereign—but in vain.

Isabella, in the meantime, was deluded with no false hopes. She felt too surely the decay of her bodily strength, and she resolved to perform what temporal duties yet remained for her, while her faculties were still unclouded.

On the 12th of October she executed that celebrated testament which reflects so clearly the peculiar qualities of her mind and character. She begins with prescribing the arrangements for her burial. She orders her remains to be transported to Granada, to the Franciscan monastery of Santa Isabella in the Alhambra, and there deposited in a low and humble sepulcher, without other memorial than a plain inscription on it. "But," she continues, "should the king my lord prefer a sepulcher in some other place, then my will is that my body be there transported, and laid by his side; that the union we have enjoyed in this world, and, through the mercy of God, may hope again for our souls in heaven, may be represented by our bodies in the earth." Then, desirous of correcting by her example, in this last act of her life, the wasteful pomp of funeral obsequies to which the Castilians were addicted, she commands that her own should be performed in the plainest and most unostentatious manner, and that the sum saved by this economy should be distributed in alms among the poor.

She next provides for several charities, assigning, among others, marriage portions for poor maidens, and a considerable sum for the redemption of Christian captives in Barbary. She enjoins the punctual discharge of all her personal debts within a year; she retrenches superfluous offices in the royal household, and revokes all such grants, whether in the forms of lands or annuities, as she conceives to have been made without sufficient warrant. She inculcates on her successors the importance of maintaining the integrity of the royal domains, and, above all, of never divesting themselves of their title to the important fortress of Gibraltar.

After this, she comes to the succession of the crown, which she settles on the infanta Joanna as "queen proprietor," and the archduke Philip as her husband. She gives them much good counsel respecting their future administration; enjoining them, as they would secure the love and obedience of their subjects, to conform in all respects to the laws and usages of the realm, to appoint no foreigner to office—an error into which Philip's connections, she saw, would be very likely to betray them—and to make no laws or ordinances "which necessarily require the consent of cortes," during their absence from the kingdom. She recommends to them the same conjugal harmony which had ever subsisted between her and her husband; she beseeches them to show the latter all the deference and filial affection "due to him beyond every other parent, for his eminent virtues"; and finally inculcates on them the most tender regard for the liberties and welfare of their subjects.

She next comes to the great question proposed by the cortes of 1503, respecting the government of the realm in the absence or incapacity of Joanna. She declares that, after mature deliberation, and with the advice of many of the prelates and nobles of the kingdom, she appoints King Ferdinand her husband to be the sole regent of Castile, in that exigency, until the majority of her grandson Charles; being led to this, she adds, "by the consideration of the magnanimity and illustrious qualities of the king my lord, as well as his large experience, and the great profit which will redound to the state from his wise and beneficent rule." She expresses her sincere conviction that his past conduct affords a sufficient guarantee for his faithful administration, but, in compliance with established usage, requires the customary oath from him on entering on the duties of the office.

She then makes a specific provision for her husband's personal maintenance, which, "although less than she could wish, and far less than he deserves, considering the eminent services he has rendered the state," she settles at one-half of all the net proceeds and profits accruing from the newly discovered countries in the west; together with ten millions of maravedis annually, assigned on the alcavalas of the grand-masterships of the military orders.

After some additional regulations, respecting the descent of the crown on failure of Johanna's lineal heirs, she recommends in the kindest and most emphatic terms to her successors the various members of her household, and her personal friends, among whom we find the names of the marquis and marchioness of Moya (Beatrice de Bobadilla, the companion of her youth), and Garcilasso de la Vega, the accomplished minister at the papal court.

And lastly, concluding in the same beautiful strain of conjugal tenderness in which she began, she says, "I beseech the king my lord that he will accept all my jewels, or such as he shall select, so that, seeing them, he may be reminded of the singular love I always bore him while living, and that I am now waiting for him in a better world; by which remembrance he may be encouraged to live the more justly and holily in this."

Six executors were named to the will. The two principal were the king and the primate Ximenes, who had full powers to act in conjunction with any one of the others.

I have dwelt the more minutely on the details of Isabella's testament, from the evidence it affords of her constancy in her dying hour to the principles which had governed her through life; of her expansive and sagacious policy; her prophetic insight into the evils to result from her death—evils, alas! which no fore-cast could avert; her scrupulous attention to all her personal obligations; and that warm attachment to her friends which could never falter while a pulse beat in her bosom.

After performing this duty, she daily grew weaker, the powers of her mind seeming to brighten as those of her body declined. The concerns of her government still occupied her thoughts; and several public measures, which she had postponed through urgency of other business, or growing infirmities, pressed so heavily on her heart that she made them the subject of a codicil to her former will. It was executed November 23d, 1504, only three days before her death.

Three of the provisions contained in it are too remarkable to pass unnoticed. The first concerns the codification of the laws. For this purpose, the queen appoints a commission to make a new digest of the statutes and pragmaticas, the contradictory tenor of which still occasioned much embarrassment in Castilian jurisprudence. This was a subject she always had much at heart; but no nearer approach had been made to it than the valuable though insufficient work of Montalvo, in the early part of her reign; and, notwithstanding her precautions, none more effectual was destined to take place till the reign of Philip the Second.

The second item had reference to the natives of the New World. Gross abuses had arisen there since the partial revival of the repartimientos, although, Las Casas says, "intelligence of this was carefully kept from the ears of the queen." Some vague apprehension of the truth, however, appears to have forced itself on her; and she enjoins her successors, in the most earnest manner, to quicken the good work of converting and civilizing the poor Indians, to treat them with the greatest gentleness, and redress any wrongs they may have suffered in their persons or property.

Lastly, she expresses her doubts as to the legality of the revenue drawn from the alcavalas, constituting the principal income of the crown. She directs a commission to ascertain whether it were originally intended to be perpetual, and if this were done with the free consent of the people; enjoining her heirs, in that event, to collect the tax so that it should press least heavily on her subjects. Should it be found otherwise, however, she directs that the legislature be summoned to devise proper measures for supplying the wants of the crown—"measures depending for their validity on the good pleasure of the subjects of the realm."

Such were the dying words of this admirable woman; displaying the same respect for the rights and liberties of the nation which she had shown through life, and striving to secure the blessings of her benign administration to the most distant and barbarous regions under her sway. These two documents were a precious legacy bequeathed to her people, to guide them when the light of her personal example should be withdrawn forever.

The queen's signature to the codicil, which still exists among the manuscripts of the Royal Library at Madrid, shows, by its irregular and scarcely legible characters, the feeble state to which she was then reduced. She had now adjusted all her worldly concerns, and she prepared to devote herself, during the brief space which remained, to those of a higher nature. It was but the last act of a life of preparation. She had the misfortune, common to persons of her rank, to be separated in her last moments from those whose filial tenderness might have done so much to soften the bitterness of death. But she had the good fortune, most rare, to have secured for this trying hour the solace of disinterested friendship; for she beheld around her the friends of her childhood, formed and proved in the dark season of adversity.

As she saw them bathed in tears around her bed, she calmly said, "Do not weep for me, nor waste your time in fruitless prayers for my recovery, but pray rather for the salvation of my soul." On receiving the extreme unction, she refused to have her feet exposed, as was usual on that occasion; a circumstance which, occurring at a time when there can be no suspicion of affectation, is often noticed by Spanish writers as a proof of that sensitive delicacy and decorum which distinguished her through life. At length, having received the sacraments, and performed all the offices of a sincere and devout Christian, she gently expired, a little before noon, on Wednesday, November 26th, 1504, in the fifty-fourth year of her age, and thirtieth of her reign.

"My hand," says Peter Martyr, in a letter written on the same day to the archbishop of Granada, "falls powerless by my side, for very sorrow. The world has lost its noblest ornament; a loss to be deplored not only by Spain, which she has so long carried forward in the career of glory, but by every nation in Christendom; for she was the mirror of every virtue, the shield of the innocent, and an avenging sword to the wicked. I know none of her sex, in ancient or modern times, who in my judgment is at all worthy to be named with this incomparable woman."

No time was lost in making preparations for transporting the queen's body unembalmed to Granada, in strict conformity to her orders. It was escorted by a numerous cortège of cavaliers and ecclesiastics, among whom was the faithful Martyr. The procession began its mournful march the day following her death, taking the route through Arevalo, Toledo, and Jaen. Scarcely had it left Medina del Campo when a tremendous tempest set in, which continued with little interruption during the whole journey. The roads were rendered nearly impassable; the bridges swept away, the small streams swollen to the size of the Tagus, and the level country buried under a deluge of water. Neither sun nor stars were seen during their whole progress. The horses and mules were borne down by the torrents, and the riders in several instances perished with them. "Never," exclaims Martyr, "did I encounter such perils in the whole of my hazardous pilgrimage to Egypt."

At length, on the 18th of December, the melancholy and wayworn cavalcade reached the place of its destination; and, amidst the wild strife of the elements, the peaceful remains of Isabella were laid, with simple solemnities, in the Franciscan monastery of the Alhambra. Here, under the shadow of those venerable Moslem towers, and in the heart of the capital which her noble constancy had recovered for her country, they continued to repose till after the death of Ferdinand, when they were removed to be laid by his side in the stately mausoleum of the cathedral church of Granada.

I shall defer the review of Queen Isabella's administration until it can be made in conjunction with that of Ferdinand's, and shall confine myself at present to such considerations on the prominent traits of her character as have been suggested by the preceding history of her life.

Her person, as mentioned in the early part of the narrative, was of the middle height, and well proportioned. She had a clear, fresh complexion, with light blue eyes and auburn hair—a style of beauty exceedingly rare in Spain. Her features were regular, and universally allowed to be uncommonly handsome. The illusion which attaches to rank, more especially when united with engaging manners, might lead us to suspect some exaggeration in the encomiums so liberally lavished on her. But they would seem to be in a great measure justified by the portraits that remain of her, which combine a faultless symmetry of features with singular sweetness and intelligence of expression.

Her manners were most gracious and pleasing. They were marked by natural dignity and modest reserve, tempered by an affability which flowed from the kindliness of her disposition. She was the last person to be approached with undue familiarity; yet the respect which she imposed was mingled with the strongest feelings of devotion and love. She showed great tact in accommodating herself to the peculiar situation and character of those around her. She appeared in arms at the head of her troops, and shrunk from none of the hardships of war. During the reforms introduced into the religious houses, she visited the nunneries in person, taking her needlework with her, and passing the day in the society of the inmates. When traveling in Galicia, she attired herself in the costume of the country, borrowing for that purpose the jewels and other ornaments of the ladies there, and returning them with liberal additions. By this condescending and captivating deportment, as well as by her higher qualities, she gained an ascendancy over her turbulent subjects which no king of Spain could ever boast.

She spoke the Castilian with much elegance and correctness. She had an easy fluency of discourse, which, though generally of a serious complexion, was occasionally seasoned with agreeable sallies, some of which have passed into proverbs. She was temperate even to abstemiousness in her diet, seldom or never tasting wine; and so frugal in her table, that the daily expenses for herself and family did not exceed the moderate sum of forty ducats. She was equally simple and economical in her apparel. On all public occasions, indeed, she displayed a royal magnificence; but she had no relish for it in private, and she freely gave away her clothes and jewels, as presents to her friends. Naturally of a sedate though cheerful temper, she had little taste for the frivolous amusements which make up so much of a court life; and, if she encouraged the presence of minstrels and musicians in her palace, it was to wean her young nobility from the coarser and less intellectual pleasures to which they were addicted.

Among her moral qualities, the most conspicuous, perhaps, was her magnanimity. She betrayed nothing little or selfish, in thought or action. Her schemes were vast, and executed in the same noble spirit in which they were conceived. She never employed doubtful agents or sinister measures, but the most direct and open policy. She scorned to avail herself of advantages offered by the perfidy of others. Where she had once given her confidence, she gave her hearty and steady support; and she was scrupulous to redeem any pledge she had made to those who ventured in her cause, however unpopular. She sustained Ximenes in all his obnoxious but salutary reforms. She seconded Columbus in the prosecution of his arduous enterprise, and shielded him from the calumny of his enemies. She did the same good service to her favorite, Gonsalvo de Cordova; and the day of her death was felt, and, as it proved, truly felt, by both, as the last of their good fortune. Artifice and duplicity were so abhorrent to her character, and so averse from her domestic policy, that when they appear in the foreign relations of Spain it is certainly not imputable to her. She was incapable of harboring any petty distrust or latent malice; and, although stern in the execution and exaction of public justice, she made the most generous allowance, and even sometimes advances, to those who had personally injured her.

But the principle which gave a peculiar coloring to every feature of Isabella's mind was piety. It shone forth from the very depths of her soul with a heavenly radiance which illuminated her whole character. Fortunately, her earliest years had been passed in the rugged school of adversity, under the eye of a mother who implanted in her serious mind such strong principles of religion as nothing in after-life had power to shake. At an early age, in the flower of youth and beauty, she was introduced to her brother's court; but its blandishments, so dazzling to a young imagination, had no power over hers; for she was surrounded by a moral atmosphere of purity,

Driving far off each thing of sin and guilt.

Such was the decorum of her manners, that, though encompassed by false friends and open enemies, not the slightest reproach was breathed on her fair name in this corrupt and calumnious court.

She gave a liberal portion of her time to private devotions, as well as to the public exercises of religion. She expended large sums in useful charities, especially in the erection of hospitals and churches, and the more doubtful endowments of monasteries. Her piety was strikingly exhibited in that unfeigned humility which, although the very essence of our faith, is so rarely found; and most rarely in those whose great powers and exalted stations seem to raise them above the level of ordinary mortals. A remarkable illustration of this is afforded in the queen's correspondence with Talavera, in which her meek and docile spirit is strikingly contrasted with the Puritanical intolerance of her confessor. Yet Talavera, as we have seen, was sincere and benevolent at heart. Unfortunately, the royal conscience was at times committed to very different keeping; and that humility which, as we have repeatedly had occasion to notice, made her defer so reverentially to her ghostly advisers, led, under the fanatic Torquemada, the confessor of her early youth, to those deep blemishes on her administration, the establishment of the Inquisition and the exile of the Jews.

But, though blemishes of the deepest dye on her administration, they are certainly not to be regarded as such on her moral character. It will be difficult to condemn her, indeed, without condemning the age; for these very acts are not only excused, but extolled by her contemporaries, as constituting her strongest claims to renown, and to the gratitude of her country. They proceeded from the principle, openly avowed by the court of Rome, that zeal for the purity of the faith could atone for every crime. This immoral maxim, flowing from the head of the Church, was echoed in a thousand different forms by the subordinate clergy, and greedily received by a superstitious people. It was not to be expected that a solitary woman, filled with natural diffidence of her own capacity on such subjects, should array herself against those venerated counselors whom she had been taught from her cradle to look to as the guides and guardians of her conscience.

However mischievous the operations of the Inquisition may have been in Spain, its establishment, in point of principle, was not worse than many other measures which have passed with far less censure, though in a much more advanced and civilized age. Where, indeed, during the sixteenth and the greater part of the seventeenth century, was the principle of persecution abandoned by the dominant party, whether Catholic or Protestant? And where that of toleration asserted, except by the weaker? It is true, to borrow Isabella's own expression in her letter to Talavera, the prevalence of a bad custom cannot constitute its apology. But it should serve much to mitigate our condemnation of the queen, that she fell into no greater error, in the imperfect light in which she lived, than was common to the greatest minds in a later and far riper period.

Isabella's actions, indeed, were habitually based on principle. Whatever errors of judgment be imputed to her, she most anxiously sought in all situations to discern and discharge her duty. Faithful in the dispensation of justice, no bribe was large enough to ward off the execution of the law. No motive, not even conjugal affection, could induce her to make an unsuitable appointment to public office. No reverence for the ministers of religion could lead her to wink at their misconduct; nor could the deference she entertained for the head of the Church allow her to tolerate his encroachments on the rights of her crown. She seemed to consider herself especially bound to preserve entire the peculiar claims and privileges of Castile, after its union under the same sovereign with Aragon. And although, "while her own will was law," says Peter Martyr, "she governed in such a manner that it might appear the joint action of both Ferdinand and herself," yet she was careful never to surrender into his hands one of those prerogatives which belonged to her as queen proprietor of the kingdom.

Isabella's measures were characterized by that practical good sense without which the most brilliant parts may work more to the woe than to the weal of mankind. Though engaged all her life in reforms, she had none of the failings so common in reformers. Her plans, though vast, were never visionary. The best proof of this is, that she lived to see most of them realized.

She was quick to discern objects of real utility. She saw the importance of the new discovery of printing, and liberally patronized it, from the first moment it appeared. She had none of the exclusive, local prejudices too common with her countrymen. She drew talent from the most remote quarters to her dominions, by munificent rewards. She imported foreign artisans for her manufactures, foreign engineers and officers for the discipline of her army, and foreign scholars to imbue her martial subjects with more cultivated tastes. She consulted the useful, in all her subordinate regulations; in her sumptuary laws, for instance, directed against the fashionable extravagances of dress, and the ruinous ostentation so much affected by the Castilians in their weddings and funerals. Lastly, she showed the same perspicacity in the selection of her agents; well knowing that the best measures become bad in incompetent hands.

But, although the skillful selection of her agents was an obvious cause of Isabella's success, yet another, even more important, is to be found in her own vigilance and untiring exertions. During the first busy and bustling years of her reign, these exertions were of incredible magnitude. She was almost always in the saddle, for she made all her journeys on horseback; and she traveled with a rapidity which made her always present on the spot where her presence was needed. She was never intimidated by the weather, or the state of her own health; and this reckless exposure undoubtedly contributed much to impair her excellent constitution.

She was equally indefatigable in her mental application. After assiduous attention to business through the day, she was often known to sit up all night dictating despatches to her secretaries. In the midst of these overwhelming cares, she found time to supply the defects of early education by learning Latin, so as to understand it without difficulty, whether written or spoken, and indeed, in the opinion of a competent judge, to attain a critical accuracy in it. As she had little turn for light amusements, she sought relief from graver cares by some useful occupation appropriate to her sex; and she left ample evidence of her skill in this way, in the rich specimens of embroidery, wrought with her own fair hands, with which she decorated the churches. She was careful to instruct her daughters in these more humble departments of domestic duty; for she thought nothing too humble to learn which was useful.

With all her high qualifications, Isabella would have been still unequal to the achievement of her grand designs, without possessing a degree of fortitude rare in either sex; not the courage which implies contempt of personal danger—though of this she had a larger share than falls to most men; nor that which supports its possessor under the extremities of bodily pain—though of this she gave ample evidence, since she endured the greatest suffering her sex is called to bear, without a groan; but that moral courage which sustains the spirit in the dark hour of adversity, and, gathering light from within to dispel the darkness, imparts its own cheering influence to all around. This was shown remarkably in the stormy season which ushered in her accession, as well as through the whole of the Moorish war. It was her voice that decided never to abandon Alhama. Her remonstrances compelled the king and nobles to return to the field, when they had quitted it after an ineffectual campaign. As dangers and difficulties multiplied, she multiplied resources to meet them; and, when her soldiers lay drooping under the evils of some protracted siege, she appeared in the midst, mounted on her war-horse, with her delicate limbs cased in knightly mail, and, riding through their ranks, breathed new courage into their hearts by her own intrepid bearing. To her personal efforts, indeed, as well as counsels, the success of this glorious war may be mainly imputed; and the unsuspicious testimony of the Venetian minister, Navagiero, a few years later, shows that the nation so considered it. "Queen Isabel," says he, "by her singular genius, masculine strength of mind, and other virtues most unusual in our own sex as well as hers, was not merely of great assistance in, but the chief cause of, the conquest of Granada. She was, indeed, a most rare and virtuous lady, one of whom the Spaniards talk far more than of the king, sagacious as he was and uncommon for his time."

Happily, these masculine qualities in Isabella did not extinguish the softer ones which constitute the charm of her sex. Her heart overflowed with affectionate sensibility to her family and friends. She watched over the declining days of her aged mother, and ministered to her sad infirmities with all the delicacy of filial tenderness. We have seen abundant proofs how fondly and faithfully she loved her husband to the last, though this love was not always as faithfully requited. For her children she lived more than for herself; and for them too she died, for it was their loss and their afflictions which froze the current of her blood before age had time to chill it. Her exalted state did not remove her above the sympathies of friendship. With her friends she forgot the usual distinctions of rank, sharing in their joys, visiting and consoling them in sorrow and sickness, and condescending in more than one instance to assume the office of executrix on their decease. Her heart, indeed, was filled with benevolence to all mankind. In the most fiery heat of war, she was engaged in devising means for mitigating its horrors. She is said to have been the first to introduce the benevolent institution of camp hospitals; and we have seen, more than once, her lively solicitude to spare the effusion of blood even of her enemies. But it is needless to multiply examples of this beautiful but familiar trait in her character.

It is in these more amiable qualities of her sex that Isabella's superiority becomes most apparent over her illustrious namesake, Elizabeth of England, whose history presents some features parallel to her own. Both were disciplined in early life by the teachings of that stern nurse of wisdom, adversity. Both were made to experience the deepest humiliation at the hands of their nearest relative, who should have cherished and protected them. Both succeeded in establishing themselves on the throne after the most precarious vicissitudes. Each conducted her kingdom, through a long and triumphant reign, to a height of glory which it had never before reached. Both lived to see the vanity of all earthly grandeur, and to fall the victim of an inconsolable melancholy; and both left behind an illustrious name, unrivaled in the subsequent annals of their country.

But with these few circumstances of their history the resemblance ceases. Their characters afford scarcely a point of contact. Elizabeth, inheriting a large share of the bold and bluff King Harry's temperament, was haughty, arrogant, coarse, and irascible; while with these fiercer qualities she mingled deep dissimulation and strange irresolution. Isabella, on the other hand, tempered the dignity of royal station with the most bland and courteous manners. Once resolved, she was constant in her purposes, and her conduct in public and private life was characterized by candor and integrity. Both may be said to have shown that magnanimity which is implied by the accomplishment of great objects in the face of great obstacles. But Elizabeth was desperately selfish; she was incapable of forgiving, not merely a real injury, but the slightest affront to her vanity; and she was merciless in exacting retribution. Isabella, on the other hand, lived only for others—was ready at all times to sacrifice self to considerations of public duty, and, far from personal resentments, showed the greatest condescension and kindness to those who had most sensibly injured her; while her benevolent heart sought every means to mitigate the authorized severities of the law, even towards the guilty.

Both possessed rare fortitude. Isabella, indeed, was placed in situations which demanded more frequent and higher displays of it than her rival; but no one will doubt a full measure of this quality in the daughter of Henry the Eighth. Elizabeth was better educated, and every way more highly accomplished, than Isabella. But the latter knew enough to maintain her station with dignity; and she encouraged learning by munificent patronage. The masculine powers and passions of Elizabeth seemed to divorce her in a great measure from the peculiar attributes of her sex; at least from those which constitute its peculiar charm; for she had abundance of its foibles—a coquetry and love of admiration which age could not chill; a levity, most careless, if not criminal; and a fondness for dress and tawdry magnificence of ornament, which was ridiculous, or disgusting, according to the different periods of life in which it was indulged. Isabella, on the other hand, distinguished through life for decorum of manners, and purity beyond the breath of calumny, was content with the legitimate affection which she could inspire within the range of her domestic circle. Far from a frivolous affectation of ornament or dress, she was most simple in her own attire, and seemed to set no value on her jewels but as they could serve the necessities of the state; when they could be no longer useful in this way, she gave them away, as we have seen, to her friends.

Both were uncommonly sagacious in the selection of their ministers; though Elizabeth was drawn into some errors in this particular by her levity, as was Isabella by religious feeling. It was this, combined with her excessive humility, which led to the only grave errors in the administration of the latter. Her rival fell into no such error; and she was a stranger to the amiable qualities which led to them. Her conduct was certainly not controlled by religious principle; and, though the bulwark of the Protestant faith, it might be difficult to say whether she were at heart most a Protestant or a Catholic. She viewed religion in its connection with the state—in other words, with herself; and she took measures for enforcing conformity to her own views, not a whit less despotic, and scarcely less sanguinary, than those countenanced for conscience' sake by her more bigoted rival.

This feature of bigotry, which has thrown a shade over Isabella's otherwise beautiful character, might lead to a disparagement of her intellectual power compared with that of the English queen. To estimate this aright, we must contemplate the results of their respective reigns. Elizabeth found all the materials of prosperity at hand, and availed herself of them most ably to build up a solid fabric of national grandeur. Isabella created these materials. She saw the faculties of her people locked up in a deathlike lethargy, and she breathed into them the breath of life for those great and heroic enterprises which terminated in such glorious consequences to the monarchy. It is when viewed from the depressed position of her early days that the achievements of her reign seem scarcely less than miraculous. The masculine genius of the English queen stands out relieved beyond its natural dimensions by its separation from the softer qualities of her sex; while her rival's, like some vast but symmetrical edifice, loses in appearance somewhat of its actual grandeur from the perfect harmony of its proportions.

The circumstances of their deaths, which were somewhat similar, displayed the great dissimilarity of their characters. Both pined amidst their royal state, a prey to incurable despondency, rather than any marked bodily distemper. In Elizabeth it sprung from wounded vanity, a sullen conviction that she had outlived the admiration on which she had so long fed—and even the solace of friendship and the attachment of her subjects. Nor did she seek consolation where alone it was to be found, in that sad hour. Isabella, on the other hand, sank under a too acute sensibility to the sufferings of others. But, amidst the gloom which gathered around her, she looked with the eye of faith to the brighter prospects which unfolded of the future; and, when she resigned her last breath, it was amidst the tears and universal lamentations of her people.

It is in this undying, unabated attachment of the nation, indeed, that we see the most unequivocal testimony to the virtues of Isabella. In the downward progress of things in Spain, some of the most ill-advised measures of her administration have found favor and been perpetuated, while the more salutary have been forgotten. This may lead to a misconception of her real merits. In order to estimate these, we must listen to the voice of her contemporaries, the eyewitnesses of the condition in which

she found the state, and in which she left it. We shall then see
but one judgment formed of her, whether by foreigners or natives. The French and Italian writers equally join in celebrating
the triumphant glories of her reign, and her magnanimity, wisdom, and purity of character. Her own subjects extol her as
"the most brilliant exemplar of every virtue," and mourn over
the day of her death as "the last of the prosperity and happiness
of their country"; while those who had nearer access to her person are unbounded in their admiration of those amiable qualities
whose full power is revealed only in the unrestrained intimacies
of domestic life. The judgment of posterity has ratified the
sentence of her own age. The most enlightened Spaniards of the
present day, by no means insensible to the errors of her government, but more capable of appreciating its merits than those of
a less instructed age, bear honorable testimony to her deserts;
and, while they pass over the bloated magnificence of succeeding
monarchs, who arrest the popular eye, dwell with enthusiasm on
Isabella's character, as the most truly great in their line of
princes.

CHAPTER XXIV

The Deaths of Gonsalvo and Ferdinand

1513-1516

Notwithstanding the good order which King Ferdinand maintained in Castile by his energetic conduct, as well as by his policy
of diverting the effervescing spirits of the nation to foreign enterprise, he still experienced annoyance from various causes. Among
these were Maximilian's pretensions to the regency, as paternal
grandfather of the heir apparent. The emperor, indeed, had more
than once threatened to assert his preposterous claims to Castile
in person; and, although this Quixotic monarch, who had been
tilting against windmills all his life, failed to excite any powerful
sensation, either by his threats or his promises, it furnished a

plausible pretext for keeping alive a faction hostile to the interests of the Catholic king.

In the winter of 1509 an arrangement was made with the emperor, through the mediation of Louis the Twelfth, by which he finally relinquished his pretensions to the regency of Castile, in consideration of the aid of three hundred lances, and the transfer to him of the fifty thousand ducats which Ferdinand was to receive from Pisa. No bribe was too paltry for a prince whose means were as narrow as his projects were vast and chimerical. Even after this pacification, the Austrian party contrived to disquiet the king, by maintaining the archduke Charles's pretensions to the government in the name of his unfortunate mother; until at length the Spanish monarch came to entertain not merely distrust, but positive aversion, for his grandson; while the latter, as he advanced in years, was taught to regard Ferdinand as one who excluded him from his rightful inheritance by a most flagrant act of usurpation.

Ferdinand's suspicious temper found other grounds for uneasiness, where there was less warrant for it, in his jealousy of his illustrious subject Gonsalvo de Cordova. This was particularly the case when circumstances had disclosed the full extent of that general's popularity. After the defeat of Ravenna, the pope and the other allies of Ferdinand urged him in the most earnest manner to send the Great Captain into Italy, as the only man capable of checking the French arms and restoring the fortunes of the league. The king, trembling for the immediate safety of his own dominions, gave a reluctant assent, and ordered Gonsalvo to hold himself in readiness to take command of an army to be instantly raised for Italy. (May, 1512.)

These tidings were received with enthusiasm by the Castilians. Men of every rank pressed forward to serve under a chief whose service was itself sufficient passport to fame. "It actually seemed," says Martyr, "as if Spain were to be drained of all her noble and generous blood. Nothing appeared impossible, or even difficult, under such a leader. Hardly a cavalier in the land but would have thought it a reproach to remain behind. Truly marvelous," he adds, "is the authority which he has acquired over all orders of men!"

Such was the zeal with which men enlisted under his banner, that great difficulty was found in completing the necessary levies for Navarre, then menaced by the French. The king, alarmed at this, and relieved from apprehensions of immediate danger to Naples, by subsequent advices from that country, sent orders greatly reducing the number of forces to be raised. But this had little effect, since every man who had the means preferred acting as a volunteer under the Great Captain to any other service, however gainful; and many a poor cavalier was there, who expended his little all, or incurred a heavy debt, in order to appear in the field in a style becoming the chivalry of Spain.

Ferdinand's former distrust of his general was now augmented tenfold by this evidence of his unbounded popularity. He saw in imagination much more danger to Naples from such a subject than from any enemy, however formidable. He had received intelligence, moreover, that the French were in full retreat towards the north. He hesitated no longer, but sent instructions to the Great Captain at Cordova to disband his levies, as the expedition would be postponed till after the present winter; at the same time inviting such as chose to enlist in the service of Navarre. (August, 1512.)

These tidings were received with indignant feelings by the whole army. The officers refused, nearly to a man, to engage in the proposed service. Gonsalvo, who understood the motives of this change in the royal purpose, was deeply sensible of what he regarded as a personal affront. He, however, enjoined on his troops implicit obedience to the king's commands. Before dismissing them, as he knew that many had been drawn into expensive preparations far beyond their means, he distributed largesses among them, amounting to the immense sum, if we may credit his biographers, of one hundred thousand ducats. "Never stint your hand," said he to his steward, who remonstrated on the magnitude of the donative; "there is no mode of enjoying one's property like giving it away." He then wrote a letter to the king, in which he gave free vent to his indignation, bitterly complaining of the ungenerous requital of his services, and asking leave to retire to his duchy of Terranova in Naples, since he could be no longer useful in Spain. This request was not calculated to lull Ferdinand's suspicions. He answered, however, "in the soft and pleasant style which he knew so well how to assume," says Zurita; and, after specifying his motives for relinquishing, however reluctantly, the expedition, he recommended

Gonsalvo's return to Loja, at least until some more definite arrangement could be made respecting the affairs of Italy.

Thus condemned to his former seclusion, the Great Captain resumed his late habits of life, freely opening his mansion to persons of merit, interesting himself in plans for ameliorating the condition of his tenantry and neighbors, and in this quiet way winning a more unquestionable title to human gratitude than when piling up the bloodstained trophies of victory. Alas for humanity, that it should have deemed otherwise!

Another circumstance which disquieted the Catholic king was the failure of issue by his present wife. The natural desire of offspring was further stimulated by hatred of the house of Austria, which made him eager to abridge the ample inheritance about to descend on his grandson Charles. It must be confessed that it reflects little credit on his heart or his understanding that he should have been so ready to sacrifice to personal resentment those noble plans for the consolidation of the monarchy which had so worthily occupied the attention both of himself and of Isabella in his early life. His wishes had nearly been realized. Queen Germaine was delivered of a son, March 3d, 1509. Providence, however, as if unwilling to defeat the glorious consummation of the union of the Spanish kingdoms, so long desired and nearly achieved, permitted the infant to live only a few hours.

Ferdinand repined at the blessing denied him, now more than ever. In order to invigorate his constitution, he resorted to artificial means. The medicines which he took had the opposite effect. At least from this time, the spring of 1513, he was afflicted with infirmities before unknown to him. Instead of his habitual equanimity and cheerfulness, he became impatient, irritable, and frequently a prey to morbid melancholy. He lost all relish for business, and even for amusements, except field-sports, to which he devoted the greater part of his time. The fever which consumed him made him impatient of long residence in any one place, and during these last years of his life the court was in perpetual migration. The unhappy monarch, alas! could not fly from disease, or from himself.

In the summer of 1515 he was found one night by his attendants in a state of insensibility, from which it was difficult to rouse him. He exhibited flashes of his former energy after this, however. On one occasion he made a journey to Aragon, in order to preside at the deliberations of the cortes, and enforce the grant of supplies, to which the nobles, from selfish considerations, made resistance. The king failed, indeed, to bend their intractable tempers, but he displayed on the occasion all his wonted address and resolution.

On his return to Castile, which, perhaps from the greater refinement and deference of the people, seems to have been always a more agreeable residence to him than his own kingdom of Aragon, he received intelligence very vexatious, in the irritable state of his mind. He learned that the Great Captain was preparing to embark for Flanders, with his friend the count of Ureña, the marquis of Priego his nephew, and his future son-in-law, the count of Cabra. Some surmised that Gonsalvo designed to take command of the papal army in Italy; others, to join himself with the archduke Charles, and introduce him, if possible, into Castile. Ferdinand, clinging to power more tenaciously as it was ready to slip of itself from his grasp, had little doubt that the latter was his purpose. He sent orders therefore to the south to prevent the meditated embarkation, and, if necessary, to seize Gonsalvo's person. But the latter was soon to embark on a voyage where no earthly arm could arrest him.

In the autumn of 1515 he was attacked by a quartan fever. Its approaches at first were mild. His constitution, naturally good, had been invigorated by the severe training of a military life; and he had been so fortunate that, notwithstanding the free exposure of his person to danger, he had never received a wound. But, although little alarm was occasioned at first by his illness, he found it impossible to throw it off; and he removed to his residence in Granada, in hopes of deriving benefit from its salubrious climate. Every effort to rally the declining powers of nature proved unavailing; and on the 2d of December, 1515, he expired in his own palace at Granada, in the arms of his wife, and his beloved daughter Elvira.

The death of this illustrious man diffused universal sorrow throughout the nation. All envy and unworthy suspicion died with him. The king and the whole court went into mourning. Funeral services were performed in his honor in the royal chapel and all the principal churches of the kingdom. Ferdinand addressed a letter of consolation to his duchess, in which he lamented the death of one "who had rendered him inestimable services, and to whom he had ever borne such sincere affection"! His obsequies were celebrated with great magnificence in the ancient Moorish capital, under the superintendence of the count of Tendilla, the son and successor of Gonsalvo's old friend, the late governor of Granada. His remains, first deposited in the Franciscan monastery, were afterwards removed, and laid beneath a sumptuous mausoleum in the church of San Geronimo; and more than a hundred banners and royal pennons, waving in melancholy pomp around the walls of the chapel, proclaimed the glorious achievements of the warrior who slept beneath. His noble wife, Doña Maria Manrique, survived him but a few days. His daughter Elvira inherited the princely titles and estates of her father, which, by her marriage with her kinsman, the count of Cabra, were perpetuated in the house of Cordova.

Gonsalvo, or, as he is called in Castilian, Gonzalo Hernandez de Cordova, was sixty-two years old at the time of his death. His countenance and person are represented to have been extremely handsome; his manners, elegant and attractive, were stamped with that lofty dignity which so often distinguishes his countrymen. "He still bears," says Martyr, speaking of him in the last years of his life, "the same majestic port as when in the height of his former authority; so that everyone who visits him acknowledges the influence of his noble presence, as fully as when, at the head of armies, he gave laws to Italy."

His splendid military successes, so gratifying to Castilian pride, have made the name of Gonsalvo as familiar to his countrymen as that of the Cid, which, floating down the stream of popular melody, has been treasured up as a part of the national history. His shining qualities, even more than his exploits, have been often made the theme of fiction; and fiction, as usual, has dealt with them in a fashion to leave only confused and erroneous conceptions of both. More is known of the Spanish hero, for instance, to foreign readers from Florian's agreeable novel, than from any authentic record of his actions. Yet Florian, by dwelling only on the dazzling and popular traits of his hero, has depicted him as the very personification of romantic chivalry. This certainly was not his character, which might be said to have been formed after a riper period of civilization than the age of chivalry. At least, it had none of the nonsense of that age—its fanciful vagaries, reckless adventure, and wild romantic gallantry. His characteristics were prudence, coolness, steadiness of purpose, and intimate knowledge of man. He understood, above all, the temper of his own countrymen. He may be said in some degree to have formed their military character; their patience of severe training and hardship, their unflinching obedience, their inflexible spirit under reverses, and their decisive energy in the hour of action. It is certain that the Spanish soldier under his hands assumed an entirely new aspect from that which he had displayed in the romantic wars of the peninsula.

Gonsalvo was untainted with the coarser vices characteristic of the time. He discovered none of that griping avarice which was too often the reproach of his countrymen in these wars. His hand and heart were liberal as the day. He betrayed none of the cruelty and licentiousness which disgrace the age of chivalry. On all occasions he was prompt to protect women from injury or insult. Although his distinguished manners and rank gave him obvious advantages with the sex, he never abused them; and he has left a character, unimpeached by any historian, of unblemished morality in his domestic relations. This was a rare virtue in the sixteenth century.

Gonsalvo's fame rests on his military prowess; yet his character would seem in many respects better suited to the calm and cultivated walks of civil life. His government of Naples exhibited much discretion and sound policy; and there, as afterwards in his retirement, his polite and liberal manners secured not merely the good will, but the strong attachment, of those around him. His early education, like that of most of the noble cavaliers who came forward before the improvements introduced under Isabella, was taken up with knightly exercises more than intellectual accomplishments. He was never taught Latin, and had no pretensions to scholarship; but he honored and nobly recompensed it in others. His solid sense and liberal taste supplied all deficiencies in himself, and led him to select friends and companions from among the most enlightened and virtuous of the community.

On this fair character there remains one foul reproach. This is his breach of faith in two memorable instances; first to the young duke of Calabria, and afterwards to Caesar Borgia, both of whom he betrayed into the hands of King Ferdinand, their personal enemy, in violation of his most solemn pledges. True, it was in obedience to his master's commands, and not to serve his own purposes; and true also, this want of faith was the besetting sin of the age. But history has no warrant to tamper with right and wrong, or to brighten the character of its favorites by diminishing one shade of the abhorrence which attaches to their vices. They should rather be held up in their true deformity, as the more conspicuous from the very greatness with which they are associated. It may be remarked, however, that the reiterated and unsparing opprobrium with which foreign writers, who have been little sensible to Gonsalvo's merits, have visited these offenses, affords tolerable evidence that they are the only ones of any magnitude that can be charged on him.

As to the imputation of disloyalty, we have elsewhere had occasion to notice its apparent groundlessness. It would be strange, indeed, if the ungenerous treatment which he had experienced ever since his return from Naples had not provoked feelings of indignation in his bosom. Nor would it be surprising, under these circumstances, if he had been led to regard the archduke Charles's pretensions to the regency, as he came of age, with a favorable eye. There is no evidence, however, of this, or of any act unfriendly to Ferdinand's interests. His whole public life, on the contrary, exhibited the truest loyalty; and the only stains that darken his fame were incurred by too unhesitating devotion to the wishes of his master. He is not the first nor the last statesman who has reaped the royal recompense of ingratitude for serving his king with greater zeal than he had served his Maker.

Ferdinand's health, in the meantime, had declined so sensibly that it was evident he could not long survive the object of his jealousy. His disease had now settled into a dropsy, accompanied with a distressing affection of the heart. He found difficulty in breathing, complained that he was stifled in the crowded cities, and passed most of his time, even after the weather became cold, in the fields and forests, occupied, as far as his strength permitted, with the fatiguing pleasures of the chase. As the winter advanced, he bent his steps towards the south. He passed some time, in December, at a country seat of the duke of Alva, near Placencia, where he hunted the stag. He then resumed his journey to Andalusia, but fell so ill on the way, at the little village of Madrigalejo, near Truxillo, that it was found impossible to advance farther. (January, 1516.)

The king seemed desirous of closing his eyes to the danger of his situation as long as possible. He would not confess, nor even admit his confessor into his chamber. He showed similar jealousy of his grandson's envoy, Adrian of Utrecht. This person, the preceptor of Charles, and afterwards raised through his means to the papacy, had come into Castile some weeks before, with the ostensible view of making some permanent arrangement with Ferdinand in regard to the regency. The real motive, as the powers which he brought with him subsequently proved, was that he might be on the spot when the king died, and assume the reins of government. Ferdinand received the minister with cold civility; and an agreement was entered into, by which the regency was guaranteed to the monarch, during not only Joanna's life, but his own. Concessions to a dying man cost nothing. Adrian, who was at Guadalupe at this time, no sooner heard of Ferdinand's illness than he hastened to Madrigalejo. The king, however, suspected the motives of his visit. "He has come to see me die," said he, and, refusing to admit him into his presence, ordered the mortified envoy back again to Guadalupe.

At length the medical attendants ventured to inform the king of his real situation, conjuring him if he had any affairs of moment to settle, to do it without delay. He listened to them with composure, and from that moment seemed to recover all his customary fortitude and equanimity. After receiving the sacrament, and attending to his spiritual concerns, he called his attendants around his bed, to advise with them respecting the disposition of the government. Among those present at this time were his faithful followers the duke of Alva and the marquis of Denia, his majordomo, with several bishops and members of his council.

The king, it seems, had made several wills. By one, executed at Burgos in 1512, he had committed the government of Castile and Aragon to the infante Ferdinand during his brother Charles's absence. This young prince had been educated in Spain under the eye of his grandfather, who entertained a strong affection for him. The counselors remonstrated in the plainest terms against this disposition of the regency. Ferdinand, they said, was too young to take the helm into his own hands. His appointment would be sure to create new factions in Castile; it would raise him up to be in a manner a rival of his brother, and kindle ambitious desires in his bosom, which could not fail to end in his disappointment, and perhaps destruction.

The king, who would never have made such a devise in his better days, was more easily turned from his purpose now than he would once have been. "To whom then," he asked, "shall I leave the regency?" "To Ximenes, archbishop of Toledo," they replied. Ferdinand turned away his face, apparently in displeasure, but after a few moments' silence rejoined, "It is well; he is certainly a good man, with honest intentions. He has no importunate friends or family to provide for. He owes everything to Queen Isabella and myself; and, as he has always been true to the interests of our family, I believe he will always remain so."

He, however, could not so readily abandon the idea of some splendid establishment for his favorite grandson; and he proposed to settle on him the grand-masterships of the military orders. But to this his attendants again objected, on the same grounds as before; adding that this powerful patronage was too great for any subject, and imploring him not to defeat the object which the late queen had so much at heart, of incorporating it with the crown. "Ferdinand will be left very poor, then," exclaimed the king, with tears in his eyes. "He will have the good will of his brother," replied one of his honest counselors, "the best legacy your Highness can leave him."

The testament, as finally arranged, settled the succession of Aragon and Naples on his daughter Joanna and her heirs. The administration of Castile during Charles's absence was intrusted to Ximenes, and that of Aragon to the king's natural son, the archbishop of Saragossa, whose good sense and popular manners made him acceptable to the people. He granted several places in the kingdom of Naples to the infante Ferdinand, with an annual stipend of fifty thousand ducats, chargeable on the public revenues. To his queen Germaine he left the yearly income of thirty thousand gold florins, stipulated by the marriage settlement, with five thousand a year more during widowhood. The will contained, besides, several appropriations for pious and charitable purposes, but nothing worthy of particular note. Notwithstanding the simplicity of the various provisions of the testament, it was so long, from the formalities and periphrases with which it was encumbered, that there was scarce time to transcribe it in season for the royal signature. On the evening of the 22d of January, 1516, he executed the instrument; and a few hours later, between one and two of the morning of the 23d, Ferdinand breathed his last. The scene of this event was a small house belonging to the friars of Guadalupe. "In so wretched a tenement," exclaims Martyr, in his usual moralizing vein, "did this lord of so many lands close his eyes upon the world."

Ferdinand was nearly sixty-four years old, of which forty-one had elapsed since he first swayed the scepter of Castile, and thirty-seven since he held that of Aragon. A long reign; long enough, indeed, to see most of those whom he had honored and trusted of his subjects gathered to the dust, and a succession of contemporary monarchs come and disappear like shadows. He died deeply lamented by his native subjects, who entertained a partiality natural towards their own hereditary sovereign. The event was regarded with very different feelings by the Castilian nobles, who calculated their gains on the transfer of the reins from such old and steady hands into those of a young and inexperienced master. The commons, however, who had felt the good effect of this curb on the nobility, in their own personal security, held his memory in reverence as that of a national benefactor.

Ferdinand's remains were interred, agreeably to his orders, in Granada. A few of his most faithful adherents accompanied them; the greater part being deterred by a prudent caution of giving umbrage to Charles. The funeral train, however, was swelled by contributions from the various towns through which it passed. At Cordova, especially, it is worthy of note that the marquis of Priego, who had slender obligations to Ferdinand, came out with all his household to pay the last melancholy honors to his remains. They were received with military respect in Granada, where the people, while they gazed on the sad spectacle, says Zurita, were naturally affected as they called to mind the pomp and splendor of his triumphal entry on the first occupation of the Moorish capital.

By his dying injunctions, all unnecessary ostentation was interdicted at his funeral. His body was laid by the side of Isabella's in the monastery of the Alhambra; and the year following, when the royal chapel of the metropolitan church was completed, they were both transported thither. A magnificent mausoleum of white marble was erected over them by their grandson Charles the Fifth. It was executed in a style worthy of the age. The sides were adorned with figures of angels and saints, richly sculptured in bas-relief. On the top reposed the effigies of the illustrious pair, whose titles and merits were commemorated in the following brief and not very felicitous inscription:

MAHOMETICÆ SECTÆ PROSTRATORES, ET HÆRETICÆ PERVICACIÆ EXTINCTORES, FERNANDUS ARAGONUM, ET HELISABETA CAS-TELLÆ, VIR ET UXOR UNANIMES, CATHOLICI APPELLATI, MAR-MOREO CLAUDUNTUR HOC TUMULO.

King Ferdinand's personal appearance has been elsewhere noticed. "He was of the middle size," says a contemporary, who knew him well. "His complexion was fresh; his eyes bright and animated; his nose and mouth small and finely formed, and his teeth white; his forehead lofty and serene; with flowing hair of a bright chestnut color. His manners were courteous, and his countenance seldom clouded by anything like spleen or melancholy. He was grave in speech and action, and had a marvelous dignity of presence. His whole demeanor, in fine, was truly that of a great king." For this flattering portrait Ferdinand must have sat at an earlier and happier period of his life.

His education, owing to the troubled state of the times, had been neglected in his boyhood, though he was early instructed in all the generous pastimes and exercises of chivalry. He was esteemed one of the most perfect horsemen of his court. He led an active life, and the only kind of reading he appeared to relish was history. It was natural that so busy an actor on the great political theater should have found peculiar interest and instruction in this study.

He was naturally of an equable temper, and inclined to moderation in all things. The only amusement for which he cared much was hunting, especially falconry, and that he never carried to excess till his last years. He was indefatigable in application to business. He had no relish for the pleasures of the table, and, like Isabella, was temperate even to abstemiousness in his diet. He was frugal in his domestic and personal expenditure; partly, no doubt, from a willingness to rebuke the opposite spirit of wastefulness and ostentation in his nobles. He lost no good opportunity of doing this. On one occasion, it is said, he turned to a gallant of the court noted for his extravagance in dress, and, laying his hand on his own doublet, exclaimed, "Excellent stuff this; it has lasted me three pair of sleeves!" This spirit of economy was carried so far as to bring on him the reproach of parsimony. And parsimony, though not so pernicious on the whole as the opposite vice of prodigality, has always found far less favor with the multitude, from the appearance of disinterestedness which the latter carries with it. Prodigality in a king, however, who draws not on his own resources, but on the public, forfeits even this equivocal claim to applause. But, in truth, Ferdinand was rather frugal than parsimonious. His income was moderate; his enterprises numerous and vast. It was impossible that he could meet them without husbanding his resources with the most careful economy. No one has accused him of attempting to enrich his exchequer by the venal sale of offices, like Louis the Twelfth, or by griping extortion, like another royal contemporary, Henry the Seventh. He amassed no treasure, and, indeed, died so poor that he left scarcely enough in his coffers to defray the charges of his funeral.

Ferdinand was devout; at least he was scrupulous in regard to the exterior of religion. He was punctual in attendance on mass, careful to observe all the ordinances and ceremonies of his Church, and left many tokens of his piety, after the fashion of the time, in sumptuous edifices and endowments for religious purposes. Although not a superstitious man for the age, he is certainly obnoxious to the reproach of bigotry; for he cooperated with Isabella in all her exceptionable measures in Castile, and spared no effort to fasten the odious yoke of the Inquisition on Aragon, and subsequently, though happily with less success, on Naples.

Ferdinand has incurred the more serious charge of hypocrisy. His Catholic zeal was observed to be marvelously efficacious in furthering his temporal interests. His most objectionable enterprises, even, were covered with a veil of religion. In this, however, he did not materially differ from the practice of the age. Some of the most scandalous wars of that period were ostensibly at the bidding of the Church, or in defense of Christendom against the infidel. This ostentation of a religious motive was indeed very usual with the Spanish and Portuguese. The crusading spirit, nourished by their struggle with the Moors, and subsequently by their African and American expeditions, gave such a religious tone habitually to their feelings as shed an illusion over their actions and enterprises, frequently disguising their true character even from themselves.

It will not be so easy to acquit Ferdinand of the reproach of perfidy which foreign writers have so deeply branded on his name, and which those of his own nation have sought rather to palliate than to deny. It is but fair to him, however, even here, to take a glance at the age. He came forward when government was in a state of transition from the feudal forms to those which it has assumed in modern times; when the superior strength of the great vassals was circumvented by the superior policy of the reigning princes. It was the dawn of the triumph of intellect over the brute force which had hitherto controlled the movements of nations, as of individuals. The same policy which these monarchs had pursued in their own domestic relations they introduced into those with foreign states, when, at the close of the fifteenth century, the barriers that had so long kept them asunder were broken down. Italy was the first field on which the great powers were brought into anything like a general collision. It was the country, too, in which this crafty policy had been first studied and reduced to a regular system. A single extract from the political manual of that age may serve as a key to the whole science, as then understood. "A prudent prince," says Machiavelli, "will not, and ought not to, observe his engagements when it would operate to his disadvantage, and the causes no longer exist which induced him to make them." Sufficient evidence of the practical application of the maxim may be found in the manifold treaties of the period, so contradictory, or, what is to the same purpose for our present argument, so confirmatory, of one another in their tenor, as clearly to show the impotence of all engagements. There were no less than four several treaties in the course of three years, solemnly stipulating the marriage of the archduke Charles and Claude of France. Louis the Twelfth violated his engagements, and the marriage after all never took place.

Such was the school in which Ferdinand was to make trial of his skill with his brother monarchs. He had an able instructor in his father, John the Second of Aragon, and the result showed that the lessons were not lost on him. "He was vigilant, wary, and subtile," writes a French contemporary, "and few histories make mention of his being outwitted in the whole course of his life." He played the game with more adroitness than his opponents, and he won it. Success, as usual, brought on him the reproaches of the losers. This is particularly true of the French, whose master, Louis the Twelfth, was more directly pitted against him. Yet Fedinand does not appear to be a whit more obnoxious to the charge of unfairness than his opponent. If he deserted his allies when it suited his convenience, he, at least, did not deliberately plot their destruction and betray them into the hands of their deadly enemy, as his rival did with Venice, in the league of Cambray. The partition of Naples, the most scandalous transaction of the period, he shared equally with Louis; and if the latter has escaped the reproach of the usurpation of Navarre, it was because the premature death of his general deprived him of the pretext and means for achieving it. Yet Louis the Twelfth, the "father of his people," has gone down to posterity with a high and honorable reputation.

Ferdinand, unfortunately for his popularity, had nothing of the frank and cordial temper, the genial expansion of the soul, which begets love. He carried the same cautious and impenetrable frigidity into private life that he showed in public. "No one," says a writer of the time, "could read his thoughts by any change of his countenance." Calm and calculating, even in trifles, it was too obvious that everything had exclusive reference to self. He seemed to estimate his friends only by the amount of services they could render him. He was not always mindful of these services. Witness his ungenerous treatment of Columbus, the Great Captain, Navarro, Ximenes—the men who shed the brightest luster and the most substantial benefits on his reign. Witness also his insensibility to the virtues and long attachment of Isabella, whose memory he could so soon dishonor by a union with one every way unworthy to be her successor.

Ferdinand's connection with Isabella, while it reflected infinite glory on his reign, suggests a contrast most unfavorable to his character. Hers was all magnanimity, disinterestedness, and deep devotion to the interests of her people. His was the spirit of egotism. The circle of his views might be more or less expanded, but self was the steady, unchangeable center. Her heart beat with the generous sympathies of friendship, and the purest constancy to the first, the only object of her love. We have seen the measure of his sensibilities in other relations. They were not more refined in this; and he proved himself unworthy of the admirable woman with whom his destinies were united, by indulging in those vicious gallantries too generally sanctioned by the age. Ferdinand, in fine, a shrewd and politic prince, "surpassing," as a French writer, not his friend, has remarked, "all the statesmen of his time in the science of the cabinet," may be taken as the representative of the peculiar genius of the age; while Isabella, discarding all the petty artifices of state policy, and pursuing the noblest ends by the noblest means, stands far above her age.

In his illustrious consort Ferdinand may be said to have lost his good genius. From that time his fortunes were under a cloud. Not that victory sat less constantly on his banner; but at home he had lost

> *All that should accompany old age,*
> *As honor, love, obedience, troops of friends.*

His ill-advised marriage disgusted his Castilian subjects. He ruled over them, indeed, but more in severity than in love. The beauty of his young queen opened new sources of jealousy; while the disparity of their ages, and her fondness for frivolous pleasure, as little qualified her to be his partner in prosperity as his solace in declining years. His tenacity of power drew him into vulgar squabbles with those most nearly allied to him by blood, which settled into a mortal aversion. Finally, bodily infirmity broke the energies of his mind, sour suspicions corroded his heart, and he had the misfortune to live long after he had lost all that could make life desirable.

Let us turn from this gloomy picture to the brighter season of the morning and meridian of his life; when he sat with Isabella on the united thrones of Castile and Aragon, strong in the love of his own subjects, and in the fear and respect of his enemies. We shall then find much in his character to admire; his impartial justice in the administration of the laws; his watchful solicitude to shield the weak from the oppression of the strong; his wise economy, which achieved great results without burdening his people with oppressive taxes; his sobriety and moderation; the decorum, and respect for religion, which he maintained among his subjects; the industry he promoted by wholesome laws and his own example; his consummate sagacity, which crowned all his enterprises with brilliant success, and made him the oracle of the princes of the age.

Machiavelli, indeed, the most deeply read of his time in human character, imputes Ferdinand's successes, in one of his letters, to "cunning and good luck, rather than superior wisdom." He was indeed fortunate; and the "star of Austria," which rose as his declined, shone not with a brighter or steadier luster. But success through a long series of years sufficiently of itself attests good conduct. "The winds and waves," says Gibbon, truly enough, "are always on the side of the most skillful mariner." The Florentine statesman has recorded a riper and more deliberate judgment, in the treatise which he intended as a mirror for the rulers of the time. "Nothing," says he, "gains estimation for a prince like great enterprises. Our own age has furnished a splendid example of this in Ferdinand of Aragon. We may call him a new king, since from a feeble one he has made himself the most renowned and glorious monarch of Christendom; and, if we ponder well his manifold achievements, we must acknowledge all of them very great, and some truly extraordinary."

Other eminent foreigners of the time join in this lofty strain of panegyric. The Castilians, mindful of the general security and prosperity they had enjoyed under his reign, seem willing to bury his frailties in his grave. While his own hereditary subjects, exulting with patriotic pride in the glory to which he had raised their petty state, and touched with grateful recollections of his mild, paternal government, deplore his loss in strains of national sorrow, as the last of the revered line who was to preside over the destinies of Aragon as a separate and independent kingdom.

History of the
Conquest of Mexico

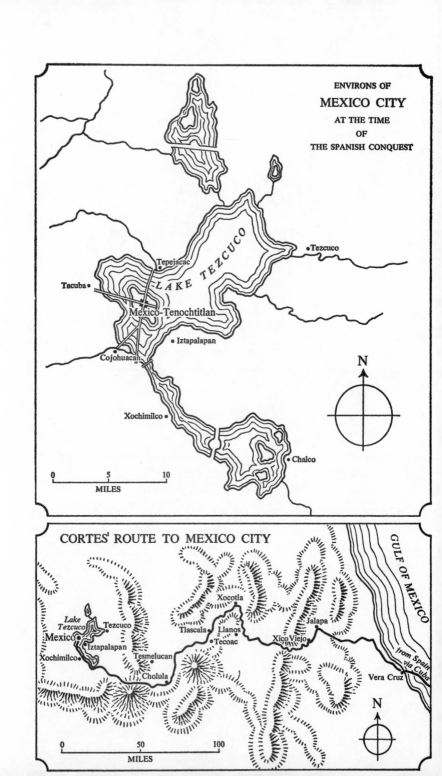

ENVIRONS OF
MEXICO CITY
AT THE TIME
OF
THE SPANISH CONQUEST

• Tezcuco

LAKE TEZCUCO

Tepejacac

Tacuba •

Mexico-Tenochtitlan

• Iztapalapan

Cojohuacan

N

Xochimilco •

• Chalco

0   5   10
MILES

CORTES' ROUTE TO MEXICO CITY

GULF OF MEXICO

Xocotla

Lake Tezcuco   Tezcuco

Mexico •

Tlascala   Llanos

Jalapa

Iztapalapan   • Tecoac   Xico Viejo

Xochimilco •

Tesmelucan   *from Spain via Cuba*

Cholula

Vera Cruz

N

0   50   100
MILES

BOOK II

CHAPTER II

Hernando Cortes

1518

HERNANDO CORTES was born at Medellin, a town in the southeast corner of Estremadura, in 1485. He came of an ancient and respectable family; and historians have gratified the national vanity by tracing it up to the Lombard kings, whose descendants crossed the Pyrenees and established themselves in Aragon under the Gothic monarchy. This royal genealogy was not found out till Cortes had acquired a name which would confer distinction on any descent, however noble. His father, Martin Cortes de Monroy, was a captain of infantry, in moderate circumstances, but a man of unblemished honor; and both he and his wife, Doña Catalina Pizarro Altamirano, appear to have been much regarded for their excellent qualities.

In his infancy Cortes is said to have had a feeble constitution, which strengthened as he grew older. At fourteen, he was sent to Salamanca, as his father, who conceived great hopes from his quick and showy parts, proposed to educate him for the law, a profession which held out better inducements to the young aspirant than any other. The son, however, did not conform to these views. He showed little fondness for books, and, after loitering away two years at college, returned home, to the great chagrin of his parents. Yet his time had not been wholly misspent, since he had laid up a little store of Latin, and learned to write good prose, and even verses "of some estimation, considering"—as an old writer quaintly remarks—"Cortes as the author." He now passed his days in the idle, unprofitable manner of one who, too willful to be guided by others, proposes no object to himself. His buoyant spirits were continually breaking out in troublesome frolics and capricious humors, quite at vari-

ance with the orderly habits of his father's household. He showed
a particular inclination for the military profession, or rather for
the life of adventure to which in those days it was sure to lead.
And when, at the age of seventeen, he proposed to enroll himself
under the banners of the Great Captain, his parents, probably
thinking a life of hardship and hazard abroad preferable to one
of idleness at home, made no objection.

The youthful cavalier, however, hesitated whether to seek his
fortunes under that victorious chief, or in the New World, where
gold as well as glory was to be won, and where the very dangers
had a mystery and romance in them inexpressibly fascinating to
a youthful fancy. It was in this direction, accordingly, that the
hot spirits of that day found a vent, especially from that part of
the country where Cortes lived, the neighborhood of Seville and
Cadiz, the focus of nautical enterprise. He decided on this latter
course, and an opportunity offered in the splendid armament
fitted out under Don Nicolas de Ovando, successor to Columbus.
An unlucky accident defeated the purpose of Cortes.

As he was scaling a high wall, one night, which gave him
access to the apartment of a lady with whom he was engaged in
an intrigue, the stones gave way, and he was thrown down with
much violence and buried under the ruins. A severe contusion,
though attended with no other serious consequences, confined
him to his bed till after the departure of the fleet.

Two years longer he remained at home, profiting little, as it
would seem, from the lesson he had received. At length he availed
himself of another opportunity presented by the departure of a
small squadron of vessels bound to the Indian islands. He was
nineteen years of age when he bade adieu to his native shores
in 1504—the same year in which Spain lost the best and greatest
in her long line of princes, Isabella the Catholic.

The vessel in which Cortes sailed was commanded by one
Alonso Quintero. The fleet touched at the Canaries, as was
common in the outward passage. While the other vessels were
detained there taking in supplies, Quintero secretly stole out by
night from the island, with the design of reaching Hispaniola and
securing the market before the arrival of his companions. A
furious storm which he encountered, however, dismasted his
ship, and he was obliged to return to port and refit. The convoy
consented to wait for their unworthy partner, and after a short

detention they all sailed in company again. But the faithless Quintero, as they drew near the Islands, availed himself once more of the darkness of the night, to leave the squadron with the same purpose as before. Unluckily for him, he met with a succession of heavy gales and headwinds, which drove him from his course, and he wholly lost his reckoning. For many days the vessel was tossed about, and all on board were filled with apprehensions, and no little indignation against the author of their calamities. At length they were cheered one morning with the sight of a white dove, which, wearied by its flight, lighted on the topmast. The biographers of Cortes speak of it as a miracle. Fortunately it was no miracle, but a very natural occurrence, showing incontestably that they were near land. In a short time, by taking the direction of the bird's flight, they reached the island of Hispaniola; and, on coming into port, the worthy master had the satisfaction to find his companions arrived before him, and their cargoes already sold.

Immediately on landing, Cortes repaired to the house of the governor, to whom he had been personally known in Spain. Ovando was absent on an expedition into the interior, but the young man was kindly received by the secretary, who assured him there would be no doubt of his obtaining a liberal grant of land to settle on. "But I came to get gold," replied Cortes, "not to till the soil, like a peasant."

On the governor's return, Cortes consented to give up his roving thoughts, at least for a time, as the other labored to convince him that he would be more likely to realize his wishes from the slow, indeed, but sure, returns of husbandry, where the soil and the laborers were a free gift to the planter, than by taking his chance in the lottery of adventure, in which there were so many blanks to a prize. He accordingly received a grant of land, with a repartimiento of Indians, and was appointed notary of the town or settlement of Açua. His graver pursuits, however, did not prevent his indulgence of the amorous propensities which belong to the sunny clime where he was born; and this frequently involved him in affairs of honor, from which, though an expert swordsman, he carried away scars that accompanied him to his grave. He occasionally, moreover, found the means of breaking up the monotony of his way of life by engaging in the military expeditions which, under the command of Ovando's lieutenant, Diego Velasquez, were employed to suppress the insurrections of the natives. In this school the young adventurer first studied the wild tactics of Indian warfare; he became familiar with toil and danger, and with those deeds of cruelty which have too often, alas! stained the bright scutcheons of the Castilian chivalry in the New World. He was only prevented by illness—a most fortunate one, on this occasion—from embarking in Nicuessa's expedition, which furnished a tale of woe not often matched in the annals of Spanish discovery. Providence reserved him for higher ends.

At length, in 1511, when Velasquez undertook the conquest of Cuba, Cortes willingly abandoned his quiet life for the stirring scenes there opened, and took part in the expedition. He displayed, throughout the invasion, an activity and courage that won him the approbation of the commander; while his free and cordial manners, his good humor and lively sallies of wit, made him the favorite of the soldiers. "He gave little evidence," says a contemporary, "of the great qualities which he afterwards showed." It is probable these qualities were not known to himself; while to a common observer his careless manners and jocund repartees might well seem incompatible with anything serious or profound; as the real depth of the current is not suspected under the light play and sunny sparkling of the surface.

After the reduction of the island, Cortes seems to have been held in great favor by Velasquez, now appointed its governor. According to Las Casas, he was made one of his secretaries. He still retained the same fondness for gallantry, for which his handsome person afforded obvious advantages, but which had more than once brought him into trouble in earlier life. Among the families who had taken up their residence in Cuba was one of the name of Xuarez, from Granada in Old Spain. It consisted of a brother, and four sisters remarkable for their beauty. With one of them, named Catalina, the susceptible heart of the young soldier became enamored. How far the intimacy was carried is not quite certain. But it appears he gave his promise to marry her—a promise which, when the time came, and reason, it may be, had got the better of passion, he showed no alacrity in keeping. He resisted, indeed, all remonstrances to this effect, from the lady's family, backed by the governor, and somewhat sharpened, no doubt, in the latter by the particular interest he took in one of the fair sisters, who is said not to have repaid it with ingratitude.

Whether the rebuke of Velasquez or some other cause of disgust rankled in the breast of Cortes, he now became cold towards his patron, and connected himself with a disaffected party tolerably numerous in the island. They were in the habit of meeting at his house and brooding over their causes of discontent, chiefly founded, it would appear, on what they conceived an ill requital of their services in the distribution of lands and offices. It may well be imagined that it could have been no easy task for the ruler of one of these colonies, however discreet and well intentioned, to satisfy the indefinite cravings of speculators and adventurers, who swarmed, like so many famished harpies, in the track of discovery in the New World.

The malcontents determined to lay their grievances before the higher authorities in Hispaniola, from whom Velasquez had received his commission. The voyage was one of some hazard, as it was to be made in an open boat, across an arm of the sea eighteen leagues wide; and they fixed on Cortes, with whose fearless spirit they were well acquainted, as the fittest man to undertake it. The conspiracy got wind, and came to the governor's ears before the departure of the envoy, whom he instantly caused to be seized, loaded with fetters, and placed in strict confinement. It is even said he would have hung him, but for the interposition of his friends. The fact is not incredible. The governors of these little territories, having entire control over the fortunes of their subjects, enjoyed an authority far more despotic than that of the sovereign himself. They were generally men of rank and personal consideration; their distance from the mother country withdrew their conduct from searching scrutiny, and, when that did occur, they usually had interest and means of corruption at command sufficient to shield them from punishment. The Spanish colonial history, in its earlier stages, affords striking instances of the extraordinary assumption and abuse of powers by these petty potentates; and the sad fate of Vasquez Nuñez de Balboa, the illustrious discoverer of the Pacific, though the most signal, is by no means a solitary example, that the greatest services could be requited by persecution and an ignominious death.

The governor of Cuba, however, although irascible and suspicious in his nature, does not seem to have been vindictive, nor particularly cruel. In the present instance, indeed, it may well be doubted whether the blame would not be more reasonably charged on the unfounded expectations of his followers than on himself.

Cortes did not long remain in durance. He contrived to throw back one of the bolts of his fetters, and, after extricating his limbs, succeeded in forcing open a window with the irons so as to admit of his escape. He was lodged on the second floor of the building, and was able to let himself down to the pavement without injury, and unobserved. He then made the best of his way to a neighboring church, where he claimed the privilege of sanctuary.

Velasquez, though incensed at his escape, was afraid to violate the sanctity of the place by employing force. But he stationed a guard in the neighborhood, with orders to seize the fugitive if he should forget himself so far as to leave the sanctuary. In a few days this happened. As Cortes was carelessly standing without the walls in front of the building, an alguacil suddenly sprang on him from behind and pinioned his arms, while others rushed in and secured him. This man, whose name was Juan Escudero, was afterwards hung by Cortes for some offense in New Spain.

The unlucky prisoner was again put in irons, and carried on board a vessel to sail the next morning for Hispaniola, there to undergo his trial. Fortune favored him once more. He succeeded, after much difficulty and no little pain, in passing his feet through the rings which shackled them. He then came cautiously on deck, and, covered by the darkness of the night, stole quietly down the side of the ship into a boat that lay floating below. He pushed off from the vessel with as little noise as possible. As he drew near the shore, the stream became rapid and turbulent. He hesitated to trust his boat to it, and, as he was an excellent swimmer, prepared to breast it himself, and boldly plunged into the water. The current was strong, but the arm of a man struggling for life was stronger; and, after buffeting the waves till he was nearly exhausted, he succeeded in gaining a landing; when he sought refuge in the same sanctuary which had protected him before. The facility with which Cortes a second time effected his escape may lead one to doubt the fidelity of his guards; who perhaps looked on him as the victim of persecution, and felt the influence of those popular manners which seem to have gained him friends in every society into which he was thrown.

For some reason not explained—perhaps from policy—he now relinquished his objections to the marriage with Catalina Xuarez. He thus secured the good offices of her family. Soon afterwards the governor himself relented, and became reconciled to his unfortunate enemy. A strange story is told in connection with this event. It is said his proud spirit refused to accept the proffers of reconciliation made him by Velasquez; and that one evening, leaving the sanctuary, he presented himself unexpectedly before the latter in his own quarters, when on a military excursion at some distance from the capital. The governor, startled by the sudden apparition of his enemy completely armed before him, with some dismay inquired the meaning of it. Cortes answered by insisting on a full explanation of his previous conduct. After some hot discussion the interview terminated amicably; the parties embraced, and, when a messenger arrived to announce the escape of Cortes, he found him in the apartments of his Excellency, where, having retired to rest, both were actually sleeping in the same bed! The anecdote is repeated without distrust by more than one biographer of Cortes. It is not very probable, however, that a haughty, irascible man like Velasquez should have given such uncommon proofs of condescension and familiarity to one, so far beneath him in station, with whom he had been so recently in deadly feud; nor, on the other hand, that Cortes should have had the silly temerity to brave the lion in his den, where a single nod would have sent him to the gibbet—and that, too, with as little compunction or fear of consequences as would have attended the execution of an Indian slave.

The reconciliation with the governor, however brought about, was permanent. Cortes, though not re-established in the office of secretary, received a liberal repartimiento of Indians, and an ample territory in the neighborhood of St. Jago, of which he was soon after made alcalde. He now lived almost wholly on his estate, devoting himself to agriculture with more zeal than formerly. He stocked his plantation with different kinds of cattle, some of which were first introduced by him into Cuba. He wrought, also, the gold-mines which fell to his share, and which in this island promised better returns than those in Hispaniola. By this course of industry he found himself, in a few years, master of some two or three thousand castellanos, a large sum for one in his situation. "God, who alone knows at what cost of Indian lives it was obtained," exclaims Las Casas, "will take account of it!" His days glided smoothly away in these tranquil pursuits, and in the society of his beautiful wife, who, however ineligible as a connection, from the inferiority of her condition, appears to have fulfilled all the relations of a faithful and affectionate partner. Indeed, he was often heard to say at this time, as the good bishop above quoted remarks, "that he lived as happily with her as if she had been the daughter of a duchess." Fortune gave him the means in after-life of verifying the truth of his assertion.

Such was the state of things, when Alvarado returned with the tidings of Grijalva's discoveries and the rich fruits of his traffic with the natives. The news spread like wildfire throughout the island; for all saw in it the promise of more important results than any hitherto obtained. The governor, as already noticed, resolved to follow up the track of discovery with a more considerable armament; and he looked around for a proper person to share the expense of it and to take the command.

Several hidalgos presented themselves, whom, from want of proper qualifications, or from his distrust of their assuming an independence of their employer, he, one after another, rejected. There were two persons in St. Jago in whom he placed great confidence—Amador de Lares, the contador, or royal treasurer, and his own secretary, Andres de Duero. Cortes was also in close intimacy with both these persons; and he availed himself of it to prevail on them to recommend him as a suitable person to be intrusted with the expedition. It is said he reinforced the proposal by promising a liberal share of the proceeds of it. However this may be, the parties urged his selection by the governor with all the eloquence of which they were capable. That officer had had ample experience of the capacity and courage of the candidate. He knew, too, that he had acquired a fortune which would enable him to cooperate materially in fitting out the armament. His popularity in the island would speedily attract followers to his standard. All past animosities had long since been buried in oblivion, and the confidence he was now to repose in him would insure his fidelity and gratitude. He lent a willing ear, therefore, to the recommendation of his counselors, and, sending for Cortes, announced his purpose of making him Captain-General of the Armada.

Cortes had now attained the object of his wishes—the object for which his soul had panted ever since he had set foot in the New World. He was no longer to be condemned to a life of mercenary drudgery, nor to be cooped up within the precincts of a petty island; but he was to be placed on a new and independent theater of action, and a boundless prospective was opened to his view, which might satisfy not merely the wildest cravings of avarice, but, to a bold, aspiring spirit like his, the far more importunate cravings of ambition. He fully appreciated the importance of the late discoveries, and read in them the existence of the great empire in the far West, dark hints of which had floated, from time to time, to the islands, and of which more certain glimpses had been caught by those who had reached the continent. This was the country intimated to the "Great Admiral" in his visit to Honduras in 1502, and which he might have reached had he held on a northern course, instead of striking to the south in quest of an imaginary strait. As it was, "he had but opened the gate," to use his own bitter expression, "for others to enter." The time had at length come when they were to enter it; and the young adventurer, whose magic lance was to dissolve the spell which had so long hung over these mysterious regions, now stood ready to assume the enterprise.

From this hour the deportment of Cortes seemed to undergo a change. His thoughts, instead of evaporating in empty levities or idle flashes of merriment, were wholly concentrated on the great object to which he was devoted. His elastic spirits were shown in cheering and stimulating the companions of his toilsome duties, and he was roused to a generous enthusiasm, of which even those who knew him best had not conceived him capable. He applied at once all the money in his possession to fitting out the armament. He raised more by the mortgage of his estates, and by giving his obligations to some wealthy merchants of the place, who relied for their reimbursement on the success of the expedition; and, when his own credit was exhausted, he availed himself of that of his friends.

The funds thus acquired he expended in the purchase of vessels, provisions, and military stores, while he invited recruits by offers of assistance to such as were too poor to provide for themselves, and by the additional promise of a liberal share of the anticipated profits.

All was now bustle and excitement in the little town of St. Jago. Some were busy in refitting the vessels and getting them ready for the voyage; some in providing naval stores; others in converting their own estates into money in order to equip themselves; everyone seemed anxious to contribute in some way or other to the success of the expedition. Six ships, some of them of a large size, had already been procured; and three hundred recruits enrolled themselves in the course of a few days, eager to seek their fortunes under the banner of this daring and popular chieftain.

How far the governor contributed towards the expenses of the outfit is not very clear. If the friends of Cortes are to be believed, nearly the whole burden fell on him; since, while he supplied the squadron without remuneration, the governor sold many of his own stores at an exorbitant profit. Yet it does not seem probable that Velasquez, with such ample means at his command, should have thrown on his deputy the burden of the expedition, nor that the latter—had he done so—could have been in a condition to meet these expenses, amounting, as we are told, to more than twenty thousand gold ducats. Still it cannot be denied that an ambitious man like Cortes, who was to reap all the glory of the enterprise, would very naturally be less solicitous to count the gains of it, than his employer, who, inactive at home, and having no laurels to win, must look on the pecuniary profits as his only recompense. The question gave rise, some years later, to a furious litigation between the parties, with which it is not necessary at present to embarrass the reader.

It is due to Velasquez to state that the instructions delivered by him for the conduct of the expedition cannot be charged with a narrow or mercenary spirit. The first object of the voyage was to find Grijalva, after which the two commanders were to proceed in company together. Reports had been brought back by Cordova, on his return from the first visit to Yucatan, that six Christians were said to be lingering in captivity in the interior of the country. It was supposed they might belong to the party of the unfortunate Nicuessa, and orders were given to find them out, if possible, and restore them to liberty. But the great object of the expedition was barter with the natives. In pursuing this, special care was to be taken that they should receive no wrong, but be treated with kindness and humanity. Cortes was to bear in mind, above all things, that the object which the Spanish monarch had most at heart was the conversion of the Indians. He was to impress on them the grandeur and goodness of his royal master, to invite them "to give in their allegiance to him, and to manifest it by regaling him with such comfortable presents of gold, pearls, and precious stones as, by showing their own good will, would secure his favor and protection." He was to make an accurate survey of the coast, sounding its bays and inlets for the benefit of future navigators. He was to acquaint himself with the natural products of the country, with the character of its different races, their institutions and progress in civilization; and he was to send home minute accounts of all these, together with such articles as he should obtain in his intercourse with them. Finally, he was to take *the most careful care* to omit nothing that might redound to the service of God or his sovereign.

Such was the general tenor of the instructions given to Cortes; and they must be admitted to provide for the interests of science and humanity, as well as for those which had reference only to a commercial speculation. It may seem strange, considering the discontent shown by Velasquez with his former captain, Grijalva, for not colonizing, that no directions should have been given to that effect here. But he had not yet received from Spain the warrant for investing his agents with such powers; and that which had been obtained from the Hieronymite fathers in Hispaniola conceded only the right to traffic with the natives. The commission at the same time recognized the authority of Cortes as Captain-General of the expedition.

CHAPTER III

Cortes Embarks

1519

The importance given to Cortes by his new position, and, perhaps, a somewhat more lofty bearing, gradually gave uneasiness to the naturally suspicious temper of Velasquez, who became apprehensive that his officer, when away where he would have the power, might also have the inclination, to throw off his dependence on him altogether. An accidental circumstance at this time heightened these suspicions. A mad fellow, his jester, one of those crack-brained wits—half wit, half fool—who formed in those days a common appendage to every great man's establishment, called out to the governor, as he was taking his usual walk one morning with Cortes towards the port, "Have a care, master Velasquez, or we shall have to go a hunting, some day or other, after this same captain of ours!" "Do you hear what the rogue says?" exclaimed the governor to his companion. "Do not heed him," said Cortes: "he is a saucy knave, and deserves a good whipping." The words sank deep, however, in the mind of Velasquez—as, indeed, true jests are apt to stick.

There were not wanting persons about his Excellency who fanned the latent embers of jealousy into a blaze. These worthy gentlemen, some of them kinsmen of Velasquez, who probably felt their own deserts somewhat thrown into the shade by the rising fortunes of Cortes, reminded the governor of his ancient quarrel with that officer, and of the little probability that affronts so keenly felt at the time could ever be forgotten. By these and similar suggestions, and by misconstructions of the present conduct of Cortes, they wrought on the passions of Velasquez to such a degree that he resolved to intrust the expedition to other hands.

He communicated his design to his confidential advisers,

Lares and Duero, and these trusty personages reported it without delay to Cortes, although, "to a man of half his penetration," says Las Casas, "the thing would have been readily divined from the governor's altered demeanor." The two functionaries advised their friend to expedite matters as much as possible, and to lose no time in getting his fleet ready for sea, if he would retain the command of it. Cortes showed the same prompt decision on this occasion which more than once afterwards in a similar crisis gave the direction to his destiny.

He had not yet got his complement of men, nor of vessels, and was very inadequately provided with supplies of any kind. But he resolved to weigh anchor that very night. He waited on his officers, informed them of his purpose, and probably of the cause of it; and at midnight, when the town was hushed in sleep, they all went quietly on board, and the little squadron dropped down the bay. First, however, Cortes had visited the person whose business it was to supply the place with meat, and relieved him of all his stock on hand, notwithstanding his complaint that the city must suffer for it on the morrow, leaving him, at the same time, in payment, a massive gold chain of much value, which he wore round his neck.

Great was the amazement of the good citizens of St. Jago when, at dawn, they saw that the fleet, which they knew was so ill prepared for the voyage, had left its moorings and was busily getting under way. The tidings soon came to the ears of his Excellency, who, springing from his bed, hastily dressed himself, mounted his horse, and, followed by his retinue, galloped down to the quay. Cortes, as soon as he descried their approach, entered an armed boat, and came within speaking-distance of the shore. "And is it thus you part from me?" exclaimed Velasquez; "a courteous way of taking leave, truly!" "Pardon me," answered Cortes; "time presses, and there are some things that should be done before they are even thought of. Has your Excellency any commands?" But the mortified governor had no commands to give; and Cortes, politely waving his hand, returned to his vessel, and the little fleet instantly made sail for the port of Macaca, about fifteen leagues distant. (November 18, 1518.) Velasquez rode back to his house to digest his chagrin as he best might; satisfied, probably, that he had made at least two blunders—one in appointing Cortes to the command, the other in attempting to deprive him of it. For, if it be true that by giving our confidence by halves we can scarcely hope to make a friend, it is equally true that by withdrawing it when given we shall make an enemy.

This clandestine departure of Cortes has been severely criticized by some writers, especially by Las Casas. Yet much may be urged in vindication of his conduct. He had been appointed to the command by the voluntary act of the governor, and this had been fully ratified by the authorities of Hispaniola. He had at once devoted all his resources to the undertaking, incurring, indeed, a heavy debt in addition. He was now to be deprived of his commission, without any misconduct having been alleged or at least proved against him. Such an event must overwhelm him in irretrievable ruin, to say nothing of the friends from whom he had so largely borrowed, and the followers who had embarked their fortunes in the expedition on the faith of his commanding it. There are few persons, probably, who, under these circumstances, would have felt called tamely to acquiesce in the sacrifice of their hopes to a groundless and arbitrary whim. The most to have been expected from Cortes was that he should feel obliged to provide faithfully for the interests of his employer in the conduct of the enterprise. How far he felt the force of this obligation will appear in the sequel.

From Macaca, where Cortes laid in such stores as he could obtain from the royal farms, and which, he said, he considered as "a loan from the king," he proceeded to Trinidad; a more considerable town, on the southern coast of Cuba. Here he landed, and, erecting his standard in front of his quarters, made proclamation, with liberal offers to all who would join the expedition. Volunteers came in daily, and among them more than a hundred of Grijalva's men, just returned from their voyage and willing to follow up the discovery under an enterprising leader. The fame of Cortes attracted, also, a number of cavaliers of family and distinction, some of whom, having accompanied Grijalva, brought much information valuable for the present expedition. Among these hidalgos may be mentioned Pedro de Alvarado and his brothers, Cristóval de Olid, Alonso de Avila, Juan Velasquez de Leon, a near relation of the governor, Alonso Hernandez de Puertocarrero, and Gonzalo de Sandoval—all of them men who took a most important part in the Conquest.

Their presence was of great moment, as giving consideration to the enterprise; and, when they entered the little camp of the adventurers, the latter turned out to welcome them amidst lively strains of music and joyous salvos of artillery.

Cortes meanwhile was active in purchasing military stores and provisions. Learning that a trading-vessel laden with grain and other commodities for the mines was off the coast, he ordered out one of his caravels to seize her and bring her into port. He paid the master in bills for both cargo and ship, and even persuaded this man, named Sedeño, who was wealthy, to join his fortunes to the expedition. He also despatched one of his officers, Diego de Ordaz, in quest of another ship, of which he had tidings, with instructions to seize it in like manner, and to meet him with it off Cape St. Antonio, the westerly point of the island. By this he effected another object, that of getting rid of Ordaz, who was one of the governor's household, and an inconvenient spy on his own actions.

While thus occupied, letters from Velasquez were received by the commander of Trinidad, requiring him to seize the person of Cortes and to detain him, as he had been deposed from the command of the fleet, which was given to another. This functionary communicated his instructions to the principal officers in the expedition, who counseled him not to make the attempt, as it would undoubtedly lead to a commotion among the soldiers, that might end in laying the town in ashes. Verdugo thought it prudent to conform to this advice.

As Cortes was willing to strengthen himself by still further reinforcements, he ordered Alvarado with a small body of men to march across the country to the Havana, while he himself would sail round the westerly point of the island and meet him there with the squadron. In this port he again displayed his standard, making the usual proclamation. He caused all the large guns to be brought on shore, and, with the small arms and crossbows, to be put in order. As there was abundance of cotton raised in this neighborhood, he had the jackets of the soldiers thickly quilted with it, for a defense against the Indian arrows, from which the troops in the former expeditions had grievously suffered. He distributed his men into eleven companies, each under the command of an experienced officer; and it was observed that, although several of the cavaliers in the service were the personal friends and even kinsmen of Velasquez, he appeared to treat them all with perfect confidence.

His principal standard was of black velvet, embroidered with gold, and emblazoned with a red cross amidst flames of blue and white, with this motto in Latin beneath: "Friends, let us follow the cross; and under this sign, if we have faith, we shall conquer." He now assumed more state in his own person and way of living, introducing a greater number of domestics and officers into his household, and placing it on a footing becoming a man of high station. This state he maintained through the rest of his life.

Cortes at this time was thirty-three, or perhaps thirty-four, years of age. In stature he was rather above the middle size. His complexion was pale; and his large dark eyes gave an expression of gravity to his countenance, not to have been expected in one of his cheerful temperament. His figure was slender, at least until later life; but his chest was deep, his shoulders broad, his frame muscular and well proportioned. It presented the union of agility and vigor which qualified him to excel in fencing, horsemanship, and the other generous exercises of chivalry. In his diet he was temperate, careless of what he ate, and drinking little; while to toil and privation he seemed perfectly indifferent. His dress, for he did not disdain the impression produced by such adventitious aids, was such as to set off his handsome person to advantage; neither gaudy nor striking, but rich. He wore few ornaments, and usually the same; but those were of great price. His manners, frank and soldier-like, concealed a most cool and calculating spirit. With his gayest humor there mingled a settled air of resolution, which made those who approached him feel they must obey, and which infused something like awe into the attachment of his most devoted followers. Such a combination, in which love was tempered by authority, was the one probably best calculated to inspire devotion in the rough and turbulent spirits among whom his lot was to be cast.

The character of Cortes seems to have undergone some change with change of circumstances; or, to speak more correctly, the new scenes in which he was placed called forth qualities which before lay dormant in his bosom. There are some hardy natures that require the heats of excited action to unfold their energies;

like the plants which, closed to the mild influence of a temperate latitude, come to their full growth, and give forth their fruits, only in the burning atmosphere of the tropics. Such is the portrait left to us by his contemporaries of this remarkable man; the instrument selected by Providence to scatter terror among the barbarian monarchs of the Western World, and lay their empires in the dust.

Before the preparations were fully completed at the Havana, the commander of the place, Don Pedro Barba, received despatches from Velasquez ordering him to apprehend Cortes and to prevent the departure of his vessels; while another epistle from the same source was delivered to Cortes himself, requesting him to postpone his voyage till the governor could communicate with him, as he proposed, in person. "Never," exclaims Las Casas, "did I see so little knowledge of affairs shown, as in this letter of Diego Velasquez—that he should have imagined that a man who had so recently put such an affront on him would defer his departure at his bidding!" It was, indeed, hoping to stay the flight of the arrow by a word, after it had left the bow.

The Captain-General, however, during his short stay, had entirely conciliated the good will of Barba. And, if that officer had had the inclination, he knew he had not the power, to enforce his principal's orders, in the face of a resolute soldiery, incensed at this ungenerous persecution of their commander, and "all of whom," in the words of the honest chronicler who bore part in the expedition, "officers and privates, would have cheerfully laid down their lives for him." Barba contented himself, therefore, with explaining to Velasquez the impracticability of the attempt, and at the same time endeavored to tranquilize his apprehensions by asserting his own confidence in the fidelity of Cortes. To this the latter added a communication of his own, couched "in the soft terms he knew so well how to use," in which he implored his Excellency to rely on his devotion to his interests, and concluded with the comfortable assurance that he and the whole fleet, God willing, would sail on the following morning.

Accordingly, on the 10th of February, 1519, the little squadron got under way, and directed its course towards Cape St. Antonio, the appointed place of rendezvous. When all were brought together, the vessels were found to be eleven in number; one of them, in which Cortes himself went, was of a hundred tons' burden, three others were from seventy to eighty tons; the remainder were caravels and open brigantines. The whole was put under the direction of Antonio de Alaminos, as chief pilot; a veteran navigator, who had acted as pilot to Columbus in his last voyage, and to Cordova and Grijalva in the former expeditions to Yucatan.

Landing on the Cape and mustering his forces, Cortes found they amounted to one hundred and ten mariners, five hundred and fifty-three soldiers, including thirty-two crossbowmen, and thirteen arquebusiers, besides two hundred Indians of the island, and a few Indian women for menial offices. He was provided with ten heavy guns, four lighter pieces called falconets, and with a good supply of ammunition. He had besides sixteen horses. They were not easily procured; for the difficulty of transporting them across the ocean in the flimsy craft of that day made them rare and incredibly dear in the Islands. But Cortes rightfully estimated the importance of cavalry, however small in number, both for their actual service in the field, and for striking terror into the savages. With so paltry a force did he enter on a conquest which even his stout heart must have shrunk from attempting with such means, had he but foreseen half its real difficulties!

Before embarking, Cortes addressed his soldiers in a short but animated harangue. He told them they were about to enter on a noble enterprise, one that would make their name famous to after-ages. He was leading them to countries more vast and opulent than any yet visited by Europeans. "I hold out to you a glorious prize," continued the orator, "but it is to be won by incessant toil. Great things are achieved only by great exertions, and glory was never the reward of sloth. If I have labored hard and staked my all on this undertaking, it is for the love of that renown which is the noblest recompense of man. But, if any among you covet riches more, be but true to me, as I will be true to you and to the occasion, and I will make you masters of such as our countrymen have never dreamed of! You are few in number, but strong in resolution; and, if this does not falter, doubt not but that the Almighty, who has never deserted the Spaniard in his contest with the infidel, will shield you, though encompassed by a cloud of enemies; for your cause is a *just cause,* and you are to fight under the banner of the cross. Go forward, then," he concluded, "with alacrity and confidence, and carry to a glorious issue the work so auspiciously begun."

The rough eloquence of the general, touching the various chords of ambition, avarice, and religious zeal, sent a thrill through the bosoms of his martial audience; and, receiving it with acclamations, they seemed eager to press forward under a chief who was to lead them not so much to battle, as to triumph.

Cortes was well satisfied to find his own enthusiasm so largely shared by his followers. Mass was then celebrated with the solemnities usual with the Spanish navigators when entering on their voyages of discovery. The fleet was placed under the immediate protection of St. Peter, the patron saint of Cortes, and, weighing anchor, took its departure on the eighteenth day of February, 1519, for the coast of Yucatan.

FROM CHAPTER VII

Management of Cortes

1519

There is no situation which tries so severely the patience and discipline of the soldier as a life of idleness in camp, where his thoughts, instead of being bent on enterprise and action, are fastened on himself and the inevitable privations and dangers of his condition. This was particularly the case in the present instance, where, in addition to the evils of a scanty subsistence, the troops suffered from excessive heat, swarms of venomous insects, and the other annoyances of a sultry climate. They were, moreover, far from possessing the character of regular forces, trained to subordination under a commander whom they had long been taught to reverence and obey. They were soldiers of fortune, embarked with him in an adventure in which all seemed to have an equal stake, and they regarded their captain—the captain of a day—as little more than an equal.

There was a growing discontent among the men at their longer residence in this strange land. They were still more dissatisfied on learning the general's intention to remove to the neighborhood of the port discovered by Montejo. "It was time to return," they said, "and report what had been done to the governor of Cuba, and not linger on these barren shores until they had brought the whole Mexican empire on their heads!" Cortes evaded their importunities as well as he could, assuring them there was no cause for despondency. "Everything so far had gone on prosperously, and, when they had taken up a more favorable position, there was no reason to doubt they might still continue the same profitable intercourse with the natives."

While this was passing, five Indians made their appearance in the camp one morning, and were brought to the general's tent. Their dress and whole appearance were different from those of the Mexicans. They wore rings of gold, and gems of bright blue stone in their ears and nostrils, while a gold leaf delicately wrought was attached to the under lip. Marina was unable to comprehend their language, but, on her addressing them in Aztec, two of them, it was found, could converse in that tongue. They said they were natives of Cempoalla, the chief town of the Totonacs, a powerful nation who had come upon the great plateau many centuries back, and, descending its eastern slope, settled along the sierras and broad plains which skirt the Mexican Gulf towards the north. Their country was one of the recent conquests of the Aztecs, and they experienced such vexatious oppressions from their conquerors as made them very impatient of the yoke. They informed Cortes of these and other particulars. The fame of the Spaniards had reached their master, who sent these messengers to request the presence of the wonderful strangers in his capital.

This communication was eagerly listened to by the general, who, it will be remembered, was possessed of none of those facts, laid before the reader, respecting the internal condition of the kingdom, which he had no reason to suppose other than strong and united. An important truth now flashed on his mind, as his quick eye descried in this spirit of discontent a potent lever, by the aid of which he might hope to overturn this barbaric empire. He received the mission of the Totonacs most graciously, and, after informing himself, as far as possible, of their dispositions and resources, dismissed them with presents, promising soon to pay a visit to their lord.

Meanwhile, his personal friends, among whom may be particularly mentioned Alonso Hernandez Puertocarrero, Cristobal de Olid, Alonso de Avila, Pedro de Alvarado and his brothers, were very busy in persuading the troops to take such measures as should enable Cortes to go forward in those ambitious plans for which he had no warrant from the powers of Velasquez. "To return now," they said, "was to abandon the enterprise on the threshold, which, under such a leader, must conduct to glory and incalculable riches. To return to Cuba would be to surrender to the greedy governor the little gains they had already got. The only way was to persuade the general to establish a permanent colony in the country, the government of which would take the conduct of matters into its own hands and provide for the interests of its members. It was true, Cortes had no such authority from Velasquez. But the interests of the sovereigns, which were paramount to every other, imperatively demanded it."

These conferences could not be conducted so secretly, though held by night, as not to reach the ears of the friends of Velasquez. They remonstrated against the proceedings, as insidious and disloyal. They accused the general of instigating them, and, calling on him to take measures without delay for the return of the troops to Cuba, announced their own intention to depart, with such followers as still remained true to the governor.

Cortes, instead of taking umbrage at this high-handed proceeding, or even answering in the same haughty tone, mildly replied "that nothing was further from his desire than to exceed his instructions. He, indeed, preferred to remain in the country, and continue his profitable intercourse with the natives. But, since the army thought otherwise, he should defer to their opinion, and give orders to return, as they desired." On the following morning, proclamation was made for the troops to hold themselves in readiness to embark at once on board the fleet, which was to sail for Cuba.

Great was the sensation caused by their general's order. Even many of those before clamorous for it, with the usual caprice of men whose wishes are too easily gratified, now regretted it. The partisans of Cortes were loud in their remonstrances. "They were betrayed by the general," they cried, and, thronging round his tent, called on him to countermand his orders. "We came here," said they, "expecting to form a settlement, if the state of the country authorized it. Now it seems you have no warrant from the governor to make one. But there are interests, higher than those of Velasquez, which demand it. These territories are not his property, but were discovered for the sovereigns; and it is necessary to plant a colony to watch over their interests, instead of wasting time in idle barter, or, still worse, of returning, in the present state of affairs, to Cuba. If you refuse," they concluded, "we shall protest against your conduct as disloyal to their Highnesses."

Cortes received this remonstrance with the embarrassed air of one by whom it was altogether unexpected. He modestly requested time for deliberation, and promised to give his answer on the following day. At the time appointed, he called the troops together, and made them a brief address. "There was no one," he said, "if he knew his own heart, more deeply devoted than himself to the welfare of his sovereigns and the glory of the Spanish name. He had not only expended his all, but incurred heavy debts, to meet the charges of this expedition, and had hoped to reimburse himself by continuing his traffic with the Mexicans. But, if the soldiers thought a different course advisable, he was ready to postpone his own advantage to the good of the state." He concluded by declaring his willingness to take measures for settling a colony *in the name of the Spanish sovereigns,* and to nominate a magistracy to preside over it.

For the alcaldes he selected Puertocarrero and Montejo, the former cavalier his fast friend, and the latter the friend of Velasquez, and chosen for that very reason; a stroke of policy which perfectly succeeded. The regidores, alguacil, treasurer, and other functionaries were then appointed, all of them his personal friends and adherents. They were regularly sworn into office, and the new city received the title of Villa Rica de Vera Cruz, "The Rich Town of the True Cross"; a name which was considered as happily intimating that union of spiritual and temporal interests to which the arms of the Spanish adventurers in the New World were to be devoted. Thus, by a single stroke of the pen, as it were, the camp was transformed into a civil community, and the whole framework and even title of the city were arranged, before the site of it had been settled.

The new municipality were not slow in coming together; when Cortes presented himself, cap in hand, before that august body, and, laying the powers of Velasquez on the table, respectfully tendered   the resignation of his office of Captain-General, "which, indeed," he said, "had necessarily expired, since the authority of the governor was now superseded by that of the magistracy of Villa Rica de Vera Cruz." He then, with a profound obeisance, left the apartment.

The council, after a decent time spent in deliberation, again requested his presence. "There was no one," they said, "who, on mature reflection, appeared to them so well qualified to take charge of the interests of the community, both in peace and in war, as himself; and they unanimously named him, in behalf of their Catholic Highnesses, Captain-General and Chief Justice of the colony." He was further empowered to draw, on his own account, one-fifth of the gold and silver which might hereafter be obtained by commerce or conquest from the natives. Thus clothed with supreme civil and military jurisdiction, Cortes was not backward in asserting his authority. He found speedy occasion for it.

The transactions above described had succeeded each other so rapidly that the governor's party seemed to be taken by surprise, and had formed no plan of opposition. When the last measure was carried, however, they broke forth into the most indignant and opprobrious invectives, denouncing the whole as a systematic conspiracy against Velasquez. These accusations led to recrimination from the soldiers of the other side, until from words they nearly proceeded to blows. Some of the principal cavaliers, among them Velasquez de Leon, a kinsman of the governor, Escobar, his page, and Diego de Ordaz, were so active in instigating these turbulent movements that Cortes took the bold measure of putting them all in irons and sending them on board the vessels. He then dispersed the common file by detaching many of them with a strong party under Alvarado to forage the neighboring country and bring home provisions for the destitute camp.

During their absence, every argument that cupidity or ambition could suggest was used to win the refractory to his views. Promises, and even gold, it is said, were liberally lavished; till, by degrees, their understandings were opened to a clearer view of the merits of the case. And when the foraging party reappeared with abundance of poultry and vegetables, and the cravings of the stomach—that great laboratory of disaffection, whether in camp or capital—were appeased, good humor returned with good cheer, and the rival factions embraced one another as companions in arms, pledged to a common cause. Even the high-mettled hidalgos on board the vessels did not long withstand the general tide of reconciliation, but one by one gave in their adhesion to the new government. What is more remarkable is that this forced conversion was not a hollow one, but from this time forward several of these very cavaliers became the most steady and devoted partisans of Cortes.

Such was the address of this extraordinary man, and such the ascendancy which in a few months he had acquired over these wild and turbulent spirits! By this ingenious transformation of a military into a civil community, he had secured a new and effectual basis for future operations. He might now go forward without fear of check or control from a superior—at least from any other superior than the crown, under which alone he held his commission. In accomplishing this, instead of incurring the charge of usurpation or of transcending his legitimate powers, he had transferred the responsibility, in a great measure, to those who had imposed on him the necessity of action. By this step, moreover, he had linked the fortunes of his followers indissolubly with his own. They had taken their chance with him, and, whether for weal or for woe, must abide the consequences. He was no longer limited to the narrow concerns of a sordid traffic, but, sure of their cooperation, might now boldly meditate, and gradually disclose, those lofty schemes which he had formed in his own bosom for the conquest of an empire. . . .

FROM CHAPTER VIII

Despatches to Spain and the Sinking of the Fleet

1519

Cortes now resolved to put a plan in execution which he had been some time meditating. He knew that all the late acts of the colony, as well as his own authority, would fall to the ground without the royal sanction. He knew, too, that the interest of Velasquez, which was great at court, would, so soon as he was acquainted with his secession, be wholly employed to circumvent and crush him. He resolved to anticipate his movements, and to send a vessel to Spain with despatches addressed to the emperor himself, announcing the nature and extent of his discoveries, and to obtain, if possible, the confirmation of his proceedings. In order to conciliate his master's good will, he further proposed to send him such a present as should suggest lofty ideas of the importance of his own services to the crown. To effect this, the royal fifth he considered inadequate. He conferred with his officers, and persuaded them to relinquish their share of the treasure. At his instance, they made a similar application to the soldiers; representing that it was the earnest wish of the general, who set the example by resigning his own fifth, equal to the share of the crown. It was but little that each man was asked to surrender, but the whole would make a present worthy of the monarch for whom it was intended. By this sacrifice they might hope to secure his indulgence for the past and his favor for the future; a temporary sacrifice, that would be well repaid by the security of the rich possessions which awaited them in Mexico. A paper was then circulated among the soldiers, which all who were disposed to relinquish their shares were requested to sign. Those who declined should have their claims respected, and receive the amount due to them. No one refused to sign; thus furnishing another example of the extraordinary power obtained by Cortes over these rapacious spirits, who, at his call, surrendered up the very treasures which had been the great object of their hazardous enterprise!

He accompanied this present with a letter to the emperor, in which he gave a full account of all that had befallen him since his departure from Cuba; of his various discoveries, battles, and traffic with the natives; their conversion to Christianity; his strange perils and sufferings; many particulars respecting the lands he had visited, and such as he could collect in regard to the great Mexican monarchy and its sovereign. He stated his difficulties with the governor of Cuba, the proceedings of the army in reference to colonization, and besought the emperor to confirm their acts, as well as his own authority, expressing his entire confidence that he should be able, with the aid of his brave followers, to place the Castilian crown in possession of this great Indian empire.

This was the celebrated *First Letter,* as it is called, of Cortes, which has hitherto eluded every search that has been made for it in the libraries of Europe. Its existence is fully established by references to it, both in his own subsequent letters, and in the writings of contemporaries. Its general purport is given by his chaplain, Gomara. The importance of the document has doubtless been much overrated; and, should it ever come to light, it will probably be found to add little of interest to the matter contained in the letter from Vera Cruz, which has formed the basis of the preceding portion of our narrative. Cortes had no sources of information beyond those open to the authors of the latter document. He was even less full and frank in his communications, if it be true that he suppressed all notice of the discoveries of his two immediate predecessors.

The magistrates of the Villa Rica, in their epistle, went over the same ground with Cortes; concluding with an emphatic representation of the misconduct of Velasquez, whose venality, extortion, and selfish devotion to his personal interests, to the exclusion of those of his sovereigns as well as of his own followers, they placed in a most clear and unenviable light. They implored the government not to sanction his interference with the new colony, which would be fatal to its welfare, but to commit the undertaking to Hernando Cortes, as the man most capable, by his experience and conduct, of bringing it to a glorious termination.

With this letter went also another in the name of the citizen-soldiers of Villa Rica, tendering their dutiful submission to the sovereigns, and requesting the confirmation of their proceedings, above all, that of Cortes as their general.

The selection of the agents for the mission was a delicate matter, as on the result might depend the future fortunes of the colony and its commander. Cortes intrusted the affair to two cavaliers on whom he could rely: Francisco de Montejo, the ancient partisan of Velasquez, and Alonso Hernandez de Puerto-carrero. The latter officer was a near kinsman of the count of Medellin, and it was hoped his high connections might secure a favorable influence at court.

Together with the treasure, which seemed to verify the assertion that "the land teemed with gold as abundantly as that whence Solomon drew the same precious metal for his temple," several Indian manuscripts were sent. Some were of cotton, others of the Mexican agave. Their unintelligible characters, says a chronicler, excited little interest in the Conquerors. As evidence of intellectual culture, however, they formed higher objects of interest to a philosophic mind than those costly fabrics which attested only the mechanical ingenuity of the nation. Four Indian slaves were added as specimens of the natives. They had been rescued from the cages in which they were confined for sacrifice. One of the best vessels of the fleet was selected for the voyage, manned by fifteen seamen, and placed under the direction of the pilot Alaminos. He was directed to hold his course through the Bahama channel, north of Cuba, or Fernandina, as it was then called, and on no account to touch at that island, or any other in the Indian Ocean. With these instructions, the good ship took its departure on the 26th of July, freighted with the treasures and the good wishes of the community of the Villa Rica de Vera Cruz.

After a quick run the emissaries made the island of Cuba, and, in direct disregard of orders, anchored before Marien, on the northern side of the island. This was done to accommodate Montejo, who wished to visit a plantation owned by him in the neighborhood. While off the port, a sailor got on shore, and, crossing the island to St. Jago, the capital, spread everywhere tidings of the expedition, until they reached the ears of Velasquez. It was the first intelligence which had been received of the armament since its departure; and, as the governor listened to the recital, it would not be easy to paint the mingled emotions of curiosity, astonishment, and wrath which agitated his bosom. In the first sally of passion, he poured a storm of invective on the heads of his secretary and treasurer, the friends of Cortes, who had recommended him as the leader of the expedition. After somewhat relieving himself in this way, he despatched two fast-sailing vessels to Marien with orders to seize the rebel ship, and, in case of her departure, to follow and overtake her.

But before the ships could reach that port the bird had flown, and was far on her way across the broad Atlantic. Stung with mortification at this fresh disappointment, Velasquez wrote letters of indignant complaint to the government at home, and to the Hieronymite fathers in Hispaniola, demanding redress. He obtained little satisfaction from the latter. He resolved, however, to take the matter into his own hands, and set about making formidable preparations for another squadron, which should be more than a match for that under his rebellious officer. He was indefatigable in his exertions, visiting every part of the island, and straining all his resources to effect his purpose. The preparations were on a scale that necessarily consumed many months.

Meanwhile the little vessel was speeding her prosperous way across the waters, and, after touching at one of the Azores, came safely into the harbor of St. Lucar, in the month of October. However long it may appear in the more perfect nautical science of our day, it was reckoned a fair voyage for that. Of what befell the commissioners on their arrival, their reception at court, and the sensation caused by their intelligence, I defer the account to a future chapter.

Shortly after the departure of the commissioners, an affair occurred of a most unpleasant nature. A number of persons, with the priest Juan Diaz at their head, ill-affected, from some cause or other, towards the administration of Cortes, or not relishing the hazardous expedition before them, laid a plan to seize one of the vessels, make the best of their way to Cuba, and report to the governor the fate of the armament. It was conducted with so much secrecy that the party had got their provisions, water, and everything necessary for the voyage, on board, without detection; when the conspiracy was betrayed, on the very night they were to sail, by one of their own number, who repented the part he had taken in it. The general caused the persons implicated to be instantly apprehended. An examination was instituted. The guilt of the parties was placed beyond a doubt. Sentence of death was passed on two of the ringleaders; another, the pilot, was condemned to lose his feet, and several others to be whipped. The priest, probably the most guilty of the whole, claiming the usual benefit of clergy, was permitted to escape. One of those condemned to the gallows was named Escudero, the very alguacil who, the reader may remember, so stealthily apprehended Cortes before the sanctuary in Cuba. The general, on signing the death-warrants, was heard to exclaim, "Would that I had never learned to write!" It was not the first time, it was remarked, that the exclamation had been uttered in similar circumstances.

The arrangements being now finally settled at the Villa Rica, Cortes sent forward Alvarado, with a large part of the army, to Cempoalla, where he soon after joined them with the remainder. The late affair of the conspiracy seems to have made a deep impression on his mind. It showed him that there were timid spirits in the camp on whom he could not rely, and who, he feared, might spread the seeds of disaffection among their companions. Even the more resolute, on any occasion of disgust or disappointment hereafter, might falter in purpose, and, getting possession of the vessels, abandon the enterprise. This was already too vast, and the odds were too formidable, to authorize expectation of success with diminution of numbers. Experience showed that this was always to be apprehended while means of escape were at hand. The best chance for success was to cut off these means. He came to the daring resolution to destroy the fleet, without the knowledge of his army.

When arrived at Cempoalla, he communicated his design to a few of his devoted adherents, who entered warmly into his views. Through them he readily persuaded the pilots, by means of those golden arguments which weigh more than any other with ordinary minds, to make such a report of the condition of the fleet as suited his purpose. The ships, they said, were grievously racked by the heavy gales they had encountered, and, what was worse, the worms had eaten into their sides and bottoms until most of them were not seaworthy, and some, indeed, could scarcely now be kept afloat.

Cortes received the communication with surprise; "for he could well dissemble," observes Las Casas, with his usual friendly comment, "when it suited his interests." "If it be so," he exclaimed, "we must make the best of it! Heaven's will be done!" He then ordered five of the worst conditioned to be dismantled, their cordage, sails, iron, and whatever was movable, to be brought on shore, and the ships to be sunk. A survey was made of the others, and, on a similar report, four more were condemned in the same manner. Only one small vessel remained!

When the intelligence reached the troops in Cempoalla, it caused the deepest consternation. They saw themselves cut off by a single blow from friends, family, country! The stoutest hearts quailed before the prospect of being thus abandoned on a hostile shore, a handful of men arrayed against a formidable empire. When the news arrived of the destruction of the five vessels first condemned, they had acquiesced in it as a necessary measure, knowing the mischievous activity of the insects in these tropical seas. But, when this was followed by the loss of the remaining four, suspicions of the truth flashed on their minds. They felt they were betrayed. Murmurs, at first deep, swelled louder and louder, menacing open mutiny. "Their general," they said, "had led them like cattle to be butchered in the shambles!" The affair wore a most alarming aspect. In no situation was Cortes ever exposed to greater danger from his soldiers.

His presence of mind did not desert him at this crisis. He called his men together, and, employing the tones of persuasion rather than authority, assured them that a survey of the ships showed they were not fit for service. If he had ordered them to be destroyed, they should consider, also, that his was the greatest sacrifice, for they were his property—all, indeed, he possessed in the world. The troops, on the other hand, would derive one great advantage from it, by the addition of a hundred able-bodied recruits, before required to man the vessels. But, even if the fleet had been saved, it could have been of little service in their present expedition; since they would not need it if they succeeded, while they would be too far in the interior to profit by it if they failed. He besought them to turn their thoughts in another direction. To be thus calculating chances and means of escape was unworthy of brave souls. They had set their hands to the work; to look back, as they advanced, would be their ruin. They had only to resume their former confidence in themselves and their general, and success was certain. "As for me," he concluded, "I have chosen my part. I will remain here, while there is one to bear me company. If there be any so craven as to shrink from sharing the dangers of our glorious enterprise, let them go home, in God's name. There is still one vessel left. Let them take that and return to Cuba. They can tell there how they deserted their commander and their comrades, and patiently wait till we return loaded with the spoils of the Aztecs."

The politic orator had touched the right chord in the bosoms of the soldiers. As he spoke, their resentment gradually died away. The faded visions of future riches and glory, rekindled by his eloquence, again floated before their imaginations. The first shock over, they felt ashamed of their temporary distrust. The enthusiasm for their leader revived, for they felt that under his banner only they could hope for victory; and, as he concluded, they testified the revulsion of their feelings by making the air ring with their shouts, "To Mexico! to Mexico!"

The destruction of his fleet by Cortes is, perhaps, the most remarkable passage in the life of this remarkable man. History, indeed, affords examples of a similar expedient in emergencies somewhat similar; but none where the chances of success were so precarious and defeat would be so disastrous. Had he failed, it might well seem an act of madness. Yet it was the fruit of deliberate calculation. He had set fortune, fame, life itself, all upon the cast, and must abide the issue. There was no alternative in his mind but to succeed or perish. The measure he adopted greatly increased the chance of success. But to carry it into execution, in the face of an incensed and desperate soldiery, was an act of resolution that has few parallels in history.

BOOK III

Interview with Montezuma and Entrance into the Capital

1519

With the first faint streak of dawn, the Spanish general was up, mustering his followers. They gathered, with beating hearts, under their respective banners, as the trumpet sent forth its spirit-stirring sounds across water and woodland, till they died away in distant echoes among the mountains. The sacred flames on the altars of numberless teocallis, dimly seen through the gray mists of morning, indicated the site of the capital, till temple, tower, and palace were fully revealed in the glorious illumination which the sun, as he rose above the eastern barrier, poured over the beautiful valley. It was the eighth of November, 1519, a conspicuous day in history, as that on which the Europeans first set foot in the capital of the Western World.

Cortes with his little body of horse formed a sort of advanced guard to the army. Then came the Spanish infantry, who in a summer's campaign had acquired the discipline and the weather-beaten aspect of veterans. The baggage occupied the center; and the rear was closed by the dark files of Tlascalan warriors. The whole number must have fallen short of seven thousand; of which less than four hundred were Spaniards.

For a short distance, the army kept along the narrow tongue of land that divides the Tezcucan from the Chalcan waters, when it entered on the great dike, which, with the exception of an angle near the commencement, stretches in a perfectly straight line across the salt floods of Tezcuco to the gates of the capital. It was the same causeway, or rather the basis of that, which still forms the great southern avenue of Mexico. The Spaniards had occasion more than ever to admire the mechanical science of the Aztecs, in the geometrical precision with which the work was executed, as well as the solidity of its construction. It was composed of huge stones well laid in cement, and wide enough, throughout its whole extent, for ten horsemen to ride abreast.

They saw, as they passed along, several large towns, resting on piles, and reaching far into the water—a kind of architecture which found great favor with the Aztecs, being in imitation of that of their metropolis. The busy population obtained a good subsistence from the manufacture of salt, which they extracted from the waters of the great lake. The duties on the traffic in this article were a considerable source of revenue to the crown.

Everywhere the Conquerors beheld the evidence of a crowded and thriving population, exceeding all they had yet seen. The temples and principal buildings of the cities were covered with a hard white stucco, which glistened like enamel in the level beams of the morning. The margin of the great basin was more thickly gemmed than that of Chalco with towns and hamlets. The water was darkened by swarms of canoes filled with Indians, who clambered up the sides of the causeway and gazed with curious astonishment on the strangers. And here, also, they beheld those fairy islands of flowers, overshadowed occasionally by trees of considerable size, rising and falling with the gentle undulation of the billows. At the distance of half a league from the capital, they encountered a solid work or curtain of stone, which traversed the dike. It was twelve feet high, was strengthened by towers at the extremities, and in the center was a battlemented gateway, which opened a passage to the troops. It was called the Fort of Xoloc, and became memorable in after-times as the position occupied by Cortes in the famous siege of Mexico.

Here they were met by several hundred Aztec chiefs, who came out to announce the approach of Montezuma and to welcome the Spaniards to his capital. They were dressed in the fanciful gala costume of the country, with the maxtlatl, or cotton sash, around their loins, and a broad mantle of the same material, or of the brilliant feather-embroidery, flowing gracefully down their shoulders. On their necks and arms they displayed collars and bracelets of turquoise mosaic, with which delicate plumage was curiously mingled, while their ears, underlips, and occasionally their noses, were garnished with pendants formed of precious stones, or crescents of fine gold. As each cacique made the usual formal salutation of the country separately to the general, the tedious ceremony delayed the march more than an hour. After this, the army experienced no further interruption till it reached a bridge near the gates of the city. It was built of wood, since replaced by one of stone, and was thrown across an opening of the dike, which furnished an outlet to the waters when agitated by the winds or swollen by a sudden influx in the rainy season. It was a drawbridge; and the Spaniards, as they crossed it, felt how truly they were committing themselves to the mercy of Montezuma, who, by thus cutting off their communications with the country, might hold them prisoners in his capital.

In the midst of these unpleasant reflections, they beheld the glittering retinue of the emperor emerging from the great street which led then, as it still does, through the heart of the city. Amidst a crowd of Indian nobles, preceded by three officers of state bearing golden wands, they saw the royal palanquin blazing with burnished gold. It was borne on the shoulders of nobles, and over it a canopy of gaudy feather-work, powdered with jewels and fringed with silver, was supported by four attendants of the same rank. They were barefooted, and walked with a slow, measured pace, and with eyes bent on the ground. When the train had come within a convenient distance, it halted, and Montezuma, descending from his litter, came forward, leaning on the arms of the lords of Tezcuco and Iztapalapan, his nephew and brother, both of whom . . . had already been made known to the Spaniards. As the monarch advanced under the canopy, the obsequious attendants strewed the ground with cotton tapestry, that his imperial feet might not be contaminated by the rude soil. His subjects of high and low degree, who lined the sides of the causeway, bent forward with their eyes fastened on the ground as he passed, and some of the humbler class prostrated themselves before him. Such was the homage paid to the Indian despot, showing that the slavish forms of Oriental adulation were to be found among the rude inhabitants of the Western World.

Montezuma wore the girdle and ample square cloak, tilmatli, of his nation. It was made of the finest cotton, with the embroidered ends gathered in a knot round his neck. His feet were defended by sandals having soles of gold, and the leathern thongs which bound them to his ankles were embossed with the same metal. Both the cloak and sandals were sprinkled with pearls and precious stones, among which the emerald and the chalchivitl— a green stone of higher estimation than any other among the Aztecs—were conspicuous. On his head he wore no other ornament than a panache of plumes of the royal green, which floated down his back, the badge of military, rather than of regal, rank.

He was at this time about forty years of age. His person was tall and thin, but not ill made. His hair, which was black and straight, was not very long; to wear it short was considered unbecoming persons of rank. His beard was thin; his complexion somewhat paler than is often found in his dusky, or rather copper-colored, race. His features, though serious in their expression, did not wear the look of melancholy, indeed, of dejection, which characterizes his portrait, and which may well have settled on them at a later period. He moved with dignity, and his whole demeanor, tempered by an expression of benignity not to have been anticipated from the reports circulated of his character, was worthy of a great prince. Such is the portrait left to us of the celebrated Indian emperor in this his first interview with the white men.

The army halted as he drew near. Cortes, dismounting, threw his reins to a page, and, supported by a few of the principal cavaliers, advanced to meet him. The interview must have been one of uncommon interest to both. In Montezuma, Cortes beheld the lord of the broad realms he had traversed, whose magnificence and power had been the burden of every tongue. In the Spaniard, on the other hand, the Aztec prince saw the strange being whose history seemed to be so mysteriously connected with his own; the predicted one of his oracles; whose achievements proclaimed him something more than human. But, whatever may have been the monarch's feelings, he so far suppressed them as to receive his guest with princely courtesy, and to express his satisfaction at personally seeing him in his capital. Cortes responded by the most profound expressions of respect, while he made ample acknowledgments for the substantial proofs which the emperor had given the Spaniards of his munificence. He then hung round Montezuma's neck a sparkling chain of colored crystal, accompanying this with a movement as if to embrace him, when he was restrained by the two Aztec lords, shocked at the menaced profanation of the sacred person of their master. After the interchange of these civilities, Montezuma appointed his brother to conduct the Spaniards to their residence in the capital, and, again entering his litter, was borne off amidst prostrate crowds in the same state in which he had come. The Spaniards quickly followed, and, with colors flying and music playing, soon made their entrance into the southern quarter of Tenochtitlan.

Here, again, they found fresh cause for admiration in the grandeur of the city and the superior style of its architecture. The dwellings of the poorer class were, indeed, chiefly of reeds and mud. But the great avenue through which they were now marching was lined with the houses of the nobles, who were encouraged by the emperor to make the capital their residence. They were built of a red porous stone drawn from quarries in the neighborhood, and, though they rarely rose to a second story, often covered a large space of ground. The flat roofs, azoteas, were protected by stone parapets, so that every house was a fortress. Sometimes these roofs resembled parterres of flowers, so thickly were they covered with them, but more frequently these were cultivated in broad terraced gardens, laid out between the edifices. Occasionally a great square or marketplace intervened, surrounded by its porticoes of stone and stucco; or a pyramidal temple reared its colossal bulk, crowned with its tapering sanctuaries, and altars blazing with inextinguishable fires. The great street facing the southern causeway, unlike most others in the place, was wide, and extended some miles in nearly a straight line, as before noticed, through the center of the city. A spectator standing at one end of it, as his eye ranged along the deep vista of temples, terraces, and gardens, might clearly discern the other, with the blue mountains in the distance, which, in the transparent atmosphere of the tableland, seemed almost in contact with the buildings.

But what most impressed the Spaniards was the throngs of people who swarmed through the streets and on the canals, filling every doorway and window and clustering on the roofs of the buildings. "I well remember the spectacle," exclaims Bernal Diaz: "it seems now, after so many years, as present to my mind as if it were but yesterday." But what must have been the sensations of the Aztecs themselves, as they looked on the portentous pageant! as they heard, now for the first time, the well-cemented pavement ring under the iron tramp of the horses—the strange animals which fear had clothed in such supernatural terrors; as they gazed on the children of the East, revealing their celestial origin in their fair complexions; saw the bright falchions and bonnets of steel, a metal to them unknown, glancing like meteors in the sun, while sounds of unearthly music—at least, such as their rude instruments had never wakened—floated in the air! But every other emotion was lost in that of deadly hatred, when they beheld their detested enemy the Tlascalan stalking, in defiance, as it were, through their streets, and staring around with looks of ferocity and wonder, like some wild animal of the forest who had strayed by chance from his native fastnesses into the haunts of civilization.

As they passed down the spacious street, the troops repeatedly traversed bridges suspended above canals, along which they saw the Indian barks gliding swiftly with their little cargoes of fruits and vegetables for the markets of Tenochtitlan. At length they halted before a broad area near the center of the city, where rose the huge pyramidal pile dedicated to the patron war-god of the Aztecs, second only, in size as well as sanctity, to the temple of Cholula, and covering the same ground now in part occupied by the great cathedral of Mexico.

Facing the western gate of the enclosure of the temple, stood a low range of stone buildings, spreading over a wide extent of ground, the palace of Axayacatl, Montezuma's father, built by that monarch about fifty years before. It was appropriated as the barracks of the Spaniards. The emperor himself was in the courtyard, waiting to receive them. Approaching Cortes, he took from a vase of flowers, borne by one of his slaves, a massy collar, in which the shell of a species of crawfish, much prized by the Indians, was set in gold and connected by heavy links of the same metal. From this chain depended eight ornaments, also of gold, made in resemblance of the same shellfish, a span in length each, and of delicate workmanship; for the Aztec goldsmiths were confessed to have shown skill in their craft not inferior to their brethren of Europe. Montezuma, as he hung the gorgeous collar round the general's neck, said, "This palace belongs to you, Malinche" (the epithet by which he always addressed him), "and your brethren. Rest after your fatigues, for you have much need to do so, and in a little while I will visit you again." So saying, he withdrew with his attendants, evincing in this act a delicate consideration not to have been expected in a barbarian.

Cortes' first care was to inspect his new quarters. The building, though spacious, was low, consisting of one floor, except, indeed, in the center, where it rose to an additional story. The apartments were of great size, and afforded accommodations, according to the testimony of the Conquerors themselves, for the whole army! The hardy mountaineers of Tlascala were, probably, not very fastidious, and might easily find a shelter in the outbuildings, or under temporary awnings in the ample courtyards. The best apartments were hung with gay cotton draperies, the floors covered with mats or rushes. There were, also, low stools made of single pieces of wood elaborately carved, and in most of the apartments beds made of the palm-leaf, woven into a thick mat, with coverlets, and sometimes canopies, of cotton. These mats were the only beds used by the natives, whether of high or low degree.

After a rapid survey of this gigantic pile, the general assigned his troops their respective quarters, and took as vigilant precautions for security as if he had anticipated a siege instead of a friendly entertainment. The place was encompassed by a stone wall of considerable thickness, with towers or heavy buttresses at intervals, affording a good means of defense. He planted his cannon so as to command the approaches, stationed his sentinels along the works, and, in short, enforced in every respect as strict military discipline as had been observed in any part of the march. He well knew the importance to his little band, at least for the present, of conciliating the good will of the citizens; and, to avoid all possibility of collision, he prohibited any soldier from leaving his quarters without orders, under pain of death. Having taken these precautions, he allowed his men to partake of the bountiful collation which had been prepared for them.

They had been long enough in the country to become reconciled to, if not to relish, the peculiar cooking of the Aztecs. The appetite of the soldier is not often dainty, and on the present occasion it cannot be doubted that the Spaniards did full justice to the savory productions of the royal kitchen. During the meal they were served by numerous Mexican slaves, who were, indeed, distributed through the palace, anxious to do the bidding of the strangers. After the repast was concluded, and they had taken their siesta, not less important to a Spaniard than food itself, the presence of the emperor was again announced.

Montezuma was attended by a few of his principal nobles. He was received with much deference by Cortes; and, after the parties had taken their seats, a conversation commenced between them, through the aid of Doña Marina, while the cavaliers and Aztec chieftains stood around in respectful silence.

Montezuma made many inquiries concerning the country of the Spaniards, their sovereign, the nature of his government, and especially their own motives in visiting Anahuac. Cortes explained these motives by the desire to see so distinguished a monarch and to declare to him the true Faith professed by the Christians. With rare discretion, he contented himself with dropping this hint, for the present, allowing it to ripen in the mind of the emperor, till a future conference. The latter asked whether those white men who in the preceding year had landed on the eastern shores of his empire were their countrymen. He showed himself well informed of the proceedings of the Spaniards from their arrival in Tabasco to the present time, information of which had been regularly transmitted in the hieroglyphical paintings. He was curious, also, in regard to the rank of his visitors in their own country; inquiring if they were the kinsmen of the sovereign. Cortes replied, they were kinsmen of one another, and subjects of their great monarch, who held them all in peculiar estimation. Before his departure, Montezuma made himself acquainted with the names of the principal cavaliers, and the position they occupied in the army.

At the conclusion of the interview, the Aztec prince commanded his attendants to bring forward the presents prepared for his guests. They consisted of cotton dresses, enough to supply every man, it is said, including the allies, with a suit! And he did not fail to add the usual accompaniment of gold chains and other ornaments, which he distributed in profusion among the Spaniards. He then withdrew with the same ceremony with which he had entered, leaving everyone deeply impressed with his munificence and his affability, so unlike what they had been taught to expect by what they now considered an invention of the enemy.

That evening the Spaniards celebrated their arrival in the Mexican capital by a general discharge of artillery. The thunders of the ordnance, reverberating among the buildings and shaking them to their foundations, the stench of the sulphureous vapor that rolled in volumes above the walls of the encampment, reminding the inhabitants of the explosions of the great "volcan," filled the hearts of the superstitious Aztecs with dismay. It proclaimed to them that their city held in its bosom those dread beings whose path had been marked with desolation, and who could call down the thunderbolts to consume their enemies! It was doubtless the policy of Cortes to strengthen this superstitious feeling as far as possible, and to impress the natives, at the outset, with a salutary awe of the supernatural powers of the Spaniards.

On the following morning, the general requested permission to return the emperor's visit, by waiting on him in his palace. This was readily granted, and Montezuma sent his officers to conduct the Spaniards to his presence. Cortes dressed himself in his richest habit, and left the quarters attended by Alvarado, Sandoval, Velasquez, and Ordaz, together with five or six of the common file.

The royal habitation was at no great distance. It stood on the ground, to the southwest of the cathedral, since covered in part by the Casa del Estado, the palace of the dukes of Monteleone, the descendants of Cortes. It was a vast, irregular pile of low stone buildings, like that garrisoned by the Spaniards. So spacious was it, indeed, that, as one of the Conquerors assures us, although he had visited it more than once, for the express purpose, he had been too much fatigued each time by wandering through the apartments ever to see the whole of it. It was built of the red porous stone of the country, tetzontli, was ornamented with marble, and on the façade over the principal entrance were sculptured the arms or device of Montezuma, an eagle bearing an ocelot in his talons.

In the courts through which the Spaniards passed, fountains of crystal water were playing, fed from the copious reservoir on the distant hill of Chapoltepec, and supplying in their turn more than a hundred baths in the interior of the palace. Crowds of Aztec nobles were sauntering up and down in these squares, and in the outer halls, loitering away their hours in attendance on the court. The apartments were of immense size, though not lofty. The ceilings were of various sorts of odoriferous wood ingeniously carved; the floors covered with mats of the palm-leaf. The walls were hung with cotton richly stained, with the skins of wild animals, or gorgeous draperies of feather-work wrought in imitation of birds, insects, and flowers, with the nice art and glowing radiance of colors that might compare with the tapestries of Flanders. Clouds of incense rolled up from censers and diffused intoxicating odors through the apartments. The Spaniards might well have fancied themselves in the voluptuous precincts of an Eastern harem, instead of treading the halls of a wild barbaric chief in the Western World.

On reaching the hall of audience, the Mexican officers took off their sandals, and covered their gay attire with a mantle of nequen, a coarse stuff made of the fibers of the maguey, worn only by the poorest classes. This act of humiliation was imposed on all, except the members of his own family, who approached the sovereign. Thus barefooted, with downcast eyes and formal obeisance, they ushered the Spaniards into the royal presence.

They found Montezuma seated at the further end of a spacious saloon and surrounded by a few of his favorite chiefs. He received them kindly, and very soon Cortes, without much ceremony, entered on the subject which was uppermost in his thoughts. He was fully aware of the importance of gaining the royal convert, whose example would have such an influence on the conversion of his people. The general, therefore, prepared to display the whole store of his theological science, with the most winning arts of rhetoric he could command, while the interpretation was conveyed through the silver tones of Marina, as inseparable from him, on these occasions, as his shadow.

He set forth, as clearly as he could, the ideas entertained by the Church in regard to the holy mysteries of the Trinity, the Incarnation, and the Atonement. From this he ascended to the origin of things, the creation of the world, the first pair, paradise, and the fall of man. He assured Montezuma that the idols he worshiped were Satan under different forms. A sufficient proof of it was the bloody sacrifices they imposed, which he contrasted with the pure and simple rite of the mass. Their worship would sink him in perdition. It was to snatch his soul, and the souls of his people, from the flames of eternal fire by opening to them a purer faith, that the Christians had come to his land. And he earnestly besought him not to neglect the occasion, but to secure his salvation by embracing the cross, the great sign of human redemption.

The eloquence of the preacher was wasted on the insensible heart of his royal auditor. It doubtless lost somewhat of its efficacy, strained through the imperfect interpretation of so recent a neophyte as the Indian damsel. But the doctrines were too abstruse in themselves to be comprehended at a glance by the rude intellect of a barbarian. And Montezuma may have, perhaps, thought it was not more monstrous to feed on the flesh of a fellow-creature than on that of the Creator himself. He was, besides, steeped in the superstitions of his country from his cradle. He had been educated in the straitest sect of her religion, had been himself a priest before his election to the throne, and was now the head both of the religion and the state. Little probability was there that such a man would be open to argument or persuasion, even from the lips of a more practiced polemic than the Spanish commander. How could he abjure the faith that was intertwined with the dearest affections of his heart and the very elements of his being? How could he be false to the gods who had raised him to such prosperity and honors, and whose shrines were intrusted to his especial keeping?

He listened, however, with silent attention, until the general had concluded his homily. He then replied that he knew the Spaniards had held this discourse wherever they had been. He doubted not their God was, as they said, a good being. His gods, also, were good to him. Yet what his visitor said of the creation of the world was like what he had been taught to believe. It was not worth while to discourse further of the matter. His ancestors, he said, were not the original proprietors of the land. They had occupied it but a few ages, and had been led there by a great Being, who, after giving them laws and ruling over the nation for a time, had withdrawn to the regions where the sun rises. He had declared, on his departure, that he or his descendants would again visit them and resume his empire. The wonderful deeds of the Spaniards, their fair complexions, and the quarter whence they came, all showed they were his descendants. If Montezuma had resisted their visit to his capital, it was because he had heard such accounts of their cruelties—that they sent the lightning to consume his people, or crushed them to pieces under the hard feet of the ferocious animals on which they rode. He was now convinced that these were idle tales; that the Spaniards were kind and generous in their natures; they were mortals, of a different race, indeed, from the Aztecs, wiser, and more valiant —and for this he honored them.

"You, too," he added, with a smile, "have been told, perhaps, that I am a god, and dwell in palaces of gold and silver. But you see it is false. My houses, though large, are of stone and wood like those of others; and as to my body," he said, baring his tawny arm, "you see it is flesh and bone like yours. It is true, I have a great empire inherited from my ancestors; lands, and gold, and silver. But your sovereign beyond the waters is, I know, the rightful lord of all. I rule in his name. You, Malinche, are his ambassador; you and your brethren shall share these things with me. Rest now from your labors. You are here in your own dwellings, and everything shall be provided for your subsistence. I will see that your wishes shall be obeyed in the same way as my own." As the monarch concluded these words, a few natural tears suffused his eyes, while the image of ancient independence, perhaps, flitted across his mind.

Cortes, while he encouraged the idea that his own sovereign was the great Being indicated by Montezuma, endeavored to comfort the monarch by the assurance that his master had no desire to interfere with his authority, otherwise than, out of pure concern for his welfare, to effect his conversion and that of his people to Christianity. Before the emperor dismissed his visitors he consulted his munificent spirit, as usual, by distributing rich stuffs and trinkets of gold among them, so that the poorest soldier, says Bernal Diaz, one of the party, received at least two heavy collars of the precious metal for his share. The iron hearts of the Spaniards were touched with the emotion displayed by Montezuma, as well as by his princely spirit of liberality. As they passed him, the cavaliers, with bonnet in hand, made him the most profound obeisance, and "on the way home," continues the same chronicler, "we could discourse of nothing but the gentle breeding and courtesy of the Indian monarch, and of the respect we entertained for him."

Speculations of a graver complexion must have pressed on the mind of the general, as he saw around him the evidences of a civilization, and consequently power, for which even the exaggerated reports of the natives—discredited from their apparent exaggeration—had not prepared him. In the pomp and burdensome ceremonial of the court he saw that nice system of subordination and profound reverence for the monarch which characterize the semi-civilized empires of Asia. In the appearance of the capital, its massy yet elegant architecture, its luxurious social accommodations, its activity in trade, he recognized the proofs of the intellectual progress, mechanical skill, and enlarged resources of an old and opulent community; while the swarms in the streets attested the existence of a population capable of turning these resources to the best account.

In the Aztec he beheld a being unlike either the rude republican Tlascalan or the effeminate Cholulan, but combining the courage of the one with the cultivation of the other. He was in the heart of a great capital, which seemed like an extensive fortification, with its dikes and its drawbridges, where every house might be easily converted into a castle. Its insular position removed it from the continent, from which, at the mere nod of the sovereign, all communication might be cut off, and the whole warlike population be at once precipitated on him and his handful of followers. What could superior science avail against such odds?

As to the subversion of Montezuma's empire, now that he had seen him in his capital, it must have seemed a more doubtful enterprise than ever. The recognition which the Aztec prince had made of the feudal supremacy, if I may so say, of the Spanish sovereign, was not to be taken too literally. Whatever show of deference he might be disposed to pay the latter under the influence of his present—perhaps temporary—delusion, it was not to be supposed that he would so easily relinquish his actual power and possessions, or that his people would consent to it. Indeed, his sensitive apprehensions in regard to this very subject, on the coming of the Spaniards, were sufficient proof of the tenacity with which he clung to his authority. It is true that Cortes had a strong lever for future operations in the superstitious reverence felt for himself both by prince and people. It was undoubtedly his policy to maintain this sentiment unimpaired in both, as far as possible. . . .

BOOK IV

CHAPTER III

Seizure of Montezuma

1519

The Spaniards had been now a week in Mexico. During this time they had experienced the most friendly treatment from the emperor. But the mind of Cortes was far from easy. He felt that it was quite uncertain how long this amiable temper would last. A hundred circumstances might occur to change it. Montezuma might very naturally feel the maintenance of so large a body too burdensome on his treasury. The people of the capital might become dissatisfied at the presence of so numerous an armed force within their walls. Many causes of disgust might arise betwixt the soldiers and the citizens. Indeed, it was scarcely possible that a rude, licentious soldiery, like the Spaniards, could be long kept in subjection without active employment. The danger was even greater with the Tlascalans, a fierce race now brought into daily contact with the nation who held them in loathing and detestation. Rumors were already rife among the allies, whether well founded or not, of murmurs among the Mexicans, accompanied by menaces of raising the bridges.

Even should the Spaniards be allowed to occupy their present quarters unmolested, it was not advancing the great object of the expedition. Cortes was not a whit nearer gaining the capital, so essential to his meditated subjugation of the country; and any day he might receive tidings that the crown, or, what he most feared, the governor of Cuba, had sent a force of superior strength to wrest from him a conquest but half achieved. Disturbed by these anxious reflections, he resolved to extricate himself from his embarrassment by one bold stroke. But he first submitted the affair to a council of the officers in whom he most confided, desirous to divide with them the responsibility of the act, and, no doubt, to interest them more heartily in its execution by making it in some measure the result of their combined judgments.

When the general had briefly stated the embarrassments of their position, the council was divided in opinion. All admitted the necessity of some instant action. One party were for retiring secretly from the city, and getting beyond the causeways before their march could be intercepted. Another advised that it should be done openly, with the knowledge of the emperor, of whose good will they had had so many proofs. But both these measures seemed alike impolitic. A retreat under these circumstances, and so abruptly made, would have the air of a flight. It would be construed into distrust of themselves; and anything like timidity on their part would be sure not only to bring on them the Mexicans, but the contempt of their allies, who would, doubtless, join in the general cry.

As to Montezuma, what reliance could they place on the protection of a prince so recently their enemy, and who, in his altered bearing, must have taken counsel of his fears rather than his inclinations?

Even should they succeed in reaching the coast, their situation would be little better. It would be proclaiming to the world that, after all their lofty vaunts, they were unequal to the enterprise. Their only hopes of their sovereign's favor, and of pardon for their irregular proceedings, were founded on success. Hitherto, they had only made the discovery of Mexico; to retreat would be to leave conquest and the fruits of it to another. In short, to stay and to retreat seemed equally disastrous.

In this perplexity, Cortes proposed an expedient which none but the most daring spirit, in the most desperate extremity, would have conceived. This was to march to the royal palace and bring Montezuma to the Spanish quarters, by fair means if they could persuade him, by force if necessary—at all events, to get possession of his person. With such a pledge, the Spaniards would be secure from the assault of the Mexicans, afraid by acts of violence to compromise the safety of their prince. If he came by his own consent, they would be deprived of all apology for doing so. As long as the emperor remained among the Spaniards, it would be easy, by allowing him a show of sovereignty, to rule in his name, until they had taken measures for securing their safety and the success of their enterprise. The idea of employing a sovereign as a tool for the government of his own kingdom, if a new one in the age of Cortes, is certainly not so in ours.

A plausible pretext for the seizure of the hospitable monarch —for the most barefaced action seeks to veil itself under some show of decency—was afforded by a circumstance of which Cortes had received intelligence at Cholula. He had left, as we have seen, a faithful officer, Juan de Escalante, with a hundred and fifty men, in garrison at Vera Cruz, on his departure for the capital. He had not been long absent when his lieutenant received a message from an Aztec chief named Quauhpopoca, governor of a district to the north of the Spanish settlement, declaring his desire to come in person and tender his allegiance to the Spanish authorities at Vera Cruz. He requested that four of the white men might be sent to protect him against certain unfriendly tribes through which his road lay. This was not an uncommon request, and excited no suspicion in Escalante. The four soldiers were sent; and on their arrival two of them were murdered by the false Aztec. The other two made their way back to the garrison.

The commander marched at once, with fifty of his men, and several thousand Indian allies, to take vengeance on the cacique. A pitched battle followed. The allies fled from the redoubted Mexicans. The few Spaniards stood firm, and with the aid of their firearms and the blessed Virgin, who was distinctly seen hovering over their ranks in the van, they made good the field against the enemy. It cost them dear, however; since seven or eight Christians were slain, and among them the gallant Escalante himself, who died of his injuries soon after his return to the fort. The Indian prisoners captured in the battle spoke of the whole proceeding as having taken place at the instigation of Montezuma.

One of the Spaniards fell into the hands of the natives, but soon after perished of his wounds. His head was cut off and sent to the Aztec emperor. It was uncommonly large and covered with hair; and, as Montezuma gazed on the ferocious features, rendered more horrible by death, he seemed to read in them the dark lineaments of the destined destroyers of his house. He turned from it with a shudder, and commanded that it should be taken from the city, and not offered at the shrine of any of his gods.

Although Cortes had received intelligence of this disaster at Cholula, he had concealed it within his own breast, or communicated it to very few only of his most trusty officers, from apprehension of the ill effect it might have on the spirits of the common soldiers.

The cavaliers whom Cortes now summoned to the council were men of the same mettle with their leader. Their bold, chivalrous spirits seemed to court danger for its own sake. If one or two, less adventurous, were startled by the proposal he made, they were soon overruled by the others, who, no doubt, considered that a desperate disease required as desperate a remedy.

That night Cortes was heard pacing his apartment to and fro, like a man oppressed by thought or agitated by strong emotion. He may have been ripening in his mind the daring scheme for the morrow. In the morning the soldiers heard mass as usual, and Father Olmedo invoked the blessing of Heaven on their hazardous enterprise. Whatever might be the cause in which he was embarked, the heart of the Spaniard was cheered with the conviction that the saints were on his side!

Having asked an audience from Montezuma, which was readily granted, the general made the necessary arrangements for his enterprise. The principal part of his force was drawn up in the courtyard, and he stationed a considerable detachment in the avenues leading to the palace, to check any attempt at rescue by the populace. He ordered twenty-five or thirty of the soldiers to drop in at the palace, as if by accident, in groups of three or four at a time, while the conference was going on with Montezuma. He selected five cavaliers, in whose courage and coolness he placed most trust, to bear him company: Pedro de Alvarado, Gonzalo de Sandoval, Francisco de Lujo, Velasquez de Leon, and Alonso de Avila—brilliant names in the annals of the Conquest. All were clad, as well as the common soldiers, in complete armor, a circumstance of too familiar occurrence to excite suspicion.

The little party were graciously received by the emperor, who soon, with the aid of the interpreters, became interested in a sportive conversation with the Spaniards, while he indulged his natural munificence by giving them presents of gold and jewels. He paid the Spanish general the particular compliment of offering him one of his daughters as his wife; an honor which the latter respectfully declined, on the ground that he was already accommodated with one in Cuba, and that his religion forbade a plurality.

When Cortes perceived that a sufficient number of his soldiers were assembled, he changed his playful manner, and in a serious tone briefly acquainted Montezuma with the treacherous proceedings in the tierra caliente, and the accusation of him as their author. The emperor listened to the charge with surprise, and disavowed the act, which he said could only have been imputed to him by his enemies. Cortes expressed his belief in his declaration, but added that, to prove it true, it would be necessary to send for Quauhpopoca and his accomplices, that they might be examined and dealt with according to their deserts. To this Montezuma made no objection. Taking from his wrist, to which it was attached, a precious stone, the royal signet, on which was cut the figure of the war-god, he gave it to one of his nobles, with orders to show it to the Aztec governor, and require his instant presence in the capital, together with all those who had been accessory to the murder of the Spaniards. If he resisted, the officer was empowered to call in the aid of the neighboring towns to enforce the mandate.

When the messenger had gone, Cortes assured the monarch that this prompt compliance with his request convinced him of his innocence. But it was important that his own sovereign should be equally convinced of it. Nothing would promote this so much as for Montezuma to transfer his residence to the palace occupied by the Spaniards, till on the arrival of Quauhpopoca the affair could be fully investigated. Such an act of condescension would, of itself, show a personal regard for the Spaniards, incompatible with the base conduct alleged against him, and would fully absolve him from all suspicion!

Montezuma listened to this proposal, and the flimsy reasoning with which it was covered, with looks of profound amazement. He became pale as death; but in a moment his face flushed with resentment, as, with the pride of offended dignity, he exclaimed,

"When was it ever heard that a great prince, like myself, voluntarily left his own palace to become a prisoner in the hands of strangers!"

Cortes assured him he would not go as a prisoner. He would experience nothing but respectful treatment from the Spaniards, would be surrounded by his own household, and hold intercourse with his people as usual. In short, it would be but a change of residence, from one of his palaces to another, a circumstance of frequent occurrence with him. It was in vain. "If I should consent to such a degradation," he answered, "my subjects never would!" When further pressed, he offered to give up one of his sons and two of his daughters to remain as hostages with the Spaniards, so that he might be spared this disgrace.

Two hours passed in this fruitless discussion, till a high-mettled cavalier, Velasquez de Leon, impatient of the long delay, and seeing that the attempt, if not the deed, must ruin them, cried out, "Why do we waste words on this barbarian? We have gone too far to recede now. Let us seize him, and, if he resists, plunge our swords into his body!" The fierce tone and menacing gestures with which this was uttered alarmed the monarch, who inquired of Marina what the angry Spaniard said. The interpreter explained it in as gentle a manner as she could, beseeching him "to accompany the white men to their quarters, where he would be treated with all respect and kindness, while to refuse them would but expose himself to violence, perhaps to death." Marina, doubtless, spoke to her sovereign as she thought, and no one had better opportunity of knowing the truth than herself.

This last appeal shook the resolution of Montezuma. It was in vain that the unhappy prince looked around for sympathy or support. As his eyes wandered over the stern visages and iron forms of the Spaniards, he felt that his hour was indeed come; and, with a voice scarcely audible from emotion, he consented to accompany the strangers—to quit the palace whither he was never more to return. Had he possessed the spirit of the first Montezuma, he would have called his guards around him, and left his lifeblood on the threshold, sooner than have been dragged a dishonored captive across it. But his courage sank under circumstances. He felt he was the instrument of an irresistible Fate!

No sooner had the Spaniards got his consent, than orders were given for the royal litter. The nobles who bore and attended it could scarcely believe their senses when they learned their master's purpose. But pride now came to Montezuma's aid, and, since he must go, he preferred that it should appear to be with his own free will. As the royal retinue, escorted by the Spaniards, marched through the street with downcast eyes and dejected mien, the people assembled in crowds, and a rumor rang among them that the emperor was carried off by force to the quarters of the white men. A tumult would have soon arisen but for the intervention of Montezuma himself, who called out to the people to disperse, as he was visiting his friends of his own accord; thus sealing his ignominy by a declaration which deprived his subjects of the only excuse for resistance. On reaching the quarters, he sent out his nobles with similar assurances to the mob, and renewed orders to return to their homes.

He was received with ostentatious respect by the Spaniards, and selected the suite of apartments which best pleased him. They were soon furnished with fine cotton tapestries, feather-work, and all the elegancies of Indian upholstery. He was attended by such of his household as he chose, his wives and his pages, and was served with his usual pomp and luxury at his meals. He gave audience, as in his own palace, to his subjects, who were admitted to his presence, few, indeed, at a time, under the pretext of greater order and decorum. From the Spaniards themselves he met with a formal deference. No one, not even the general himself, approached him without doffing his casque and rendering the obeisance due to his rank. Nor did they ever sit in his presence, without being invited by him to do so.

With all this studied ceremony and show of homage, there was one circumstance which too clearly proclaimed to his people that their sovereign was a prisoner. In the front of the palace a patrol of sixty men was established, and the same number in the rear. Twenty of each corps mounted guard at once, maintaining a careful watch, day and night. Another body, under command of Velasquez de Leon, was stationed in the royal ante-chamber. Cortes punished any departure from duty, or relaxation of vigilance, in these sentinels, with the utmost severity. He felt, as indeed every Spaniard must have felt, that the escape of the emperor now would be their ruin. Yet the task of this uninter-mitting watch sorely added to their fatigues. "Better this dog of a king should die," cried a soldier one day, "than that we should wear out our lives in this manner." The words were uttered in the hearing of Montezuma, who gathered something of their import, and the offender was severely chastised by order of the general. Such instances of disrespect, however, were very rare. Indeed, the amiable deportment of the monarch, who seemed to take pleasure in the society of his jailers, and who never allowed a favor or attention from the meanest soldier to go unrequited, inspired the Spaniards with as much attachment as they were capable of feeling—for a barbarian.

Things were in this posture, when the arrival of Quauhpopoca from the coast was announced. He was accompanied by his son and fifteen Aztec chiefs. He had traveled all the way, borne, as became his high rank, in a litter. On entering Montezuma's presence, he threw over his dress the coarse robe of nequen, and made the usual humiliating acts of obeisance. The poor parade of courtly ceremony was the more striking when placed in contrast with the actual condition of the parties.

The Aztec governor was coldly received by his master, who referred the affair (had he the power to do otherwise?) to the examination of Cortes. It was, doubtless, conducted in a sufficiently summary manner. To the general's query, whether the cacique was the subject of Montezuma, he replied, "And what other sovereign could I serve?" implying that his sway was universal. He did not deny his share in the transaction, nor did he seek to shelter himself under the royal authority till sentence of death was passed on him and his followers, when they all laid the blame of their proceedings on Montezuma. They were condemned to be burnt alive in the area before the palace. The funeral piles were made of heaps of arrows, javelins, and other weapons, drawn by the emperor's permission from the arensals round the great teocalli, where they had been stored to supply means of defense in times of civic tumult or insurrection. By this politic precaution Cortes proposed to remove a ready means of annoyance in case of hostilities with the citizens.

To crown the whole of these extraordinary proceedings, Cortes, while preparations for the execution were going on, entered the emperor's apartment, attended by a soldier bearing fetters in his hands. With a severe aspect, he charged the monarch with being the original contriver of the violence offered to the Spaniards, as was now proved by the declaration of his own instruments. Such a crime, which merited death in a subject, could not be atoned for, even by a sovereign, without some punishment. So saying, he ordered the soldier to fasten the fetters on Montezuma's ankles. He coolly waited till it was done, then, turning his back on the monarch, quitted the room.

Montezuma was speechless under the infliction of this last insult. He was like one struck down by a heavy blow, that deprives him of all his faculties. He offered no resistance. But, though he spoke not a word, low, ill-suppressed moans, from time to time, intimated the anguish of his spirit. His attendants, bathed in tears, offered him their consolations. They tenderly held his feet in their arms, and endeavored, by inserting their shawls and mantles, to relieve them from the pressure of the iron. But they could not reach the iron which had penetrated into his soul. He felt that he was no more a king.

Meanwhile, the execution of the dreadful doom was going forward in the courtyard. The whole Spanish force was under arms, to check any interruption that might be offered by the Mexicans. But none was attempted. The populace gazed in silent wonder, regarding it as the sentence of the emperor. The manner of the execution, too, excited less surprise, from their familiarity with similar spectacles, aggravated, indeed, by additional horrors, in their own diabolical sacrifices. The Aztec lord and his companions, bound hand and foot to the blazing piles, submitted without a cry or a complaint to their terrible fate. Passive fortitude is the virtue of the Indian warrior; and it was the glory of the Aztec, as of the other races on the North American continent, to show how the spirit of the brave man may triumph over torture and the agonies of death.

When the dismal tragedy was ended, Cortes re-entered Montezuma's apartment. Kneeling down, he unclasped his shackles with his own hand, expressing at the same time his regret that so disagreeable a duty as that of subjecting him to such a punishment had been imposed on him. This last indignity had entirely crushed the spirit of Montezuma; and the monarch whose frown, but a week since, would have made the nations of Anahuac tremble to their remotest borders, was now craven enough to thank his deliverer for his freedom, as for a great and unmerited boon!

Not long after, the Spanish general, conceiving that his royal captive was sufficiently humbled, expressed his willingness that he should return, if he inclined, to his own palace. Montezuma declined it; alleging, it is said, that his nobles had more than once importuned him to resent his injuries by taking arms against the Spaniards, and that, were he in the midst of them, it would be difficult to avoid it, or to save his capital from bloodshed and anarchy. The reason did honor to his heart, if it was the one which influenced him. It is probable that he did not care to trust his safety to those haughty and ferocious chieftains, who had witnessed the degradation of their master, and must despise his pusillanimity, as a thing unprecedented in an Aztec monarch. It is also said that, when Marina conveyed to him the permission of Cortes, the other interpreter, Aguilar, gave him to understand the Spanish officers never would consent that he should avail himself of it.

Whatever were his reasons, it is certain that he declined the offer; and the general, in a well-feigned or real ecstasy, embraced him, declaring "that he loved him as a brother, and that every Spaniard would be zealously devoted to his interests, since he had shown himself so mindful of theirs!" Honeyed words, "which," says the shrewd old chronicler who was present, "Montezuma was wise enough to know the worth of."

The events recorded in this chapter are certainly some of the most extraordinary on the page of history. That a small body of men, like the Spaniards, should have entered the palace of a mighty prince, have seized his person in the midst of his vassals, have borne him off a captive to their quarters—that they should have put to an ignominious death before his face his high officers, for executing, probably, his own commands, and have crowned the whole by putting the monarch in irons like a common malefactor—that this should have been done, not to a driveling dotard in the decay of his fortunes, but to a proud monarch in the plenitude of his power, in the very heart of his capital, surrounded by thousands and tens of thousands, who trembled at his nod and would have poured out their blood like water in his defense—that all this should have been done by a mere handful of adventurers, is a thing too extravagant, altogether too improbable, for the pages of romance! It is, nevertheless, literally true. Yet we shall not be prepared to acquiesce in the judgments of contemporaries who regarded these acts with admiration.

We may well distrust any grounds on which it is attempted to justify the kidnaping of a friendly sovereign—by those very persons, too, who were reaping the full benefit of his favors.

To view the matter differently, we must take the position of the Conquerors and assume with them the original right of conquest. Regarded from this point of view, many difficulties vanish. If conquest were a duty, whatever was necessary to effect it was right also. Right and expedient become convertible terms. And it can hardly be denied that the capture of the monarch was expedient, if the Spaniards would maintain their hold on the empire.

The execution of the Aztec governor suggests other considerations. If he were really guilty of the perfidious act imputed to him by Cortes, and if Montezuma disavowed it, the governor deserved death, and the general was justified by the law of nations in inflicting it. It is by no means so clear, however, why he should have involved so many in this sentence; most, perhaps all, of whom must have acted under his authority. The cruel manner of the death will less startle those who are familiar with the established penal codes in most civilized nations in the sixteenth century.

But, if the governor deserved death, what pretense was there for the outrage on the person of Montezuma? If the former was guilty, the latter surely was not. But, if the cacique only acted in obedience to orders, the responsibility was transferred to the sovereign who gave the orders. They could not both stand in the same category.

It is vain, however, to reason on the matter on any abstract principles of right and wrong, or to suppose that the Conquerors troubled themselves with the refinements of casuistry. Their standard of right and wrong, in reference to the natives, was a very simple one. Despising them as an outlawed race, without God in the world, they, in common with their age, held it to be their "mission" (to borrow the cant phrase of our own day) to conquer and to convert. The measures they adopted certainly facilitated the first great work of conquest. By the execution of the caciques they struck terror not only into the capital, but throughout the country. It proclaimed that not a hair of a Spaniard was to be touched with impunity! By rendering Montezuma contemptible in his own eyes and those of his subjects, Cortes deprived him of the support of his people and forced him to lean on the arm of the stranger. It was a politic proceeding—to which few men could have been equal who had a touch of humanity in their natures.

A good criterion of the moral sense of the actors in these events is afforded by the reflections of Bernal Diaz, made some fifty years, it will be remembered, after the events themselves, when the fire of youth had become extinct, and the eye, glancing back through the vista of half a century, might be supposed to be unclouded by the passions and prejudices which throw their mist over the present. "Now that I am an old man," says the veteran, "I often entertain myself with calling to mind the heroical deeds of early days, till they are as fresh as the events of yesterday. I think of the seizure of the Indian monarch, his confinement in irons, and the execution of his officers, till all these things seem actually passing before me. And, as I ponder on our exploits, I feel that it was not of ourselves that we performed them, but that it was the providence of God which guided us. Much food is there here for meditation!" There is so, indeed, and for a meditation not unpleasing, as we reflect on the advance, in speculative morality at least, which the nineteenth century has made over the sixteenth. But should not the consciousness of this teach us charity? Should it not make us the more distrustful of applying the standard of the present to measure the actions of the past?

FROM CHAPTER VIII

The Uprising and Return to Mexico City

1520

While Cortes was occupied with new schemes of discovery and conquest, he received such astounding intelligence from Mexico as compelled him to concentrate all his faculties and his forces on that one point. The city was in a state of insurrection. No sooner had the struggle with his rival been decided, than

Cortes despatched a courier with the tidings to the capital. In less than a fortnight the messenger returned with a letter from Alvarado, conveying the alarming information that the Mexicans were in arms and had vigorously assaulted the Spaniards in their own quarters. The enemy, he added, had burned the brigantines, by which Cortes had secured the means of retreat in case of the destruction of the bridges. They had attempted to force the defenses, and had succeeded in partially undermining them, and they had overwhelmed the garrison with a tempest of missiles, which had killed several and wounded a great number. The letter concluded with beseeching the commander to hasten to the relief of his men, if he would save them or keep his hold on the capital.

These tidings were a heavy blow to the general—the heavier, it seemed, coming as they did in the hour of triumph, when he had thought to have all his enemies at his feet. There was no room for hesitation. To lose his footing in the capital, the noblest city in the Western World, would be to lose the country itself, which looked up to it as its head. He opened the matter fully to his soldiers, calling on all who would save their countrymen to follow him. All declared their readiness to go; showing an alacrity, says Diaz, which some would have been slow to manifest had they foreseen the future.

Cortes now made preparations for instant departure. He countermanded the orders previously given to Velasquez and Ordaz, and directed them to join him with their forces at Tlascala. He called the troops from Vera Cruz, leaving only a hundred men in garrison there, under command of one Rodrigo Rangre; for he could not spare the services of Sandoval at this crisis. He left his sick and wounded at Cempoalla, under charge of a small detachment, directing that they should follow as soon as they were in marching order. Having completed these arrangements, he set out from Cempoalla, well supplied with provisions by its hospitable cacique, who attended him some leagues on his way. The Totonac chief seems to have had an amiable facility of accommodating himself to the powers that were in the ascendant.

Nothing worthy of notice occurred during the first part of the march. The troops everywhere met with a friendly reception from the peasantry, who readily supplied their wants. For some time before reaching Tlascala, the route lay through a country thinly settled; and the army experienced considerable suffering from want of food, and still more from that of water. Their distress increased to an alarming degree, as, in the hurry of their forced march, they traveled with the meridian sun beating fiercely on their heads. Several faltered by the way, and, throwing themselves down by the roadside, seemed incapable of further effort, and almost indifferent to life.

In this extremity, Cortes sent forward a small detachment of horse to procure provisions in Tlascala, and speedily followed in person. On arriving, he found abundant supplies already prepared by the hospitable natives. They were sent back to the troops; the stragglers were collected one by one; refreshments were administered; and the army, restored in strength and spirits, entered the republican capital.

Here they gathered little additional news respecting the events in Mexico, which a popular rumor attributed to the secret encouragement and machinations of Montezuma. Cortes was commodiously lodged in the quarters of Maxixca, one of the four chiefs of the republic. They readily furnished him with two thousand troops. There was no want of heartiness, when the war was with their ancient enemy the Aztec.

The Spanish commander, on reviewing his forces after the junction with his two captains, found that they amounted to about a thousand foot, and one hundred horse, besides the Tlascalan levies. In the infantry were nearly a hundred arquebusiers, with as many crossbowmen; and the part of the army brought over by Narvaez was admirably equipped. It was inferior, however, to his own veterans in what is better than any outward appointments—military training, and familiarity with the peculiar service in which they were engaged.

Leaving these friendly quarters, the Spaniards took a more northerly route, as more direct than that by which they had before penetrated into the valley. It was the road to Tezcuco. It still compelled them to climb the same bold range of the Cordilleras, which attains its greatest elevation in the two mighty volcans at whose base they had before traveled. The sides of the sierra were clothed with dark forests of pine, cypress, and cedar, through which glimpses now and then opened into fathomless dells and valleys, whose depths, far down in the sultry climate of the tropics, were lost in a glowing wilderness of vegetation.

From the crest of the mountain range the eye traveled over the broad expanse of country, which they had lately crossed, far away to the green plains of Cholula. Towards the west, they looked down on the Mexican Valley, from a point of view wholly different from that which they had before occupied, but still offering the same beautiful spectacle, with its lakes trembling in the light, its gay cities and villas floating on their bosom, its burnished teocallis touched with fire, its cultivated slopes and dark hills of porphyry stretching away in dim perspective to the verge of the horizon. At their feet lay the city of Tezcuco, which, modestly retiring behind her deep groves of cypress, formed a contrast to her more ambitious rival on the other side of the lake, who seemed to glory in the unveiled splendors of her charms, as Mistress of the Valley.

As they descended into the populous plains, their reception by the natives was very different from that which they had experienced on the preceding visit. There were no groups of curious peasantry to be seen gazing at them as they passed, and offering their simple hospitality. The supplies they asked were not refused, but granted with an ungracious air, that showed the blessing of the giver did not accompany them. This air of reserve became still more marked as the army entered the suburbs of the ancient capital of the Acolhuans. No one came forth to greet them, and the population seemed to have dwindled away—so many of them were withdrawn to the neighboring scene of hostilities at Mexico. Their cold reception was a sensible mortification to the veterans of Cortes, who, judging from the past, had boasted to their new comrades of the sensation their presence would excite among the natives. The cacique of the place, who, as it may be remembered, had been created through the influence of Cortes, was himself absent. The general drew an ill omen from all these circumstances, which even raised an uncomfortable apprehension in his mind respecting the fate of the garrison in Mexico.

But his doubts were soon dispelled by the arrival of a messenger in a canoe from that city, whence he had escaped through the remissness of the enemy, or, perhaps, with their connivance. He brought despatches from Alvarado, informing his commander that the Mexicans had for the last fortnight desisted from active hostilities and converted their operations into a blockade. The

garrison had suffered greatly, but Alvarado expressed his conviction that the siege would be raised, and tranquillity restored,
on the approach of his countrymen. Montezuma sent a messenger, also, to the same effect. At the same time, he exculpated
himself from any part in the late hostilities, which he said had
been conducted not only without his privity, but contrary to his
inclination and efforts.

The Spanish general, having halted long enough to refresh
his wearied troops, took up his march along the southern margin
of the lake, which led him over the same causeway by which he
had before entered the capital. It was the day consecrated to
St. John the Baptist, the 24th of June, 1520. But how different
was the scene from that presented on his former entrance! No
crowds now lined the roads, no boats swarmed on the lake, filled
with admiring spectators. A single pirogue might now and then
be seen in the distance, like a spy stealthily watching their movements, and darting away the moment it had attracted notice. A
deathlike stillness brooded over the scene,—a stillness that spoke
louder to the heart than the acclamations of multitudes.

Cortes rode on moodily at the head of his battalions, finding
abundant food for meditation, doubtless, in this change of circumstances. As if to dispel these gloomy reflections, he ordered
his trumpets to sound, and their clear, shrill notes, borne across
the waters, told the inhabitants of the beleaguered fortress that
their friends were at hand. They were answered by a joyous peal
of artillery, which seemed to give a momentary exhilaration to
the troops, as they quickened their pace, traversed the great
drawbridges, and once more found themselves within the walls
of the imperial city.

The appearance of things here was not such as to allay their
apprehensions. In some places they beheld the smaller bridges
removed, intimating too plainly, now that their brigantines were
destroyed, how easy it would be to cut off their retreat. The
town seemed even more deserted than Tezcuco. Its once
busy and crowded population had mysteriously vanished. And,
as the Spaniards defiled through the empty streets, the tramp
of their horses' feet upon the pavement was answered by
dull and melancholy echoes that fell heavily on their hearts. With
saddened feelings they reached the great gates of the palace of
Axayacatl. The gates were thrown open, and Cortes and his

veterans, rushing in, were cordially embraced by their companions in arms, while both parties soon forgot the present in the interesting recapitulation of the past.

The first inquiries of the general were respecting the origin of the tumult. The accounts were various. Some imputed it to the desire of the Mexicans to release their sovereign from confinement; others to the design of cutting off the garrison while crippled by the absence of Cortes and their countrymen. All agreed, however, in tracing the immediate cause to the violence of Alvarado. It was common for the Aztecs to celebrate an annual festival in May, in honor of their patron war-god. It was called the "incensing of Huitzilopochtli," and was commemorated by sacrifice, religious songs, and dances, in which most of the nobles engaged, for it was one of the great festivals which displayed the pomp of the Aztec ritual. As it was held in the court of the teocalli, in the immediate neighborhood of the Spanish quarters, and as a part of the temple itself was reserved for a Christian chapel, the caciques asked permission of Alvarado to perform their rites there. They requested also, it is said, to be allowed the presence of Montezuma. This latter petition Alvarado declined, in obedience to the injunctions of Cortes; but acquiesced in the former, on condition that the Aztecs should celebrate no human sacrifices and should come without weapons.

They assembled accordingly on the day appointed, to the number of six hundred, at the smallest computation. They were dressed in their most magnificent gala costumes, with their graceful mantles of feather-work sprinkled with precious stones, and their necks, arms, and legs ornamented with collars and bracelets of gold. They had that love of gaudy splendor which belongs to semi-civilized nations, and on these occasions displayed all the pomp and profusion of their barbaric wardrobes.

Alvarado and his soldiers attended as spectators, some of them taking their station at the gates as if by chance, and others mingling in the crowd. They were all armed—a circumstance which, as it was usual, excited no attention. The Aztecs were soon engrossed by the exciting movement of the dance, accompanied by their religious chant and wild, discordant minstrelsy. While thus occupied, Alvarado and his men, at a concerted signal, rushed with drawn swords on their victims. Unprotected by armor or weapons of any kind, they were hewn down without resistance by their assailants, who in their bloody work, says a contemporary, showed no touch of pity or compunction. Some fled to the gates, but were caught on the long pikes of the soldiers. Others, who attempted to scale the coatepantli, or Wall of Serpents, as it was called, which surrounded the area, shared the like fate, or were cut to pieces, or shot by the ruthless soldiery. The pavement, says a writer of the age, ran with streams of blood, like water in a heavy shower. Not an Aztec, of all that gay company, was left alive! It was repeating the dreadful scene of Cholula, with the disgraceful addition that the Spaniards, not content with slaughtering their victims, rifled them of the precious ornaments on their persons! On this sad day fell the flower of the Aztec nobility. Not a family of note but had morning and desolation brought within its walls. And many a doleful ballad, rehearsing the tragic incidents of the story, and adapted to the plaintive national airs, continued to be chanted by the natives long after the subjugation of the country.

Various explanations have been given of this atrocious deed. But few historians have been content to admit that of Alvarado himself. According to this, intelligence had been obtained through his spies—some of them Mexicans—of an intended rising of the Indians. The celebration of this festival was fixed on as the period for its execution, when the caciques would be met together and would easily rouse the people to support them. Alvarado, advised of all this, had forbidden them to wear arms at their meeting. While affecting to comply, they had secreted their weapons in the neighboring arsenals, whence they could readily withdraw them. But his own blow, by anticipating theirs, defeated the design, and, as he confidently hoped, would deter the Aztecs from a similar attempt in future.

Such is the account of the matter given by Alvarado. But, if true, why did he not verify his assertion by exposing the arms thus secreted? Why did he not vindicate his conduct in the eyes of the Mexicans generally, by publicly avowing the treason of the nobles, as was done by Cortes at Cholula? The whole looks much like an apology devised after the commission of the deed, to cover up its atrocity.

Some contemporaries assign a very different motive for the massacre, which, according to them, originated in the cupidity of the Conquerors, as shown by their plundering the bodies of their victims. Bernal Diaz, who, though not present, had conversed familiarly with those who were, vindicates them from the charge of this unworthy motive. According to him, Alvarado struck the blow in order to intimidate the Aztecs from any insurrectionary movement. But whether he had reason to apprehend such, or even affected to do so before the massacre, the old chronicler does not inform us.

On reflection, it seems scarcely possible that so foul a deed, and one involving so much hazard to the Spaniards themselves, should have been perpetrated from the mere desire of getting possession of the baubles worn on the persons of the natives. It is more likely this was an afterthought, suggested to the rapacious soldiery by the display of the spoil before them. It is not improbable that Alvarado may have gathered rumors of a conspiracy among the nobles—rumors, perhaps, derived through the Tlascalans, their inveterate foes, and for that reason very little deserving of credit. He proposed to defeat it by imitating the example of his commander at Cholula. But he omitted to imitate his leader in taking precautions against the subsequent rising of the populace. And he grievously miscalculated when he confounded the bold and warlike Aztec with the effeminate Cholulan.

No sooner was the butchery accomplished, than the tidings spread like wildfire through the capital. Men could scarcely credit their senses. All they had hitherto suffered, the desecration of their temples, the imprisonment of their sovereign, the insults heaped on his person, all were forgotten in this one act. Every feeling of long-smothered hostility and rancor now burst forth in the cry for vengeance. Every former sentiment of superstitious dread was merged in that of inextinguishable hatred. It required no effort of the priests—though this was not wanting—to fan these passions into a blaze. The city rose in arms to a man; and on the following dawn, almost before the Spaniards could secure themselves in their defenses, they were assaulted with desperate fury. Some of the assailants attempted to scale the walls; others succeeded in partially undermining and setting fire to the works. Whether they would have succeeded in carrying the place by storm is doubtful. But, at the prayers of the garrison, Montezuma himself interfered, and, mounting the battlements, addressed the populace, whose fury he endeavored to mitigate by urging considerations for his own safety. They respected their monarch so far as to desist from further attempts to storm the fortress, but changed their operations into a regular blockade. They threw up works around the palace to prevent the egress of the Spaniards. They suspended the tianguez, or market, to preclude the possibility of their enemy's obtaining supplies; and they then quietly sat down, with feelings of sullen desperation, waiting for the hour when famine should throw their victims into their hands.

The condition of the besieged, meanwhile, was sufficiently distressing. Their magazines of provisions, it is true, were not exhausted; but they suffered greatly from want of water, which, within the enclosure, was exceedingly brackish, for the soil was saturated with the salt of the surrounding element. In this extremity, they discovered, it is said, a spring of fresh water in the area. Such springs were known in some other parts of the city; but, discovered first under these circumstances, it was accounted as nothing less than a miracle. Still they suffered much from their past encounters. Seven Spaniards, and many Tlascalans, had fallen, and there was scarcely one of either nation who had not received several wounds. In this situation, far from their own countrymen, without expectation of succor from abroad, they seemed to have no alternative before them but a lingering death by famine, or one more dreadful on the altar of sacrifice. From this gloomy state they were relieved by the coming of their comrades.

Cortes calmly listened to the explanation made by Alvarado. But, before it was ended, the conviction must have forced itself on his mind that he had made a wrong selection for this important post. Yet the mistake was natural. Alvarado was a cavalier of high family, gallant and chivalrous, and his warm personal friend. He had talents for action, was possessed of firmness and intrepidity, while his frank and dazzling manners made the Tonatiuh an especial favorite with the Mexicans. But underneath this showy exterior the future conqueror of Guatemala concealed a heart rash, rapacious, and cruel. He was altogether destitute of that moderation which, in the delicate position he occupied, was a quality of more worth than all the rest.

When Alvarado had concluded his answers to the several interrogatories of Cortes, the brow of the latter darkened, as he said to his lieutenant, "You have done badly. You have been false to your trust. Your conduct has been that of a madman!" And, turning abruptly on his heel, he left him in undisguised displeasure.

Yet this was not a time to break with one so popular, and, in many respects, so important to him, as this captain, much less to inflict on him the punishment he merited. The Spaniards were like mariners laboring in a heavy tempest, whose bark nothing but the dexterity of the pilot and the hearty cooperation of the crew can save from foundering. Dissensions at such a moment must be fatal. Cortes, it is true, felt strong in his present resources. He now found himself at the head of a force which could scarcely amount to less than twelve hundred and fifty Spaniards, and eight thousand native warriors, principally Tlascalans. But, though relying on this to overawe resistance, the very augmentation of numbers increased the difficulty of subsistence. Discontented with himself, disgusted with his officer, and embarrassed by the disastrous consequences in which Alvarado's intemperance had involved him, he became irritable, and indulged in a petulance by no means common; for, though a man of lively passions by nature, he held them habitually under control.

On the day that Cortes arrived, Montezuma had left his own quarters to welcome him. But the Spanish commander, distrusting, as it would seem, however unreasonably, his good faith, received him so coldly that the Indian monarch withdrew, displeased and dejected, to his apartment. As the Mexican populace made no show of submission, and brought no supplies to the army, the general's ill humor with the emperor continued. When, therefore, Montezuma sent some of the nobles to ask an interview with Cortes, the latter, turning to his own officers, haughtily exclaimed, "What have I to do with this dog of a king who suffers us to starve before his eyes?"

His captains, among whom were Olid, De Avila, and Velasquez de Leon, endeavored to mitigate his anger, reminding him, in respectful terms, that had it not been for the emperor the garrison might even now have been overwhelmed by the enemy. This remonstrance only chafed him the more. "Did not the dog," he asked, repeating the opprobrious epithet, "betray us in his communications with Narvaez? And does he not now suffer his markets to be closed, and leave us to die of famine?" Then, turning fiercely to the Mexicans, he said, "Go tell your master and his people to open the markets, or we will do it for them, at their cost!" The chiefs, who had gathered the import of his previous taunt on their sovereign, from his tone and gesture, or perhaps from some comprehension of his language, left his presence swelling with resentment, and, in communicating his message, took care it should lose none of its effect.

Shortly after, Cortes, at the suggestion, it is said, of Montezuma, released his brother Cuitlahua, lord of Iztapalapan, who, it will be remembered, had been seized on suspicion of cooperating with the chief of Tezcuco in his meditated revolt. It was thought he might be of service in allaying the present tumult and bringing the populace to a better state of feeling. But he returned no more to the fortress. He was a bold, ambitious prince, and the injuries he had received from the Spaniards rankled deep in his bosom. He was presumptive heir to the crown, which, by the Aztec laws of succession, descended much more frequently in a collateral than in a direct line. The people welcomed him as the representative of their sovereign, and chose him to supply the place of Montezuma during his captivity. Cuitlahua willingly accepted the post of honor and of danger. He was an experienced warrior, and exerted himself to reorganize the disorderly levies and to arrange a more efficient plan of operations. The effect was soon visible.

Cortes meanwhile had so little doubt of his ability to overawe the insurgents, that he wrote to that effect to the garrison of Villa Rica by the same despatches in which he informed them of his safe arrival in the capital. But scarcely had his messenger been gone half an hour, when he returned breathless with terror and covered with wounds. "The city," he said, "was all in arms! The drawbridges were raised, and the enemy would soon be upon them!" He spoke truth. It was not long before a hoarse, sullen sound became audible, like that of the roaring of distant waters. It grew louder and louder; till, from the parapet surrounding the enclosure, the great avenues which led to it might be seen dark with the masses of warriors, who came rolling on in a confused tide towards the fortress. At the same time, the terraces and azoteas or flat roofs, in the neighborhood, were thronged with combatants brandishing their missiles, who seemed to have risen up as if by magic! It was a spectacle to appall the stoutest. But the dark storm to which it was the prelude, and which gathered deeper and deeper round the Spaniards during the remainder of their residence in the capital, must form the subject of a separate Book.

BOOK V

CHAPTER I

Fury of the Mexicans

1520

The palace of Axayacatl, in which the Spaniards were quartered, was, as the reader may remember, a vast, irregular pile of stone buildings, having but one floor, except in the center, where another story was added, consisting of a suite of apartments which rose like turrets on the main building of the edifice. A vast area stretched around, encompassed by a stone wall of no great height. This was supported by towers or bulwarks at certain intervals, which gave it some degree of strength, not, indeed, as compared with European fortifications, but sufficient to resist the rude battering enginery of the Indians. The parapet had been pierced here and there with embrasures for the artillery, which consisted of thirteen guns; and smaller apertures were made in other parts for the convenience of the arquebusiers. The Spanish forces found accommodations within the great building; but the numerous body of Tlascalan auxiliaries could have had no other shelter than what was afforded by barracks or sheds hastily constructed for the purpose in the spacious courtyard. Most of them, probably, bivouacked under the open sky, in a climate milder than that to which they were accustomed among the rude hills of their native land. Thus crowded into a small and compact compass, the whole army could be assembled at a moment's notice; and, as the Spanish commander was careful to enforce the strictest discipline and vigilance, it was scarcely possible that he could be taken by surprise. No sooner, therefore, did the trumpet call to arms, as the approach of the enemy was announced, than every soldier was at his post, the cavalry mounted, the artillery men at their guns, and the archers and arquebusiers stationed so as to give the assailants a warm reception.

On they came, with the companies, or irregular masses, into which the multitude was divided, rushing forward each in its own dense column, with many a gay banner displayed, and many a bright gleam of light reflected from helmet, arrow, and spearhead, as they were tossed about in their disorderly array. As they drew near the enclosure, the Aztecs set up a hideous yell, or rather that shrill whistle used in fight by the nations of Anahuac, which rose far above the sound of shell and atabal and their other rude instruments of warlike melody. They followed this by a tempest of missiles—stones, darts, and arrows—which fell thick as rain on the besieged, while volleys of the same kind descended from the crowded terraces in the neighborhood.

The Spaniards waited until the foremost column had arrived within the best distance for giving effect to their fire, when a general discharge of artillery and arquebuses swept the ranks of the assailants and mowed them down by hundreds. The Mexicans were familiar with the report of these formidable engines as they had been harmlessly discharged on some holiday festival; but never till now had they witnessed their murderous power. They stood aghast for a moment, as with bewildered looks they staggered under the fury of the fire; but, soon rallying, the bold barbarians uttered a piercing cry, and rushed forward over the prostrate bodies of their comrades. A second and a third volley checked their career, and threw them into disorder, but still they pressed on, letting off clouds of arrows; while their comrades on the roofs of the houses took more deliberate aim at the combatants in the courtyard. The Mexicans were particularly expert in the use of the sling; and the stones which they hurled from their elevated positions on the heads of their enemies did even greater execution than the arrows. They glanced, indeed, from the mail-covered bodies of the cavaliers, and from those who were sheltered under the cotton panoply, or escaupil. But some of the soldiers, especially the veterans of Cortes, and many of their Indian allies, had but slight defenses, and suffered greatly under this stony tempest.

The Aztecs, meanwhile, had advanced close under the walls of the intrenchment, their ranks broken and disordered and their limbs mangled by the unintermitting fire of the Christians.

But they still pressed on, under the very muzzles of the guns. They endeavored to scale the parapet, which, from its moderate height, was in itself a work of no great difficulty. But the moment they showed their heads above the rampart they were shot down by the unerring marksmen within, or stretched on the ground by a blow of a Tlascalan maquahuitl. Nothing daunted, others soon appeared to take the place of the fallen, and strove by raising themselves on the writhing bodies of their dying comrades, or by fixing their spears in the crevices of the wall, to surmount the barrier. But the attempt proved equally vain.

Defeated here, they tried to effect a breach in the parapet by battering it with heavy pieces of timber. The works were not constructed on those scientific principles by which one part is made to overlook and protect another. The besiegers, therefore, might operate at their pleasure, with but little molestation from the garrison within, whose guns could not be brought into a position to bear on them, and who could mount no part of their own works for their defense without exposing their persons to the missiles of the whole besieging army. The parapet, however, proved too strong for the efforts of the assailants. In their despair, they endeavored to set the Christian quarters on fire, shooting burning arrows into them, and climbing up so as to dart their firebrands through the embrasures. The principal edifice was of stone. But the temporary defenses of the Indian allies, and other parts of the exterior works, were of wood. Several of these took fire, and the flame spread rapidly among the light, combustible materials. This was a disaster for which the besieged were wholly unprepared. They had little water, scarcely enough for their own consumption. They endeavored to extinguish the flames by heaping on earth. But in vain. Fortunately, the great building was of materials which defied the destroying element. But the fire raged in some of the outworks, connected with the parapet, with a fury which could only be checked by throwing down a part of the wall itself, thus laying open a formidable breach. This, by the general's order, was speedily protected by a battery of heavy guns, and a file of arquebusiers, who kept up an incessant volley through the opening on the assailants.

The fight now raged with fury on both sides. The walls around the palace belched forth an unintermitting sheet of flame and smoke. The groans of the wounded and dying were lost in the fiercer battle-cries of the combatants, the roar of the artillery, the sharper rattle of the musketry, and the hissing sound of Indian missiles. It was the conflict of the European with the American; of civilized man with the barbarian; of the science of the one with the rude weapons and warfare of the other. And as the ancient walls of Tenochtitlan shook under the thunders of the artillery, it announced that the white man, the destroyer, had set his foot within her precincts.

Night at length came, and drew her friendly mantle over the contest. The Aztec seldom fought by night. It brought little repose, however, to the Spaniards, in hourly expectation of an assault; and they found abundant occupation in restoring the breaches in their defenses and in repairing their battered armor. The beleaguering host lay on their arms through the night, giving token of their presence, now and then, by sending a stone or shaft over the battlements, or by a solitary cry of defiance from some warrior more determined than the rest, till all other sounds were lost in the vague, indistinct murmurs which float upon the air in the neighborhood of a vast assembly.

The ferocity shown by the Mexicans seems to have been a thing for which Cortes was wholly unprepared. His past experience, his uninterrupted career of victory with a much feebler force at his command, had led him to underrate the military efficiency, as well as the valor, of the Indians. The apparent facility with which the Mexicans had acquiesced in the outrages on their sovereign and themselves had led him to hold their courage, in particular, too lightly. He could not believe the present assault to be anything more than a temporary ebullition of the populace, which would soon waste itself by its own fury. And he proposed, on the following day, to sally out and inflict such chastisement on his foes as should bring them to their senses and show who was master in the capital.

With early dawn, the Spaniards were up and under arms; but not before their enemies had given evidence of their hostility by the random missiles which from time to time were sent into the enclosure. As the gray light of morning advanced, it showed the besieging army, far from being diminished in numbers, filling up the great square and neighboring avenues in more dense array than on the preceding evening. Instead of a confused, disorderly rabble, it had the appearance of something like a regular force, with its battalions distributed under their respective banners, the devices of which showed a contribution from the principal cities and districts in the valley. High above the rest was conspicuous an ancient standard of Mexico, with its well-known cognizance, an eagle pouncing on an ocelot, emblazoned on a rich mantle of feather-work. Here and there priests might be seen mingling in the ranks of the besiegers, and, with frantic gestures, animating them to avenge their insulted deities.

The greater part of the enemy had little clothing save the maxtlatl, or sash round the loins. They were variously armed, with long spears tipped with copper or flint, or sometimes merely pointed and hardened in the fire. Some were provided with slings, and others with darts having two or three points, with long strings attached to them, by which, when discharged, they could be torn away again from the body of the wounded. This was a formidable weapon, much dreaded by the Spaniards. Those of a higher order wielded the terrible maquahuitl, with its sharp and brittle blades of obsidian. Amidst the motley bands of warriors were seen many whose showy dress and air of authority intimated persons of high military consequence. Their breasts were protected by plates of metal, over which was thrown the gay surcoat of feather-work. They wore casques resembling in their form the head of some wild and ferocious animal, crested with bristly hair, or overshadowed by tall and graceful plumes of many a brilliant color. Some few were decorated with the red fillet bound round the hair, having tufts of cotton attached to it, which denoted by their number that of the victories they had won, and their pre-eminent rank among the warriors of the nation. The motley assembly plainly showed that priest, warrior, and citizen had all united to swell the tumult.

Before the sun had shot his beams into the Castilian quarters, the enemy were in motion, evidently preparing to renew the assault of the preceding day. The Spanish commander determined to anticipate them by a vigorous sortie, for which he had already made the necessary dispositions. A general discharge of ordnance and musketry sent death far and wide into the enemy's ranks, and, before they had time to recover from their confusion, the gates were thrown open, and Cortes, sallying out at the head of his cavalry, supported by a large body of infantry and several thousand Tlascalans, rode at full gallop against them. Taken thus by surprise, it was scarcely possible to offer much resistance. Those who did were trampled down under the horses' feet, cut to pieces with the broadswords, or pierced with the lances of the riders. The infantry followed up the blow, and the rout for the moment was general.

But the Aztecs fled only to take refuge behind a barricade, or strong work of timber and earth, which had been thrown across the great street through which they were pursued. Rallying on the other side, they made a gallant stand, and poured in turn a volley of their light weapons on the Spaniards, who, saluted with a storm of missiles at the same time from the terraces of the houses, were checked in their career and thrown into some disorder.

Cortes, thus impeded, ordered up a few pieces of heavy ordnance, which soon swept away the barricades and cleared a passage for the army. But it had lost the momentum acquired in its rapid advance. The enemy had time to rally and to meet the Spaniards on more equal terms. They were attacked in flank, too, as they advanced, by fresh battalions, who swarmed in from the adjoining streets and lanes. The canals were alive with boats filled with warriors, who with their formidable darts searched every crevice or weak place in the armor of proof, and made havoc on the unprotected bodies of the Tlascalans. By repeated and vigorous charges, the Spaniards succeeded in driving the Indians before them; though many, with a desperation which showed they loved vengeance better than life, sought to embarrass the movements of their horses by clinging to their legs, or, more successfully, strove to pull the riders from their saddles. And woe to the unfortunate cavalier who was thus dismounted— to be despatched by the brutal maquahuitl, or to be dragged on board a canoe to the bloody altar of sacrifice!

But the greatest annoyance which the Spaniards endured was from the missiles from the azoteas, consisting often of large stones, hurled with a force that would tumble the stoutest rider from his saddle. Galled in the extreme by these discharges, against which even their shields afforded no adequate protection, Cortes ordered fire to be set to the buildings. This was no very difficult matter, since, although chiefly of stone, they were filled with mats, cane-work, and other combustible materials, which were soon in a blaze. But the buildings stood separated from one another by canals and drawbridges, so that the flames did not easily communicate to the neighboring edifices. Hence the labor of the Spaniards was incalculably increased, and their progress in the work of destruction—fortunately for the city—was comparatively slow. They did not relax their efforts, however, till several hundred houses had been consumed, and the miseries of a conflagration, in which the wretched inmates perished equally with the defenders, were added to the other horrors of the scene.

The day was now far spent. The Spaniards had been everywhere victorious. But the enemy, though driven back on every point, still kept the field. When broken by the furious charges of the cavalry, he soon rallied behind the temporary defenses, which, at different intervals, had been thrown across the streets, and, facing about, renewed the fight with undiminished courage, till the sweeping away of the barriers by the cannon of the assailants left a free passage for the movements of their horse. Thus the action was a succession of rallying and retreating, in which both parties suffered much, although the loss inflicted on the Indians was probably tenfold greater than that of the Spaniards. But the Aztecs could better afford the loss of a hundred lives than their antagonists that of one. And, while the Spaniards showed an array broken and obviously thinned in numbers, the Mexican army, swelled by the tributary levies which flowed in upon it from the neighboring streets, exhibited, with all its losses, no sign of diminution. At length, sated with carnage, and exhausted by toil and hunger, the Spanish commander drew off his men, and sounded a retreat.

On his way back to his quarters, he beheld his friend the secretary Duero, in a street adjoining, unhorsed, and hotly engaged with a body of Mexicans, against whom he was desperately defending himself with his poniard. Cortes, roused at the sight, shouted his war-cry, and, dashing into the midst of the enemy, scattered them like chaff by the fury of his onset; then, recovering his friend's horse, he enabled him to remount, and the two cavaliers, striking their spurs into their steeds, burst through their opponents and joined the main body of the army. Such displays of generous gallantry were not uncommon in these engagements, which called forth more feats of personal adventure than battles with antagonists better skilled in the science of war.

The chivalrous bearing of the general was emulated in full measure by Sandoval, De Leon, Olid, Alvarado, Ordaz, and his other brave companions, who won such glory under the eye of their leader as prepared the way for the independent commands which afterwards placed provinces and kingdoms at their disposal.

The undaunted Aztecs hung on the rear of their retreating foes, annoying them at every step by fresh flights of stones and arrows; and, when the Spaniards had re-entered their fortress, the Indian host encamped around it, showing the same dogged resolution as on the preceding evening. Though true to their ancient habits of inaction during the night, they broke the stillness of the hour by insulting cries and menaces, which reached the ears of the besieged. "The gods have delivered you, at last, into our hands," they said; "Huitzilopochtli has long cried for his victims. The stone of sacrifice is ready. The knives are sharpened. The wild beasts in the palace are roaring for their offal. And the cages," they added, taunting the Tlascalans with their leanness, "are waiting for the false sons of Anahuac, who are to be fattened for the festival!" These dismal menaces, which sounded fearfully in the ears of the besieged, who understood too well their import, were mingled with piteous lamentations for their sovereign, whom they called on the Spaniards to deliver up to them.

Cortes suffered much from a severe wound which he had received in the hand in the late action. But the anguish of his mind must have been still greater as he brooded over the dark prospect before him. He had mistaken the character of the Mexicans. Their long and patient endurance had been a violence to their natural temper, which, as their whole history proves, was arrogant and ferocious beyond that of most of the races of Anahuac. The restraint which, in deference to their monarch more than to their own fears, they had so long put on their natures, being once removed, their passions burst forth with accumulated violence. The Spaniards had encountered in the Tlascalan an open enemy, who had no grievance to complain of, no wrong to redress. He fought under the vague apprehension only of some coming evil to his country. But the Aztec, hitherto the proud lord of the land, was goaded by insult and injury, till he had reached that pitch of self-devotion which made life cheap in comparison with revenge. Armed thus with the energy of despair, the savage is almost a match for the civilized man; and a whole nation, moved to its depths by a common feeling, which swallows up all selfish considerations of personal interest and safety, becomes, whatever be its resources, like the earthquake and the tornado, the most formidable among the agencies of nature.

Considerations of this kind may have passed through the mind of Cortes, as he reflected on his own impotence to restrain the fury of the Mexicans, and resolved, in despite of his late supercilious treatment of Montezuma, to employ his authority to allay the tumult—an authority so successfully exerted in behalf of Alvarado at an earlier stage of the insurrection. He was the more confirmed in his purpose on the following morning, when the assailants, redoubling their efforts, succeeded in scaling the works in one quarter and effecting an entrance into the enclosure. It is true, they were met with so resolute a spirit that not a man of those who entered was left alive. But, in the impetuosity of the assault, it seemed, for a few moments, as if the place was to be carried by storm.

Cortes now sent to the Aztec emperor to request his interposition with his subjects in behalf of the Spaniards. But Montezuma was not in the humor to comply. He had remained moodily in his quarters ever since the general's return. Disgusted with the treatment he had received, he had still further cause for mortification in finding himself the ally of those who were the open enemies of his nation. From his apartment he had beheld the tragical scenes in his capital, and seen another, the presumptive heir to his throne, taking the place which he should have occupied at the head of his warriors and fighting the battles of his country. Distressed by his position, indignant at those who had placed him in it, he coldly answered, "What have I to do with Malinche? I do not wish to hear from him. I desire only to die. To what a state has my willingness to serve him reduced me!" When urged still further to comply by Olid and Father Olmedo, he added, "It is of no use. They will neither believe me, nor the false words and promises of Malinche. You will never leave these walls alive." On being assured, however, that the Spaniards would willingly depart if a way were opened to them by their enemies, he at length—moved, probably, more by the desire to spare the blood of his subjects than of the Christians—consented to expostulate with his people.

In order to give the greater effect to his presence, he put on his imperial robes. The tilmatli, his mantle of white and blue, flowed over his shoulders, held together by its rich clasp of the green chalchivitl. The same precious gem, with emeralds of uncommon size, set in gold, profusely ornamented other parts of his dress. His feet were shod with the golden sandals, and his brows covered by the copilli, or Mexican diadem, resembling in form the pontifical tiara. Thus attired, and surrounded by a guard of Spaniards and several Aztec nobles, and preceded by the golden wand, the symbol of sovereignty, the Indian monarch ascended the central turret of the palace. His presence was instantly recognized by the people, and, as the royal retinue advanced along the battlements, a change, as if by magic, came over the scene. The clang of instruments, the fierce cries of the assailants, were hushed, and a deathlike stillness pervaded the whole assembly, so fiercely agitated, but a few moments before, by the wild tumult of war! Many prostrated themselves on the ground; others bent the knee; and all turned with eager expectation towards the monarch whom they had been taught to reverence with slavish awe, and from whose countenance they had been wont to turn away as from the intolerable splendors of divinity. Montezuma saw his advantage; and, while he stood thus confronted with his awe-struck people, he seemed to recover all his former authority and confidence, as he felt himself to be still a king. With a calm voice, easily heard over the silent assembly, he is said by the Castilian writers to have thus addressed them:

"Why do I see my people here in arms against the palace of my fathers? Is it that you think your sovereign a prisoner, and wish to release him? If so, you have acted rightly. But you are mistaken. I am no prisoner. The strangers are my guests. I remain with them only from choice, and can leave them when I list. Have you come to drive them from the city? That is unnecessary. They will depart of their own accord, if you will open a way for them. Return to your homes, then. Lay down your arms. Show your obedience to me who have a right to it. The white men shall go back to their own land; and all shall be well again within the walls of Tenochtitlan."

As Montezuma announced himself the friend of the detested strangers, a murmur ran through the multitude; a murmur of contempt for the pusillanimous prince who could show himself so insensible to the insults and injuries for which the nation was in arms. The swollen tide of their passions swept away all the barriers of ancient reverence, and, taking a new direction, descended on the head of the unfortunate monarch, so far degenerated from his warlike ancestors. "Base Aztec," they exclaimed, "woman, coward! the white men have made you a woman—fit only to weave and spin!" These bitter taunts were soon followed by still more hostile demonstrations. A chief, it is said, of high rank, bent a bow or brandished a javelin with an air of defiance against the emperor, when, in an instant, a cloud of stones and arrows descended on the spot where the royal train was gathered. The Spaniards appointed to protect his person had been thrown off their guard by the respectful deportment of the people during their lord's address. They now hastily interposed their bucklers. But it was too late. Montezuma was wounded by three of the missiles, one of which, a stone, fell with such violence on his head, near the temple, as brought him senseless to the ground. The Mexicans, shocked at their own sacrilegious act, experienced a sudden revulsion of feeling, and, setting up a dismal cry, dispersed, panic-struck, in different directions. Not one of the multitudinous array remained in the great square before the palace!

The unhappy prince, meanwhile, was borne by his attendants to his apartments below. On recovering from the insensibility caused by the blow, the wretchedness of his condition broke upon him. He had tasted the last bitterness of degradation. He had been reviled, rejected, by his people. The meanest of the rabble had raised their hands against him. He had nothing more to live for. It was in vain that Cortes and his officers endeavored to soothe the anguish of his spirit and fill him with better thoughts. He spoke not a word in answer. His wound, though dangerous, might still, with skillful treatment, not prove mortal. But Montezuma refused all the remedies prescribed for it. He tore off the bandages as often as they were applied, maintaining, all the while, the most determined silence. He sat with eyes dejected, brooding over his fallen fortunes, over the image of ancient majesty and present humiliation. He had survived his honor.

But a spark of his ancient spirit seemed to kindle in his bosom as it was clear he did not mean to survive his disgrace. From this painful scene the Spanish general and his followers were soon called away by the new dangers which menaced the garrison.

FROM CHAPTER II

Storming of the Great Temple

1520

Opposite to the Spanish quarters, at only a few rods' distance, stood the great teocalli of Huitzilopochtli. This pyramida mound, with the sanctuaries that crowned it, rising altogether to the height of near a hundred and fifty feet, afforded an elevated position that completely commanded the palace of Axayacatl, occupied by the Christians. A body of five or six hundred Mexicans, many of them nobles and warriors of the highest rank, had got possession of the teocalli, whence they discharged such a tempest of arrows on the garrison that no one could leave his defenses for a moment without imminent danger; while the Mexicans, under shelter of the sanctuaries, were entirely covered from the fire of the besieged. It was obviously necessary to dislodge the enemy, if the Spaniards would remain longer in their quarters.

Cortes assigned this service to his chamberlain, Escobar, giving him a hundred men for the purpose, with orders to storm the teocalli and set fire to the sanctuaries. But that officer was thrice repulsed in the attempt, and, after the most desperate efforts, was obliged to return with considerable loss and without accomplishing his object.

Cortes, who saw the immediate necessity of carrying the place, determined to lead the storming party himself. He was then suffering much from the wound in his left hand, which had disabled it for the present. He made the arm serviceable, however, by fastening his buckler to it, and, thus crippled, sallied out at the head of three hundred chosen cavaliers and several thousand of his auxiliaries.

In the courtyard of the temple he found a numerous body of Indians prepared to dispute his passage. He briskly charged them; but the flat smooth stones of the pavement were so slippery that the horses lost their footing and many of them fell. Hastily dismounting, they sent back the animals to their quarters, and, renewing the assault, the Spaniards succeeded without much difficulty in dispersing the Indian warriors and opening a free passage for themselves to the teocalli. This building, as the reader may remember, was a huge pyramidal structure, about three hundred feet square at the base. A flight of stone steps on the outside, at one of the angles of the mound, led to a platform, or terraced walk, which passed round the building until it reached a similar flight of stairs directly over the preceding, that conducted to another landing as before. As there were five bodies or divisions of the teocalli, it became necessary to pass round its whole extent four times, or nearly a mile, in order to reach the summit, which, it may be recollected, was an open area, crowned only by the two sanctuaries dedicated to the Aztec deities.

Cortes, having cleared a way for the assault, sprang up the lower stairway, followed by Alvarado, Sandoval, Ordaz, and the other gallant cavaliers of his little band, leaving a file of arquebusiers and a strong corps of Indian allies to hold the enemy in check at the foot of the monument. On the first landing, as well as on the several galleries above, and on the summit, the Aztec warriors were drawn up to dispute his passage. From their elevated position they showered down volleys of lighter missiles, together with heavy stones, beams, and burning rafters, which, thundering along the stairway, overturned the ascending Spaniards and carried desolation through their ranks. The more fortunate, eluding or springing over these obstacles, succeeded in gaining the first terrace; where, throwing themselves on their enemies, they compelled them, after a short resistance, to fall back. The assailants pressed on, effectually supported by a brisk fire of the musketeers from below, which so much galled the Mexicans in their exposed situation that they were glad to take shelter on the broad summit of the teocalli.

Cortes and his comrades were close upon their rear, and the

two parties soon found themselves face to face on this aerial battlefield, engaged in mortal combat in presence of the whole city, as well as of the troops in the courtyard, who paused, as if by mutual consent, from their own hostilities, gazing in silent expectation on the issue of those above. The area, though somewhat smaller than the base of the teocalli, was large enough to afford a fair field of fight for a thousand combatants. It was paved with broad, flat stones. No impediment occurred over its surface, except the huge sacrificial block, and the temples of stone which rose to the height of forty feet, at the farther extremity of the arena. One of these had been consecrated to the cross. The other was still occupied by the Mexican war-god. The Christian and the Aztec contended for their religions under the very shadow of their respective shrines; while the Indian priests, running to and fro, with their hair wildly streaming over their sable mantles, seemed hovering in mid-air, like so many demons of darkness urging on the work of slaughter!

The parties closed with the desperate fury of men who had no hope but in victory. Quarter was neither asked nor given; and to fly was impossible. The edge of the area was unprotected by parapet or battlement. The least slip would be fatal; and the combatants, as they struggled in mortal agony, were sometimes seen to roll over the sheer sides of the precipice together. Cortes himself is said to have had a narrow escape from this dreadful fate. Two warriors, of strong, muscular frames, seized on him, and were dragging him violently towards the brink of the pyramid. Aware of their intention, he struggled with all his force, and, before they could accomplish their purpose, succeeded in tearing himself from their grasp and hurling one of them over the walls with his own arm! The story is not improbable in itself, for Cortes was a man of uncommon agility and strength. It has been often repeated; but not by contemporary history.

The battle lasted with unintermitting fury for three hours. The number of the enemy was double that of the Christians; and it seemed as if it were a contest which must be determined by numbers and brute force, rather than by superior science. But it was not so. The invulnerable armor of the Spaniard, his sword of matchless temper, and his skill in the use of it, gave him advantages which far outweighed the odds of physical strength and numbers. After doing all that the courage of despair could enable men to do, resistance grew fainter and fainter on the side of the Aztecs. One after another they had fallen. Two or three priests only survived, to be led away in triumph by the victors. Every other combatant was stretched a corpse on the bloody arena, or had been hurled from the giddy heights. Yet the loss of the Spaniards was not inconsiderable. It amounted to forty-five of their best men; and nearly all the remainder were more or less injured in the desperate conflict.

The victorious cavaliers now rushed towards the sanctuaries. The lower story was of stone; the two upper were of wood. Penetrating into their recesses, they had the mortification to find the image of the Virgin and the cross removed. But in the other edifice they still beheld the grim figure of Huitzilopochtli, with his censer of smoking hearts, and the walls of his oratory reeking with gore—not improbably of their own countrymen! With shouts of triumph the Christians tore the uncouth monster from his niche, and tumbled him, in the presence of the horror-struck Aztecs, down the steps of the teocalli. They then set fire to the accursed building. The flames speedily ran up the slender towers, sending forth an ominous light over city, lake, and valley, to the remotest hut among the mountains. It was the funeral pyre of paganism, and proclaimed the fall of that sanguinary religion which had so long hung like a dark cloud over the fair regions of Anahuac!

Having accomplished this good work, the Spaniards descended the winding slopes of the teocalli with more free and buoyant step, as if conscious that the blessing of Heaven now rested on their arms. They passed through the dusky files of Indian warriors in the courtyard, too much dismayed by the appalling scenes they had witnessed to offer resistance, and reached their own quarters in safety. That very night they followed up the blow by a sortie on the sleeping town, and burned three hundred houses, the horrors of conflagration being made still more impressive by occurring at the hour when the Aztecs, from their own system of warfare, were least prepared for them.

Hoping to find the temper of the natives somewhat subdued by these reverses, Cortes now determined, with his usual policy, to make them a vantage-ground for proposing terms of accommodation. He accordingly invited the enemy to a parley, and, as the principal chiefs, attended by their followers, assembled in the great square, he mounted the turret before occupied by Montezuma, and made signs that he would address them. Marina, as usual, took her place by his side, as his interpreter. The multitude gazed with earnest curiosity on the Indian girl, whose influence with the Spaniards was well known, and whose connection with the general, in particular, had led the Aztecs to designate him by her Mexican name of Malinche. Cortes, speaking through the soft, musical tones of his mistress, told his audience they must now be convinced that they had nothing further to hope from opposition to the Spaniards. They had seen their gods trampled in the dust, their altars broken, their dwellings burned, their warriors falling on all sides. "All this," continued he, "you have brought on yourselves by your rebellion. Yet, for the affection the sovereign whom you have so unworthily treated still bears you, I would willingly stay my hand, if you will lay down your arms and return once more to your obedience. But, if you do not," he concluded, "I will make your city a heap of ruins, and leave not a soul alive to mourn over it!"

But the Spanish commander did not yet comprehend the character of the Aztecs, if he thought to intimidate them by menaces. Calm in their exterior, and slow to move, they were the more difficult to pacify when roused; and now that they had been stirred to their inmost depths, it was no human voice that could still the tempest. It may be, however, that Cortes did not so much misconceive the character of the people. He may have felt that an authoritative tone was the only one he could assume with any chance of effect in his present position, in which milder and more conciliatory language would, by intimating a consciousness of inferiority, have too certainly defeated its own object.

It was true, they answered, he had destroyed their temples, broken in pieces their gods, massacred their countrymen. Many more, doubtless, were yet to fall under their terrible swords. But they were content so long as for every thousand Mexicans they could shed the blood of a single white man! "Look out," they continued, "on our terraces and streets; see them still thronged with warriors as far as your eyes can reach. Our numbers are scarcely diminished by our losses. Yours, on the contrary, are lessening every hour. You are perishing from hunger and sickness. Your provisions and water are failing. You must soon fall into our hands. *The bridges are broken down, and you cannot escape!* There will be too few of you left to glut the vengeance of our gods!" As they concluded, they sent a volley of arrows over the battlements, which compelled the Spaniards to descend and take refuge in their defenses.

The fierce and indomitable spirit of the Aztecs filled the besieged with dismay. All, then, that they had done and suffered, their battles by day, their vigils by night, the perils they had braved, even the victories they had won, were of no avail. It was too evident that they had no longer the spring of ancient superstition to work upon in the breasts of the natives, who, like some wild beast that has burst the bonds of his keeper, seemed now to swell and exult in the full consciousness of their strength. The annunciation respecting the bridges fell like a knell on the ears of the Christians. All that they had heard was too true; and they gazed on one another with looks of anxiety and dismay. . . .

CHAPTER III

Noche Triste

1520

There was no longer any question as to the expediency of evacuating the capital. The only doubt was as to the time of doing so, and the route. The Spanish commander called a council of officers to deliberate on these matters. It was his purpose to retreat on Tlascala, and in that capital to decide, according to circumstances, on his future operations. After some discussion, they agreed on the causeway of Tlacopan as the avenue by which to leave the city. It would, indeed, take them back by a circuitous route, considerably longer than either of those by which they had approached the capital. But, for that reason, it would be less likely to be guarded, as least suspected; and the causeway itself, being shorter than either of the other entrances, would sooner place the army in comparative security on the main land.

There was some difference of opinion in respect to the hour of departure. The daytime, it was argued by some, would be preferable, since it would enable them to see the nature and extent of their danger and to provide against it. Darkness would be much more likely to embarrass their own movements than those of the enemy, who were familiar with the ground. A thousand impediments would occur in the night, which might prevent their acting in concert, or obeying, or even ascertaining, the orders of the commander. But, on the other hand, it was urged that the night presented many obvious advantages in dealing with a foe who rarely carried his hostilities beyond the day. The late active operations of the Spaniards had thrown the Mexicans off their guard, and it was improbable they would anticipate so speedy a departure of their enemies. With celerity and caution they might succeed, therefore, in making their escape from the town, possibly over the causeway, before their retreat should be discovered; and, could they once get beyond that pass of peril, they felt little apprehension for the rest.

These views were fortified, it is said, by the counsels of a soldier named Botello, who professed the mysterious science of judicial astrology. He had gained credit with the army by some predictions which had been verified by the events; those lucky hits which make chance pass for calculation with the credulous multitude. This man recommended to his countrymen by all means to evacuate the place in the night, as the hour most propitious to them, although he should perish in it. The event proved the astrologer better acquainted with his own horoscope than with that of others.

It is possible Botello's predictions had some weight in determining the opinion of Cortes. Superstition was the feature of the age, and the Spanish general, as we have seen, had a full measure of its bigotry. Seasons of gloom, moreover, dispose the mind to a ready acquiescence in the marvelous. It is, however, quite as probable that he made use of the astrologer's opinion, finding it coincided with his own, to influence that of his men and inspire them with higher confidence. At all events, it was decided to abandon the city that very night.

The general's first care was to provide for the safe transportation of the treasure. Many of the common soldiers had converted their share of the prize, as we have seen, into gold chains, collars, or other ornaments, which they easily carried about their persons. But the royal fifth, together with that of Cortes himself, and much of the rich booty of the principal cavaliers, had been converted into bars and wedges of solid gold, and deposited in one of the strong apartments of the palace. Cortes delivered the share belonging to the crown to the royal officers, assigning them one of the strongest horses, and a guard of Castilian soldiers, to transport it. Still, much of the treasure, belonging both to the crown and to individuals, was necessarily abandoned, from the want of adequate means of conveyance. The metal lay scattered in shining heaps along the floor, exciting the cupidity of the soldiers. "Take what you will of it," said Cortes to his men. "Better you should have it, than these Mexican hounds. But be careful not to overload yourselves. He travels safest in the dark night who travels lightest." His own more wary followers took heed to his counsel, helping themselves to a few articles of least bulk, though, it might be, of greatest value. But the troops of Narvaez, pining for riches of which they had heard so much and hitherto seen so little, showed no such discretion. To them it seemed as if the very mines of Mexico were turned up before them, and, rushing on the treacherous spoil, they greedily loaded themselves with as much of it, not merely as they could accommodate about their persons, but as they could stow away in wallets, boxes, or any other means of conveyance at their disposal.

Cortes next arranged the order of march. The van, composed of two hundred Spanish foot, he placed under the command of the valiant Gonzalo de Sandoval, supported by Diego de Ordaz, Francisco de Lujo, and about twenty other cavaliers. The rear guard, constituting the strength of the infantry, was intrusted to Pedro de Alvarado and Velasquez de Leon. The general himself took change of the "battle," or center, in which went the baggage, some of the heavy guns, most of which, however, remained in the rear, the treasure, and the prisoners. These consisted of a son and two daughters of Montezuma, Cacama, the deposed lord of Tezcuco, and several other nobles, whom Cortes retained as important pledges in his future negotiations with the enemy. The Tlascalans were distributed pretty equally among the three divisions; and Cortes had under his immediate command a hundred picked soldiers, his own veterans most attached to his service, who, with Cristoval de Olid, Francisco de Morla, Alonso de Avila, and two or three other cavaliers, formed a select corps, to act wherever occasion might require.

The general had already superintended the construction of a portable bridge to be laid over the open canals in the causeway. This was given in charge to an officer named Magarino, with forty soldiers under his orders, all pledged to defend the passage to the last extremity. The bridge was to be taken up when the entire army had crossed one of the breaches, and transported to the next. There were three of these openings in the causeway, and most fortunate would it have been for the expedition if the foresight of the commander had provided the same number of bridges. But the labor would have been great, and time was short.

At midnight the troops were under arms, in readiness for the march. Mass was performed by Father Olmedo, who invoked the protection of the Almighty through the awful perils of the night. The gates were thrown open, and on the first of July, 1520, the Spaniards for the last time sallied forth from the walls of the ancient fortress, the scene of so much suffering and such indomitable courage.

The night was cloudy, and a drizzling rain, which fell without intermission, added to the obscurity. The great square before the palace was deserted, as, indeed, it had been since the fall of Montezuma. Steadily, and as noiselessly as possible, the Spaniards held their way along the great street of Tlacopan, which so lately had resounded with the tumult of battle. All was now hushed in silence; and they were only reminded of the past by the occasional presence of some solitary corpse, or a dark heap of the slain, which too plainly told where the strife had been hottest. As they passed along the lanes and alleys which opened into the great street, or looked down the canals, whose polished surface gleamed with a sort of ebon luster through the obscurity of night, they easily fancied that they discerned the shadowy forms of their foe lurking in ambush and ready to spring on them. But it was only fancy; and the city slept undisturbed even by the prolonged echoes of the tramp of the horses and the hoarse rumbling of the artillery and baggage-trains. At length, a lighter space beyond the dusky line of buildings showed the van of the army that it was emerging on the open causeway.

They might well have congratulated themselves on having thus escaped the dangers of an assault in the city itself, and that a brief time would place them in comparative safety on the opposite shore. But the Mexicans were not all asleep.

As the Spaniards drew near the spot where the street opened on the causeway, and were preparing to lay the portable bridge across the uncovered breach, which now met their eyes, several Indian sentinels, who had been stationed at this, as at the other approaches to the city, took the alarm, and fled, rousing their countrymen by their cries. The priests, keeping their night-watch on the summit of the teocallis, instantly caught the tidings and sounded their shells, while the huge drum in the desolate temple of the war-god sent forth those solemn tones, which, heard only in seasons of calamity, vibrated through every corner of the capital. The Spaniards saw that no time was to be lost. The bridge was brought forward and fitted with all possible expedition. Sandoval was the first to try its strength, and, riding across, was followed by his little body of chivalry, his infantry, and Tlascalan allies, who formed the first division of the army. Then came Cortes and his squadrons, with the baggage, ammunition-wagons, and a part of the artillery. But before they had time to defile across the narrow passage, a gathering sound was heard, like that of a mighty forest agitated by the winds. It grew louder and louder, while on the dark waters of the lake was heard a plashing noise, as of many oars. Then came a few stones and arrows striking at random among the hurrying troops. They fell every moment faster and more furious, till they thickened into a terrible tempest, while the very heavens were rent with the yells and war-cries of myriads of combatants, who seemed all at once to be swarming over land and lake!

The Spaniards pushed steadily on through this arrowy sleet, though the barbarians, dashing their canoes against the sides of the causeway, clambered up and broke in upon their ranks. But the Christians, anxious only to make their escape, declined all combat except for self-preservation. The cavaliers, spurring forward their steeds, shook off their assailants and rode over their prostrate bodies, while the men on foot with their good swords or the butts of their pieces drove them headlong again down the sides of the dike.

But the advance of several thousand men, marching, probably, on a front of not more than fifteen or twenty abreast, necessarily required much time, and the leading files had already reached the second breach in the causeway before those in the rear had entirely traversed the first. Here they halted, as they had no means of effecting a passage, smarting all the while under unintermitting volleys from the enemy, who were clustered thick on the waters around this second opening. Sorely distressed, the vanguard sent repeated messages to the rear to demand the portable bridge. At length the last of the army had crossed, and Magarino and his sturdy followers endeavored to raise the ponderous framework. But it stuck fast in the sides of the dike. In vain they strained every nerve. The weight of so many men and horses, and above all of the heavy artillery, had wedged the timbers so firmly in the stones and earth that it was beyond their power to dislodge them. Still they labored amidst a torrent of missiles, until, many of them slain, and all wounded, they were obliged to abandon the attempt.

The tidings soon spread from man to man, and no sooner was their dreadful import comprehended than a cry of despair arose, which for a moment drowned all the noise of conflict. All means of retreat were cut off. Scarcely hope was left. The only hope was in such desperate exertions as each could make for himself. Order and subordination were at an end. Intense danger produced intense selfishness. Each thought only of his own life. Pressing forward, he trampled down the weak and the wounded, heedless whether it were friend or foe. The leading files, urged on by the rear, were crowded on the brink of the gulf. Sandoval, Ordaz, and the other cavaliers dashed into the water. Some succeeded in swimming their horses across. Others failed, and some, who reached the opposite bank, being overturned in the ascent, rolled headlong with their steeds into the lake. The infantry followed pellmell, heaped promiscuously on one another, frequently pierced by the shafts or struck down by the war-clubs of the Aztecs; while many an unfortunate victim was dragged half stunned on board their canoes, to be reserved for a protracted but more dreadful death.

The carnage raged fearfully along the length of the causeway. Its shadowy bulk presented a mark of sufficient distinctness for the enemy's missiles, which often prostrated their own countrymen in the blind fury of the tempest. Those nearest the dike, running their canoes alongside, with a force that shattered them to pieces, leaped on the land, and grappled with the Christians, until both came rolling down the side of the causeway together. But the Aztec fell among his friends, while his antagonist was borne away in triumph to the sacrifice. The struggle was long and deadly. The Mexicans were recognized by their white cotton tunics, which showed faint through the darkness. Above the combatants rose a wild and discordant clamor, in which horrid shouts of vengeance were mingled with groans of agony, with invocations of the saints and the blessed Virgin, and with the screams of women; for there were several women, both natives and Spaniards, who had accompanied the Christian camp. Among these, one named Maria de Estrada is particularly noticed for the courage she displayed, battling with broadsword and target like the stanchest of the warriors.

The opening in the causeway, meanwhile, was filled up with the wreck of matter which had been forced into it, ammunition wagons, heavy guns, bales of rich stuffs scattered over the waters, chests of solid ingots, and bodies of men and horses, till over this dismal ruin a passage was gradually formed, by which those in the rear were enabled to clamber to the other side. Cortes, it is said, found a place that was fordable, where, halting, with the water up to his saddle-girths, he endeavored to check the confusion, and lead his followers by a safer path to the opposite bank. But his voice was lost in the wild uproar, and finally, hurrying on with the tide, he pressed forward with a few trusty cavaliers, who remained near his person, to the van; but not before he had seen his favorite page, Juan de Salazar, struck down, a corpse, by his side. Here he found Sandoval and his companions, halting before the third and last breach, endeavoring to cheer on their followers to surmount it. But their resolution faltered. It was wide and deep; though the passage was not so closely beset by the enemy as the preceding ones. The cavaliers again set the example by plunging into the water. Horse and foot followed as they could, some swimming, others with dying grasp clinging to the manes and tails of the struggling animals. Those fared best, as the general had predicted, who traveled lightest; and many were the unfortunate wretches who, weighed down by the fatal gold which they loved so well, were buried with it in the salt floods of the lake. Cortes, with his gallant comrades, Olid, Morla, Sandoval, and some few others, still kept in the advance, leading his broken remnant off the fatal causeway. The din of battle lessened in the distance; when the rumor reached them that the rear guard would be wholly overwhelmed without speedy relief. It seemed almost an act of desperation; but the generous hearts of the Spanish cavaliers did not stop to calculate danger when the cry for succor reached them. Turning their horses' bridles, they galloped back to the theater of action, worked their way through the press, swam the canal, and placed themselves in the thick of the mêlée on the opposite bank.

The first gray of the morning was now coming over the waters. It showed the hideous confusion of the scene which had been shrouded in the obscurity of night. The dark masses of combatants, stretching along the dike, were seen struggling for mastery, until the very causeway on which they stood appeared to tremble, and reel to and fro, as if shaken by an earthquake; while the bosom of the lake, as far as the eye could reach, was darkened by canoes crowded with warriors, whose spears and bludgeons, armed with blades of "volcanic glass," gleamed in the morning light.

The cavaliers found Alvarado unhorsed, and defending himself with a poor handful of followers against an overwhelming tide of the enemy. His good steed, which had borne him through many a hard fight, had fallen under him. He was himself wounded in several places, and was striving in vain to rally his scattered column, which was driven to the verge of the canal by the fury of the enemy, then in possession of the whole rear of the causeway, where they were reinforced every hour by fresh combatants from the city. The artillery in the earlier part of the engagement had not been idle, and its iron shower, sweeping along the dike, had mowed down the assailants by hundreds. But nothing could resist their impetuosity. The front ranks, pushed on by those behind, were at length forced up to the pieces, and, pouring over them like a torrent, overthrew men and guns in one general ruin. The resolute charge of the Spanish cavaliers, who had now arrived, created a temporary check, and gave time for their countrymen to make a feeble rally. But they were speedily borne down by the returning flood. Cortes and his companions were compelled to plunge again into the lake—

though all did not escape. Alvarado stood on the brink for a moment, hesitating what to do. Unhorsed as he was, to throw himself into the water, in the face of the hostile canoes that now swarmed around the opening, afforded but a desperate chance of safety. He had but a second for thought. He was a man of powerful frame, and despair gave him unnatural energy. Setting his long lance firmly on the wreck which strewed the bottom of the lake, he sprung forward with all his might, and cleared the wide gap at a leap! Aztecs and Tlascalans gazed in stupid amazement, exclaiming, as they beheld the incredible feat, "This is truly the Tonatiuh—the child of the Sun!" The breadth of the opening is not given. But it was so great that the valorous captain Diaz, who well remembered the place, says the leap was impossible to any man. Other contemporaries, however, do not discredit the story. It was, beyond doubt, matter of popular belief at the time; it is to this day familiarly known to every inhabitant of the capital; and the name of the Salto de Alvarado, "Alvarado's Leap," given to the spot, still commemorates an exploit which rivaled those of the demi-gods of Grecian fable.

Cortes and his companions now rode forward to the front, where the troops, in a loose, disorderly manner, were marching off the fatal causeway. A few only of the enemy hung on their rear, or annoyed them by occasional flights of arrows from the lake. The attention of the Aztecs was diverted by the rich spoil that strewed the battleground; fortunately for the Spaniards, who, had their enemy pursued with the same ferocity with which he had fought, would, in their crippled condition, have been cut off, probably, to a man. But little molested, therefore, they were allowed to defile through the adjacent village, or suburbs, it might be called, of Popotla.

The Spanish commander there dismounted from his jaded steed, and, sitting down on the steps of an Indian temple, gazed mournfully on the broken files as they passed before him. What a spectacle did they present! The cavalry, most of them dismounted, were mingled with the infantry, who dragged their feeble limbs along with difficulty; their shattered mail and tattered garments dripping with the salt ooze, showing through their rents many a bruise and ghastly wound; their bright arms soiled, their proud crests and banners gone, the baggage, artillery, all, in short, that constitutes the pride and panoply of glorious war, forever lost. Cortes, as he looked wistfully on their thin and disordered ranks, sought in vain for many a familiar face, and missed more than one dear companion who had stood side by side with him through all the perils of the Conquest. Though accustomed to control his emotions, or, at least, to conceal them, the sight was too much for him. He covered his face with his hands, and the tears, which trickled down, revealed too plainly the anguish of his soul.

He found some consolation, however, in the sight of several of the cavaliers on whom he most relied. Alvarado, Sandoval, Olid, Ordaz, Avila, were yet safe. He had the inexpressible satisfaction, also, of learning the safety of the Indian interpreter, Marina, so dear to him, and so important to the army. She had been committed, with a daughter of a Tlascalan chief, to several of that nation. She was fortunately placed in the van, and the faithful escort had carried her securely through all the dangers of the night. Aguilar, the other interpreter, had also escaped. And it was with no less satisfaction that Cortes learned the safety of the shipbuilder, Martin Lopez. The general's solicitude for the fate of this man, so indispensable, as he proved, to the success of his subsequent operations, showed that, amidst all his affliction, his indomitable spirit was looking forward to the hour of vengeance.

Meanwhile, the advancing column had reached the neighboring city of Tlacopan (Tacuba), once the capital of an independent principality. There it halted in the great street, as if bewildered and altogether uncertain what course to take; like a herd of panic-struck deer, who, flying from the hunters, with the cry of hound and horn still ringing in their ears, look wildly around for some glen or copse in which to plunge for concealment. Cortes, who had hastily mounted and rode on to the front again, saw the danger of remaining in a populous place, where the inhabitants might sorely annoy the troops from the azoteas, with little risk to themselves. Pushing forward, therefore, he soon led them into the country. There he endeavored to reform his disorganized battalions and bring them to something like order.

Hard by, at no great distance on the left, rose an eminence, looking towards a chain of mountains which fences in the valley on the west. It was called the Hill of Otoncalpolco, and sometimes the Hill of Montezuma. It was crowned with an Indian teocalli, with its large outworks of stone covering an ample space, and by its strong position, which commanded the neighboring plain, promised a good place of refuge for the exhausted troops. But the men, disheartened and stupefied by their late reverses, seemed for the moment incapable of further exertion; and the place was held by a body of armed Indians. Cortes saw the necessity of dislodging them if he would save the remains of his army from entire destruction. The event showed he still held a control over their wills stronger than circumstances themselves. Cheering them on, and supported by his gallant cavaliers, he succeeded in infusing into the most sluggish something of his own intrepid temper, and led them up the ascent in face of the enemy. But the latter made slight resistance, and, after a few feeble volleys of missiles which did little injury, left the ground to the assailants.

It was covered by a building of considerable size, and furnished ample accommodations for the diminished numbers of the Spaniards. They found there some provisions; and more, it is said, were brought to them, in the course of the day, from some friendly Otomi villages in the neighborhood. There was, also, a quantity of fuel in the courts, destined to the uses of the temple. With this they made fires to dry their drenched garments, and busily employed themselves in dressing one another's wounds, stiff and extremely painful from exposure and long exertion. Thus refreshed, the weary soldiers threw themselves down on the floor and courts of the temple, and soon found the temporary oblivion which nature seldom denies even in the greatest extremity of suffering.

There was one eye in that assembly, however, which we may well believe did not so speedily close. For what agitating thoughts must have crowded on the mind of their commander, as he beheld his poor remnant of followers thus huddled together in this miserable bivouac! And this was all that survived of the brilliant array with which but a few weeks since he had entered the capital of Mexico! Where now were his dreams of conquest and empire? And what was he but a luckless adventurer, at whom the finger of scorn would be uplifted as a madman? Whichever way he turned, the horizon was almost equally gloomy, with scarcely one light spot to cheer him. He had still a weary journey before him, through perilous and unknown paths, with guides of whose fidelity he could not be assured. And how could he rely on his reception at Tlascala, the place of his destination—the land of his ancient enemies, where, formerly as a foe, and now as a friend, he had brought desolation to every family within its borders?

Yet these agitating and gloomy reflections, which might have crushed a common mind, had no power over that of Cortes; or, rather, they only served to renew his energies and quicken his perceptions, as the war of the elements purifies and gives elasticity to the atmosphere. He looked with an unblenching eye on his past reverses; but, confident in his own resources, he saw a light through the gloom which others could not. Even in the shattered relics which lay around him, resembling in their haggard aspect and wild attire a horde of famished outlaws, he discerned the materials out of which to reconstruct his ruined fortunes. In the very hour of discomfiture and general despondency, there is no doubt that his heroic spirit was meditating the plan of operations which he afterwards pursued with such dauntless constancy.

The loss sustained by the Spaniards on this fatal night, like every other event in the history of the Conquest, is reported with the greatest discrepancy. If we believe Cortes' own letter, it did not exceed one hundred and fifty Spaniards and two thousand Indians. But the general's bulletins, while they do full justice to the difficulties to be overcome and the importance of the results, are less scrupulous in stating the extent either of his means or of his losses. Thoan Cano, one of the cavaliers present, estimates the slain at eleven hundred and seventy Spaniards and eight thousand allies. But this is a greater number than we have allowed for the whole army. Perhaps we may come nearest the truth by taking the computation of Gomara, who was the chaplain of Cortes, and who had free access, doubtless, not only to the general's papers, but to other authentic sources of information. According to him, the number of Christians killed and missing was four hundred and fifty, and that of natives four thousand. This, with the loss sustained in the conflicts of the previous week, may have reduced the former to something more than a third, and the latter to a fourth, or perhaps fifth, of the original force with which they entered the capital. The brunt of the action fell on the rear guard, few of whom escaped. It was formed chiefly of the soldiers of Narvaez, who fell the victims, in some measure, of their cupidity. Forty-six of the cavalry were cut off, which with previous losses reduced the number in this branch of the service to twenty-three, and some of these in very poor condition. The greater part of the treasure, the baggage, the general's papers, including his accounts, and a minute diary of transactions since leaving Cuba—which, to posterity at least, would have been of more worth than the gold—had been swallowed up by the waters. The ammunition, the beautiful little train of artillery with which Cortes had entered the city, were all gone. Not a musket even remained, the men having thrown them away, eager to disencumber themselves of all that might retard their escape on that disastrous night. Nothing, in short, of their military apparatus was left, but their swords, their crippled cavalry, and a few damaged crossbows, to assert the superiority of the European over the barbarian.

The prisoners, including, as already noticed, the children of Montezuma and the cacique of Tezcuco, all perished by the hands of their ignorant countrymen, it is said, in the indiscriminate fury of the assault. There were, also, some persons of consideration among the Spaniards whose names were inscribed on the same bloody roll of slaughter. Such was Francisco de Morla, who fell by the side of Cortes on returning with him to the rescue. But the greatest loss was that of Juan Velasquez de Leon, who, with Alvarado, had command of the rear. It was the post of danger on that night, and he fell, bravely defending it, at an early part of the retreat. He was an excellent officer, possessed of many knightly qualities, though somewhat haughty in his bearing, being one of the best-connected cavaliers in the army. The near relation of the governor of Cuba, he looked coldly, at first, on the pretensions of Cortes; but, whether from a conviction that the latter had been wronged, or from personal preference, he afterwards attached himself zealously to his leader's interests. The general requited this with a generous confidence, assigning him, as we have seen, a separate and independent command, where misconduct, or even a mistake, would have been fatal to the expedition. Velasquez proved himself worthy of the trust; and there was no cavalier in the army, with the exception, perhaps, of Sandoval and Alvarado, whose loss would have been so deeply deplored by the commander. Such were the disastrous results of this terrible passage of the causeway; more disastrous than those occasioned by any other reverse which has stained the Spanish arms in the New World; and which have branded the night on which it happened, in the national annals, with the name of the noche triste, "the sad or melancholy night."

FROM CHAPTER IV

Battle of Otumba

1520

The Mexicans, during the day which followed the retreat of the Spaniards, remained, for the most part, quiet in their own capital, where they found occupation in cleansing the streets and causeways from the dead, which lay festering in heaps that might have bred a pestilence. They may have been employed, also, in paying the last honors to such of their warriors as had fallen, solemnizing the funeral rites by the sacrifice of their wretched prisoners, who, as they contemplated their own destiny, may well have envied the fate of their companions who left their bones on the battlefield. It was most fortunate for the Spaniards, in their extremity, that they had this breathing-time allowed them by the enemy. But Cortes knew that he could not calculate on its continuance, and, feeling how important it was to get the start of his vigilant foe, he ordered his troops to be in readiness to resume their march by midnight. Fires were left burning, the better to deceive the enemy; and at the appointed hour the little army, without sound of drum or trumpet, but with renewed spirits, sallied forth from the gates of the teocalli, within whose hospitable walls they had found such seasonable succor. The place is now indicated by a Christian church, dedicated to the Virgin, under the title of Nuestra Señora de los Remedios, whose miraculous image—the very same, *it is said,* brought over by the followers of Cortes—still extends her beneficent sway over the neighboring capital; and the traveler who pauses within the precincts of the consecrated fane may feel that he is standing on the spot made memorable by the refuge it afforded to the Conquerors in the hour of their deepest despondency.

It was arranged that the sick and wounded should occupy the center, transported on litters, or on the backs of the tamanes, while those who were strong enough to keep their seats should mount behind the cavalry. The able-bodied soldiers were ordered to the front and rear, while others protected the flanks, thus affording all the security possible to the invalids.

The retreating army held on its way unmolested under cover of the darkness. But, as morning dawned, they beheld parties of the natives moving over the heights, or hanging at a distance, like a cloud of locusts, on their rear. They did not belong to the capital, but were gathered from the neighboring country, where the tidings of their rout had already penetrated. The charm which had hitherto covered the white men was gone. The dread Teules were no longer invincible.

The Spaniards, under the conduct of their Tlascalan guides, took a circuitous route to the north, passing through Quauhtitlan, and round lake Tzompanco (Zumpango), thus lengthening their march, but keeping at a distance from the capital. From the eminences, as they passed along, the Indians rolled down heavy stones, mingled with volleys of darts and arrows, on the heads of the soldiers. Some were even bold enough to descend into the plain and assault the extremities of the column. But they were soon beaten off by the horse, and compelled to take refuge among the hills, where the ground was too rough for the riders to follow. Indeed, the Spaniards did not care to do so, their object being rather to fly than to fight.

In this way they slowly advanced, halting at intervals to drive off their assailants when they became too importunate, and greatly distressed by their missiles and their desultory attacks. At night, the troops usually found shelter in some town or hamlet, whence the inhabitants, in anticipation of their approach, had been careful to carry off all the provisions. The Spaniards were soon reduced to the greatest straits for subsistence. Their principal food was the wild cherry, which grew in the woods or by the roadside. Fortunate were they if they found a few ears of corn unplucked. More frequently nothing was left but the stalks; and with them, and the like unwholesome fare, they were fain to supply the cravings of appetite. When a horse happened to be killed, it furnished an extraordinary banquet; and Cortes himself records the fact of his having made one of a party who thus sumptuously regaled themselves, devouring the animal even to his hide.

The wretched soldiers, faint with famine and fatigue, were sometimes seen to drop down lifeless on the road. Others loitered behind, unable to keep up with the march, and fell into the hands of the enemy, who followed in the track of the army like a flock of famished vultures, eager to pounce on the dying and the dead. Others, again, who strayed too far, in their eagerness to procure sustenance, shared the same fate. The number of these, at length, and the consciousness of the cruel lot for which they were reserved, compelled Cortes to introduce stricter discipline, and to enforce it by sterner punishments than he had hitherto done— though too often ineffectually, such was the indifference to danger, under the overwhelming pressure of present calamity.

In their prolonged distresses, the soldiers ceased to set a value on those very things for which they had once been content to hazard life itself. More than one who had brought his golden treasure safe through the perils of the noche triste now abandoned it as an intolerable burden; and the rude Indian peasant gleaned up, with wondering delight, the bright fragments of the spoils of the capital.

Through these weary days Cortes displayed his usual serenity and fortitude. He was ever in the post of danger, freely exposing himself in encounters with the enemy; in one of which he received a severe wound in the head that afterwards gave him much trouble. He fared no better than the humblest soldier, and strove, by his own cheerful countenance and counsels, to fortify the courage of those who faltered, assuring them that their sufferings would soon be ended by their arrival in the hospitable "land of bread." His faithful officers cooperated with him in these efforts; and the common file, indeed, especially his own veterans, must be allowed, for the most part, to have shown a full measure of the constancy and power of endurance so characteristic of their nation—justifying the honest boast of an old chronicler, "that there was no people so capable of supporting hunger as the Spaniards, and none of them who were ever more severely tried than the soldiers of Cortes." A similar fortitude was shown by the Tlascalans, trained in a rough school that made them familiar with hardship and privations. Although they sometimes threw themselves on the ground, in the extremity of famine, imploring their gods not to abandon them, they did their duty as warriors, and, far from manifesting coldness towards the Spaniards as the cause of their distresses, seemed only the more firmly knit to them by the sense of a common suffering.

On the seventh morning, the army had reached the mountain rampart which overlooks the plains of Otompan, or Otumba, as commonly called, from the Indian city—now a village—situated in them. The distance from the capital is hardly nine leagues. But the Spaniards had traveled more than thrice that distance, in their circuitous march round the lakes. This had been performed so slowly that it consumed a week, two nights of which had been passed in the same quarters, from the absolute necessity of rest. It was not, therefore, till the seventh of July that they reached the heights commanding the plains which stretched far away towards the territory of Tlascala, in full view of the venerable pyramids of Teotihuacan, two of the most remarkable monuments of the antique American civilization now existing north of the Isthmus. During all the preceding day they had seen parties of the enemy hovering like dark clouds above the highlands, brandishing their weapons, and calling out, in vindictive tones, "Hasten on! You will soon find yourselves where you cannot escape!" words of mysterious import, which they were made fully to comprehend on the following morning. . . .

As the army was climbing the mountain steeps which shut in the Valley of Otompan, the vedettes came in with the intelligence that a powerful body was encamped on the other side, apparently awaiting their approach. The intelligence was soon confirmed by their own eyes, as they turned the crest of the sierra, and saw spread out, below, a mighty host, filling up the whole depth of the valley, and giving to it the appearance, from the white cotton mail of the warriors, of being covered with snow. It consisted of levies from the surrounding country, and especially the populous territory of Tezcuco, drawn together at the instance of Cuitlahua, Montezuma's successor, and now concentrated on this point to dispute the passage of the Spaniards. Every chief of note had taken the field with his whole array gathered under his standard, proudly displaying all the pomp and rude splendor of his military equipment. As far as the eye could reach, were to be seen shields and waving banners, fantastic helmets, forests of shining spears, the bright feather-mail of the chief, and the coarse cotton panoply of his followers, all mingled together in wild confusion and tossing to and fro like the billows of a troubled ocean. It was a sight to fill the stoutest heart among the Christians with dismay, heightened by the previous expectation of soon reaching the friendly land which was to terminate their wearisome pilgrimage. Even Cortes, as he contrasted the tremendous array before him with his own diminished squadrons, wasted by disease and enfeebled by hunger and fatigue, could not escape the conviction that his last hour had arrived.

But his was not the heart to despond; and he gathered strength from the very extremity of his situation. He had no room for hesitation; for there was no alternative left to him. To escape was impossible. He could not retreat on the capital, from which he had been expelled. He must advance—cut through the enemy, or perish. He hastily made his dispositions for the fight. He gave his force as broad a front as possible, protecting it on each flank by his little body of horse, now reduced to twenty. Fortunately, he had not allowed the invalids, for the last two days, to mount behind the riders, from a desire to spare the horses, so that these were now in tolerable condition; and, indeed, the whole army had been refreshed by halting, as we have seen, two nights and a day in the same place, a delay, however, which had allowed the enemy time to assemble in such force to dispute its progress.

Cortes instructed his cavaliers not to part with their lances, and to direct them at the face. The infantry were to thrust, not strike, with their swords; passing them at once through the bodies of their enemies. They were, above all, to aim at the leaders, as the general well knew how much depends on the life of the commander in the wars of barbarians, whose want of subordination makes them impatient of any control but that to which they are accustomed.

He then addressed to his troops a few words of encouragement, as customary with him on the eve of an engagement. He reminded them of the victories they had won with odds nearly as discouraging as the present; thus establishing the superiority

of science and discipline over numbers. Numbers, indeed, were
of no account, where the arm of the Almighty was on their side.
And he bade them have full confidence that He who had carried
them safely through so many perils would not now abandon
them and His own good cause to perish by the hand of the infidel. His address was brief, for he read in their looks that
settled resolve which rendered words unnecessary. The circumstances of their position spoke more forcibly to the heart of
every soldier than any eloquence could have done, filling it
with that feeling of desperation which makes the weak arm
strong and turns the coward into a hero. After they had earnestly
commended themselves, therefore, to the protection of God, the
Virgin, and St. James, Cortes led his battalions straight against
the enemy.

It was a solemn moment, that in which the devoted little band,
with steadfast countenances and their usual intrepid step, descended on the plain, to be swallowed up, as it were, in the vast
ocean of their enemies. The latter rushed on with impetuosity
to meet them, making the mountains ring to their discordant
yells and battle-cries, and sending forth volleys of stones and
arrows which for a moment shut out the light of day. But, when
the leading files of the two armies closed, the superiority of the
Christians was felt, as their antagonists, falling back before the
charges of cavalry, were thrown into confusion by their own
numbers who pressed on them from behind. The Spanish infantry followed up the blow, and a wide lane was opened in the
ranks of the enemy, who, receding on all sides, seemed willing
to allow a free passage for their opponents. But it was to return
on them with accumulated force, as rallying they poured upon
the Christians, enveloping the little army on all sides, which,
with its bristling array of long swords and javelins, stood firm
—in the words of a contemporary—like an islet against which
the breakers, roaring and surging, spend their fury in vain. The
struggle was desperate of man against man. The Tlascalan
seemed to renew his strength, as he fought almost in view of
his own native hills; as did the Spaniard, with the horrible doom
of the captive before his eyes. Well did the cavaliers do their
duty on that day; charging, in little bodies of four or five abreast,
deep into the enemy's ranks, riding over the broken files, and by
this temporary advantage giving strength and courage to the

infantry. Not a lance was there which did not reek with the blood of the infidel. Among the rest, the young captain Sandoval is particularly commemorated for his daring prowess. Managing his fiery steed with easy horsemanship, he darted, when least expected, into the thickest of the mêlée, overturning the stanchest warriors, and rejoicing in danger, as if it were his natural element.

But these gallant displays of heroism served only to ingulf the Spaniards deeper and deeper in the mass of the enemy, with scarcely any more chance of cutting their way through his dense and interminable battalions than of hewing a passage with their swords through the mountains. Many of the Tlascalans and some of the Spaniards had fallen, and not one but had been wounded. Cortes himself had received a second cut on the head, and his horse was so much injured that he was compelled to dismount, and take one from the baggage train, a strong-boned animal, who carried him well through the turmoil of the day. The contest had now lasted several hours. The sun rode high in the heavens, and shed an intolerable fervor over the plain. The Christians, weakened by previous sufferings, and faint with loss of blood, began to relax in their desperate exertions. Their enemies, constantly supported by fresh relays from the rear, were still in good heart, and, quick to perceive their advantage, pressed with redoubled force on the Spaniards. The horse fell back, crowded on the foot; and the latter, in vain seeking a passage amidst the dusky throngs of the enemy, who now closed up the rear, were thrown into some disorder. The tide of battle was setting rapidly against the Christians. The fate of the day would soon be decided; and all that now remained for them seemed to be to sell their lives as dearly as possible.

At this critical moment, Cortes, whose restless eye had been roving round the field in quest of any object that might offer him the means of arresting the coming ruin, rising in his stirrups, descried at a distance, in the midst of the throng, the chief who from his dress and military cortège he knew must be the commander of the barbarian forces. He was covered with a rich surcoat of feather-work; and a panache of beautiful plumes, gorgeously set in gold and precious stones, floated above his head. Rising above this, and attached to his back, between the shoulders, was a short staff bearing a golden net for a banner—

the singular, but customary, symbol of authority for an Aztec commander. The cacique, whose name was Cihuaca, was borne on a litter, and a body of young warriors, whose gay and ornamented dresses showed them to be the flower of the Indian nobles, stood round as a guard of his person and the sacred emblem.

The eagle eye of Cortes no sooner fell on this personage than it lighted up with triumph. Turning quickly round to the cavaliers at his side, among whom were Sandoval, Olid, Alvarado, and Avila, he pointed out the chief, exclaiming, "There is our mark! Follow and support me!" Then, crying his war-cry, and striking his iron heel into his weary steed, he plunged headlong into the thickest of the press. His enemies fell back, taken by surprise and daunted by the ferocity of the attack. Those who did not were pierced through with his lance or borne down by the weight of his charger. The cavaliers followed close in the rear. On they swept with the fury of a thunderbolt, cleaving the solid ranks asunder, strewing their path with the dying and the dead, and bounding over every obstacle in their way. In a few minutes they were in the presence of the Indian commander, and Cortes, overturning his supporters, sprang forward with the strength of a lion, and, striking him through with his lance, hurled him to the ground. A young cavalier, Juan de Salamanca, who had kept close by his general's side, quickly dismounted and despatched the fallen chief. Then, tearing away his banner, he presented it to Cortes, as a trophy to which he had the best claim. It was all the work of a moment. The guard, overpowered by the suddenness of the onset, made little resistance, but, flying, communicated their own panic to their comrades. The tidings of the loss soon spread over the field. The Indians, filled with consternation, now thought only of escape. In their blind terror, their numbers augmented their confusion. They trampled on one another, fancying it was the enemy in their rear.

The Spaniards and Tlascalans were not slow to avail themselves of the marvelous change in their affairs. Their fatigue, their wounds, hunger, thirst, all were forgotten in the eagerness for vengeance; and they followed up the flying foe, dealing death at every stroke, and taking ample retribution for all they had suffered in the bloody marshes of Mexico. Long did they pursue, till, the enemy having abandoned the field, they returned, sated with slaughter, to glean the booty which he had left. It was great, for the ground was covered with the bodies of chiefs, at whom the Spaniards, in obedience to the general's instructions, had particularly aimed; and their dresses displayed all the barbaric pomp of ornament in which the Indian warrior delighted. When his men had thus indemnified themselves, in some degree, for their late reverses, Cortes called them again under their banners; and, after offering up a grateful acknowledgment to the Lord of Hosts for their miraculous preservation, they renewed their march across the now deserted valley. The sun was declining in the heavens, but, before the shades of evening had gathered around, they reached an Indian temple on an eminence, which afforded a strong and commodious position for the night.

Such was the famous battle of Otompan—or Otumba, as commonly called, from the Spanish corruption of the name. It was fought on the eighth of July, 1520. The whole amount of the Indian force is reckoned by Castilian writers at two hundred thousand! that of the slain at twenty thousand! Those who admit the first part of the estimate will find no difficulty in receiving the last. It is about as difficult to form an accurate calculation of the numbers of a disorderly savage multitude as of the pebbles on the beach or the scattered leaves in autumn. Yet it was, undoubtedly, one of the most remarkable victories ever achieved in the New World. And this, not merely on account of the disparity of the forces, but of their unequal condition. For the Indians were in all their strength, while the Christians were wasted by disease, famine, and long-protracted sufferings; without cannon or firearms, and deficient in the military apparatus which had so often struck terror into their barbarian foe—deficient even in the terrors of a victorious name. But they had discipline on their side, desperate resolve, and implicit confidence in their commander. That they should have triumphed against such odds furnishes an inference of the same kind as that established by the victories of the European over the semi-civilized hordes of Asia.

Yet even here all must not be referred to superior discipline and tactics. For the battle would certainly have been lost had it not been for the fortunate death of the Indian general. And, although the selection of the victim may be called the result of calculation, yet it was by the most precarious chance that he was thrown in the way of the Spaniards. It is, indeed, one among many examples of the influence of fortune in determining the fate of military operations. The star of Cortes was in the ascendant. Had it been otherwise, not a Spaniard would have survived that day to tell the bloody tale of the battle of Otumba.

BOOK VI

Situation in Spain

1521

At the very time when Cortes was occupied with reconnoitering the valley, preparatory to his siege of the capital, a busy faction in Castile was laboring to subvert his authority and defeat his plans of conquest altogether. The fame of his brilliant exploits had spread not only through the isles, but to Spain and many parts of Europe, where a general admiration was felt for the invincible energy of the man who with his single arm, as it were, could so long maintain a contest with the powerful Indian empire. The absence of the Spanish monarch from his dominions, and the troubles of the country, can alone explain the supine indifference shown by the government to the prosecution of this great enterprise. To the same causes it may be ascribed that no action was had in regard to the suits of Velasquez and Narvaez, backed as they were by so potent an advocate as Bishop Fonseca, president of the Council of the Indies. The reins of government had fallen into the hands of Adrian of Utrecht, Charles's preceptor, and afterwards Pope—a man of learning, and not without sagacity, but slow and timid in his policy, and altogether incapable of that decisive action which suited the bold genius of his predecessor, Cardinal Ximenes.

In the spring of 1521, however, a number of ordinances passed the Council of the Indies, which threatened an important innovation in the affairs of New Spain. It was decreed that the Royal Audience of Hispaniola should abandon the proceeding already instituted against Narvaez for his treatment of the commissioner Ayllon; that that unfortunate commander should be released from his confinement at Vera Cruz; and that an arbitrator should be sent to Mexico with authority to investigate the affairs and conduct of Cortes and to render ample justice to the governor of Cuba. There were not wanting persons at court who looked with dissatisfaction on these proceedings, as an unworthy requital of the services of Cortes, and who thought the present moment, at any rate, not the most suitable for taking measures which might discourage the general and perhaps render him desperate. But the arrogant temper of the bishop of Burgos overruled all objections; and the ordinances, having been approved by the Regency, were signed by that body, April 11, 1521. A person named Tapia, one of the functionaries of the Audience at St. Domingo, was selected as the new commissioner to be despatched to Vera Cruz. Fortunately, circumstances occurred which postponed the execution of the design for the present, and permitted Cortes to go forward unmolested in his career of conquest.

But, while thus allowed to remain, for the present at least, in possession of authority, he was assailed by a danger nearer home, which menaced not only his authority, but his life. This was a conspiracy in the army, of a more dark and dangerous character than any hitherto formed there. It was set on foot by a common soldier, named Antonio Villafaña, a native of Old Castile, of whom nothing is known but his share in this transaction. He was one of the troop of Narvaez—that leaven of disaffection, which had remained with the army, swelling with discontent on every light occasion, and ready at all times to rise into mutiny. They had voluntarily continued in the service after the secession of their comrades at Tlascala; but it was from the same mercenary hopes with which they had originally embarked in the expedition—and in these they were destined still to be disappointed. They had little of the true spirit of adventure which distinguished the old companions of Cortes; and they found the barren laurels of victory but a sorry recompense for all their toils and sufferings.

With these men were joined others, who had causes of personal disgust with the general; and others, again, who looked with distrust on the result of the war. The gloomy fate of their countrymen who had fallen into the enemy's hands filled them with dismay. They felt themselves the victims of a chimerical spirit in their leader, who, with such inadequate means, was urging to extremity so ferocious and formidable a foe; and they shrank with something like apprehension from thus pursuing the enemy into his own haunts, where he would gather tenfold energy from despair.

These men would have willingly abandoned the enterprise and returned to Cuba; but how could they do it? Cortes had control over the whole route from the city to the seacoast; and not a vessel could leave its ports without his warrant. Even if he were put out of the way, there were others, his principal officers, ready to step into his place and avenge the death of their commander. It was necessary to embrace these, also, in the scheme of destruction; and it was proposed, therefore, together with Cortes, to assassinate Sandoval, Olid, Alvarado, and two or three others most devoted to his interests. The conspirators would then raise the cry of liberty, and doubted not that they should be joined by the greater part of the army, or enough, at least, to enable them to work their own pleasure. They proposed to offer the command, on Cortes' death, to Francisco Verdugo, a brother-in-law of Velasquez. He was an honorable cavalier, and not privy to their design. But they had little doubt that he would acquiesce in the command thus in a manner forced upon him, and this would secure them the protection of the governor of Cuba, who, indeed, from his own hatred of Cortes, would be disposed to look with a lenient eye on their proceedings.

The conspirators even went so far as to appoint the subordinate officers, an alguacil mayor in place of Sandoval, a quartermaster-general to succeed Olid, and some others. The time fixed for the execution of the plot was soon after the return of Cortes from his expedition. A parcel, pretended to have come by a fresh arrival from Castile, was to be presented to him while at table, and, when he was engaged in breaking open the letters, the conspirators were to fall on him and his officers and despatch them with their poniards. Such was the iniquitous scheme devised for the destruction of Cortes and the expedition. But a conspiracy, to be successful, especially when numbers are concerned, should allow but little time to elapse between its conception and its execution.

On the day previous to that appointed for the perpetration of the deed, one of the party, feeling a natural compunction at the commission of the crime, went to the general's quarters and solicited a private interview with him. He threw himself at his commander's feet, and revealed all the particulars relating to the conspiracy, adding that in Villafaña's possession a paper would be found, containing the names of his accomplices. Cortes, thunderstruck at the disclosure, lost not a moment in profiting by it. He sent for Alvarado, Sandoval, and one or two other officers marked out by the conspirator, and, after communicating the affair to them, went at once with them to Villafaña's quarters, attended by four alguacils.

They found him in conference with three or four friends, who were instantly taken from the apartment and placed in custody. Villafaña, confounded at this sudden apparition of his commander, had barely time to snatch a paper, containing the signatures of the confederates, from his bosom, and attempt to swallow it. But Cortes arrested his arm, and seized the paper. As he glanced his eye rapidly over the fatal list, he was much moved at finding there the names of more than one who had some claim to consideration in the army. He tore the scroll in pieces, and ordered Villafaña to be taken into custody. He was immediately tried by a military court hastily got together, at which the general himself presided. There seems to have been no doubt of the man's guilt. He was condemned to death, and, after allowing him time for confession and absolution, the sentence was executed by hanging him from the window of his own quarters.

Those ignorant of the affair were astonished at the spectacle; and the remaining conspirators were filled with consternation when they saw that their plot was detected, and anticipated a similar fate for themselves. But they were mistaken. Cortes pursued the matter no further. A little reflection convinced him that to do so would involve him in the most disagreeable, and even dangerous, perplexities. And, however much the parties implicated in so foul a deed might deserve death, he could ill afford the loss even of the guilty, with his present limited numbers. He resolved, therefore, to content himself with the punishment of the ringleader.

He called his troops together, and briefly explained to them the nature of the crime for which Villafaña had suffered. He had made no confession, he said, and the guilty secret had perished with him. He then expressed his sorrow that any should have been found in their ranks capable of so base an act, and stated his own unconsciousness of having wronged any individual among them; but, if he had done so, he invited them frankly to declare it, as he was most anxious to afford them all the redress in his power. But there was no one of his audience, whatever might be his grievances, who cared to enter his complaint at such a moment; least of all were the conspirators willing to do so, for they were too happy at having, as they fancied, escaped detection, to stand forward now in the ranks of the malcontents. The affair passed off, therefore, without further consequences. . . .

According to the plan of operations settled by Cortes, Sandoval, with his division, was to take a southern direction, while Alvarado and Olid would make the northern circuit of the lakes. These two cavaliers, after getting possession of Tacuba, were to advance to Chapoltepec and demolish the great aqueduct there, which supplied Mexico with water. On the tenth of May they commenced their march; but at Acolman, where they halted for the night, a dispute arose between the soldiers of the two divisions, respecting their quarters. From words they came to blows, and a defiance was even exchanged between the leaders, who entered into the angry feelings of their followers. Intelligence of this was soon communicated to Cortes, who sent at once to the fiery chiefs, imploring them, by their regard for him and the common cause, to lay aside their differences, which must end in their own ruin and that of the expedition. His remonstrance prevailed, at least, so far as to establish a show of reconciliation between the parties. But Olid was not a man to forget, or easily to forgive; and Alvarado, though frank and liberal, had an impatient temper much more easily excited than appeased. They were never afterwards friends.

The Spaniards met with no opposition on their march. The principal towns were all abandoned by the inhabitants, who had gone to strengthen the garrison of Mexico, or taken refuge with their families among the mountains. Tacuba was in like manner deserted, and the troops once more established themselves in their old quarters in the lordly city of the Tepanecs.

Their first undertaking was to cut off the pipes that conducted the water from the royal streams of Chapoltepec to feed the numerous tanks and fountains which sparkled in the courtyards of the capital. The aqueduct, partly constructed of brickwork and partly of stone and mortar, was raised on a strong though narrow dike, which transported it across an arm of the lake; and the whole work was one of the most pleasing monuments of Mexican civilization. The Indians, well aware of its importance, had stationed a large body of troops for its protection. A battle followed, in which both sides suffered considerably, but the Spaniards were victorious. A part of the aqueduct was demolished, and during the siege no water found its way again to the capital through this channel.

On the following day the combined forces descended on the fatal causeway, to make themselves masters, if possible, of the nearest bridge. They found the dike covered with a swarm of warriors, as numerous as on the night of their disaster, while the surface of the lake was dark with the multitude of canoes. The intrepid Christians strove to advance under a perfect hurricane of missiles from the water and the land, but they made slow progress. Barricades thrown across the causeway embarrassed the cavalry and rendered it nearly useless. The sides of the Indian boats were fortified with bulwarks, which shielded the crews from the arquebuses and crossbows; and, when the warriors on the dike were hard pushed by the pikemen, they threw themselves fearlessly into the water, as if it were their native element, and, reappearing along the sides of the dike, shot off their arrows and javelins with fatal execution. After a long and obstinate struggle, the Christians were compelled to fall back on their own quarters with disgrace, and—including the allies— with nearly as much damage as they had inflicted on the enemy. Olid, disgusted with the result of the engagement, inveighed against his companion as having involved them in it by his wanton temerity, and drew off his forces the next morning to his own station at Cojohuacan.

The camps, separated by only two leagues, maintained an easy communication with each other. They found abundant employment in foraging the neighboring country for provisions, and in repelling the active sallies of the enemy; on whom they took their revenge by cutting off his supplies. But their own position was precarious, and they looked with impatience for the arrival of the brigantines under Cortes. It was in the latter part of May that Olid took up his quarters at Cojohuacan; and from that time may be dated the commencement of the siege of Mexico.

FROM CHAPTER V

The Naval Battle

1521

No sooner had Cortes received intelligence that his two officers had established themselves in their respective posts, than he ordered Sandoval to march on Iztapalapan. The cavalier's route led him through a country for the most part friendly; and at Chalco his little body of Spaniards was swelled by the formidable muster of Indian levies who awaited there his approach. After this junction, he continued his march without opposition till he arrived before the hostile city, under whose walls he found a large force drawn up to receive him. A battle followed, and the natives, after maintaining their ground sturdily for some time, were compelled to give way, and to seek refuge either on the water, or in that part of the town which hung over it. The remainder was speedily occupied by the Spaniards.

Meanwhile, Cortes had set sail with his flotilla, intending to support his lieutenant's attack by water. On drawing near the southern shore of the lake, he passed under the shadow of an insulated peak, since named from him the "Rock of the Marquis." It was held by a body of Indians, who saluted the fleet, as it passed, with showers of stones and arrows. Cortes, resolving to punish their audacity, and to clear the lake of his troublesome enemy, instantly landed with a hundred and fifty of his followers. He placed himself at their head, scaled the steep ascent, in the face of a driving storm of missiles, and, reaching the summit, put the garrison to the sword. There was a number of women and children, also, gathered in the place, whom he spared.

On the top of the eminence was a blazing beacon, serving to notify to the inhabitants of the capital when the Spanish fleet weighed anchor. Before Cortes had regained his brigantine, the canoes and piraguas of the enemy had left the harbors of Mexico, and were seen darkening the lake for many a rood. There were several hundred of them, all crowded with warriors, and advancing rapidly by means of their oars over the calm bosom of the waters.

Cortes, who regarded his fleet, to use his own language, as "the key of the war," felt the importance of striking a decisive blow in the first encounter with the enemy. It was with chagrin, therefore, that he found his sails rendered useless by the want of wind. He calmly awaited the approach of the Indian squadron, which, however, lay on their oars at something more than musket-shot distance, as if hesitating to encounter these leviathans of their waters. At this moment, a light air from land rippled the surface of the lake; it gradually freshened into a breeze, and Cortes, taking advantage of the friendly succor, which he may be excused, under all the circumstances, for regarding as especially sent him by Heaven, extended his line of battle, and bore down, under full press of canvas, on the enemy.

The latter no sooner encountered the bows of their formidable opponents than they were overturned and sent to the bottom by the shock, or so much damaged that they speedily filled and sank. The water was covered with the wreck of broken canoes, and with the bodies of men struggling for life in the waves and vainly imploring their companions to take them on board their overcrowded vessels. The Spanish fleet, as it dashed through the mob of boats, sent off its volleys to the right and left with a terrible effect, completing the discomfiture of the Aztecs. The latter made no attempt at resistance, scarcely venturing a single flight of arrows, but strove with all their strength to regain the port from which they had so lately issued. They were no match in the chase, any more than in the fight, for their terrible antagonist, who, borne on the wings of the wind, careered to and fro at his pleasure, dealing death widely around him, and making the shores ring with the thunders of his ordnance. A few only of the Indian flotilla succeeded in recovering the port, and, gliding up the canals, found a shelter in the bosom of the city, where the heavier burden of the brigantines made it impossible for them to follow. This victory, more complete than even the sanguine temper of Cortes had prognosticated, proved the superiority of the Spaniards, and left them, henceforth, undisputed masters of the Aztec sea. . . .

FROM CHAPTER VII

The Siege

1521

Cortes now steadily pursued the plan he had laid down for the devastation of the city. Day after day the several armies entered by their respective quarters, Sandoval probably directing his operations against the northeastern district. The buildings, made of the porous tetzontli, though generally low, were so massy and extensive, and the canals were so numerous, that their progress was necessarily slow. They, however, gathered fresh accessions of strength every day from the numbers who flocked to the camp from the surrounding country, and who joined in the work of destruction with a hearty good will which showed their eagerness to break the detested yoke of the Aztecs. The latter raged with impotent anger as they beheld their lordly edifices, their temples, all they had been accustomed to venerate, thus ruthlessly swept away; their canals, constructed with so much labor and what to them seemed science, filled up with rubbish; their flourishing city, in short, turned into a desert, over which the insulting foe now rode triumphant. They heaped many a taunt on the Indian allies. "Go on," they said, bitterly: "the more you destroy, the more you will have to build up again hereafter. If we conquer, you shall build for us; and if your white friends conquer, they will make you do as much for them." The event justified the prediction.

In their rage they rushed blindly on the corps which covered the Indian pioneers. But they were as often driven back by the impetuous charge of the cavalry, or received on the long pikes of Chinantla, which did good service to the besiegers in their operations. At the close of day, however, when the Spaniards drew off their forces, taking care to send the multitudinous host of confederates first from the ground, the Mexicans usually rallied for a more formidable attack. Then they poured out from every lane and byway, like so many mountain streams, sweeping over the broad level cleared by the enemy, and falling impetuously on their flanks and rear. At such times they inflicted considerable loss in their turn, till an ambush, which Cortes laid for them among the buildings adjoining the great temple, did them so much mischief that they were compelled to act with more reserve.

At times the war displayed something of a chivalrous character, in the personal rencontres of the combatants. Challenges passed between them, and especially between the native warriors. These combats were usually conducted on the azoteas, whose broad and level surface afforded a good field of fight. On one occasion, a Mexican of powerful frame, brandishing a sword and buckler which he had won from the Christians, defied his enemies to meet him in single fight. A young page of Cortes', named Nuñez, obtained his master's permission to accept the vaunting challenge of the Aztec, and, springing on the azotea, succeeded, after a hard struggle, in discomfiting his antagonist, who fought at a disadvantage with weapons in which he was unpracticed, and, running him through the body, brought off his spoils in triumph and laid them at the general's feet.

The division of Cortes had now worked its way as far north as the great street of Tacuba, which opened a communication with Alvarado's camp, and near which stood the palace of Guatemozin. It was a spacious stone pile, that might well be called a fortress. Though deserted by its royal master, it was held by a strong body of Aztecs, who made a temporary defense, but of little avail against the battering enginery of the besiegers. It was soon set on fire, and its crumbling walls were leveled in the dust, like those other stately edifices of the capital, the boast and admiration of the Aztecs, and some of the fairest fruits of their civilization. "It was a sad thing to witness their destruction," exclaims Cortes; "but it was part of our plan of operations, and we had no alternative."

These operations had consumed several weeks, so that it was now drawing towards the latter part of July. During this time the blockade had been maintained with the utmost rigor, and the wretched inhabitants were suffering all the extremities of famine. Some few stragglers were taken, from time to time, in the neighborhood of the Christian camp, whither they had wandered in search of food. They were kindly treated, by command of Cortes, who was in hopes to induce others to follow their example, and thus to afford a means of conciliating the inhabitants, which might open the way to their submission. But few were found willing to leave the shelter of the capital, and they preferred to take their chance with their suffering countrymen rather than trust themselves to the mercies of the besiegers.

From these few stragglers, however, the Spaniards heard a dismal tale of woe respecting the crowded population in the interior of the city. All the ordinary means of sustenance had long since failed, and they now supported life as they could, by means of such roots as they could dig from the earth, by gnawing the bark of trees, by feeding on the grass—on anything, in short, however, loathsome, that could allay the craving of appetite. Their only drink was the brackish water of the soil saturated with the salt lake. Under this unwholesome diet, and the diseases engendered by it, the population was gradually wasting away. Men sickened and died every day, in all the excruciating torments produced by hunger, and the wan and emaciated survivors seemed only to be waiting for their time.

The Spaniards had visible confirmation of all this as they penetrated deeper into the city and approached the district of Tlatelolco, now occupied by the besieged. They found the ground turned up in quest of roots and weeds, the trees stripped of their green stems, their foliage, and their bark. Troops of famished Indians flitted in the distance, gliding like ghosts among the scenes of their former residence. Dead bodies lay unburied in the streets and courtyards, or filled up the canals. It was a sure sign of the extremity of the Aztecs; for they held the burial of the dead as a solemn and imperative duty. In the early part of the siege they had religiously attended to it. In its later stages they were still careful to withdraw the dead from the public eye, by bringing their remains within the houses. But the number of these, and their own sufferings, had now so fearfully increased that they had grown indifferent to this, and they suffered their friends and their kinsmen to lie and molder on the spot where they drew their last breath!

As the invaders entered the dwellings, a more appalling spectacle presented itself—the floors covered with the prostrate forms of the miserable inmates, some in the agonies of death, others festering in their corruption; men, women, and children inhaling the poisonous atmosphere, and mingled promiscuously together; mothers with their infants in their arms perishing of hunger before their eyes, while they were unable to afford them the nourishment of nature; men crippled by their wounds, with their bodies frightfully mangled, vainly attempting to crawl away, as the enemy entered. Yet even in this state they scorned to ask for mercy, and glared on the invaders with the sullen ferocity of the wounded tiger that the huntsmen have tracked to his forest cave. The Spanish commander issued strict orders that mercy should be shown to these poor and disabled victims. But the Indian allies made no distinction. An Aztec, under whatever circumstances, was an enemy; and, with hideous shouts of triumph, they pulled down the burning buildings on their heads, consuming the living and the dead in one common funeral pile!

Yet the sufferings of the Aztecs, terrible as they were, did not incline them to submission. There were many, indeed, who, from greater strength of constitution, or from the more favorable circumstances in which they were placed, still showed all their wonted energy of body and mind, and maintained the same undaunted and resolute demeanor as before. They fiercely rejected all the overtures of Cortes, declaring they would rather die than surrender, and adding, with a bitter tone of exultation, that the invaders would be at least disappointed in their expectations of treasure, for it was buried where they could never find it!

The women, it is said, shared in this desperate—it should rather be called heroic—spirit. They were indefatigable in nursing the sick and dressing their wounds; they aided the warriors in battle, by supplying them with the Indian ammunition of stones and arrows, prepared their slings, strung their bows, and displayed, in short, all the constancy and courage shown by the noble maidens of Saragossa in our day, and by those of Carthage in the days of antiquity.

Cortes had now entered one of the great avenues leading to the market-place of Tlatelolco, the quarter towards which the movements of Alvarado were also directed. A single canal only lay in his way; but this was of great width and stoutly defended by the Mexican archery. At this crisis, the army one evening, while in their intrenchments on the causeway, were surprised by an uncommon light that arose from the huge teocalli in that part of the city which, being at the north, was the most distant from their own position. This temple, dedicated to the dread war-god, was inferior only to the pyramid in the great square; and on it the Spaniards had more than once seen their unhappy countrymen led to slaughter. They now supposed that the enemy were employed in some of their diabolical ceremonies—when the flame, mounting higher and higher, showed that the sanctuaries themselves were on fire. A shout of exultation at the sight broke forth from the assembled soldiers, as they assured one another that their countrymen under Alvarado had got possession of the building.

It was indeed true. That gallant officer, whose position on the western causeway placed him near the district of Tlatelolco, had obeyed his commander's instructions to the letter, razing every building to the ground in his progress, and filling up the ditches with their ruins. He at length found himself before the great teocalli in the neighborhood of the market. He ordered a company, under a cavalier named Gutierre de Badajoz, to storm the place, which was defended by a body of warriors, mingled with priests, still more wild and ferocious than the soldiery. The garrison, rushing down the winding terraces, fell on the assailants with such fury as compelled them to retreat in confusion and with some loss. Alvarado ordered another detachment to their support. This last was engaged, at the moment, with a body of Aztecs, who hung on its rear as it wound up the galleries of the teocalli. Thus hemmed in between two enemies, above and below, the position of the Spaniards was critical. With sword and buckler, they plunged desperately on the ascending Mexicans, and drove them into the courtyard below, where Alvarado plied them with such lively volleys of musketry as soon threw them into disorder and compelled them to abandon the ground. Being thus rid of annoyance in the rear, the Spaniards returned to the charge. They drove the enemy up the heights of the pyramid, and, reaching the broad summit, a fierce encounter followed in mid-air—such an encounter as takes place where death is the certain consequence of defeat. It ended, as usual, in the discomfiture of the Aztecs, who were either slaughtered on the spot still wet with the blood of their own victims, or pitched headlong down the sides of the pyramid.

The area was covered with the various symbols of the barbarous worship of the country, and with two lofty sanctuaries, before whose grinning idols were displayed the heads of several Christian captives who had been immolated on their altars. Although overgrown by their long, matted hair and bushy beards, the Spaniards could recognize, in the livid countenances, their comrades who had fallen into the hands of the enemy. Tears fell from their eyes as they gazed on the melancholy spectacle and thought of the hideous death which their countrymen had suffered. They removed the sad relics with decent care, and after the Conquest deposited them in consecrated ground, on a spot since covered by the Church of the Martyrs.

They completed their work by firing the sanctuaries, that the place might be no more polluted by these abominable rites. The flame crept slowly up the lofty pinnacles, in which stone was mingled with wood, till at length, bursting into one bright blaze, it shot up its spiral volume to such a height that it was seen from the most distant quarters of the valley. It was this which had been hailed by the soldiery of Cortes, and it served as the beacon-light to both friend and foe, intimating the progress of the Christian arms.

The commander-in-chief and his division, animated by the spectacle, made, in their entrance on the following day, more determined efforts to place themselves alongside of their companions under Alvarado. The broad canal, above noticed as the only impediment now lying in his way, was to be traversed; and on the farther side the emaciated figures of the Aztec warriors were gathered in numbers to dispute the passage, like the gloomy shades that wander—an ancient poets tell us—on the banks of the infernal river. They poured down, however, a storm of missiles, which were no shades, on the heads of the Indian laborers while occupied with filling up the wide gap with the ruins of the surrounding buildings. Still they toiled on in defiance of the arrowy shower, fresh numbers taking the place of those who fell. And when at length the work was completed, the cavalry rode over the rough plain at full charge against the enemy, fol-

lowed by the deep array of spearmen, who bore down all opposition with their invincible phalanx.

The Spaniards now found themselves on the same ground
with Alvarado's division. Soon afterwards, that chief, attended
by several of his staff, rode into their lines, and cordially embraced his countrymen and companions in arms, for the first
time since the beginning of the siege. They were now in the
neighborhood of the market. Cortes, taking with him a few of
his cavaliers, galloped into it. It was a vast enclosure, as the
reader has already seen, covering many an acre. Its dimensions
were suited to the immense multitudes who gathered there from
all parts of the valley in the flourishing days of the Aztec monarchy. It was surrounded by porticoes and pavilions for the
accommodation of the artisans and traders who there displayed their various fabrics and articles of merchandise. The flat
roofs of the piazzas were now covered with crowds of men and
women, who gazed in silent dismay on the steel-clad horsemen,
that profaned these precincts with their presence for the first
time since their expulsion from the capital. The multitude, composed for the most part, probably, of unarmed citizens, seemed
taken by surprise; at least, they made no show of resistance; and
the general, after leisurely viewing the ground, was permitted to
ride back unmolested to the army.

On arriving there, he ascended the teocalli, from which the
standard of Castile, supplanting the memorials of Aztec superstition, was now triumphantly floating. The Conqueror, as he
strode among the smoking embers on the summit, calmly surveyed the scene of desolation below. The palaces, the temples,
the busy marts of industry and trade, the glittering canals, covered with their rich freights from the surrounding country, the
royal pomp of groves and gardens, all the splendors of the imperial city, the capital of the Western World, forever gone—
and in their place a barren wilderness! How different the spectacle which the year before had met his eye, as it wandered over
the same scenes from the heights of the neighboring teocalli,
with Montezuma at his side! Seven-eighths of the city were laid
in ruins, with the occasional exception, perhaps, of some colossal
temple which it would have required too much time to demolish.
The remaining eighth, comprehending the district of Tlatelolco,

was all that now remained to the Aztecs, whose population—still large after all its losses—was crowded into a compass that would hardly have afforded accommodations for a third of their numbers. It was the quarter lying between the great northern and western causeways, and is recognized in the modern capital as the Barrio de San Jago and its vicinity. It was the favorite residence of the Indians after the Conquest, though at the present day thinly covered with humble dwellings, forming the straggling suburbs, as it were, of the metropolis. Yet it still affords some faint vestiges of what it was in its prouder days; and the curious antiquary, and occasionally the laborer, as he turns up the soil, encounters a glittering fragment of obsidian, or the moldering head of a lance or arrow, or some other warlike relic, attesting that on this spot the retreating Aztecs made their last stand for the independence of their country.

On the day following, Cortes, at the head of his battalions, made a second entry into the great tianguez. But this time the Mexicans were better prepared for his coming. They were assembled in considerable force in the spacious square. A sharp encounter followed; but it was short. Their strength was not equal to their spirit, and they melted away before the rolling fire of musketry, and left the Spaniards masters of the enclosure.

The first act was to set fire to some temples, of no great size, within the market-place, or more probably on its borders. As the flames ascended, the Aztecs, horror-struck, broke forth into piteous lamentations at the destruction of the deities on whom they relied for protection.

The general's next step was at the suggestion of a soldier named Sotelo, a man who had served under the Great Captain in the Italian wars, where he professed to have gathered knowledge of the science of engineering, as it was then practiced. He offered his services to construct a sort of catapult, a machine for discharging stones of great size, which might take the place of the regular battering-train in demolishing the buildings. As the ammunition, notwithstanding the liberal supplies which from time to time had found their way into the camp, now began to fail, Cortes eagerly acceded to a proposal so well suited to his exigencies. Timber and stone were furnished, and a number of hands were employed, under the direction of the self-styled engineer, in constructing the ponderous apparatus, which was erected on a solid platform of masonry, thirty paces square and seven or eight feet high, that covered the center of the marketplace. This was a work of the Aztec princes, and was used as a scaffolding on which mountebanks and jugglers might exhibit their marvelous feats for the amusement of the populace, who took great delight in these performances.

The erection of the machine consumed several days, during which hostilities were suspended, while the artisans were protected from interruption by a strong corps of infantry. At length the work was completed; and the besieged, who with silent awe had beheld from the neighboring azoteas the progress of the mysterious engine which was to lay the remainder of their capital in ruins, now looked with terror for its operation. A stone of huge size was deposited on the timber. The machinery was set in motion; and the rocky fragment was discharged with a tremendous force from the catapult. But, instead of taking the direction of the Aztec buildings, it rose high and perpendicularly into the air, and, descending whence it sprung, broke the ill-omened machine into splinters! It was a total failure.

The Aztecs were released from their apprehensions, and the soldiery made many a merry jest on the catastrophe, somewhat at the expense of their commander, who testified no little vexation at the disappointment, and still more at his own credulity.

CHAPTER VIII

The Final Conquest

1521

There was no occasion to resort to artificial means to precipitate the ruin of the Aztecs. It was accelerated every hour by causes more potent than those arising from mere human agency. There they were—pent up in their close and suffocating quarters, nobles, commoners, and slaves, men, women, and children, some in houses, more frequently in hovels—for this part of the city was not the best—others in the open air in canoes, or in the streets, shivering in the cold rains of night, and scorched by the burning heat of day. An old chronicler mentions the fact of two women of rank remaining three days and nights up to their necks in the water among the reeds, with only a handful of maize for their support. The ordinary means of sustaining life were long since gone. They wandered about in search of anything, however unwholesome or revolting, that might mitigate the fierce gnawings of hunger. Some hunted for insects and worms on the borders of the lake, or gathered the salt weeds and moss from its bottom, while at times they might be seen casting a wistful look at the green hills beyond, which many of them had left to share the fate of their brethren in the capital.

To their credit, it is said by the Spanish writers that they were not driven, in their extremity, to violate the laws of nature by feeding on one another. But, unhappily, this is contradicted by the Indian authorities, who state that many a mother, in her agony, devoured the offspring which she had no longer the means of supporting. This is recorded of more than one siege in history; and it is the more probable here, where the sensibilities must have been blunted by familiarity with the brutal practices of the national superstition.

But all was not sufficient, and hundreds of famished wretches died every day from extremity of suffering. Some dragged themselves into the houses, and drew their last breath alone and in silence. Others sank down in the public streets. Wherever they died, there they were left. There was no one to bury or to remove them. Familiarity with the spectacle made men indifferent to it. They looked on in dumb despair, waiting for their own turn. There was no complaint, no lamentation, but deep, unutterable woe.

If in other quarters of the town the corpses might be seen scattered over the streets, here they were gathered in heaps. "They lay so thick," says Bernal Diaz, "that one could not tread except among the bodies." "A man could not set his foot down," says Cortes, yet more strongly, "unless on the corpse of an Indian." They were piled one upon another, the living mingled with the dead. They stretched themselves on the bodies of their friends, and lay down to sleep there. Death was everywhere. The city was a vast charnel-house, in which all was hastening to decay and decomposition. A poisonous steam arose from the mass of putrefaction, under the action of alternate rain and heat, which so tainted the whole atmosphere that the Spaniards, including the general himself, in their brief visits to the quarter, were made ill by it, and it bred a pestilence that swept off even greater numbers than the famine.

Men's minds were unsettled by these strange and accumulated horrors. They resorted to all the superstitious rites prescribed by their religion, to stay the pestilence. They called on their priests to invoke the gods in their behalf. But the oracles were dumb, or gave only gloomy responses. Their deities had deserted them, and in their place they saw signs of celestial wrath, telling of still greater woes in reserve. Many, after the siege, declared that, among other prodigies, they beheld a stream of light, of a blood-red color, coming from the north in the direction of Tepejacac, with a rushing noise like that of a whirlwind, which swept round the district of Tlatelolco, darting out sparkles and flakes of fire, till it shot far into the center of the lake! In the disordered state of their nerves, a mysterious fear took possession of their senses. Prodigies were of familiar occurrence, and the most familiar phenomena of nature were converted into prodigies. Stunned by their calamities, reason was bewildered, and they became the sport of the wildest and most superstitious fancies.

In the midst of these awful scenes, the young emperor of the Aztecs remained, according to all accounts, calm and courageous. With his fair capital laid in ruins before his eyes, his nobles and faithful subjects dying around him, his territory rent away, foot by foot, till scarce enough remained for him to stand on, he rejected every invitation to capitulate, and showed the same indomitable spirit as at the commencement of the siege. When Cortes, in the hope that the extremities of the besieged would incline them to listen to an accommodation, persuaded a noble prisoner to bear to Guatemozin his proposals to that effect, the fierce young monarch, according to the general, ordered him at once to be sacrificed. It is a Spaniard, we must remember, who tells the story.

Cortes, who had suspended hostilities for several days, in the vain hope that the distresses of the Mexicans would bend them to submission, now determined to drive them to it by a general assault. Cooped up as they were within a narrow quarter of the city, their position favored such an attempt. He commanded Alvarado to hold himself in readiness, and directed Sandoval—who, besides the causeway, had charge of the fleet, which lay off the Tlatelolcan district—to support the attack by a cannonade on the houses near the water. He then led his forces into the city, or rather across the horrid waste that now encircled it.

On entering the Indian precincts, he was met by several of the chiefs, who, stretching forth their emaciated arms, exclaimed, "You are the children of the Sun. But the Sun is swift in his course. Why are you, then, so tardy? Why do you delay so long to put an end to our miseries? Rather kill us at once, that we may go to our god Huitzilopochtli, who waits for us in heaven to give us rest from our sufferings!"

Cortes was moved by their piteous appeal, and answered that he desired not their death, but their submission. "Why does your master refuse to treat with me," he said, "when a single hour will suffice for me to crush him and all his people?" He then urged them to request Guatemozin to confer with him, with the assurance that he might do it in safety, as his person should not be molested.

The nobles, after some persuasion, undertook the mission; and it was received by the young monarch in a manner which showed—if the anecdote before related of him be true—that misfortune had at length asserted some power over his haughty spirit. He consented to the interview, though not to have it take place on that day, but the following, in the great square of Tlatelolco. Cortes, well satisfied, immediately withdrew from the city and resumed his position on the causeway.

The next morning he presented himself at the place appointed, having previously stationed Alvarado there with a strong corps of infantry, to guard against treachery. The stone platform in the center of the square was covered with mats and carpets, and a banquet was prepared to refresh the famished monarch and his nobles. Having made these arrangements, he awaited the hour of the interview.

But Guatemozin, instead of appearing himself, sent his nobles, the same who had brought to him the general's invitation, and who now excused their master's absence on the plea of illness. Cortes, though disappointed, gave a courteous reception to the

envoys, considering that it might still afford the means of opening a communication with the emperor. He persuaded them,
without much entreaty, to partake of the good cheer spread before them, which they did with a voracity that told how severe
had been their abstinence. He then dismissed them with a seasonable supply of provisions for their master, pressing him to consent to an interview, without which it was impossible their differences could be adjusted.

The Indian envoys returned in a short time, bearing with them
a present of fine cotton fabrics, of no great value, from Guatemozin, who still declined to meet the Spanish general. Cortes,
though deeply chagrined, was unwilling to give up the point. "He
will surely come," he said to the envoys, "when he sees that I
suffer you to go and come unharmed, you who have been my
steady enemies, no less than himself, throughout the war. He
has nothing to fear from me." He again parted with them, promising to receive their answer the following day.

On the next morning the Aztec chiefs, entering the Christian
quarters, announced to Cortes that Guatemozin would confer
with him at noon in the market-place. The general was punctual
at the hour; but without success. Neither monarch nor ministers
appeared there. It was plain that the Indian prince did not care
to trust the promises of his enemy. A thought of Montezuma
may have passed across his mind. After he had waited three
hours, the general's patience was exhausted, and, as he learned
that the Mexicans were busy in preparations for defense, he
made immediate dispositions for the assault.

The confederates had been left without the walls; for he did
not care to bring them within sight of the quarry before he was
ready to slip the leash. He now ordered them to join him, and,
supported by Alvarado's division, marched at once into the
enemy's quarters. He found them prepared to receive him. Their
most able-bodied warriors were thrown into the van, covering
their feeble and crippled comrades. Women were seen occasionally mingling in the ranks, and, as well as children, thronged
the azoteas, where, with famine-stricken visages and haggard
eyes, they scowled defiance and hatred on their invaders.

As the Spaniards advanced, the Mexicans set up a fierce war-
cry, and sent off clouds of arrows with their accustomed spirit,
while the women and boys rained down darts and stones from

their elevated position on the terraces. But the missiles were sent by hands too feeble to do much damage; and, when the squadrons closed, the loss of strength became still more sensible in the Aztecs. Their blows fell feebly and with doubtful aim, though some, it is true, of stronger constitution, or gathering strength from despair, maintained to the last a desperate fight.

The arquebusiers now poured in a deadly fire. The brigantines replied by successive volleys, in the opposite quarter. The besieged, hemmed in, like deer surrounded by the huntsmen, were brought down on every side. The carnage was horrible. The ground was heaped up with slain, until the maddened combatants were obliged to climb over the human mounds to get at one another. The miry soil was saturated with blood, which ran off like water and dyed the canals themselves with crimson. All was uproar and terrible confusion. The hideous yells of the barbarians, the oaths and execrations of the Spaniards, the cries of the wounded, the shrieks of women and children, the heavy blows of the Conquerors, the death-struggle of their victims, the rapid, reverberating echoes of musketry, the hissing of innumerable missiles, the crash and crackling of blazing buildings, crushing hundreds in their ruins, the blinding volumes of dust and sulphurous smoke shrouding all in their gloomy canopy, made a scene appalling even to the soldiers of Cortes, steeled as they were by many a rough passage of war, and by long familiarity with blood and violence. "The piteous cries of the women and children, in particular," says the general, "were enough to break one's heart." He commanded that they should be spared, and that all who asked it should receive quarter. He particularly urged this on the confederates, and placed Spaniards among them to restrain their violence. But he had set an engine in motion too terrible to be controlled. It were as easy to curb the hurricane in its fury, as the passions of an infuriated horde of savages. "Never did I see so pitiless a race," he exclaims, "or anything wearing the form of man so destitute of humanity." They made no distinction of sex or age, and in this hour of vengeance seemed to be requiting the hoarded wrongs of a century. At length, sated with slaughter, the Spanish commander sounded a retreat. It was full time, if, according to his own statement—we may hope it is an exaggeration—forty thousand souls had perished! Yet their fate was to be envied, in comparison with that of those who survived.

Through the long night which followed, no movement was perceptible in the Aztec quarter. No light was seen there, no sound was heard, save the low moaning of some wounded or dying wretch, writhing in his agony. All was dark and silent— the darkness of the grave. The last blow seemed to have completely stunned them. They had parted with hope, and sat in sullen despair, like men waiting in silence the stroke of the executioner. Yet, for all this, they showed no disposition to submit. Every new injury had sunk deeper into their souls, and filled them with a deeper hatred of their enemy. Fortune, friends, kindred, home—all were gone. They were content to throw away life itself, now that they had nothing more to live for.

Far different was the scene in the Christian camp, where, elated with their recent successes, all was alive with bustle and preparation for the morrow. Bonfires were seen blazing along the causeways, lights gleamed from tents and barracks, and the sounds of music and merriment, borne over the waters, proclaimed the joy of the soldiers at the prospect of so soon terminating their wearisome campaign.

On the following morning the Spanish commander again mustered his forces, having decided to follow up the blow of the preceding day before the enemy should have time to rally, and at once to put an end to the war. He had arranged with Alvarado, on the evening previous, to occupy the market-place of Tlatelolco; and the discharge of an arquebuse was to be the signal for a simultaneous assault. Sandoval was to hold the northern causeway, and, with the fleet, to watch the movements of the Indian emperor, and to intercept the flight to the mainland, which Cortes knew he meditated. To allow him to effect this would be to leave a formidable enemy in his own neighborhood, who might at any time kindle the flame of insurrection throughout the country. He ordered Sandoval, however, to do no harm to the royal person, and not to fire on the enemy at all, except in self-defense.

It was the memorable thirteenth of August, 1521, the day of St. Hippolytus—from this circumstance selected as the patron saint of modern Mexico—that Cortes led his warlike array for the last time across the black and blasted environs which lay around the Indian capital. On entering the Aztec precincts, he paused, willing to afford its wretched inmates one more chance of escape before striking the fatal blow. He obtained an interview with some of the principal chiefs, and expostulated with them on the conduct of their prince. "He surely will not," said the general, "see you all perish, when he can so easily save you." He then urged them to prevail on Guatemozin to hold a conference with him, repeating the assurances of his personal safety.

The messengers went on their mission, and soon returned with the cihuacoatl at their head, a magistrate of high authority among the Mexicans. He said, with a melancholy air, in which his own disappointment was visible, that "Guatemozin was ready to die where he was, but would hold no interview with the Spanish commander"; adding, in a tone of resignation, "it is for you to work your pleasure." "Go, then," replied the stern Conqueror, "and prepare your countrymen for death. Their hour is come."

He still postponed the assault for several hours. But the impatience of his troops at this delay was heightened by the rumor that Guatemozin and his nobles were preparing to escape with their effects in the piraguas and canoes which were moored on the margin of the lake. Convinced of the fruitlessness and impolicy of further procrastination, Cortes made his final dispositions for the attack, and took his own station on an azotea which commanded the theater of operations.

When the assailants came into the presence of the enemy, they found them huddled together in the utmost confusion, all ages and sexes, in masses so dense that they nearly forced one another over the brink of the causeways into the water below. Some had climbed on the terraces, others feebly supported themselves against the walls of the buildings. Their squalid and tattered garments gave a wildness to their appearance which still further heightened the ferocity of their expression, as they glared on their enemy with eyes in which hate was mingled with despair. When the Spaniards had approached within bowshot, the Aztecs let off a flight of impotent missiles, showing to the last the resolute spirit, though they had lost the strength, of their better days. The fatal signal was then given by the discharge of an arquebuse—speedily followed by peals of heavy ordnance, the rattle of firearms, and the hellish shouts of the confederates as they sprang upon their victims. It is unnecessary to stain the page with a repetition of the horrors of the preceding day. Some of the wretched Aztecs threw themselves into the water and were picked up by the canoes. Others sank and were suffocated in the canals. The number of these became so great that a bridge was made of their dead bodies, over which the assailants could climb to the opposite banks. Others again, especially the women, begged for mercy, which, as the chroniclers assure us, was everywhere granted by the Spaniards, and, contrary to the instructions and entreaties of Cortes, everywhere refused by the confederates.

While this work of butchery was going on, numbers were observed pushing off in the barks that lined the shore, and making the best of their way across the lake. They were constantly intercepted by the brigantines, which broke through the flimsy array of boats, sending off their volleys to the right and left, as the crews of the latter hotly assailed them. The battle raged as fiercely on the lake as on the land. Many of the Indian vessels were shattered and overturned. Some few, however, under cover of the smoke, which rolled darkly over the waters, succeeded in clearing themselves of the turmoil, and were fast nearing the opposite shore.

Sandoval had particularly charged his captains to keep an eye on the movements of any vessel in which it was at all probable that Guatemozin might be concealed. At this crisis, three or four of the largest piraguas were seen skimming over the water and making their way rapidly across the lake. A captain, named Garci Holguin, who had command of one of the best sailers in the fleet, instantly gave them chase. The wind was favorable, and every moment he gained on the fugitives, who pulled their oars with a vigor that despair alone could have given. But it was in vain; and, after a short race, Holguin, coming alongside of one of the piraguas, which, whether from its appearance or from information he had received, he conjectured might bear the Indian emperor, ordered his men to level their crossbows at the boat. But, before they could discharge them, a cry arose from those in it that their lord was on board. At the same moment a young warrior, armed with buckler and maquahuitl, rose up, as if to beat off the assailants. But, as the Spanish captain ordered his men not to shoot, he dropped his weapons, and exclaimed, "I am

Guatemozin. Lead me to Malinche; I am his prisoner; but let no harm come to my wife and my followers."

Holguin assured him that his wishes should be respected, and assisted him to get on board the brigantine, followed by his wife and attendants. These were twenty in number, consisting of Coanaco, the deposed lord of Tezcuco, the lord of Tlacopan, and several other caciques and dignitaries, whose rank, probably, had secured them some exemption from the general calamities of the siege. When the captives were seated on the deck of his vessel, Holguin requested the Aztec prince to put an end to the combat by commanding his people in the other canoes to surrender. But, with a dejected air, he replied, "It is not necessary. They will fight no longer, when they see that their prince is taken." He spoke truth. The news of Guatemozin's capture spread rapidly through the fleet, and on shore, where the Mexicans were still engaged in conflict with their enemies. It ceased, however, at once. They made no further resistance; and those on the water quickly followed the brigantines, which conveyed their captive monarch to land. It seemed as if the fight had been maintained thus long the better to divert the enemy's attention and cover their master's retreat.

Meanwhile, Sandoval, on receiving tidings of the capture, brought his own brigantine alongside of Holguin's and demanded the royal prisoner to be surrendered to him. But the captain claimed him as his prize. A dispute arose between the parties, each anxious to have the glory of the deed, and perhaps the privilege of commemorating it on his escutcheon. The controversy continued so long that it reached the ears of Cortes, who, in his station on the azotea, had learned with no little satisfaction the capture of his enemy. He instantly sent orders to his wrangling officers to bring Guatemozin before him, that he might adjust the difference between them. He charged them, at the same time, to treat their prisoner with respect. He then made preparations for the interview, caused the terrace to be carpeted with crimson cloth and matting, and a table to be spread with provisions, of which the unhappy Aztecs stood so much in need. His lovely Indian mistress, Doña Marina, was present to act as interpreter. She had stood by his side through all the troubled scenes of the Conquest, and she was there now to witness its triumphant termination.

Guatemozin, on landing, was escorted by a company of infantry to the presence of the Spanish commander. He mounted the azotea with a calm and steady step, and was easily to be distinguished from his attendant nobles, though his full, dark eye was no longer lighted up with its accustomed fire, and his features wore an expression of passive resignation, that told little of the fierce and fiery spirit that burned within. His head was large, his limbs well proportioned, his complexion fairer than that of his bronze-colored nation, and his whole deportment singularly mild and engaging.

Cortes came forward with a dignified and studied courtesy to receive him. The Aztec monarch probably knew the person of his conqueror, for he first broke silence by saying, "I have done all that I could to defend myself and my people. I am now reduced to this state. You will deal with me, Malinche, as you list." Then, laying his hand on the hilt of a poniard stuck in the general's belt, he added, with vehemence, "Better despatch me with this, and rid me of life at once." Cortes was filled with admiration at the proud bearing of the young barbarian, showing in his reverses a spirit worthy of an ancient Roman. "Fear not," he replied: "you shall be treated with all honor. You have defended your capital like a brave warrior. A Spaniard knows how to respect valor even in an enemy." He then inquired of him where he had left the princess his wife; and, being informed that she still remained under protection of a Spanish guard on board the brigantine, the general sent to have her escorted to his presence.

She was the youngest daughter of Montezuma, and was hardly yet on the verge of womanhood. On the accession of her cousin Guatemozin to the throne, she had been wedded to him as his lawful wife. She is celebrated by her contemporaries for her personal charms; and the beautiful princess Tecuichpo is still commemorated by the Spaniards, since from her by a subsequent marriage are descended some of the illustrious families of their own nation. She was kindly received by Cortes, who showed her the respectful attentions suited to her rank. Her birth, no doubt, gave her an additional interest in his eyes, and he may have felt some touch of compunction as he gazed on the daughter of the unfortunate Montezuma. He invited his royal captives to partake of the refreshments which their exhausted condition rendered so necessary. Meanwhile the Spanish commander made his dispositions for the night, ordering Sandoval to escort the prisoners to Cojohuacan, whither he proposed himself immediately to follow. The other captains, Olid and Alvarado, were to draw off their forces to their respective quarters. It was impossible for them to continue in the capital, where the poisonous effluvia from the unburied carcasses loaded the air with infection. A small guard only was stationed to keep order in the wasted suburbs. It was the hour of vespers when Guatemozin surrendered, and the siege might be considered as then concluded. The evening set in dark, and the rain began to fall before the several parties had evacuated the city.

During the night, a tremendous tempest, such as the Spaniards had rarely witnessed, and such as is known only within the tropics, burst over the Mexican Valley. The thunder, reverberating from the rocky amphitheater of hills, bellowed over the waste of waters, and shook the teocallis and crazy tenements of Tenochtitlan—the few that yet survived—to their foundations. The lightning seemed to cleave asunder the vault of heaven, as its vivid flashes wrapped the whole scene in a ghastly glare, for a moment, to be again swallowed up in darkness. The war of elements was in unison with the fortunes of the ruined city. It seemed as if the deities of Anahuac, scared from their ancient abodes, were borne along shrieking and howling in the blast, as they abandoned the fallen capital to its fate!

On the day following the surrender, Guatemozin requested the Spanish commander to allow the Mexicans to leave the city and to pass unmolested into the open country. To this Cortes readily assented, as, indeed, without it he could take no steps for purifying the capital. He gave his orders, accordingly, for the evacuation of the place, commanding that no one, Spaniard or confederate, should offer violence to the Aztecs or in any way obstruct their departure. The whole number of these is variously estimated at from thirty to seventy thousand, besides women and children, who had survived the sword, pestilence, and famine. It is certain they were three days in defiling along the several causeways—a mournful train; husbands and wives, parents and children, the sick and the wounded, leaning on one another for support, as they feebly tottered along, squalid, and but half covered with rags, that disclosed at every step hideous gashes, some recently received, others festering from long neglect, and carrying with them an atmosphere of contagion. Their wasted forms and famine-stricken faces told the whole history of the siege; and, as the straggling files gained the opposite shore, they were observed to pause from time to time, as if to take one more look at the spot so lately crowned by the imperial city, once their pleasant home, and endeared to them by many a glorious recollection.

On the departure of the inhabitants, measures were immediately taken to purify the place, by means of numerous fires kept burning day and night, especially in the infected quarter of Tlatelolco, and by collecting the heaps of dead, which lay moldering in the streets, and consigning them to the earth. Of the whole number who perished in the course of the siege it is impossible to form any probable computation. The accounts range widely, from one hundred and twenty thousand, the lowest estimate, to two hundred and forty thousand. The number of the Spaniards who fell was comparatively small, but that of the allies must have been large, if the historian of Tezcuco is correct in asserting that thirty thousand perished of his own countrymen alone. That the number of those destroyed within the city was immense cannot be doubted, when we consider that, besides its own redundant population, it was thronged with that of the neighboring towns, who, distrusting their strength to resist the enemy, sought protection within its walls.

The booty found there—that is, the treasures of gold and jewels, the only booty of much value in the eyes of the Spaniards —fell far below their expectations. It did not exceed, according to the general's statement, a hundred and thirty thousand castellanos of gold, including the sovereign's share, which, indeed, taking into account many articles of curious and costly workmanship, voluntarily relinquished by the army, greatly exceeded his legitimate fifth. Yet the Aztecs must have been in possession of a much larger treasure, if it were only the wreck of that recovered from the Spaniards on the night of the memorable flight from Mexico. Some of the spoil may have been sent away from the capital, some spent in preparations for defense, and more of it buried in the earth, or sunk in the water of the lake. Their menaces were not without a meaning. They had, at least, the satisfaction of disappointing the avarice of their enemies.

Cortes had no further occasion for the presence of his Indian allies. He assembled the chiefs of the different squadrons, thanked them for their services, noticed their valor in flattering terms, and, after distributing presents among them, with the assurance that his master the emperor would recompense their fidelity yet more largely, dismissed them to their own homes. They carried off a liberal share of the spoils of which they had plundered the dwellings—not of a kind to excite the cupidity of of the Spaniards—and returned in triumph, short-sighted triumph! at the success of their expedition and the downfall of the Aztec dynasty.

Great, also, was the satisfaction of the Spaniards at this brilliant termination of their long and laborious campaign. They were, indeed, disappointed at the small amount of treasure found in the conquered city. But the soldier is usually too much absorbed in the present to give much heed to the future; and, though their discontent showed itself afterwards in a more clamorous form, they now thought only of their triumph, and abandoned themselves to jubilee. Cortes celebrated the event by a banquet, as sumptuous as circumstances would permit, to which all the cavaliers and officers were invited. Loud and long was their revelry, which was carried to such an excess as provoked the animadversion of Father Olmedo, who intimated that this was not the fitting way to testify their sense of the favors shown them by the Almighty. Cortes admitted the justice of the rebuke, but craved some indulgence for a soldier's license in the hour of victory. The following day was appointed for the commemoration of their successes in a more suitable manner.

A procession of the whole army was then formed, with Father Olmedo at its head. The soiled and tattered banners of Castile, which had waved over many a field of battle, now threw their shadows on the peaceful array of the soldiery, as they slowly moved along, rehearsing the litany, and displaying the image of the Virgin and the blessed symbol of man's redemption. The reverend father pronounced a discourse, in which he briefly reminded the troops of their great cause for thankfulness to Providence for conducting them safe through their long and perilous pilgrimage; and, dwelling on the responsibility incurred by their present position, he besought them not to abuse the rights of conquest, but to treat the unfortunate Indians with humanity. The sacrament was then administered to the commander-in-chief and the principal cavaliers, and the services concluded with a solemn thanksgiving to the God of battles, who had enabled them to carry the banner of the cross triumphant over this barbaric empire.

Thus, after a siege of nearly three months' duration, unmatched in history for the constancy and courage of the besieged, seldom surpassed for the severity of its sufferings, fell the renowned capital of the Aztecs. Unmatched, it may be truly said, for constancy and courage, when we recollect that the door of capitulation on the most honorable terms was left open to them throughout the whole blockade, and that, sternly rejecting every proposal of their enemy, they, to a man, preferred to die rather than surrender. More than three centuries had elapsed since the Aztecs, a poor and wandering tribe from the far Northwest, had come on the plateau. There they built their miserable collection of huts on the spot—as tradition tells us—prescribed by the oracle. Their conquests, at first confined to their immediate neighborhood, gradually covered the valley, then, crossing the mountains, swept over the broad extent of the tableland, descended its precipitous sides, and rolled onwards to the Mexican Gulf and the distant confines of Central America. Their wretched capital, meanwhile, keeping pace with the enlargement of territory, had grown into a flourishing city, filled with buildings, monuments of art, and a numerous population, that gave it the first rank among the capitals of the Western World. At this crisis came over another race from the remote East, strangers like themselves, whose coming had also been predicted by the oracle, and, appearing on the plateau, assailed them in the very zenith of their prosperity, and blotted them out from the map of nations forever! The whole story has the air of fable rather than of history! a legend of romance—a tale of the genii!

Yet we cannot regret the fall of an empire which did so little to promote the happiness of its subjects or the real interests of humanity. Notwithstanding the luster thrown over its latter days by the glorious defense of its capital, by the mild munificence of Montezuma, by the dauntless heroism of Guatemozin, the Aztecs were emphatically a fierce and brutal race, little calculated, in their best aspects, to excite our sympathy and regard. Their civilization, such as it was, was not their own, but reflected, perhaps imperfectly, from a race whom they had succeeded in the land. It was, in respect to the Aztecs, a generous graft on a vicious stock, and could have brought no fruit to perfection. They ruled over their wide domains with a sword, instead of a scepter. They did nothing to ameliorate the condition or in any way promote the progress of their vassals. Their vassals were serfs, used only to minister to their pleasure, held in awe by armed garrisons, ground to the dust by imposts in peace, by military conscriptions in war. They did not, like the Romans, whom they resembled in the nature of their conquests, extend the rights of citizenship to the conquered. They did not amalgamate them into one great nation, with common rights and interests. They held them as aliens—even those who in the valley were gathered round the very walls of the capital. The Aztec metropolis, the heart of the monarchy, had not a sympathy, not a pulsation, in common with the rest of the body politic. It was a stranger in its own land.

The Aztecs not only did not advance the condition of their vassals, but, morally speaking, they did much to degrade it. How can a nation where human sacrifices prevail, and especially when combined with cannibalism, further the march of civilization? How can the interests of humanity be consulted, where man is leveled to the rank of the brutes that perish? The influence of the Aztecs introduced their gloomy superstition into lands before unacquainted with it, or where, at least, it was not established in any great strength. The example of the capital was contagious. As the latter increased in opulence, the religious celebrations were conducted with still more terrible magnificence; in the same manner as the gladiatorial shows of the Romans increased in pomp with the increasing splendor of the capital. Men became familiar with scenes of horror and the most loathsome abominations. Women and children—the whole nation—became familiar with and assisted at them. The heart was hardened, the manners were made ferocious, the feeble light of civilization, transmitted from a milder race, was growing fainter and fainter, as thousands and thousands of miserable victims, throughout the empire, were yearly fattened in its cages, sacrificed on its altars, dressed and served at its banquets! The whole land was converted into vast human shambles! The empire of the Aztecs did not fall before its time.

Whether these unparalleled outrages furnish a sufficient plea to the Spaniards for their invasion, whether, with the Protestant, we are content to find a warrant for it in the natural rights and demands of civilization, or, with the Roman Catholic, in the good pleasure of the pope—on the one or other of which grounds the conquests by most Christian nations in the East and the West have been defended—it is unnecessary to discuss, as it has already been considered in a former chapter. It is more material to inquire whether, assuming the right, the Conquest of Mexico was conducted with a proper regard to the claims of humanity. And here we must admit that, with all allowance for the ferocity of the age and the laxity of its principles, there are passages which every Spaniard who cherishes the fame of his countrymen would be glad to see expunged from their history; passages not to be vindicated on the score of self-defense, or of necessity of any kind, and which must forever leave a dark spot on the annals of the Conquest. And yet, taken as a whole, the invasion, up to the capture of the capital, was conducted on principles less revolting to humanity than most, perhaps than any, of the other conquests of the Castilian crown in the New World.

It may seem slight praise to say that the followers of Cortes used no bloodhounds to hunt down their wretched victims, as in some other parts of the continent, nor exterminated a peaceful and submissive population in mere wantonness of cruelty, as in the islands. Yet it is something that they were not so far infected by the spirit of the age, and that their swords were rarely stained with blood unless it was indispensable to the success of their enterprise. Even in the last siege of the capital, the sufferings of the Aztecs, terrible as they were, do not imply any unusual cruelty in the victors; they were not greater than those inflicted on their own countrymen at home, in many a memorable instance, by the most polished nations, not merely of ancient times, but of our own. They were the inevitable consequences which follow from war when, instead of being confined to its legitimate field, it is brought home to the hearthstone, to the peaceful community of the city—its burghers untrained to arms, its women and children yet more defenseless. In the present instance, indeed, the sufferings of the besieged were in a great degree to be charged on themselves—on their patriotic but desperate self-devotion. It was not the desire, as certainly it was not the interest, of the Spaniards to destroy the capital or its inhabitants. When any of these fell into their hands, they were kindly entertained, their wants supplied, and every means taken to infuse into them a spirit of conciliation; and this, too, it should be remembered, in despite of the dreadful doom to which they consigned their Christian captives. The gates of a fair capitulation were kept open, though unavailingly, to the last hour.

The right of conquest necessarily implies that of using whatever force may be necessary for overcoming resistance to the assertion of that right. For the Spaniards to have done otherwise than they did would have been to abandon the siege, and, with it, the conquest of the country. To have suffered the inhabitants, with their high-spirited monarch, to escape, would but have prolonged the miseries of war by transferring it to another and more inaccessible quarter. They literally, so far as the success of the expedition was concerned, had no choice. If our imagination is struck with the amount of suffering in this and in similar scenes of the Conquest, it should be borne in mind that it was a natural result of the great masses of men engaged in the conflict. The amount of suffering does not of itself show the amount of cruelty which caused it; and it is but justice to the Conquerors of Mexico to say that the very brilliancy and importance of their exploits have given a melancholy celebrity to their misdeeds, and thrown them into somewhat bolder relief than strictly belongs to them. It is proper that thus much should be stated, not to excuse their excesses, but that we may be enabled to make a more impartial estimate of their conduct as compared with that of other nations under similar circumstances, and that we may not visit them with peculiar obloquy for evils which necessarily flow from the condition of war. I have not drawn a veil over these evils; for the historian should not shrink from depicting in their true colors the atrocities of a condition over which success is apt to throw a false halo of glory, but which, bursting asunder the strong bonds of human fellowship, purchases its triumphs by arming the hand of man against his brother, makes a savage of the civilized, and kindles the fires of hell in the bosom of the savage.

Whatever may be thought of the Conquest in a moral view, regarded as a military achievement it must fill us with astonishment. That a handful of adventurers, indifferently armed and equipped, should have landed on the shores of a powerful empire inhabited by a fierce and warlike race, and, in defiance of the reiterated prohibitions of its sovereign, have forced their way into the interior; that they should have done this without knowledge of the language or of the land, without chart or compass to guide them, without any idea of the difficulties they were to encounter, totally uncertain whether the next step might bring them on a hostile nation or on a desert, feeling their way along in the dark, as it were; that, though nearly overwhelmed in their first encounter with the inhabitants, they should have still pressed on to the capital of the empire, and, having reached it, thrown themselves unhesitatingly into the midst of their enemies; that, so far from being daunted by the extraordinary spectacle there exhibited of power and civilization, they should have been but the more confirmed in their original design; that they should have seized the monarch, have executed his ministers before the eyes of his subjects, and, when driven forth with ruin from the gates, have gathered their scattered wreck together, and, after a system of operations pursued with consummate policy and daring, have succeeded in overturning the capital and establishing their sway over the country; that all this should have been so effected by a mere handful of indigent adventurers, is a fact little short of the miraculous—too startling for the probabilities demanded by fiction, and without a parallel in the pages of history.

Yet this must not be understood too literally; for it would be unjust to the Aztecs themselves, at least to their military prowess, to regard the Conquest as directly achieved by the Spaniards alone. This would indeed be to arm the latter with the charmed shield of Ruggiero, and the magic lance of Astolfo, overturning its hundreds at a touch. The Indian empire was in a manner conquered by Indians. The first terrible encounter of the Spaniards with the Tlascalans, which had nearly proved their ruin, did in fact insure their success. It secured to them a strong native support on which to retreat in the hour of trouble, and round which they could rally the kindred races of the land for one great and overwhelming assault. The Aztec monarchy fell by the hands of its own subjects, under the direction of European sagacity and science. Had it been united, it might have bidden defiance to the invaders. As it was, the capital was dissevered from the rest of the country, and the bolt, which might have passed off comparatively harmless had the empire been cemented by a common principle of loyalty and patriotism, now found its way into every crack and crevice of the ill-compacted fabric and buried it in its own ruins. Its fate may serve as a striking proof that a government which does not rest on the sympathies of its subjects cannot long abide; that human institutions, when not connected with human prosperity and progress, must fall—if not before the increasing light of civilization, by the hand of violence; by violence from within, if not from without. And who shall lament their fall?

BOOK VII

The Final Years of Cortes

1530–1547

Early in the spring of 1530, Cortes embarked for New Spain. He was accompanied by the marchioness, his wife, together with his aged mother, who had the good fortune to live to see her son's elevation, and by a magnificent retinue of pages and attendants, such as belonged to the household of a powerful noble. How different from the forlorn condition in which, twenty-six years before, he had been cast loose, as a wild adventurer, to seek his bread upon the waters!

The first point of his destination was Hispaniola, where he was to remain until he received tidings of the organization of the new government that was to take charge of Mexico. In the preceding chapter it was stated that the administration of the country had been intrusted to a body called the Royal Audience; one of whose first duties it was to investigate the charges brought against Cortes. Nuñez de Guzman, his avowed enemy, was placed at the head of this board; and the investigation was conducted with all the rancor of personal hostility. A remarkable document still exists, called the Pesquisa Secreta, or "Secret Inquiry," which contains a record of the proceedings against Cortes. It was prepared by the secretary of the Audience, and signed by the several members. The document is very long, embracing nearly a hundred folio pages. The name and the testimony of every witness are given, and the whole forms a mass of loathsome details, such as might better suit a prosecution in a petty municipal court than that of a great officer of the crown.

The charges are eight in number; involving, among other crimes, that of a deliberate design to cast off his allegiance to the crown; that of the murder of two of the commissioners who had been sent out to supersede him; of the murder of his own wife, Catalina Xuarez; of extortion, and of licentious practices—of offenses, in short, which, from their private nature, would seem to have little to do with his conduct as a public man. The testimony is vague and often contradictory; the witnesses are for the most part obscure individuals, and the few persons of consideration among them appear to have been taken from the ranks of his decided enemies. When it is considered that the inquiry was conducted in the absence of Cortes, before a court the members of which were personally unfriendly to him, and that he was furnished with no specification of the charges, and had no opportunity, consequently, of disproving them, it is impossible, at this distance of time, to attach any importance to this paper as a legal document. When it is added that no action was taken on it by the government to whom it was sent, we may be disposed to regard it simply as a monument of the malice of his enemies. It has been drawn by the curious antiquary from the obscurity to which it had been so long consigned in the Indian archives at Seville; but it can be of no further use to the historian than to show that a great name in the sixteenth century exposed its possessor to calumnies as malignant as it has at any time since.

The high-handed measures of the Audience, and the oppressive conduct of Guzman, especially towards the Indians, excited general indignation in the colony and led to serious apprehensions of an insurrection. It became necessary to supersede an administration so reckless and unprincipled. But Cortes was detained two months at the island, by the slow movements of the Castilian court, before tidings reached him of the appointment of a new Audience for the government of the country. The person selected to preside over it was the bishop of St. Domingo, a prelate whose acknowledged wisdom and virtue gave favorable augury for the conduct of his administration. After this, Cortes resumed his voyage, and landed at Villa Rica on the 15th of July, 1530.

After remaining for a time in the neighborhood, where he received some petty annoyances from the Audience, he proceeded to Tlascala, and publicly proclaimed his powers as Captain-General of New Spain and the South Sea. An edict issued by the empress during her husband's absence had interdicted Cortes from approaching within ten leagues of the Mexican capital while the present authorities were there. The empress was afraid of a collision between the parties. Cortes, however, took up his residence on the opposite side of the lake, at Tezcuco.

No sooner was his arrival there known in the metropolis than multitudes, both of Spaniards and natives, crossed the lake to pay their respects to their old commander, to offer him their services, and to complain of their manifold grievances. It seemed as if the whole population of the capital was pouring into the neighboring city, where the marquis maintained the state of an independent potentate. The members of the Audience, indignant at the mortifying contrast which their own diminished court presented, imposed heavy penalties on such of the natives as should be found in Tezcuco, and, affecting to consider themselves in danger, made preparations for the defense of the city. But these belligerent movements were terminated by the arrival of the new Audience; though Guzman had the address to maintain his hold on a northern province, where he earned a reputation for cruelty and extortion unrivaled even in the annals of the New World.

Everything seemed now to assure a tranquil residence to Cortes. The new magistrates treated him with marked respect, and took his advice on the most important measures of government. Unhappily, this state of things did not long continue; and a misunderstanding arose between the parties, in respect to the enumeration of the vassals assigned by the crown to Cortes, which the marquis thought was made on principles prejudicial to his interests and repugnant to the intentions of the grant. He was still further displeased by finding that the Audience were intrusted, by their commission, with a concurrent jurisdiction with himself in military affairs. This led occasionally to an interference, which the proud spirit of Cortes, so long accustomed to independent rule, could ill brook. After submitting to it for a time, he left the capital in disgust, no more to return there, and took up his residence in his city of Cuernavaca.

It was the place won by his own sword from the Aztecs previous to the siege of Mexico. It stood on the southern slope of the Cordilleras, and overlooked a wide expanse of country, the fairest and most flourishing portion of his domain. He had erected a stately palace on the spot, and henceforth made this city his favorite residence. It was well situated for superintending his vast estates, and he now devoted himself to bringing them into proper cultivation. He introduced the sugar-cane from Cuba, and it grew luxuriantly in the rich soil of the neighboring lowlands. He imported large numbers of merino sheep and other cattle, which found abundant pastures in the country around Tehuantepec. His lands were thickly sprinkled with groves of mulberry trees, which furnished nourishment for the silkworm. He encouraged the cultivation of hemp and flax, and, by his judicious and enterprising husbandry, showed the capacity of the soil for the culture of valuable products before unknown in the land; and he turned these products to the best account, by the erection of sugar-mills, and other works for the manufacture of the raw material. He thus laid the foundation of an opulence for his family, as substantial, if not as speedy, as that derived from the mines. Yet this latter source of wealth was not neglected by him, and he drew gold from the region of Tehuantepec, and silver from that of Zacatecas. The amount derived from these mines was not so abundant as at a later day. But the expense of working them, on the other hand, was much less in the earlier stages of the operation, when the metal lay so much nearer the surface.

But this tranquil way of life did not long content his restless and adventurous spirit; and it sought a vent by availing itself of his new charter of discovery to explore the mysteries of the great Southern Ocean. In 1527, two years before his return to Spain, he had sent a little squadron to the Moluccas. The expedition was attended with some important consequences; but, as they do not relate to Cortes, an account of it will find a more suitable place in the maritime annals of Spain, where it has been given by the able hand which has done so much for the country in this department.

Cortes was preparing to send another squadron of four vessels in the same direction, when his plans were interrupted by his visit to Spain; and his unfinished little navy, owing to the malice of the Royal Audience, who drew off the hands employed in building it, went to pieces on the stocks. Two other squadrons were now fitted out by Cortes, in the years 1532 and 1533, and sent on a voyage of discovery to the Northwest. They were unfortunate, though in the latter expedition the California penin-

sula was reached, and a landing effected on its southern extremity at Santa Cruz, probably the modern port of La Paz.
One of the vessels, thrown on the coast of New Galicia, was
seized by Guzman, the old enemy of Cortes, who ruled over
that territory, the crew were plundered, and the ship was detained as a lawful prize. Cortes, indignant at the outrage, demanded justice from the Royal Audience; and, as that body was
too feeble to enforce its own decrees in his favor, he took redress
into his own hands.

He made a rapid but difficult march on Chiametla, the scene
of Guzman's spoliation; and, as the latter did not care to face
his incensed antagonist, Cortes recovered his vessel, though not
the cargo. He was then joined by the little squadron which he
had fitted out from his own port of Tehuantepec—a port which
in the sixteenth century promised to hold the place since occupied by that of Acapulco. The vessels were provided with everything requisite for planting a colony in the newly discovered region, and transported four hundred Spaniards and *three hundred
negro slaves,* which Cortes had assembled for that purpose. With
this intention he crossed the gulf, the Adriatic—to which an old
writer compares it—of the Western World.

Our limits will not allow us to go into the details of this disastrous expedition, which was attended with no important results
either to its projector or to science. It may suffice to say that, in
the prosecution of it, Cortes and his followers were driven to
the last extremity by famine; that he again crossed the gulf, was
tossed about by terrible tempests, without a pilot to guide him,
was thrown upon the rocks, where his shattered vessel nearly
went to pieces, and, after a succession of dangers and disasters
as formidable as any which he had ever encountered on land,
succeeded, by means of his indomitable energy, in bringing his
crazy bark safe into the same port of Santa Cruz from which
he had started.

While these occurrences were passing, the new Royal Audience, after a faithful discharge of its commission, had been
superseded by the arrival of a viceroy, the first ever sent to New
Spain. Cortes, though invested with similar powers, had the title
only of Governor. This was the commencement of the system,
afterwards pursued by the crown, of intrusting the colonial administration to some individual whose high rank and personal

consideration might make him the fitting representative of majesty. The jealousy of the court did not allow the subject clothed with such ample authority to remain long enough in the same station to form dangerous schemes of ambition, but at the expiration of a few years he was usually recalled, or transferred to some other province of the vast colonial empire. The person now sent to Mexico was Don Antonio de Mendoza, a man of moderation and practical good sense, and one of that illustrious family who in the preceding reign furnished so many distinguished ornaments to the Church, to the camp, and to letters.

The long absence of Cortes had caused the deepest anxiety in the mind of his wife, the marchioness of the Valley. She wrote to the viceroy immediately on his arrival, beseeching him to ascertain, if possible, the fate of her husband, and, if he could be found, to urge his return. The viceroy, in consequence, despatched two ships in search of Cortes, but whether they reached him before his departure from Santa Cruz is doubtful. It is certain that he returned safe, after his long absence, to Acapulco, and was soon followed by the survivors of his wretched colony.

Undismayed by these repeated reverses, Cortes, still bent on some discovery worthy of his reputation, fitted out three more vessels, and placed them under the command of an officer named Ulloa. This expedition, which took its departure in July, 1539, was attended with more important results. Ulloa penetrated to the head of the gulf, then, returning and winding round the coast of the peninsula, doubled its southern point, and ascended as high as the twenty-eighth or twenty-ninth degree of north latitude on its western borders. After this, sending home one of the squadron, the bold navigator held on his course to the north, but was never more heard of.

Thus ended the maritime enterprises of Cortes, sufficiently disastrous in a pecuniary view, since they cost him three hundred thousand castellanos of gold, without the return of a ducat. He was even obliged to borrow money, and to pawn his wife's jewels, to procure funds for the last enterprise; thus incurring a debt which, increased by the great charges of his princely establishment, hung about him during the remainder of his life. But, though disastrous in an economical view, his generous efforts added important contributions to science. In the course of these expeditions, and those undertaken by Cortes previous to his visit to Spain, the Pacific had been coasted from the Bay of Panama to the Rio Colorado. The great peninsula of California had been circumnavigated as far as to the isle of Cedros, or Cerros, into which the name has since been corrupted. This vast tract, which had been supposed to be an archipelago of islands, was now discovered to be a part of the continent; and its general outline, as appears from the maps of the time, was nearly as well understood as at the present day. Lastly, the navigator had explored the recesses of the Californian Gulf, or Sea of Cortes, as, in honor of the great discoverer, it is with more propriety named by the Spaniards; and he had ascertained that, instead of the outlet before supposed to exist towards the north, this unknown ocean was locked up within the arms of the mighty continent. These were results that might have made the glory and satisfied the ambition of a common man; but they are lost in the brilliant renown of the former achievements of Cortes.

Notwithstanding the embarrassments of the marquis of the Valley, he still made new efforts to enlarge the limits of discovery, and prepared to fit out another squadron of five vessels, which he proposed to place under the command of a natural son, Don Luis. But the viceroy Mendoza, whose imagination had been inflamed by the reports of an itinerant monk respecting an El Dorado in the north, claimed the right of discovery in that direction. Cortes protested against this, as an unwarrantable interference with his own powers. Other subjects of collision arose between them; till the marquis, disgusted with this perpetual check on his authority and his enterprises, applied for redress to Castile. He finally determined to go there to support his claims in person, and to obtain, if possible, remuneration for the heavy charges he had incurred by his maritime expeditions, as well as for the spoliation of his property by the Royal Audience during his absence from the country; and, lastly, to procure an assignment of his vassals on principles more conformable to the original intentions of the grant. With these objects in view he bade adieu to his family, and, taking with him his eldest son and heir, Don Martin, then only eight years of age, he embarked at Mexico in 1540, and, after a favorable voyage, again set foot on the shores of his native land.

The emperor was absent from the country. But Cortes was honorably received in the capital, where ample accommodations were provided for him and his retinue. When he attended the Royal Council of the Indies to urge his suit, he was distinguished by uncommon marks of respect. The president went to the door of the hall to receive him, and a seat was provided for him among the members of the Council. But all evaporated in this barren show of courtesy. Justice, proverbially slow in Spain, did not mend her gait for Cortes; and at the expiration of a year he found himself no nearer the attainment of his object than on the first week after his arrival in the capital.

In the following year, 1541, we find the marquis of the Valley embarked as a volunteer in the memorable expedition against Algiers. Charles the Fifth, on his return to his dominions, laid siege to that stronghold of the Mediterranean corsairs. Cortes accompanied the forces destined to meet the emperor, and embarked on board the vessel of the Admiral of Castile. But a furious tempest scattered the navy, and the admiral's ship was driven a wreck upon the coast. Cortes and his son escaped by swimming, but the former, in the confusion of the scene, lost the inestimable set of jewels noticed in the preceding chapter; "a loss," says an old writer, "that made the expedition fall more heavily on the marquis of the Valley than on any other man in the kingdom, except the emperor."

It is not necessary to recount the particulars of this disastrous siege, in which Moslem valor, aided by the elements, set at defiance the combined forces of the Christians. A council of war was called, and it was decided to abandon the enterprise and return to Castile. This determination was indignantly received by Cortes, who offered, with the support of the army, to reduce the place himself; and he only expressed the regret that he had not a handful of those gallant veterans by his side who had served him in the Conquest of Mexico. But his offers were derided, as those of a romantic enthusiast. He had not been invited to take part in the discussions of the council of war. It was a marked indignity; but the courtiers, weary of the service, were too much bent on an immediate return to Spain, to hazard the opposition of a man who, when he had once planted his foot, was never known to raise it again till he had accomplished his object.

On arriving in Castile, Cortes lost no time in laying his suit before the emperor. His applications were received by the monarch with civility—a cold civility, which carried no conviction of its sincerity. His position was materially changed since his former visit to the country. More than ten years had elapsed, and he was now too well advanced in years to give promise of serviceable enterprise in future. Indeed, his undertakings of late had been singularly unfortunate. Even his former successes suffered the disparagement natural to a man of declining fortunes. They were already eclipsed by the magnificent achievements in Peru, which had poured a golden tide into the country, that formed a striking contrast to the streams of wealth that as yet had flowed in but scantily from the silver mines of Mexico. Cortes had to learn that the gratitude of a court has reference to the future much more than to the past. He stood in the position of an importunate suitor whose claims, however just, are too large to be readily allowed. He found, like Columbus, that it was possible to deserve too greatly.

In the month of February, 1544, he addressed a letter to the emperor—it was the last he ever wrote him—soliciting his attention to his suit. He begins by proudly alluding to his past services to the crown. "He had hoped that the toils of youth would have secured him repose in his old age. For forty years he had passed his life with little sleep, bad food, and with his arms constantly by his side. He had freely exposed his person to peril, and spent his substance in exploring distant and unknown regions, that he might spread abroad the name of his sovereign and bring under his scepter many great and powerful nations. All this he had done, not only without assistance from home, but in the face of obstacles thrown in his way by rivals and by enemies who thirsted like leeches for his blood. He was now old, infirm, and embarrassed with debt. Better had it been for him not to have known the liberal intentions of the emperor, as intimated by his grants; since he should then have devoted himself to the care of his estates, and not have been compelled, as he now was, to contend with the officers of the crown, against whom it was more difficult to defend himself than to win the land from the enemy." He concludes with beseeching his sovereign to "order the Council of the Indies, with the other tribunals which had cognizance of his suits, to come to a decision; since he was too old to wander about like a vagrant, but ought rather, during the brief remainder of his life, to stay at home and settle his account with Heaven, occupied with the concerns of his soul, rather than with his substance."

This appeal to his sovereign, which has something in it touching from a man of the haughty spirit of Cortes, had not the effect to quicken the determination of his suit. He still lingered at the court from week to week, and from month to month, beguiled by the deceitful hopes of the litigant, tasting all that bitterness of the soul which arises from hope deferred. After three years more, passed in this unprofitable and humiliating occupation, he resolved to leave his ungrateful country and return to Mexico.

He had proceeded as far as Seville, accompanied by his son, when he fell ill of an indigestion, caused, probably, by irritation and trouble of mind. This terminated in dysentery, and his strength sank so rapidly under the disease that it was apparent his mortal career was drawing towards its close. He prepared for it by making the necessary arrangements for the settlement of his affairs. He had made his will some time before; and he now executed it. It is a very long document, and in some respects a remarkable one.

The bulk of his property was entailed to his son, Don Martin, then fifteen years of age. In the testament he fixes his majority at twenty-five; but at twenty his guardians were to allow him his full income, to maintain the state becoming his rank. In a paper accompanying the will, Cortes specified the names of the agents to whom he had committed the management of his vast estates scattered over many different provinces; and he requests his executors to confirm the nomination, as these agents have been selected by him from a knowledge of their peculiar qualifications. Nothing can better show the thorough supervision which, in the midst of pressing public concerns, he had given to the details of his widely extended property.

He makes a liberal provision for his other children, and a generous allowance to several old domestics and retainers in his household. By another clause he gives away considerable sums in charity, and he applies the revenues of his estates in the city of Mexico to establish and permanently endow three public institutions—a hospital in the capital, which was to be dedicated to Our Lady of the Conception, a college in Cojohuacan for the education of missionaries to preach the gospel among the natives, and a convent, in the same place, for nuns. To the chapel of this convent, situated in his favorite town, he orders that his own body shall be transported for burial, in whatever quarter of the world he may happen to die.

After declaring that he has taken all possible care to ascertain the amount of the tributes formerly paid by his Indian vassals to their native sovereigns, he enjoins on his heir that, in case those which they have hitherto paid shall be found to exceed the right valuation, he shall restore them a full equivalent. In another clause he expresses a doubt whether it is right to exact personal service from the natives, and commands that a strict inquiry shall be made into the nature and value of such services as he had received, and that in all cases a fair compensation shall be allowed for them. Lastly, he makes this remarkable declaration: "It has long been a question whether one can conscientiously hold property in Indian slaves. Since this point has not yet been determined, I enjoin it on my son Martin and his heirs that they spare no pains to come to an exact knowledge of the truth; as a matter which deeply concerns the conscience of each of them, no less than mine."

Such scruples of conscience, not to have been expected in Cortes, were still less likely to be met with in the Spaniards of a later generation. The state of opinion in respect to the great question of slavery, in the sixteenth century, at the commencement of the system, bears some resemblance to that which exists in our time, when we may hope it is approaching its conclusion. Las Casas and the Dominicans of the former age, the abolitionists of their day, thundered out their uncompromising invectives against the system on the broad ground of natural equity and the rights of man. The great mass of proprietors troubled their heads little about the question of right, but were satisfied with the expediency of the institution. Others, more considerate and conscientious, while they admitted the evil, found an argument for its toleration in the plea of necessity, regarding the constitution of the white man as unequal, in a sultry climate, to the labor of cultivating the soil. In one important respect the condition of slavery in the sixteenth century differed materially from its condition in the nineteenth. In the former, the seeds of the evil, but lately sown, might have been, with comparatively little difficulty, eradicated. But in our time they have struck their roots deep into the social system, and cannot be rudely handled without shaking the very foundations of the political fabric. It is easy to conceive that a man who admits all the wretchedness of the institution and its wrong to humanity may nevertheless hesitate to adopt a remedy until he is satisfied that the remedy itself is not worse than the disease. That such a remedy will come with time, who can doubt, that has confidence in the ultimate prevalence of the right and the progressive civilization of his species?

Cortes names as his executors, and as guardians of his children, the duke of Medina Sidonia, the marquis of Astorga, and the count of Aguilar. For his executors in Mexico, he appoints his wife, the marchioness, the archbishop of Toledo, and two other prelates. The will was executed at Seville, October 11th, 1547.

Finding himself much incommoded, as he grew weaker, by the presence of visitors, to which he was necessarily exposed at Seville, he withdrew to the neighboring village of Castilleja de la Cuesta, attended by his son, who watched over his dying parent with filial solicitude. Cortes seems to have contemplated his approaching end with a composure not always to be found in those who have faced death with indifference on the field of battle. At length, having devoutly confessed his sins and received the sacrament, he expired on the 2d of December, 1547, in the sixty-third year of his age.

The inhabitants of the neighboring country were desirous to show every mark of respect to the memory of Cortes. His funeral obsequies were celebrated with due solemnity by a long train of Andalusian nobles and of the citizens of Seville, and his body was transported to the chapel of the monastery of San Isidro, in that city, where it was laid in the family vault of the duke of Medina Sidonia. . . .

History of the
Conquest of Peru

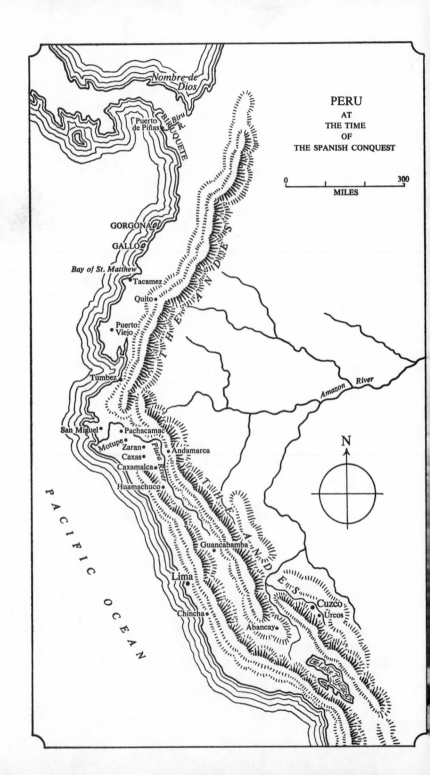

PERU
AT
THE TIME
OF
THE SPANISH CONQUEST

0   300
MILES

Nombre-de Dios

Biru R.

BIRUQUETE

Puerto de Piñas

GORGONA

GALLO

Bay of St. Matthew

Tacamez

Quito

Puerto Viejo

THE ANDES

Tumbez

Amazon River

San Miguel

Pachacamac

Motupe

Zaran   Andamarca

Caxas

Caxamalca

Piura River

Huamachuco

THE ANDES

N

PACIFIC OCEAN

Guancabamba

Lima

DES

Cuzco

Chincha

Urcos

Abancay

Lake

BOOK II

Rumors of Peru

1511–1524

FLOATING RUMORS had reached the Spaniards, from time to time, of countries in the far west, teeming with the metal they so much coveted; but the first distinct notice of Peru was about the year 1511, when Vasco Nuñez de Balboa, the discoverer of the Southern Sea, was weighing some gold which he had collected from the natives. A young barbarian chieftain, who was present, struck the scales with his fist, and, scattering the glittering metal around the apartment, exclaimed, "If this is what you prize so much that you are willing to leave your distant homes and risk even life itself for it, I can tell you of a land where they eat and drink out of golden vessels, and gold is as cheap as iron is with you." It was not long after this startling intelligence that Balboa achieved the formidable adventure of scaling the mountain-rampart of the isthmus which divides the two mighty oceans from each other; when, armed with sword and buckler, he rushed into the waters of the Pacific, and cried out, in the true chivalrous vein, that "he claimed this unknown sea, with all that it contained, for the King of Castile, and that he would make good the claim against all, Christian or infidel, who dared to gainsay it"! All the broad continent and sunny isles washed by the waters of the Southern Ocean! Little did the bold cavalier comprehend the full import of his magnificent vaunt.

On this spot he received more explicit tidings of the Peruvian empire, heard proofs recounted of its civilization, and was shown drawings of the llama, which, to the European eye, seemed a species of the Arabian camel. But, although he steered his caravel for these golden realms, and even pushed his discoveries some twenty leagues south of the Gulf of St. Michael, the adventure was not reserved for him. The illustrious discoverer was doomed to fall a victim to that miserable jealousy with which a little spirit regards the achievements of a great one.

The Spanish colonial domain was broken up into a number of petty governments, which were dispensed sometimes to court favorites, though, as the duties of the post, at this early period, were of an arduous nature, they were more frequently reserved for men of some practical talent and enterprise. Columbus, by virtue of his original contract with the crown, had jurisdiction over the territories discovered by himself, embracing some of the principal islands, and a few places on the continent. This jurisdiction differed from that of other functionaries, inasmuch as it was hereditary; a privilege found in the end too considerable for a subject, and commuted, therefore, for a title and a pension. These colonial governments were multiplied with the increase of empire, and by the year 1524, the period at which our narrative properly commences, were scattered over the islands, along the Isthmus of Darien, the broad tract of Tierra Firme, and the recent conquests in Mexico. Some of these governments were of no great extent; others, like that of Mexico, were of the dimensions of a kingdom; and most had an indefinite range for discovery assigned to them in their immediate neighborhood, by which each of the petty potentates might enlarge his territorial sway and enrich his followers and himself. This politic arrangement best served the ends of the crown, by affording a perpetual incentive to the spirit of enterprise. Thus living on their own little domains at a long distance from the mother-country, these military rulers held a sort of viceregal sway, and too frequently exercised it in the most oppressive and tyrannical manner—oppressive to the native, and tyrannical towards their own followers. It was the natural consequence, when men originally low in station, and unprepared by education for office, were suddenly called to the possession of a brief, but in its nature irresponsible, authority. It was not till after some sad experience of these results that measures were taken to hold these petty tyrants in check by means of regular tribunals, or Royal Audiences, as they were termed, which, composed of men of character and learning, might interpose the arm of the law, or at least the voice of remonstrance, for the protection of both colonist and native.

Among the colonial governors who were indebted for their situation to their rank at home was Don Pedro Arias de Avila, or Pedrarias, as usually called. He was married to a daughter of Doña Beatriz de Bobadilla, the celebrated Marchioness of Moya, best known as the friend of Isabella the Catholic. He was a man of some military experience and considerable energy of character. But, as it proved, he was of a malignant temper; and the base qualities which might have passed unnoticed in the obscurity of private life were made conspicuous, and perhaps created in some measure, by sudden elevation to power; as the sunshine, which operates kindly on a generous soil and stimulates it to production, calls forth from the unwholesome marsh only foul and pestilent vapors. This man was placed over the territory of Castilla del Oro, the ground selected by Nuñez de Balboa for the theater of his discoveries. Success drew on this latter the jealousy of his superior, for it was crime enough in the eyes of Pedrarias to deserve too well. The tragical history of this cavalier belongs to a period somewhat earlier than that with which we are to be occupied. It has been traced by abler hands than mine, and, though brief, forms one of the most brilliant passages in the annals of the American conquerors.

But, though Pedrarias was willing to cut short the glorious career of his rival, he was not insensible to the important consequences of his discoveries. He saw at once the unsuitableness of Darien for prosecuting expeditions on the Pacific, and, conformably to the original suggestion of Balboa, in 1519 he caused his rising capital to be transferred from the shores of the Atlantic to the ancient site of Panama, some distance east of the present city of that name. This most unhealthy spot, the cemetery of many an unfortunate colonist, was favorably situated for the great object of maritime enterprise; and the port, from its central position, afforded the best point of departure for expeditions, whether to the north or south, along the wide range of undiscovered coast that lined the Southern Ocean. Yet in this new and more favorable position several years were suffered to elapse before the course of discovery took the direction of Peru. This was turned exclusively towards the north, or rather west, in obedience to the orders of the government, which had ever at heart the detection of a strait that, as was supposed, must intersect some part or other of the long-extended isthmus. Armament after armament was fitted out with this chimerical object; and Pedrarias saw his domain extending every year farther and farther without deriving any considerable advantage from his acquisitions. Veragua, Costa Rica, Nicaragua, were successively occupied; and his brave cavaliers forced a way across forest and mountain and warlike tribes of savages, till, at Honduras, they came in collision with the companions of Cortes, the Conquerors of Mexico, who had descended from the great northern plateau on the regions of Central America, and thus completed the survey of this wild and mysterious land.

It was not till 1522 that a regular expedition was despatched in the direction south of Panama, under the conduct of Pascual de Andagoya, a cavalier of much distinction in the colony. But that officer penetrated only to the Puerto de Piñas, the limit of Balboa's discoveries, when the bad state of his health compelled him to re-embark and abandon his enterprise at its commencement.

Yet the floating rumors of the wealth and civilization of a mighty nation at the south were continually reaching the ears and kindling the dreamy imaginations of the colonists; and it may seem astonishing that an expedition in that direction should have been so long deferred. But the exact position and distance of this fairy realm were matter of conjecture. The long tract of intervening country was occupied by rude and warlike races; and the little experience which the Spanish navigators had already had of the neighboring coast and its inhabitants, and, still more, the tempestuous character of the seas—for their expeditions had taken place at the most unpropitious seasons of the year—enhanced the apparent difficulties of the undertaking and made even their stout hearts shrink from it.

Such was the state of feeling in the little community of Panama for several years after its foundation. Meanwhile, the dazzling conquest of Mexico gave a new impulse to the ardor of discovery, and in 1524 three men were found in the colony in whom the spirit of adventure triumphed over every consideration of difficulty and danger that obstructed the prosecution of the enterprise. One among them was selected as fitted by his character to conduct it to a successful issue. That man was Francisco Pizarro; and, as he held the same conspicuous post in the Conquest of Peru that was occupied by Cortes in that of Mexico, it will be necessary to take a brief review of his early history.

FROM CHAPTER II

Francisco Pizarro

1524–1525

Francisco Pizarro was born at Truxillo, a city of Estremadura, in Spain. The period of his birth is uncertain; but probably it was not far from 1471. He was an illegitimate child, and that his parents should not have taken pains to perpetuate the date of his birth is not surprising. Few care to make a particular record of their transgressions. His father, Gonzalo Pizarro, was a colonel of infantry, and served with some distinction in the Italian campaigns under the Great Captain, and afterwards in the wars of Navarre. His mother, named Francisca Gonzales, was a person of humble condition in the town of Truxillo.

But little is told of Francisco's early years, and that little not always deserving of credit. According to some, he was deserted by both his parents, and left as a foundling at the door of one of the principal churches of the city. It is even said that he would have perished, had he not been nursed by a sow. This is a more discreditable fountain of supply than that assigned to the infant Romulus. The early history of men who have made their names famous by deeds in after-life, like the early history of nations, affords a fruitful field for invention.

It seems certain that the young Pizarro received little care from either of his parents, and was suffered to grow up as nature dictated. He was neither taught to read nor write, and his principal occupation was that of a swineherd. But this torpid way of life did not suit the stirring spirit of Pizarro, as he grew older, and listened to the tales, widely circulated and so captivating to a youthful fancy, of the New World. He shared in the popular enthusiasm, and availed himself of a favorable moment to abandon his ignoble charge and escape to Seville, the pórt where the Spanish adventurers embarked to seek their fortunes in the West. Few of them could have turned their backs on their native land with less cause for regret than Pizarro.

In what year this important change in his destiny took place we are not informed. The first we hear of him in the New World is at the island of Hispaniola, in 1510, where he took part in the expedition to Uraba in Tierra Firme, under Alonso de Ojeda, a cavalier whose character and achievements find no parallel but in the pages of Cervantes. Hernando Cortes, whose mother was a Pizarro, and related, it is said, to the father of Francis, was then in St. Domingo, and prepared to accompany Ojeda's expedition, but was prevented by a temporary lameness. Had he gone, the fall of the Aztec empire might have been postponed for some time longer, and the scepter of Montezuma have descended in peace to his posterity. Pizarro shared in the disastrous fortunes of Ojeda's colony, and by his discretion obtained so far the confidence of his commander as to be left in charge of the settlement when the latter returned for supplies to the islands. The lieutenant continued at his perilous post for nearly two months, waiting deliberately until death should have thinned off the colony sufficiently to allow the miserable remnant to be embarked in the single small vessel that remained to it.

After this, we find him associated with Balboa, the discoverer of the Pacific, and cooperating with him in establishing the settlement at Darien. He had the glory of accompanying this gallant cavalier in his terrible march across the mountains, and of being among the first Europeans, therefore, whose eyes were greeted with the long-promised vision of the Southern Ocean.

After the untimely death of his commander, Pizarro attached himself to the fortunes of Pedrarias, and was employed by that governor in several military expeditions, which, if they afforded nothing else, gave him the requisite training for the perils and privations that lay in the path of the future Conqueror of Peru.

In 1515 he was selected, with another cavalier, named Morales, to cross the isthmus and traffic with the natives on the shores of the Pacific. And there, while engaged in collecting his booty of gold and pearls from the neighboring islands, as his eye ranged along the shadowy line of coast till it faded in the distance, his imagination may have been first fired with the idea of, one day, attempting the conquest of the mysterious regions beyond the mountains. On the removal of the seat of government across the isthmus to Panama, Pizarro accompanied Pedrarias, and his name became conspicuous among the cavalriers who extended the line of conquest to the north over the martial tribes of Veragua. But all these expeditions, whatever glory they may have brought him, were productive of very little gold, and at the age of fifty the captain Pizarro found himself in possession only of a tract of unhealthy land in the neighborhood of the capital, and of such repartimientos of the natives as were deemed suited to his military services. The New World was a lottery, where the great prizes were so few that the odds were much against the player; yet in the game he was content to stake health, fortune, and, too often, his fair fame.

Such was Pizarro's situation when, in 1522, Andagoya returned from his unfinished enterprise to the south of Panama, bringing back with him more copious accounts than any hitherto received of the opulence and grandeur of the countries that lay beyond. It was at this time, too, that the splendid achievements of Cortes made their impression on the public mind and gave a new impulse to the spirit of adventure. The southern expeditions became a common topic of speculation among the colonists of Panama. But the region of gold, as it lay behind the mighty curtain of the Cordilleras, was still veiled in obscurity. No idea could be formed of its actual distance; and the hardships and difficulties encountered by the few navigators who had sailed in that direction gave a gloomy character to the undertaking, which had hitherto deterred the most daring from embarking in it. There is no evidence that Pizarro showed any particular alacrity in the cause. Nor were his own funds such as to warrant any expectation of success without great assistance from others. He found this in two individuals of the colony, who took too important a part in the subsequent transactions not to be particularly noticed.

One of them, Diego de Almagro, was a soldier of fortune, somewhat older, it seems probable, than Pizarro; though little is known of his birth, and even the place of it is disputed. It is supposed to have been the town of Almagro in New Castile, whence his own name, for want of a better source, was derived; for, like Pizarro, he was a foundling. Few particulars are known of him till the present period of our history; for he was one of those whom the working of turbulent times first throws upon the surface—less fortunate, perhaps, than if left in their original obscurity. In his military career, Almagro had earned the reputation of a gallant soldier. He was frank and liberal in his disposition, somewhat hasty and ungovernable in his passions, but, like men of a sanguine temperament, after the first sallies had passed away, not difficult to be appeased. He had, in short, the good qualities and the defects incident to an honest nature not improved by the discipline of early education or self-control.

The other member of the confederacy was Hernando de Luque, a Spanish ecclesiastic, who exercised the functions of vicar at Panama, and had formerly filled the office of schoolmaster in the Cathedral of Darien. He seems to have been a man of singular prudence and knowledge of the world, and by his respectable qualities had acquired considerable influence in the little community to which he belonged, as well as the control of funds, which made his cooperation essential to the success of the present enterprise.

It was arranged among the three associates that the two cavaliers should contribute their little stock towards defraying the expenses of the armament, but by far the greater part of the funds was to be furnished by Luque. Pizarro was to take command of the expedition, and the business of victualing and equipping the vessels was assigned to Almagro. The associates found no difficulty in obtaining the consent of the governor to their undertaking. After the return of Andagoya, he had projected another expedition, but the officer to whom it was to be intrusted died. Why he did not prosecute his original purpose, and commit the affair to an experienced captain like Pizarro, does not appear. He was probably not displeased that the burden of the enterprise should be borne by others, so long as a good share of the profits went into his own coffers. This he did not overlook in his stipulations.

Thus fortified with the funds of Luque and the consent of the governor, Almagro was not slow to make preparations for the voyage. Two small vessels were purchased, the larger of which had been originally built by Balboa for himself, with a view to this same expedition. Since his death, it had lain dismantled in the harbor of Panama. It was now refitted as well as circumstances would permit, and put in order for sea, while the stores and provisions were got on board with an alacrity which did more credit, as the event proved, to Almagro's zeal than to his forecast.

There was more difficulty in obtaining the necessary complement of hands; for a general feeling of distrust had gathered round expeditions in this direction, which could not readily be overcome. But there were many idle hangers-on in the colony, who had come out to mend their fortunes, and were willing to take their chance of doing so, however desperate. From such materials as these, Almagro assembled a body of somewhat more than a hundred men; and, everything being ready, Pizarro assumed the command, and, weighing anchor, took his departure from the little port of Panama about the middle of November, 1524. Almagro was to follow in a second vessel of inferior size, as soon as it could be fitted out.

The time of year was the most unsuitable that could have been selected for the voyage; for it was the rainy season, when the navigation to the south, impeded by contrary winds, is made doubly dangerous by the tempests that sweep over the coast. But this was not understood by the adventurers. After touching at the Isle of Pearls, the frequent resort of navigators, at a few leagues' distance from Panama, Pizarro held his way across the Gulf of St. Michael, and steered almost due south for the Puerto de Piñas, a headland in the province of Biruquete, which marked the limit of Andagoya's voyage. Before his departure, Pizarro had obtained all the information which he could derive from that officer in respect to the country, and the route he was to follow. But the cavalier's own experience had been too limited to enable him to be of much assistance.

Doubling the Puerto de Piñas, the little vessel entered the river Biru, the misapplication of which name is supposed by some to have given rise to that of the empire of the Incas. After sailing up this stream for a couple of leagues, Pizarro came to anchor, and, disembarking his whole force except the sailors, proceeded at the head of it to explore the country. The land spread out into a vast swamp, where the heavy rains had settled in pools of stagnant water, and the muddy soil afforded no footing to the traveler. This dismal morass was fringed with woods, through whose thick and tangled undergrowth they found it difficult to penetrate; and, emerging from them, they came out on a hilly country, so rough and rocky in its character that their feet were cut to the bone, and the weary soldier, encumbered with his heavy mail or thick-padded doublet of cotton, found it difficult to drag one foot after the other. The heat at times was oppressive; and, fainting with toil and famished for want of food, they sank down on the earth from mere exhaustion. Such was the ominous commencement of the expedition to Peru. . . .

FROM CHAPTER III

Gallo

1524

At length they found a secure haven in the island of Gallo, already visited by Ruiz. As they were now too strong in numbers to apprehend an assault, the crews landed, and, experiencing no molestation from the natives, they continued on the island for a fortnight, refitting their damaged vessels, and recruiting themselves after the fatigues of the ocean. Then, resuming their voyage, the captains stood towards the south until they reached the bay of St. Matthew. As they advanced along the coast, they were struck, as Ruiz had been before, with the evidences of a higher civilization constantly exhibited in the general aspect of the country and its inhabitants. The hand of cultivation was visible in every quarter. The natural appearance of the coast, too, had something in it more inviting; for instead of the eternal labyrinth of mangrove-trees, with their complicated roots snarled into formidable coils under the water, as if to waylay and entangle the voyager, the low margin of the sea was covered with a stately growth of ebony, and with a species of mahogany, and other hard woods that take the most brilliant and variegated polish. The sandalwood, and many balsamic trees of unknown names, scattered their sweet odors far and wide, not in an atmosphere tainted with vegetable corruption, but on the pure breezes of the ocean, bearing health as well as fragrance on their wings. Broad patches of cultivated land intervened, disclosing hillsides covered with the yellow maize and the potato, or checkered, in the lower levels, with blooming plantations of cacao.

The villages became more numerous; and, as the vessels rode at anchor off the port of Tacamez, the Spaniards saw before them a town of two thousand houses or more, laid out into streets, with a numerous population clustering around it in the suburbs. The men and women displayed many ornaments of gold and precious stones about their persons, which may seem strange, considering that the Peruvian Incas claimed a monopoly of jewels for themselves and the nobles on whom they condescended to bestow them. But, although the Spaniards had now reached the outer limits of the Peruvian empire, it was not Peru, but Quito, and that portion of it but recently brought under the scepter of the Incas, where the ancient usages of the people could hardly have been effaced under the oppressive system of the American despots. The adjacent country was, moreover, particularly rich in gold, which, collected from the washings of the streams, still forms one of the staple products of Barbacoas. Here, too, was the fair River of Emeralds, so called from the quarries of the beautiful gem on its borders, from which the Indian monarchs enriched their treasury.

The Spaniards gazed with delight on these undeniable evidences of wealth, and saw in the careful cultivation of the soil a comfortable assurance that they had at length reached the land which had so long been seen in brilliant, though distant, perspective before them. But here again they were doomed to be disappointed by the warlike spirit of the people, who, conscious of their own strength, showed no disposition to quail before the invaders. On the contrary, several of their canoes shot out, loaded with warriors, who, displaying a gold mask as their ensign, hovered round the vessels with looks of defiance, and, when pursued, easily took shelter under the lee of the land.

A more formidable body mustered along the shore, to the number, according to the Spanish accounts, of at least ten thousand warriors, eager, apparently, to come to close action with the invaders. Nor could Pizarro, who had landed with a party of his men in the hope of a conference with the natives, wholly prevent hostilities; and it might have gone hard with the Spaniards, hotly pressed by their resolute enemy so superior in numbers, but for a ludicrous accident reported by the historians as happening to one of the cavaliers. This was a fall from his horse, which so astonished the barbarians, who were not prepared for this division of what seemed one and the same being into two, that, filled with consternation, they fell back, and left a way open for the Christians to regain their vessels!

A council of war was now called. It was evident that the forces of the Spaniards were unequal to a contest with so numerous and well-appointed a body of natives; and, even if they should prevail here, they could have no hope of stemming the torrent which must rise against them in their progress—for the country was becoming more and more thickly settled, and towns and hamlets started into view at every new headland which they doubled. It was better, in the opinion of some—the faint-hearted —to abandon the enterprise at once, as beyond their strength. But Almagro took a different view of the affair. "To go home," he said, "with nothing done, would be ruin, as well as disgrace. There was scarcely one but had left creditors at Panama, who looked for payment to the fruits of this expedition. To go home now would be to deliver themselves at once into their hands. It would be to go to prison. Better to roam a freeman, though in the wilderness, than to lie bound with fetters in the dungeons of Panama. The only course for them," he concluded, "was the one lately pursued. Pizarro might find some more commodious place where he could remain with part of the force while he himself went back for recruits to Panama. The story they had now to tell of the riches of the land, as they had seen them with their own eyes, would put their expedition in a very different light, and could not fail to draw to their banner as many volunteers as they needed."

But this recommendation, however judicious, was not altogether to the taste of the latter commander, who did not relish the part, which constantly fell to him, of remaining behind in the swamps and forests of this wild country. "It is all very well," he said to Almagro, "for you, who pass your time pleasantly enough, careering to and fro in your vessel, or snugly sheltered in a land of plenty at Panama; but it is quite another matter for those who stay behind to droop and die of hunger in the wilderness." To this Almagro retorted with some heat, professing his own willingness to take charge of the brave men who would remain with him, if Pizarro declined it. The controversy assuming a more angry and menacing tone, from words they would have soon come to blows, as both, laying their hands on their swords, were preparing to rush on each other, when the treasurer Ribera, aided by the pilot Ruiz, succeeded in pacifying them. It required but little effort on the part of these cooler counselors to convince the cavaliers of the folly of a conduct which must at once terminate the expedition in a manner little creditable to its projectors. A reconciliation consequently took place, sufficient, at least in outward show, to allow the two commanders to act together in concert. Almagro's plan was then adopted; and it only remained to find out the most secure and convenient spot for Pizarro's quarters.

Several days were passed in touching at different parts of the coast, as they retraced their course; but everywhere the natives appeared to have caught the alarm, and assumed a menacing, and from their numbers a formidable, aspect. The more northerly region, with its unwholesome fens and forests, where nature wages a war even more relentless than man, was not to be thought of. In this perplexity, they decided on the little island of Gallo, as being, on the whole, from its distance from the shore, and from the scantiness of its population, the most eligible spot for them in their forlorn and destitute condition.

But no sooner was the resolution of the two captains made known than a feeling of discontent broke forth among their followers, especially those who were to remain with Pizarro on the island. "What!" they exclaimed, "were they to be dragged to that obscure spot to die by hunger? The whole expedition had been a cheat and a failure, from beginning to end. The golden countries, so much vaunted, had seemed to fly before them as they advanced; and the little gold they had been fortunate enough to glean had all been sent back to Panama to entice other fools to follow their example. What had they got in return for all their sufferings? The only treasures they could boast were their bows and arrows, and they were now to be left to die on this dreary island, without so much as a rood of consecrated ground to lay their bones in!"

In this exasperated state of feeling, several of the soldiers wrote back to their friends, informing them of their deplorable condition, and complaining of the cold-blooded manner in which they were to be sacrificed to the obstinate cupidity of their leaders. But the latter were wary enough to anticipate this movement, and Almagro defeated it by seizing all the letters in the vessels and thus cutting off at once the means of communication with their friends at home. Yet this act of unscrupulous violence, like most other similar acts, fell short of its purpose; for a soldier named Sarabia had the ingenuity to evade it by introducing a letter into a ball of cotton, which was to be taken to Panama as a specimen of the products of the country and presented to the governor's lady.

The letter, which was signed by several of the disaffected soldiery besides the writer, painted in gloomy colors the miseries of their condition, accused the two commanders of being the authors of this, and called on the authorities at Panama to interfere by sending a vessel to take them from the desolate spot while some of them might still be found surviving the horrors of their confinement. The epistle concluded with a stanza, in which the two leaders were stigmatized as partners in a slaughterhouse—one being employed to drive in the cattle for the other to butcher. The verses, which had a currency in their day among the colonists to which they were certainly not entitled by their poetical merits, may be thus rendered into corresponding doggerel:

> *Look out, Señor Governor,*
> *For the drover while he's near,*
> *Since he goes home to get the sheep*
> *For the butcher, who stays here.*

FROM CHAPTER IV

Stern Resolution of Pizarro

1527–1528

Not long after Almagro's departure, Pizarro sent off the remaining vessel, under the pretext of its being put in repair at Panama. It probably relieved him of a part of his followers, whose mutinous spirit made them an obstacle rather than a help in his forlorn condition, and with whom he was the more willing to part from the difficulty of finding subsistence on the barren spot which he now occupied.

Great was the dismay occasioned by the return of Almagro and his followers in the little community of Panama; for the letter surreptitiously conveyed in the ball of cotton fell into the hands for which it was intended, and the contents soon got abroad, with the usual quantity of exaggeration. The haggard and dejected mien of the adventurers, of itself, told a tale sufficiently disheartening, and it was soon generally believed that the few ill-fated survivors of the expedition were detained against their will by Pizarro, to end their days with their disappointed leader on his desolate island.

Pedro de los Rios, the governor, was so much incensed at the result of the expedition, and the waste of life it had occasioned to the colony, that he turned a deaf ear to all the applications of Luque and Almagro for further countenance in the affair; he derided their sanguine anticipations of the future, and finally resolved to send an officer to the isle of Gallo, with orders to bring back every Spaniard whom he should find still living in that dreary abode. Two vessels were immediately despatched for the purpose, and placed under charge of a cavalier named Tafur, a native of Cordova.

Meanwhile, Pizarro and his followers were experiencing all the miseries which might have been expected from the character of the barren spot on which they were imprisoned. They were, indeed, relieved from all apprehensions of the natives, since these had quitted the island on its occupation by the white men; but they had to endure the pains of hunger even in a greater degree than they had formerly experienced in the wild woods of the neighboring continent. Their principal food was crabs and such shellfish as they could scantily pick up along the shores. Incessant storms of thunder and lightning, for it was the rainy season, swept over the devoted island and drenched them with a perpetual flood. Thus, half naked, and pining with famine, there were few in that little company who did not feel the spirit of enterprise quenched within them, or who looked for any happier termination of their difficulties than that afforded by a return to Panama. The appearance of Tafur, therefore, with his two vessels, well stored with provisions, was greeted with all the rapture that the crew of a sinking wreck might feel on the arrival of some unexpected succor; and the only thought, after satisfying the immediate cravings of hunger, was to embark and leave the detested isle forever.

But by the same vessel letters came to Pizarro from his two confederates, Luque and Almagro, beseeching him not to despair in his present extremity, but to hold fast to his original purpose. To return under the present circumstances would be to seal the fate of the expedition; and they solemnly engaged, if he would remain firm at his post, to furnish him in a short time with the necessary means for going forward.

A ray of hope was enough for the courageous spirit of Pizarro. It does not appear that he himself had entertained, at any time, thoughts of returning. If he had, these words of encouragement entirely banished them from his bosom, and he prepared to stand the fortune of the cast on which he had so desperately ventured. He knew, however, that solicitations or remonstrances would avail little with the companions of his enterprise; and he probably did not care to win over the more timid spirits who, by perpetually looking back, would only be a clog on his future movements. He announced his own purpose, however, in a laconic but decided manner, characteristic of a man more accustomed to act than to talk, and well calculated to make an impression on his rough followers.

Drawing his sword, he traced a line with it on the sand from east to west. Then, turning towards the south, "Friends and comrades!" he said, "on that side are toil, hunger, nakedness, the drenching storm, desertion, and death; on this side, ease and pleasure. There lies Peru with its riches; here, Panama and its poverty. Choose, each man, what best becomes a brave Castilian. For my part, I go to the south." So saying, he stepped across the line. He was followed by the brave pilot Ruiz; next by Pedro de Candia, a cavalier, born, as his name imports, in one of the isles of Greece. Eleven others successively crossed the line, thus intimating their willingness to abide the fortunes of their leader, for good or for evil. Fame, to quote the enthusiastic language of an ancient chronicler, has commemorated the names of this little band, "who thus, in the face of difficulties unexampled in history, with death rather than riches for their reward, preferred it all to abandoning their honor, and stood firm by their leader as an example of loyalty to future ages."

But the act excited no such admiration in the mind of Tafur, who looked on it as one of gross disobedience to the commands of the governor, and as little better than madness, involving the certain destruction of the parties engaged in it. He refused to give any sanction to it himself by leaving one of his vessels with the adventurers to prosecute their voyage, and it was with great difficulty that he could be persuaded even to allow them a part of the stores which he had brought for their support. This had no influence on their determination, and the little party, bidding adieu to their returning comrades, remained unshaken in their purpose of abiding the fortunes of their commander.

There is something striking to the imagination in the spectacle of these few brave spirits thus consecrating themselves to a daring enterprise, which seemed as far above their strength as any recorded in the fabulous annals of knight-errantry. A handful of men, without food, without clothing, almost without arms, without knowledge of the land to which they were bound, without vessel to transport them, were here left on a lonely rock in the ocean with the avowed purpose of carrying on a crusade against a powerful empire, staking their lives on its success. What is there in the legends of chivalry that surpasses it? This was the crisis of Pizarro's fate. There are moments in the lives of men, which, as they are seized or neglected, decide their future destiny. Had Pizarro faltered from his strong purpose, and yielded to the occasion, now so temptingly presented, for extricating himself and his broken band from their desperate position, his name would have been buried with his fortunes, and the conquest of Peru would have been left for other and more successful adventurers. But his constancy was equal to the occasion, and his conduct here proved him competent to the perilous post he had assumed, and inspired others with a confidence in him which was the best assurance of success.

In the vessel that bore back Tafur and those who seceded from the expedition the pilot Ruiz was also permitted to return, in order to cooperate with Luque and Almagro in their application for further succor.

Not long after the departure of the ships, it was decided by Pizarro to abandon his present quarters, which had little to recommend them, and which, he reflected, might now be exposed to annoyance from the original inhabitants, should they take courage and return on learning the diminished number of the white men. The Spaniards, therefore, by his orders, constructed a rude boat or raft, on which they succeeded in transporting themselves to the little island of Gorgona, twenty-five leagues to the north of their present residence. It lay about five leagues from the continent, and was uninhabited. It had some advantages over the isle of Gallo; for it stood higher above the sea, and was partially covered with wood, which afforded shelter to a species of pheasant, and the hare or rabbit of the country, so that the Spaniards, with their crossbows, were enabled to procure a tolerable supply of game. Cool streams that issued from the living rock furnished abundance of water, though the drenching rains that fell without intermission left them in no danger of perishing by thirst. From this annoyance they found some protection in the rude huts which they constructed; though here, as in their former residence, they suffered from the no less intolerable annoyance of venomous insects, which multiplied and swarmed in the exhalations of the rank and stimulated soil. In this dreary abode Pizarro omitted no means by which to sustain the drooping spirits of his men. Morning prayers were duly said, and the evening hymn to the Virgin was regularly chanted; the festivals of the Church were carefully commemorated, and every means taken by their commander to give a kind of religious character to his enterprise, and to inspire his rough followers with a confidence in the protection of Heaven, that might support them in their perilous circumstances.

In these uncomfortable quarters, their chief employment was to keep watch on the melancholy ocean, that they might hail the first signal of the anticipated succor. But many a tedious month passed away, and no sign of it appeared. All around was the same wide waste of waters, except to the eastward, where the frozen crest of the Andes, touched with the ardent sun of the equator, glowed like a ridge of fire along the whole extent of the great continent. Every speck in the distant horizon was carefully noticed, and the drifting timber or masses of seaweed, heaving to and fro on the bosom of the waters, was converted by their imaginations into the promised vessel; till, sinking under successive disappointments, hope gradually gave way to doubt, and doubt settled into despair.

Meanwhile the vessel of Tafur had reached the port of Panama. The tidings which she brought of the inflexible obstinacy of Pizarro and his followers filled the governor with indignation. He could look on it in no other light than as an act of suicide, and steadily refused to send further assistance to men who were obstinately bent on their own destruction. Yet Luque and Almagro were true to their engagements. They represented to the governor that, if the conduct of their comrade was rash, it was at least in the service of the crown and in prosecuting the great work of discovery. Rios had been instructed, on his taking the government, to aid Pizarro in the enterprise; and to desert him now would be to throw away the remaining chance of success, and to incur the responsibility of his death and that of the brave men who adhered to him. These remonstrances, at length, so far operated on the mind of that functionary that he reluctantly consented that a vessel should be sent to the island of Gorgona, but with no more hands than were necessary to work her, and with positive instructions to Pizarro to return in six months and report himself at Panama, whatever might be the future results of his expedition.

Having thus secured the sanction of the executive, the two associates lost no time in fitting out a small vessel with stores and a supply of arms and ammunition, and despatched it to the island. The unfortunate tenants of this little wilderness, who had now occupied it for seven months, hardly dared to trust their senses when they descried the white sails of the friendly bark coming over the waters. And although, when the vessel anchored off the shore, Pizarro was disappointed to find that it brought no additional recruits for the enterprise, yet he greeted it with joy, as affording the means of solving the great problem of the existence of the rich southern empire, and of thus opening the way for its future conquest. Two of his men were so ill that it was determined to leave them in the care of some of the friendly Indians who had continued with him through the whole of his sojourn, and to call for them on his return. Taking with him the rest of his hardy followers and the natives of Tumbez, he embarked, and, speedily weighing anchor, bade adieu to the "Hell," as it was called by the Spaniards, which had been the scene of so much suffering and such undaunted resolution.

Every heart was now elated with hope, as they found themselves once more on the waters, under the guidance of the good pilot Ruiz, who, obeying the directions of the Indians, proposed to steer for the land of Tumbez. . . .

On leaving Tumbez, the adventurers steered directly for Panama, touching only, on their way, at the ill-fated island of Gorgona, to take on board their two companions who were left there too ill to proceed with them. One had died; and, receiving the other, Pizarro and his gallant little band continued their voyage, and, after an absence of at least eighteen months, found themselves once more safely riding at anchor in the harbor of Panama.

The sensation caused by their arrival was great, as might have been expected. For there were few, even among the most sanguine of their friends, who did not imagine that they had long since paid for their temerity, and fallen victims to the climate or the natives, or miserably perished in a watery grave. Their joy was proportionably great, therefore, as they saw the wanderers now returned, not only in health and safety, but with certain tidings of the fair countries which had so long eluded their grasp. It was a moment of proud satisfaction to the three associates, who, in spite of obloquy, derision, and every impediment which the distrust of friends or the coldness of government could throw in their way, had persevered in their great enterprise until they had established the truth of what had been so generally denounced as a chimera. It is the misfortune of those daring spirits who conceive an idea too vast for their own generation to comprehend, or, at least, to attempt to carry out, that they pass for visionary dreamers. Such had been the fate of Luque and his associates. The existence of a rich Indian empire at the south, which in their minds, dwelling long on the same idea and alive to all the arguments in its favor, had risen to the certainty of conviction, had been derided by the rest of their countrymen as a mere mirage of the fancy, which, on nearer approach, would melt into air; while the projectors who staked their fortunes on the adventure were denounced as madmen. But their hour of triumph, their slow and hard-earned triumph, had now arrived.

Yet the governor, Pedro de los Rios, did not seem, even at this moment, to be possessed with a conviction of the magnitude of the discovery—or perhaps he was discouraged by its very magnitude. When the associates now with more confidence applied to him for patronage in an undertaking too vast for their individual resources, he coldly replied, "He had no desire to build up other states at the expense of his own; nor would he be led to throw away more lives than had already been sacrificed by the cheap display of gold and silver toys and a few Indian sheep!"

Sorely disheartened by this repulse from the only quarter whence effectual aid could be expected, the confederates, without funds, and with credit nearly exhausted by their past efforts, were perplexed in the extreme. Yet to stop now—what was it but to abandon the rich mine which their own industry and perseverance had laid open, for others to work at pleasure? In this extremity the fruitful mind of Luque suggested the only expedient by which they could hope for success. This was to apply to the crown itself. No one was so much interested in the result of the expedition. It was for the government, indeed, that discoveries were to be made, that the country was to be conquered. The government alone was competent to provide the requisite means, and was likely to take a much broader and more liberal view of the matter than a petty colonial officer.

But who was there qualified to take charge of this delicate mission? Luque was chained by his professional duties to Panama; and his associates, unlettered soldiers, were much better fitted for the business of the camp than of the court. Almagro, blunt, though somewhat swelling and ostentatious in his address, with a diminutive stature and a countenance naturally plain, now much disfigured by the loss of an eye, was not so well qualified for the mission as his companion in arms, who, possessing a good person and altogether a commanding presence, was plausible, and, with all his defects of education, could, where deeply interested, be even eloquent in discourse. The ecclesiastic, however, suggested that the negotiation should be committed to the Licentiate Corral, a respectable functionary, then about to return on some public business to the mother-country. But to this Almagro strongly objected. No one, he said, could conduct the affair so well as the party interested in it. He had a high opinion of Pizarro's prudence, his discernment of character, and his cool, deliberate policy. He knew enough of his comrade to have confidence that his presence of mind would not desert him even in the new, and therefore embarrassing, circumstances in which he would be placed at court. No one, he said, could tell the story of their adventures with such effect as the man who had been the chief actor in them. No one could so well paint the unparalleled sufferings and sacrifices which they had encountered; no other could tell so forcibly what had been done, what yet remained to do, and what assistance would be necessary to carry it into execution. He concluded, with characteristic frankness, by strongly urging his confederate to undertake the mission.

Pizarro felt the force of Almagro's reasoning, and, though with undisguised reluctance, acquiesced in a measure which was less to his taste than an expedition to the wilderness. But Luque came into the arrangement with more difficulty. "God grant, my children," exclaimed the ecclesiastic, "that one of you may not defraud the other of his blessing!" Pizarro engaged to consult the interests of his associates equally with his own. But Luque, it is clear, did not trust Pizarro.

There was some difficulty in raising the funds necessary for putting the envoy in condition to make a suitable appearance at court; so low had the credit of the confederates fallen, and so little confidence was yet placed in the result of their splendid discoveries. Fifteen hundred ducats were at length raised; and Pizarro, in the spring of 1528, bade adieu to Panama, accompanied by Pedro de Candia. He took with him, also, some of the natives, as well as two or three llamas, various nice fabrics of cloth, with many ornaments and vases of gold and silver, as specimens of the civilization of the country, and vouchers for his wonderful story.

BOOK III

The Third Expedition

1528–1531

Pizarro and his officer, having crossed the isthmus, embarked at Nombre de Dios for the old country, and, after a good passage, reached Seville early in the summer of 1528. There happened to be at that time in port a person well known in the history of Spanish adventure as the Bachelor Enciso. He had taken an active part in the colonization of Tierra Firme, and had a pecuniary claim against the early colonists of Darien, of whom Pizarro was one. Immediately on the landing of the latter, he was seized by Enciso's orders and held in custody for the debt. Pizarro, who had fled from his native land as a forlorn and houseless adventurer, after an absence of more than twenty years, passed, most of them, in unprecedented toil and suffering, now found himself on his return the inmate of a prison. Such was the commencement of those brilliant fortunes which, as he had trusted, awaited him at home. The circumstance excited general indignation; and no sooner was the court advised of his arrival in the country, and the great purpose of his mission, than orders, were sent for his release, with permission to proceed at once on his journey.

Pizarro found the emperor at Toledo, which he was soon to quit, in order to embark for Italy. Spain was not the favorite residence of Charles the Fifth in the earlier part of his reign. He was now at that period of it when he was enjoying the full flush of his triumphs over his gallant rival of France, whom he had defeated and taken prisoner at the great battle of Pavia; and the victor was at this moment preparing to pass into Italy to receive the imperial crown from the hands of the Roman pontiff. Elated by his successes and his elevation to the German throne, Charles made little account of his hereditary kingdom, as his ambition found so splendid a career thrown open to it on the wide field of European politics. He had hitherto received too inconsiderable returns from his transatlantic possessions to give them the attention they deserved. But, as the recent acquisition of Mexico and the brilliant anticipations in respect to the southern continent were pressed upon his notice, he felt their importance as likely to afford him the means of prosecuting his ambitious and most expensive enterprises.

Pizarro, therefore, who had now come to satisfy the royal eyes, by visible proofs, of the truth of the golden rumors which from time to time had reached Castile, was graciously received by the emperor. Charles examined the various objects which his officer exhibited to him with great attention. He was particularly interested by the appearance of the llama, so remarkable as the only beast of burden yet known on the new continent; and the fine fabrics of woollen cloth which were made from its shaggy sides gave it a much higher value, in the eyes of the sagacious monarch, than what it possessed as an animal for domestic labor. But the specimens of gold and silver manufacture, and the wonderful tale which Pizarro had to tell of the abundance of the precious metals, must have satisfied even the cravings of royal cupidity.

Pizarro, far from being embarrassed by the novelty of his situation, maintained his usual self-possession, and showed that decorum and even dignity in his address which belong to the Castilian. He spoke in a simple and respectful style, but with the earnestness and natural eloquence of one who had been an actor in the scenes he described, and who was conscious that the impression he made on his audience was to decide his future destiny. All listened with eagerness to the account of his strange adventures by sea and land, his wanderings in the forests, or in the dismal and pestilent swamps on the seacoast, without food, almost without raiment, with feet torn and bleeding at every step, with his few companions becoming still fewer by disease and death, and yet pressing on with unconquerable spirit to extend the empire of Castile and the name and power of her sovereign; but when he painted his lonely condition on the desolate island, abandoned by the government at home, deserted by all but a handful of devoted followers, his royal auditor, though not easily moved, was affected to tears. On his departure from Toledo, Charles commended the affairs of his vassal in the most favorable terms to the consideration of the Council of the Indies.

There was at this time another man at court, who had come there on a similar errand from the New World, but whose splendid achievements had already won for him a name that threw the rising reputation of Pizarro comparatively into the shade. The man was Hernando Cortes, the Conqueror of Mexico. He had come home to lay an empire at the feet of his sovereign, and to demand in return the redress of his wrongs and the recompense of his great services. He was at the close of his career, as Pizarro was at the commencement of his; the Conqueror of the North and of the South; the two men appointed by Providence to overturn the most potent of the Indian dynasties, and to open the golden gates by which the treasures of the New World were to pass into the coffers of Spain.

Notwithstanding the emperor's recommendation, the business of Pizarro went forward at the tardy pace with which affairs are usually conducted in the court of Castile. He found his limited means gradually sinking under the expenses incurred by his present situation, and he represented that unless some measures were speedily taken in reference to his suit, however favorable they might be in the end, he should be in no condition to profit by them. The queen, accordingly, who had charge of the business, on her husband's departure, expedited the affair, and on the twenty-sixth of July, 1529, she executed the memorable Capitulation which defined the powers and privileges of Pizarro.

The instrument secured to that chief the right of discovery and conquest in the province of Peru, or New Castile—as the country was then called, in the same manner as Mexico had received the name of New Spain—for the distance of two hundred leagues south of Santiago. He was to receive the titles and rank of governor and captain-general of the province, together with those of adelantado and alguacil mayor, for life; and he was to have a salary of seven hundred and twenty-five thousand maravedis, with the obligation of maintaining certain officers and military retainers, corresponding with the dignity of his station. He was to have the right to erect certain fortresses, with the absolute

government of them; to assign encomiendas of Indians, under
the limitations by law; and, in fine, to exercise nearly all the
prerogatives incident to the authority of a viceroy.

His associate, Almagro, was declared commander of the fortress of Tumbez, with an annual rent of three hundred thousand
maravedis, and with the further rank and privileges of an hidalgo.
The reverend Father Luque received the reward of his services
in the bishopric of Tumbez, and he was also declared Protector
of the Indians of Peru. He was to enjoy the yearly stipend of a
thousand ducats—to be derived, like the other salaries and
gratuities in this instrument, from the revenues of the conquered
territory.

Nor were the subordinate actors in the expedition forgotten.
Ruiz received the title of Grand Pilot of the Southern Ocean,
with a liberal provision; Candia was placed at the head of the
artillery; and the remaining eleven companions on the desolate
island were created hidalgos and cavalleros, and raised to certain
municipal dignities—in prospect.

Several provisions of a liberal tenor were also made, to encourage emigration to the country. The new settlers were to be
exempted from some of the most onerous but customary taxes,
as the alcabala, or to be subject to them only in a mitigated form.
The tax on the precious metals drawn from mines was to be
reduced, at first, to one-tenth, instead of the fifth imposed on
the same metals when obtained by barter or by rapine.

It was expressly enjoined on Pizarro to observe the existing
regulations for the good government and protection of the natives; and he was required to carry out with him a specified number of ecclesiastics, with whom he was to take counsel in the
conquest of the country, and whose efforts were to be dedicated
to the service and conversion of the Indians; while lawyers and
attorneys, on the other hand, whose presence was considered as
boding ill to the harmony of the new settlements, were strictly
prohibited from setting foot in them.

Pizarro, on his part, was bound, in six months from the date
of the instrument, to raise a force, well equipped for the service,
of two hundred and fifty men, of whom one hundred might be
drawn from the colonies; and the government engaged to furnish
some trifling assistance in the purchase of artillery and military
stores. Finally, he was to be prepared, in six months after his

return to Panama, to leave that port and embark on his expedition.

Such are some of the principal provisions of this Capitulation, by which the Castilian government, with the sagacious policy which it usually pursued on the like occasions, stimulated the ambitious hopes of the adventurer by high-sounding titles and liberal promises of reward contingent on his success, but took care to stake nothing itself on the issue of the enterprise. It was careful to reap the fruits of his toil, but not to pay the cost of them.

A circumstance that could not fail to be remarked in these provisions was the manner in which the high and lucrative posts were accumulated on Pizarro, to the exclusion of Almagro, who, if he had not taken as conspicuous a part in personal toil and exposure, had at least divided with him the original burden of the enterprise, and, by his labors in another direction, had contributed quite as essentially to its success. Almagro had willingly conceded the post of honor to his confederate; but it had been stipulated, on Pizarro's departure for Spain, that, while he solicited the office of governor and captain-general for himself, he should secure that of adelantado for his companion. In like manner, he had engaged to apply for the see of Tumbez for the vicar of Panama, and the office of alguacil mayor for the pilot Ruiz. The bishopric took the direction that was concerted, for the soldier could scarcely claim the miter of the prelate; but the other offices, instead of their appropriate distribution, were all concentrated in himself. Yet it was in reference to his application for his friends that Pizarro had promised on his departure to deal fairly and honorably by them all.

It is stated by the military chronicler, Pedro Pizarro, that his kinsman did, in fact, urge the suit strongly in behalf of Almagro, but that he was refused by the government, on the ground that offices of such paramount importance could not be committed to different individuals. The ill effects of such an arrangement had been long since felt in more than one of the Indian colonies, where it had led to rivalry and fatal collision. Pizarro, therefore, finding his remonstrances unheeded, had no alternative but to combine the offices in his own person, or to see the expedition fall to the ground. This explanation of the affair has not received the sanction of other contemporary historians. The apprehensions expressed by Luque, at the time of Pizarro's assuming the mission, of some such result as actually occurred, founded, doubtless, on a knowledge of his associate's character, may warrant us in distrusting the alleged vindication of his conduct; and our distrust will not be diminished by familiarity with his subsequent career. Pizarro's virtue was not of a kind to withstand temptation—though of a much weaker sort than now thrown in his path.

The fortunate cavalier was also honored with the habit of St. Jago; and he was authorized to make an important innovation in his family escutcheon—for by the father's side he might claim his armorial bearings. The black eagle and the two pillars emblazoned on the royal arms were incorporated with those of the Pizarros; and an Indian city, with a vessel in the distance on the waters, and the llama of Peru, revealed the theater and the character of his exploits; while the legend announced that "under the auspices of Charles, and by the industry, the genius, and the resources of Pizarro, the country had been discovered and reduced to tranquillity"—thus modestly intimating both the past and prospective services of the Conqueror.

These arrangements having been thus completed to Pizarro's satisfaction, he left Toledo for Truxillo, his native place, in Estremadura, where he thought he should be most likely to meet with adherents for his new enterprise, and where it doubtless gratified his vanity to display himself in the palmy, or at least promising, state of his present circumstances. If vanity be ever pardonable, it is certainly in a man who, born in an obscure station in life, without family, interest, or friends to back him, has carved out his own fortunes in the world, and, by his own resources, triumphed over all the obstacles which nature and accident had thrown in his way. Such was the condition of Pizarro as he now revisited the place of his nativity, where he had hitherto been known only as a poor outcast, without a home to shelter, a father to own him, or a friend to lean upon. But he now found both friends and followers, and some who were eager to claim kindred with him and take part in his future fortunes. Among these were four brothers. Three of them, like himself, were illegitimate—one of whom, named Francisco Martin de Alcantara, was related to him by the mother's side, the other two, named

Gonzalo and Juan Pizarro, were descended from the father. "They were all poor, and proud as they were poor," says Oviedo, who had seen them; "and their eagerness for gain was in proportion to their poverty."

The remaining and eldest brother, named Hernando, was a legitimate son—"legitimate," continues the same caustic authority, "by his pride, as well as by his birth." His features were plain, even disagreeably so; but his figure was good. He was large of stature, and, like his brother Francis, had on the whole an imposing presence. In his character he combined some of the worst defects incident to the Castilian. He was jealous in the extreme; impatient, not merely of affront, but of the least slight, and implacable in his resentment. He was decisive in his measures, and unscrupulous in their execution. No touch of pity had power to arrest his arm. His arrogance was such that he was constantly wounding the self-love of those with whom he acted; thus begetting an ill will which unnecessarily multiplied obstacles in his path. In this he differed from his brother Francis, whose plausible manners smoothed away difficulties and conciliated confidence and cooperation in his enterprise. Unfortunately, the evil counsels of Hernando exercised an influence over his brother which more than compensated the advantages derived from his singular capacity for business.

Notwithstanding the general interest which Pizarro's adventures excited in his country, that chief did not find it easy to comply with the provisions of the Capitulation in respect to the amount of his levies. Those who were most astonished by his narrative were not always most inclined to take part in his fortunes. They shrank from the unparalleled hardships which lay in the path of the adventurer in that direction; and they listened with visible distrust to the gorgeous pictures of the golden temples and gardens of Tumbez, which they looked upon as indebted in some degree, at least, to the coloring of his fancy, with the obvious purpose of attracting followers to his banner. It is even said that Pizarro would have found it difficult to raise the necessary funds, but for the seasonable aid of Cortes, a native of Estremadura like himself, his companion in arms in early days, and, according to report, his kinsman. No one was in a better condition to hold out a helping hand to a brother adventurer, and probably no one felt greater sympathy in Pizarro's fortunes, or greater confidence in his eventual success, than the man who had so lately trod the same career with renown.

The six months allowed by the Capitulation had elapsed, and Pizarro had assembled somewhat less than his stipulated complement of men, with which he was preparing to embark in a little squadron of three vessels at Seville; but before they were wholly ready he received intelligence that the officers of the Council of the Indies proposed to inquire into the condition of the vessels and ascertain how far the requisitions had been complied with.

Without loss of time, therefore, Pizarro, afraid, if the facts were known, that his enterprise might be nipped in the bud, slipped his cables, and, crossing the bar of San Lucar, in January, 1530, stood for the isle of Gomera—one of the Canaries—where he ordered his brother Hernando, who had charge of the remaining vessels, to meet him.

Scarcely had he gone, before the officers arrived to institute the search. But when they objected the deficiency of men they were easily—perhaps willingly—deceived by the pretext that the remainder had gone forward in the vessel with Pizarro. At all events, no further obstacles were thrown in Hernando's way, and he was permitted, with the rest of the squadron, to join his brother, according to agreement, at Gomera.

After a prosperous voyage, the adventurers reached the northern coast of the great southern continent, and anchored off the port of Santa Marta. Here they received such discouraging reports of the countries to which they were bound, of forests teeming with insects and venomous serpents, of huge alligators that swarmed on the banks of the streams, and of hardships and perils such as their own fears had never painted, that several of Pizarro's men deserted, and their leader, thinking it no longer safe to abide in such treacherous quarters, set sail at once for Nombre de Dios.

Soon after his arrival there, he was met by his two associates, Luque and Almagro, who had crossed the mountains for the purpose of hearing from his own lips the precise import of the Capitulation with the crown. Great, as might have been expected, was Almagro's discontent at learning the result of what he regarded as the perfidious machinations of his associate. "Is it thus," he exclaimed, "that you have dealt with the friend who shared equally with you in the trials, the dangers, and the cost of the enterprise, and this, notwithstanding your solemn engagements on your departure to provide for his interests as faithfully as your own? How could you allow me to be thus dishonored in the eyes of the world by so paltry a compensation, which seems to estimate my services as nothing in comparison with your own?"

Pizarro, in reply, assured his companion that he had faithfully urged his suit, but that the government refused to confide powers which intrenched so closely on one another to different hands. He had no alternative but to accept all himself or to decline all; and he endeavored to mitigate Almagro's displeasure by representing that the country was large enough for the ambition of both, and that the powers conferred on himself were, in fact, conferred on Almagro, since all that he had would ever be at his friend's disposal, as if it were his own. But these honeyed words did not satisfy the injured party; and the two captains soon after returned to Panama with feelings of estrangement, if not hostility, towards one another, which did not augur well for their enterprise.

Still, Almagro was of a generous temper, and might have been appeased by the politic concessions of his rival, but for the interference of Hernando Pizarro, who, from the first hour of their meeting, showed little respect for the veteran, which, indeed, the diminutive person of the latter was not calculated to inspire, and who now regarded him with particular aversion as an impediment to the career of his brother.

Almagro's friends—and his frank and liberal manners had secured him many—were no less disgusted than himself with the overbearing conduct of this new ally. They loudly complained that it was quite enough to suffer from the perfidy of Pizarro, without being exposed to the insults of his family, who had now come over with him to fatten on the spoils of conquest which belonged to their leader. The rupture soon proceeded to such a length that Almagro avowed his intention to prosecute the expedition without further cooperation with his partner, and actually entered into negotiations for the purchase of vessels for that object. But Luque, and the Licentiate Espinosa, who had fortunately come over at that time from St. Domingo, now interposed to repair a breach which must end in the ruin of the enterprise and the probable destruction of those most interested in its success. By their mediation, a show of reconciliation was at length effected between the parties, on Pizarro's assurance that he would relinquish the dignity of adelantado in favor of his rival, and petition the emperor to confirm him in the possession of it—an assurance, it may be remarked, not easy to reconcile with his former assertion in respect to the avowed policy of the crown in bestowing this office. He was, moreover, to apply for a distinct government for his associate, so soon as he had become master of the country assigned to himself, and was to solicit no office for either of his own brothers until Almagro had been first provided for. Lastly, the former contract in regard to the division of the spoil into three equal shares between the three original associates was confirmed in the most explicit manner. The reconciliation thus effected among the parties answered the temporary purpose of enabling them to go forward in concert in the expedition. But it was only a thin scar that had healed over the wound, which, deep and rankling within, waited only fresh cause of irritation to break out with a virulence more fatal than ever.

No time was now lost in preparing for the voyage. It found little encouragement, however, among the colonists of Panama, who were too familiar with the sufferings on the former expeditions to care to undertake another, even with the rich bribe that was held out to allure them. A few of the old company were content to follow out the adventure to its close; and some additional stragglers were collected from the province of Nicaragua —a shoot, it may be remarked, from the colony of Panama. But Pizarro made slender additions to the force brought over with him from Spain, though this body was in better condition, and, in respect to arms, ammunition, and equipment generally, was on a much better footing, than his former levies. The whole number did not exceed one hundred and eighty men, with twenty-seven horses for the cavalry. He had provided himself with three vessels, two of them of a good size, to take the place of those which he had been compelled to leave on the opposite side of the Isthmus at Nombre de Dios; an armament small for the conquest of an empire, and far short of that prescribed by the Capitulation with the crown. With this the intrepid chief proposed to commence operations, trusting to his own successes, and the exertions of Almagro, who was to remain behind for the present, to muster reinforcements.

On St. John the Evangelist's day, the banners of the company and the royal standard were consecrated in the cathedral church of Panama; a sermon was preached before the little army by Fray Juan de Vargas, one of the Dominicans selected by the government for the Peruvian mission; and mass was performed, and the sacrament administered to every soldier previous to his engaging in the crusade against the infidel. Having thus solemnly invoked the blessing of Heaven on the enterprise, Pizarro and his followers went on board their vessels, which rode at anchor in the Bay of Panama, and early in January, 1531, sallied forth on his third and last expedition for the conquest of Peru. . . .

FROM CHAPTER III

March into the Interior

1532

On the 24th of September, 1532, five months after landing at Tumbez, Pizarro marched out at the head of his little body of adventurers from the gates of San Miguel, having enjoined it on the colonists to treat their Indian vassals with humanity and to conduct themselves in such a manner as would secure the good will of the surrounding tribes. Their own existence, and with it the safety of the army and the success of the undertaking, depended on this course. In the place were to remain the royal treasurer, the veedor, or inspector of metals, and other officers of the crown; and the command of the garrison was intrusted to the contador, Antonio Navarro. Then, putting himself at the head of his troops, the chief struck boldly into the heart of the country in the direction where, as he was informed, lay the camp of the Inca. It was a daring enterprise, thus to venture with a handful of followers into the heart of a powerful empire, to present himself face to face before the Indian monarch in his own camp, encompassed by the flower of his victorious army! Pizarro had already experienced more than once the difficulty of maintaining his ground against the rude tribes of the north, so much inferior in strength and numbers to the warlike legions of Peru. But the hazard of the game, as I have already more than once had occasion to remark, constituted its great charm with the Spaniard. The brilliant achievements of his countrymen, on the like occasions, with means so inadequate, inspired him with confidence in his own good star, and this confidence was one source of his success. Had he faltered for a moment, had he stopped to calculate chances, he must inevitably have failed; for the odds were too great to be combated by sober reason. They were only to be met triumphantly by the spirit of the knight-errant.

After crossing the smooth waters of the Piura, the little army continued to advance over a level district intersected by streams that descended from the neighboring Cordilleras. The face of the country was shagged over with forests of gigantic growth, and occasionally traversed by ridges of barren land, that seemed like shoots of the adjacent Andes, breaking up the surface of the region into little sequestered valleys of singular loveliness. The soil, though rarely watered by the rains of heaven, was naturally rich, and wherever it was refreshed with moisture, as on the margins of the streams, it was enameled with the brightest verdure. The industry of the inhabitants, moreover, had turned these streams to the best account, and canals and aqueducts were seen crossing the low lands in all directions, and spreading over the country, like a vast network, diffusing fertility and beauty around them. The air was scented with the sweet odors of flowers, and everywhere the eye was refreshed by the sight of orchards laden with unknown fruits, and of fields waving with yellow grain and rich in luscious vegetables of every description that teem in the sunny clime of the equator. The Spaniards were among a people who had carried the refinements of husbandry to a greater extent than any yet found on the American continent; and, as they journeyed through this paradise of plenty, their condition formed a pleasing contrast to what they had before endured in the dreary wilderness of the mangroves.

Everywhere, too, they were received with confiding hospitality by the simple people; for which they were no doubt indebted, in a great measure, to their own inoffensive deportment. Every

Spaniard seemed to be aware that his only chance of success lay in conciliating the good opinion of the inhabitants among whom he had so recklessly cast his fortunes. In most of the hamlets, and in every place of considerable size, some fortress was to be found, or royal caravansary, destined for the Inca on his progresses, the ample halls of which furnished abundant accommodations for the Spaniards; who were thus provided with quarters along their route at the charge of the very government which they were preparing to overturn.

On the fifth day after leaving San Miguel, Pizarro halted in one of these delicious valleys, to give his troops repose and to make a more complete inspection of them. Their number amounted in all to one hundred and seventy-seven, of which sixty-seven were cavalry. He mustered only three arquebusiers in his whole company, and a few crossbow-men, altogether not exceeding twenty. The troops were tolerably well equipped, and in good condition. But the watchful eye of their commander noticed with uneasiness that, notwithstanding the general heartiness in the cause manifested by his followers, there were some among them whose countenances lowered with discontent, and who, although they did not give vent to it in open murmurs, were far from moving with their wonted alacrity. He was aware that if this spirit became contagious it would be the ruin of the enterprise; and he thought it best to exterminate the gangrene at once, and at whatever cost, than to wait until it had infected the whole system. He came to an extraordinary resolution.

Calling his men together, he told them that "a crisis had now arrived in their affairs, which it demanded all their courage to meet. No man should think of going forward in the expedition who could not do so with his whole heart, or who had the least misgiving as to its success. If any repented of his share in it, it was not too late to turn back. San Miguel was but poorly garrisoned, and he should be glad to see it in greater strength. Those who chose might return to this place, and they should be entitled to the same proportion of lands and Indian vassals as the present residents. With the rest, were they few or many, who chose to take their chance with him, he should pursue the adventure to the end."

It was certainly a remarkable proposal for a commander who was ignorant of the amount of disaffection in his ranks, and who could not safely spare a single man from his force, already far too feeble for the undertaking. Yet, by insisting on the wants of the little colony of San Miguel, he afforded a decent pretext for the secession of the malcontents, and swept away the barrier of shame which might have still held them in the camp. Notwithstanding the fair opening thus afforded, there were but few, nine in all, who availed themselves of the general's permission. Four of these belonged to the infantry, and five to the horse. The rest loudly declared their resolve to go forward with their brave leader; and, if there were some whose voices were faint amidst the general acclamation, they at least relinquished the right of complaining hereafter, since they had voluntarily rejected the permission to return. This stroke of policy in their sagacious captain was attended with the best effects. He had winnowed out the few grains of discontent which, if left to themselves, might have fermented in secret till the whole mass had swelled into mutiny. Cortes had compelled his men to go forward heartily in his enterprise by burning their vessels and thus cutting off the only means of retreat. Pizarro, on the other hand, threw open the gates to the disaffected and facilitated their departure. Both judged right, under their peculiar circumstances, and both were perfectly successful.

Feeling himself strengthened, instead of weakened, by his loss, Pizarro now resumed his march, and on the second day arrived before a place called Zaran, situated in a fruitful valley among the mountains. Some of the inhabitants had been drawn off to swell the levies of Atahuallpa. The Spaniards had repeated experience on their march of the oppressive exactions of the Inca, who had almost depopulated some of the valleys to obtain reinforcements for his army. The curaca of the Indian town where Pizarro now arrived received him with kindness and hospitality, and the troops were quartered as usual in one of the royal tambos or caravansaries, which were found in all the principal places.

Yet the Spaniards saw no signs of their approach to the royal encampment, though more time had already elapsed than was originally allowed for reaching it. Shortly before entering Zaran, Pizarro had heard that a Peruvian garrison was established in a place called Caxas, lying among the hills, at no great distance from his present quarters. He immediately despatched a small party under Hernando de Soto in that direction, to reconnoiter the ground, and bring him intelligence of the actual state of things, at Zaran, where he would halt until his officer's return.

Day after day passed on, and a week had elapsed before tidings were received of his companions, and Pizarro was becoming seriously alarmed for their fate, when on the eighth morning Soto appeared, bringing with him an envoy from the Inca himself. He was a person of rank, and was attended by several followers of inferior condition. He had met the Spaniards at Caxas, and now accompanied them on their return, to deliver his sovereign's message, with a present to the Spanish commander. The present consisted of two fountains, made of stone, in the form of fortresses; some fine stuffs of woollen embroidered with gold and silver; and a quantity of goose-flesh, dried and seasoned in a peculiar manner, and much used as a perfume, in a pulverized state, by the Peruvian nobles. The Indian ambassador came charged also with his master's greeting to the strangers, whom Atahuallpa welcomed to his country and invited to visit him in his camp among the mountains.

Pizarro well understood that the Inca's object in this diplomatic visit was less to do him courtesy than to inform himself of the strength and condition of the invaders. But he was well pleased with the embassy, and dissembled his consciousness of its real purpose. He caused the Peruvian to be entertained in the best manner the camp could afford, and paid him the respect, says one of the Conquerors, due to the ambassador of so great a monarch. Pizarro urged him to prolong his visit for some days, which the Indian envoy declined, but made the most of his time while there, by gleaning all the information he could in respect to the use of every strange article which he saw, as well as the object of the white men's visit to the land, and the quarter whence they came.

The Spanish captain satisfied his curiosity in all these particulars. The intercourse with the natives, it may be here remarked, was maintained by means of two of the youths who had accompanied the Conquerors on their return home from their preceding voyage. They had been taken by Pizarro to Spain, and, as much pains had been bestowed on teaching them the Castilian, they now filled the office of interpreters and opened an easy communication with their countrymen. It was of inestimable service; and well did the Spanish commander reap the fruits of his forecast.

On the departure of the Peruvian messenger, Pizarro presented him with a cap of crimson cloth, some cheap but showy ornaments of glass, and other toys, which he had brought for the purpose from Castile. He charged the envoy to tell his master that the Spaniards came from a powerful prince who dwelt far beyond the waters; that they had heard much of the fame of Atahuallpa's victories, and were come to pay their respects to him, and to offer their services by aiding him with their arms against his enemies; and he might be assured they would not halt on the road longer than was necessary, before presenting themselves before him.

Pizarro now received from Soto a full account of his late expedition. That chief, on entering Caxas, found the inhabitants mustered in hostile array, as if to dispute his passage. But the cavalier soon convinced them of his pacific intentions, and, laying aside their menacing attitude, they received the Spaniards with the same courtesy which had been shown them in most places on their march.

Here Soto found one of the royal officers, employed in collecting the tribute for the government. From this functionary he learned that the Inca was quartered with a large army at Caxamalca, a place of considerable size on the other side of the Cordillera, where he was enjoying the luxury of the warm baths, supplied by natural springs, for which it was then famous, as it is at the present day. The cavalier gathered, also, much important information in regard to the resources and the general policy of government, the state maintained by the Inca, and the stern severity with which obedience to the law was everywhere enforced. He had some opportunity of observing this for himself, as, on entering the village, he saw several Indians hanging dead by their heels, having been executed for some violence offered to the Virgins of the Sun, of whom there was a convent in the neighborhood.

From Caxas, De Soto had passed to the adjacent town of Guancabamba, much larger, more populous, and better built than the preceding. The houses, instead of being made of clay baked in the sun, were many of them constructed of solid stone, so nicely put together that it was impossible to detect the line of junction. A river which passed through the town was traversed by a bridge, and the highroad of the Incas which crossed this district was far superior to that which the Spaniards had seen on the seaboard. It was raised in many places, like a causeway, paved with heavy stone flags, and bordered by trees that afforded a grateful shade to the passenger, while streams of water were conducted through aqueducts along the sides to slake his thirst. At certain distances, also, they noticed small houses, which, they were told, were for the accommodation of the traveler, who might thus pass without inconvenience from one end of the kingdom to the other. In another quarter they beheld one of those magazines destined for the army, filled with grain and with articles of clothing; and at the entrance of the town was a stone building, occupied by a public officer, whose business it was to collect the tolls or duties on various commodities brought into the place or carried out of it. These accounts of De Soto not only confirmed all that the Spaniards had heard of the Indian empire, but greatly raised their ideas of its resources and domestic policy. They might well have shaken the confidence of hearts less courageous.

Pizarro, before leaving his present quarters, despatched a messenger to San Miguel with particulars of his movements, sending at the same time the articles received from the Inca, as well as those obtained at different places on the route. The skill shown in the execution of some of these fabrics sent to Castile excited great admiration there. The fine woollen cloths, especially, with their rich embroidery, were pronounced equal to textures of silk, from which it was not easy to distinguish them. The material was probably the delicate wool of the vicuña, none of which had then been seen in Europe.

Pizarro, having now acquainted himself with the most direct route to Caxamalca—the Caxamarca of the present day—resumed his march, taking a direction nearly south. The first place of any size at which he halted was Motupe, pleasantly situated in a fruitful valley, among hills of no great elevation, which cluster round the base of the Cordilleras. The place was deserted by its curaca, who, with three hundred of its warriors, had gone to join the standard of their Inca. Here the general, notwithstanding his avowed purpose to push forward without delay, halted four days. The tardiness of his movements can be explained only by the hope which he may have still entertained of being joined by further reinforcements before crossing the Cordilleras. None such appeared, however; and, advancing across a country in which tracts of sandy plain were occasionally relieved by a broad expanse of verdant meadow, watered by natural streams and still more abundantly by those brought through artificial channels, the troops at length arrived at the borders of a river. It was broad and deep, and the rapidity of the current opposed more than ordinary difficulty to the passage. Pizarro, apprehensive lest this might be disputed by the natives on the opposite bank, ordered his brother Hernando to cross over with a small detachment under cover of night and secure a safe landing for the rest of the troops. At break of day Pizarro made preparations for his own passage, by hewing timber in the neighboring woods and constructing a sort of floating bridge, on which before nightfall the whole company passed in safety, the horses swimming, being led by the bridle. It was a day of severe labor, and Pizarro took his own share in it freely, like a common soldier, having ever a word of encouragement to say to his followers.

On reaching the opposite side, they learned from their comrades that the people of the country, instead of offering resistance, had fled in dismay. One of them, having been taken and brought before Hernando Pizarro, refused to answer the questions put to him respecting the Inca and his army; till, being put to the torture, he stated that Atahuallpa was encamped, with his whole force, in three seperate divisions, occupying the high grounds and plains of Caxamalca. He further stated that the Inca was aware of the approach of the white men and of their small number, and that he was purposely decoying them into his own quarters, that he might have them more completely in his power.

This account, when reported by Hernando to his brother, caused the latter much anxiety. As the timidity of the peasantry, however, gradually wore off, some of them mingled with the troops, and among them the curaca or principal person of the village. He had himself visited the royal camp, and he informed the general that Atahuallpa lay at the strong town of Huamachuco, twenty leagues or more south of Caxamalca, with an army of at least fifty thousand men.

These contradictory statements greatly perplexed the chieftain; and he proposed to one of the Indians who had borne him company during a great part of the march, to go as a spy into the Inca's quarters and bring him intelligence of his actual position, and, as far as he could learn them, of his intentions towards the Spaniards. But the man positively declined this dangerous service, though he professed his willingness to go as an authorized messenger of the Spanish commander.

Pizarro acquiesced in this proposal, and instructed his envoy to assure the Inca that he was advancing with all convenient speed to meet him. He was to acquaint the monarch with the uniformly considerate conduct of the Spaniards towards his subjects in their progress through the land, and to assure him that they were now coming in full confidence of finding in him the same amicable feelings towards themselves. The emissary was practically instructed to observe if the strong passes on the road were defended, or if any preparations of a hostile character were to be discerned. This last intelligence he was to communicate to the general by means of two or three nimble-footed attendants who were to accompany him on his mission.

Having taken this precaution, the wary commander again resumed his march, and at the end of three days reached the base of the mountain-rampart behind which lay the ancient town of Caxamalca. Before him rose the stupendous Andes, rock piled upon rock, their skirts below dark with evergreen forests, varied here and there by terraced patches of cultivated garden, with the peasant's cottage clinging to their shaggy sides, and their crests of snow glittering high in the heavens—presenting altogether such a wild chaos of magnificence and beauty as no other mountain scenery in the world can show. Across this tremendous rampart, through a labyrinth of passes, easily capable of defense by a handful of men against an army, the troops were now to march. To the right ran a broad and level road, with its border of friendly shades, and wide enough for two carriages to pass abreast. It was one of the great routes leading to Cuzco, and seemed by its pleasant and easy access to invite the way-worn soldier to choose it in preference to the dangerous mountain defiles. Many were accordingly of opinion that the army should take this course and abandon the original destination to Caxamalca. But such was not the decision of Pizarro.

The Spaniards had everywhere proclaimed their purpose, he said, to visit the Inca in his camp. This purpose had been communicated to the Inca himself. To take an opposite direction now would only be to draw on them the imputation of cowardice, and to incur Atahuallpa's contempt. No alternative remained but to march straight across the sierra to his quarters. "Let every one of you," said the bold cavalier, "take heart and go forward like a good soldier, nothing daunted by the smallness of your numbers. For in the greatest extremity God ever fights for his own; and doubt not he will humble the pride of the heathen, and bring him to the knowledge of the true faith, the great end and object of the Conquest."

Pizarro, like Cortes, possessed a good share of that frank and manly eloquence which touches the heart of the soldier more than the parade of rhetoric or the finest flow of elocution. He was a soldier himself, and partook in all the feelings of the soldier, his joys, his hopes, and his disappointments. He was not raised by rank and education above sympathy with the humblest of his followers. Every chord in their bosoms vibrated with the same pulsations as his own, and the conviction of this gave him a mastery over them. "Lead on," they shouted, as he finished his brief but animating address, "lead on wherever you think best. We will follow with good will, and you shall see that we can do our duty in the cause of God and the King!" There was no longer hesitation. All thoughts were now bent on the instant passage of the Cordilleras.

CHAPTER IV

Passage of the Andes and Embassy to the Inca

1532

That night Pizarro held a council of his principal officers, and it was determined that he should lead the advance, consisting of forty horse and sixty foot, and reconnoiter the ground; while the rest of the company, under his brother Hernando, should occupy their present position till they received further orders.

At early dawn the Spanish general and his detachment were under arms and prepared to breast the difficulties of the sierra. These proved even greater than had been foreseen. The path had been conducted in the most judicious manner round the rugged and precipitous sides of the mountains, so as best to avoid the natural impediments presented by the ground. But it was necessarily so steep, in many places, that the cavalry were obliged to dismount, and, scrambling up as they could, to lead their horses by the bridle. In many places, too, where some huge crag or eminence overhung the road, this was driven to the very verge of the precipice; and the traveler was compelled to wind along the narrow ledge of rock, scarcely wide enough for his single steed, where a misstep would precipitate him hundreds, nay, thousands of feet into the dreadful abyss! The wild passes of the sierra, practicable for the half-naked Indian, and even for the sure and circumspect mule—an animal that seems to have been created for the roads of the Cordilleras—were formidable to the man-at-arms encumbered with his panoply of mail. The tremendous fissures or quebradas, so frightful in this mountain chain, yawned open, as if the Andes had been split asunder by some terrible convulsion, showing a broad expanse of the primitive rock on their sides, partially mantled over with the spontaneous vegetation of ages; while their obscure depths furnished a channel for the torrents, that, rising in the heart of the sierra, worked their way gradually into light and spread over the savannas and green valleys of the tierra caliente on their way to the great ocean.

Many of these passes afforded obvious points of defense; and the Spaniards, as they entered the rocky defiles, looked with apprehension lest they might rouse some foe from his ambush. This apprehension was heightened as, at the summit of a steep and narrow gorge, in which they were engaged, they beheld a strong work, rising like a fortress, and frowning, as it were, in gloomy defiance on the invaders. As they drew near this building, which was of solid stone, commanding an angle of the road, they almost expected to see the dusky forms of the warriors rise over the battlements, and to receive their tempest of missiles on their bucklers; for it was in so strong a position that a few resolute men might easily have held there an army at bay. But they had the satisfaction to find the place untenanted, and their spirits were greatly raised by the conviction that the Indian monarch did not intend to dispute their passage, when it would have been easy to do so with success.

Pizarro now sent orders to his brother to follow without delay, and, after refreshing his men, continued his toilsome ascent, and before nightfall reached an eminence crowned by another fortress, of even greater strength than the preceding. It was built of solid masonry, the lower part excavated from the living rock, and the whole work executed with skill not inferior to that of the European architect.

Here Pizarro took up his quarters for the night. Without waiting for the arrival of the rear, on the following morning he resumed his march, leading still deeper into the intricate gorges of the sierra. The climate had gradually changed, and the men and horses, especially the latter, suffered severely from the cold, so long accustomed as they had been to the sultry climate of the tropics. The vegetation also had changed its character; and the magnificent timber which covered the lower level of the country had gradually given way to the funereal forest of pine, and, as they rose still higher, to the stunted growth of numberless Alpine plants, whose hardy natures found a congenial temperature in the icy atmosphere of the more elevated regions. These dreary solitudes seemed to be nearly abandoned by the brute creation as well as by man. The light-footed vicuña, roaming in its native state, might be sometimes seen looking down from some airy cliff, where the foot of the hunter dared not venture. But instead of the feathered tribes whose gay plumage sparkled in the deep glooms of the tropical forests, the adventurers now beheld only the great bird of the Andes, the loathsome condor, which, sailing high above the clouds, followed with doleful cries in the track of the army, as if guided by instinct in the path of blood and carnage.

At length they reached the crest of the Cordillera, where it spreads out into a bold and bleak expanse, with scarcely a vestige of vegetation, except what is afforded by the pajonal, a dried yellow grass, which, as it is seen from below, encircling the base of the snow-covered peaks, looks, with its brilliant straw-color lighted up in the rays of an ardent sun, like a setting of gold round pinnacles of burnished silver. The land was sterile, as usual in mining districts, and they were drawing near the once famous gold quarries on the way to Caxamalca:

Rocks rich in gems, and mountains big with mines,
That on the high equator ridgy rise.

Here Pizarro halted for the coming up of the rear. The air was sharp and frosty; and the soldiers, spreading their tents, lighted fires, and, huddling round them, endeavored to find some repose after their laborious march.

They had not been long in these quarters, when a messenger arrived, one of those who had accompanied the Indian envoy sent by Pizarro to Atahuallpa. He informed the general that the road was free from enemies, and that an embassy from the Inca was on its way to the Castilian camp. Pizarro now sent back to quicken the march of the rear, as he was unwilling that the Peruvian envoy should find him with his present diminished numbers. The rest of the army were not far distant, and not long after reached the encampment.

In a short time the Indian embassy also arrived, which consisted of one of the Inca nobles and several attendants, bringing a welcome present of llamas to the Spanish commander. The Peruvian bore, also, the greetings of his master, who wished to know when the Spaniards would arrive at Caxamalca, that he might provide suitable refreshments for them. Pizarro learned that the Inca had left Huamachuco, and was now lying with a small force in the neighborhood of Caxamalca, at a place celebrated for its natural springs of warm water. The Peruvian was an intelligent person, and the Spanish commander gathered from him many particulars respecting the late contests which had distracted the empire.

As the envoy vaunted in lofty terms the military prowess and resources of his sovereign, Pizarro thought it politic to show that it had no power to overawe him. He expressed his satisfaction at the triumphs of Atahuallpa, who, he acknowledged, had raised himself high in the rank of Indian warriors. But he was as inferior, he added with more policy than politeness, to the monarch who ruled over the white men, as the petty curacas of the country were inferior to him. This was evident from the ease with which a few Spaniards had overrun this great continent, subduing one nation after another that had offered resistance to their arms. He had been led by the fame of Atahuallpa to visit his dominions and to offer him his services in his wars, and, if he were received by the Inca in the same friendly spirit with which he came, he was willing, for the aid he could render him, to postpone awhile his passage across the country to the opposite seas. The Indian, according to the Castilian accounts, listened with awe to this strain of glorification from the Spanish commander. Yet it is possible that the envoy was a better diplomatist than they imagined, and that he understood it was only the game of brag at which he was playing with his more civilized antagonist.

On the succeeding morning, at an early hour, the troops were again on their march, and for two days were occupied in threading the airy defiles of the Cordilleras. Soon after beginning their descent on the eastern side, another emissary arrived from the Inca, bearing a message of similar import to the preceding, and a present, in like manner, of Peruvian sheep. This was the same noble that had visited Pizarro in the valley. He now came in more state, quaffing chicha—the fermented juice of the maize —from golden goblets borne by his attendants, which sparkled in the eyes of the rapacious adventurers.

While he was in the camp, the Indian messenger, originally sent by Pizarro to the Inca, returned, and no sooner did he behold the Peruvian, and the honorable reception which he met with from the Spaniards, than he was filled with wrath, which would have vented itself in personal violence, but for the interposition of the by-standers. It was hard, he said, that this Peruvian dog should be thus courteously treated, when he himself had nearly lost his life on a similar mission among his countrymen. On reaching the Inca's camp he had been refused admission to his presence, on the ground that he was keeping a fast and could not be seen. They had paid no respect to his assertion that he came as an envoy from the white men, and would, probably, not have suffered him to escape with life, if he had not assured them that any violence offered to him would be retaliated in full measure on the persons of the Peruvian envoys now in the Spanish quarters. There was no doubt, he continued, of the hostile intentions of Atahuallpa; for he was surrounded with a powerful army, strongly encamped about a league from Caxamalca, while that city was entirely evacuated by its inhabitants.

To all this the Inca's envoy coolly replied that Pizarro's messenger might have reckoned on such a reception as he had found, since he seemed to have taken with him no credentials of his mission. As to the Inca's fast, that was true; and, although he would doubtless have seen the messenger had he known there was one from the strangers, yet it was not safe to disturb him at these solemn seasons, when engaged in his religious duties. The troops by whom he was surrounded were not numerous, considering that the Inca was at that time carrying on an important war; and as to Caxamalca, it was abandoned by the inhabitants in order to make room for the white men, who were so soon to occupy it.

This explanation, however plausible, did not altogether satisfy the general; for he had too deep a conviction of the cunning of Atahuallpa, whose intentions towards the Spaniards he had long greatly distrusted. As he proposed, however, to keep on friendly relations with the monarch for the present, it was obviously not his cue to manifest suspicion. Affecting, therefore, to give full credit to the explanation of the envoy, he dismissed him with reiterated assurances of speedily presenting himself before the Inca.

The descent of the sierra, though the Andes are less precipitous on their eastern side than towards the west, was attended with difficulties almost equal to those of the upward march; and the Spaniards felt no little satisfaction when, on the seventh day, they arrived in view of the valley of Caxamalca, which, enameled with all the beauties of cultivation, lay unrolled like a rich and variegated carpet of verdure, in strong contrast with the dark forms of the Andes, that rose up everywhere around it. The valley is of an oval shape, extending about five leagues in length by three in breadth. It was inhabited by a population of a superior character to any which the Spaniards had met on the other side of the mountains, as was argued by the superior style of their attire and the greater cleanliness and comfort visible both in their persons and dwellings. As far as the eye could reach, the level tract exhibited the show of a diligent and thrifty husbandry. A broad river rolled through the meadows, supplying facilities for copious irrigation by means of the usual canals and subterraneous aqueducts. The land, intersected by verdant hedgerows, was checkered with patches of various cultivation;

for the soil was rich, and the climate, if less stimulating than that of the sultry regions of the coast, was more favorable to the hardy products of the temperate latitudes. Below the adventurers, with its white houses glittering in the sun, lay the little city of Caxamalca, like a sparkling gem on the dark skirts of the sierra. At the distance of about a league farther, across the valley, might be seen columns of vapor rising up towards the heavens, indicating the place of the famous hot baths, much frequented by the Peruvian princes. And here, too, was a spectacle less grateful to the eyes of the Spaniards; for along the slope of the hills a white cloud of pavilions was seen covering the ground, as thick as snowflakes, for the space, apparently, of several miles. "It filled us all with amazement," exclaims one of the Conquerors, "to behold the Indians occupying so proud a position! So many tents, so well appointed, as were never seen in the Indies till now! The spectacle caused something like confusion and even fear in the stoutest bosom. But it was too late to turn back, or to betray the least sign of weakness, since the natives in our own company would, in such case, have been the first to rise upon us. So, with as bold a countenance as we could, after coolly surveying the ground, we prepared for our entrance into Caxamalca."

What were the feelings of the Peruvian monarch we are not informed, when he gazed on the martial cavalcade of the Christians, as, with banners streaming, and bright panoplies glistening in the rays of the evening sun, it emerged from the dark depths of the sierra and advanced in hostile array over the fair domain which, to this period, had never been trodden by other foot than that of the red man. It might be, as several of the reports had stated, that the Inca had purposely decoyed the adventurers into the heart of his populous empire, that he might envelop them with his legions and the more easily become master of their property and persons. Or was it from a natural feeling of curiosity, and relying on their professions of friendship, that he had thus allowed them, without any attempt at resistance, to come into his presence? At all events, he could hardly have felt such confidence in himself as not to look with apprehension, mingled with awe, on the mysterious strangers, who, coming from an unknown world and possessed of such wonderful gifts, had made their way across mountain and valley in spite of every obstacle which man and nature had opposed to them.

Pizarro, meanwhile, forming his little corps into three divisions, now moved forward, at a more measured pace, and in order of battle, down the slopes that led towards the Indian city. As he drew near, no one came out to welcome him; and he rode through the streets without meeting with a living thing, or hearing a sound, except the echoes, sent back from the deserted dwellings, of the tramp of the soldiery.

It was a place of considerable size, containing about ten thousand inhabitants, somewhat more, probably, than the population assembled at this day within the walls of the modern city of Caxamalca. The houses, for the most part, were built of clay, hardened in the sun; the roofs thatched or of timber. Some of the more ambitious dwellings were of hewn stone; and there was a convent in the place, occupied by the Virgins of the Sun, and a temple dedicated to the same tutelar deity, which last was hidden in the deep embowering shades of a grove on the skirts of the city. On the quarter towards the Indian camp was a square— if square it might be called, which was almost triangular in form—of an immense size, surrounded by low buildings. These consisted of capacious halls, with wide doors or openings communicating with the square. They were probably intended as a sort of barracks for the Inca's soldiers. At the end of the plaza, looking towards the country, was a fortress of stone, with a stairway leading from the city, and a private entrance from the adjoining suburbs. There was still another fortress on the rising ground which commanded the town, built of hewn stone and encompassed by three circular walls—or rather one and the same wall, which wound up spirally around it. It was a place of great strength, and the workmanship showed a better knowledge of masonry, and gave a higher impression of the architectural science of the people, than anything the Spaniards had yet seen.

It was late in the afternoon of the fifteenth of November, 1532, when the Conquerors entered the city of Caxamalca. The weather, which had been fair during the day, now threatened a storm, and some rain mingled with hail—for it was unusually cold—began to fall. Pizarro, however, was so anxious to ascertain the dispositions of the Inca that he determined to send an embassy at once to his quarters. He selected for this Hernando de Soto with fifteen horse, and, after his departure, conceiving that the number was too small in case of any unfriendly demonstrations by the Indians, he ordered his brother Hernando to follow with twenty additional troopers. This captain and one other of his party have left us an account of the excursion.

Between the city and the imperial camp was a causeway, built in a substantial manner across the meadowland that intervened. Over this the cavalry galloped at a rapid pace, and before they had gone a league they came in front of the Peruvian encampment, where it spread along the gentle slope of the mountains. The lances of the warriors were fixed in the ground before their tents, and the Indian soldiers were loitering without, gazing with silent astonishment at the Christian cavalcade, as with clangor of arms and shrill blast of trumpet it swept by, like some fearful apparition on the wings of the wind.

The party soon came to a broad but shallow stream, which, winding through the meadow, formed a defense for the Inca's position. Across it was a wooden bridge; but the cavaliers, distrusting its strength, preferred to dash through the waters, and without difficulty gained the opposite bank. A battalion of Indian warriors was drawn up under arms on the farther side of the bridge, but they offered no molestation to the Spaniards; and these latter had strict orders from Pizarro—scarcely necessary in their present circumstances—to treat the natives with courtesy. One of the Indians pointed out the quarter occupied by the Inca.

It was an open courtyard, with a light building or pleasure-house in the center, having galleries running round it, and opening in the rear on a garden. The walls were covered with a shining plaster, both white and colored, and in the area before the edifice was seen a spacious tank or reservoir of stone, fed by aqueducts that supplied it with both warm and cold water. A basin of hewn stone—it may be of a more recent construction—still bears, on the spot, the name of the "Inca's bath." The court was filled with Indian nobles, dressed in gaily ornamented attire, in attendance on the monarch, and with women of the royal household. Amidst this assembly it was not difficult to distinguish the person of Atahuallpa, though his dress was simpler than that of his attendants. But he wore on his head the crimson borla or fringe, which, surrounding the forehead, hung down as low as the eyebrow. This was the well-known badge of Peruvian sovereignty, and had been assumed by the monarch only since the defeat of his brother Huascar. He was seated on a low stool or cushion, somewhat after the Morisco or Turkish fashion, and his nobles and principal officers stood around him with great ceremony, holding the stations suited to their rank.

The Spaniards gazed with much interest on the prince, of whose cruelty and cunning they had heard so much, and whose valor had secured to him the possession of the empire. But his countenance exhibited neither the fierce passions nor the sagacity which had been ascribed to him; and, though in his bearing he showed a gravity and a calm consciousness of authority well becoming a king, he seemed to discharge all expression from his features, and to discover only the apathy so characteristic of the American races. On the present occasion this must have been in part, at least, assumed. For it is impossible that the Indian prince should not have contemplated with curious interest a spectacle so strange, and, in some respects, appalling, as that of these mysterious strangers, for which no previous description could have prepared him.

Hernando Pizarro and Soto, with two or three only of their followers, slowly rode up in front of the Inca; and the former, making a respectful obeisance, but without dismounting, informed Atahuallpa that he came as an ambassador from his brother, the commander of the white men, to acquaint the monarch with their arrival in his city of Caxamalca. They were the subjects of a mighty prince across the waters, and had come, he said, drawn thither by the report of his great victories, to offer their services, and to impart to him the doctrines of the true faith which they professed; and he brought an invitation from the general to Atahuallpa that the latter would be pleased to visit the Spaniards in their present quarters.

To all this the Inca answered not a word; nor did he make even a sign of acknowledgment that he comprehended it; though it was translated for him by Felipillo, one of the interpreters already noticed. He remained silent, with his eyes fastened on the ground; but one of his nobles, standing by his side, answered, "It is well." This was an embarrassing situation for the Spaniards, who seemed to be as far from ascertaining the real disposition of the Peruvian monarch towards themselves as when the mountains were between them.

In a courteous and respectful manner, Hernando Pizarro again broke the silence by requesting the Inca to speak to them himself and to inform them what was his pleasure. To this Atahuallpa condescended to reply, while a faint smile passed over his features, "Tell your captain that I am keeping a fast, which will end tomorrow morning. I will then visit him, with my chieftains. In the mean time, let him occupy the public buildings on the square, and no other, till I come, when I will order what shall be done."

Soto, one of the party present at this interview, as before noticed, was the best mounted and perhaps the best rider in Pizarro's troop. Observing that Atahuallpa looked with some interest on the fiery steed that stood before him, champing the bit and pawing the ground with the natural impatience of a war-horse, the Spaniard gave him the rein, and, striking his iron heel into his side, dashed furiously over the plain, then, wheeling him round and round, displayed all the beautiful movements of his charger, and his own excellent horsemanship. Suddenly checking him in full career, he brought the animal almost on his haunches, so near the person of the Inca that some of the foam that flecked his horse's sides was thrown on the royal garments. But Atahuallpa maintained the same marble composure as before, though several of his soldiers, whom De Soto passed in the course, were so much disconcerted by it that they drew back in manifest terror—an act of timidity for which they paid dearly, *if*, as the Spaniards assert, Atahuallpa caused them to be put to death that same evening for betraying such unworthy weakness to the strangers.

Refreshments were now offered by the royal attendants to the Spaniards, which they declined, being unwilling to dismount. They did not refuse, however, to quaff the sparkling chicha from golden vases of extraordinary size, presented to them by the dark-eyed beauties of the harem. Taking then a respectful leave of the Inca, the cavaliers rode back to Caxamalca, with many moody speculations on what they had seen: on the state and opulence of the Indian monarch; on the strength of his military array, their excellent appointments, and the apparent discipline in their ranks—all arguing a much higher degree of civilization, and consequently of power, than any thing they had witnessed in the lower regions of the country. As they contrasted all this with their own diminutive force, too far advanced, as they now were, for succor to reach them, they felt they had done rashly in throwing themselves into the midst of so formidable an emperor, and were filled with gloomy forebodings of the result. Their comrades in the camp soon caught the infectious spirit of despondency, which was not lessened as night came on, and they beheld the watch-fires of the Peruvians lighting up the sides of the mountains and glittering in the darkness, "as thick," says one who saw them, "as the stars of heaven."

Yet there was one bosom in that little host which was not touched with the feeling either of fear or dejection. That was Pizarro's, who secretly rejoiced that he had now brought matters to the issue for which he had so long panted. He saw the necessity of kindling a similar feeling in his followers, or all would be lost. Without unfolding his plans, he went round among his men, beseeching them not to show faint hearts at this crisis, when they stood face to face with the foe whom they had been so long seeking. "They were to rely on themselves, and on that Providence which had carried them safe through so many fearful trials. It would not now desert them; and if numbers, however great, were on the side of their enemy, it mattered little, when the arm of Heaven was on theirs." The Spanish cavalier acted under the combined influence of chivalrous adventure and religious zeal. The latter was the more effective in the hour of peril; and Pizarro, who understood well the characters he had to deal with, by presenting the enterprise as a crusade, kindled the dying embers of enthusiasm in the bosoms of his followers, and restored their faltering courage.

He then summoned a council of his officers, to consider the plan of operations, or rather to propose to them the extraordinary plan on which he had himself decided. This was to lay an ambuscade for the Inca and take him prisoner in the face of his whole army! It was a project full of peril—bordering, as it might well seem, on desperation. But the circumstances of the Spaniards were desperate. Whichever way they turned, they were menaced by the most appalling dangers; and better was it bravely to confront the danger than weakly to shrink from it, when there was no avenue for escape.

To fly was now too late. Whither could they fly? At the first signal of retreat, the whole army of the Inca would be upon them. Their movements would be anticipated by a foe far better acquainted with the intricacies of the sierra than themselves; the passes would be occupied, and they would be hemmed in on all sides; while the mere fact of this retrograde movement would diminish their confidence and with it their effective strength, while it doubled that of their enemy.

Yet to remain long inactive in their present position seemed almost equally perilous. Even supposing that Atahuallpa should entertain friendly feelings towards the Christians, they could not confide in the continuance of such feelings. Familiarity with the white men would soon destroy the idea of anything supernatural, or even superior, in their natures. He would feel contempt for their diminutive numbers. Their horses, their arms and showy appointments, would be an attractive bait in the eye of the barbaric monarch, and when conscious that he had the power to crush their possessors he would not be slow in finding a pretext for it. A sufficient one had already occurred in the high-handed measures of the Conquerors on their march through his dominions.

But what reason had they to flatter themselves that the Inca cherished such a disposition towards them? He was a crafty and unscrupulous prince, and, if the accounts they had repeatedly received on their march were true, had ever regarded the coming of the Spaniards with an evil eye. It was scarcely possible he should do otherwise. His soft messages had only been intended to decoy them across the mountains, where, with the aid of his warriors, he might readily overpower them. They were entangled in the toils which the cunning monarch had spread for them.

Their only remedy, then, was to turn the Inca's arts against himself; to take him, if possible, in his own snare. There was no time to be lost; for any day might bring back the victorious legions who had recently won his battles at the south, and thus make the odds against the Spaniards far greater than now.

Yet to encounter Atahuallpa in the open field would be attended with great hazard; and, even if victorious, there would be little probability that the person of the Inca, of so much importance, would fall into their hands. The invitation he had so unsuspiciously accepted to visit them in their quarters afforded the best means for securing this desirable prize. Nor was the enterprise so desperate, considering the great advantages afforded by the character and weapons of the invaders and the unexpectedness of the assault. The mere circumstance of acting on a concerted plan would alone make a small number more than a match for a much larger one. But it was not necessary to admit the whole of the Indian force into the city before the attack; and the person of the Inca once secured, his followers, astounded by so strange an event, were they few or many, would have no heart for further resistance; and with the Inca once in his power, Pizarro might dictate laws to the empire.

In this daring project of the Spanish chief it was easy to see that he had the brilliant exploit of Cortes in his mind when he carried off the Aztec monarch in his capital. But that was not by violence—at least not by open violence—and it received the sanction, compulsory though it were, of the monarch himself. It was also true that the results in that case did not altogether justify a repetition of the experiment, since the people rose in a body to sacrifice both the prince and his kidnapers. Yet this was owing, in part at least, to the indiscretion of the latter. The experiment in the outset was perfectly successful; and could Pizarro once become master of the person of Atahuallpa he trusted to his own discretion for the rest. It would at least extricate him from his present critical position, by placing in his power an inestimable guarantee for his safety; and if he could not make his own terms with the Inca at once, the arrival of reinforcements from home would, in all probability, soon enable him to do so.

Pizarro having concerted his plans for the following day, the council broke up, and the chief occupied himself with providing for the security of the camp during the night. The approaches to the town were defended; sentinels were posted at different points, especially on the summit of the fortress, where they were to observe the position of the enemy and to report any movement that menaced the tranquillity of the night. After these precautions, the Spanish commander and his followers withdrew to their appointed quarters—but not to sleep. At least, sleep must have come late to those who were aware of the decisive plan for the

morrow; that morrow which was to be the crisis of their fate—
to crown their ambitious schemes with full success, or consign
them to irretrievable ruin!

FROM CHAPTER V

The Desperate Plan of Pizarro

1532

The clouds of the evening had passed away, and the sun rose
bright on the following morning, the most memorable epoch
in the annals of Peru. It was Saturday, the sixteenth of November, 1532. The loud cry of the trumpet called the Spaniards to
arms with the first streak of dawn; and Pizarro, briefly acquaint-
ing them with the plan of the assault, made the necessary dispositions.

The plaza, as mentioned in the preceding chapter, was defended on its three sides by low ranges of buildings, consisting
of spacious halls with wide doors or vomitories opening into the
square. In these halls he stationed his cavalry in two divisions,
one under his brother Hernando, the other under De Soto. The
infantry he placed in another of the buildings, reserving twenty
chosen men to act with himself as occasion might require. Pedro
de Candia, with a few soldiers and the artillery—comprehending
under this imposing name two small pieces of ordnance, called
falconets—he established in the fortress. All received orders
to wait at their posts till the arrival of the Inca. After his entrance into the great square, they were still to remain under
cover, withdrawn from observation, till the signal was given by
the discharge of a gun, when they were to cry their war-cries, to
rush out in a body from their covert, and, putting the Peruvians
to the sword, bear off the person of the Inca. The arrangement
of the immense halls, opening on a level with the plaza, seemed
to be contrived on purpose for a coup de théâtre. Pizarro particularly inculcated order and implicit obedience, that in the

hurry of the moment there should be no confusion. Everything depended on their acting with concert, coolness, and celerity.

The chief next saw that their arms were in good order, and that the breastplates of their horses were garnished with bells, to add by their noise to the consternation of the Indians. Refreshments were, also, liberally provided, that the troops should be in condition for the conflict. These arrangements being completed, mass was performed with great solemnity by the ecclesiastics who attended the expedition; the God of battles was invoked to spread his shield over the soldiers who were fighting to extend the empire of the Cross; and all joined with enthusiasm in the chant, "Exsurge, Domine," "Rise, O Lord! and judge thine own cause." One might have supposed them a company of martyrs about to lay down their lives in defense of their faith, instead of a licentious band of adventurers meditating one of the most atrocious acts of perfidy on the record of history! Yet, whatever were the vices of the Castilian cavalier, hypocrisy was not among the number. He felt that he was battling for the Cross, and under this conviction, exalted as it was at such a moment as this into the predominant impulse, he was blind to the baser motives which mingled with the enterprise. With feelings thus kindled to a flame of religious ardor, the soldiers of Pizarro looked forward with renovated spirits to the coming conflict; and the chieftain saw with satisfaction that in the hour of trial his men would be true to their leader and themselves.

It was late in the day before any movement was visible in the Peruvian camp, where much preparation was making to approach the Christian quarters with due state and ceremony. A message was received from Atahuallpa, informing the Spanish commander that he should come with his warriors fully armed, in the same manner as the Spaniards had come to his quarters the night preceding. This was not an agreeable intimation to Pizarro, though he had no reason, probably, to expect the contrary. But to object might imply distrust, or perhaps disclose, in some measure, his own designs. He expressed his satisfaction, therefore, at the intelligence, assuring the Inca that, come as he would, he would be received by him as a friend and brother.

It was noon before the Indian procession was on its march, when it was seen occupying the great causeway for a long extent. In front came a large body of attendants, whose office seemed to be to sweep away every particle of rubbish from the road. High above the crowd appeared the Inca, borne on the shoulders of his principal nobles, while others of the same rank marched by the sides of his litter, displaying such a dazzling show of ornaments on their persons that, in the language of one of the Conquerors, "they blazed like the sun." But the greater part of the Inca's forces mustered along the fields that lined the road, and were spread over the broad meadows as far as the eye could reach.

When the royal procession had arrived within half a mile of the city, it came to a halt; and Pizarro saw with surprise that Atahuallpa was preparing to pitch his tents, as if to encamp there. A messenger soon after arrived, informing the Spaniards that the Inca would occupy his present station the ensuing night, and enter the city on the following morning.

This intelligence greatly disturbed Pizarro, who had shared in the general impatience of his men at the tardy movements of the Peruvians. The troops had been under arms since daylight, the cavalry mounted, and the infantry at their post, waiting in silence the coming of the Inca. A profound stillness reigned throughout the town, broken only at intervals by the cry of the sentinel from the summit of the fortress, as he proclaimed the movements of the Indian army. Nothing, Pizarro well knew, was so trying to the soldier as prolonged suspense, in a critical situation like the present; and he feared lest his ardor might evaporate, and be succeeded by that nervous feeling natural to the bravest soul at such a crisis, and which, if not fear, is near akin to it. He returned an answer, therefore, to Atahuallpa, deprecating his change of purpose, and adding that he had provided everything for his entertainment, and expected him that night to sup with him.

This message turned the Inca from his purpose; and, striking his tents again, he resumed his march, first advising the general that he should leave the greater part of his warriors behind, and enter the place with only a few of them, and without arms, as he preferred to pass the night at Caxamalca. At the same time he ordered accommodations to be provided for himself and his retinue in one of the large stone buildings, called, from a serpent sculptured on the walls, "the House of the Serpent." No tidings could have been more grateful to the Spaniards. It seemed as if the Indian monarch was eager to rush into the snare that had been spread for him! The fanatical cavalier could not fail to discern in it the immediate finger of Providence.

It is difficult to account for this wavering conduct of Atahuallpa, so different from the bold and decided character which history ascribes to him. There is no doubt that he made his visit to the white men in perfect good faith; though Pizarro was probably right in conjecturing that this amiable disposition stood on a very precarious footing. There is as little reason to suppose that he distrusted the sincerity of the strangers; or he would not thus unnecessarily have proposed to visit them unarmed. His original purpose of coming with all his force was doubtless to display his royal state, and perhaps, also, to show greater respect for the Spaniards; but when he consented to accept their hospitality and pass the night in their quarters, he was willing to dispense with a great part of his armed soldiery and visit them in a manner that implied entire confidence in their good faith. He was too absolute in his own empire easily to suspect; and he probably could not comprehend the audacity with which a few men, like those now assembled in Caxamalca, meditated an assault on a powerful monarch in the midst of his victorious army. He did not know the character of the Spaniard.

It was not long before sunset when the van of the royal procession entered the gates of the city. First came some hundreds of the menials, employed to clear the path of every obstacle, and singing songs of triumph as they came, "which in our ears," says one of the Conquerors, "sounded like the songs of hell"! Then followed other bodies of different ranks, and dressed in different liveries. Some wore a showy stuff, checkered white and red, like the squares of a chessboard. Others were clad in pure white, bearing hammers or maces of silver or copper; and the guards, together with those in immediate attendance on the prince, were distinguished by a rich azure livery, and a profusion of gay ornaments, while the large pendants attached to the ears indicated the Peruvian noble.

Elevated high above his vassals came the Inca Atahuallpa, borne on a sedan or open litter, on which was a sort of throne made of massive gold of inestimable value. The palanquin was lined with the richly colored plumes of tropical birds and studded with shining plates of gold and silver. The monarch's attire was much richer than on the preceding evening. Round his neck was suspended a collar of emeralds of uncommon size and brilliancy. His short hair was decorated with golden ornaments, and the imperial borla encircled his temples. The bearing of the Inca was sedate and dignified; and from his lofty station he looked down on the multitudes below with an air of composure, like one accustomed to command.

As the leading files of the procession entered the great square, larger, says an old chronicler, than any square in Spain, they opened to the right and left for the royal retinue to pass. Everything was conducted with admirable order. The monarch was permitted to traverse the plaza in silence, and not a Spaniard was to be seen. When some five or six thousand of his people had entered the place, Atahuallpa halted, and, turning round with an inquiring look, demanded, "Where are the strangers?"

At this moment Fray Vicente de Valverde, a Dominican friar, Pizarro's chaplain, and afterwards Bishop of Cuzco, came forward with his breviary, or, as other accounts say, a Bible, in one hand, and a crucifix in the other, and, approaching the Inca, told him that he came by order of his commander to expound to him the doctrines of the true faith, for which purpose the Spaniards had come from a great distance to his country. The friar then explained, as clearly as he could, the mysterious doctrine of the Trinity, and, ascending high in his account, began with the creation of man, thence passed to his fall, to his subsequent redemption by Jesus Christ, to the crucifixion, and the ascension, when the Savior left the Apostle Peter as his vicegerent upon earth. This power had been transmitted to the successors of the apostle, good and wise men, who, under the title of popes, held authority over all powers and potentates on earth. One of the last of these popes had commissioned the Spanish emperor, the most mighty monarch in the world, to conquer and convert the natives in this Western hemisphere; and his general, Francisco Pizarro, had now come to execute this important mission. The friar concluded with beseeching the Peruvian monarch to receive him kindly, to abjure the errors of his own faith, and embrace that of the Christians now proffered to him, the only one by which he could hope for salvation, and, furthermore, to acknowledge himself a tributary of the Emperor Charles the Fifth, who, in that event, would aid and protect him as his loyal vassal.

Whether Atahuallpa possessed himself of every link in the curious chain of argument by which the monk connected Pizarro with St. Peter, may be doubted. It is certain, however, that he must have had very incorrect notions of the Trinity, if, as Garcilasso states, the interpreter Felipillo explained it by saying that "the Christians believed in three Gods and one God, and that made four." But there is no doubt he perfectly comprehended that the drift of the discourse was to persuade him to resign his scepter and acknowledge the supremacy of another.

The eyes of the Indian monarch flashed fire, and his dark brow grew darker, as he replied, "I will be no man's tributary. I am greater than any prince upon earth. Your emperor may be a great prince; I do not doubt it, when I see that he has sent his subjects so far across the waters; and I am willing to hold him as a brother. As for the pope of whom you speak, he must be crazy to talk of giving away countries which do not belong to him. For my faith," he continued, "I will not change it. Your own God, as you say, was put to death by the very men whom he created. But mine," he concluded, pointing to his Deity—then, alas! sinking in glory behind the mountains—"my God still lives in the heavens and looks down on his children."

He then demanded of Valverde by what authority he had said these things. The friar pointed to the book which he held, as his authority. Atahuallpa, taking it, turned over the pages a moment, then, as the insult he had received probably flashed across his mind, he threw it down with vehemence, and exclaimed, "Tell your comrades that they shall give me an account of their doings in my land. I will not go from here till they have made me full satisfaction for all the wrongs they have committed."

The friar, greatly scandalized by the indignity offered to the sacred volume, stayed only to pick it up, and, hastening to Pizarro, informed him of what had been done, exclaiming, at the same time, "Do you not see that while we stand here wasting our breath in talking with this dog, full of pride as he is, the fields are filling with Indians? Set on, at once; I absolve you." Pizarro saw that the hour had come. He waved a white scarf in the air, the appointed signal. The fatal gun was fired from the fortress. Then, springing into the square, the Spanish captain and his followers shouted the old war-cry of "St. Jago and at them." It was answered by the battle-cry of every Spaniard in the city, as, rushing from the avenues of the great halls in which they were concealed, they poured into the plaza, horse and foot, each in his own dark column, and threw themselves into the midst of the Indian crowd. The latter, taken by surprise, stunned by the report of artillery and muskets, the echoes of which reverberated like thunder from the surrounding buildings, and blinded by the smoke which rolled in sulphurous volumes along the square, were seized with a panic. They knew not whither to fly for refuge from the coming ruin. Nobles and commoners—all were trampled down under the fierce charge of the cavalry, who dealt their blows, right and left, without sparing; while their swords, flashing through the thick gloom, carried dismay into the hearts of the wretched natives, who now for the first time saw the horse and his rider in all their terrors. They made no resistance—as, indeed, they had no weapons with which to make it. Every avenue to escape was closed, for the entrance to the square was choked up with the dead bodies of men who had perished in vain efforts to fly; and such was the agony of the survivors under the terrible pressure of their assailants that a large body of Indians, by their convulsive struggles, burst through the wall of stone and dried clay which formed part of the boundary of the plaza! It fell, leaving an opening of more than a hundred paces, through which multitudes now found their way into the country, still hotly pursued by the cavalry, who, leaping the fallen rubbish, hung on the rear of the fugitives, striking them down in all directions.

Meanwhile the fight, or rather massacre, continued hot around the Inca, whose person was the great object of the assault. His faithful nobles, rallying about him, threw themselves in the way of the assailants, and strove, by tearing them from their saddles, or at least by offering their own bosoms as a mark for their vengeance, to shield their beloved master. It is said by some authorities that they carried weapons concealed under their clothes. If so, it availed them little, as it is not pretended that they used them. But the most timid animal will defend itself when at bay. That the Indians did not do so in the present instance is proof that they had no weapons to use. Yet they still continued to force back the cavaliers, clinging to their horses with dying grasp, and, as one was cut down, another taking the place of his fallen comrade with a loyalty truly affecting.

The Indian monarch, stunned and bewildered, saw his faithful subjects falling around him without fully comprehending his situation. The litter on which he rode heaved to and fro, as the mighty press swayed backwards and forwards; and he gazed on the overwhelming ruin, like some forlorn mariner, who, tossed about in his bark by the furious elements, sees the lightning's flash and hears the thunder bursting around him with the consciousness that he can do nothing to avert his fate. At length, weary with the work of destruction, the Spaniards, as the shades of evening grew deeper, felt afraid that the royal prize might, after all, elude them; and some of the cavaliers made a desperate attempt to end the affray at once by taking Atahuallpa's life. But Pizarro, who was nearest his person, called out, with stentorian voice, "Let no one who values his life strike at the Inca"; and, stretching out his arm to shield him, received a wound on the hand from one of his own men—the only wound received by a Spaniard in the action.

The struggle now became fiercer than ever round the royal litter. It reeled more and more, and at length, several of the nobles who supported it having been slain, it was overturned, and the Indian prince would have come with violence to the ground, had not his fall been broken by the efforts of Pizarro and some other of the cavaliers, who caught him in their arms. The imperial borla was instantly snatched from his temples by a soldier named Estete, and the unhappy monarch, strongly secured, was removed to a neighboring building, where he was carefully guarded.

All attempt at resistance now ceased. The fate of the Inca soon spread over town and country. The charm which might have held the Peruvians together was dissolved. Every man thought only of his own safety. Even the soldiery encamped on the adjacent fields took the alarm, and, learning the fatal tidings, were seen flying in every direction before their pursuers, who in the heat of triumph showed no touch of mercy. At length night, more pitiful than man, threw her friendly mantle over the fugitives, and the scattered troops of Pizarro rolled once more at the sound of the trumpet in the bloody square of Caxamalca.

The number of slain is reported, as usual, with great discrepancy. Pizarro's secretary says two thousand natives fell. A

descendant of the Incas—a safer authority than Garcilasso—
swells the number to ten thousand. Truth is generally found
somewhere between the extremes. The slaughter was incessant,
for there was nothing to check it. That there should have been
no resistance will not appear strange when we consider the fact
that the wretched victims were without arms, and that their
senses must have been completely overwhelmed by the strange
and appalling spectacle which burst on them so unexpectedly.
"What wonder was it," said an ancient Inca to a Spaniard, who
repeats it, "what wonder that our countrymen lost their wits,
seeing blood run like water, and the Inca, whose person we all
of us adore, seized and carried off by a handful of men?" Yet,
though the massacre was incessant, it was short in duration. The
whole time consumed by it, the brief twilight of the tropics, did
not much exceed half an hour; a short period, indeed—yet long
enough to decide the fate of Peru and to subvert the dynasty of
the Incas.

That night Pizarro kept his engagement with the Inca, since
he had Atahuallpa to sup with him. The banquet was served in
one of the halls facing the great square, which a few hours before
had been the scene of slaughter, and the pavement of which was
still encumbered with the dead bodies of the Inca's subjects. The
captive monarch was placed next his conqueror. He seemed like
one who did not yet fully comprehend the extent of his calamity.
If he did, he showed an amazing fortitude. "It is the fortune of
war," he said; and, if we may credit the Spaniards, he expressed
his admiration of the adroitness with which they had contrived
to entrap him in the midst of his own troops. He added that
he had been made acquainted with the progress of the white
men from the hour of their landing, but that he had been led
to undervalue their strength from the insignificance of their
numbers. He had no doubt he should be easily able to overpower
them, on their arrival at Caxamalca, by his superior strength;
and, as he wished to see for himself what manner of men they
were, he had suffered them to cross the mountains, meaning to
select such as he chose for his own service, and, getting possession of their wonderful arms and horses, put the rest to death.

That such may have been Atahuallpa's purpose is not improbable. It explains his conduct in not occupying the mountain
passes, which afforded such strong points of defense against in-

vasion. But that a prince so astute, as by the general testimony of the Conquerors he is represented to have been, should have made so impolitic a disclosure of his hidden motive is not so probable. The intercourse with the Inca was carried on chiefly by means of the interpreter Felipillo, or little Philip, as he was called, from his assumed Christian name—a malicious youth, as it appears, who bore no good will to Atahuallpa, and whose interpretations were readily admitted by the Conquerors, eager to find some pretext for their bloody reprisals.

Atahuallpa, as elsewhere noticed, was at this time about thirty years of age. He was well made, and more robust than usual with his countrymen. His head was large, and his countenance might have been called handsome, but that his eyes, which were bloodshot, gave a fierce expression to his features. He was deliberate in speech, grave in manner, and towards his own people stern even to severity; though with the Spaniards he showed himself affable, sometimes even indulging in sallies of mirth.

Pizarro paid every attention to his royal captive, and endeavored to lighten, if he could not dispel, the gloom which, in spite of his assumed equanimity, hung over the monarch's brow. He besought him not to be cast down by his reverses, for his lot had only been that of every prince who had resisted the white men. They had come into the country to proclaim the gospel, the religion of Jesus Christ; and it was no wonder they had prevailed, when his shield was over them. Heaven had permitted that Atahuallpa's pride should be humbled, because of his hostile intentions towards the Spaniards and the insult he had offered to the sacred volume. But he bade the Inca take courage and confide in him, for the Spaniards were a generous race, warring only against those who made war on them, and showing grace to all who submitted! Atahuallpa may have thought the massacre of that day an indifferent commentary on this vaunted lenity.

Before retiring for the night, Pizarro briefly addressed his troops on their present situation. When he had ascertained that not a man was wounded, he bade them offer up thanksgivings to Providence for so great a miracle; without its care, they could never have prevailed so easily over the host of their enemies; and he trusted their lives had been reserved for still greater things. But, if they would succeed, they had much to do for themselves. They were in the heart of a powerful kingdom, encompassed by foes deeply attached to their own sovereign. They must be ever on their guard, therefore, and be prepared at any hour to be roused from their slumbers by the call of the trumpet. Having then posted his sentinels, placed a strong guard over the apartment of Atahuallpa, and taken all the precautions of a careful commander, Pizarro withdrew to repose; and, if he could really feel that in the bloody scenes of the past day he had been fighting only the good fight of the cross, he doubtless slept sounder than on the night preceding the seizure of the Inca. . . .

It was not long before Atahuallpa discovered, amidst all the show of religious zeal in his Conquerors, a lurking appetite more potent in most of their bosoms than either religion or ambition. This was the love of gold. He determined to avail himself of it to procure his own freedom. The critical posture of his affairs made it important that this should not be long delayed. His brother Huascar, ever since his defeat, had been detained as a prisoner, subject to the victor's orders. He was now at Andamarca, at no great distance from Caxamalca; and Atahuallpa feared, with good reason, that, when his own imprisonment was known, Huascar would find it easy to corrupt his guards, make his escape, and put himself at the head of the contested empire without a rival to dispute it.

In the hope, therefore, to effect his purpose by appealing to the avarice of his keepers, he one day told Pizarro that if he would set him free he would engage to cover the floor of the apartment on which they stood with gold. Those present listened with an incredulous smile; and, as the Inca received no answer, he said, with some emphasis, that "he would not merely cover the floor, but would fill the room with gold as high as he could reach"; and, standing on tiptoe, he stretched out his hand against the wall. All stared with amazement; while they regarded it as the insane boast of a man too eager to procure his liberty to weigh the meaning of his words. Yet Pizarro was sorely perplexed. As he had advanced into the country, much that he had seen, and all that he had heard, had confirmed the dazzling reports first received of the riches of Peru. Atahuallpa himself had given him the most glowing picture of the wealth of the capital, where the roofs of the temples were plated with gold, while the walls were hung with tapestry and the floors inlaid with tiles of the same precious metal. There must be some foundation for all this. At all events, it was safe to accede to the Inca's proposition; since by so doing he could collect at once all the gold at his disposal, and thus prevent its being purloined or secreted by the natives. He therefore acquiesced in Atahuallpa's offer, and, drawing a red line along the wall at the height which the Inca had indicated, he caused the terms of the proposal to be duly recorded by the notary. The apartment was about seventeen feet broad, by twenty-two feet long, and the line round the walls was nine feet from the floor. This space was to be filled with gold; but it was understood that the gold was not to be melted down into ingots, but to retain the original form of the articles into which it was manufactured, that the Inca might have the benefit of the space which they occupied. He further agreed to fill an adjoining room of smaller dimensions twice full with silver, in like manner; and he demanded two months to accomplish all this.

FROM CHAPTER VI

Gathering the Treasure

1532

Atahuallpa in his confinement continued to receive the same respectful treatment from the Spaniards as hitherto. They taught him to play with dice, and the more intricate game of chess, in which the royal captive became expert, and loved to beguile with it the tedious hours of his imprisonment. Towards his own people he maintained as far as possible his wonted state and ceremonial. He was attended by his wives and the girls of his harem, who, as was customary, waited on him at table and discharged the other menial offices about his person. A body of Indian nobles were stationed in the antechamber, but never entered the presence unbidden; and when they did enter it they submitted to the same humiliating ceremonies imposed on the greatest of his subjects. The service of his table was gold and silver plate. His dress, which he often changed, was composed of the wool of the vicuña wrought into mantles, so fine that it had the appearance of silk. He sometimes exchanged these for a robe made of the skins of bats, as soft and sleek as velvet. Round his head he wore the llautu, a woollen turban or shawl of the most delicate texture, wreathed in folds of various bright colors; and he still continued to encircle his temples with the borla, the crimson threads of which, mingled with gold, descended so as partly to conceal his eyes. The image of royalty had charms for him, when its substance had departed. No garment or utensil that had once belonged to the Peruvian sovereign could ever be used by another. When he laid it aside, it was carefully deposited in a chest, kept for the purpose, and afterwards burned. It would have been sacrilege to apply to vulgar uses that which had been consecrated by the touch of the Inca.

Not long after the arrival of the party from Pachacamac, in the latter part of May, the three emissaries returned from Cuzco. They had been very successful in their mission. Owing to the Inca's order, and the awe which the white men now inspired throughout the country, the Spaniards had everywhere met with a kind reception. They had been carried on the shoulders of the natives in the hamacas, or sedans, of the country; and, as they had traveled all the way to the capital on the great imperial road, along which relays of Indian carriers were established at stated intervals, they performed this journey of more than six hundred miles, not only without inconvenience, but with the most luxurious ease. They passed through many populous towns, and always found the simple natives disposed to venerate them as beings of a superior nature. In Cuzco they were received with public festivities, were sumptuously lodged, and had every want anticipated by the obsequious devotion of the inhabitants.

Their accounts of the capital confirmed all that Pizarro had before heard of the wealth and population of the city. Though they had remained more than a week in this place, the emissaries had not seen the whole of it. The great temple of the Sun they found literally covered with plates of gold. They had entered the interior and beheld the royal mummies, seated each in his gold-embossed chair and in robes profusely covered with ornaments. The Spaniards had the grace to respect these, as they had been previously enjoined by the Inca; but they required that the plates which garnished the walls should be all removed. The Peruvians most reluctantly acquiesced in the commands of their sovereign to desecrate the national temple, which every inhabitant of the city regarded with peculiar pride and veneration. With less reluctance they assisted the Conquerors in stripping the ornaments from some of the other edifices, where the gold, however, being mixed with a larger proportion of alloy, was of much less value.

The number of plates they tore from the temple of the Sun was seven hundred; and though of no great thickness, probably, they are compared in size to the lid of a chest, ten or twelve inches wide. A cornice of pure gold encircled the edifice, but so strongly set in the stone that it fortunately defied the efforts of the spoilers. The Spaniards complained of the want of alacrity shown by the Indians in the work of destruction, and said that there were other parts of the city containing buildings rich in gold and silver which they had not been allowed to see. In truth, their mission, which at best was a most ungrateful one, had been rendered doubly annoying by the manner in which they had executed it. The emissaries were men of a very low stamp, and, puffed up by the honors conceded to them by the natives, they looked on themselves as entitled to these, and contemned the poor Indians as a race immeasurably beneath the European. They not only showed the most disgusting rapacity, but treated the highest nobles with wanton insolence. They even went so far, it is said, as to violate the privacy of the convents, and to outrage the religious sentiments of the Peruvians by their scandalous amours with the Virgins of the Sun. The people of Cuzco were so exasperated that they would have laid violent hands on them, but for their habitual reverence for the Inca, in whose name the Spaniards had come there. As it was, the Indians collected as much gold as was necessary to satisfy their unworthy visitors, and got rid of them as speedily as possible. It was a great mistake in Pizarro to send such men. There were persons, even in his company, who, as other occasions showed, had some sense of self-respect, if not respect for the natives.

The messengers brought with them, besides silver, full two hundred cargas or loads of gold. This was an important accession to the contributions of Atahuallpa; and, although the treasure was still considerably below the mark prescribed, the monarch saw with satisfaction the time drawing nearer for the completion of his ransom.

Not long before this, an event had occurred which changed the condition of the Spaniards and had an unfavorable influence on the fortunes of the Inca. This was the arrival of Almagro at Caxamalca, with a strong reinforcement. That chief had succeeded, after great efforts, in equipping three vessels and assembling a body of one hundred and fifty men, with which he sailed from Panama the latter part of the preceding year. On his voyage he was joined by a small additional force from Nicaragua, so that his whole strength amounted to one hundred and fifty foot and fifty horse, well provided with the munitions of war. His vessels were steered by the old pilot Ruiz; but, after making the Bay of St. Matthew, he crept slowly along the coast, baffled as usual by winds and currents, and experiencing all the hardships incident to that protracted navigation. From some cause or other, he was not so fortunate as to obtain tidings of Pizarro; and so disheartened were his followers, most of whom were raw adventurers, that when arrived at Puerto Viejo they proposed to abandon the expedition and return at once to Panama. Fortunately, one of the little squadron which Almagro had sent forward to Tumbez brought intelligence of Pizarro and of the colony he had planted at San Miguel. Cheered by the tidings, the cavalier resumed his voyage, and succeeded at length, towards the close of December, 1532, in bringing his whole party safe to the Spanish settlement.

He there received the account of Pizarro's march across the mountains, his seizure of the Inca, and, soon afterwards, of the enormous ransom offered for his liberation. Almagro and his companions listened with undisguised amazement to this account of his associate, and of a change in his fortunes so rapid and wonderful that it seemed little less than magic. At the same time he received a caution from some of the colonists not to trust himself in the power of Pizarro, who was known to bear him no good will.

Not long after Almagro's arrival at San Miguel, advices were sent of it to Caxamalca, and a private note from his secretary Perez informed Pizarro that his associate had come with no purpose of cooperating with him, but with the intention to establish an independent government. Both of the Spanish captains seem to have been surrounded by mean and turbulent spirits, who sought to embroil them with each other, trusting, doubtless, to find their own account in the rupture. For once, however, their malicious machinations failed.

Pizarro was overjoyed at the arrival of so considerable a reinforcement, which would enable him to push his fortunes as he had desired, and go forward with the conquest of the country. He laid little stress on the secretary's communication, since, whatever might have been Almagro's original purpose, Pizarro knew that the richness of the vein he had now opened in the land would be certain to secure his cooperation in working it. He had the magnanimity, therefore—for there is something magnanimous in being able to stifle the suggestions of a petty rivalry in obedience to sound policy—to send at once to his ancient comrade, and invite him, with many assurances of friendship, to Caxamalca. Almagro, who was of a frank and careless nature, received the communication in the spirit in which it was made, and, after some necessary delay, directed his march into the interior. But before leaving San Miguel, having become acquainted with the treacherous conduct of his secretary, he recompensed his treason by hanging him on the spot.

Almagro reached Caxamalca about the middle of February, 1533. The soldiers of Pizarro came out to welcome their countrymen, and the two captains embraced each other with every mark of cordial satisfaction. All past differences were buried in oblivion, and they seemed only prepared to aid one another in following up the brilliant career now opened to them in the conquest of an empire.

There was one person in Caxamalca on whom this arrival of the Spaniards produced a very different impression from that made on their own countrymen. This was the Inca Atahuallpa. He saw in the newcomers only a new swarm of locusts to devour his unhappy country; and he felt that, with his enemies thus multiplying around him, the chances were diminished of recovering his freedom, or of maintaining it if recovered. A little circumstance, insignificant in itself, but magnified by superstition into something formidable, occurred at this time to cast an additional gloom over his situation.

A remarkable appearance, somewhat of the nature of a me-

teor, or it may have been a comet, was seen in the heavens by
some soldiers and pointed out to Atahuallpa. He gazed on it with
fixed attention for some minutes, and then exclaimed, with a
dejected air, that "a similar sign had been seen in the skies a
short time before the death of his father Huayna Capac." From
this day a sadness seemed to take possession of him, as he looked
with doubt and undefined dread to the future. Thus it is that in
seasons of danger the mind, like the senses, becomes morbidly
acute in its perceptions, and the least departure from the regular
course of nature, that would have passed unheeded in ordinary
times, to the superstitious eye seems pregnant with meaning, as
in some way or other connected with the destiny of the individual.

CHAPTER VII

Trial of the Inca

1533

The arrival of Almagro produced a considerable change in
Pizarro's prospects, since it enabled him to resume active operations and push forward his conquests in the interior. The only
obstacle in his way was the Inca's ransom, and the Spaniards had
patiently waited, till the return of the emissaries from Cuzco
swelled the treasure to a large amount, though still below the
stipulated limit. But now their avarice got the better of their for-
bearance, and they called loudly for the immediate division of
the gold. To wait longer would only be to invite the assault of
their enemies, allured by a bait so attractive. While the treasure
remained uncounted, no man knew its value, nor what was to be
his own portion. It was better to distribute it at once, and let
everyone possess and defend his own. Several, moreover, were
now disposed to return home and take their share of the gold
with them, where they could place it in safety. But these were
few; while much the larger part were only anxious to leave their
present quarters and march at once to Cuzco. More gold, they

thought, awaited them in that capital than they could get here by prolonging their stay; while every hour was precious, to prevent the inhabitants from secreting their treasures, of which design they had already given indication.

Pizarro was especially moved by the last consideration; and he felt that without the capital he could not hope to become master of the empire. Without further delay, the division of the treasure was agreed upon.

Yet, before making this, it was necessary to reduce the whole to ingots of a uniform standard, for the spoil was composed of an infinite variety of articles, in which the gold was of very different degrees of purity. These articles consisted of goblets, ewers, salvers, vases of every shape and size, ornaments and utensils for the temples and the royal palaces, tiles and plates for the decoration of the public edifices, curious imitations of different plants and animals. Among the plants, the most beautiful was the Indian corn, in which the golden ear was sheathed in its broad leaves of silver, from which hung a rich tassel of threads of the same precious metal. A fountain was also much admired, which sent up a sparkling jet of gold, while birds and animals of the same material played in the waters at its base. The delicacy of the workmanship of some of these, and the beauty and ingenuity of the design, attracted the admiration of better judges than the rude Conquerors of Peru.

Before breaking up these specimens of Indian art, it was determined to send a quantity, which should be deducted from the royal fifth, to the emperor. It would serve as a sample of the ingenuity of the natives, and would show him the value of his conquests. A number of the most beautiful articles was selected, of the value of a hundred thousand ducats, and Hernando Pizarro was appointed to be the bearer of them to Spain. He was to obtain an audience of Charles, and at the same time that he laid the treasures before him he was to give an account of the proceedings of the Conquerors, and to seek a further augmentation of their powers and dignities.

No man in the army was better qualified for this mission, by his address and knowledge of affairs, than Hernando Pizarro; no one would be so likely to urge his suit with effect at the haughty Castilian court. But other reasons influenced the selection of him at the present juncture.

His former jealousy of Almagro still rankled in his bosom, and he had beheld that chief's arrival at the camp with feelings of disgust, which he did not care to conceal. He looked on him as coming to share the spoils of victory and defraud his brother of his legitimate honors. Instead of exchanging the cordial greeting proffered by Almagro at their first interview, the arrogant cavalier held back in sullen silence. His brother Francis was greatly displeased at conduct which threatened to renew their ancient feud, and he induced Hernando to accompany him to Almagro's quarters and make some acknowledgment for his uncourteous behavior. But, notwithstanding this show of reconciliation, the general thought the present a favorable opportunity to remove his brother from the scene of operations, where his factious spirit more than counterbalanced his eminent services.

The business of melting down the plate was intrusted to the Indian goldsmiths, who were thus required to undo the work of their own hands. They toiled day and night, but such was the quantity to be recast that it consumed a full month. When the whole was reduced to bars of a uniform standard, they were nicely weighed, under the superintendence of the royal inspectors. The total amount of the gold was found to be one million three hundred and twenty-six thousand five hundred and thirty-nine pesos de oro, which, allowing for the greater value of money in the sixteenth century, would be equivalent, probably, at the present time, to near *three millions and a half of pounds sterling*, or somewhat less than *fifteen millions and a half of dollars*. The quantity of silver was estimated at fifty-one thousand six hundred and ten marks. History affords no parallel of such a booty— and that, too, in the most convertible form, in ready money, as it were—having fallen to the lot of a little band of military adventurers, like the Conquerors of Peru. The great object of the Spanish expeditions in the New World was gold. It is remarkable that their success should have been so complete. Had they taken the track of the English, the French, or the Dutch, on the shores of the northern continent, how different would have been the result! It is equally worthy of remark that the wealth thus suddenly acquired, by diverting them from the slow but surer and more permanent sources of national prosperity, has in the end glided from their grasp and left them among the poorest of the nations of Christendom.

A new difficulty now arose in respect to the division of the treasure. Almagro's followers claimed to be admitted to a share of it; which, as they equaled and, indeed, somewhat exceeded in number Pizarro's company, would reduce the gains of these last very materially. "We were not here, it is true," said Almagro's soldiers to their comrades, "at the seizure of the Inca, but we have taken our turn in mounting guard over him since his capture, have helped you to defend your treasures, and now give you the means of going forward and securing your conquests. It is a common cause," they urged, "in which all are equally embarked, and the gains should be shared equally between us."

But this way of viewing the matter was not at all palatable to Pizarro's company, who alleged that Atahuallpa's contract had been made exclusively with them; that they had seized the Inca, had secured the ransom, had incurred, in short, all the risk of the enterprise, and were not now disposed to share the fruits of it with every one who came after them. There was much force, it could not be denied, in this reasoning, and it was finally settled between the leaders that Almagro's followers should resign their pretensions for a stipulated sum of no great amount, and look to the career now opened to them for carving out their fortunes for themselves.

This delicate affair being thus harmoniously adjusted, Pizarro prepared, with all solemnity, for a division of the imperial spoil. The troops were called together in the great square, and the Spanish commander, "with the fear of God before his eyes," says the record, "invoked the assistance of Heaven to do the work before him conscientiously and justly." The appeal may seem somewhat out of place at the distribution of spoil so unrighteously acquired; yet in truth, considering the magnitude of the treasure, and the power assumed by Pizarro to distribute it according to the respective deserts of the individuals, there were few acts of his life involving a heavier responsibility. On his present decision might be said to hang the future fortunes of each one of his followers—poverty or independence during the remainder of his days.

The royal fifth was first deducted, including the remittance already sent to Spain. The share appropriated by Pizarro amounted to fifty-seven thousand two hundred and twenty-two pesos of gold, and two thousand three hundred and fifty marks of silver. He had besides this the great chair or throne of the Inca, of solid gold, and valued at twenty-five thousand pesos de oro. To his brother Hernando were paid thirty-one thousand and eighty pesos of gold, and two thousand three hundred and fifty marks of silver. De Soto received seventeen thousand seven hundred and forty pesos of gold, and seven hundred and twenty-four marks of silver. Most of the remaining cavalry, sixty in number, received each eight thousand eight hundred and eighty pesos of gold, and three hundred and sixty-two marks of silver, though some had more, and a few considerably less. The infantry mustered in all one hundred and five men. Almost one-fifth of them were allowed, each, four thousand four hundred and forty pesos of gold, and one hundred and eighty marks of silver, half of the compensation of the troopers. The remainder received one-fourth part less; though here again there were exceptions, and some were obliged to content themselves with a much smaller share of the spoil.

The new church of San Francisco, the first Christian temple in Peru, was endowed with two thousand two hundred and twenty pesos of gold. The amount assigned to Almagro's company was not excessive, if it was not more than twenty thousand pesos; and that reserved for the colonists of San Miguel, which amounted only to fifteen thousand pesos, was unaccountably small. There were among them certain soldiers who, at an early period of the expedition, as the reader may remember, abandoned the march and returned to San Miguel. These, certainly, had little claim to be remembered in the division of booty. But the greater part of the colony consisted of invalids, men whose health had been broken by their previous hardships, but who still, with a stout and willing heart, did good service in their military post on the seacoast. On what grounds they had forfeited their claims to a more ample remuneration it is not easy to explain.

Nothing is said, in the partition, of Almagro himself, who, by the terms of the original contract, might claim an equal share of the spoil with his associate. As little notice is taken of Luque, the remaining partner. Luque himself was, indeed, no longer to be benefited by worldly treasure. He had died a short time before Almagro's departure from Panama; too soon to learn the

full success of the enterprise, which, but for his exertions, must
have failed; too soon to become acquainted with the achievements and the crimes of Pizarro. But the Licentiate Espinosa,
whom he represented, and who, it appears, had advanced the
funds for the expedition, was still living at St. Domingo, and
Luque's pretensions were explicitly transferred to him. Yet it is
unsafe to pronounce, at this distance of time, on the authority
of mere negative testimony; and it must be admitted to form
a strong presumption in favor of Pizarro's general equity in the
distribution, that no complaint of it has reached us from any
of the parties present, nor from contemporary chroniclers.

The division of the ransom being completed by the Spaniards,
there seemed to be no further obstacle to their resuming active
operations and commencing the march to Cuzco. But what was
to be done with Atahuallpa? In the determination of this question, whatever was expedient was just. To liberate him would
be to set at large the very man who might prove their most dangerous enemy—one whose birth and royal station would rally
round him the whole nation, place all the machinery of government at his control, and all its resources—one, in short, whose
bare word might concentrate all the energies of his people against
the Spaniards, and thus delay for a long period, if not wholly defeat, the conquest of the country. Yet to hold him in captivity
was attended with scarcely less difficulty; since to guard so important a prize would require such a division of their force as
must greatly cripple its strength, and how could they expect, by
any vigilance, to secure their prisoner against rescue in the perilous passes of the mountains?

The Inca himself now loudly demanded his freedom. The
proposed amount of the ransom had, indeed, not been fully paid.
It may be doubted whether it ever would have been, considering
the embarrassments thrown in the way by the guardians of the
temples, who seemed disposed to secrete the treasures, rather
than despoil these sacred depositories to satisfy the cupidity of
the strangers. It was unlucky, too, for the Indian monarch that
much of the gold, and that of the best quality, consisted of flat
plates or tiles, which, however valuable, lay in a compact form
that did little towards swelling the heap. But an immense amount
had been already realized, and it would have been a still greater

one, the Inca might allege, but for the impatience of the Spaniards. At all events, it was a magnificent ransom, such as was never paid by prince or potentate before.

These considerations Atahuallpa urged on several of the cavaliers, and especially on Hernando de Soto, who was on terms of more familiarity with him than Pizarro. De Soto reported Atahuallpa's demands to his leader; but the latter evaded a direct reply. He did not disclose the dark purposes over which his mind was brooding. Not long afterwards he caused the notary to prepare an instrument in which he fully acquitted the Inca of further obligation in respect to the ransom. This he commanded to be publicly proclaimed in the camp, while at the same time he openly declared that the safety of the Spaniards required that the Inca should be detained in confinement until they were strengthened by additional reinforcements.

Meanwhile the old rumors of a meditated attack by the natives began to be current among the soldiers. They were repeated from one to another, gaining something by every repetition. An immense army, it was reported, was mustering at Quito, the land of Atahuallpa's birth, and thirty thousand Caribs were on their way to support it. The Caribs were distributed by the early Spaniards rather indiscriminately over the different parts of America, being invested with peculiar horrors as a race of cannibals.

It was not easy to trace the origin of these rumors. There was in the camp a considerable number of Indians, who belonged to the party of Huascar, and who were, of course, hostile to Atahuallpa. But his worst enemy was Felipillo, the interpreter from Tumbez, already mentioned in these pages. This youth had conceived a passion for, or, as some say, had been detected in an intrigue with, one of the royal concubines. The circumstance had reached the ears of Atahuallpa, who felt himself deeply outraged by it. "That such an insult should have been offered by so base a person was an indignity," he said, "more difficult to bear than his imprisonment"; and he told Pizarro "that, by the Peruvian law, it could be expiated, not by the criminal's own death alone, but by that of his whole family and kindred." But Felipillo was too important to the Spaniards to be dealt with so summarily; nor did they probably attach such consequence to an offense which, if report be true, they had countenanced by their own example. Felipillo, however, soon learned the state of the Inca's feelings towards himself, and from that moment he regarded him with deadly hatred. Unfortunately, his malignant temper found ready means for its indulgence.

The rumors of a rising among the natives pointed to Atahuallpa as the author of it. Challcuchima was examined on the subject, but avowed his entire ignorance of any such design, which he pronounced a malicious slander. Pizarro next laid the matter before the Inca himself, repeating to him the stories in circulation, with the air of one who believed them. "What treason is this," said the general, "that you have meditated against me— me, who have ever treated you with honor, confiding in your words, as in those of a brother?" "You jest," replied the Inca, who perhaps did not feel the weight of this confidence; "you are always jesting with me. How could I or my people think of conspiring against men so valiant as the Spaniards? Do not jest with me thus, I beseech you." "This," continues Pizarro's secretary, "he said in the most composed and natural manner, smiling all the while to dissemble his falsehood, so that we were all amazed to find such cunning in a barbarian."

But it was not with cunning, but with the consciousness of innocence, as the event afterwards proved, that Atahuallpa thus spoke to Pizarro. He readily discerned, however, the causes, perhaps the consequences, of the accusation. He saw a dark gulf opening beneath his feet; and he was surrounded by strangers, on none of whom he could lean for counsel or protection. The life of the captive monarch is usually short; and Atahuallpa might have learned the truth of this, when he thought of Huascar. Bitterly did he now lament the absence of Hernando Pizarro, for, strange as it may seem, the haughty spirit of this cavalier had been touched by the condition of the royal prisoner, and he had treated him with a deference which won for him the peculiar regard and confidence of the Indian. Yet the latter lost no time in endeavoring to efface the general's suspicions and to establish his own innocence. "Am I not," said he to Pizarro, "a poor captive in your hands? How could I harbor the designs you impute to me, when I should be the first victim of the outbreak? And you little know my people, if you think that such a movement would be made without my orders; when the very birds in my dominions," said he, with somewhat of an hyperbole, "would scarcely venture to fly contrary to my will."

But these protestations of innocence had little effect on the troops; among whom the story of a general rising of the natives continued to gain credit every hour. A large force, it was said, was already gathered at Huamachuco, not a hundred miles from the camp, and their assault might be hourly expected. The treasure which the Spaniards had acquired afforded a tempting prize, and their own alarm was increased by the apprehension of losing it. The patrols were doubled. The horses were kept saddled and bridled. The soldiers slept on their arms; Pizarro went the rounds regularly to see that every sentinel was on his post. The little army, in short, was in a state of preparation for instant attack.

Men suffering from fear are not likely to be too scrupulous as to the means of removing the cause of it. Murmurs, mingled with gloomy menaces, were now heard against the Inca, the author of these machinations. Many began to demand his life, as necessary to the safety of the army. Among these the most vehement were Almagro and his followers. They had not witnessed the seizure of Atahuallpa. They had no sympathy with him in his fallen state. They regarded him only as an encumbrance, and their desire now was to push their fortunes in the country, since they had got so little of the gold of Caxamalca. They were supported by Riquelme, the treasurer, and by the rest of the royal officers. These men had been left at San Miguel by Pizarro, who did not care to have such official spies on his movements. But they had come to the camp with Almagro, and they loudly demanded the Inca's death, as indispensable to the tranquillity of the country and the interests of the crown.

To these dark suggestions Pizarro turned—or seemed to turn—an unwilling ear, showing visible reluctance to proceed to extreme measures with his prisoner. There were some few, and among others Hernando de Soto, who supported him in these views, and who regarded such measures as not at all justified by the evidence of Atahuallpa's guilt. In this state of things, the Spanish commander determined to send a small detachment to Huamachuco, to reconnoiter the country and ascertain what ground there was for the rumors of an insurrection. De Soto was placed at the head of the expedition, which, as the distance was not great, would occupy but a few days.

After that cavalier's departure, the agitation among the soldiers, instead of diminishing, increased to such a degree that Pizarro, unable to resist their importunities, consented to bring Atahuallpa to instant trial. It was but decent, and certainly safer, to have the forms of a trial. A court was organized, over which the two captains, Pizarro and Almagro, were to preside as judges. An attorney-general was named to prosecute for the crown, and counsel was assigned to the prisoner.

The charges preferred against the Inca, drawn up in the form of interrogatories, were twelve in number. The most important were, that he had usurped the crown and assassinated his brother Huascar; that he had squandered the public revenues since the conquest of the country by the Spaniards, and lavished them on his kindred and his minions; that he was guilty of idolatry, and of adulterous practices, indulging openly in a plurality of wives; finally, that he had attempted to excite an insurrection against the Spaniards.

These charges, most of which had reference to national usages, or to the personal relations of the Inca, over which the Spanish conquerors had clearly no jurisdiction, are so absurd that they might well provoke a smile, did they not excite a deeper feeling. The last of the charges was the only one of moment in such a trial; and the weakness of this may be inferred from the care taken to bolster it up with the others. The mere specification of the articles must have been sufficient to show that the doom of the Inca was already sealed.

A number of Indian witnesses were examined, and their testimony, filtrated through the interpretation of Felipillo, received, it is said, when necessary, a very different coloring from that of the original. The examination was soon ended, and "a warm discussion," as we are assured by one of Pizarro's own secretaries, "took place in respect to the probable good or evil that would result from the death of Atahuallpa." It was a question of expediency. He was found guilty—whether of all the crimes alleged we are not informed—and he was sentenced to be burnt alive in the great square of Caxamalca. The sentence was to be carried into execution that very night. They were not even to wait for the return of De Soto, when the information he would bring would go far to establish the truth or the falsehood of the reports respecting the insurrection of the natives. It was desirable to obtain the countenance of Father Valverde to these proceedings, and a copy of the judgment was submitted to the friar for his signature, which he gave without hesitation, declaring that, "in his opinion, the Inca, at all events, deserved death."

Yet there were some few in that martial conclave who resisted these high-handed measures. They considered them as a poor requital of all the favors bestowed on them by the Inca, who hitherto had received at their hands nothing but wrong. They objected to the evidence as wholly insufficient; and they denied the authority of such a tribunal to sit in judgment on a sovereign prince in the heart of his own dominions. If he were to be tried, he should be sent to Spain, and his cause brought before the emperor, who alone had power to determine it.

But the great majority—and they were ten to one—overruled these objections, by declaring there was no doubt of Atahuallpa's guilt, and they were willing to assume the responsibility of his punishment. A full account of the proceedings would be sent to Castile, and the emperor should be informed who were the loyal servants of the crown, and who were its enemies. The dispute ran so high that for a time it menaced an open and violent rupture; till, at length, convinced that resistance was fruitless, the weaker party, silenced, but not satisfied, contented themselves with entering a written protest against these proceedings, which would leave an indelible stain on the names of all concerned in them.

When the sentence was communicated to the Inca, he was greatly overcome by it. He had, indeed, for some time, looked to such an issue as probable, and had been heard to intimate as much to those about him. But the probability of such an event is very different from its certainty—and that, too, so sudden and speedy. For a moment, the overwhelming conviction of it unmanned him, and he exclaimed, with tears in his eyes, "What have I done, or my children, that I should meet such a fate? And from your hands, too," said he, addressing Pizarro; "you, who have met with friendship and kindness from my people, with whom I have shared my treasures, who have received nothing but benefits from my hands!" In the most piteous tones, he then implored that his life might be spared, promising any guarantee that might be required for the safety of every Spaniard in the army—promising double the ransom he had already paid, if time were only given him to obtain it.

An eye-witness assures us that Pizarro was visibly affected, as he turned away from the Inca, to whose appeal he had no power to listen in opposition to the voice of the army and to his own sense of what was due to the security of the country. Atahuallpa, finding he had no power to turn his Conqueror from his purpose, recovered his habitual self-possession, and from that moment submitted himself to his fate with the courage of an Indian warrior.

The doom of the Inca was proclaimed by sound of trumpet in the great square of Caxamalca; and, two hours after sunset, the Spanish soldiery assembled by torchlight in the plaza to witness the execution of the sentence. It was on the twenty-ninth of August, 1533. Atahuallpa was led out chained hand and foot —for he had been kept in irons ever since the great excitement had prevailed in the army respecting an assault. Father Vicente de Valverde was at his side, striving to administer consolation, and, if possible, to persuade him at this last hour to abjure his superstition and embrace the religion of his Conquerors. He was willing to save the soul of his victim from the terrible expiation in the next world to which he had so cheerfully consigned his mortal part in this.

During Atahuallpa's confinement, the friar had repeatedly expounded to him the Christian doctrines, and the Indian monarch discovered much acuteness in apprehending the discourse of his teacher. But it had not carried conviction to his mind, and, though he listened with patience, he had shown no disposition to renounce the faith of his fathers. The Dominican made a last appeal to him in this solemn hour; and, when Atahuallpa was bound to the stake, with the fagots that were to kindle his funeral pile lying around him, Valverde, holding up the cross, besought him to embrace it and be baptized, promising that, by so doing, the painful death to which he had been sentenced should be commuted for the milder form of the garrote—a mode of punishment by strangulation, used for criminals in Spain.

The unhappy monarch asked if this were really so, and, on its being confirmed by Pizarro, he consented to abjure his own religion and receive baptism. The ceremony was performed by Father Valverde, and the new convert received the name of Juan de Atahuallpa—the name of Juan being conferred in honor of John the Baptist, on whose day the event took place.

Atahuallpa expressed a desire that his remains might be transported to Quito, the place of his birth, to be preserved with those of his maternal ancestors. Then, turning to Pizarro, as a last request, he implored him to take compassion on his young children and receive them under his protection. Was there no other one in that dark company who stood grimly around him, to whom he could look for the protection of his offspring? Perhaps he thought there was no other so competent to afford it, and that the wishes so solemnly expressed in that hour might meet with respect even from his Conqueror. Then, recovering his stoical bearing, which for a moment had been shaken, he submitted himself calmly to his fate—while the Spaniards, gathering around, muttered their Credos for the salvation of his soul! Thus by the death of a vile malefactor perished the last of the Incas!

I have already spoken of the person and the qualities of Atahuallpa. He had a handsome countenance, though with an expression somewhat too fierce to be pleasing. His frame was muscular and well proportioned; his air commanding; and his deportment in the Spanish quarters had a degree of refinement, the more interesting that it was touched with melancholy. He is accused of having been cruel in his wars and bloody in his revenge. It may be true, but the pencil of an enemy would be likely to overcharge the shadows of the portrait. He is allowed to have been bold, high-minded, and liberal. All agree that he showed singular penetration and quickness of perception. His exploits as a warrior had placed his valor beyond dispute. The best homage to it is the reluctance shown by the Spaniards to restore him to freedom. They dreaded him as an enemy, and they had done him too many wrongs to think that he could be their friend. Yet his conduct towards them from the first had been most friendly; and they repaid it with imprisonment, robbery, and death.

The body of the Inca remained on the place of execution through the night. The following morning it was removed to the church of San Francisco, where his funeral obsequies were performed with great solemnity. Pizarro and the principal cavaliers went into mourning, and the troops listened with devout attention to the service of the dead from the lips of Father Valverde. The ceremony was interrupted by the sound of loud cries and wailing, as of many voices at the doors of the church. These were suddenly thrown open, and a number of Indian women, the wives and sisters of the deceased, rushing up the great aisle, surrounded the corpse. This was not the way, they cried, to celebrate the funeral rites of an Inca; and they declared their intention to sacrifice themselves on his tomb and bear him company to the land of spirits. The audience, outraged by this frantic behavior, told the intruders that Atahuallpa had died in the faith of a Christian, and that the God of the Christians abhorred such sacrifices. They then caused the women to be excluded from the church, and several, retiring to their own quarters, laid violent hands on themselves, in the vain hope of accompanying their beloved lord to the bright mansions of the Sun.

Atahuallpa's remains, notwithstanding his request, were laid in the cemetery of San Francisco. But from thence, as is reported, after the Spaniards left Caxamalca, they were secretly removed, and carried, as he had desired, to Quito. The colonists of a later time supposed that some treasures might have been buried with the body. But, on excavating the ground, neither treasure nor remains were to be discovered.

A day or two after these tragic events, Hernando de Soto returned from his excursion. Great was his astonishment and indignation at learning what had been done in his absence. He sought out Pizarro at once, and found him, says the chronicler, "with a great felt hat, by way of mourning, slouched over his eyes," and in his dress and demeanor exhibiting all the show of sorrow. "You have acted rashly," said De Soto to him bluntly; "Atahuallpa has been basely slandered. There was no enemy at Huamachuco; no rising among the natives. I have met with nothing on the road but demonstrations of good will, and all is quiet. If it was necessary to bring the Inca to trial, he should have been taken to Castile and judged by the emperor. I would have pledged myself to see him safe on board the vessel." Pizarro confessed that he had been precipitate, and said that he had been deceived by Riquelme, Valverde, and the others. These charges soon reached the ears of the treasurer and the Dominican, who, in their turn, exculpated themselves, and upbraided Pizarro to his face, as the only one responsible for the deed. The dispute ran high; and the parties were heard by the by-standers to give one another the lie! This vulgar squabble among the leaders, so soon after the event, is the best commentary on the inquity of their own proceedings and the innocence of the Inca.

The treatment of Atahuallpa, from first to last, forms undoubtedly one of the darkest chapters in Spanish colonial history. There may have been massacres perpetrated on a more extended scale, and executions accompanied with a greater refinement of cruelty. But the bloodstained annals of the Conquest afford no such example of coldhearted and systematic persecution, not of an enemy, but of one whose whole deportment had been that of a friend and a benefactor.

From the hour that Pizarro and his followers had entered within the sphere of Atahuallpa's influence, the hand of friendship had been extended to them by the natives. Their first act, on crossing the mountains, was to kidnap the monarch and massacre his people. The seizure of his person might be vindicated, by those who considered the end as justifying the means, on the ground that it was indispensable to secure the triumphs of the Cross. But no such apology can be urged for the massacre of the unarmed and helpless population—as wanton as it was wicked.

The long confinement of the Inca had been used by the Conquerors to wring from him his treasures with the hard gripe of avarice. During the whole of this dismal period he had conducted himself with singular generosity and good faith. He had opened a free passage to the Spaniards through every part of his empire, and had furnished every facility for the execution of their plans. When these were accomplished, and he remained an encumbrance on their hands, notwithstanding their engagement, expressed or implied, to release him—and Pizarro, as we have seen, by a formal act acquitted his captive of any further obligation on the score of the ransom—he was arraigned before a mock tribunal, and, under pretenses equally false and frivolous, was condemned to an excruciating death. From first to last, the policy of the Spanish Conquerors towards their unhappy victim is stamped with barbarity and fraud.

It is not easy to acquit Pizarro of being in a great degree responsible for this policy. His partisans have labored to show that it was forced on him by the necessity of the case, and that in the death of the Inca, especially, he yielded reluctantly to the importunities of others. But, weak as is this apology, the historian who has the means of comparing the various testimony of the period will come to a different conclusion. To him it will appear that Pizarro had probably long felt the removal of Atahuallpa to be essential to the success of his enterprise. He foresaw the odium that would be incurred by the death of his royal captive without sufficient grounds; while he labored to establish these, he still shrank from the responsibility of the deed, and preferred to perpetrate it in obedience to the suggestions of others, rather than his own. Like many an unprincipled politician, he wished to reap the benefit of a bad act and let others bear the blame of it.

Almagro and his followers are reported by Pizarro's secretaries to have first insisted on the Inca's death. They were loudly supported by the treasurer and the royal officers, who considered it as indispensable to the interests of the crown; and, finally, the rumors of a conspiracy raised the same cry among the soldiers, and Pizarro, with all his tenderness for his prisoner, could not refuse to bring him to trial. The form of a trial was necessary to give an appearance of fairness to the proceedings. That it was only form is evident from the indecent haste with which it was conducted—the examination of evidence, the sentence, and the execution being all on the same day. The multiplication of the charges, designed to place the guilt of the accused on the strongest ground, had, from their very number, the opposite effect, proving only the determination to convict him. If Pizarro had felt the reluctance to his conviction which he pretended, why did he send De Soto, Atahuallpa's best friend, away, when the inquiry was to be instituted? Why was the sentence so summarily executed, as not to afford opportunity, by that cavalier's return, of disproving the truth of the principal charge—the only one, in fact, with which the Spaniards had any concern? The solemn farce of mourning and deep sorrow affected by Pizarro, who by these honors to the dead would intimate the sincere regard he had entertained for the living, was too thin a veil to impose on the most credulous.

It is not intended by these reflections to exculpate the rest of the army, and especially its officers, from their share in the infamy of the transaction. But Pizarro, as commander of the army, was mainly responsible for its measures. For he was not a man to allow his own authority to be wrested from his grasp, or to yield timidly to the impulses of others. He did not even yield to his own. His whole career shows him, whether for good or for evil, to have acted with a cool and calculating policy.

A story has been often repeated, which refers the motives of Pizarro's conduct, in some degree at least, to personal resentment. The Inca had requested one of the Spanish soldiers to write the name of God on his nail. This the monarch showed to several of his guards successively, and, as they read it, and each pronounced the same word, the sagacious mind of the barbarian was delighted with what seemed to him little short of a miracle —to which the science of his own nation afforded no analogy. On showing the writing to Pizarro, that chief remained silent; and the Inca, finding he could not read, conceived a contempt for the commander who was even less informed than his soldiers. This he did not wholly conceal, and Pizarro, aware of the cause of it, neither forgot nor forgave it. The anecdote is reported not on the highest authority. It may be true; but it is unnecessary to look for the motives of Pizarro's conduct in personal pique, when so many proofs are to be discerned of a dark and deliberate policy.

Yet the arts of the Spanish chieftain failed to reconcile his countrymen to the atrocity of his proceedings. It is singular to observe the difference between the tone assumed by the first chroniclers of the transaction, while it was yet fresh, and that of those who wrote when the lapse of a few years had shown the tendency of public opinion. The first boldly avow the deed as demanded by expediency, if not necessity; while they deal in no measured terms of reproach with the character of their unfortunate victim. The latter, on the other hand, while they extenuate the errors of the Inca, and do justice to his good faith, are unreserved in their condemnation of the Conquerors, on whose conduct, they say, Heaven set the seal of its own reprobation, by bringing them all to an untimely and miserable end. The sentence of contemporaries has been fully ratified by that of posterity; and the persecution of Atahuallpa is regarded with justice as having left a stain, never to be effaced, on the Spanish arms in the New World.

BOOK IV

CHAPTER I

Civil Wars of the Conquerors

1535-1537

While the events recorded in the preceding chapter were passing, the Marshal Almagro was engaged in his memorable expedition to Chili. He had set out, as we have seen, with only part of his forces, leaving his lieutenant to follow him with the remainder. During the first part of the way he profited by the great military road of the Incas, which stretched across the tableland far towards the south. But as he drew near to Chili the Spanish commander became entangled in the defiles of the mountains, where no vestige of a road was to be discerned. Here his progress was impeded by all the obstacles which belong to the wild scenery of the Cordilleras: deep and ragged ravines, round whose sides a slender sheep-path wound up to a dizzy height over the precipices below; rivers rushing in fury down the slopes of the mountains and throwing themselves in stupendous cataracts into the yawning abyss; dark forests of pine that seemed to have no end, and then again long reaches of desolate tableland, without so much as a bush or shrub to shelter the shivering traveler from the blast that swept down from the frozen summits of the sierra.

The cold was so intense that many lost the nails of their fingers, their fingers themselves, and sometimes their limbs. Others were blinded by the dazzling waste of snow, reflecting the rays of a sun made intolerably brilliant in the thin atmosphere of these elevated regions. Hunger came, as usual, in the train of woes; for in these dismal solitudes no vegetation that would suffice for the food of man was visible, and no living thing, except only the great bird of the Andes hovering over their heads in expectation of his banquet. This was too frequently afforded by the number of wretched Indians who, unable, from the scantiness of their clothing, to encounter the severity of the climate, perished by the way. Such was the pressure of hunger that the miserable survivors fed on the dead bodies of their countrymen, and the Spaniards forced a similar sustenance from the carcasses of their horses, literally frozen to death in the mountain passes. Such were the terrible penalties which nature imposed on those who rashly intruded on these her solitary and most savage haunts.

Yet their own sufferings do not seem to have touched the hearts of the Spaniards with any feeling of compassion for the weaker natives. Their path was everywhere marked by burnt and desolated hamlets, the inhabitants of which were compelled to do them service as beasts of burden. They were chained together in gangs of ten or twelve, and no infirmity or feebleness of body excused the unfortunate captive from his full share of the common toil, till he sometimes dropped dead, in his very chains, from mere exhaustion! Alvarado's company are accused of having been more cruel than Pizarro's; and many of Almagro's men, it may be remembered, were recruited from that source. The commander looked with displeasure, it is said, on these enormities, and did what he could to repress them. Yet he did not set a good example in his own conduct, if it be true that he caused no less than thirty Indian chiefs to be burnt alive for the massacre of three of his followers! The heart sickens at the recital of such atrocities perpetrated on an unoffending people, or, at least, guilty of no other crime than that of defending their own soil too well.

There is something in the possession of superior strength most dangerous, in a moral view, to its possessor. Brought in contact with semi-civilized man, the European, with his endowments and effective force so immeasurably superior, holds him as little higher than the brute, and as born equally for his service. He feels that he has a natural right, as it were, to his obedience, and that this obedience is to be measured, not by the powers of the barbarian, but by the will of his conqueror. Resistance becomes a crime to be washed out only in the blood of the victim. The tale of such atrocities is not confined to the Spaniard. Wherever the civilized man and the savage have come in contact, in the East or in the West, the story has been too often written in blood.

From the wild chaos of mountain scenery the Spaniards emerged on the green vale of Coquimbo, about the thirtieth degree of south latitude. Here they halted, to refresh themselves in its abundant plains, after their unexampled sufferings and fatigues. Meanwhile Almagro despatched an officer with a strong party in advance, to ascertain the character of the country towards the south. Not long after, he was cheered by the arrival of the remainder of his forces under his lieutenant Rodrigo de Orgoñez. This was a remarkable person, intimately connected with the subsequent fortunes of Almagro.

He was a native of Oropesa, had been trained in the Italian wars, and held the rank of ensign in the army of the Constable of Bourbon at the famous sack of Rome. It was a good school in which to learn his iron trade and to steel the heart against any too ready sensibility to human suffering. Orgoñez was an excellent soldier—true to his commander, prompt, fearless, and unflinching in the execution of his orders. His services attracted the notice of the crown, and shortly after this period he was raised to the rank of marshal of New Toledo. Yet it may be doubted whether his character did not qualify him for an executive and subordinate station, rather than for one of higher responsibility.

Almagro received also the royal warrant conferring on him his new powers and territorial jurisdiction. The instrument had been detained by the Pizarros to the very last moment. His troops, long since disgusted with their toilsome and unprofitable march, were now clamorous to return. Cuzco, they said, undoubtedly fell within the limits of his government, and it was better to take possession of its comfortable quarters than to wander like outcasts in this dreary wilderness. They reminded their commander that thus only could he provide for the interests of his son Diego. This was an illegitimate son of Almagro, on whom his father doted with extravagant fondness, justified more than usual by the promising character of the youth.

After an absence of about two months, the officer sent on the exploring expedition returned, bringing unpromising accounts of the southern regions of Chili. The only land of promise for the Castilian was one that teemed with gold. He had penetrated to the distance of a hundred leagues, to the limits, probably, of the conquests of the Incas on the river Maule. The Spaniards had fortunately stopped short of the land of Arauco, where the blood of their countrymen was soon after to be poured out like water, and which still maintains a proud independence amidst the general humiliation of the Indian races around it.

Almagro now yielded, with little reluctance, to the renewed importunities of the soldiers, and turned his face towards the north. It is unnecessary to follow his march in detail. Disheartened by the difficulties of the mountain passage, he took the road along the coast, which led him across the great desert of Atacama. In crossing this dreary waste, which stretches for nearly a hundred leagues to the northern borders of Chili, with hardly a green spot in its expanse to relieve the fainting traveler, Almagro and his men experienced as great sufferings, though not of the same kind, as those which they had encountered in the passes of the Cordilleras. Indeed, the captain would not easily be found at this day who would venture to lead his army across this dreary region. But the Spaniard of the sixteenth century had a strength of limb and a buoyancy of spirit which raised him to a contempt of obstacles almost justifying the boast of the historian that "he contended indifferently at the same time with man, with the elements, and with famine!"

After traversing the terrible desert, Almagro reached the ancient town of Arequipa, about sixty leagues from Cuzco. Here he learned with astonishment the insurrection of the Peruvians, and, further, that the young Inca Manco still lay with a formidable force at no great distance from the capital. He had once been on friendly terms with the Peruvian prince, and he now resolved, before proceeding farther, to send an embassy to his camp and arrange an interview with him in the neighborhood of Cuzco.

Almagro's emissaries were well received by the Inca, who alleged his grounds of complaint against the Pizarros, and named the vale of Yucay as the place where he would confer with the marshal. The Spanish commander accordingly resumed his march, and, taking one-half of his force, whose whole number fell somewhat short of five hundred men, he repaired in person to the place of rendezvous; while the remainder of his army established their quarters at Urcos, about six leagues from the capital.

The Spaniards in Cuzco, startled by the appearance of this fresh body of troops in their neighborhood, doubted, when they learned the quarter whence they came, whether it betided them good or evil. Hernando Pizarro marched out of the city with a small force, and, drawing near to Urcos, heard with no little uneasiness of Almagro's purpose to insist on his pretensions to Cuzco. Though much inferior in strength to his rival, he determined to resist him.

Meanwhile, the Peruvians, who had witnessed the conference between the soldiers of the opposite camps, suspected some secret understanding between the parties, which would compromise the safety of the Inca. They communicated their distrust to Manco, and the latter, adopting the same sentiments, or perhaps from the first meditating a surprise of the Spaniards, suddenly fell upon the latter in the valley of Yucay with a body of fifteen thousand men. But the veterans of Chili were too familiar with Indian tactics to be taken by surprise; and, though a sharp engagement ensued, which lasted more than an hour, in which Orgoñez had a horse killed under him, the natives were finally driven back with great slaughter, and the Inca was so far crippled by the blow that he was not likely for the present to give further molestation.

Almagro, now joining the division left at Urcos, saw no further impediment to his operations on Cuzco. He sent at once an embassy to the municipality of the place, requiring the recognition of him as its lawful governor, and presenting at the same time a copy of his credentials from the crown. But the question of jurisdiction was not one easy to be settled, depending as it did on a knowledge of the true parallels of latitude, not very likely to be possessed by the rude followers of Pizarro. The royal grant had placed under his jurisdiction all the country extending two hundred and seventy leagues south of the river of Santiago, situated one degree and twenty minutes north of the equator. Two hundred and seventy leagues on the meridian, by our measurement, would fall more than a degree short of Cuzco, and, indeed, would barely include the city of Lima itself. But the Spanish leagues, of only seventeen and a half to a degree, would remove the southern boundary to nearly half a degree beyond the capital of the Incas, which would thus fall within the jurisdiction of Pizarro. Yet the division line ran so close to the disputed ground that the true result might reasonably be doubted, where no careful scientific observations had been made to obtain it; and each party was prompt to assert, as always happens in such cases, that its own claim was clear and unquestionable.

Thus summoned by Almagro, the authorities of Cuzco, unwilling to give umbrage to either of the contending chiefs, decided that they must wait until they could take counsel—which they promised to do at once—with certain pilots better instructed than themselves in the position of the Santiago. Meanwhile, a truce was arranged between the parties, both solemnly engaging to abstain from hostile measures and to remain quiet in their present quarters.

The weather now set in cold and rainy. Almagro's soldiers, greatly discontented with their position, flooded as it was by the waters, were quick to discover that Hernando Pizarro was busily employed in strengthening himself in the city, contrary to agreement. They also learned with dismay that a large body of men, sent by the governor from Lima, under command of Alonso de Alvarado, was on the march to relieve Cuzco. They exclaimed that they were betrayed, and that the truce had been only an artifice to secure their inactivity until the arrival of the expected succors. In this state of excitement, it was not very difficult to persuade their commander—too ready to surrender his own judgment to the rash advisers around him—to violate the treaty and take possession of the capital.

Under cover of a dark and stormy night (April 8th, 1537), he entered the place without opposition, made himself master of the principal church, established strong parties of cavalry at the head of the great avenues to prevent surprise, and detached Orgoñez with a body of infantry to force the dwelling of Hernando Pizarro. That captain was lodged with his brother Gonzalo in one of the large halls built by the Incas for public diversions, with immense doors of entrance that opened on the plaza. It was garrisoned by about twenty soldiers, who, as the gates were burst open, stood stoutly to the defense of their leader. A smart struggle ensued, in which some lives were lost, till at length Orgoñez, provoked by the obstinate resistance, set fire to the combustible roof of the building. It was speedily in flames, and the burning rafters falling on the heads of the inmates, they forced their reluctant leader to an unconditional surrender.

Scarcely had the Spaniards left the building, when the whole roof fell in with a tremendous crash.

Almagro was now master of Cuzco. He ordered the Pizarros, with fifteen or twenty of the principal cavaliers, to be secured and placed in confinement. Except so far as required for securing his authority, he does not seem to have been guilty of acts of violence to the inhabitants, and he installed one of Pizarro's most able officers, Gabriel de Rojas, in the government of the city. The municipality, whose eyes were now open to the validity of Almagro's pretensions, made no further scruple to recognize his title to Cuzco.

The marshal's first step was to send a message to Alonso de Alvarado's camp, advising that officer of his occupation of the city, and requiring his obedience to him, as its legitimate master. Alvarado was lying, with a body of five hundred men, horse and foot, at Xauxa, about thirteen leagues from the capital. He had been detached several months previously for the relief of Cuzco, but had, most unaccountably, and, as it proved, most unfortunately for the Peruvian capital, remained at Xauxa, with the alleged motive of protecting that settlement and the surrounding country against the insurgents. He now showed himself loyal to his commander; and when Almagro's ambassadors reached his camp he put them in irons, and sent advice of what had been done to the governor at Lima.

Almagro, offended by the detention of his emissaries, prepared at once to march against Alonso de Alvarado and take more effectual measures to bring him to submission. His lieutenant, Orgoñez, strongly urged him before his departure to strike off the heads of the Pizarros, alleging "that, while they lived, his commander's life would never be safe," and concluding with the Spanish proverb, "Dead men never bite." But the marshal, though he detested Hernando in his heart, shrank from so violent a measure; and, independently of other considerations, he had still an attachment for his old associate, Francisco Pizarro, and was unwilling to sever the ties between them forever. Contenting himself, therefore, with placing his prisoners under strong guard in one of the stone buildings belonging to the House of the Sun, he put himself at the head of his forces and left the capital in quest of Alvarado.

That officer had now taken up a position on the farther side of the Rio de Abancay, where he lay, with the bulk of his little army, in front of a bridge, by which its rapid waters are traversed, while a strong detachment occupied a spot commanding a ford lower down the river. But in this detachment was a cavalier of much consideration in the army, Pedro de Lerma, who, from some pique against his commander, had entered into treasonable correspondence with the opposite party. By his advice, Almagro, on reaching the border of the river, established himself against the bridge in face of Alvarado, as if prepared to force a passage, thus concentrating his adversary's attention on that point. But when darkness had set in he detached a large body under Orgoñez to pass the ford and operate in concert with Lerma. Orgoñez executed this commission with his usual promptness. The ford was crossed, though the current ran so swiftly that several of his men were swept away by it and perished in the waters. Their leader received a severe wound himself in the mouth, as he was gaining the opposite bank, but, nothing daunted, he cheered on his men and fell with fury on the enemy. He was speedily joined by Lerma and such of the soldiers as he had gained over, and, unable to distinguish friend from foe, the enemy's confusion was complete.

Meanwhile, Alvarado, roused by the noise of the attack on this quarter, hastened to the support of his officer, when Almagro, seizing the occasion, pushed across the bridge, dispersed the small body left to defend it, and, falling on Alvarado's rear, that general saw himself hemmed in on all sides. The struggle did not last long; and the unfortunate chief, uncertain on whom he could rely, surrendered with all his force—those only excepted who had already deserted to the enemy. Such was the battle of Abancay, as it was called, from the river on whose banks it was fought, on the twelfth of July, 1537. Never was a victory more complete or achieved with less cost of life; and Almagro marched back, with an array of prisoners scarcely inferior to his own army in number, in triumph to Cuzco.

While the events related in the preceding pages were passing, Francisco Pizarro had remained at Lima, anxiously awaiting the arrival of the reinforcements which he had requested, to enable him to march to the relief of the beleaguered capital of the Incas. His appeal had not been unanswered. Among the rest was a corps of two hundred and fifty men, led by the Licentiate Gaspar de Espinosa, one of the three original associates, it may be remembered, who engaged in the conquest of Peru. He had now left his own residence at Panama, and came in person, for the first time, it would seem, to revive the drooping fortunes of his confederates. Pizarro received also a vessel laden with provisions, military stores, and other necessary supplies, besides a rich wardrobe for himself, from Cortes, the Conqueror of Mexico, who generously stretched forth his hand to aid his kinsman in the hour of need.

With a force amounting to four hundred and fifty men, half of them cavalry, the governor quitted Lima and began his march on the Inca capital. He had not advanced far when he received tidings of the return of Almagro, the seizure of Cuzco, and the imprisonment of his brothers; and before he had time to recover from this astounding intelligence he learned the total defeat and capture of Alvarado. Filled with consternation at these rapid successes of his rival, he now returned in all haste to Lima, which he put in the best posture of defense, to secure it against the hostile movements not unlikely, as he thought, to be directed against that capital itself. Meanwhile, far from indulging in impotent sallies of resentment, or in complaints of his ancient comrade, he only lamented that Almagro should have resorted to these violent measures for the settlement of their dispute, and this less—if we may take his word for it—from personal considerations than from the prejudice it might do to the interests of the crown.

But, while busily occupied with warlike preparations, he did not omit to try the effect of negotiation. He sent an embassy to Cuzco, consisting of several persons in whose discretion he placed the greatest confidence, with Espinosa at their head, as the party most interested in an amicable arrangement.

The licentiate, on his arrival, did not find Almagro in as favorable a mood for an accommodation as he could have wished. Elated by his recent successes, he now aspired not only to the possession of Cuzco, but of Lima itself, as falling within the limits of his jurisdiction. It was in vain that Espinosa urged the propriety, by every argument which prudence could suggest, of moderating his demands. His claims upon Cuzco, at least, were not to be shaken, and he declared himself ready to peril his life in maintaining them. The licentiate coolly replied by quoting the pithy Castilian proverb, "El vencido vencido, y el vencidor perdido": "The vanquished vanquished, and the victor undone."

What influence the temperate arguments of the licentiate might eventually have had on the heated imagination of the soldier is doubtful; but, unfortunately for the negotiation, it was abruptly terminated by the death of Espinosa himself, which took place most unexpectedly, though, strange to say, in those times, without the imputation of poison. He was a great loss to the parties in the existing fermentation of their minds; for he had the weight of character which belongs to wise and moderate counsels, and a deeper interest than any other man in recommending them.

The name of Espinosa is memorable in history from his early connection with the expedition to Peru, which, but for the seasonable though secret application of his funds, could not then have been compassed. He had long been a resident in the Spanish colonies of Tierra Firme and Panama, where he had served in various capacities, sometimes as a legal functionary presiding in the courts of justice, and not unfrequently as an efficient leader in the early expeditions of conquest and discovery. In these manifold vocations he acquired a high reputation for probity, intelligence, and courage, and his death at the present crisis was undoubtedly the most unfortunate event that could have befallen the country.

All attempt at negotiation was now abandoned; and Almagro announced his purpose to descend to the seacoast, where he could plant a colony and establish a port for himself. This would secure him the means, so essential, of communicating with the mother-country, and here he would resume negotiations for the settlement of his dispute with Pizarro. Before quitting Cuzco, he sent Orgoñez with a strong force against the Inca, not caring to leave the capital exposed in his absence to further annoyance from that quarter.

But the Inca, discouraged by his late discomfiture, and unable, perhaps, to rally in sufficient strength for resistance, abandoned his stronghold at Tambo and retreated across the mountains. He was hotly pursued by Orgoñez over hill and valley, till, deserted by his followers, and with only one of his wives to bear him company, the royal fugitive took shelter in the remote fast-nesses of the Andes.

Before leaving the capital, Orgoñez again urged his com-mander to strike off the heads of the Pizarros and then march at once upon Lima. By this decisive step he would bring the war to an issue, and forever secure himself from the insidious mach-inations of his enemies. But in the meantime a new friend had risen up to the captive brothers. This was Diego de Alvarado, brother of that Pedro who, as mentioned in a preceding chapter, had conducted the unfortunate expedition to Quito. After his brother's departure, Diego had attached himself to the fortunes of Almagro, had accompanied him to Chili, and, as he was a cavalier of birth, and possessed of some truly noble qualities, he had gained deserved ascendancy over his commander. Alvarado had frequently visited Hernando Pizarro in his confinement, where, to beguile the tediousness of captivity, he amused himself with gaming—the passion of the Spaniard. They played deep, and Alvarado lost the enormous sum of eighty thousand gold cas-tellanos. He was prompt in paying the debt, but Hernando Pizarro peremptorily declined to receive the money. By this politic generosity he secured an important advocate in the coun-cil of Almagro. It stood him now in good stead. Alvarado repre-sented to the marshal that such a measure as that urged by Orgo-ñez would not only outrage the feelings of his followers, but would ruin his fortunes by the indignation it must excite at court. When Almagro acquiesced in these views, as in truth most grateful to his own nature, Orgoñez, chagrined at his deter-mination, declared that the day would come when he would re-pent this mistaken lenity. "A Pizarro," he said, "was never known to forget an injury; and that which they had already received from Almagro was too deep for them to forgive." Prophetic words!

On leaving Cuzco, the marshal gave orders that Gonzalo Pizarro and the other prisoners should be detained in strict custody. Hernando he took with him, closely guarded, on his march. Descending rapidly towards the coast, he reached the pleasant vale of Chincha in the latter part of August. Here he occupied himself with laying the foundations of a town bearing his own name, which might serve as a counterpart to the City of the Kings—thus bidding defiance, as it were, to his rival on his own borders. While occupied in this manner, he received the unwelcome tidings that Gonzalo Pizarro, Alonso de Alvarado, and the other prisoners, having tampered with their guards, had effected their escape from Cuzco, and he soon after heard of their safe arrival in the camp of Pizarro.

Chafed by this intelligence, the marshal was not soothed by the insinuations of Orgoñez, that it was owing to his ill-advised lenity; and it might have gone hard with Hernando, but that Almagro's attention was diverted by the negotiation which Francisco Pizarro now proposed to resume.

After some correspondence between the parties, it was agreed to submit the arbitration of the dispute to a single individual, Fray Francisco de Bovadilla, a Brother of the Order of Mercy. Though living in Lima, and, as might be supposed, under the influence of Pizarro, he had a reputation for integrity that disposed Almagro to confide the settlement of the question exclusively to him. In this implicit confidence in the friar's impartiality, Orgoñez, of a less sanguine temper than his chief, did not participate.

An interview was arranged between the rival chiefs. It took place at Mala, November 13th, 1537; but very different was the deportment of the two commanders towards each other from that which they had exhibited at their former meetings. Almagro, indeed, doffing his bonnet, advanced in his usual open manner to salute his ancient comrade; but Pizarro, hardly condescending to return the salute, haughtily demanded why the marshal had seized upon his city of Cuzco and imprisoned his brothers. This led to a recrimination on the part of his associate. The discussion assumed the tone of an angry altercation, till Almagro, taking a hint—or what he conceived to be such—from an attendant, that some treachery was intended, abruptly quitted the apartment, mounted his horse, and galloped back to his quarters at Chincha. The conference closed, as might have been anticipated from the heated temper of their minds when they began it, by widening the breach it was intended to heal. The friar, now left wholly to himself, after some deliberation, gave his award. He decided that a vessel, with a skillful pilot on board, should be sent to determine the exact latitude of the river of Santiago, the northern boundary of Pizarro's territory, by which all the measurements were to be regulated. In the meantime, Cuzco was to be delivered up by Almagro, and Hernando Pizarro to be set at liberty, on condition of his leaving the country in six weeks for Spain. Both parties were to retire within their undisputed territories, and to abandon all further hostilities.

This award, as may be supposed, highly satisfactory to Pizarro, was received by Almagro's men with indignation and scorn. They had been sold, they cried, by their general, broken, as he was, by age and infirmities. Their enemies were to occupy Cuzco and its pleasant places, while they were to be turned over to the barren wilderness of Charcas. Little did they dream that under this poor exterior were hidden the rich treasures of Potosi. They denounced the umpire as a hireling of the governor, and murmurs were heard among the troops, stimulated by Orgoñez, demanding the head of Hernando. Never was that cavalier in greater danger. But his good genius in the form of Alvarado again interposed to protect him. His life in captivity was a succession of reprieves.

Yet his brother, the governor, was not disposed to abandon him to his fate. On the contrary, he was now prepared to make every concession to secure his freedom. Concessions, that politic chief well knew, cost little to those who are not concerned to abide by them. After some preliminary negotiation, another award, more equitable, or, at all events, more to the satisfaction of the discontented party, was given. The principal articles of it were, that, until the arrival of some definite instructions on the point from Castile, the city of Cuzco, with its territory, should remain in the hands of Almagro; and that Hernando Pizarro should be set at liberty, on the condition, above stipulated, of leaving the country in six weeks. When the terms of this agreement were communicated to Orgoñez, that officer intimated his opinion of them by passing his finger across his throat, and exclaiming, "What has my fidelity to my commander cost me!"

Almagro, in order to do greater honor to his prisoner, visited him in person and announced to him that he was from that moment free. He expressed a hope, at the same time, that "all past differences would be buried in oblivion, and that henceforth they should live only in the recollection of their ancient friendship." Hernando replied, with apparent cordiality, that "he desired nothing better for himself." He then swore in the most solemn manner, and pledged his knightly honor—the latter, perhaps, a pledge of quite as much weight in his own mind as the former—that he would faithfully comply with the terms stipulated in the treaty. He was next conducted by the marshal to his quarters, where he partook of a collation in company with the principal officers; several of whom, together with Diego Almagro, the general's son, afterwards escorted the cavalier to his brother's camp, which had been transferred to the neighboring town of Mala. Here the party received a most cordial greeting from the governor, who entertained them with a courtly hospitality, and lavished many attentions, in particular, on the son of his ancient associate. In short, such, on their return, was the account of their reception, that it left no doubt in the mind of Almagro that all was at length amicably settled. He did not know Pizarro.

CHAPTER II

Trial and Execution of Almagro

1537–1538

Scarcely had Almagro's officers left the governor's quarters, when the latter, calling his little army together, briefly recapitulated the many wrongs which had been done him by his rival, the seizure of his capital, the imprisonment of his brothers, the assault and defeat of his troops; and he concluded with the declaration—heartily echoed back by his military audience—that the time had now come for revenge. All the while that the negotiations were pending, Pizarro had been busily occupied with military preparations. He had mustered a force considerably larger than that of his rival, drawn from various quarters, but most of them familiar with service. He now declared that, as he was too old to take charge of the campaign himself, he should devolve that duty on his brothers; and he released Hernando from all his engagements to Almagro, as a measure justified by necessity. That cavalier, with graceful pertinacity, intimated his design to abide by the pledges he had given, but at length yielded a reluctant assent to the commands of his brother, as to a measure imperatively demanded by his duty to the crown.

The governor's next step was to advise Almagro that the treaty was at an end. At the same time, he warned him to relinquish his pretensions to Cuzco and withdraw into his own territory, or the responsibility of the consequences would lie on his own head.

After reposing in his false security, Almagro was now fully awakened to the consciousness of the error he had committed; and the warning voice of his lieutenant may have risen to his recollection. The first part of the prediction was fulfilled. And what should prevent the latter from being so? To add to his distress, he was laboring at this time under a grievous malady, the result of early excesses, which shattered his constitution and made him incapable alike of mental and bodily exertion.

In this forlorn condition, he confided the management of his affairs to Orgoñez, on whose loyalty and courage he knew he might implicitly rely. The first step was to secure the passes of the Guaitara, a chain of hills that hemmed in the valley of Zangalla, where Almagro was at present established. But, by some miscalculation, the passes were not secured in season; and the active enemy, threading the dangerous defiles, effected a passage across the sierra, where a much inferior force to his own might have taken him at a disadvantage. The fortunes of Almagro were on the wane.

His thoughts were now turned towards Cuzco, and he was anxious to get possession of this capital before the arrival of the enemy. Too feeble to sit on horseback, he was obliged to be carried in a litter; and when he reached the ancient town of Bilcas, not far from Guamanga, his indisposition was so severe that he was compelled to halt and remain there three weeks before resuming his march.

The governor and his brothers, in the meantime, after traversing the pass of Guaitara, descended into the valley of Ica, where Pizarro remained a considerable while, to get his troops into order and complete his preparations for the campaign. Then, taking leave of the army, he returned to Lima, committing the prosecution of the war, as he had before announced, to his younger and more active brothers. Hernando, soon after quitting

Ica, kept along the coast as far as Nasca, proposing to penetrate the country by a circuitous route in order to elude the enemy, who might have greatly embarrassed him in some of the passes of the Cordilleras. But, unhappily for himself, this plan of operations, which would have given him such manifest advantage, was not adopted by Almagro; and his adversary, without any other impediment than that arising from the natural difficulties of the march, arrived, in the latter part of April, 1538, in the neighborhood of Cuzco.

Almagro, however, was already in possession of that capital, which he had reached ten days before. A council of war was held by him respecting the course to be pursued. Some were for making good the defense of the city. Almagro would have tried what could be done by negotiation. But Orgoñez bluntly replied, "It is too late: you have liberated Hernando Pizarro, and nothing remains but to fight him." The opinion of Orgoñez finally prevailed, to march out and give the enemy battle on the plains. The marshal, still disabled by illness from taking the command, devolved it on his trusty lieutenant, who, mustering his forces, left the city, and took up a position at Las Salinas, less than a league distant from Cuzco. The place received its name from certain pits or vats in the ground, used for the preparation of salt, that was obtained from a natural spring in the neighborhood. It was an injudicious choice of ground, since its broken character was most unfavorable to the free action of cavalry, in which the strength of Almagro's force consisted. But, although repeatedly urged by the officers to advance into the open country, Orgoñez persisted in his position, as the most favorable for defense, since the front was protected by a marsh, and by a little stream that flowed over the plain. His forces amounted in all to about five hundred, more than half of them horse. His infantry was deficient in firearms, the place of which was supplied by the long pike. He had also six small cannon, or falconets, as they were called, which, with his cavalry, formed into two equal divisions, he disposed on the flanks of his infantry. Thus prepared, he calmly awaited the approach of the enemy.

It was not long before the bright arms and banners of the Spaniards under Hernando Pizarro were seen emerging from the mountain passes. The troops came forward in good order, and like men whose steady step showed that they had been spared in the march and were now fresh for action. They advanced slowly across the plain, and halted on the opposite border of the little stream which covered the front of Orgoñez. Here Hernando, as the sun had set, took up his quarters for the night, proposing to defer the engagement till daylight.

The rumors of the approaching battle had spread far and wide over the country; and the mountains and rocky heights around were thronged with multitudes of natives, eager to feast their eyes on a spectacle where, whichever side were victorious, the defeat would fall on their enemies. The Castilian women and children, too, with still deeper anxiety, had thronged out from Cuzco to witness the deadly strife in which brethren and kindred were to contend for mastery. The whole number of the combatants was insignificant; though not as compared with those usually engaged in these American wars. It is not, however, the number of the players, but the magnitude of the stake, that gives importance and interest to the game; and in this bloody game they were to play for the possession of an empire.

The night passed away in silence, unbroken by the vast assembly which covered the surrounding hilltops. Nor did the soldiers of the hostile camps, although keeping watch within hearing of one another, and with the same blood flowing in their veins, attempt any communication. So deadly was the hate in their bosoms!

The sun rose bright, as usual in this beautiful climate, on Saturday, the twenty-sixth day of April, 1538. But long before his beams were on the plain the trumpet of Hernando Pizarro had called his men to arms. His forces amounted in all to about seven hundred. They were drawn from various quarters, the veterans of Pizarro, the followers of Alonso de Alvarado—many of whom, since their defeat, had found their way back to Lima—and the late reinforcement from the isles, most of them seasoned by many a toilsome march in the Indian campaigns, and many a hard-fought field. His mounted troops were inferior to those of Almagro; but this was more than compensated by the strength of his infantry, comprehending a well-trained corps of arquebusiers, sent from St. Domingo, whose weapons were of the improved construction recently introduced from Flanders. They were of a large caliber, and threw double-headed shot, consisting of bullets linked together by an iron chain. It was doubtless a clumsy weapon compared with modern firearms, but, in hands accustomed to wield it, proved a destructive instrument.

Hernando Pizarro drew up his men in the same order of battle as that presented by the enemy—throwing his infantry into the center, and disposing his horse on the flanks; one corps of which he placed under command of Alonso de Alvarado, and took charge of the other himself. The infantry was headed by his brother Gonzalo, supported by Pedro de Valdivia, the future hero of Arauco, whose disastrous story forms the burden of romance as well as of chronicle.

Mass was said, as if the Spaniards were about to fight what they deemed the good fight of the faith, instead of imbruing their hands in the blood of their countrymen. Hernando Pizarro then made a brief address to his soldiers. He touched on the personal injuries he and his family had received from Almagro; reminded his brother's veterans that Cuzco had been wrested from their possession; called up the glow of shame on the brows of Alvarado's men as he talked of the rout of Abancay; and, pointing out the Inca metropolis that sparkled in the morning sunshine, he told them that there was the prize of the victor. They answered his appeal with acclamations; and, the signal being given, Gonzalo Pizarro, heading his battalion of infantry, led it straight across the river. The water was neither broad nor deep, and the soldiers found no difficulty in gaining a landing, as the enemy's horse was prevented by the marshy ground from approaching the borders. But, as they worked their way across the morass, the heavy guns of Orgoñez played with effect on the leading files, and threw them into disorder. Gonzalo and Valdivia threw themselves into the midst of their followers, menacing some, encouraging others, and at length led them gallantly forward to the firm ground. Here the arquebusiers, detaching themselves from the rest of the infantry, gained a small eminence, whence, in their turn, they opened a galling fire on Orgoñez, scattering his array of spearmen, and sorely annoying the cavalry on the flanks.

Meanwhile, Hernando, forming his two squadrons of horse into one column, crossed under cover of this well-sustained fire, and, reaching the firm ground, rode at once against the enemy. Orgoñez, whose infantry was already much crippled, advancing his horse, formed the two squadrons into one body, like his antagonist, and spurred at full gallop against the assailants. The shock was terrible; and it was hailed by the swarms of Indian spectators on the surrounding heights with a fiendish yell of triumph, that rose far above the din of battle, till it was lost in distant echoes among the mountains.

The struggle was desperate. For it was not that of the white man against the defenseless Indian, but of Spaniard against Spaniard; both parties cheering on their comrades with their battle-cries of "El Rey y Almagro," or "El Rey y Pizarro"— while they fought with a hate to which national antipathy was as nothing—a hate strong in proportion to the strength of the ties that had been rent asunder.

In this bloody field well did Orgoñez do his duty, fighting like one to whom battle was the natural element. Singling out a cavalier whom, from the color of the sobre-vest on his armor, he erroneously supposed to be Hernando Pizarro, he charged him in full career, and overthrew him with his lance. Another he ran through in like manner, and a third he struck down with his sword, as he was prematurely shouting "Victory!" But, while thus doing the deeds of a paladin of romance, he was hit by a chain-shot from an arquebuse, which, penetrating the bars of his visor, grazed his forehead and deprived him for a moment of reason. Before he had fully recovered, his horse was killed under him, and, though the fallen cavalier succeeded in extricating himself from the stirrups, he was surrounded, and soon overpowered by numbers. Still refusing to deliver up his sword, he asked "if there was no knight to whom he could surrender." One Fuentes, a menial of Pizarro, presenting himself as such, Orgoñez gave his sword into his hands—and the dastard, drawing his dagger, stabbed his defenseless prisoner to the heart! His head, then struck off, was stuck on a pike, and displayed, a bloody trophy, in the great square of Cuzco, as the head of a traitor. Thus perished as loyal a cavalier, as decided in council, and as bold in action, as ever crossed to the shores of America.

The fight had now lasted more than an hour, and the fortune of the day was turning against the followers of Almagro. Orgoñez being down, their confusion increased. The infantry, unable to endure the fire of the arquebusiers, scattered and took refuge behind the stone walls that here and there straggled across the country. Pedro de Lerma, vainly striving to rally the cavalry, spurred his horse against Hernando Pizarro, with whom he had a personal feud. Pizarro did not shrink from the encounter. The lances of both the knights took effect. That of Hernando penetrated the thigh of his opponent, while Lerma's weapon, glancing by his adversary's saddle-bow, struck him with such force above the groin that it pierced the joints of his mail, slightly wounding the cavalier, and forcing his horse back on his haunches. But the press of the fight soon parted the combatants, and, in the turmoil that ensued, Lerma was unhorsed, and left on the field, covered with wounds.

There was no longer order, and scarcely resistance, among the followers of Almagro. They fled, making the best of their way to Cuzco, and happy was the man who obtained quarter when he asked it. Almagro himself, too feeble to sit so long on his horse, reclined on a litter, and from a neighboring eminence surveyed the battle, watching its fluctuations with all the interest of one who felt that honor, fortune, life itself, hung on the issue. With agony not to be described, he had seen his faithful followers, after their hard struggle, borne down by their opponents, till, convinced that all was lost, he succeeded in mounting a mule, and rode off for a temporary refuge to the fortress of Cuzco. Thither he was speedily followed, taken, and brought in triumph to the capital, where, ill as he was, he was thrown into irons and confined in the same apartment of the stone building in which he had imprisoned the Pizarros.

The action lasted not quite two hours. The number of killed, variously stated, was probably not less than a hundred and fifty—one of the combatants calls it two hundred—a great number, considering the shortness of the time, and the small amount of the forces engaged. No account is given of the wounded. Wounds were the portion of the cavalier. Pedro de Lerma is said to have received seventeen, and yet was taken alive from the field! The loss fell chiefly on the followers of Almagro. But the slaughter was not confined to the heat of the action. Such was the deadly animosity of the parties that several were murdered in cold blood, like Orgoñez, after they had surrendered. Pedro de Lerma himself, while lying on his sick couch in the quarters of a friend in Cuzco, was visited by a soldier, named Samaniego, whom he had once struck for an act of disobedience. This person entered the solitary chamber of the

wounded man, took his place by his bedside, and then, up-
braiding him for the insult, told him that he had come to wash
it away in his blood! Lerma in vain assured him that, when
restored to health, he would give him the satisfaction he desired.
The miscreant, exclaiming, "Now is the hour!" plunged his
sword into his bosom. He lived several years to vaunt this atrocious exploit, which he proclaimed as a reparation to his honor.
It is some satisfaction to know that the insolence of this vaunt
cost him his life. Such anecdotes, revolting as they are, illustrate
not merely the spirit of the times, but that peculiarly ferocious
spirit which is engendered by civil wars—the most unforgiving
in their character of any, but wars of religion.

In the hurry of the flight of one party, and the pursuit by the
other, all pouring towards Cuzco, the field of battle had been
deserted. But it soon swarmed with plunderers, as the Indians,
descending like vultures from the mountains, took possession of
the bloody ground, and, despoiling the dead, even to the minutest
article of dress, left their corpses naked on the plain. It has been
thought strange that the natives should not have availed themselves of their superior numbers to fall on the victors after they
had been exhausted by the battle. But the scattered bodies of
the Peruvians were without a leader; they were broken in spirits,
moreover, by recent reverses, and the Castilians, although weakened for the moment by the struggle, were in far greater strength
in Cuzco than they had ever been before.

Indeed, the number of troops now assembled within its walls,
amounting to full thirteen hundred, composed, as they were, of
the most discordant materials, gave great uneasiness to Hernando Pizarro. For there were enemies glaring on each other
and on him with deadly though smothered rancor, and friends, if
not so dangerous, not the less troublesome from their craving
and unreasonable demands. He had given the capital up to pillage, and his followers found good booty in the quarters of
Almagro's officers. But this did not suffice the more ambitious
cavaliers; and they clamorously urged their services, and demanded to be placed in charge of some expedition, nothing
doubting that it must prove a golden one. All were in quest of an
El Dorado. Hernando Pizarro acquiesced as far as possible in
these desires, most willing to relieve himself of such importunate
creditors. The expeditions, it is true, usually ended in disaster;

but the country was explored by them. It was the lottery of adventure; the prizes were few, but they were splendid; and, in the excitement of the game, few Spaniards paused to calculate the chances of success.

Among those who left the capital was Diego, the son of Almagro. Hernando was mindful to send him, with a careful escort, to his brother the governor, desirous to remove him at this crisis from the neighborhood of his father. Meanwhile, the marshal himself was pining away in prison under the combined influence of bodily illness and distress of mind. Before the battle of Salinas, it had been told to Hernando Pizarro that Almagro was like to die. "Heaven forbid," he exclaimed, "that this should come to pass before he falls into my hands!" Yet the gods seemed now disposed to grant but half of this pious prayer, since his captive seemed about to escape him just as he had come into his power. To console the unfortunate chief, Hernando paid him a visit in his prison, and cheered him with the assurance that he only waited for the governor's arrival to set him at liberty; adding "that if Pizarro did not come soon to the capital he himself would assume the responsibility of releasing him, and would furnish him with a conveyance to his brother's quarters." At the same time, with considerate attention to his comfort, he inquired of the marshal "what mode of conveyance would be best suited to his state of health." After this he continued to send him delicacies from his own table to revive his faded appetite. Almagro, cheered by these kind attentions and by the speedy prospect of freedom, gradually mended in health and spirits.

He little dreamed that all this while a process was industriously preparing against him. It had been instituted immediately on his capture, and everyone, however humble, who had any cause of complaint against the unfortunate prisoner, was invited to present it. The summons was readily answered; and many an enemy now appeared in the hour of his fallen fortunes, like the base reptiles crawling into light amidst the ruins of some noble edifice; and more than one who had received benefits from his hands were willing to court the favor of his enemy by turning on their benefactor. From these loathsome sources a mass of accusations was collected which spread over four thousand folio pages! Yet Almagro was the idol of his soldiers!

Having completed the process (July 8th, 1538), it was not

difficult to obtain a verdict against the prisoner. The principal charges on which he was pronounced guilty were those of levying war against the crown and thereby occasioning the death of many of his Majesty's subjects, of entering into conspiracy with the Inca, and, finally, of dispossessing the royal governor of the city of Cuzco. On these charges he was condemned to suffer death as a traitor, by being publicly beheaded in the great square of the city. Who were the judges, or what was the tribunal that condemned him, we are not informed. Indeed, the whole trial was a mockery; if that can be called a trial where the accused himself is not even aware of the accusation.

The sentence was communicated by a friar deputed for the purpose to Almagro. The unhappy man, who all the while had been unconsciously slumbering on the brink of a precipice, could not at first comprehend the nature of his situation. Recovering from the first shock, "It was impossible," he said, "that such wrong could be done him—he would not believe it." He then besought Hernando Pizarro to grant him an interview. That cavalier, not unwilling, it would seem, to witness the agony of his captive, consented; and Almagro was so humbled by his misfortunes that he condescended to beg for his life with the most piteous supplications. He reminded Hernando of his ancient relations with his brother, and the good offices he had rendered him and his family in the earlier part of their career. He touched on his acknowledged services to his country, and besought his enemy "to spare his gray hairs, and not to deprive him of the short remnant of an existence from which he had now nothing more to fear." To this the other coldly replied that "he was surprised to see Almagro demean himself in a manner so unbecoming a brave cavalier; that his fate was no worse than had befallen many a soldier before him; and that, since God had given him the grace to be a Christian, he should employ his remaining moments in making up his account with Heaven."

But Almagro was not to be silenced. He urged the service he had rendered Hernando himself. "This was a hard requital," he said, "for having spared his life so recently under similar circumstances, and that, too, when he had been urged again and again by those around him to take it away." And he concluded by menacing his enemy with the vengeance of the emperor, who would never suffer this outrage on one who had rendered such signal services to the crown to go unrequited. It was all in vain; and Hernando abruptly closed the conference by repeating that "his doom was inevitable, and he must prepare to meet it."

Almagro, finding that no impression was to be made on his iron-hearted conqueror, now seriously addressed himself to the settlement of his affairs. By the terms of the royal grant he was empowered to name his successor. He accordingly devolved his office on his son, appointing Diego de Alvarado, on whose integrity he had great reliance, administrator of the province during his minority. All his property and possessions in Peru, of whatever kind, he devised to his master the emperor, assuring him that a large balance was still due to him in his unsettled accounts with Pizarro. By this politic bequest he hoped to secure the monarch's protection for his son, as well as a strict scrutiny into the affairs of his enemy.

The knowledge of Almagro's sentence produced a deep sensation in the community of Cuzco. All were amazed at the presumption with which one armed with a little brief authority ventured to sit in judgment on a person of Almagro's station. There were few who did not call to mind some generous or good-natured act of the unfortunate veteran. Even those who had furnished materials for the accusation, now startled by the tragic result to which it was to lead, were heard to denounce Hernando's conduct as that of a tyrant. Some of the principal cavaliers, and among them Diego de Alvarado, to whose intercession, as we have seen, Hernando Pizarro, when a captive, had owed his own life, waited on that commander and endeavored to dissuade him from so high-handed and atrocious a proceeding. It was in vain. But it had the effect of changing the mode of the execution, which, instead of the public square, was now to take place in prison.

On the day appointed, a strong corps of arquebusiers was drawn up in the plaza. The guards were doubled over the houses where dwelt the principal partisans of Almagro. The executioner, attended by a priest, stealthily entered his prison; and the unhappy man, after confessing and receiving the sacrament, submitted without resistance to the garrote. Thus obscurely, in the gloomy silence of a dungeon, perished the hero of a hundred battles! His corpse was removed to the great square of the city, where, in obedience to the sentence, the head was severed from the body. A herald proclaimed aloud the nature of the crimes for which he had suffered; and his remains, rolled in their bloody shroud, were borne to the house of his friend Hernan Ponce de Leon, and the next day laid with all due solemnity in the church of Our Lady of Mercy. The Pizarros appeared among the principal mourners. It was remarked that their brother had paid similar honors to the memory of Atahuallpa.

Almagro, at the time of his death, was probably not far from seventy years of age. But this is somewhat uncertain; for Almagro was a foundling, and his early history is lost in obscurity. He had many excellent qualities by nature; and his defects, which were not few, may reasonably be palliated by the circumstances of his situation. For what extenuation is not authorized by the position of a *foundling*—without parents, or early friends, or teacher to direct him—his little bark set adrift on the ocean of life, to take its chance among the rude billows and breakers, without one friendly hand stretched forth to steer or to save it! The name of "foundling" comprehends an apology for much, very much, that is wrong in after-life.

He was a man of strong passions, and not too well used to control them. But he was neither vindictive nor habitually cruel. I have mentioned one atrocious outrage which he committed on the natives. But insensibility to the rights of the Indian he shared with many a better-instructed Spaniard. Yet the Indians, after his conviction, bore testimony to his general humanity, by declaring that they had no such friend among the white men. Indeed, far from being vindictive, he was placable, and easily yielded to others. The facility with which he yielded, the result of good-natured credulity, made him too often the dupe of the crafty; and it showed, certainly, a want of that self-reliance which belongs to great strength of character. Yet his facility of temper, and the generosity of his nature, made him popular with his followers. No commander was ever more beloved by his soldiers. His generosity was often carried to prodigality. When he entered on the campaign of Chili, he lent a hundred thousand gold ducats to the poorer cavaliers to equip themselves, and afterwards gave them up the debt. He was profuse to ostentation. But his extravagance did him no harm among the roving spirits of the camp, with whom prodigality is apt to gain more favor than a strict and well-regulated economy.

He was a good soldier, careful and judicious in his plans, patient and intrepid in their execution. His body was covered with the scars of his battles, till the natural plainness of his person was converted almost into deformity. He must not be judged by his closing campaign, when, depressed by disease, he yielded to the superior genius of his rival, but by his numerous expeditions by land and by water for the conquest of Peru and the remote Chili. Yet it may be doubted whether he possessed those uncommon qualities, either as a warrior or as a man, that, in ordinary circumstances, would have raised him to distinction. He was one of the three, or, to speak more strictly, of the two, associates who had the good fortune and the glory to make one of the most splendid discoveries in the Western World. He shares largely in the credit of this with Pizarro; for when he did not accompany that leader in his perilous expeditions he contributed no less to their success by his exertions in the colonies.

Yet his connection with that chief can hardly be considered a fortunate circumstance in his career. A partnership between individuals for discovery and conquest is not likely to be very scrupulously observed, especially by men more accustomed to govern others than to govern themselves. If causes for discord do not arise before, they will be sure to spring up on division of the spoil. But this association was particularly ill assorted. For the free, sanguine, and confiding temper of Almagro was no match for the cool and crafty policy of Pizarro; and he was invariably circumvented by his companion whenever their respective interests came in collision.

Still, the final ruin of Almagro may be fairly imputed to himself. He made two capital blunders. The first was his appeal to arms by the seizure of Cuzco. The determination of a boundary line was not to be settled by arms. It was a subject for arbitration; and if arbitrators could not be trusted it should have been referred to the decision of the crown. But, having once appealed to arms, he should not then have resorted to negotiation—above all, to negotiation with Pizarro. This was his second and greatest error. He had seen enough of Pizarro to know that he was not to be trusted. Almagro did trust him; and he paid for it with his life.

FROM CHAPTER V

Assassination of Pizarro

1541

After the execution of Almagro, his followers, to the number of several hundred, remained scattered through the country, but, however scattered, still united by a common sentiment of indignation against the Pizarros, the murderers, as they regarded them, of their leader. The governor was less the object of these feelings than his brother Hernando, as having been less instrumental in the perpetration of the deed. Under these circumstances, it was clearly Pizarro's policy to do one of two things— to treat the opposite faction either as friends or as open enemies. He might conciliate the most factious by acts of kindness, efface the remembrance of past injury, if he could, by present benefits —in short, prove to them that his quarrel had been with their leader, not with themselves, and that it was plainly for their interest to come again under his banner. This would have been the most politic as well as the most magnanimous course, and, by augmenting the number of his adherents, would have greatly strengthened his power in the land. But, unhappily, he had not the magnanimity to pursue it. It was not in the nature of a Pizarro to forgive an injury, or the man whom he had injured. As he would not, therefore, try to conciliate Almagro's adherents, it was clearly the governor's policy to regard them as enemies— not the less so for being in disguise—and to take such measures as should disqualify them for doing mischief. He should have followed the counsel of his more prudent brother Hernando, and distributed them in different quarters, taking care that no great number should assemble at any one point, or, above all, in the neighborhood of his own residence.

But the governor despised the broken followers of Almagro too heartily to stoop to precautionary measures. He suffered the son of his rival to remain in Lima, where his quarters soon became the resort of the disaffected cavaliers. The young man was well known to most of Almagro's soldiers, having been trained along with them in the camp under his father's eye, and, now that his parent was removed, they naturally transferred their allegiance to the son who survived him.

That the young Almagro, however, might be less able to maintain this retinue of unprofitable followers, he was deprived by Pizarro of a great part of his Indians and lands, while he was excluded from the government of New Toledo, which had been settled on him by his father's testament. Stripped of all means of support, without office or employment of any kind, the men of Chili, for so Almagro's adherents continued to be called, were reduced to the utmost distress. So poor were they, as is the story of the time, that twelve cavaliers who lodged in the same house could muster only one cloak among them all; and, with the usual feeling of pride that belongs to the poor *hidalgo,* unwilling to expose their poverty, they wore this cloak by turns, those who had no right to it remaining at home. Whether true or not, the anecdote well illustrates the extremity to which Almagro's faction was reduced. And this distress was rendered yet more galling by the effrontery of their enemies, who, enriched by their forfeitures, displayed before their eyes all the insolent bravery of equipage and apparel that could annoy their feelings.

Men thus goaded by insult and injury were too dangerous to be lightly regarded. But, although Pizarro received various intimations intended to put him on his guard, he gave no heed to them. "Poor devils!" he would exclaim, speaking with contemptuous pity of the men of Chili; "they have had bad luck enough. We will not trouble them further." And so little did he consider them that he went freely about, as usual, riding without attendants to all parts of the town and to its immediate environs.

News now reached the colony of the appointment of a judge by the crown to take cognizance of the affairs of Peru. Pizarro, although alarmed by the intelligence, sent orders to have him well entertained on his landing, and suitable accommodations prepared for him on the route. The spirits of Almagro's followers were greatly raised by the tidings. They confidently looked to this high functionary for the redress of their wrongs; and two of their body, clad in suits of mourning, were chosen to go to the north, where the judge was expected to land, and to lay their grievances before him.

But months elapsed, and no tidings came of his arrival, till at length a vessel coming into port announced that most of the squadron had foundered in the heavy storms on the coast, and that the commissioner had probably perished with them. This was disheartening intelligence to the men of Chili, whose "miseries," to use the words of their young leader, "had become too grievous to be borne." Symptoms of disaffection had already begun openly to manifest themselves. The haughty cavaliers did not always doff their bonnets on meeting the governor in the street; and on one occasion three ropes were found suspended from the public gallows, with labels attached to them, bearing the names of Pizarro, Velasquez the judge, and Picado the governor's secretary. This last functionary was peculiarly odious to Almagro and his followers. As his master knew neither how to read nor write, all his communications passed through Picado's hands; and, as the latter was of a hard and arrogant nature, greatly elated by the consequence which his position gave him, he exercised a mischievous influence on the governor's measures. Almagro's poverty-stricken followers were the objects of his open ridicule, and he revenged the insult now offered him by riding before their young leader's residence, displaying a tawdry magnificence in his dress, sparkling with gold and silver, and with the inscription, "For the Men of Chili," set in his bonnet. It was a foolish taunt; but the poor cavaliers who were the object of it, made morbidly sensitive by their sufferings, had not the philosophy to despise it.

At length, disheartened by the long-protracted coming of Vaca de Castro, and still more by the recent reports of his loss, Almagro's faction, despairing of redress from a legitimate authority, determined to take it into their own hands. They came to the desperate resolution of assassinating Pizarro. The day named for this was Sunday, the twenty-sixth of June, 1541. The conspirators, eighteen or twenty in number, were to assemble in Almagro's house, which stood in the great square next to the cathedral, and when the governor was returning from mass they were to issue forth and fall on him in the street. A white flag, unfurled at the same time from an upper window in the house, was to be the signal for the rest of their comrades to move to the support of those immediately engaged in the execution of the deed.

These arrangements could hardly have been concealed from Almagro, since his own quarters were to be the place of rendezvous. Yet there is no good evidence of his having taken part in the conspiracy. He was, indeed, too young to make it probable that he took a leading part in it. He is represented by contemporary writers to have given promise of many good qualities, though, unhappily, he was not placed in a situation favorable for their development. He was the son of an Indian woman of Panama, but from early years had followed the troubled fortunes of his father, to whom he bore much resemblance in his free and generous nature, as well as in the violence of his passions. His youth and inexperience disqualified him from taking the lead in the perplexing circumstances in which he was placed, and made him little more than a puppet in the hands of others.

The most conspicuous of his advisers was Juan de Herrada, or Rada, as his name is more usually spelt—a cavalier of respectable family, who, having early enlisted as a common soldier, had gradually risen to the highest posts in the army by his military talents. At this time he was well advanced in years; but the fires of youth were not quenched in his bosom, and he burned with desire to avenge the wrongs done to his ancient commander. The attachment which he had ever felt for the elder Almagro he seems to have transferred in full measure to his son; and it was apparently with reference to him, even more than to himself, that he devised this audacious plot and prepared to take the lead in the execution of it.

There was one, however, in the band of conspirators who felt some compunctions of conscience at the part he was acting, and who relieved his bosom by revealing the whole plot to his confessor. The latter lost no time in reporting it to Picado, by whom in turn it was communicated to Pizarro. But, strange to say, it made little more impression on the governor's mind than the vague warnings he had so frequently received. "It is a device of the priest," said he: "he wants a miter." Yet he repeated the story to the judge Velasquez, who, instead of ordering the conspirators to be seized and the proper steps taken for learning the truth of the accusation, seemed to be possessed with the same infatuation as Pizarro; and he bade the governor be under no apprehension, "for no harm should come to him while the rod of justice," not a metaphorical badge of authority in Castile, "was in his hands." Still, to obviate every possibility of danger, it was deemed prudent for Pizarro to abstain from going to mass on Sunday, and to remain at home on pretense of illness.

On the day appointed, Rada and his companions met in Almagro's house, and waited with anxiety for the hour when the governor should issue from the church. But great was their consternation when they learned that he was not there, but was detained at home, as currently reported, by illness. Little doubting that their design was discovered, they felt their own ruin to be the inevitable consequence, and that, too, without enjoying the melancholy consolation of having struck the blow for which they had incurred it. Greatly perplexed, some were for disbanding, in the hope that Pizarro might, after all, be ignorant of their design. But most were for carrying it into execution at once, by assaulting him in his own house. The question was summarily decided by one of the party, who felt that in this latter course lay their only chance of safety. Throwing open the doors, he rushed out, calling on his comrades "to follow him, or he would proclaim the purpose for which they had met." There was no longer hesitation, and the cavaliers issued forth, with Rada at their head, shouting, as they went, "Long live the king! Death to the tyrant!"

It was the hour of dinner, which, in this primitive age of the Spanish colonies, was at noon. Yet numbers, roused by the cries of the assailants, came out into the square to inquire the cause. "They are going to kill the marquis," some said, very coolly; others replied, "It is Picado." No one stirred in their defense. The power of Pizarro was not seated in the hearts of his people.

As the conspirators traversed the plaza, one of the party made a circuit to avoid a little pool of water that lay in their path. "What!" exclaimed Rada, "afraid of wetting your feet, when you are to wade up to your knees in blood!" And he ordered the man to give up the enterprise and go home to his quarters. The anecdote is characteristic.

The governor's palace stood on the opposite side of the square. It was approached by two courtyards. The entrance to the outer one was protected by a massive gate, capable of being made good against a hundred men or more. But it was left open, and the assailants, hurrying through to the inner court, still shouting their fearful battle-cry, were met by two domestics loitering in the yard. One of these they struck down. The other, flying in all haste towards the house, called out, "Help, help! the men of Chili are all coming to murder the marquis!"

Pizarro at this time was at dinner, or, more probably, had just dined. He was surrounded by a party of friends, who had dropped in, it seems, after mass, to inquire after the state of his health, some of whom had remained to partake of his repast. Among these was Don Martinez de Alcantara, Pizarro's half-brother by the mother's side, the judge Velasquez, the bishop elect of Quito, and several of the principal cavaliers in the place, to the number of fifteen or twenty. Some of them, alarmed by the uproar in the courtyard, left the saloon, and, running down to the first landing on the stairway, inquired into the cause of the disturbance. No sooner were they informed of it by the cries of the servant than they retreated with precipitation into the house; and, as they had no mind to abide the storm unarmed, or at best imperfectly armed, as most of them were, they made their way to a corridor that overlooked the gardens, into which they easily let themselves down without injury. Velasquez, the judge, the better to have the use of his hands in the descent, held his rod of office in his mouth, thus taking care, says a caustic old chronicler, not to falsify his assurance that "no harm should come to Pizarro while the rod of justice was in his hands"!

Meanwhile, the marquis, learning the nature of the tumult, called out to Francisco de Chaves, an officer high in his confidence, and who was in the outer apartment opening on the staircase, to secure the door, while he and his brother Alcantara buckled on their armor. Had this order, coolly given, been as coolly obeyed, it would have served them all, since the entrance could easily have been maintained against a much larger force, till the report of the cavaliers who had fled had brought support to Pizarro. But, unfortunately, Chaves, disobeying his commander, half opened the door, and attempted to enter into a parley with the conspirators. The latter had now reached the head of the stairs, and cut short the debate by running Chaves through the body and tumbling his corpse down into the area below. For a moment they were kept at bay by the attendants of the slaughtered cavalier, but these, too, were quickly despatched; and Rada and his companions, entering the apartment, hurried across it, shouting out, "Where is the marquis? Death to the tyrant!"

Martinez de Alcantara, who in the adjoining room was assisting his brother to buckle on his mail, no sooner saw that the entrance to the antechamber had been gained than he sprang to the doorway of the apartment, and, assisted by two young men, pages of Pizarro, and by one or two cavaliers in attendance, endeavored to resist the approach of the assailants. A desperate struggle now ensued. Blows were given on both sides, some of which proved fatal, and two of the conspirators were slain, while Alcantara and his brave companions were repeatedly wounded.

At length, Pizarro, unable, in the hurry of the moment, to adjust the fastenings of his cuirass, threw it away, and, enveloping one arm in his cloak, with the other seized his sword and sprang to his brother's assistance. It was too late; for Alcantara was already staggering under the loss of blood, and soon fell to the ground. Pizarro threw himself on his invaders, like a lion roused in his lair, and dealt his blows with as much rapidity and force as if age had no power to stiffen his limbs. "What ho!" he cried, "traitor! have you come to kill me in my own house?" The conspirators drew back for a moment, as two of their body fell under Pizarro's sword; but they quickly rallied, and, from their superior numbers, fought at great advantage by relieving one another in the assault. Still, the passage was narrow, and the struggle lasted for some minutes, till both of Pizarro's pages were stretched by his side, when Rada, impatient of the delay, called out, "Why are we so long about it? Down with the tyrant!" and taking one of his companions, Narvaez, in his arms, he thrust him against the marquis. Pizarro, instantly grappling with his opponent, ran him through with his sword. But at that moment he received a wound in the throat, and, reeling, he sank on the floor, while the swords of Rada and several of the conspirators were plunged into his body. "Jesu!" exclaimed the dying man, and, tracing a cross with his finger on the bloody floor, he bent down his head to kiss it, when a stroke more friendly than the rest put an end to his existence.

The conspirators, having accomplished their bloody deed, rushed into the street, and, brandishing their dripping weapons, shouted out, "The tyrant is dead! The laws are restored! Long live our master the emperor, and his governor, Almagro!" The men of Chili, roused by the cheering cry, now flocked in from every side to join the banner of Rada, who soon found himself at the head of nearly three hundred followers, all armed and prepared to support his authority. A guard was placed over the houses of the principal partisans of the late governor, and their persons were taken into custody. Pizarro's house, and that of his secretary Picado, were delivered up to pillage, and a large booty in gold and silver was found in the former. Picado himself took refuge in the dwelling of Riquelme, the treasurer; but his hiding-place was detected—betrayed, according to some accounts, by the looks, though not the words, of the treasurer himself—and he was dragged forth and committed to a secure prison. The whole city was thrown into consternation, as armed bodies hurried to and fro on their several errands; and all who were not in the faction of Almagro trembled lest they should be involved in the proscription of their enemies. So great was the disorder that the Brothers of Mercy, turning out in a body, paraded the streets in solemn procession, with the host elevated in the air, in hopes by the presence of the sacred symbol to calm the passions of the multitude.

But no other violence was offered by Rada and his followers than to apprehend a few suspected persons and to seize upon horses and arms wherever they were to be found. The municipality was then summoned to recognize the authority of Almagro; the refractory were ejected without ceremony from their offices, and others, of the Chili faction, were substituted. The claims of the new aspirant were fully recognized; and young Almagro, parading the streets on horseback and escorted by a well-armed body of cavaliers, was proclaimed by sound of trumpet governor and captain-general of Peru.

Meanwhile, the mangled bodies of Pizarro and his faithful adherents were left weltering in their blood. Some were for dragging forth the governor's corpse to the market-place and fixing his head upon a gibbet. But Almagro was secretly prevailed on to grant the entreaties of Pizarro's friends and allow his interment. This was stealthily and hastily performed, in the fear of momentary interruption. A faithful attendant and his wife, with a few black domestics, wrapped the body in a cotton cloth and removed it to the cathedral. A grave was hastily dug in an obscure corner, the services were hurried through, and, in secrecy, and in darkness dispelled only by the feeble glimmering of a few tapers furnished by these humble menials, the remains of Pizzaro, rolled in their bloody shroud, were consigned to their kindred dust. Such was the miserable end of the Conqueror of Peru—of the man who but a few hours before had lorded it over the land with as absolute a sway as was possessed by its hereditary Incas. Cut off in the broad light of day, in the heart of his own capital, in the very midst of those who had been his companions in arms and shared with him his triumphs and his spoils, he perished like a wretched outcast. "There was none even," in the expressive language of the chronicler, "to say, God forgive him!" . . .

History of
Philip the Second

BOOK I

Abdication of Charles the Fifth

1555

IN A FORMER work I have endeavored to portray the period when the different provinces of Spain were consolidated into one empire under the rule of Ferdinand and Isabella; when, by their wise and beneficent policy, the nation emerged from the obscurity in which it had so long remained behind the Pyrenees, and took its place as one of the great members of the European commonwealth. I now propose to examine a later period in the history of the same nation—the reign of Philip the Second; when, with resources greatly enlarged, and territory extended by a brilliant career of discovery and conquest, it had risen to the zenith of its power, but when, under the mischievous policy of the administration, it had excited the jealousy of its neighbors, and already disclosed those germs of domestic corruption which gradually led to its dismemberment and decay.

By the marriage of Ferdinand and Isabella, most of the states of the peninsula became united under one common rule; and in 1516 the scepter of Spain, with its dependencies both in the Old and the New World, passed into the hands of their grandson, Charles the Fifth, who, though he shared the throne nominally with his mother, Joanna, became, in consequence of her incapacity, the real sovereign of this vast empire. He had before inherited, through his father, Philip the Handsome, that fair portion of the ducal realm of Burgundy which comprehended Franche-Comté and the Netherlands. In 1519 he was elected to the imperial crown of Germany. Not many years elapsed before his domain was still further enlarged by the barbaric empires of Mexico and Peru; and Spain then first realized the magnificent vaunt, since so often repeated, that the sun never set within the borders of her dominions.

Yet the importance of Spain did not rise with the importance of her acquisitions. She was, in a manner, lost in the magnitude of these acquisitions. Some of the rival nations which owned the sway of Charles, in Europe, were of much greater importance than Spain, and attracted much more attention from their contemporaries. In the earlier period of that monarch's reign there was a moment when a contest was going forward in Castile, of the deepest interest to mankind. Unfortunately, the "War of the Comunidades," as it was termed, was soon closed by the ruin of the patriots; and on the memorable field of Villalar the liberties of Spain received a blow from which they were destined not to recover for centuries. From that fatal hour—the bitter fruit of the jealousy of castes and the passions of the populace—an unbroken tranquillity reigned throughout the country; such a tranquillity as naturally flows not from a free and well-conducted government, but from a despotic one. In this political tranquillity, however, the intellect of Spain did not slumber. Sheltered from invasion by the barrier of the Pyrenees, her people were allowed to cultivate the arts of peace, so long as they did not meddle with politics or religion—in other words, with the great interests of humanity; while the more adventurous found a scope for their prowess in European wars, or in exploring the boundless regions of the Western world.

While there was so little passing in Spain to attract the eye of the historian, Germany became the theater of one of those momentous struggles which have had a permanent influence on the destinies of mankind. It was in this reign that the great battle of religious liberty was begun; and the attention and personal presence of Charles were necessarily demanded most in the country where that battle was to be fought. But a small part of his life was passed in Spain in comparison with what he spent in other parts of his dominions. His early attachments, his lasting sympathies, were with the people of the Netherlands; for Flanders was the place of his birth. He spoke the language of that country more fluently than the Castilian; although he knew the various languages of his dominions so well that he could address his subjects from every quarter in their native dialect. In the same manner, he could accommodate himself to their peculiar national manners and tastes. But this flexibility was foreign to the genius of the Spaniard. Charles brought nothing from Spain but a religious zeal, amounting to bigotry, which took deep root in a melancholy temperament inherited from his mother. His tastes were all Flemish. He introduced the gorgeous ceremonial of the Burgundian court into his own palace, and into the household of his son. He drew his most trusted and familiar counselors from Flanders; and this was one great cause of the troubles which at the beginning of his reign distracted Castile. There was little to gratify the pride of the Spaniard in the position which he occupied at the imperial court. Charles regarded Spain chiefly for the resources she afforded for carrying on his ambitious enterprises. When he visited her, it was usually to draw supplies from the cortes. The Spaniards understood this, and bore less affection to his person than to many of their monarchs far inferior to him in the qualities for exciting it. They hardly regarded him as one of the nation. There was, indeed, nothing national in the reign of Charles. His most intimate relations were with Germany; and as the Emperor Charles the Fifth of Germany, not as King Charles the First of Spain, he was known in his own time and stands recorded on the pages of history.

When Charles ascended the throne, at the beginning of the sixteenth century, Europe may be said to have been in much the same condition, in one respect, as she was at the beginning of the eighth. The Turk menaced her on the east, in the same manner as the Arab had before menaced her on the west. The hour seemed to be fast approaching which was to decide whether Christianity or Mahometanism should hold the ascendant. The Ottoman tide of conquest rolled up to the very walls of Vienna; and Charles, who, as head of the empire, was placed on the frontier of Christendom, was called on to repel it. When thirty-two years of age, he marched against the formidable Solyman, drove him to an ignominious retreat, and, at less cost of life than is often expended in a skirmish, saved Europe from an invasion. He afterwards crossed the sea to Tunis, then occupied by a horde of pirates, the scourge of the Mediterranean. He beat them in a bloody battle, slew their chief, and liberated ten thousand captives from their dungeons. All Europe rang with the praises of the young hero who thus consecrated his arms to the service of the cross and stood forward as the true champion of Christendom.

But from this high position Charles was repeatedly summoned to other contests, of a more personal and far less honorable character. Such was his long and bloody quarrel with Francis the First. It was hardly possible that two princes so well matched in years, power, pretensions, and, above all, love of military glory, with dominions touching on one another through their whole extent, could long remain without cause of rivalry and collision. Such rivalry did exist from the moment that the great prize of the empire was adjudged to Charles; and through the whole of their long struggle, with the exception of a few reverses, the superior genius of the emperor triumphed over his bold but less politic adversary.

There was still a third contest, on which the strength of the Spanish monarch was freely expended through the greater part of his reign—his contest with the Lutheran princes of Germany. Here, too, for a long time, fortune favored him. But it is easier to contend against man than against a great moral principle. The principle of reform had struck too deep into the mind of Germany to be eradicated by force or by fraud. Charles for a long time, by a course of crafty policy, succeeded in baffling the Protestant league, and by the decisive victory at Muhlberg seemed at last to have broken it altogether. But his success only ministered to his ruin. The very man on whom he bestowed the spoils of victory turned them against his benefactor. Charles, ill in body and mind, and glad to escape from his enemies under cover of the night and a driving tempest, was at length compelled to sign the treaty of Passau, which secured to the Protestants those religious immunities against which he had contended through his whole reign.

Not long after, he experienced another humiliating reverse from France, then ruled by a younger rival, Henry the Second, the son of Francis. The good star of Charles—the star of Austria—seemed to have set; and, as he reluctantly raised the siege of Metz, he was heard bitterly to exclaim, "Fortune is a strumpet, who reserves her favors for the young!"

With spirits greatly depressed by his reverses, and still more by the state of his health, which precluded him from taking part in the manly and martial exercises to which he had been accustomed, he felt that he had no longer the same strength as formerly to bear up under the toils of empire. When but little more than thirty years of age, he had been attacked by the gout, and of late had been so sorely afflicted with that disorder that he had nearly lost the use of his limbs. The man who, cased in steel, had passed whole days and nights in the saddle, indifferent to the weather and the season, could now hardly drag himself along with the aid of his staff. For days he was confined to his bed; and he did not leave his room for weeks together. His mind became oppressed with melancholy, which was to some extent a constitutional infirmity. His chief pleasure was in listening to books, especially of a religious character. He denied himself to all except his most intimate and trusted counselors. He lost his interest in affairs; and for whole months, according to one of his biographers, who had access to his person, he refused to receive any public communication, or to subscribe any document, or even letter. One cannot understand how the business of the nation could have been conducted in such a state of things. After the death of his mother, Joanna, his mind became more deeply tinctured with those gloomy fancies which in her amounted to downright insanity. He imagined he heard her voice calling on him to follow her. His thoughts were now turned from secular concerns to those of his own soul; and he resolved to put in execution a plan for resigning his crown and withdrawing to some religious retreat, where he might prepare for his latter end. This plan he had conceived many years before, in the full tide of successful ambition. So opposite were the elements at work in the character of this extraordinary man!

Although he had chosen the place of his retreat, he had been deterred from immediately executing his purpose by the forlorn condition of his mother and the tender age of his son. The first obstacle was now removed by the death of Joanna, after a reign —a nominal reign—of half a century, in which the cloud that had settled on her intellect at her husband's death was never dispelled.

The age of Philip, his son and heir, was also no longer an objection. From early boyhood he had been trained to the duties of his station, and, when very young, had been intrusted with the government of Castile. His father had surrounded him with able and experienced counselors, and their pupil, who showed a discretion far beyond his years, had largely profited by their lessons. He had now entered his twenty-ninth year, an age when the character is formed, and when, if ever, he might be supposed qualified to assume the duties of government. His father had already ceded to him the sovereignty of Naples and Milan, on occasion of the prince's marriage with Mary of England. He was on a visit to that country, when Charles, having decided on the act of abdication, sent to require his son's attendance at Brussels, where the ceremony was to be performed. The different provinces of the Netherlands were also summoned to send their deputies, with authority to receive the emperor's resignation and to transfer their allegiance to his successor. As a preliminary step, on the twenty-second of October, 1555, he conferred on Philip the grand-mastership—which, as lord of Flanders, was vested in himself—of the toison d'or, the order of the Golden Fleece, of Burgundy, the proudest and most coveted, at that day, of all the military orders of knighthood.

Preparations were then made for conducting the ceremony of abdication with all the pomp and solemnity suited to so august an occasion. The great hall of the royal palace of Brussels was selected for the scene of it. The walls of the spacious apartment were hung with tapestry, and the floor was covered with rich carpeting. A scaffold was erected at one end of the room, to the height of six or seven steps. On it was placed a throne, or chair of state, for the emperor, with other seats for Philip and for the great Flemish lords who were to attend the person of their sovereign. Above the throne was suspended a gorgeous canopy, on which were emblazoned the arms of the ducal house of Burgundy. In front of the scaffolding, accommodations were provided for the deputies of the provinces, who were to be seated on benches arranged according to their respective rights of precedence.

On the twenty-fifth of October, the day fixed for the ceremony, Charles the Fifth executed an instrument by which he ceded to his son the sovereignty of the Netherlands. Mass was then performed; and the emperor, accompanied by Philip and a numerous retinue, proceeded in state to the great hall, where the deputies were already assembled.

Charles was at this time in the fifty-sixth year of his age. His

form was slightly bent—but it was by disease more than by time
—and on his countenance might be traced the marks of anxiety
and rough exposure. Yet it still wore that majesty of expression
so conspicuous in his portraits by the inimitable pencil of Titian.
His hair, once of a light color, approaching to yellow, had begun
to turn before he was forty, and, as well as his beard, was now
gray. His forehead was broad and expansive; his nose aquiline.
His blue eyes and fair complexion intimated his Teutonic
descent. The only feature in his countenance decidedly bad was
his lower jaw, protruding with its thick, heavy lip, so characteristic of the physiognomies of the Austrian dynasty.

In stature he was about the middle height. His limbs were
strongly knit, and once well formed, though now the extremities
were sadly distorted by disease. The emperor leaned for support
on a staff with one hand, while with the other he rested on the
arm of William of Orange, who, then young, was destined at a
later day to become the most formidable enemy of his house.
The grave demeanor of Charles was rendered still more impressive by his dress; for he was in mourning for his mother; and the
sable hue of his attire was relieved only by a single ornament, the
superb collar of the Golden Fleece, which hung from his neck.

Behind the emperor came Philip, the heir of his vast dominions. He was of a middle height, of much the same proportions as his father, whom he resembled also in his lineaments,
except that those of the son wore a more somber and perhaps a
sinister expression; while there was a reserve in his manner, in
spite of his efforts to the contrary, as if he would shroud his
thoughts from observation. The magnificence of his dress cor-
responded with his royal station, and formed a contrast to that
of his father, who was quitting the pomp and grandeur of the
world, on which the son was about to enter.

Next to Philip came Mary, the emperor's sister, formerly
queen of Hungary. She had filled the post of Regent of the Low
Countries for nearly twenty years, and now welcomed the hour
when she was to resign the burden of sovereignty to her nephew,
and withdraw, like her imperial brother, into private life. Another sister of Charles, Eleanor, widow of the French king
Francis the First, also took part in these ceremonies, previous to
her departure for Spain, whither she was to accompany the emperor.

After these members of the imperial family came the nobility of the Netherlands, the knights of the Golden Fleece, the royal counselors, and the great officers of the household, all splendidly attired in their robes of state and proudly displaying the insignia of their orders. When the emperor had mounted his throne, with Philip on his right hand, the Regent Mary on his left, and the rest of his retinue disposed along the seats prepared for them on the platform, the president of the council of Flanders addressed the assembly. He briefly explained the object for which they had been summoned, and the motives which had induced their master to abdicate the throne; and he concluded by requiring them, in their sovereign's name, to transfer their allegiance from himself to Philip, his son and rightful heir.

After a pause, Charles rose to address a few parting words to his subjects. He stood with apparent difficulty, and rested his right hand on the shoulder of the prince of Orange—intimating by this preference on so distinguished an occasion the high favor in which he held the young nobleman. In the other hand he held a paper, containing some hints for his discourse, and occasionally cast his eyes on it, to refresh his memory. He spoke in the French language.

He was unwilling, he said, to part from his people without a few words from his own lips. It was now forty years since he had been intrusted with the scepter of the Netherlands. He was soon after called to take charge of a still more extensive empire, both in Spain and in Germany, involving a heavy responsibility for one so young. He had, however, endeavored earnestly to do his duty to the best of his abilities. He had been ever mindful of the interests of the dear land of his birth, but, above all, of the great interests of Christianity. His first object had been to maintain these inviolate against the infidel. In this he had been thwarted, partly by the jealousy of neighboring powers, and partly by the factions of the heretical princes of Germany.

In the performance of his great work, he had never consulted his ease. His expeditions, in war and in peace, to France, England, Germany, Italy, Spain, and Flanders, had amounted to no less than forty. Four times he had crossed the Spanish seas, and eight times the Mediterranean. He had shrunk from no toil, while he had the strength to endure it. But a cruel malady had deprived him of that strength. Conscious of his inability to discharge the duties of his station, he had long since come to the resolution to relinquish it. From this he had been diverted only by the situation of his unfortunate parent and by the inexperience of his son. These objections no longer existed; and he should not stand excused, in the eye of Heaven or of the world, if he should insist on still holding the reins of government when he was incapable of managing them—when every year his incapacity must become more obvious.

He begged them to believe that this and no other motive induced him to resign the scepter which he had so long swayed. They had been to him dutiful and loving subjects; and such, he doubted not, they would prove to his successor. Above all things, he besought them to maintain the purity of the faith. If anyone, in these licentious times, had admitted doubts into his bosom, let such doubts be extirpated at once. "I know well," he concluded, "that, in my long administration, I have fallen into many errors and committed some wrongs. But it was from ignorance; and, if there be any here whom I have wronged, they will believe that it was not intended, and grant me their forgiveness."

While the emperor was speaking, a breathless silence pervaded the whole audience. Charles had ever been dear to the people of the Netherlands—the land of his birth. They took a national pride in his achievements, and felt that his glory reflected a peculiar luster on themselves. As they now gazed for the last time on that revered form, and listened to the parting admonitions from his lips, they were deeply affected, and not a dry eye was to be seen in the assembly.

After a short interval, Charles, turning to Philip, who, in an attitude of deep respect, stood awaiting his commands, thus addressed him: "If the vast possessions which are now bestowed on you had come by inheritance, there would be abundant cause for gratitude. How much more, when they come as a free gift, in the lifetime of your father! But, however large the debt, I shall consider it all repaid, if you only discharge your duty to your subjects. So rule over them that men shall commend and not censure me for the part I am now acting. Go on as you have begun. Fear God; live justly; respect the laws; above all, cherish the interests of religion; and may the Almighty bless you with a son to whom, when old and stricken with disease, you may be able to resign your kingdom with the same good will with which I now resign mine to you."

As he ceased, Philip, much affected, would have thrown himself at his father's feet, assuring him of his intention to do all in his power to merit such goodness; but Charles, raising his son, tenderly embraced him, while the tears flowed fast down his cheeks. Everyone, even the most stoical, was touched by this affecting scene; "and nothing," says one who was present, "was to be heard throughout the hall but sobs and ill-suppressed moans." Charles, exhausted by his efforts, and deadly pale, sank back upon his seat; while, with feeble accents, he exclaimed, as he gazed on his people, "God bless you! God bless you!"

After these emotions had somewhat subsided, Philip arose, and, delivering himself in French, briefly told the deputies of the regret which he felt at not being able to address them in their native language, and to assure them of the favor and high regard in which he held them. This would be done for him by the bishop of Arras.

This was Antony Perennot, better known as Cardinal Granvelle, son of the famous minister of Charles the Fifth, and destined himself to a still higher celebrity as the minister of Philip the Second. In clear and fluent language, he gave the deputies the promise of their new sovereign to respect the laws and liberties of the nation; invoking them, on his behalf, to aid him with their counsels, and, like loyal vassals, to maintain the authority of the law in his dominions. After a suitable response from the deputies, filled with sentiments of regret for the loss of their late monarch and with those of loyalty to their new one, the Regent Mary formally abdicated her authority, and the session closed. So ended a ceremony which, considering the importance of its consequences, the character of the actors, and the solemnity of the proceedings, is one of the most remarkable in history. That the crown of the monarch is lined with thorns, is a trite maxim; and it requires no philosophy to teach us that happiness does not depend on station. Yet, numerous as are the instances of those who have waded to a throne through seas of blood, there are but few who, when they have once tasted the sweets of sovereignty, have been content to resign them; still fewer who, when they have done so, have had the philosophy to conform to their change of condition and not to repent it. Charles, as the event proved, was one of these few.

On the sixteenth day of January, 1556, in the presence of such of the Spanish nobility as were at the court, he executed the deeds by which he ceded the sovereignty of Castile and Aragon, with their dependencies, to Philip. . . .

FROM CHAPTER V

War with the Pope

1555-1556

Soon after Philip's arrival in Brussels took place that memorable scene of the abdication of Charles the Fifth, which occupies the introductory pages of our narrative. By this event Philip saw himself master of the most widely extended and powerful monarchy in Europe. He was king of Spain, comprehending under that name Castile, Aragon, and Granada, which, after surviving as independent states for centuries, had been first brought under one scepter in the reign of his father, Charles the Fifth. He was king of Naples and Sicily, and duke of Milan, which important possessions enabled him to control to a great extent the nicely balanced scales of Italian politics. He was lord of Franche-Comté, and of the Low Countries, comprehending the most flourishing and populous provinces in Christendom, whose people had made the greatest progress in commerce, husbandry, and the various mechanic arts. As titular king of England, he eventually obtained an influence which, as we shall see, enabled him to direct the counsels of that country to his own purposes. In Africa he possessed the Cape de Verd Islands and the Canaries, as well as Tunis, Oran, and some other important places on the Barbary coast. He owned the Philippines and the Spice Islands in Asia. In America, besides his possessions in the West Indies, he was master of the rich empires of Mexico and Peru, and claimed a right to a boundless extent of country, that offered an inexhaustible field to the cupidity and enterprise of the Spanish adventurer. Thus the dominions of Philip stretched over every quarter of the globe. The flag of Castile was seen in the remotest latitudes—on the Atlantic, the Pacific, and the far-off Indian seas—passing from port to port, and uniting by commercial intercourse the widely scattered members of her vast colonial empire.

The Spanish army consisted of the most formidable infantry in Europe; veterans who had been formed under the eye of Charles the Fifth and of his generals, who had fought on the fields of Pavia and of Muhlberg, or who, in the New World, had climbed the Andes with Almagro and Pizarro and helped these bold chiefs to overthrow the dynasty of the Incas. The navy of Spain and Flanders combined far exceeded that of any other power in the number and size of its vessels; and if its supremacy might be contested by England on the "narrow seas," it rode the undisputed mistress of the ocean. To supply the means for maintaining this costly establishment, as well as the general machinery of government, Philip had at his command the treasures of the New World; and if the incessant enterprises of his father had drained the exchequer, it was soon replenished by the silver streams that flowed in from the inexhaustible mines of Zacatecas and Potosi.

All this vast empire, with its magnificent resources, was placed at the disposal of a single man. Philip ruled over it with an authority more absolute than that possessed by any European prince since the days of the Caesars. The Netherlands, indeed, maintained a show of independence under the shadow of their ancient institutions. But they consented to supply the necessities of the crown by a tax larger than the revenues of America. Naples and Milan were ruled by Spanish viceroys. Viceroys, with delegated powers scarcely less than those of their sovereign, presided over the American colonies, which received their laws from the parent country. In Spain itself, the authority of the nobles was gone. First assailed under Ferdinand and Isabella, it was completely broken down under Charles the Fifth. The liberties of the commons were crushed at the fatal battle of Villalar, in the beginning of that monarch's reign. Without nobles, without commons, the ancient cortes had faded into a mere legislative pageant, with hardly any other right than that of presenting petitions and of occasionally raising an ineffectual note of remonstrance against abuses. It had lost the power to redress them. Thus all authority vested in the sovereign. His will was the law of the land. From his palace at Madrid he sent forth the edicts which became the law of Spain and of her remotest colonies. It may well be believed that foreign nations watched with interest the first movements of a prince who seemed to hold in his hands the destinies of Europe, and that they regarded with no little apprehension the growth of that colossal power which had already risen to a height that cast a shadow over every other monarchy.

From his position, Philip stood at the head of the Roman Catholic princes. He was in temporal matters what the pope was in spiritual. In the existing state of Christendom, he had the same interest as the pope in putting down that spirit of religious reform which had begun to show itself, in public or in private, in every corner of Europe. He was the natural ally of the pope. He understood this well, and would have acted on it. Yet, strange to say, his very first war, after his accession, was with the pope himself. It was a war not of Philip's seeking.

The papal throne was at that time filled by Paul the Fourth, one of those remarkable men who, amidst the shadowy personages that have reigned in the Vatican and been forgotten, have vindicated to themselves a permanent place in history. He was a Neapolitan by birth, of the noble family of the Caraffas. He was bred to the religious profession, and early attracted notice by his diligent application and the fruits he gathered from it. His memory was prodigious. He was not only deeply read in theological science, but skilled in various languages, ancient and modern, several of which he spoke with fluency. His rank, sustained by his scholarship, raised him speedily to high preferment in the Church. In 1513, when thirty-six years of age, he went as nuncio to England. In 1525 he resigned his benefices, and, with a small number of his noble friends, he instituted a new religious order, called the Theatins. The object of the society was to combine, to some extent, the contemplative habits of the monk with the more active duties of the secular clergy. The members visited the sick, buried the dead, and preached frequently in public, thus performing the most important functions of the priesthood. For this last vocation, of public speaking, Caraffa was peculiarly qualified by a flow of natural eloquence which, if it did not always convince, was sure to carry away the audience by its irresistible fervor. The new order showed itself particularly zealous in enforcing reform in the Catholic clergy and in stemming the tide of heresy which now threatened to inundate the Church. Caraffa and his associates were earnest to introduce the Inquisition. A life of asceticism and penance too often extinguishes sympathy with human suffering, and leads its votaries to regard the sharpest remedies as the most effectual for the cure of spiritual error.

From this austere way of life Caraffa was called, in 1536, to a situation which engaged him more directly in worldly concerns. He was made cardinal by Paul the Third. He had, as far back as the time of Ferdinand the Catholic, been one of the royal council of Naples. The family of Caraffa, however, was of the Angevine party, and regarded the house of Aragon in the light of usurpers. The cardinal had been educated in this political creed, and even after his elevation to his new dignity he strongly urged Paul the Third to assert the claims of the holy see to the sovereignty of Naples. This conduct, which came to the ears of Charles the Fifth, so displeased that monarch that he dismissed Caraffa from the council. Afterwards, when the cardinal was named by the pope, his unfailing patron, to the archbishopric of Naples, Charles resisted the nomination, and opposed all the obstacles in his power to the collection of the episcopal revenues. These indignities sank deep into the cardinal's mind, naturally tenacious of affronts; and what at first had been only a political animosity was now sharpened into personal hatred of the most implacable character.

Such was the state of feeling when, on the death of Marcellus the Second, in 1555, Cardinal Caraffa was raised to the papal throne. His election, as was natural, greatly disgusted the emperor, and caused astonishment throughout Europe; for he had not the conciliatory manners which win the favor and the suffrages of mankind. But the Catholic Church stood itself in need of a reformer, to enable it to resist the encroaching spirit of Protestantism. This was well understood not only by the highest but by the humblest ecclesiastics; and in Caraffa they saw the man whose qualities precisely fitted him to effect such a reform.

He was, moreover, at the time of his election, in his eightieth year; and age and infirmity have always proved powerful arguments with the Sacred College, as affording the numerous competitors the best guarantees for a speedy vacancy. Yet it has more than once happened that the fortunate candidate who has owed his election mainly to his infirmities has been miraculously restored by the touch of the tiara.

Paul the Fourth—for such was the name assumed by the new pope, in gratitude to the memory of his patron—adopted a way of life, on his accession, for which his brethren of the college were not at all prepared. The austerity and self-denial of earlier days formed a strong contrast to the pomp of his present establishment and the profuse luxury of his table. When asked how he would be served, "How but as a great prince?" he answered. He usually passed three hours at his dinner, which consisted of numerous courses of the most refined and epicurean dishes. No one dined with him, though one or more of the cardinals were usually present, with whom he freely conversed; and, as he accompanied his meals with large draughts of the thick, black wine of Naples, it no doubt gave additional animation to his discourse. At such times his favorite theme was the Spaniards, whom he denounced as the scum of the earth, a race accursed of God, heretics and schismatics, the spawn of Jews and of Moors. He bewailed the humiliation of Italy, galled by the yoke of a nation so abject. But the day had come, he would thunder out, when Charles and Philip were to be called to a reckoning for their ill-gotten possessions, and be driven from the land!

Yet Paul did not waste all his hours in this idle vaporing, nor in the pleasures of the table. He showed the same activity as ever in the labors of the closet and in attention to business. He was irregular in his hours, sometimes prolonging his studies through the greater part of the night, and at others rising long before the dawn. When thus engaged, it would not have been well for anyone of his household to venture into his presence without a summons.

Paul seemed to be always in a state of nervous tension. "He is all nerve," the Venetian minister, Navagero, writes of him; "and when he walks, it is with a free, elastic step, as if he hardly touched the ground." His natural arrogance was greatly increased by his elevation to the first dignity in Christendom. He had al-

ways entertained the highest ideas of the authority of the sacer-
dotal office; and now that he was in the chair of St. Peter he
seemed to have entire confidence in his own infallibility. He
looked on the princes of Europe as not so much his sons—the
language of the Church—as his servants, bound to do his bidding. Paul's way of thinking would have better suited the twelfth
century than the sixteenth. He came into the world at least three
centuries too late. In all his acts he relied solely on himself. He
was impatient of counsel from anyone, and woe to the man who
ventured to oppose any remonstrance, still more any impediment
to the execution of his plans. He had no misgivings as to the
wisdom of these plans. An idea that had once taken possession
of his mind lay there, to borrow a cant phrase of the day, like
"a fixed fact"—not to be disturbed by argument or persuasion.
We occasionally meet with such characters, in which strength of
will and unconquerable energy in action pass for genius with the
world. They, in fact, serve as the best substitute for genius, by
the ascendancy which such qualities secure their possessors over
ordinary minds. Yet there were ways of approaching the pontiff,
for those who understood his character and who by condescending to flatter his humors could turn them to their own account.
Such was the policy pursued by some of Paul's kindred, who,
cheered by his patronage, now came forth from their obscurity
to glitter in the rays of the meridian sun.

Paul had all his life declaimed against nepotism as an opprobrious sin in the head of the Church. Yet no sooner did he put
on the tiara than he gave a glaring example of the sin he had
denounced, in the favors which he lavished on three of his own
nephews. This was the more remarkable as they were men whose
way of life had given scandal even to the Italians, not used to
be too scrupulous in their judgments.

The eldest, who represented the family, he raised to the rank
of a duke, providing him with an ample fortune from the confiscated property of the Colonnas—which illustrious house was
bitterly persecuted by Paul for its attachment to the Spanish
interests.

Another of his nephews he made a cardinal—a dignity for
which he was indifferently qualified by his former profession,
which was that of a soldier, and still less fitted by his life, which
was that of a libertine. He was a person of a busy, intriguing

disposition, and stimulated his uncle's vindictive feelings against the Spaniards, whom he himself hated for some affront which he conceived had been put upon him while in the emperor's service.

But Paul needed no prompter in this matter. He very soon showed that, instead of ecclesiastical reform, he was bent on a project much nearer to his heart—the subversion of the Spanish power in Naples. Like Julius the Second, of warlike memory, he swore to drive out the *barbarians* from Italy. He seemed to think that the thunders of the Vatican were more than a match for all the strength of the empire and of Spain. But he was not weak enough to rely wholly on his spiritual artillery in such a contest. Through the French ambassador at his court, he opened negotiations with France, and entered into a secret treaty with that power, by which each of the parties agreed to furnish a certain contingent of men and money to carry on the war for the recovery of Naples. The treaty was executed on the sixteenth of December, 1555.

In less than two months after this event, on the fifth of February, 1556, the fickle monarch of France, seduced by the advantageous offers of Charles, backed, moreover, by the ruinous state of his own finances, deserted his new ally, and signed the treaty of Vaucelles, which secured a truce for five years between his dominions and those of Philip.

Paul received the news of this treaty while surrounded by his courtiers. He treated the whole with skepticism, but expressed the pious hope that such a peace might be in store for the nations of Christendom. In private he was not so temperate. But, without expending his wrath in empty menaces, he took effectual means to bring things back to their former state—to induce the French king to renew the treaty with himself, and at once to begin hostilities. He knew the vacillating temper of the monarch he had to deal with. Cardinal Caraffa was accordingly despatched on a mission to Paris, fortified with ample powers for the arrangement of a new treaty, and with such tempting promises on the part of his holiness as might insure its acceptance by the monarch and his ministers.

The French monarchy was at that time under the scepter of Henry the Second, the son of Francis the First, to whose character his own bore no resemblance, or rather the resemblance consisted in those showy qualities which lie too near the surface to enter into what may be called character. He affected a chivalrous vein, excelled in the exercises of the tourney, and indulged in vague aspirations after military renown. In short, he fancied himself a hero, and seems to have imposed on some of his own courtiers so far as to persuade them that he was designed for one. But he had few of the qualities which enter into the character of a hero. He was as far from being a hero as he was from being a good Christian, though he thought to prove his orthodoxy by persecuting the Protestants, who were now rising into a formidable sect in the southern parts of his kingdom. He had little reliance on his own resources, leading a life of easy indulgence, and trusting the direction of his affairs to his favorites and his mistresses.

The most celebrated of these was Diana of Poictiers, created by Henry duchess of Valentinois, who preserved her personal charms and her influence over her royal lover to a much later period than usually happens. The persons of his court in whom the king most confided were the Constable Montmorency and the duke of Guise.

Anne de Montmorency, constable of France, was one of the proudest of the French nobility—proud alike of his great name, his rank, and his authority with his sovereign. He had grown gray in the service of the court, and Henry, accustomed to his society from boyhood, had learned to lean on him for the execution of his measures. Yet his judgments, though confidently given, were not always sound. His views were far from being enlarged; and, though full of courage, he showed little capacity for military affairs. A consciousness of this, perhaps, may have led him to recommend a pacific policy, suited to his own genius. He was a stanch Catholic, extremely punctilious in all the ceremonies of devotion, and, if we may credit Brantôme, would strangely mingle together the military and the religious. He repeated his Pater-Noster at certain fixed hours, whatever might be his occupation at the time. He would occasionally break off to give his orders, calling out, "Cut me down such a man!" "Hang up another!" "Run those fellows through with your lances!" "Set fire to the village!"—and so on; when, having thus relieved the military part of his conscience, he would go on with his Pater-Nosters as before.

A very different character was that of his younger rival, Francis, duke of Guise, uncle to Mary, queen of Scots, and brother to the regent. Of a bold, aspiring temper, filled with the love of glory, brilliant and popular in his address, he charmed the people by his manners and the splendor of his equipage and dress. He came to court attended usually by three or four hundred cavaliers, who formed themselves on Guise as their model. His fine person was set off by the showy costume of the time— a crimson doublet and cloak of spotless ermine, and a cap ornamented with a scarlet plume. In this dress he might often be seen, mounted on his splendid charger and followed by a gay retinue of gentlemen, riding at full gallop through the streets of Paris, and attracting the admiration of the people.

But his character was not altogether made up of such vanities. He was sagacious in counsel, and had proved himself the best captain of France. It was he who commanded at the memorable siege of Metz and foiled the efforts of the imperial forces under Charles and the duke of Alva. Caraffa found little difficulty in winning him over to his cause, as he opened to the ambitious chief the brilliant perspective of the conquest of Naples. The arguments of the wily Italian were supported by the duchess of Valentinois. It was in vain that the veteran Montmorency reminded the king of the ruinous state of the finances, which had driven him to the shameful expedient of putting up public offices to sale. The other party represented that the condition of Spain, after her long struggle, was little better; that the reins of government had now been transferred from the wise Charles to the hands of his inexperienced son; and that the cooperation of Rome afforded a favorable conjunction of circumstances, not to be neglected. Henry was further allured by Caraffa's assurance that his uncle would grant to the French monarch the investiture of Naples for one of his younger sons, and bestow Milan on another. The offer was too tempting to be resisted.

One objection occurred, in certain conscientious scruples as to the violation of the recent treaty of Vaucelles. But for this the pope, who had anticipated the objection, readily promised absolution. As the king also intimated some distrust lest the successor of Paul, whose advanced age made his life precarious, might not be inclined to carry out the treaty, Caraffa was authorized to assure him that this danger should be obviated by the creation of a batch of French cardinals, or of cardinals in the French interest.

All the difficulties being thus happily disposed of, the treaty was executed in the month of July, 1556. The parties agreed each to furnish about twelve thousand infantry, five hundred men-at-arms, and the same number of light horse. France was to contribute three hundred and fifty thousand ducats to the expenses of the war, and Rome one hundred and fifty thousand. The French troops were to be supplied with provisions by the pope, for which they were to reimburse his holiness. It was moreover agreed that the crown of Naples should be settled on a younger son of Henry, that a considerable tract on the northern frontier should be transferred to the papal territory, and that ample estates should be provided from the new conquests for the three nephews of his Holiness. In short, the system of partition was as nicely adjusted as if the quarry were actually in their possession, ready to be cut up and divided among the parties.

Finally, it was arranged that Henry should invite the Sultan Solyman to renew his former alliance with France and make a descent with his galleys on the coast of Calabria. Thus did his most Christian Majesty, with the pope for one of his allies and the Grand Turk for the other, prepare to make war on the most Catholic prince in Christendom!

Meanwhile, Paul the Fourth, elated by the prospect of a successful negotiation, threw off the little decency he had hitherto preserved in his deportment. He launched out into invectives more bitter than ever against Philip, and in a tone of defiance told such of the Spanish cardinals as were present that they might repeat his sayings to their master. He talked of instituting a legal process against the king for the recovery of Naples, which he had forfeited by omitting to pay the yearly tribute to the holy see. The pretext was ill founded, as the pope well knew. But the process went on with suitable gravity, and a sentence of forfeiture was ultimately pronounced against the Spanish monarch.

With these impotent insults, Paul employed more effectual means of annoyance. He persecuted all who showed any leaning to the Spanish interest. He set about repairing the walls of Rome and strengthening the garrisons on the frontier. His movements raised great alarm among the Romans, who had too vivid a recollection of their last war with Spain, under Clement the Seventh, to wish for another. Garcilasso de la Vega, who had represented Philip, during his father's reign, at the papal court, wrote a full account of these doings to the viceroy of Naples. Garcilasso was instantly thrown into prison. Taxis, the Spanish director of the posts, was both thrown into prison and put to the torture. Saria, the imperial ambassador, after in vain remonstrating against these outrages, waited on the pope to demand his passport, and was kept standing a full hour at the gate of the Vatican before he was admitted.

Philip had full intelligence of all these proceedings. He had long since descried the dark storm that was mustering beyond the Alps. He had provided for it at the close of the preceding year, by committing the government of Naples to the man most competent to such a crisis. This was the duke of Alva, at that time governor of Milan and commander-in-chief of the army in Italy. As this remarkable person is to occupy a large space in the subsequent pages of this narrative, it may be well to give some account of his earlier life.

Fernando Alvarez de Toledo was descended from an illustrious house in Castile, whose name is associated with some of the most memorable events in the national history. He was born in 1508, and, while a child, had the misfortune to lose his father, who perished in Africa, at the siege of Gelves. The care of the orphan devolved on his grandfather, the celebrated conqueror of Navarre. Under this veteran teacher the young Fernando received his first lessons in war, being present at more than one skirmish when quite a boy. This seems to have sharpened his appetite for a soldier's life, for we find him at the age of sixteen secretly leaving his home and taking service under the banner of the Constable Velasco, at the siege of Fontarabia. He was subsequently made governor of that place. In 1527, when not twenty years of age, he came, by his grandfather's death, into possession of the titles and large patrimonial estates of the house of Toledo.

The capacity which he displayed, as well as his high rank, soon made him an object of attention; and as Philip grew in years, the duke of Alva was placed near his person, formed one of his council, and took part in the regency of Castile. He accompanied Philip on his journeys from Spain, and, as we have seen, made one of his retinue both in Flanders and in England. The duke was of too haughty and imperious a temper to condescend to those arts which are thought to open the most ready avenues to the favor of the sovereign. He met with rivals of a finer policy and more accommodating disposition. Yet Philip perfectly comprehended his character. He knew the strength of his understanding, and did full justice to his loyalty; and he showed his confidence in his integrity by placing him in offices of the highest responsibility.

The emperor, with his usual insight into character, had early discerned the military talents of the young nobleman. He took Alva along with him on his campaigns in Germany, where from a subordinate station he rapidly rose to the first command in the army. Such was his position at the unfortunate siege of Metz, where the Spanish infantry had nearly been sacrificed to the obstinacy of Charles.

In his military career the duke displayed some of the qualities most characteristic of his countrymen. But they were those qualities which belong to a riper period of life. He showed little of that romantic and adventurous spirit of the Spanish cavalier which seemed to court peril for its own sake and would hazard all on a single cast. Caution was his prominent trait, in which he was a match for any graybeard in the army—a caution carried to such a length as sometimes to put a curb on the enterprising spirit of the emperor. Men were amazed to see so old a head on so young shoulders.

Yet this caution was attended by a courage which dangers could not daunt, and by a constancy which toil, however severe, could not tire. He preferred the surest, even though the slowest, means to attain his object. He was not ambitious of effect; never sought to startle by a brilliant coup-de-main. He would not have compromised a single chance in his own favor by appealing to the issue of a battle. He looked steadily to the end, and he moved surely towards it by a system of operations planned with the nicest forecast. The result of these operations was almost always success. Few great commanders have been more uniformly successful in their campaigns. Yet it was rare that these campaigns were marked by what is so dazzling to the imagination of the young aspirant for glory—a great and decisive victory. Such were some of the more obvious traits in the military character of the chief to whom Philip at this crisis confided the post of viceroy of Naples.

Before commencing hostilities against the Church, the Spanish monarch determined to ease his conscience by obtaining, if possible, a warrant for his proceedings from the Church itself. He assembled a body composed of theologians from Salamanca, Alcala, Valladolid, and some other places, and of jurists from his several councils, to resolve certain queries which he propounded. Among the rest, he inquired whether, in case of a defensive war with the pope, it would not be lawful to sequestrate the revenues of those persons, natives or foreigners, who had benefices in Spain, but who refused obedience to the orders of its sovereign; whether he might not lay an embargo on all revenues of the Church, and prohibit any remittance of moneys to Rome; whether a council might not be convoked to determine the validity of Paul's election, which in some particulars was supposed to have been irregular; whether inquiry might not be made into the gross abuses of ecclesiastical patronage by the Roman see, and effectual measures taken to redress them. The suggestion of an ecclesiastical council was a menace that grated unpleasantly on the pontifical ear, and was used by European princes as a sort of counterblast to the threat of excommunication. The particular objects for which this council was to be summoned were not of a kind to soothe the irritable nerves of his Holiness. The conclave of theologians and jurists made as favorable responses as the king had anticipated to his several interrogatories; and Philip, under so respectable a sanction, sent orders to his viceroy to take effectual measures for the protection of Naples.

Alva had not waited for these orders, but had busily employed himself in mustering his resources and in collecting troops from the Abruzzi and other parts of his territory. As hostilities were inevitable, he determined to strike the first blow, and carry the war into the enemy's country before he had time to cross the Neapolitan frontier. Like his master, however, the duke was willing to release himself, as far as possible, from personal responsibility before taking up arms against the head of the Church. He accordingly addressed a manifesto to the pope and the cardinals, setting forth in glowing terms the manifold grievances of his sovereign; the opprobrious and insulting language of Paul;

the indignities offered to Philip's agents and to the imperial ambassador; the process instituted for depriving his master of Naples; and lastly, the warlike demonstrations of the pope along the frontier, which left no doubt as to his designs. He conjured his Holiness to pause before he plunged his country into war. As the head of the Church, it was his duty to preserve peace, not to bring war into Christendom. He painted the inevitable evils of war, and the ruin and devastation which it must bring on the fair fields of Italy. If this were done, it would be the pope's doing, and his would be the responsibility. On the part of Naples the war would be a war of defense. For himself, he had no alternative. He was placed there to maintain the possessions of his sovereign; and, by the blessing of God, he would maintain them to the last drop of his blood.

Alva, while making this appeal to the pope, invoked the good offices of the Venetian government in bringing about a reconciliation between Philip and the Vatican. His spiritual manifesto to the pope was intrusted to a special messenger, a person of some consideration in Naples. The only reply which the hotheaded pontiff made to it was to throw the envoy into prison, and, as some state, to put him to the torture.

Meanwhile, Alva, who had not placed much reliance on the success of his appeal, had mustered a force amounting in all to twelve thousand infantry, fifteen hundred horse, and a train of twelve pieces of artillery. His infantry was chiefly made up of Neapolitans, some of whom had seen but little service. The strength of his army lay in his Spanish veterans, forming one-third of his force. The place of rendezvous was San Germano, a town on the northern frontier of the kingdom. On the first of September, 1556, Alva, attended by a gallant band of cavaliers, left the capital, and on the fourth arrived at the place appointed. The following day he crossed the borders at the head of his troops, and marched on Pontecorvo. He met with no resistance from the inhabitants, who at once threw open their gates to him. Several other places followed the example of Pontecorvo and Alva, taking possession of them, caused a scutcheon displaying the arms of the Sacred College to be hung up in the principal church of each town, with a placard announcing that he held it only for the college, until the election of a new pontiff. By this act he proclaimed to the Christian world that the object of the war, as far as Spain was concerned, was not conquest, but defense. Some historians find in it a deeper policy—that of exciting feelings of distrust between the pope and the cardinals.

Anagni, a place of some strength, refused the duke's summons to surrender. He was detained three days before his guns had opened a practicable breach in the walls. He then ordered an assault. The town was stormed and delivered up to sack—by which phrase is to be understood the perpetration of all those outrages which the ruthless code of war allowed, in that age, on the persons and property of the defenseless inhabitants, without regard to sex or age.

One or two other places which made resistance shared the fate of Anagni; and the duke of Alva, having garrisoned his new conquests with such forces as he could spare, led his victorious legions against Tivoli—a town strongly situated on elevated ground, commanding the eastern approaches to the capital. The place surrendered without attempting a defense; and Alva, willing to give his men some repose, made Tivoli his headquarters, while his army spread over the suburbs and adjacent country, which afforded good forage for his cavalry.

The rapid succession of these events, the fall of town after town, and, above all, the dismal fate of Anagni, filled the people of Rome with terror. The women began to hurry out of the city; many of the men would have followed but for the interference of Cardinal Caraffa. The panic was as great as if the enemy had been already at the gates of the capital. Amidst this general consternation, Paul seemed to be almost the only person who retained his self-possession. Navagero, the Venetian minister, was present when he received tidings of the storming of Anagni, and bears witness to the composure with which he went through the official business of the morning, as if nothing had happened. This was in public; but the shock was sufficiently strong to strike out some sparkles of his fiery temper, as those found who met him that day in private. To the Venetian agent who had come to Rome to mediate a peace, and who pressed him to enter into some terms of accommodation with the Spaniards, he haughtily replied that Alva must first recross the frontier, and then, if he had aught to solicit, prefer his petition like a dutiful son of the Church. This course was not one very likely to be adopted by the victorious general.

In an interview with two French gentlemen, who, as he had reason to suppose, were interesting themselves in the affair of a peace, he exclaimed, "Whoever would bring me into a peace with heretics is a servant of the Devil. Heaven will take vengeance on him. I will pray that God's curse may fall on him. If I find that you intermeddle in any such matter, I will cut your heads off your shoulders. Do not think this an empty threat. I have an eye in my back on you"—quoting an Italian proverb—"and if I find you playing me false, or attempting to entangle me a second time in an accursed truce, I swear to you by the eternal God, I will make your heads fly from your shoulders, come what may come of it!" "In this way," concludes the narrator, one of the parties, "his Holiness continued for nearly an hour, walking up and down the apartment, and talking all the while of his own grievances and of cutting off our heads, until he had talked himself quite out of breath."

But the valor of the pope did not expend itself in words. He instantly set about putting the capital in the best state of defense. He taxed the people to raise funds for his troops, drew in the garrisons from the neighboring places, formed a bodyguard of six or seven hundred horse, and soon had the satisfaction of seeing his Roman levies, amounting to six thousand infantry, well equipped for the war. They made a brave show, with their handsome uniforms and their banners richly emblazoned with the pontifical arms. As they passed in review before his Holiness, who stood at one of the windows of his palace, he gave them his benediction. But the edge of the Roman sword, according to an old proverb, was apt to be blunt; and these holiday troops were soon found to be no match for the hardy veterans of Spain.

Among the soldiers at the pope's disposal was a body of German mercenaries, who followed war as a trade, and let themselves out to the highest bidder. They were Lutherans, with little knowledge of the Roman Catholic religion, and less respect for it. They stared at its rites as mummeries, and made a jest of its most solemn ceremonies, directly under the eyes of the pope. But Paul, who at other times would have punished offenses like these with the gibbet and the stake, could not quarrel with his defenders, and was obliged to digest his mortification as he best might. It was remarked that the times were sadly out of joint, when the head of the Church had heretics for his allies and Catholics for his enemies.

Meanwhile the duke of Alva was lying at Tivoli. If he had taken advantage of the panic caused by his successes, he might, it was thought, without much difficulty have made himself master of the capital. But this did not suit his policy, which was rather to bring the pope to terms than to ruin him. He was desirous to reduce the city by cutting off its supplies. The possession of Tivoli, as already noticed, enabled him to command the eastern approaches to Rome, and he now proposed to make himself master of Ostia and thus destroy the communications with the coast.

Accordingly, drawing together his forces, he quitted Tivoli, and directed his march across the Campagna, south of the Roman capital. On his way he made himself master of some places belonging to the holy see, and in the early part of November arrived before Ostia and took up a position on the banks of the Tiber, where it spread into two branches, the northern one of which was called the Fiumicino, or little river. The town, or rather village, consisted of only a few straggling houses, very different from the proud Ostia whose capacious harbor was once filled with the commerce of the world. It was protected by a citadel of some strength, garrisoned by a small but picked body of troops, so indifferently provided with military stores that it was clear the government had not anticipated an attack in this quarter.

The duke ordered a number of boats to be sent round from Nettuno, a place on the coast, of which he had got possession. By means of these he formed a bridge, over which he passed a small detachment of his army, together with his battering train of artillery. The hamlet was easily taken, but, as the citadel refused to surrender, Alva laid regular siege to it. He constructed two batteries, on which he planted his heavy guns, commanding opposite quarters of the fortress. He then opened a lively cannonade on the outworks, which was returned with great spirit by the garrison.

Meanwhile he detached a considerable body of horse, under Colonna, who swept the country to the very walls of Rome. A squadron of cavalry, whose gallant bearing had filled the heart of the old pope with exultation, sallied out against the marauders.

An encounter took place not far from the city. The Romans bore themselves up bravely to the shock; but, after splintering their lances, they wheeled about, and, without striking another blow, abandoned the field to the enemy, who followed them up to the gates of the capital. They were so roughly handled in their flight that the valiant troopers could not be induced again to leave their walls, although Cardinal Caraffa—who had a narrow escape from the enemy—sallied out with a handful of his followers, to give them confidence.

During this time Alva was vigorously pressing the siege of Ostia; but, though more than a week had elapsed, the besieged showed no disposition to surrender. At length the Spanish commander, on the seventeenth of November, finding his ammunition nearly expended, and his army short of provisions, determined on a general assault. Early on the following morning, after hearing mass as usual, the duke mounted his horse, and, riding among the ranks to animate the spirits of his soldiers, gave orders for the attack. A corps of Italians was first detached, to scale the works; but they were repulsed with considerable loss. It was found impossible for their officers to rally them and bring them back to the assault. A picked body of Spanish infantry was then despatched on this dangerous service. With incredible difficulty they succeeded in scaling the ramparts, under a storm of combustibles and other missiles hurled down by the garrison, and effected an entrance into the place. But here they were met with a courage as dauntless as their own. The struggle was long and desperate. There had been no such fighting in the course of the campaign. At length, the duke, made aware of the severe loss sustained by his men, and of the impracticability of the attempt, as darkness was setting in, gave the signal for retreat. The assailants had doubtless the worst of it in the conflict; but the besieged, worn out with fatigue, with their ammunition nearly exhausted, and almost without food, did not feel themselves in condition to sustain another assault on the following day. On the nineteenth of November, therefore, the morning after the conflict, the brave garrison capitulated, and were treated with honor as prisoners of war.

The fate of the campaign seemed now to be decided. The pope, with his principal towns in the hands of the enemy, his communications cut off both with the country and the coast, may well have felt his inability to contend thus single-handed against the power of Spain. At all events, his subjects felt it, and they were not deterred by his arrogant bearing from clamoring loudly against the continuance of this ruinous war. But Paul would not hear of a peace. However crippled by his late reverses, he felt confident of repairing them all on the arrival of the French, who, as he now learned with joy, were in full march across the territory of Milan. He was not so disinclined to a truce, which might give time for their coming.

Cardinal Caraffa, accordingly, had a conference with the duke of Alva, and entered into negotiations with him for a suspension of arms. The proposal was not unwelcome to the duke, who, weakened by losses of every kind, was by no means in condition at the end of an active campaign to contend with a fresh army under the command of so practiced a leader as the duke of Guise. He did not care to expose himself a second time to an encounter with the French general, under disadvantages nearly as great as those which had foiled him at Metz.

With these amiable dispositions, a truce was soon arranged between the parties, to continue forty days. The terms were honorable to Alva, since they left him in possession of all his conquests. Having completed these arrangements, the Spanish commander broke up his camp on the southern bank of the Tiber, recrossed the frontier, and in a few days made his triumphant entry, at the head of his battalions, into the city of Naples. . . .

BOOK II

―――― ◆ ――――

Protestantism in Spain

1559

The voyage of King Philip was a short and prosperous one. On the twenty-ninth of August, 1559, he arrived off the port of Laredo. But while he was in sight of land, the weather, which had been so propitious, suddenly changed. A furious tempest arose, which scattered his little navy. Nine of the vessels foundered, and though the monarch had the good fortune, under the care of an experienced pilot, to make his escape in a boat and reach the shore in safety, he had the mortification to see the ship which had borne him go down with the rest, and with her the inestimable cargo he had brought from the Low Countries. It consisted of curious furniture, tapestries, gems, pieces of sculpture, and paintings—the rich productions of Flemish and Italian art, which his father, the emperor, had been employed many years of his life in collecting. Truly was it said of Charles that "he had sacked the land only to feed the ocean." To add to the calamity, more than a thousand persons perished in this shipwreck.

The king, without delay, took the road to Valladolid; but on arriving at that capital, whether depressed by his late disaster, or from his habitual dislike of such empty parade, he declined the honors with which the loyal inhabitants would have greeted the return of their sovereign to his dominions. Here he was cordially welcomed by his sister, the Regent Joanna, who, long since weary of the cares of sovereignty, resigned the scepter into his hands with a better will than that with which most persons would have received it. Here, too, he had the satisfaction of embracing his son Carlos, the heir to his empire. The length of Philip's absence may have allowed him to see some favorable change in the person of the young prince, though, if report be true, there was little change for the better in his disposition, which, headstrong and imperious, had already begun to make men tremble for the future destinies of their country.

Philip had not been many days in Valladolid when his presence was celebrated by one of those exhibitions which, unhappily for Spain, may be called national. This was an auto da fe, not, however, as formerly, of Jews and Moors, but of Spanish Protestants. The Reformation had been silently, but not slowly, advancing in the peninsula; and intelligence of this, as we have already seen, was one cause of Philip's abrupt departure from the Netherlands. The brief but disastrous attempt at a religious revolution in Spain is an event of too much importance to be passed over in silence by the historian.

Notwithstanding the remote position of Spain, under the imperial scepter of Charles she was brought too closely into contact with the other states of Europe not to feel the shock of the great religious reform which was shaking those states to their foundations. Her most intimate relations, indeed, were with those very countries in which the seeds of the Reformation were first planted. It was no uncommon thing for Spaniards, in the sixteenth century, to be indebted for some portion of their instruction to German universities. Men of learning, who accompanied the emperor, became familiar with the religious doctrines so widely circulated in Germany and Flanders. The troops gathered the same doctrines from the Lutheran soldiers who occasionally served with them under the imperial banners. These opinions, crude for the most part as they were, they brought back to their own country; and a curiosity was roused which prepared the mind for the reception of the great truths which were quickening the other nations of Europe. Men of higher education, on their return to Spain, found the means of disseminating these truths. Secret societies were established; meetings were held; and, with the same secrecy as in the days of the early Christians, the gospel was preached and explained to the growing congregation of the faithful. The greatest difficulty was the want of books. The enterprise of a few self-devoted proselytes at length overcame this difficulty.

A Castilian version of the Bible had been printed in Germany. Various Protestant publications, whether originating in the Cas-

tilian or translated into that language, appeared in the same
country. A copy now and then, in the possession of some private
individual, had found its way, without detection, across the
Pyrenees. These instances were rare, when a Spaniard named
Juan Hernandez, resident in Geneva, where he followed the
business of a corrector of the press, undertook, from no other
motive but zeal for the truth, to introduce a larger supply of the
forbidden fruit into his native land.

With great adroitness, he evaded the vigilance of the custom-
house officers and the more vigilant spies of the Inquisition, and
in the end succeeded in landing two large casks filled with
prohibited works, which were quickly distributed among the
members of the infant church. Other intrepid converts followed
the example of Hernandez, and with similar success; so that,
with the aid of books and spiritual teachers, the number of the
faithful multiplied daily throughout the country. Among this
number was a much larger proportion, it was observed, of
persons of rank and education than is usually found in like
cases; owing doubtless to the circumstance that it was this class
of persons who had most frequented the countries where the
Lutheran doctrines were taught. Thus the Reformed Church
grew and prospered, not indeed as it had prospered in the freer
atmospheres of Germany and Britain, but as well as it could
possibly do under the blighting influence of the Inquisition; like
some tender plant, which, nurtured in the shade, waits only for
a more genial season for its full expansion. That season was not
in reserve for it in Spain.

It may seem strange that the spread of the reformed religion
should so long have escaped the detection of the agents of the
holy office. Yet it is certain that the first notice which the Spanish inquisitors received of the fact was from their brethren
abroad. Some ecclesiastics in the train of Philip, suspecting the
heresy of several of their own countrymen in the Netherlands,
had them seized and sent to Spain, to be examined by the Inquisition. On a closer investigation, it was found that a correspondence had long been maintained between these persons and
their countrymen, of a similar persuasion with themselves, at
home. Thus the existence, though not the extent, of the Spanish
Reformation was made known.

No sooner was the alarm sounded than Paul the Fourth,

quick to follow up the scent of heresy in any quarter of his pontifical dominions, issued a brief, in February, 1558, addressed to the Spanish inquisitor-general. In this brief, his Holiness enjoins it on the head of the tribunal to spare no efforts to detect and exterminate the growing evil; and he empowers that functionary to arraign and bring to condign punishment all suspected of heresy, of whatever rank or profession—whether bishops or archbishops, nobles, kings, or emperors. Paul the Fourth was fond of contemplating himself as seated in the chair of the Innocents and the Gregories, and like them setting his pontifical foot on the necks of princes. His natural arrogance was probably not diminished by the concessions which Philip the Second had thought proper to make to him at the close of the Roman war.

Philip, far from taking umbrage at the swelling tone of this apostolical mandate, followed it up, in the same year, by a monstrous edict, borrowed from one in the Netherlands, which condemned all who bought, sold, or read prohibited works to be burned alive.

In the following January, Paul, to give greater efficacy to this edict, published another bull, in which he commanded all confessors, under pain of excommunication, to enjoin on their penitents to inform against all persons, however nearly allied to them, who might be guilty of such practices. To quicken the zeal of the informer, Philip, on his part, revived a law fallen somewhat into disuse, by which the accuser was to receive one-fourth of the confiscated property of the convicted party. And, finally, a third bull from Paul allowed the inquisitors to withhold a pardon from the recanting heretic if any doubt existed of his sincerity; thus placing the life as well as fortune of the unhappy prisoner entirely at the mercy of judges who had an obvious interest in finding him guilty. In this way the pope and the king continued to play into each other's hands, and while his Holiness artfully spread the toils, the king devised the means for driving the quarry into them.

Fortunately for these plans, the Inquisition was at this time under the direction of a man peculiarly fitted to execute them. This was Fernando Valdes, cardinal-archbishop of Seville, a person of a hard, inexorable nature, and possessed of as large a measure of fanaticism as ever fell to a grand inquisitor since the days of Torquemada. Valdes readily availed himself of the terrible machinery placed under his control. Careful not to alarm the suspected parties, his approaches were slow and stealthy. He was the chief of a tribunal which sat in darkness and which dealt by invisible agents. He worked long and silently under ground before firing the mine which was to bury his enemies in a general ruin.

His spies were everywhere abroad, mingling with the suspected and insinuating themselves into their confidence. At length, by the treachery of some, and by working on the nervous apprehensions or the religious scruples of others, he succeeded in detecting the lurking-places of the new heresy and the extent of ground which it covered. This was much larger than had been imagined, although the Reformation in Spain seemed less formidable from the number of its proselytes than from their character and position. Many of them were ecclesiastics, especially intrusted with maintaining the purity of the faith. The quarters in which the heretical doctrines most prevailed were Aragon, which held an easy communication with the Huguenots of France, and the ancient cities of Seville and Valladolid, indebted less to any local advantages than to the influence of a few eminent men who had early embraced the faith of the reformers.

At length, the preliminary information having been obtained, the proscribed having been marked out, the plan of attack settled, an order was given for the simultaneous arrest of all persons suspected of heresy, throughout the kingdom. It fell like a thunderbolt on the unhappy victims, who had gone on with their secret associations, little suspecting the ruin that hung over them. No resistance was attempted. Men and women, churchmen and laymen, persons of all ranks and professions, were hurried from their homes and lodged in the secret chambers of the Inquisition. Yet these could not furnish accommodations for the number, and many were removed to the ordinary prisons, and even to convents and private dwellings. In Seville alone eight hundred were arrested on the first day. Fears were entertained of an attempt at rescue, and an additional guard was stationed over the places of confinement. The inquisitors were in the condition of a fisherman whose cast has been so successful that the draft of fishes seems likely to prove too heavy for his net.

The arrest of one party gradually led to the detection of others. Dragged from his solitary dungeon before the secret tribunal of the Inquisition, alone, without counsel to aid or one friendly face to cheer him, without knowing the name of his accuser, without being allowed to confront the witnesses who were there to swear away his life, without even a sight of his own process, except such garbled extracts as the wily judges thought fit to communicate, is it strange that the unhappy victim, in his perplexity and distress, should have been drawn into disclosures fatal to his associates and himself? If these disclosures were not to the mind of his judges, they had only to try the efficacy of the torture—the rack, the cord, and the pulley—until, when every joint had been wrenched from its socket, the barbarous tribunal was compelled to suspend, not terminate, the application, from the inability of the sufferer to endure it. Such were the dismal scenes enacted in the name of religion, and by the ministers of religion, as well as of the Inquisition—scenes to which few of those who had once witnessed them, and escaped with life, dared ever to allude. For to reveal the secrets of the Inquisition was death.

At the expiration of eighteen months from the period of the first arrests, many of the trials had been concluded, the doom of the prisoners was sealed, and it was thought time that the prisons should disgorge their superfluous inmates. Valladolid was selected as the theater of the first auto da fe, both from the importance of the capital and the presence of the court, which would thus sanction and give greater dignity to the celebration. This event took place in May, 1559. The Regent Joanna, the young prince of Asturias, Don Carlos, and the principal grandees of the court, were there to witness the spectacle. By rendering the heir of the crown thus early familiar with the tender mercies of the holy office, it may have been intended to conciliate his favor to that institution. If such was the object, according to the report it signally failed, since the woeful spectacle left no other impressions on the mind of the prince than those of indignation and disgust.

The example of Valladolid was soon followed by autos da fe in Granada, Toledo, Seville, Barcelona—in short, in the twelve capitals in which tribunals of the holy office were established. A second celebration at Valladolid was reserved for the eighth of October in the same year, when it would be graced by the presence of the sovereign himself. Indeed, as several of the processes had been concluded some months before this period, there is reason to believe that the sacrifice of more than one of the victims had been postponed in order to give greater effect to the spectacle.

The auto da fe—"act of faith"—was the most imposing, as it was the most awful, of the solemnities authorized by the Roman Catholic Church. It was intended, somewhat profanely, as has been intimated, to combine the pomp of the Roman triumph with the terrors of the day of judgment. It may remind one quite as much of those bloody festivals prepared for the entertainment of the Caesars in the Coliseum. The religious import of the auto da fe was intimated by the circumstance of its being celebrated on a Sunday, or some other holiday of the Church. An indulgence for forty days was granted by his Holiness to all who should be present at the spectacle; as if the appetite for witnessing the scenes of human suffering required to be stimulated by a bounty—that, too, in Spain, where the amusements were, and still are, of the most sanguinary character.

The scene for this second auto da fe at Valladolid was the great square in front of the church of St. Francis. At one end a platform was raised, covered with rich carpeting, on which were ranged the seats of the inquisitors, emblazoned with the arms of the holy office. Near to this was the royal gallery, a private entrance to which secured the inmates from molestation by the crowd. Opposite to this gallery a large scaffold was erected, so as to be visible from all parts of the arena, and was appropriated to the unhappy martyrs who were to suffer in the *auto*.

At six in the morning all the bells in the capital began to toll, and a solemn procession was seen to move from the dismal fortress of the Inquisition. In the van marched a body of troops, to secure a free passage for the procession. Then came the condemned, each attended by two familiars of the holy office, and those who were to suffer at the stake by two friars, in addition, exhorting the heretic to abjure his errors. Those admitted to penitence wore a sable dress; while the unfortunate martyr was enveloped in a loose sack of yellow cloth—the san benito—with his head surmounted by a cap of pasteboard of a conical form, which, together with the cloak, was embroidered with figures of flames and of devils fanning and feeding them; all emblematical of the destiny of the heretic's soul in the world to come, as well as of his body in the present. Then came the magistrates of the city, the judges of the courts, the ecclesiastical orders, and the nobles of the land, on horseback. These were followed by the members of the dread tribunal, and the fiscal, bearing a standard of crimson damask, on one side of which were displayed the arms of the Inquisition, and on the other the insignia of its founders, Sixtus the Fifth and Ferdinand the Catholic. Next came a numerous train of familiars, well mounted, among whom were many of the gentry of the province, proud to act as the bodyguard of the holy office. The rear was brought up by an immense concourse of the common people, stimulated on the present occasion, no doubt, by the loyal desire to see their new sovereign, as well as by the ambition to share in the triumphs of the auto da fe. The number thus drawn together from the capital and the country, far exceeding what was usual on such occasions, is estimated by one present at full two hundred thousand.

As the multitude defiled into the square, the inquisitors took their place on the seats prepared for their reception. The condemned were conducted to the scaffold, and the royal station was occupied by Philip, with the different members of his household. At his side sat his sister, the late regent, his son, Don Carlos, his nephew, Alexander Farnese, several foreign ambassadors, and the principal grandees and higher ecclesiastics in attendance on the court. It was an august assembly of the greatest and the proudest in the land. But the most indifferent spectator, who had a spark of humanity in his bosom, might have turned with feelings of admiration from this array of worldly power, to the poor martyr, who, with no support but what he drew from within, was prepared to defy this power and to lay down his life in vindication of the rights of conscience. Some there may have been, in that large concourse, who shared in these sentiments. But their number was small indeed in comparison with those who looked on the wretched victim as the enemy of God, and his approaching sacrifice as the most glorious triumph of the cross.

The ceremonies began with a sermon, "the sermon of the faith," by the bishop of Zamora. The subject of it may well be

guessed, from the occasion. It was no doubt plentifully larded
with texts of Scripture, and, unless the preacher departed from
the fashion of the time, with passages from the heathen writers,
however much out of place they may seem in an orthodox discourse.

When the bishop had concluded, the grand inquisitor administered an oath to the assembled multitude, who on their
knees solemnly swore to defend the Inquisition, to maintain the
purity of the faith, and to inform against anyone who should
swerve from it. As Philip repeated an oath of similar import,
he suited the action to the word, and, rising from his seat, drew
his sword from its scabbard, as if to announce himself the determined champion of the holy office. In the earlier *autos* of the
Moorish and Jewish infidels, so humiliating an oath had never
been exacted from the sovereign.

After this, the secretary of the tribunal read aloud an instrument reciting the grounds for the conviction of the prisoners,
and the respective sentences pronounced against them. Those
who were to be admitted to penitence, each, as his sentence was
proclaimed, knelt down, and, with his hands on the missal,
solemnly adjured his errors, and was absolved by the grand
inquisitor. The absolution, however, was not so entire as to
relieve the offender from the penalty of his transgressions in this
world. Some were doomed to perpetual imprisonment in the
cells of the Inquisition, others to lighter penances. All were
doomed to the confiscation of their property—a point of too
great moment to the welfare of the tribunal ever to be omitted.
Besides this, in many cases the offender, and, by a glaring per-
version of justice, his immediate descendants, were rendered
forever ineligible to public office of any kind, and their names
branded with perpetual infamy. Thus blighted in fortune and
in character, they were said, in the soft language of the Inquisition, to be *reconciled*.

As these unfortunate persons were remanded, under a strong
guard, to their prisons, all eyes were turned on the little company
of martyrs, who, clothed in the ignominious garb of the san
benito, stood awaiting the sentence of their judges, with cords
round their necks, and in their hands a cross, or sometimes an
inverted torch, typical of their own speedy dissolution. The
interest of the spectators was still further excited, in the present

instance, by the fact that several of these victims were not only illustrious for their rank, but yet more so for their talents and virtues. In their haggard looks, their emaciated forms, and too often, alas! their distorted limbs, it was easy to read the story of their sufferings in their long imprisonment, for some of them had been confined in the dark cells of the Inquisition much more than a year. Yet their countenances, though haggard, far from showing any sign of weakness or fear, were lighted up with the glow of holy enthusiasm, as of men prepared to seal their testimony with their blood.

When that part of the process showing the grounds of their conviction had been read, the grand inquisitor consigned them to the hands of the corregidor of the city, beseeching him to deal with the prisoners *in all kindness and mercy;* a honeyed but most hypocritical phrase, since no choice was left to the civil magistrate but to execute the terrible sentence of the law against heretics, the preparation for which had been made by him a week before.

The whole number of convicts amounted to thirty, of whom sixteen were *reconciled,* and the remainder *relaxed* to the secular arm—in other words, turned over to the civil magistrate for execution. There were few of those thus condemned who, when brought to the stake, did not so far shrink from the dreadful doom that awaited them as to consent to purchase a commutation of it by confession before they died; in which case they were strangled by the garrote before their bodies were thrown into the flames. . . .

BOOK IV

The Ottoman Empire

1559–1563

There are two methods of writing history—one by following down the stream of time and exhibiting events in their chronological order, the other by disposing of these events according to their subjects. The former is the most obvious; and where the action is simple and continuous, as in biography, for the most part, or in the narrative of some grand historical event, which concentrates the interest, it is probably the best. But when the story is more complicated, covering a wide field and embracing great variety of incident, the chronological system, however easy for the writer, becomes tedious and unprofitable to the reader. He is hurried along from one scene to another without fully apprehending any; and as the thread of the narrative is perpetually broken by sudden transition, he carries off only such scraps in his memory as it is hardly possible to weave into a connected and consistent whole. Yet this method, as the most simple and natural, is the one most affected by the early writers —by the old Castilian chroniclers more particularly, who form the principal authorities in the present work. Their wearisome pages, mindful of no order but that of time, are spread over as miscellaneous a range of incidents, and having as little relation to one another, as the columns of a newspaper.

To avoid this inconvenience, historians of a later period have preferred to conduct their story on more philosophical principles, having regard rather to the nature of the events described than to the precise time of their occurrence. And thus the reader, possessed of one action, its causes and its consequences, before passing on to another, is enabled to treasure up in his memory distinct impressions of the whole.

In conformity to this plan, I have detained the reader in the Netherlands until he had seen the close of Margaret's administration, and the policy which marked the commencement of her successor's. During this period, Spain was at peace with her European neighbors, most of whom were too much occupied with their domestic dissensions to have leisure for foreign war. France, in particular, was convulsed by religious feuds, in which Philip, as the champion of the faith, took not only the deepest interest, but an active part. To this I shall return hereafter.

But, while at peace with her Christian brethren, Spain was engaged in perpetual hostilities with the Moslems, both of Africa and Asia. The relations of Europe with the East were altogether different in the sixteenth century from what they are in our day. The Turkish power lay like a dark cloud on the Eastern horizon, to which every eye was turned with apprehension; and the same people for whose protection European nations are now willing to make common cause were viewed by them, in the sixteenth century, in the light of a common enemy.

It was fortunate for Islamism that, as the standard of the prophet was falling from the feeble grasp of the Arabs, it was caught up by a nation like the Turks, whose fiery zeal urged them to bear it still onward in the march of victory. The Turks were to the Arabs what the Romans were to the Greeks. Bold, warlike, and ambitious, they had little of that love of art which had been the dominant passion of their predecessors, and still less of that refinement which, with the Arabs, had degenerated into effeminacy and sloth. Their form of government was admirably suited to their character. It was an unmixed despotism. The sovereign, if not precisely invested with the theocratic character of the caliphs, was hedged round with so much sanctity that resistance to his authority was an offense against religion as well as law. He was placed at an immeasurable distance above his subjects. No hereditary aristocracy was allowed to soften the descent and interpose a protecting barrier for the people. All power was derived from the sovereign, and, on the death of its proprietor, returned to him. In the eye of the sultan, his vassals were all equal, and all equally his slaves.

The theory of an absolute government would seem to imply perfection in the head of it. But, as perfection is not the lot of humanity, it was prudently provided by the Turkish constitution that the sultan should have the benefit of a council to advise him. It consisted of three or four great officers, appointed by himself, with the grand vizier at their head. This functionary was possessed of an authority far exceeding that of the prime minister of any European prince. All the business of state may be said to have passed through his hands. The persons chosen for this high office were usually men of capacity and experience; and in a weak reign they served by their large authority to screen the incapacity of the sovereign from the eyes of his subjects, while they preserved the state from detriment. It might be thought that powers so vast as those bestowed on the vizier might have rendered him formidable, if not dangerous, to his master. But his master was placed as far above him as above the meanest of his subjects. He had unlimited power of life and death; and how little he was troubled with scruples in the exercise of this power is abundantly shown in history. The bowstring was too often the only warrant for the deposition of a minister.

But the most remarkable of the Turkish institutions, the one which may be said to have formed the keystone of the system, was that relating to the Christian population of the empire. Once in five years a general conscription was made, by means of which all the children of Christian parents who had reached the age of seven, and gave promise of excellence in mind or body, were taken from their homes and brought to the capital. They were then removed to different quarters, and placed in seminaries where they might receive such instruction as would fit them for the duties of life. Those giving greatest promise of strength and endurance were sent to places prepared for them in Asia Minor. Here they were subjected to a severe training, to abstinence, to privations of every kind, and to the strict discipline which should fit them for the profession of a soldier. From this body was formed the famous corps of the janizaries.

Another portion were placed in school in the capital or the neighboring cities, where, under the eye of the sultan, as it were, they were taught various manly accomplishments, with such a smattering of science as Turkish, or rather Arabian, scholarship could supply. When their education was finished, some went into the sultan's bodyguard, where a splendid provision was made for their maintenance. Others, intended for civil life, entered on a career which might lead to the highest offices in the state.

As all these classes of Christian youths were taken from their parents at that tender age when the doctrines of their own faith could hardly have taken root in their minds, they were without difficulty won over to the faith of the Koran; which was further commended to their choice as the religion of the state, the only one which opened to them the path of preferment. Thus set apart from the rest of the community, and cherished by royal favor, the new converts, as they rallied round the throne of their sovereign, became more stanch in their devotion to his interests, as well as to the interests of the religion they had adopted, than even the Turks themselves.

This singular institution bore hard on the Christian population, who paid this heavy tax of their own offspring. But it worked well for the monarchy, which, acquiring fresh vigor from the constant infusion of new blood into its veins, was slow in exhibiting any signs of decrepitude or decay.

The most important of these various classes was that of the janizaries, whose discipline was far from terminating with the school. Indeed, their whole life may be said to have been passed in war, or in preparation for it. Forbidden to marry, they had no families to engage their affections, which, as with the monks and friars in Christian countries, were concentrated on their own order, whose prosperity was inseparably connected with that of the state. Proud of the privileges which distinguished them from the rest of the army, they seemed desirous to prove their title to them by their thorough discipline and by their promptness to execute the most dangerous and difficult services. Their post was always the post of danger. It was their proud vaunt that they had never fled before an enemy. Clad in their flowing robes, so little suited to the warrior, armed with the arquebuse and the scimitar—in their hands more than a match for the pike or sword of the European—with the heron's plume waving above their heads, their dense array might ever be seen bearing down in the thickest of the fight; and more than once, when the fate of the empire trembled in the balance, it was this invincible corps that turned the scale and by their intrepid conduct decided the fortune of the day. Gathering fresh reputation with age, so long as their discipline remained unimpaired they were a match for the best soldiers of Europe. But in time this admirable organization experienced a change. One sultan allowed them to marry; another, to bring their sons into the corps; a third opened the ranks to Turks as well as Christians; until, forfeiting their peculiar character, the janizaries became confounded with the militia of the empire. These changes occurred in the time of Philip the Second; but their consequences were not fully unfolded till the following century.

It was fortunate for the Turks, considering the unlimited power lodged in the hands of their rulers, that these should have so often been possessed of the courage and capacity for using it for the advancement of the nation. From Othman the First, the founder of the dynasty, to Solyman the Magnificent, the contemporary of Philip, the Turkish throne was filled by a succession of able princes, who, bred to war, were every year enlarging the boundaries of the empire and adding to its resources. By the middle of the sixteenth century, besides their vast possessions in Asia, they held the eastern portions of Africa. In Europe, together with the countries at this day acknowledging their scepter, they were masters of Greece; and Solyman, overrunning Transylvania and Hungary, had twice carried his victorious banners up to the walls of Vienna. The battleground of the cross and the crescent was transferred from the west to the east of Europe; and Germany in the sixteenth century became what Spain and the Pyrenees had been in the eighth, the bulwark of Christendom.

Nor was the power of Turkey on the sea less formidable than on the land. Her fleet rode undisputed mistress of the Levant; for Venice, warned by the memorable defeat at Prevesa in 1538, and by the loss of Cyprus and other territories, hardly ventured to renew the contest. That wily republic found that it was safer to trust to diplomacy than to arms, in her dealings with the Ottomans.

The Turkish navy, sweeping over the Mediterranean, combined with the corsairs of the Barbary coast—who, to some extent, owed allegiance to the Porte—and made frequent descents on the coasts of Italy and Spain, committing worse ravages than those of the hurricane. From these ravages France only was exempt; for her princes, with an unscrupulous policy which caused general scandal in Christendom, by an alliance with the Turks, protected her territories somewhat at the expense of her honor.

The northern coast of Africa, at this time, was occupied by various races, who, however they may have differed in other respects, all united in obedience to the Koran. Among them was a large infusion of Moors descended from the Arab tribes who had once occupied the south of Spain, and who, on its reconquest by the Christians, had fled that country rather than renounce the religion of their fathers. Many even of the Moors then living were among the victims of this religious persecution; and they looked with longing eyes on the beautiful land of their inheritance, and with feelings of unquenchable hatred on the Spaniards who had deprived them of it.

The African shore was studded with towns—some of them, like Algiers, Tunis, Tripoli, having a large extent of territory adjacent—which owned the sway of some Moslem chief, who ruled them in sovereign state, or, it might be, acknowledging, for the sake of protection, a qualified allegiance to the Sultan. These rude chiefs, profiting by their maritime position, followed the dreadful trade of the corsair. Issuing from their strongholds, they fell on the unprotected merchantman, or, descending on the opposite coasts of Andalusia and Valencia, sacked the villages and swept off the wretched inhabitants into slavery.

The Castilian government did what it could for the protection of its subjects. Fortified posts were established along the shores. Watchtowers were raised on the heights, to give notice of the approach of an enemy. A fleet of galleys, kept constantly on duty, rode off the coasts to intercept the corsairs. The war was occasionally carried into the enemy's country. Expeditions were fitted out to sweep the Barbary shores or to batter down the strongholds of the pirates. Other states, whose territories bordered on the Mediterranean, joined in these expeditions; among them Tuscany, Rome, Naples, Sicily—the two last the dependencies of Spain—and above all Genoa, whose hardy seamen did good service in these maritime wars. To these should be added the Knights of St. John, whose little island of Malta, with its iron defenses, boldly bidding defiance to the enemy, was thrown into the very jaws, as it were, of the African coast. Pledged by their vows to perpetual war with the infidel, these brave knights, thus stationed on the outposts of Christendom, were the first to sound the alarm of an invasion, as they were foremost to repel it.

The Mediterranean in that day presented a very different spectacle from what it shows at present—swarming, as it does, with the commerce of many a distant land, and its shores glittering with towns and villages that echo to the sounds of peaceful and protected industry. Long tracts of deserted territory might then be seen on its borders, with the blackened ruins of many a hamlet, proclaiming too plainly the recent presence of the corsair. The condition of the peasantry of the south of Spain, in that day, was not unlike that of our New England ancestors, whose rural labors might at any time be broken by the war-whoop of the savage, as he burst on the peaceful settlement, sweeping off its wretched inmates—those whom he did not massacre—to captivity in the wilderness. The trader, instead of pushing out to sea, crept timidly along the shore, under the protecting wings of its fortresses, fearful lest the fierce enemy might dart on him unawares and bear him off to the dungeons of Africa. Or, if he ventured out into the open deep, it was under a convoy of well-armed galleys, or, armed to the teeth himself, prepared for war.

Scarcely a day passed without some conflict between Christian and Moslem on the Mediterranean waters. Not unfrequently, instead of a Moor, the command was intrusted to some Christian renegade, who, having renounced his country and his religion for the roving life of a corsair, felt, like most apostates, a keener hatred than even its natural enemies for the land he had abjured. In these encounters there were often displayed, on both sides, such deeds of heroism as, had they been performed on a wider theater of action, would have covered the actors with immortal glory. By this perpetual warfare a race of hardy and experienced seamen was formed in the countries bordering on the Mediterranean; and more than one name rose to eminence for nautical science as well as valor, with which it would not be easy to find a parallel in other quarters of Christendom. Such were the Dorias of Genoa—a family to whom the ocean seemed their native element, and whose brilliant achievements on its waters, through successive generations, shed an undying luster on the arms of the republic.

The corsair's life was full of maritime adventure. Many a tale of tragic interest was told of his exploits, and many a sad recital of the sufferings of the Christian captive, tugging at the oar, or pining in the dungeons of Tripoli and Algiers. Such tales formed the burden of the popular minstrelsy of the period, as well as of more elegant literature—the drama, and romantic fiction. But fact was stranger than fiction. It would have been difficult to exaggerate the number of the Christian captives, or the amount of their sufferings. On the conquest of Tunis by Charles the Fifth, in 1535, ten thousand of these unhappy persons, as we are assured, walked forth from its dungeons, and knelt, with tears of gratitude and joy, at the feet of their liberator. Charitable associations were formed in Spain for the sole purpose of raising funds to ransom the Barbary prisoners. But the ransom demanded was frequently exorbitant, and the efforts of these benevolent fraternities made but a feeble impression on the whole number of captives.

Thus the war between the cross and the crescent was still carried on along the shores of the Mediterranean, when the day of the Crusades was past in most of the other quarters of Christendom. The existence of the Spaniard—as I have often had occasion to remark—was one long crusade; and in the sixteenth century he was still doing battle with the infidel as stoutly as in the heroic days of the Cid. The furious contests with the petty pirates of Barbary engendered in his bosom feelings of even keener hostility than that which grew up in his contests with the Arabs, where there was no skulking, predatory foe, but army was openly arrayed against army and they fought for the sovereignty of the peninsula. The feeling of religious hatred rekindled by the Moors of Africa extended in some degree to the Morisco population, who still occupied those territories on the southern borders of the monarchy which had belonged to their ancestors, the Spanish Arabs. This feeling was increased by the suspicion, not altogether without foundation, of a secret correspondence between the Moriscoes and their brethren on the Barbary coast. These mingled sentiments of hatred and suspicion sharpened the sword of persecution, and led to most disastrous consequences, which before long will be unfolded to the reader. . . .

BOOK V

FROM CHAPTER V

Don John of Austria

1569

As Don John of Austria is to occupy an important place, not only in the war with the Moriscoes, but in some of the most memorable scenes in the remainder of this history, it will be proper to acquaint the reader with what is known of the earlier part of his career. Yet it is precisely over this part of it that a veil of mystery hangs, which no industry of the historian has been able wholly to remove.

It seems probable that he was born in the year 1547. The twenty-fourth of February is assigned by common consent—I hardly know on what ground—as the day of his birth. It was also, it may be remembered, the birthday of his father, Charles the Fifth. His mother, Barbara Blomberg, was an inhabitant of Ratisbon, in Germany. She is described as a beautiful young girl, who attracted the emperor's notice several years after the death of the Empress Isabella. The Spanish chroniclers claim a noble descent for Barbara. Indeed, it would go hard but a Spaniard could make out a pedigree for his hero. Yet there are several circumstances which suggest the idea that the mother of Don John must have occupied a very humble position.

Subsequently to her connection with Charles she married a German named Kegell, on whom the emperor bestowed the office of commissary. The only other notice, so far as I am aware, which Charles took of his former mistress, was the settlement on her of a yearly pension of two hundred florins, which he made the day before his death. It was certainly not a princely legacy, and infers that the object of it must have been in a humble condition in life to have rendered it important to her comfort. We are led to the same conclusion by the mystery thrown around the birth of the child, forming so strong a contrast to the publicity given to the birth of the emperor's natural daughter, Margaret of Parma, whose mother could boast that in her veins flowed some of the best blood of the Netherlands.

For three years the boy, who received the name of Geronimo, remained under his mother's roof, when, by Charles's order, he was placed in the hands of a Fleming named Maffi, a musician in the imperial band. This man transferred his residence to Leganes, a village in Castile, not far from Madrid. The instrument still exists that contains the agreement by which Maffi, after acknowledging the receipt of a hundred florins, engages for fifty florins annually to bring up the child with as much care as if he were his own. It was a moderate allowance, certainly, for the nature of one who was some day to come before the world as the son of an emperor. It showed that Charles was fond of a bargain—though at the expense of his own offspring.

No instruction was provided for the child except such as he could pick up from the parish priest, who, as he knew as little as Maffi did of the secret of Geronimo's birth, probably bestowed no more attention on him than on the other lads of the village. And we cannot doubt that a boy of his lively temper must have preferred passing his days in the open fields, to confinement in the house and listening to the homilies of his teacher. As he grew in years, he distinguished himself above his young companions by his courage. He took the lead in all their rustic sports, and gave token of his belligerent propensities by making war on the birds in the orchards, on whom he did great execution with his little crossbow.

Four years were passed in this hardy way of life, which, if it did nothing else for the boy, had the advantage of strengthening his constitution for the serious trials of manhood, when the emperor thought it was time to place him in a situation where he would receive a better training than could be found in the cottage of a peasant. He was accordingly transferred to the protection of Luis Quixada, Charles's trusty major-domo, who received the child into his family at Villagarcia, in the neighborhood of Valladolid. The emperor showed his usual discernment in the selection of a guardian for his son. Quixada, with his zeal for the faith, his loyalty, his nice sentiment of honor, was the very type of the Castilian hidalgo in his best form; while he possessed

all those knightly qualities which made him the perfect mirror
of the antique chivalry. His wife, Doña Magdalena de Ulloa,
sister of the marquis of Mota, was a lady yet more illustrious for
her virtues than for her rank. She had naturally the most to do
with the training of the boy's earlier years; and under her discipline it was scarcely possible that one of so generous a nature
should fail to acquire the courtly breeding and refinement of
taste which shed a luster over the stern character of the soldier.

However much Quixada may have reposed on his wife's discretion, he did not think proper to try it, in the present instance,
by communicating to her the secret of Geronimo's birth. He
spoke of him as the son of a great man, his dear friend, expressing his desire that his wife would receive him as her own child.
This was the less difficult, as Magdalena had no children of her
own. The solicitude shown by her lord may possibly have suggested to her the idea that the boy was more nearly related to
him than he chose to acknowledge—in short, that he was the offspring of some intrigue of Quixada previous to his marriage. But
an event which took place not long after the child's introduction
into the family is said to have awakened in her suspicions of an
origin more in accordance with the truth. The house at Villagarcia took fire; and, as it was in the night, the flames gained
such head that they were not discovered till they burst through
the windows. The noise in the street roused the sleeping inmates; and Quixada, thinking first of his charge, sprang from his
bed, and, rushing into Geronimo's apartment, snatched up the
affrighted child and bore him in his arms to a place of safety.
He then re-entered the house, and, forcing his way through the
smoke and flames, succeeded in extricating his wife from her
perilous situation. This sacrifice of love to loyalty is panegyrized
by a Castilian chronicler as "a rare achievement, far transcending any act of heroism of which antiquity could boast." Whether
Magdalena looked with the same complacency on the proceeding we are not informed. Certain it is, however, that the interest
shown by her husband in the child had no power to excite any
feeling of jealousy in her bosom. On the contrary, it seemed
rather to strengthen her own interest in the boy, whose uncommon beauty and affectionate disposition soon called forth all the
tenderness of her nature. She took him to her heart, and treated
him with all the fondness of a mother—a feeling warmly re-

ciprocated by the object of it, who, to the day of his death, regarded her with the truest feelings of filial love and reverence.

In 1558, the year after his retirement to Yuste, Charles the Fifth, whether from a wish to see his son, or, as is quite as probable, in the hope of making Quixada more contented with his situation, desired his major-domo to bring his family to the adjoining village of Cuacos. While there, the young Geronimo must doubtless sometimes have accompanied his mother, as he called Doña Magdalena, in her visits to the monastery. Indeed, his biographer assures us that the sight of him operated like a panacea on the emperor's health. We find no allusion to him, however, in any of the letters from Yuste; and, if he did go there, we may be sure that Charles had sufficient control over himself not to betray, by any indiscreet show of fondness, his relationship to the child. One tradition respecting him lingered to a late period among the people of Cuacos, where the peasants, it is said, pelted him with stones as he was robbing their orchards. It was the first lesson in war of the future hero of Lepanto.

There is no reason to doubt that the boy witnessed the obsequies of the emperor. One who was present tells us that he saw him there, dressed in full mourning, and standing by the side of Quixada, for whose page he passed among the brethren of the convent. We may well believe that a spectacle so solemn and affecting as these funeral ceremonies must have sunk deep into his young mind, and heightened the feelings of veneration with which he always regarded the memory of his father. It was perhaps the appearance of Geronimo as one of the mourners that first suggested the idea of his relationship to the emperor. We find a letter from Quixada to Philip, dated soon after, in which he speaks of rumors on the subject as current in the neighborhood.

Among the testamentary papers of Charles was found one in an envelope sealed with his private seal, and addressed to his son, Philip, or, in case of his death, to his grandson, Carlos, or whoever might be in possession of the crown. It was dated in 1554, before his retirement to Yuste. It acknowledged his connection with a German maiden, and the birth of a son named Geronimo. The mother's name was not given. He pointed out the quarter where information could be got respecting the child, who was then living with the violin-player at Leganes. He expressed the wish that he should be trained up for the ecclesiastical profession, and that, when old enough, he should enter a convent of one of the reformed orders. Charles would not, however, have any constraint put on the inclinations of the boy, and in case of his preferring a secular life he would have a suitable estate settled on him in the kingdom of Naples, with an annual income of between thirty and forty thousand ducats. Whatever course Geronimo might take, the emperor requested that he should receive all the honor and consideration due to him as his son. His letter concluded by saying that, although for obvious reasons he had not inserted these directions in his will, he wished them to be held of the same validity as if he had. Philip seems from the first to have so regarded them, though, as he was then in Flanders, he resolved to postpone the public acknowledgment of his brother till his return to Spain.

Meanwhile, the rumors in regard to Geronimo's birth had reached the ears of the regent, Joanna. With natural curiosity, she ordered her secretary to write to Quixada and ascertain the truth of the report. The trusty hidalgo endeavored to evade the question by saying that some years since a friend of his had intrusted a boy to his care, but, as no allusion whatever was made to the child in the emperor's will, the story of their relationship to each other should be treated as idle gossip. The reply did not satisfy Joanna, who seems to have settled it in her own mind that the story was well founded. She took an occasion soon after to write to Doña Magdalena, during her husband's absence from home, expressing her wish that the lady would bring the boy where she could see him. The place selected was at an auto da fe about to be celebrated in Valladolid. Doña Magdalena, reluctant as she was, felt herself compelled to receive the request from such a source as a command which she had no right to disobey. One might have thought that a ceremony so heart-rending and appalling in its character as an auto da fe would be the last to be selected for the indulgence of any feeling of a light and joyous nature. But the Spaniard of that and of a much later age regarded this as the sweetest sacrifice that could be offered to the Almighty; and he went to it with the same indifference to the sufferings of the victim—probably with the same love of excitement—which he would have felt in going to a bull-fight.

On the day which had been named, Magdalena and her

charge took their seats on the carpeted platform reserved for persons of rank, in full view of the scaffold appropriated to the martyrs who were to suffer for conscience' sake. It was in the midst of the august company here assembled that the son of Charles the Fifth was to receive his first lesson in the school of persecution; that he was to learn to steel his heart against sympathy with human suffering; to learn, above all, that compassion for the heretic was a crime of the deepest dye. It was a terrible lesson for one so young—of an age when the mind is most open to impressions; and the bitter fruits of it were to be discerned ere long in the war with the Moriscoes.

As the royal train approached the place occupied by Doña Magdalena, the regent paused and looked around for the boy. Magdalena had thrown her mantle about him, to conceal him as much as possible from the public eye. She now drew it aside; and Joanna looked so long and earnestly on the child that he shrank abashed from her gaze. It was not, however, before she had recognized in his bright blue eyes, his ample forehead, and the rich yellow locks that clustered round his head, some of the peculiarities of the Austrian line, though happily without the deformity of the protruding lip, which was no less its characteristic. Her heart yearned with the tenderness of a sister, as she felt convinced that the same blood flowed in his veins as in her own; and, stooping down, she threw her arms around his neck, and, kissing him, called him by the endearing name of brother. She would have persuaded him to go with her and sit by her side. But the boy, clinging closely to his foster-mother, refused to leave her for the stranger lady.

This curious scene attracted the attention of the surrounding spectators, which was hardly diverted from the child by the appearance of the prisoners on the scaffold to receive their sentences. When these had been pronounced, and the wretched victims led away to execution, the multitude pressed so eagerly round Magdalena and the boy that it was with difficulty the guards could keep them back, till the regent, seeing the awkwardness of their situation, sent one of her train, the count of Osorno, to their relief; and that nobleman, forcing his way through the crowd, carried off Geronimo in his arms to the royal carriage.

It was not long before all mystery was dispelled by the public acknowledgment of the child as the son of the emperor. One of the first acts of Philip after his return to Spain, in 1559, was to arrange an interview with his brother. The place assigned for the meeting was an extensive park, not far from Valladolid, in the neighborhood of the convent of La Espina, a spot much resorted to by the Castilian princes of the older time for the pleasures of the chase.

On the appointed day, Quixada, richly dressed, and mounted on the best horse in his stables, rode forth, at the head of his vassals, to meet the king, with the little Geronimo, simply attired and on a common palfrey, by his side. They had gone but a few miles when they heard through the woods the sound of horses' hoofs, announcing the approach of the royal cavalcade. Quixada halted, and, alighting, drew near to Geronimo, with much deference in his manner, and, dropping on one knee, begged permission to kiss his hand. At the same time he desired his ward to dismount, and take the charger which he had himself been riding. Geronimo was sorely bewildered by what he would have thought a merry jest on the part of his guardian, had not his sedate and dignified character forbidden the supposition. Recovering from his astonishment, he complied with his guardian's directions; and the vision of future greatness must have flashed on his mind, if, as we are told, when preparing to mount, he turned round to Quixada, and with an affected air of dignity told him that, "since things were so, he might hold the stirrup for him."

They had not proceeded far when they came in sight of the royal party. Quixada pointed out the king to his ward, adding that his majesty had something of importance to communicate to him. They then dismounted; and the boy, by his guardian's instructions, drawing near to Philip, knelt down and begged leave to kiss his majesty's hand. The king, graciously extending it, looked intently on the youth, and at length broke silence by asking "if he knew who was his father." Geronimo, disconcerted by the abruptness of the question, and indeed, if the reports of his origin had ever reached his ears, ignorant of their truth, cast his eyes on the ground and made no answer. Philip, not displeased with his embarrassment, was well satisfied, doubtless, to read in his intelligent countenance and noble mien an assurance that he would do no discredit to his birth. Alighting from his horse, he embraced Geronimo, exclaiming, "Take courage, my child; you are descended from a great man. The Emperor Charles the Fifth, now in glory, is your father as well as mine." Then, turning to the lords who stood around, he presented the boy to them as the son of their late sovereign, and his own brother. The courtiers, with the ready instinct of their tribe, ever prompt to worship the rising sun, pressed eagerly forward to pay their obeisance to Geronimo. The scene was concluded by the king's buckling a sword on his brother's side and throwing around his neck the sparkling collar of the Golden Fleece.

The tidings of this strange event soon spread over the neighborhood, for there were many more witnesses of the ceremony than those who took part in it; and the king and his retinue found, on their return, a multitude of people gathering along the route, eager to get a glimpse of this newly discovered gem of royalty. The sight of the handsome youth called forth a burst of noisy enthusiasm from the populace, and the air rang with their tumultuous vivas as the royal party rode through the streets of the ancient city of Valladolid. Philip expressed his satisfaction at the events of the day, by declaring that "he had never met better sport in his life, or brought back game so much to his mind."

Having thus publicly acknowledged his brother, the king determined to provide for him an establishment suited to his condition. He assigned him for his residence one of the best mansions in Madrid. He was furnished with a numerous band of retainers, and as great state was maintained in his household as in that of a prince of the blood. The count of Priego acted as his chief major-domo; Don Luis Carrillo, the eldest son of that noble, was made captain of the guard; and Don Luis de Cordova master of the horse. In short, nobles and cavaliers of the best blood in Castile did not disdain to hold offices in the service of the peasant boy. With one or two exceptions, of little importance, he enjoyed all the privileges that belonged to the royal infantes. He did not, like them, have apartments in the palace; and he was to be addressed by the title of "Excellency," instead of "Highness," which was their peculiar prerogative. The distinction was not always scrupulously observed.

A more important change took place in his name, which from

Geronimo was now converted into John of Austria—a lofty name, which intimated his descent from the imperial house of Hapsburg, and on which his deeds in after-life shed a luster greater than the proudest title that sovereignty could confer.

Luis Quixada kept the same place after his pupil's elevation as before. He continued to be his ayo, or governor, and removed with Doña Magdalena to Madrid, where he took up his residence in the house of Don John. Thus living in the most intimate personal relations with him, Quixada maintained his influence unimpaired till the hour of his own death.

Philip fully appreciated the worth of the faithful hidalgo, who was fortunate in thus enjoying the favor of the son in as great a degree as he had done that of the father—and, as it would seem, with a larger recompense for his services. He was master of the horse to Don Carlos, the heir to the crown; he held the important post of president of the Council of the Indies; and he possessed several lucrative benefices in the military order of Calatrava. In one of his letters to the king, we find Quixada remarking that he had endeavored to supply the deficiencies of his pupil's early education by training him in a manner better suited to his destinies in after-life. We cannot doubt that in the good knight's estimate of what was essential to such a training the exercises of chivalry must have found more favor than the monastic discipline recommended by the emperor. However this may have been, Philip resolved to give his brother the best advantages for a liberal education by sending him to the University of Alcala, which, founded by the great Ximenes a little more than a century before, now shared with the older school of Salamanca the glory of being the most famous seat of science in the peninsula. Don John had for his companions his two nephews, Don Carlos, and Alexander Farnese, the son of Margaret of Parma. They formed a triumvirate each member of which was to fill a large space in the pages of history—Don Carlos from his errors and misfortunes, and the two others from their military achievements. They were all of nearly the same age. Don John, according to a writer of the time, stood foremost among the three for the comeliness, or rather beauty, of his person, no less than for the charm of his manners; while his soul was filled with those nobler qualities which gave promise of the highest excellence.

His biographers tell us that Don John gave due attention to his studies; but the studies which found most favor in his eyes were those connected with the art of war. He was perfect in all chivalrous accomplishments; and he sighed for some field on which he could display them. The knowledge of his real parentage fired his soul with a generous ambition, and he longed by some heroic achievement to vindicate his claim to his illustrious descent.

At the end of three years, in 1564, he left the university. The following year was that of the famous siege of Malta; and all Christendom hung in suspense on the issue of the desperate conflict which a handful of warriors, on their lonely isle, were waging against the whole strength of the Ottoman empire. The sympathies of Don John were roused in behalf of the Christian knights; and he resolved to cast his own fortunes into the scale with theirs, and win his maiden laurels under the banner of the cross. He did not ask the permission of his brother. That, he knew, would be refused to him. He withdrew secretly from the court, and with only a few attendants took his way to Barcelona, whence an armament was speedily to sail to carry succor to the besieged. Everywhere on the route he was received with the respect due to his rank. At Saragossa he was lodged with the archbishop, under whose roof he was detained by illness. While there he received a letter from the king, who had learned the cause of his departure, commanding him to return, as he was altogether too young to take part in this desperate strife. Don John gave little heed to the royal orders. He pushed on to Barcelona, where he had the mortification to find that the fleet had sailed. He resolved to cross the mountains and take ship at Marseilles. The viceroy of Catalonia could not dissuade the hotheaded youth from his purpose, when another despatch came from court, in which Philip, in a more peremptory tone than before, repeated his orders for his brother to return, under pain of his severe displeasure. A letter from Quixada had warned him of the certain disgrace which awaited him if he continued to trifle with the royal commands. Nothing remained but to obey; and Don John, disappointed in his scheme of ambition, returned to the capital.

This adventure caused a great sensation throughout the country. The young nobles and cavaliers about the court, fired by

Don John's example, which seemed like a rebuke on their own sluggishness, had hastened to buckle on their armor and follow him to the war. The common people, peculiarly sensible in Spain to deeds of romantic daring, were delighted with the adventurous spirit of the young prince, which gave promise that he was one day to take his place among the heroes of the nation. This was the beginning of the popularity of John of Austria with his countrymen, who in time came to regard him with feelings little short of idolatry. Even Philip, however necessary he may have thought it to rebuke the insubordination of his brother, must in his heart have been pleased with the generous spirit he had exhibited. At least, the favor with which he continued to regard the offender showed that the royal displeasure was of no long continuance.

The sudden change in the condition of Don John might remind one of some fairy-tale, where the poor peasant boy finds himself all at once converted by enchantment into a great prince. A wiser man than he might well have had his head turned by such a rapid revolution of the wheel of fortune; and Philip may naturally have feared that the idle dalliance of a court, to which his brother was now exposed, might corrupt his simple nature and seduce him from the honorable path of duty. Great, therefore, must have been his satisfaction when he saw that, far from this, the elevation of the youth had only served to give a wider expansion to his views and to fill his bosom with still higher and nobler aspirations.

The discreet conduct of Don John in regard to his nephew, Don Carlos, when the latter would have engaged him in his wild and impracticable schemes, established him still more firmly in the royal favor.

In the spring of the year 1568 an opportunity occurred for Philip to gratify his brother's ambition, by intrusting him with the command of a fleet then fitting out, in the port of Carthagena, against the Barbary corsairs, who had been making alarming depredations of late on the Spanish commerce. But, while giving him this appointment, the king was careful to supply the lack of experience in his brother by naming as second in command an officer in whose abilities he perfectly confided. This was Antonio de Zuñiga y Requesens, grand commander of St. James, an eminent personage, who will come frequently before the reader in the progress of the narrative. Requesens, who at this time filled the post of ambassador at Rome, was possessed of the versatility of talent so important in an age when the same individual was often required to exchange the duties of the cabinet for those of the camp. While Don John appeared before the public as the captain of the fleet, the actual responsibility for the conduct of the expedition rested on his lieutenant.

On the third of June, Don John sailed out of port, at the head of as brave an armament as ever floated on the waters of the Mediterranean. The prince's own vessel was a stately galley, gorgeously fitted up, and decorated with a profusion of paintings, the subjects of which, drawn chiefly from ancient history and mythology, were of didactic import, intended to convey some useful lesson to the young commander. The moral of each picture was expressed by some pithy maxim inscribed beneath it in Latin. Thus, to whatever quarter Don John turned his eyes, they were sure to fall on some homily for his instruction; so that his galley might be compared to a volume richly filled with illustrations, that serve to impress the contents on the reader's memory.

The cruise was perfectly successful; and Don John, on his return to port, some eight months later, might boast that, in more than one engagement, he had humbled the pride of the corsairs, and so far crippled them that it would be long before they could resume their depredations; that, in fine, he had vindicated the honor of his country's flag throughout the Mediterranean.

His return to Madrid was welcomed with the honors of a triumph. Courtier and commoner, men of all classes, in short, vied with each other in offering up the sweet incense of adulation, filling his young mind with lofty visions of the future, that beckoned him forward in the path of glory.

When the insurrection of the Moriscoes broke out, in 1568, the eyes of men naturally turned on Don John of Austria, as the person who would most likely be sent to suppress it. But Philip thought it would be safer to trust the command to those who, from their long residence in the neighborhood, were better acquainted with the character of the country and of its inhabitants. When, however, the dissensions of the rival chiefs made it necessary to send someone invested with such powers as might enable him to overawe this factious spirit and enforce greater concert of action, the council of state recommended Don John to the command. Their recommendation was approved by the king, if indeed it was not originally made at his suggestion.

Still, the "prudent" monarch was careful not to invest his brother with that independent command which the public supposed him to possess. On the contrary, his authority was restricted within limits almost as narrow as those which had curbed it in the Mediterranean. A council of war was appointed, by whose opinions Don John was to be guided in every question of moment. In case of a division of opinion, the question was to be referred to the decision of Philip.

The chief members of this body, in whom the supreme power was virtually lodged, were the marquis of Mondejar, who from this time does not appear to have taken the field in person; the duke of Sesa, grandson of the Great Captain, Gonsalvo de Cordova, and endowed with no small portion of the military talent of his ancestor; the archbishop of Granada, a prelate possessed of as large a measure of bigotry as ever fell to the lot of a Spanish ecclesiastic; Deza, president of the audience, who hated the Moriscoes with the fierce hatred of an inquisitor; and, finally, Don John's faithful ayo, Quixada, who had more influence over him than was enjoyed by any other, and who had come to witness the first of his pupil's campaigns, destined, alas! to be the closing one of his own.

There could hardly have been a more unfortunate device than the contrivance of so cumbrous a machinery as this council, opposed as it was, from its very nature, to the despatch so indispensable to the success of military operations. The mischief was increased by the necessity of referring every disputed point to the decision of the king. As this was a contingency that often occurred, the young prince soon found almost as many embarrassments thrown in his way by his friends as by his foes—embarrassments which nothing but an uncommon spirit of determination on his own part could have overcome.

On the sixth of April, 1569, Don John took leave of the king, then at Aranjuez, and hastened towards the south. His coming was eagerly expected by the inhabitants of Granada: by the Christians, from their hopes that it would remedy the disorders in the army and bring the war to a speedy conclusion; by the

Moriscoes, from the protection they anticipated he would afford them against the violence of the Spaniards. Preparations were made in the capital for giving him a splendid reception. The program of the ceremonies was furnished by Philip himself. At some miles from the city, Don John was met by the count of Tendilla, at the head of a small detachment of infantry, wearing uniforms partly of the Castilian fashion, partly of the Morisco— presenting altogether a strange and picturesque spectacle, in which silks, velvets, and rich embroidery floated gaily amidst the iron mail and burnished weapons of the warrior. As the prince proceeded along his route, he was met by a long train of ecclesiastical and civic functionaries, followed by the principal cavaliers and citizens of Granada. At their head were the arch- bishop and the president, the latter of whom was careful to assert his rank by walking on the right of the prelate. Don John showed them both the greatest deference; and, as they drew near, he dismounted from his horse, and, embracing the two church- men, stood with hat in hand, for some moments, while con- versing with them. As their train came up, the president pre- sented the most eminent persons to the prince, who received them with that frank and graceful courtesy which won the hearts of all who approached him. He then resumed his route, escorted on either side by the president and the archbishop. The neigh- boring fields were covered with spectators, and on the plains of Beyro he found a large body of troops, not less than ten thou- sand, drawn up to receive him. As he approached, they greeted him with salvoes of musketry, delivered with admirable preci- sion. As Don John glanced over their beautiful array and beheld their perfect discipline and appointments, his eyes brightened and his cheek flushed with a soldier's pride.

Hardly had he entered the gates of Granada when he was sur- rounded by a throng of women, who gathered about him in an attitude of supplication. They were the widows, the mothers, and the daughters of those who had so miserably perished in the massacres of the Alpujarras. They were clad in mourning, some of them so scantily as too plainly to reveal their poverty. Falling on their knees, with tears streaming from their eyes, and their words rendered almost inarticulate by their sobs, they demanded justice—justice on the murderers of their kindred. They had seen their friends fall, they said, beneath the blows of their executioners; but the pain with which their hearts were then rent was not so great as what they now felt on learning that the cruel acts of these miscreants were to go unpunished. Don John endeavored to calm their agitation by expressions of the deepest sympathy for their misfortunes—expressions of which none who saw his countenance could doubt the truth; and he promised that he would do all in his power to secure them justice.

A livelier scene awaited him as the procession held its way along the streets of the ancient capital. Everywhere the houses were gaily decorated with tapestries of cloth of gold. The multitude who thronged the avenues filled the air with their loyal acclamations. Bright eyes glanced from balconies and windows, where the noblest matrons and maidens of Granada, in rich attire, were gathered to look upon the splendid pageant and the young hero who was the object of it. In this state he moved along until he reached the palace of the royal audience, where, by the king's command, apartments had been sumptuously fitted up for his accommodation.

The following day, a deputation waited on Don John from the principal Moriscoes of the city, claiming his protection against the injuries and insults to which they were exposed whenever they went abroad. They complained especially of the Spanish troops quartered on them, and of the manner in which they violated the sanctity of their dwellings by the foulest outrages. Don John replied in a tone that expressed little of the commiseration which he had shown to the female petitioners on the preceding day. He told the Moriscoes that he had been sent to restore order to Granada, and that those who had proved loyal would find themselves protected in all their rights. Those, on the contrary, who had taken part in the late rebellion would be chastised with unsparing rigor. He directed them to state their grievances in a memorial, with a caution to set down nothing which they could not prove, or it would go hard with them. The unfortunate Moriscoes found that they were to expect such justice only as comes from the hand of an enemy.

The first session of the council showed how defective was the system for conducting the war. In the discussions that ensued, Mondejar remarked that the contest, in his opinion, was virtually at an end; that the Moriscoes, for the most part, were in so favorable a mood that he would undertake, if the affair were placed in his hands, to bring them all to submission in a very short time. This proposal was treated with contempt by the haughty president, who denounced them as a false-hearted race, on whose promises no one could rely. The war, he said, would never be ended so long as the Moriscoes of the capital were allowed to communicate with their countrymen in the mountains and to furnish them with secret intelligence respecting what was passing in the Christian camp. The first step was to remove them all from Granada into the interior; the second, to make such an example of the miscreants who had perpetrated the massacres in the Alpujarras as should strike terror into the hearts of the infidels and deter them from any further resistance to authority. In this division of opinion the members took different sides according to the difference of their tempers. The commander-in-chief and Quixada both leaned to Mondejar's opinion. After a protracted discussion, it became necessary to refer the question to the king, who was by no means distinguished for the promptness with which he came to his conclusions. All this required much time, during which active operations could not be resumed.

Yet Don John did not pass it idly. He examined the state of the works in Granada and its neighborhood; he endeavored to improve the condition of the army, and to quell the spirit of insubordination which had risen in some portions of it; finally, he sent his commands for enforcing levies, not merely in Andalusia and the adjoining provinces, but in Castile. The appeal was successful; and the great lords in the south, more particularly, gathering their retainers, hastened to Granada, to draw their swords under this popular chieftain.

Meanwhile, the delay was attended with most mischievous consequences, as it gave the enemy time to recover from the disasters of the previous campaign. Aben-Humeya had returned . . . to his mountain-throne, where he soon found himself in greater strength than before. Even the "Moriscoes of the peace," as they were called, who had resumed their allegiance to the crown, exasperated by the outrages of the Spanish soldiery and the contempt which they showed for the safe-conduct of the marquis of Mondejar, now came in great numbers to Aben-Humeya's camp, offering their services and promising to stand by him to the last. Other levies he drew from Africa. The

Moslem princes to whom he had applied for succor, though
refusing to embark openly in his cause, as he had desired, allowed such of their subjects as chose to join his standard. In
consequence, a considerable body of Barbary Moors crossed the
sea and entered into the service of the Morisco chief. They were
a fierce, intrepid race, accustomed to a life of wild adventure,
and possessing a better acquaintance with military tactics than
belonged to the Spanish mountaineers.

While strengthened by these recruits, Aben-Humeya drew a
much larger revenue than formerly from his more extended
domains. Though showy and expensive in his tastes, he did not
waste it all on the maintenance of the greater state which he now
assumed in his way of living. He employed it freely in the pay
of foreign levies, and in procuring arms and munitions for his
own troops; and he profited by his experience in the last campaign, and by the example of his African mercenaries, to introduce a better system of tactics among his Morisco warriors. The
policy he adopted, as before, was to avoid pitched battles, and to
confine himself chiefly to the guerrilla warfare better suited to
the genius of the mountaineer. He fell on small detachments of
Spaniards who were patrolling the country, cut off the convoys,
and thus greatly straitened the garrisons in their supplies. He
made forays into the Christian territories, penetrating even into
the vega, and boldly carried the war up to the walls of Granada.

His ravages in this quarter, it is true, did not continue long
after the arrival of Don John, who took effectual measures for
protecting the capital from insult. But the prince was greatly
chagrined by seeing the rapid extension of the Morisco domain.
Yet he could take no decisive measures to check it until the
council had determined on some plan of operations. He was
moreover fettered by the king's orders not to take the field in
person, but to remain and represent him in Granada, where he
would find enough to do in regulating the affairs and providing
for the safety of the city. Philip seems to have feared that Don
John's adventurous spirit would lead him to some rash act,
that might unnecessarily expose him to danger. He appears,
indeed, as we may gather from numerous passages in his letters,
to have been more concerned for the safety of his brother than
for the success of the campaign. He may have thought, too, that
it was better to trust the war to the hands of the veteran chief,

the marquis of Los Velez, who could boast so much larger experience than Don John, and who had possessed the king with a high idea of his military talents.

This nobleman still held the command of the country east of the Alpujarras, in which lay his own large property. He had, as we have seen, a hard and arrogant nature, which could ill brook the paramount authority of the young commander-in-chief, to whom he rarely condescended to write, preferring to make his communications directly to the king. Philip, prompted by his appetite for power, winked at this irregular proceeding, which enabled him to take a more direct part in the management of affairs than he could otherwise have done. It was a most injudicious step, and was followed, as we shall see, by disastrous consequences.

The marquis, without waiting for orders, resolved to open the campaign by penetrating into the Alpujarras with the small force he had under his command. But a body of some four hundred troops, which he had caused to occupy the pass of Ravaha, was cut off by the enemy; and the haughty chieftain reluctantly obeyed the orders of Don John to abandon his design. Aben-Humeya's success encouraged him to attack the marquis in his new quarters at Verja. It was a well-concerted enterprise, but unfortunately, before the time arrived for its execution, it was betrayed by a prisoner to the Spanish commander. It consequently failed. Aben-Humeya penetrated into the heart of the town, where he found himself in the midst of an ambuscade, and with difficulty, after a heavy loss, effected his retreat. But if the victory remained with the Spaniards, the fruits of it fell to the Moriscoes. The spirit shown by the Moslem prince gave new life to his countrymen, and more than counterbalanced the effects of his defeat. The rich and populous country of the Rio de Almanzora rose in arms. The marquis of Los Velez found it expedient to abandon his present position, and to transfer his quarters to Adra, a seaport on the Mediterranean, which would afford him greater facilities for receiving reinforcements and supplies.

The spirit of insurrection now spread rapidly over other parts of the Alpujarras, and especially along the sierra of Bentomiz, which stretches from the neighborhood of Alhama towards the south. Here the mountaineers, who had hitherto taken no part in the troubles of the country, ranging themselves under the crimson banner of Aben-Humeya, broke forth into open rebellion. The inhabitants of Velez and of the more important city of Malaga were filled with consternation, trembling lest the enemy should descend on them from the mountains and deluge their streets with blood. They hastily mustered the militia of the country, and made preparations for their defense.

Fortunately, at this conjuncture, they were gladdened by the sight of the Grand Commander Requesens, who sailed into the harbor of Velez Malaga with a squadron from Italy, having on board several battalions of Spanish veterans who had been ordered home by the government to reinforce the army of the Alpujarras. There were no better troops in the service, seasoned as they were by many a hard campaign, and all under the most perfect discipline. The first step of Requesens—the same officer, it will be remembered, who had acted as the lieutenant of Don John of Austria in his cruise in the Mediterranean—was to request of his young general the command of the expedition against the rebels of Bentomiz. These were now gathered in great force on the lofty tableland of Fraxiliana, where they had strengthened the natural defenses of the ground by such works as rendered the approach to it nearly impracticable. The request was readily granted; and the grand commander of St. James, without loss of time, led his battalions into the heart of the sierra.

We have not space for the details. It is enough to say that the expedition was one of the best-conducted in the war. The enemy made a desperate resistance; and, had it not been for the timely arrival of the bold burghers of Malaga, the grand commander would have been driven from the field. The Morisco women fought by the side of their husbands; and, when all was lost, many threw themselves headlong from the precipices rather than fall into the hands of the Spaniards. Two thousand of the enemy were slain; and three thousand captives, with an immense booty of gold, silver, jewels, and precious stuffs, became the spoil of the victors. The spirit of rebellion was effectually crushed in the sierra of Bentomiz.

Yet it was not a bloodless victory. Full six hundred of the Christians fell on the field of battle. The loss bore most heavily on the troops from Italy. Nearly every captain in this valiant corps was wounded. The bloody roll displayed, moreover, the name of more than one cavalier as distinguished for his birth as for his bravery. Two thousand Moriscoes succeeded in making their escape to the camp of Aben-Humeya. They proved a seasonable reinforcement; for that chief was meditating an assault on Seron.

This was a strongly fortified place, perched like an eagle's eyrie on the summit of a bold cliff that looked down on the Rio de Almanzora and commanded its formidable passes. It was consequently a most important post, and at this time was held by a Spanish garrison under an officer named Mirones. Aben-Humeya sent a strong detachment against it, intending to carry it by storm. But the Moriscoes had no battering-train, and, as it soon appeared, were little skilled in the art of conducting a siege. It was resolved, therefore, to abandon the present plan of operations, and to reduce the place by the slower but surer way of blockade. Five thousand men, accordingly, sat down before the town on the eighteenth of June, and effectually cut off all communication from abroad.

The garrison succeeded in conveying intelligence of their condition to Don John, who lost no time in ordering Alonso de Carbajal to march with a body of troops and a good supply of provisions to their relief. But just after his departure Don John received information that the king had intrusted the marquis of Los Velez with the defense of Seron. He therefore, by Quixada's advice, countermanded his orders to Carbajal, and directed him to return. That officer, who had approached within a short distance of the place, reluctantly obeyed, and left Seron to its fate. The marquis of Los Velez, notwithstanding the jealousy he displayed of the interference of Don John in the affair, showed so little alacrity in providing for the safety of the beleaguered fortress that the garrison, reduced to extremity, on the eleventh of July surrendered on honorable terms. But no sooner had they given up the place than the victors, regardless of the terms of capitulation, murdered in cold blood every male over twelve years of age, and made slaves of the women and children. This foul act was said to have been perpetrated by the secret command of Aben-Humeya. The Morisco chief might allege, in vindication of his perfidy, that he had but followed the lesson set him by the Spaniards.

The loss of Seron caused deep regret to the army. Nor could this regret be mitigated by the reflection that its loss was to be attributed not so much to the valor of the Moslems as to the misconduct of their own commanders, or rather to the miserable system adopted for carrying on the war. The triumph of the Moriscoes, however, was greatly damped by the intelligence which they had received, shortly before the surrender of Seron, of disasters that had befallen their countrymen in Granada.

Philip, after much hesitation, had given his sanction to Deza's project for the removal of the Moriscoes from the capital into the interior of the country. The day appointed for carrying the measure into effect was the twenty-third of June. A large body of troops, with the principal commanders, was secretly assembled in the capital, to enforce the execution of the plan. Meanwhile, rumors were current that the Moriscoes in the city were carrying on a secret communication with their countrymen in the Alpujarras; that they supplied the mountaineers with arms and money; that the young men were leaving Granada to join their ranks; finally, that a conspiracy had been planned for an assault on the city, and even that the names of the leaders were given. It is impossible, at this time, to say what foundation there was for these charges; but the reader may recollect that similar ones had been circulated previous to the barbarous massacre in the prison of the chancery.

On the twenty-third of the month, on the eve of St. John's, an edict was published, commanding all the Morisco males in Granada between ten and sixty years of age to repair to the parish churches to which they respectively belonged, where they were to learn their fate. The women were to remain some time longer in the city, to dispose of the most valuable effects, such as could not easily be transported. This was not difficult, at the low prices for which, in their extremity, they were obliged to part with their property. We are left in ignorance of the fate of the children, who, no doubt, remained in the hands of the government, to be nurtured in the Roman Catholic faith.

Nothing could exceed the consternation of the Moriscoes on the publication of this decree, for which, though so long suspended by a thread, as it were, over their heads, they were wholly unprepared. It is not strange, as they recalled the atrocious murders perpetrated in the prison of the chancery, that they should have been led to believe that nothing less than a massacre of the whole Moorish population was now designed. It was in vain that the marquis of Mondejar endeavored to allay their fears. They were somewhat comforted by the assurance of the President Deza, given under his own hand, that their lives were in no danger. But their apprehensions on this point were not wholly quieted till Don John had pledged his royal word that no harm should come to their persons—that, in short, the great object of the government was to secure their safety. They then submitted without any attempt at resistance. Resistance, indeed, would have been hardly possible, destitute as they were of weapons or other means of defense, and surrounded on all quarters by the well-armed soldiery of Castile. They accordingly entered the churches assigned to them, at the doors of which strong guards were stationed during the night.

On the following morning the Moriscoes were marched out and formed into a procession, which was to take its way to the great hospital in the suburbs. This was a noble building, erected by the good Queen Isabella the Catholic, not long after the conquest. Here they were to stay till the arrangements were completed for forming them into divisions according to their several places of destination. It was a sad and solemn spectacle, that of this company of exiles, as they moved with slow and uncertain step, bound together by cords, and escorted, or rather driven along like a gang of convicts, by the fierce soldiery. There they were, the old and the young, the rich and the poor, now, alas! brought to the same level, the forms of most of them bowed down, less by the weight of years than of sorrow, their hands meekly folded on their breasts, their cheeks wet with tears, as they gazed for the last time on their beautiful city, the sweet home of their infancy, the proud seat of ancient empire, endeared to them by so many tender and glorious recollections.

The march was conducted in an orderly manner, with but a single interruption, which, however, was near being attended by the most disastrous consequences. A Spanish alguacil, offended at some words that fell from one of the prisoners—for so they might be called—requited them with a blow from his staff. But the youth whom he struck had the fiery blood of the Arab in his veins. Snatching up a broken tile, he dealt such a blow on the offender's head as nearly severed his ear from it. The act cost

him his life. He was speedily cut down by the Spaniards, who
rushed to the assistance of their wounded comrade. A rumor
now went round that the Moriscoes had attempted the life of
Don John, whose dress resembled in its color that of the alguacil.
The passions of the soldiery were roused. They flocked to the
scene of violence, uttering the most dreadful imprecations. Their
swords and lances glittered in the air, and in a few moments
would have been sheathed in the bodies of their terrified victims.

Fortunately, the quick eye of Don John discerned the confusion. Surrounded by a bodyguard of arquebusiers, he was there
in person to superintend the removal of the Moriscoes. Spurring
his horse forward into the midst of the tumult, and showing
himself to the troops, he exclaimed that no one had offered him
any harm. He called on them to return to their duty, and not to
dishonor him, as well as themselves, by offering violence to innocent men, for whose protection he had so solemnly pledged his
word. The soldiers, abashed by the rebuke of their young chief,
and satisfied with the vengeance they had taken on the offender,
fell back into their ranks. The trembling Moriscoes gradually recovered from their panic, the procession resumed its march, and
without further interruption reached the hospital of Isabella.

There the royal contadores were not long in ascertaining the
number of the exiles. It amounted to thirty-five hundred. That
of the women, who were soon to follow, was much greater. The
names, the ages, and the occupations of the men were all carefully registered. The following day they were marched into the
great square before the hospital, where they were distributed
into companies, each under a strong escort, to be conducted to
their various places of destination. These, far from being confined to Andalusia, reached into New Castile. In this arrangement we may trust that so much respect was paid to the dictates
of humanity as not to separate those of the same kindred from
one another. But the chroniclers give no information on the
subject—probably regarding details of this sort in regard to the
fallen race as below the dignity of history.

It was on the twenty-fifth of June, 1569, that, bidding a sad
farewell to the friends and companions of their youth, from
whom they were now to be forever parted, they set forth on
their doleful pilgrimage. The morning light had broken on the
red towers of the Alhambra, as the bands of exiles, issuing from

the gates of their beloved capital, the spot dearest to them upon earth, turned their faces towards their new homes—homes which many of them were destined never to behold. The government, with shameful indifference, had neglected to provide for the poor wanderers the most common necessaries of life. Some actually perished of hunger by the way. Others, especially those accustomed from infancy to a delicate nurture, sank down and died of fatigue. Some were seized by the soldiers, whose cupidity was roused by the sight of their helplessness, and were sold as slaves. Others were murdered by their guards in cold blood. Thus reduced far below their original number, they reached their appointed places, there to linger out the remainder of their days in the midst of a population who held them in that abhorrence with which a good Catholic of the sixteenth century regarded "the enemies of God."

But the evils which grew out of this stern policy of the government were not wholly confined to the Moriscoes. This ingenious people were so far superior to the Spaniards in the knowledge of husbandry and in the various mechanic arts that they formed the most important part of the population of Granada. The only art in which their rivals excelled them was that which thrives at the expense of every other—the art of war. Aware of this, the government had excepted some of the best artisans in the capital from the doom of exile which had fallen on their countrymen, and they had accordingly remained in the city. But their number was too small to produce the result desired; and it was not long before the quarter of the town which had been occupied by the Moriscoes exhibited a scene of woeful desolation. The light and airy edifices, which displayed in their forms the fantastic graces of Arabian architecture, fell speedily into decay. The parterres and pleasure-grounds, filled with exotics and glowing in all the exuberance of southern vegetation, became a wilderness of weeds; and the courtyards and public squares, where tanks and sparkling fountains, fed by the streams of the Sierra Nevada, shed a refreshing coolness over the atmosphere in the sultriest months of summer, were soon converted into a melancholy heap of rubbish.

The mischiefs growing out of the removal of the Moriscoes fell sorely on the army. The men had been quartered, as we have seen, in the houses of the Moriscoes. From the present occupants, for the most part needy and thriftless speculators, they met with very different fare from what they had enjoyed under the former wealthy and luxurious proprietors. The troops supplied the deficiency, as far as they could, by plundering the citizens. Hence incessant feuds arose between the people and the army, and a spirit of insubordination rapidly grew up in the latter, which made it more formidable to its friends than to its foes.

An eye-witness of these troubles closes his narrative of the removal of the Moriscoes by remarking that it was a sad spectacle to one who reflected on the former policy and prosperity of this ill-starred race; who had seen their sumptuous mansions in the day of their glory, their gardens and pleasure-grounds, the scene of many a gay revel and jocund holiday, and who now contrasted all this with the ruin into which everything had fallen. "It seems," he concludes, "as if Providence had intended to show, by the fate of this beautiful city, that the fairest things in this world are the most subject to decay." To the philosopher of the present age it may seem rather the natural result of that system of religious intolerance which had converted into enemies those who, under a beneficent rule, would have been true and loyal subjects, and who by their industry and skill would have added incalculably to the resources of the country.

FROM CHAPTER VI

Rebellion of the Moriscoes

1569

The war now took the same romantic aspect that it wore in the days of the conquest of Granada. Beacon fires were to be seen along the highest peaks of the sierra, throwing their ominous glare around for many a league, and calling the bold mountaineers to the foray. Then came the gathering of the wild militia of the country, which, pouring down on the lower levels, now in the faded green of autumn, swept away herds and flocks and bore them off in triumph to their fastnesses.

Sometimes marauders penetrated into the vega, the beautiful vega, every inch of whose soil was fertilized with human blood, and which now, as in ancient times, became the battle-ground of Christian and Moslem cavaliers. Almost always it was the former who had the advantage, as was intimated by the gory trophies, the heads and hands of the vanquished, which they bore on the points of their lances, when, amidst the shouts of the populace, they came thundering on through the gates of the capital.

Yet sometimes fortune lay in the opposite scale. The bold infidels, after scouring the vega, would burst into the suburbs, or even into the city, of Granada, filling the place with consternation. Then might be seen the terror-stricken citizens hurrying to and fro, while the great alarm-bell of the Alhambra sent forth its summons, and the chivalry, mounting in haste, shouted the old war-cry of "Saint Iago" and threw themselves on the invaders, who, after a short but bloody fray, were sure to be driven in confusion across the vega and far over the borders.

Don John on these occasions was always to be descried in the front of battle, as if rejoicing in his element and courting danger like some paladin of romance. Indeed, Philip was obliged again and again to rebuke his brother for thus wantonly exposing his life in a manner, the king intimated, wholly unbecoming his rank. But it would have been as easy to rein in the war-horse when the trumpet was sounding in his ears as to curb the spirits of the high-mettled young chieftain when his followers were mustering to the charge. In truth, it was precisely these occasions that filled him with the greatest glee; for they opened to him the only glimpses he was allowed of that career of glory for which his soul had so long panted. Every detachment that sallied forth from Granada on a warlike adventure was an object of his envy; and as he gazed on the blue mountains that rose as an impassable barrier around him, he was like the bird vainly beating its plumage against the gilded wires of its prison-house and longing to be free.

He wrote to the king in the most earnest terms, representing the forlorn condition of affairs—the Spaniards losing ground day after day, and the army under the marquis of Los Velez wasting away its energies in sloth or exerting them in unprofitable enterprises. He implored his brother not to compel him to remain thus cooped up within the walls of Granada, but to allow him to have a real as well as nominal command, and to conduct the war in person.

The views presented by Don John were warmly supported by Requesens, who wrote to Philip, denouncing in unqualified terms the incapacity of Los Velez.

Philip had no objection to receive complaints, even against those whom he most favored. He could not shut his eyes to the truth of the charges now brought against the hot-headed old chief who had so long enjoyed his confidence, but whose campaigns of late had been a series of blunders. He saw the critical aspect of affairs and the danger that the rebellion, which had struck so deep root in Granada, unless speedily crushed, would spread over the adjoining provinces. Mondejar's removal from the scene of action had not brought the remedy that Philip had expected.

Yet it was with reluctance that he yielded to his brother's wishes; whether distrusting the capacity of one so young for an independent command, or, as might be inferred from his letters, apprehending the dangers in which Don John's impetuous spirit would probably involve him. Having formed his plans, he lost no time in communicating them to his brother. The young warrior was to succeed Los Velez in the command of the eastern army, which was to be strengthened by reinforcements, while the duke of Sesa, under the direction of Don John, was to establish himself, with an efficient corps, in the Alpujarras, in such a position as to cover the approaches to Granada.

A summons was then sent to the principal towns of Andalusia, requiring them to raise fresh levies for the war, who were to be encouraged by promises of better pay than had before been given. But these promises did not weigh so much with the soldiers as the knowledge that Don John of Austria was to take charge of the expedition; and nobles and cavaliers came thronging to the war, with their well-armed retainers, in such numbers that the king felt it necessary to publish another ordinance, prohibiting any, without express permission, from joining the service.

All now was bustle and excitement in Granada, as the new

levies came in and the old ones were receiving a better organization. Indeed, Don John had been closely occupied, for some time, with introducing reforms among the troops quartered in the city, who, from causes already mentioned, had fallen into a state of the most alarming insubordination. A similar spirit had infected the officers, and to such an extent that it was deemed necessary to suspend no less than thirty-seven out of forty-five captains from their commands. Such were the difficulties under which the youthful hero was to enter on his first campaign.

Fortunately, in the retainers of the great lords and cavaliers he had a body of well-appointed and well-disciplined troops, who were actuated by higher motives than the mere love of plunder. His labors, moreover, did much to restore the ancient discipline of the regiments quartered in Granada. But the zeal with which he had devoted himself to the work of reform had impaired his health. This drew forth a kind remonstrance from Philip, who wrote to his brother not thus to overtask his strength, but to remember that he had need of his services; telling him to remind Quixada that he must watch over him more carefully. "And God grant," he concluded, "that your health may be soon reestablished." The affectionate solicitude constantly shown for his brother's welfare in the king's letters was hardly to have been expected in one of so phlegmatic a temperament and who was usually so little demonstrative in the expression of his feelings.

Before entering on his great expedition, Don John resolved to secure the safety of Granada in his absence by the reduction of "the robbers' nest," as the Spaniards called it, of Guejar. This was a fortified place near the confines of the Alpujarras, held by a warlike garrison, that frequently sallied out over the neighboring country, sometimes carrying their forays into the vega of Granada and causing a panic in the capital. Don John formed his force into two divisions, one of which he gave to the duke of Sesa, while the other he proposed to lead in person. They were to proceed by different routes, and, meeting before the place, to attack it simultaneously from opposite quarters.

The duke, marching by the most direct road across the mountains, reached Guejar first, and was not a little surprised to find that the inhabitants, who had received notice of the preparations of the Spaniards, were already evacuating the town, while the garrison was formed in order of battle to cover their retreat.

After a short skirmish with the rear guard, in which some lives were lost on both sides, the victorious Spaniards, without following up their advantage, marched into the town and took possession of the works abandoned by the enemy.

Great was the surprise of Don John, on arriving some hours later before Guejar, to see the Castilian flag floating from its ramparts; and his indignation was roused as he found that the laurels he had designed for his own brow had been thus unceremoniously snatched from him by another. "With eyes," says the chronicler, "glowing like coals of fire," he turned on the duke of Sesa and demanded an explanation of the affair. But he soon found that the blame, if blame there were, was to be laid on one whom he felt that he had not the power to rebuke. This was Luis Quixada, who, in his solicitude for the safety of his ward, had caused the army to be conducted by a circuitous route, that brought it thus late upon the field. But, though Don John uttered no word of rebuke, he maintained a moody silence, that plainly showed his vexation; and, as the soldiers remarked, not a morsel of food passed his lips until he had reached Granada.

The constant supervision maintained over him by Quixada, which, as we have seen, was encouraged by the king, was a subject of frequent remark among the troops. It must have afforded no little embarrassment and mortification to Don John—alike ill suited as it was to his age, his aspiring temper, and his station. For his station as commander-in-chief of the army made him responsible, in the eyes of the world, for the measures of the campaign. Yet, in his dependent situation, he had the power neither to decide on the plan of operations nor to carry it into execution. Not many days were to elapse before the death of his kind-hearted monitor was to relieve him from the jealous oversight that so much chafed his spirit, and to open to him an independent career of glory such as might satisfy the utmost cravings of his ambition.

FROM CHAPTER VIII

Renewal of the War

1569

The war, which Don John had flattered himself he had so happily brought to a close, now, like a fire smothered but not quenched, burst forth again with redoubled fury. The note of defiance was heard loudest among the hills of Ronda, a wild sierra on the western skirts of the Alpujarras, inhabited by a bold and untamed race, more formidable than the mountaineers of any other district of Granada. Aben-Aboo did all he could to fan the flame of insurrection in this quarter, and sent his own brother, El Galipe, to take the command.

The Spanish government, now fully aroused, made more vigorous efforts to crush the spirit of rebellion than at any time during the war. Don John was ordered to occupy Guadix, and thence to scour the country in a northerly direction. Another army, under the Grand Commander Requesens, marching from Granada, was to enter the Alpujarras from the north, and, taking a route different from that of the duke of Sesa in the previous campaign, was to carry a war of extermination into the heart of the mountains. Finally, the duke of Arcos, the worthy descendant of the great marquis of Cadiz, whose name was so famous in the first war of Granada, and whose large estates in this quarter he had inherited, was intrusted with the operations against the rebels of the Serrania de Ronda.

The grand commander executed his commission in the same remorseless spirit in which it had been dictated. Early in September, quitting Granada, he took the field at the head of five thousand men. He struck at once into the heart of the country. All the evils of war in its most horrid form followed in his train. All along his track it seemed as if the land had been swept by a conflagration. The dwellings were sacked and burned to the ground. The mulberry and olive groves were cut down; the vines were torn up by the roots; and the ripening harvests were trampled in the dust. The country was converted into a wilderness. Occasionally small bodies of the Moriscoes made a desperate stand. But for the most part, without homes to shelter or food to nourish them, they were driven, like unresisting cattle, to seek a refuge in the depths of the mountains, and in the caves in which this part of the country abounded. Their pursuers followed up the chase with the fierce glee with which the hunter tracks the wild animal of the forest to his lair. There they were huddled together, one or two hundred frequently in the same cavern. It was not easy to detect the hiding-place amidst the rocks and thickets which covered up and concealed the entrance. But when it was detected it was no difficult matter to destroy the inmates. The green bushes furnished the materials for a smoldering fire, and those within were soon suffocated by the smoke, or, rushing out, threw themselves on the mercy of their pursuers. Some were butchered on the spot; others were sent to the gibbet or the galleys; while the greater part, with a fate scarcely less terrible, were given up as the booty of the soldiers and sold into slavery.

Aben-Aboo had a narrow escape in one of these caverns, not far from Berchul, where he had secreted himself with a wife and two of his daughters. The women were suffocated, with about seventy other persons. The Morisco chief succeeded in making his escape through an aperture at the farther end, which was unknown to his enemies.

Small forts were erected at short intervals along the ruined country. No less than eighty-four of these towers were raised in different parts of the land, twenty-nine of which were to be seen in the Alpujarras and the vale of Lecrin alone. There they stood, crowning every peak and eminence in the sierra, frowning over the horrid waste, the sad memorials of the conquest. This was the stern policy of the victors. Within this rocky girdle, long held as it was by the iron soldiery of Castile, it was impossible that rebellion should again gather to a head.

The months of September and October were consumed in these operations. Meanwhile, the duke of Arcos had mustered his Andalusian levies, to the number of four thousand men, including a thousand of his own vassals. He took with him his son, a boy of not more than thirteen years of age—following in this, says the chronicler, the ancient usage of the valiant house of Ponce de Leon. About the middle of September he began his expedition into the Sierra Vermeja, or Red Sierra. It was a spot memorable in Spanish history for the defeat and death of Alonso de Aguilar, in the time of Ferdinand and Isabella, and has furnished the theme of many a plaintive romance in the beautiful minstrelsy of the South. The wife of the duke of Arcos was descended from Alonso de Aguilar, as he himself was the grandson of the good count of Ureña, who, with better fortune than his friend, survived the disasters of that day. The route of the army led directly across the fatal field. As they traversed the elevated plain of Calaluz, the soldiers saw everywhere around the traces of the fight. The ground was still covered with fragments of rusty armor, bits of broken sword-blades, and heads of spears. More touching evidence was afforded by the bones of men and horses, which, in this solitary region, had been whitening in the blasts of seventy winters. The Spaniards knew well the localities, with which they had become familiar from boyhood in the legends and traditions of the country. Here was the spot where the vanguard, under its brave commander, had made its halt in the obscurity of the night. There were the faint remains of the enemy's intrenchments, which time had nearly leveled with the dust; and there, too, the rocks still threw their dark shadows over the plain, as on the day when the valiant Alonso de Aguilar fell at their base in combat with the renowned Feri de Ben Estepar. The whole scene was brought home to the hearts of the Spaniards. As they gazed on the unburied relics lying around them, the tears, says the eloquent historian who records the incident, fell fast down their iron cheeks, and they breathed a soldier's prayer for the repose of the noble dead. But these holier feelings were soon succeeded by others of a fierce nature, and they loudly clamored to be led against the enemy.

The duke of Arcos, profiting by the errors of Alonso de Aguilar, had made his arrangements with great circumspection. He soon came in sight of the Moriscoes, full three thousand strong. But, though well posted, they made a defense little worthy of their ancient reputation, or of the notes of defiance which they had so boldly sounded at the opening of the campaign. They indeed showed mettle at first, and inflicted some loss on the Christians. But the frequent reverses of their countrymen seemed to have broken their spirits, and they were soon thrown into disorder, and fled in various directions into the more inaccessible tracts of the sierra. The Spaniards followed up the fugitives, who did not attempt to rally. Nor did they ever again assemble in any strength, so effectual were the dispositions made by the victorious general. The insurrection of the Sierra Vermeja was at an end.

The rebellion, indeed, might be said to be everywhere crushed within the borders of Granada. The more stout-hearted of the insurgents still held out among the caves and fastnesses of the Alpujarras, supporting a precarious existence until they were hunted down by detachments of the Spaniards, who were urged to the pursuit by the promise from government of twenty ducats a head for every Morisco. But nearly all felt the impracticability of further resistance. Some succeeded in making their escape to Barbary. The rest, broken in spirit, and driven to extremity by want of food in a country now turned into a desert, consented at length to accept the amnesty offered them, and tendered their submission.

On the twenty-eighth of October Don John received advices of a final edict of Philip, commanding that all the Moriscoes in the kingdom of Granada should be at once removed into the interior of the country. None were to be excepted from this decree, not even the Moriscos de la Paz, as those were called who had loyally refused to take part in the rebellion. The arrangements for this important and difficult step were made with singular prudence, and, under the general direction of Don John of Austria, the Grand Commander Requesens, and the dukes of Sesa and Arcos, were carried into effect with promptness and energy.

By the terms of the edict, the lands and houses of the exiles were to be forfeited to the crown. But their personal effects—their flocks, their herds, and their grain—would be taken, if they desired it, at a fixed valuation by the government. Every regard was to be paid to their personal convenience and security; and it was forbidden, in the removal, to separate parents from children, husbands from wives, in short, to divide the members of a family from one another—"an act of clemency," says a humane chronicler, "which they little deserved; but his majesty was willing in this to content them."

The country was divided into districts, the inhabitants of which were to be conducted, under the protection of a strong military escort, to their several places of destination. These seem to have been the territory of La Mancha, the northern borders of Andalusia, the Castiles, Estremadura, and even the remote province of Galicia. Care was taken that no settlement should be made near the borders of Murcia or Valencia, where large numbers of the Moriscoes were living in comparative quiet on the estates of the great nobles, who were exceedingly jealous of any interference with their vassals.

The first of November, All Saints' Day, was appointed for the removal of the Moriscoes throughout Granada. On that day they were gathered in the principal churches of their districts, and, after being formed into their respective divisions, began their march. The grand commander had occupied the passes of the Alpujarras with strong detachments of the military. The different columns of emigrants were placed under the direction of persons of authority and character. The whole movement was conducted with singular order—resistance being attempted in one or two places only, where the blame, it may be added, as intimated by a Castilian chronicler, was to be charged on the brutality of the soldiers. Still, the removal of the Moriscoes, on the present occasion, was attended with fewer acts of violence and rapacity than the former removal, from Granada. At least this would seem to be inferred by the silence of the chroniclers; though it is true such silence is far from being conclusive, as the chroniclers, for the most part, felt too little interest in the sufferings of the Moriscoes to make a notice of them indispensable. However this may be, it cannot be doubted that, whatever precautions may have been taken to spare the exiles any unnecessary suffering, the simple fact of their being expelled from their native soil is one that suggests an amount of misery not to be estimated. For what could be more dreadful than to be thus torn from their pleasant homes, the scenes of their childhood, where every mountain, valley, and stream were as familiar friends—a part of their own existence—to be rudely thrust into a land of strangers, of a race different from themselves in faith, language, and institutions, with no sentiment in common but that of a deadly hatred? That the removal of a whole nation should have been so quietly accomplished, proves how entirely the strength and spirit of the Moriscoes must have been broken by their reverses.

The war thus terminated, there seemed no reason for John of Austria to prolong his stay in the province. For some time he had been desirous to obtain the king's consent to his return. His ambitious spirit, impatient of playing a part on what now seemed to him an obscure field of action, pent up within the mountain barrier of the Alpujarras, longed to display itself on a bolder theater before the world. He aspired, too, to a more independent command. He addressed repeated letters to the king's ministers —to the Cardinal Espinosa and Ruy Gomez de Silva in particular—to solicit their influence in his behalf. "I should be glad," he wrote to the latter, "to serve his majesty, if I might be allowed, on some business of importance. I wish he may understand that I am no longer a boy. Thank God, I can begin to fly without the aid of others' wings, and it is full time, as I believe, that I was out of swaddling-clothes." In another letter he expresses his desire to have some place more fitting the brother of such a monarch as Philip and the son of such a father as Charles the Fifth. On more than one occasion he alludes to the command against the Turk as the great object of his ambition.

His importunity to be allowed to resign his present office had continued from the beginning of summer, some months before the proper close of the campaign. It may be thought to argue an instability of character, of which a more memorable example was afforded by him at a later period of life. At length he was rejoiced by obtaining the royal consent to resign his command and return to court.

On the eleventh of November, Don John repaired to Granada. Till the close of the month he was occupied with making the necessary arrangements preparatory to his departure. The greater part of the army was paid off and disbanded. A sufficient number was reserved to garrison the fortresses, and to furnish detachments which were to scour the country and hunt down such Moriscoes as still held out in the mountains. As Requesens was to take part in the expedition against the Ottomans, the office of captain-general was placed in the hands of the valiant duke of Arcos. On the twenty-ninth of November, Don John, having completed his preparations, quitted Granada and set forth on his journey to Madrid, where the popular chieftain was welcomed with enthusiasm by the citizens, as a conqueror returned from a victorious campaign. By Philip and his newly married bride, Anne of Austria, he was no less kindly greeted; and it was not long before the king gave a substantial proof of his contentment with his brother, by placing in his hands the baton offered by the allies of generalissimo in the war against the Turks. . . .

CHAPTER X

Battle of Lepanto

1571

As the allied fleet coasted along the Calabrian shore, it was so much baffled by rough seas and contrary winds that its progress was slow. Not long before his departure, Don John had sent a small squadron under a Spanish captain, Gil de Andrada, to collect tidings of the enemy. On his return, that commander met the Christian fleet, and reported that the Turks, with a powerful armament, were still in the Adriatic, where they had committed fearful ravages on the Venetian territories. Don John now steered his course for Corfu, which, however, he did not reach till the twenty-sixth of September. He soon had ample opportunities of seeing for himself the traces of the enemy, in the smoking hamlets and desolated fields along the coast. The allies were welcomed with joy by the islanders, who furnished them with whatever supplies they needed. Here Don John learned that the Ottoman fleet had been seen standing into the gulf of Lepanto, where it lay as if waiting the coming of the Christians.

The young commander-in-chief had now no hesitation as to the course he ought to pursue. But he chose to call a council of his principal captains before deciding. The treaty of alliance, indeed, required him to consult with the other commanders before taking any decisive step in matters of importance; and this had been strenuously urged on him by the king, ever afraid of his brother's impetuosity.

The opinions of the council were divided. Some who had had personal experience of the naval prowess of the Turks appeared to shrink from encountering so formidable an armament, and would have confined the operations of the fleet to the siege of some place belonging to the Moslems. Even Doria, whose life had been spent in fighting with the infidel, thought it was not advisable to attack the enemy in his present position, surrounded by friendly shores, whence he might easily obtain succor. It would be better, he urged, to attack some neighboring place, like Navarino, which might have the effect of drawing him from the gulf, and thus compel him to give battle in some quarter more advantageous to the allies.

But the majority of the council took a very different view of the matter. To them it appeared that the great object of the expedition was to destroy the Ottoman fleet, and that a better opportunity could not be offered than the present one, while the enemy was shut up in the gulf, from which, if defeated, he would find no means of escape. Fortunately, this was the opinion not only of the majority, but of most of those whose opinions were entitled to the greatest deference. Among these were the gallant marquis of Santa Cruz, the Grand Commander Requesens, who still remained near the person of Don John and had command of a galley in his rear, Cardona, general of the Sicilian squadron, Barbarigo, the Venetian provveditore, next in authority to the captain-general of his nation, the Roman Colonna, and Alexander Farnese, the young prince of Parma, Don John's nephew, who had come, on this memorable occasion, to take his first lesson in the art of war—an art in which he was destined to remain without a rival.

The commander-in-chief with no little satisfaction saw himself so well supported in his own judgment; and he resolved, without any unnecessary delay, to give the Turks battle in the position they had chosen. He was desirous, however, to be joined by a part of his fleet, which, baffled by the winds, and without oars, still lagged far behind. For the galley, with its numerous oars in addition to its sails, had somewhat of the properties of a modern

steamer, which so gallantly defies both wind and wave. As Don
John wished also to review his fleet before coming to action, he
determined to cross over to Comenizza, a capacious and well-
protected port on the opposite coast of Albania.

This he did on the thirtieth of September. Here the vessels
were got in readiness for immediate action. They passed in review before the commander-in-chief, and went through their
various evolutions; while the artillerymen and musketeers showed
excellent practice. Don John looked with increased confidence
to the approaching combat. An event, however, occurred at
this time which might have been attended with the worst consequences.

A Roman officer named Tortona, one of those who had been
drafted to make up the complement of the Venetian galleys, engaged in a brawl with some of his crew. This reached the ears of
Veniero, the Venetian captain-general. The old man, naturally
of a choleric temper, and still smarting from the insult which he
fancied he had received by the introduction of the allies on
board of his vessels, instantly ordered the arrest of the offender.
Tortona for a long while resisted the execution of these orders;
and when finally seized, with some of his companions, they were
all sentenced by the vindictive Veniero to be hung at the yardarm. Such a high-handed proceeding caused the deepest indignation in Don John, who regarded it, moreover, as an insult
to himself. In the first moments of his wrath he talked of retaliating on the Venetian admiral by a similar punishment. But, happily, the remonstrances of Colonna—who, as the papal commander, had in truth the most reason to complain—and the
entreaties of other friends prevailed on the angry chief to abstain
from any violent act. He insisted, however, that Veniero should
never again take his place at the council board, but should be
there represented by the provveditore Barbarigo, next in command—a man, fortunately, possessed of a better control over his
temper than was shown by his superior. Thus the cloud passed
away which threatened for a moment to break up the harmony
of the allies and to bring ruin on the enterprise.

On the third of October, Don John, without waiting longer
for the missing vessels, again put to sea, and stood for the gulf of
Lepanto. As the fleet swept down the Ionian Sea, it passed many
a spot famous in ancient story. None, we may imagine, would be

so likely to excite an interest at this time as Actium, on whose waters was fought the greatest naval battle of antiquity. But the mariner, probably, gave little thought to the past, as he dwelt on the conflict that awaited him at Lepanto. On the fifth, a thick fog enveloped the armada and shut out every object from sight. Fortunately, the vessels met with no injury, and, passing by Ithaca, the ancient home of Ulysses, they safely anchored off the eastern coast of Cephalonia. For two days their progress was thwarted by head-winds. But on the seventh, Don John, impatient of delay, again put to sea, though wind and weather were still unfavorable.

While lying off Cephalonia he had received tidings that Famagosta, the second city of Cyprus, had fallen into the hands of the enemy, and this under circumstances of unparalleled perfidy and cruelty. The place, after a defense that had cost hecatombs of lives to the besiegers, was allowed to capitulate on honorable terms. Mustapha, the Moslem commander, the same fierce chief who had conducted the siege of Malta, requested an interview at his quarters with four of the principal Venetian captains. After a short and angry conference, he ordered them all to execution. Three were beheaded. The other, a noble named Bragadino, who had held the supreme command, he caused to be flayed alive in the market-place of the city. The skin of the wretched victim was then stuffed; and with this ghastly trophy dangling from the yardarm of his galley, the brutal monster sailed back to Constantinople, to receive the reward of his services from Selim. These services were great. The fall of Famagosta secured the fall of Cyprus, which thus became permanently incorporated in the Ottoman empire.

The tidings of these shocking events filled the breast of every Venetian with an inextinguishable thirst for vengeance. The confederates entered heartily into these feelings; and all on board of the armada were impatient for the hour that was to bring them hand to hand with the enemies of the faith.

It was two hours before dawn, on Sunday, the memorable seventh of October, when the fleet weighed anchor. The wind had become lighter; but it was still contrary, and the galleys were indebted for their progress much more to their oars than their sails. By sunrise they were abreast of the Curzolari, a cluster of huge rocks, or rocky islets, which on the north defends the entrance of the gulf of Lepanto. The fleet moved laboriously along, while every eye was strained to catch the first glimpse of the hostile navy. At length the watch on the foretop of the *Real* called out, "A sail!" and soon after declared that the whole Ottoman fleet was in sight. Several others, climbing up the rigging, confirmed his report; and in a few moments more, word was sent to the same effect by Andrew Doria, who commanded on the right. There was no longer any doubt; and Don John, ordering his pennon to be displayed at the mizzen-peak, unfurled the great standard of the league, given by the pope, and directed a gun to be fired, the signal for battle. The report, as it rang along the rocky shores, fell cheerily on the ears of the confederates, who, raising their eyes towards the consecrated banner, filled the air with their shouts.

The principal captains now came on board the *Real,* to receive the last orders of the commander-in-chief. Even at this late hour there were some who ventured to intimate their doubts of the expediency of engaging the enemy in a position where he had a decided advantage. But Don John cut short the discussion. "Gentlemen," he said, "this is the time for combat, not for counsel." He then continued the dispositions he was making for the attack.

He had already given to each commander of a galley written instructions as to the manner in which the line of battle was to be formed in case of meeting the enemy. The armada was now disposed in that order. It extended on a front of three miles. Far on the right, a squadron of sixty-four galleys was commanded by the Genoese admiral, Andrew Doria—a name of terror to the Moslems. The center, or battle, as it was called, consisting of sixty-three galleys, was led by John of Austria, who was supported on the one side by Colonna, the captain-general of the pope, and on the other by the Venetian captain-general, Veniero. Immediately in the rear was the galley of the Grand Commander Requesens, who still remained near the person of his former pupil; though a difference which arose between them on the voyage, fortunately now healed, showed that the young commander-in-chief was wholly independent of his teacher in the art of war.

The left wing was commanded by the noble Venetian, Barbarigo, whose vessels stretched along the Aetolian shore, to which he approached as near as, in his ignorance of the coast, he dared to venture, so as to prevent his being turned by the enemy. Finally, the reserve, consisting of thirty-five galleys, was given to the brave marquis of Santa Cruz, with directions to act in any quarter where he thought his presence most needed. The smaller craft, some of which had now arrived, seem to have taken little part in the action, which was thus left to the galleys.

Each commander was to occupy so much space with his galley as to allow room for maneuvering it to advantage, and yet not enough to allow the enemy to break the line. He was directed to single out his adversary, to close with him at once, and board as soon as possible. The beaks of the galleys were pronounced to be a hindrance rather than a help in action. They were rarely strong enough to resist a shock from an antagonist, and they much interfered with the working and firing of the guns. Don John had the beak of his vessel cut away. The example was followed throughout the fleet, and, as it is said, with eminently good effect. It may seem strange that this discovery should have been reserved for the crisis of a battle.

When the officers had received their last instructions, they returned to their respective vessels; and Don John, going on board of a light frigate, passed rapidly through the part of the armada lying on his right, while he commanded Requesens to do the same with the vessels on his left. His object was to feel the temper of his men, and to rouse their mettle with a few words of encouragement. The Venetians he reminded of their recent injuries. The hour for vengeance, he told them, had arrived. To the Spaniards and other confederates he said, "You have come to fight the battle of the cross; to conquer or to die. But, whether you are to die or conquer, do your duty this day, and you will secure a glorious immortality." His words were received with a burst of enthusiasm which went to the heart of the commander and assured him that he could rely on his men in the hour of trial. On returning to his vessel, he saw Veniero on his quarter-deck; and they exchanged salutations in as friendly a manner as if no difference had existed between them. At this solemn hour both these brave men were willing to forget all personal animosity in a common feeling of devotion to the great cause in which they were engaged.

The Ottoman fleet came on slowly and with difficulty. For,

strange to say, the wind, which had hitherto been adverse to the Christians, after lulling for a time, suddenly shifted to the opposite quarter and blew in the face of the enemy. As the day advanced, moreover, the sun, which had shone in the eyes of the confederates, gradually shot its rays into those of the Moslems. Both circumstances were of good omen to the Christians, and the first was regarded as nothing short of a direct interposition of Heaven. Thus plowing its way along, the Turkish armament, as it came more into view, showed itself in greater strength than had been anticipated by the allies. It consisted of nearly two hundred and fifty royal galleys, most of them of the largest class, besides a number of smaller vessels in the rear, which, like those of the allies, appear scarcely to have come into action. The men on board, of every description, were computed at not less than a hundred and twenty thousand. The galleys spread out, as usual with the Turks, in the form of a regular half-moon, covering a wider extent of surface than the combined fleets, which they somewhat exceeded in number. They presented, indeed, as they drew nearer, a magnificent array, with their gilded and gaudily painted prows, and their myriads of pennons and streamers fluttering gaily in the breeze; while the rays of the morning sun glanced on the polished scimitars of Damascus, and on the superb aigrettes of jewels which sparkled in the turbans of the Ottoman chiefs.

In the center of the extended line, and directly opposite to the station occupied by the captain-general of the league, was the huge galley of Ali Pasha. The right of the armada was commanded by Mahomet Sirocco, viceroy of Egypt, a circumspect as well as courageous leader; the left, by Uluch Ali, dey of Algiers, the redoubtable corsair of the Mediterranean. Ali Pasha had experienced a difficulty like that of Don John, as several of his officers had strongly urged the inexpediency of engaging so formidable an armament as that of the allies. But Ali, like his rival, was young and ambitious. He had been sent by his master to fight the enemy; and no remonstrances, not even those of Mahomet Sirocco, for whom he had great respect, could turn him from his purpose.

He had, moreover, received intelligence that the allied fleet was much inferior in strength to what it proved. In this error he was fortified by the first appearance of the Christians; for the ex-

tremity of their left wing, commanded by Barbarigo, stretching
behind the Aetolian shore, was hidden from his view. As he
drew nearer and saw the whole extent of the Christian lines, it is
said his countenance fell. If so, he still did not abate one jot of
his resolution. He spoke to those around him with the same confidence as before, of the result of the battle. He urged his rowers
to strain every nerve. Ali was a man of more humanity in his
nature than often belonged to his nation. His galley-slaves were
all, or nearly all, Christian captives; and he addressed them in
this brief and pithy manner: "If your countrymen are to win this
day, Allah give you the benefit of it; yet if I win it, you shall certainly have your freedom. If you feel that I do well by you, do
then the like by me."

As the Turkish admiral drew nearer, he made a change in his
order of battle, by separating his wings farther from his center,
thus conforming to the dispositions of the allies. Before he had
come within cannon-shot, he fired a gun by way of challenge to
his enemy. It was answered by another from the galley of John
of Austria. A second gun discharged by Ali was as promptly replied to by the Christian commander. The distance between the
two fleets was now rapidly diminishing. At this solemn moment
a deathlike silence reigned throughout the armament of the confederates. Men seemed to hold their breath, as if absorbed in the
expectation of some great catastrophe. The day was magnificent.
A light breeze, still adverse to the Turks, played on the waters,
somewhat fretted by the contrary winds. It was nearly noon; and
as the sun, mounting through a cloudless sky, rose to the zenith,
he seemed to pause, as if to look down on the beautiful scene,
where the multitude of galleys, moving over the water, showed
like a holiday spectacle rather than a preparation for mortal
combat.

The illusion was soon dispelled by the fierce yells which rose
on the air from the Turkish armada. It was the customary war-
cry with which the Moslems entered into battle. Very different
was the scene on board of the Christian galleys. Don John might
be there seen, armed cap-à-pie, standing on the prow of the *Real*,
anxiously awaiting the conflict. In this conspicuous position,
kneeling down, he raised his eyes to Heaven, and humbly prayed
that the Almighty would be with his people on that day. His example was followed by the whole fleet. Officers and men, all

prostrating themselves on their knees and turning their eyes to the consecrated banner which floated from the *Real,* put up a petition like that of their commander. They then received absolution from the priests, of whom there were some in every vessel; and each man, as he rose to his feet, gathered new strength, as he felt assured that the Lord of Hosts would fight on his side.

When the foremost vessels of the Turks had come within cannon shot, they opened their fire on the Christians. The firing soon ran along the whole of the Turkish line, and was kept up without interruption as it advanced. Don John gave orders for trumpet and atabal to sound the signal for action; which was followed by the simultaneous discharge of such of the guns in the combined fleet as could be brought to bear on the enemy. The Spanish commander had caused the galeazzas, those mammoth warships, . . . to be towed half a mile ahead of the fleet, where they might intercept the advance of the Turks. As the latter came abreast of them, the huge galleys delivered their broadsides right and left, and their heavy ordnance produced a startling effect. Ali Pasha gave orders for his galleys to open their line and pass on either side, without engaging these monsters of the deep, of which he had had no experience. Even so their heavy guns did considerable damage to several of the nearest vessels, and created some confusion in the pasha's line of battle. They were, however, but unwieldly craft, and, having accomplished their object, seem to have taken no further part in the combat.

The action began on the left wing of the allies, which Mahomet Sirocco was desirous of turning. This had been anticipated by Barbarigo, the Venetian admiral, who commanded in that quarter. To prevent it, as we have seen, he lay with his vessels as near the coast as he dared. Sirocco, better acquainted with the soundings, saw there was space enough for him to pass, and, darting by with all the speed that oars could give him, he succeeded in doubling on his enemy. Thus placed between two fires, the extreme of the Christian left fought at terrible disadvantage. No less than eight galleys went to the bottom, and several others were captured. The brave Barbarigo, throwing himself into the heat of the fight, without availing himself of his defensive armor, was pierced in the eye by an arrow, and, reluctant to leave the glory of the field to another, was borne to his cabin. The combat still continued with unabated fury on the part of the Venetians. They fought like men who felt that the war was theirs, and who were animated not only by the thirst for glory, but for revenge.

Far on the Christian right a maneuver similar to that so successfully executed by Sirocco was attempted by Uluch Ali, the dey of Algiers. Profiting by his superiority in numbers, he endeavored to turn the right wing of the confederates. It was in this quarter that Andrew Doria commanded. He had foreseen this movement of his enemy, and he succeeded in foiling it. It was a trial of skill between the two most accomplished seamen in the Mediterranean. Doria extended his line so far to the right, indeed, to prevent being surrounded, that Don John was obliged to remind him that he left the center too much exposed. His dispositions were so far unfortunate for himself that his own line was thus weakened and afforded some vulnerable points to his assailant. These were soon detected by the eagle eye of Uluch Ali; and, like the king of birds swooping on his prey, he fell on some galleys separated by a considerable interval from their companions, and, sinking more than one, carried off the great *Capitana* of Malta in triumph as his prize.

While the combat opened thus disastrously to the allies both on the right and on the left, in the center they may be said to have fought with doubtful fortune. Don John had led his division gallantly forward. But the object on which he was intent was an encounter with Ali Pasha, the foe most worthy of his sword. The Turkish commander had the same combat no less at heart. The galleys of both were easily recognized, not only from their position, but from their superior size and richer decoration. The one, moreover, displayed the holy banner of the league; the other, the great Ottoman standard. This, like the ancient standard of the caliphs, was held sacred in its character. It was covered with texts from the Koran, emblazoned in letters of gold, and had the name of Allah inscribed upon it no less than twenty-eight thousand nine hundred times. It was the banner of the sultan, having passed from father to son since the foundation of the imperial dynasty, and was never seen in the field unless the grand seigneur or his lieutenant was there in person.

Both the chiefs urged on their rowers to the top of their speed. Their galleys soon shot ahead of the rest of the line, driven through the boiling surges as by the force of a tornado, and closed with a shock that made every timber crack and the two vessels quiver to their very keels. So powerful, indeed, was the impetus they received that the pasha's galley, which was considerably the larger and loftier of the two, was thrown so far upon its opponent that the prow reached the fourth bench of rowers. As soon as the vessels were disengaged from each other, and those on board had recovered from the shock, the work of death began. Don John's chief strength consisted in some three hundred Spanish arquebusiers, culled from the flower of his infantry. Ali, on the other hand, was provided with an equal number of janizaries. He was followed by a smaller vessel, in which two hundred more were stationed as a *corps de réserve.* He had, moreover, a hundred archers on board. The bow was still as much in use with the Turks as with the other Moslems.

The pasha opened at once on his enemy a terrible fire of cannon and musketry. It was returned with equal spirit and much more effect; for the Turks were observed to shoot over the heads of their adversaries. The Moslem galley was unprovided with the defenses which protected the sides of the Spanish vessels; and the troops, crowded together on the lofty prow, presented an easy mark to their enemy's balls. But, though numbers of them fell at every discharge, their places were soon supplied by those in reserve. They were enabled, therefore, to keep up an incessant fire, which wasted the strength of the Spaniards; and, as both Christian and Mussulman fought with indomitable spirit, it seemed doubtful to which side victory would incline.

The affair was made more complicated by the entrance of other parties into the conflict. Both Ali and Don John were supported by some of the most valiant captains in their fleets. Next to the Spanish commander, as we have seen, were Colonna and the veteran Veniero, who, at the age of seventy-six, performed feats of arms worthy of a paladin of romance. In this way a little squadron of combatants gathered round the principal leaders, who sometimes found themselves assailed by several enemies at the same time. Still the chiefs did not lose sight of one another; but, beating off their inferior foes as well as they could, each, refusing to loosen his hold, clung with mortal grasp to his antagonist.

Thus the fight raged along the whole extent of the entrance to the gulf of Lepanto. The volumes of vapor rolling heavily over the waters effectually shut out from sight whatever was passing at any considerable distance, unless when a fresher breeze dispelled the smoke for a moment, or the flashes of the heavy guns threw a transient gleam on the dark canopy of battle. If the eye of the spectator could have penetrated the cloud of smoke that enveloped the combatants, and have embraced the whole scene at a glance, he would have perceived them broken up into small detachments, separately engaged one with another, independently of the rest, and indeed ignorant of all that was doing in other quarters. The contest exhibited few of those large combinations and skillful maneuvers to be expected in a great naval encounter. It was rather an assemblage of petty actions, resembling those on land. The galleys, grappling together, presented a level arena, on which soldier and galley-slave fought hand to hand, and the fate of the engagement was generally decided by boarding. As in most hand-to-hand contests, there was an enormous waste of life. The decks were loaded with corpses, Christian and Moslem lying promiscuously together in the embrace of death. Instances are recorded where every man on board was slain or wounded. It was a ghastly spectacle, where blood flowed in rivulets down the sides of the vessels, staining the waters of the gulf for miles around.

It seemed as if a hurricane had swept over the sea and covered it with the wreck of the noble armaments which a moment before were so proudly riding on its bosom. Little had they now to remind one of their late magnificent array, with their hulls battered, their masts and spars gone or splintered by the shot, their canvas cut into shreds and floating wildly on the breeze, while thousands of wounded and drowning men were clinging to the floating fragments and calling piteously for help. Such was the wild uproar which succeeded the Sabbath-like stillness that two hours before had reigned over these beautiful solitudes.

The left wing of the confederates, commanded by Barbarigo, had been sorely pressed by the Turks, as we have seen, at the beginning of the fight. Barbarigo himself had been mortally wounded. His line had been turned. Several of his galleys had been sunk. But the Venetians gathered courage from despair. By incredible efforts, they succeeded in beating off their enemies. They became the assailants in their turn. Sword in hand, they carried one vessel after another. The Capuchin was seen in the thickest of the fight, waving aloft his crucifix and leading the boarders to the assault. The Christian galley-slaves, in some instances, broke their fetters and joined their countrymen against their masters. Fortunately, the vessel of Mahomet Sirocco, the Moslem admiral, was sunk; and though extricated from the water himself, it was only to perish by the sword of his conqueror, Giovanni Contarini. The Venetian could find in his heart no mercy for the Turk.

The fall of their commander gave the final blow to his followers. Without further attempt to prolong the fight, they fled before the avenging swords of the Venetians. Those nearest the land endeavored to escape by running their vessels ashore, where they abandoned them as prizes to the Christians. Yet many of the fugitives, before gaining the land, perished miserably in the waves. Barbarigo, the Venetian admiral, who was still lingering in agony, heard the tidings of the enemy's defeat, and, uttering a few words expressive of his gratitude to Heaven, which had permitted him to see this hour, he breathed his last.

During this time the combat had been going forward in the center between the two commanders-in-chief, Don John and Ali Pasha, whose galleys blazed with an incessant fire of artillery and musketry, that enveloped them like "a martyr's robe of flames." The parties fought with equal spirit, though not with equal fortune. Twice the Spaniards had boarded their enemy, and both times they had been repulsed with loss. Still, their superiority in the use of firearms would have given them a decided advantage over their opponents if the loss they had inflicted had not been speedily repaired by fresh reinforcements. More than once the contest between the two chieftains was interrupted by the arrival of others to take part in the fray. They soon, however, returned to each other, as if unwilling to waste their strength on a meaner enemy. Through the whole engagement both commanders exposed themselves to danger as freely as any common soldier. In such a contest even Philip must have admitted that it would be difficult for his brother to find, with honor, a place of safety. Don John received a wound in the foot. It was a slight one, however, and he would not allow it to be dressed till the action was over.

Again his men were mustered, and a third time the trumpets sounded to the attack. It was more successful than the preceding. The Spaniards threw themselves boldly into the Turkish galley. They were met with the same spirit as before by the janizaries. Ali Pasha led them on. Unfortunately, at this moment he was struck in the head by a musket ball and stretched senseless in the gangway. His men fought worthily of their ancient renown. But they missed the accustomed voice of their commander. After a short but ineffectual struggle against the fiery impetuosity of the Spaniards, they were overpowered and threw down their arms. The decks were loaded with the bodies of the dead and the dying. Beneath these was discovered the Turkish commander-in-chief, severely wounded, but perhaps not mortally. He was drawn forth by some Castilian soldiers, who, recognizing his person, would at once have despatched him. But the disabled chief, having rallied from the first effects of his wound, had sufficient presence of mind to divert them from their purpose by pointing out the place below where he had deposited his money and jewels; and they hastened to profit by the disclosure before the treasure should fall into the hands of their comrades.

Ali was not so successful with another soldier, who came up soon after, brandishing his sword and preparing to plunge it into the body of the prostrate commander. It was in vain that the latter endeavored to turn the ruffian from his purpose. He was a convict, one of those galley-slaves whom Don John had caused to be unchained from the oar and furnished with arms. He could not believe that any treasure would be worth so much as the head of the pasha. Without further hesitation, he dealt him a blow which severed it from his shoulders. Then, returning to his galley, he laid the bloody trophy before Don John. But he had miscalculated on his recompense. His commander gazed on it with a look of pity mingled with horror. He may have thought of the generous conduct of Ali to his Christian captives, and have felt that he deserved a better fate. He coldly inquired "of what use such a present could be to him," and then ordered it to be thrown into the sea. Far from the order being obeyed, it is said the head was stuck on a pike and raised aloft on board of the captured galley. At the same time the banner of the crescent was pulled down; while that of the cross, run up in its place, proclaimed the downfall of the pasha.

The sight of the sacred ensign was welcomed by the Christians with a shout of "Victory!" which rose high above the din of battle. The tidings of the death of Ali soon passed from mouth to mouth, giving fresh heart to the confederates, but falling like a knell on the ears of the Moslems. Their confidence was gone. Their fire slackened. Their efforts grew weaker and weaker. They were too far from shore to seek an asylum there, like their comrades on the right. They had no resource but to prolong the combat or to surrender. Most preferred the latter. Many vessels were carried by boarding, others were sunk by the victorious Christians. Ere four hours had elapsed, the center, like the right wing, of the Moslems might be said to be annihilated.

Still the fight was lingering on the right of the confederates, where, it will be remembered, Uluch Ali, the Algerine chief, had profited by Doria's error in extending his line so far as greatly to weaken it. Uluch Ali, attacking it on its most vulnerable quarter, had succeeded, as we have seen, in capturing and destroying several vessels, and would have inflicted still heavier losses on his enemy had it not been for the seasonable succor received from the marquis of Santa Cruz. This brave officer, who commanded the reserve, had already been of much service to Don John when the *Real* was assailed by several Turkish galleys at once during his combat with Ali Pasha; for at this juncture the marquis of Santa Cruz arriving, and beating off the assailants, one of whom he afterwards captured, enabled the commander-in-chief to resume his engagement with the pasha.

No sooner did Santa Cruz learn the critical situation of Doria than, supported by Cardona, "general" of the Sicilian squadron, he pushed forward to his relief. Dashing into the midst of the mêlée, the two commanders fell like a thunderbolt on the Algerine galleys. Few attempted to withstand the shock. But in their haste to avoid it they were encountered by Doria and his Genoese galleys. Thus beset on all sides, Uluch Ali was compelled to abandon his prizes and provide for his own safety by flight. He cut adrift the Maltese *Capitana,* which he had lashed to his stern, and on which three hundred corpses attested the desperate character of her defense. As tidings reached him of the discomfiture of the center and of the death of Ali Pasha, he felt that nothing remained but to make the best of his way from the fatal scene of action and save as many of his own ships as he could. And there were no ships in the Turkish fleet superior to his, or manned by men under more perfect discipline. For they were the famous corsairs of the Mediterranean, who had been rocked from infancy on its waters.

Throwing out his signals for retreat, the Algerine was soon to be seen, at the head of his squadron, standing towards the north, under as much canvas as remained to him after the battle, and urged forward through the deep by the whole strength of his oarsmen. Doria and Santa Cruz followed quickly in his wake. But he was borne on the wings of the wind, and soon distanced his pursuers. Don John, having disposed of his own assailants, was coming to the support of Doria, and now joined in the pursuit of the viceroy. A rocky headland, stretching far into the sea, lay in the path of the fugitive; and his enemies hoped to intercept him there. Some few of his vessels were stranded on the rocks. But the rest, near forty in number, standing more boldly out to sea, safely doubled the promontory. Then, quickening their flight, they gradually faded from the horizon, their white sails, the last thing visible, showing in the distance like a flock of Arctic sea-fowl on their way to their native homes. The confederates explained the inferior sailing of their own galleys on this occasion by the circumstance of their rowers, who had been allowed to bear arms in the fight, being crippled by their wounds.

The battle had lasted more than four hours. The sky, which had been almost without a cloud through the day, began now to be overcast, and showed signs of a coming storm. Before seeking a place of shelter for himself and his prizes, Don John reconnoitered the scene of action. He met with several vessels too much damaged for further service. These, mostly belonging to the enemy, after saving what was of any value on board, he ordered to be burnt. He selected the neighboring port of Petala, as affording the most secure and accessible harbor for the night. Before he had arrived there, the tempest began to mutter and darkness was on the water. Yet the darkness rendered only more visible the blazing wrecks, which, sending up streams of fire mingled with showers of sparks, looked like volcanoes on the deep.

FROM CHAPTER XI

Significance of Lepanto

1571

The news of the victory of Lepanto caused a profound sensation throughout Christendom; for it had been a general opinion that the Turks were invincible by sea. The confederates more particularly testified their joy by such extraordinary demonstrations as showed the extent of their previous fears. In Venice, which might be said to have gained a new lease of existence from the result of the battle, the doge, the senators, and the people met in the great square of St. Mark and congratulated one another on the triumph of their arms. By a public decree, the seventh of October was set apart to be observed forever as a national anniversary.

The joy was scarcely less in Naples, where the people had so often seen their coasts desolated by the Ottoman cruisers; and when their admiral, the marquis of Santa Cruz, returned to port with his squadron, he was welcomed with acclamations such as greet the conqueror returning from his campaign.

But even these honors were inferior to those which in Rome were paid to Colonna, the captain-general of the papal fleet. As he was borne in stately procession, with the trophies won from the enemy carried before him, and a throng of mourning captives in the rear, the spectacle recalled the splendors of the ancient Roman triumph. Pius the Fifth had, before this, announced that the victory of the Christians had been revealed to him from Heaven. But when the tidings reached him of the actual result, it so far transcended his expectations that, overcome by his emotions, the old pontiff burst into a flood of tears, exclaiming, in the words of the Evangelist, "There was a man sent from God; and his name was John."

We may readily believe that the joy with which the glad tidings were welcomed in Spain fell nothing short of that with which they were received in other parts of Christendom. While lying off Petala, Don John sent Lope de Figueroa with despatches for the king, together with the great Ottoman standard, as the most glorious trophy taken in the battle. He soon after sent a courier with further letters. It so happened that neither the one nor the other arrived at the place of their destination till some weeks after the intelligence had reached Philip by another channel. This was the Venetian minister, who on the last of October received despatches from his own government, containing a full account of the fight. Hastening with them to the palace, he found the king in his private chapel, attending vespers on the eve of All Saints. The news, it cannot be doubted, filled his soul with joy; though *it is said* that, far from exhibiting this in his demeanor, he continued to be occupied with his devotions, without the least change of countenance, till the services were concluded. He then ordered *Te Deum* to be sung. All present joined, with overflowing hearts, in pouring forth their gratitude to the Lord of Hosts for granting such a triumph to the cross.

That night there was a grand illumination in Madrid. The following day mass was said by the papal legate in presence of the king, who afterwards took part in a solemn procession to the church of St. Mary, where the people united with the court in a general thanksgiving.

In a letter from Philip to his brother, dated from the Escorial, the twenty-ninth of November, he writes to him out of the fullness of his heart, in the language of gratitude and brotherly love: "I cannot express to you the joy it has given me to learn the particulars of your conduct in the battle, of the great valor you showed in your own person, and your watchfulness in giving proper directions to others—all of which has doubtless been a principal cause of the victory. So to you, after God, I am to make my acknowledgments for it, as I now do; and happy am I that it has been reserved for one so near and so dear to me to perform this great work, which has gained such glory for you in the eyes of God and of the whole world."

The feelings of the king were fully shared by his subjects.

The enthusiasm roused throughout the country by the great victory was without bounds. "There is no man," writes one of the royal secretaries to Don John, "who does not discern the hand of the Lord in it—though it seems rather like a dream than a reality, so far does it transcend any naval encounter that the world ever heard of before." The best sculptors and painters were employed to perpetuate the memory of the glorious event. Among the number was Titian, who in the time of Charles the Fifth had passed two years in Spain, and who now, when more than ninety years of age, executed the great picture of "The Victory of the League," still hanging on the walls of the Museo at Madrid. The lofty theme proved a fruitful source of inspiration to the Castilian muse. Among hecatombs of epics and lyrics, the heroic poem of Ercilla and the sublime cancion of Fernando de Herrera perpetuate the memory of the victory of Lepanto in forms more durable than canvas or marble—as imperishable as the language itself.

While all were thus ready to render homage to the talent and bravery which had won the greatest battle of the time, men, as they grew cooler and could criticize events more carefully, were disposed to ask, where were the fruits of this great victory. Had Don John's father, Charles the Fifth, gained such a victory, it was said, he would not thus have quitted the field, but, before the enemy could recover from the blow, would have followed it up by another. Many expressed the conviction that the young generalissimo should at once have led his navy against Constantinople.

There would indeed seem to be plausible ground for criticizing his course after the action. But we must remember, in explanation of the conduct of Don John, that his situation was altogether different from that of his imperial father. He possessed no such absolute authority as the latter did over his army. The great leaders of the confederates were so nearly equal in rank that they each claimed a right to be consulted on all measures of importance. The greatest jealousy existed among the three commanders, as there did also among the troops whom they commanded. They were all united, it is true, in their hatred to the Turk. But they were all influenced, more or less, by the interests of their own states, in determining the quarter where he was to be assailed. Every rood of territory wrung from the enemy in the Levant would only serve to enlarge the domain of Venice; while the conquests in the western parts of the Mediterranean would strengthen the empire of Castile. This feeling of jealousy between the Spaniards and the Venetians was, as we have seen, so great in the early part of the expedition as nearly to bring ruin on it.

Those who censured Don John for not directing his arms against Constantinople would seem to have had but a very inadequate notion of the resources of the Porte—as shown in the course of that very year. There is a remarkable letter from the duke of Alva, written the month after the battle of Lepanto, in which he discusses the best course to be taken in order to reap the full fruits of the victory. In it he expresses the opinion that an attempt against Constantinople, or indeed any part of the Turkish dominions, unless supported by a general coalition of the great powers of Christendom, must end only in disappointment—so vast were the resources of that great empire. If this were so—and no better judge than Alva could be found in military affairs—how incompetent were the means at Don John's disposal for effecting this object—confederates held together, as the event proved, by a rope of sand, and a fleet so much damaged in the recent combat that many of the vessels were scarcely seaworthy!

In addition to this, it may be stated that Don John knew it was his brother's wish that the Spanish squadron should return to Sicily to pass the winter. If he persisted, therefore, in the campaign, he must do so on his own responsibility. He had now accomplished the great object for which he had put to sea. He had won a victory more complete than the most sanguine of his countrymen had a right to anticipate. To prolong the contest under the present circumstances would be in a manner to provoke his fate, to jeopard the glory he had already gained, and incur the risk of closing the campaign with melancholy cypress, instead of the laurel wreath of victory. Was it surprising that even an adventurous spirit like his should have shrunk from hazarding so vast a stake with the odds against him?

It is a great error to speak of the victory of Lepanto as a barren victory, which yielded no fruits to those who gained it. True, it did not strip the Turks of an inch of territory. Even the heavy loss of ships and soldiers which it cost them was repaired in the following year. But the loss of reputation—that tower of strength to the conqueror—was not to be estimated. The long and successful career of the Ottoman princes, especially of the last one, Solyman the Magnificent, had made the Turks to be thought invincible. There was not a nation in Christendom that did not tremble at the idea of a war with Turkey. The spell was now broken. Though her resources were still boundless, she lost confidence in herself. Venice gained confidence in proportion. When the hostile fleets met in the year following the battle of Lepanto, the Turks, though greatly the superior in numbers, declined the combat. For the seventy years which elapsed after the close of the present war, the Turks abandoned their efforts to make themselves masters of any of the rich possessions of the republic, which lay so temptingly around them. When the two nations came next into collision, Venice, instead of leaning on confederates, took the field single-handed, and disputed it with an intrepidity which placed her on a level with the gigantic power that assailed her. That power was already on the wane; and those who have most carefully studied the history of the Ottoman empire date the commencement of her decline from the battle of Lepanto.

BOOK VI

Domestic Affairs of Spain

1573

Seventeen years had now elapsed since Philip the Second ascended the throne of his ancestors—a period long enough to disclose the policy of his government, longer, indeed, than that of the entire reigns of some of his predecessors. In the previous portions of this work the reader has been chiefly occupied with the foreign relations of Spain, and with military details. It is now time to pause, and, before plunging anew into the stormy scenes of the Netherlands, to consider the internal administration of the country and the character and policy of the monarch who presided over it.

The most important epoch in Castilian history since the great Saracen invasion in the eighth century is the reign of Ferdinand and Isabella, when anarchy was succeeded by law, and from the elements of chaos arose that beautiful fabric of order and constitutional liberty which promised a new era for the nation. In the assertion of her rights, Isabella, to whom this revolution is chiefly to be attributed, was obliged to rely on the support of the people. It was natural that she should requite their services by aiding them in the recovery of their own rights,—especially of those which had been usurped by the rapacious nobles. Indeed, it was the obvious policy of the crown to humble the pride of the aristocracy and abate their arrogant pretensions. In this it was so well supported by the commons that the scheme perfectly succeeded. By the depression of the privileged classes and the elevation of the people, the different orders were brought more strictly within their constitutional limits; and the state made a nearer approach to a well-balanced limited monarchy than at any previous period of its history.

This auspicious revolution was soon, alas! to be followed by another, of a most disastrous kind. Charles the Fifth, who succeeded his grandfather Ferdinand, was born a foreigner—and a foreigner he remained through his whole life. He was a stranger to the feelings and habits of the Spaniards, had little respect for their institutions, and as little love for the nation. He continued to live mostly abroad; was occupied with foreign enterprises; and the only people whom he really loved were those of the Netherlands, his native land. The Spaniards requited these feelings of indifference in full measure. They felt that the glory of the imperial name shed no luster upon them. Thus estranged at heart, they were easily provoked to insurrection by his violation of their rights. The insurrection was a failure; and the blow which crushed the insurgents on the plains of Villalar deprived them forever of the few liberties which they had been permitted to retain. They were excluded from all share in the government, and were henceforth summoned to the cortes only to swear allegiance to the heir-apparent or to furnish subsidies for their master. They were indeed allowed to lay their grievances before the throne. But they had no means of enforcing redress; for, with the cunning policy of a despot, Charles would not receive their petitions until they had first voted the supplies.

The nobles, who had stood by their master in the struggle, fared no better. They found too late how short-sighted was the policy which had led them to put their faith in princes. Henceforth they could not be said to form a necessary part of the legislature. For, as they insisted on their right to be excused from bearing any share in the burdens of the state, they could take no part in voting the supplies; and, as this was almost the only purpose for which the cortes was convened, their presence was no longer required in it. Instead of the powers which were left to them untouched by Ferdinand and Isabella, they were now amused with high-sounding and empty titles, or with offices about the person of the monarch. In this way they gradually sank into the unsubstantial though glittering pageant of a court. Meanwhile, the government of Castile, assuming the powers of both making the laws and enforcing their execution, became in its essential attributes nearly as absolute as that of Turkey.

Such was the gigantic despotism which, on the death of Charles, passed into the hands of Philip the Second. The son had many qualities in common with his father. But among these was not that restless ambition of foreign conquest which was ever goading the emperor. Nor was he, like his father, urged by the love of glory to military achievement. He was of too sluggish a nature to embark readily in great enterprises. He was capable of much labor; but it was of that sedentary kind which belongs to the cabinet rather than the camp. His tendencies were naturally pacific; and up to the period at which we are now arrived he had engaged in no wars but those into which he had been drawn by the revolt of his vassals, as in the Netherlands and Granada, or those forced on him by circumstances beyond his control. Such was the war which he had carried on with the pope and the French monarchy at the beginning of his reign.

But, while less ambitious than Charles of foreign acquisitions, Philip was full as tenacious of the possessions and power which had come to him by inheritance. Nor was it likely that the regal prerogative would suffer any diminution in his reign, or that the nobles or commons would be allowed to retrieve any of the immunities which they had lost under his predecessors.

Philip understood the character of his countrymen better than his father had done. A Spaniard by birth, he was, as I have more than once had occasion to remark, a Spaniard in his whole nature. His tastes, his habits, his prejudices, were all Spanish. His policy was directed solely to the aggrandizement of Spain. The distant races whom he governed were all strangers to him. With a few exceptions, Spaniards were the only persons he placed in offices of trust. His Castilian countrymen saw with pride and satisfaction that they had a native prince on the throne, who identified his own interests with theirs. They contrasted this conduct with that of his father, and requited it with a devotion such as they had shown to few of his predecessors. They not only held him in reverence, says the Venetian minister, Contarini, but respected his laws, as something sacred and inviolable. It was the people of the Netherlands who rose up against him. For similar reasons it fared just the opposite with Charles. His Flemish countrymen remained loyal to the last. It was his Castilian subjects who were driven to rebellion.

Though tenacious of power, Philip had not the secret consciousness of strength which enabled his father, unaided as it were, to bear up so long under the burden of empire. The habitual caution of the son made him averse to taking any step of importance without first ascertaining the opinions of others. Yet he was not willing, like his ancestor the good Queen Isabella, to invoke the cooperation of the cortes, and thus awaken the consciousness of power in an arm of the government which had been so long smitten with paralysis. Such an expedient was fraught with too much danger. He found a substitute in the several councils, the members of which, appointed by the crown and removable at its pleasure, were pledged to the support of the prerogative.

Under Ferdinand and Isabella there had been a complete reorganization of these councils. Their number was increased under Charles the Fifth, to suit the increased extent of the empire. It was still further enlarged by Philip. Under him there were no less than eleven councils, among which may be particularly noticed those of war, of finance, of justice, and of state. Of these various bodies the council of state, charged with the most important concerns of the monarchy, was held in highest consideration. The number of its members varied. At the time of which I am writing, it amounted to sixteen. But the weight of the business devolved on less than half that number. It was composed of both ecclesiastics and laymen. Among the latter were some eminent jurists. A sprinkling of men of the robe, indeed, was to be found in most of the councils. Philip imitated in this the policy of Ferdinand and Isabella, who thus intended to humble the pride of the great lords, and to provide themselves with a loyal militia, whose services would be of no little advantage in maintaining the prerogative. . . .

Philip, unlike most of his predecessors, rarely took his seat in the council of state. It was his maxim that his ministers would more freely discuss measures in the absence of their master than when he was there to overawe them. The course he adopted was for a consulta, or a committee of two or three members, to wait on him in his cabinet and report to him the proceedings of the council. He more commonly, especially in the later years of his reign, preferred to receive a full report of the discussion, written so as to leave an ample margin for his own commentaries. These were eminently characteristic of the man, and were so minute as usually to cover several sheets of paper. Philip had a reserved and unsocial temper. He preferred to work alone, in the seclusion of his closet, rather than in the presence of others. This may explain the reason, in part, why he seemed so much to prefer writing to talking. Even with his private secretaries, who were always near at hand, he chose to communicate by writing; and they had as large a mass of his autograph notes in their possession as if the correspondence had been carried on from different parts of the kingdom. His thoughts too—at any rate his words—came slowly; and by writing he gained time for the utterance of them.

Philip has been accused of indolence. As far as the body was concerned, such an accusation was well founded. Even when young, he had no fondness . . . for the robust and chivalrous sports of the age. He never, like his father, conducted military expeditions in person. He thought it wiser to follow the example of his great-grandfather, Ferdinand the Catholic, who stayed at home and sent his generals to command his armies. As little did he like to travel—forming too in this respect a great contrast to the emperor. He had been years on the throne before he made a visit to his great southern capital, Seville. It was a matter of complaint in cortes that he thus withdrew himself from the eyes of his subjects. The only sport he cared for—not by any means to excess—was shooting with his gun or his crossbow such game as he could find in his own grounds at the Wood of Segovia, or Aranjuez, or some other of his pleasant country seats, none of them at a great distance from Madrid.

On a visit to such places he would take with him as large a heap of papers as if he were a poor clerk earning his bread; and after the fatigues of the chase he would retire to his cabinet and refresh himself with his despatches. It would indeed be a great mistake to charge him with sluggishness of mind. He was content to toil for hours, and long into the night, at his solitary labors. No expression of weariness or of impatience was known to escape him. A characteristic anecdote is told of him in regard to this. Having written a despatch, late at night, to be sent on the following morning, he handed it to his secretary to throw some sand over it. This functionary, who happened to be dozing, suddenly roused himself, and, snatching up the inkstand, emptied it on the paper. The king, coolly remarking that "it would have been better to use the sand," set himself down, without any complaint, to rewrite the whole of the letter. A prince so much addicted to the pen, we may well believe, must have left a large amount of autograph materials behind him. Few monarchs, in point of fact, have done so much in this way to illustrate the history of their reigns. Fortunate would it have been for the historian who was to profit by it, if the royal composition had been somewhat less diffuse and the handwriting somewhat more legible.

Philip was an economist of time, and regulated the distribution of it with great precision. In the morning he gave audience to foreign ambassadors. He afterwards heard mass. After mass came dinner, in his father's fashion. But dinner was not an affair with Philip of so much moment as it was with Charles. He was exceedingly temperate both in eating and drinking, and not unfrequently had his physician at his side, to warn him against any provocative of the gout—the hereditary disease which at a very early period had begun to affect his health. After a light repast, he gave audience to such of his subjects as desired to present their memorials. He received the petitioners graciously, and listened to all they had to say with patience—for that was his virtue. But his countenance was exceedingly grave—which, in truth, was its natural expression; and there was a reserve in his deportment which made the boldest feel ill at ease in his presence. On such occasions he would say, "Compose yourself"— a recommendation that had not always the tranquilizing effect intended. Once when a papal nuncio forgot, in his confusion, the address he had prepared, the king coolly remarked, "If you will bring it in writing, I will read it myself, and expedite your business." It was natural that men of even the highest rank should be overawed in the presence of a monarch who held the destinies of so many millions in his hands, and who surrounded himself with a veil of mystery which the most cunning politician could not penetrate.

The reserve so noticeable in his youth increased with age. He became more difficult of access. His public audiences were much less frequent. In the summer he would escape from them altogether, by taking refuge in some one of his country places. His favorite retreat was his palace-monastery of the Escorial, then slowly rising under his patronage and affording him an occupation congenial with his taste. He seems, however, to have sought the country not so much from the love of its beauties as for the retreat it afforded him from the town. When in the latter, he rarely showed himself to the public eye, going abroad chiefly in a closed carriage, and driving late so as to return to the city after dark.

Thus he lived in solitude even in the heart of his capital, knowing much less of men from his own observation than from the reports that were made to him. In availing himself of these sources of information he was indefatigable. He caused a statistical survey of Spain to be prepared for his own use. It was a work of immense labor, embracing a vast amount of curious details, such as were rarely brought together in those days. He kept his spies at the principal European courts, who furnished him with intelligence; and he was as well acquainted with what was passing in England and in France as if he had resided on the spot. . . . He knew the smallest details of the proceedings in the Netherlands, sometimes even better than Margaret herself. He employed similar means to procure information that might be of service in making appointments to ecclesiastical and civil offices.

In his eagerness for information, his ear was ever open to accusations against his ministers, which, as they were sure to be locked up in his own bosom, were not slow in coming to him. This filled his mind with suspicions. He waited till time had proved their truth, treating the object of them with particular favor till the hour of vengeance had arrived. The reader will not have forgotten the terrible saying of Philip's own historian, "His dagger followed close upon his smile."

Even to the ministers in whom Philip appeared most to confide, he often gave but half his confidence. Instead of frankly furnishing them with a full statement of facts, he sometimes made so imperfect a disclosure that, when his measures came to be taken, his counselors were surprised to find of how much they had been kept in ignorance. When he communicated to them any foreign despatches, he would not scruple to alter the original, striking out some passages and inserting others, so as best to serve his purpose. The copy, in this garbled form, was given to the council. Such was the case with a letter of Don John of Austria, containing an account of the troubles of Genoa, the original of which, with its numerous alterations in the royal handwriting, still exists in the Archives of Simancas.

But, though Philip's suspicious nature prevented him from entirely trusting his ministers—though with chilling reserve he kept at a distance even those who approached him nearest—he was kind, even liberal, to his servants, was not capricious in his humors, and seldom, if ever, gave way to those sallies of passion so common in princes clothed with absolute power. He was patient to the last degree, and rarely changed his ministers without good cause. Ruy Gomez was not the only courtier who continued in the royal service to the end of his days.

Philip was of a careful, or, to say truth, of a frugal disposition, which he may well have inherited from his father; though this did not, as with his father in later life, degenerate into parsimony. The beginning of his reign, indeed, was distinguished by some acts of uncommon liberality. One of these occurred at the close of Alva's campaigns in Italy, when the king presented that commander with a hundred and fifty thousand ducats, greatly to the discontent of the emperor. This was contrary to his usual policy. As he grew older, and the expenses of government pressed more heavily on him, he became more economical. Yet those who served him had no reason, like the emperor's servants, to complain of their master's meanness. It was observed, however, that he was slow to recompense those who served him until they had proved themselves worthy of it. Still, it was a man's own fault, says a contemporary, if he was not well paid for his services in the end.

In one particular he indulged in a most lavish expenditure. This was his household. It was formed on the Burgundian model —the most stately and magnificent in Europe. Its peculiarity consisted in the number and quality of the members who composed it. The principal officers were nobles of the highest rank, who frequently held posts of great consideration in the state. Thus, the duke of Alva was chief major-domo; the prince of Eboli was first gentleman of the bedchamber; the duke of Feria was captain of the Spanish guard. There was the grand equerry, the grand huntsman, the chief muleteer, and a host of officers, some of whom were designated by menial titles, though nobles and cavaliers of family. There were forty pages, sons of the most illustrious houses in Castile. The whole household amounted to no less than fifteen hundred persons. The king's guard consisted of three hundred men, one-third of whom were Spaniards, one-third Flemings, and the remainder Germans.

The queen had also her establishment on the same scale. She had twenty-six ladies-in-waiting, and, among other functionaries, no less than four physicians to watch over her health.

The annual cost of the royal establishment amounted to full two hundred thousand florins. The cortes earnestly remonstrated against this useless prodigality, beseeching the king to place his household on the modest scale to which the monarchs of Castile had been accustomed. And it seems singular that one usually so averse to extravagance and pomp should have so recklessly indulged in them here. It was one of those inconsistencies which we sometimes meet with in private life, when a man habitually careful of his expenses indulges himself in some which taste, or, as in this case, early habits, have made him regard as indispensable. The emperor had been careful to form the household of his son, when very young, on the Burgundian model; and Philip, thus early trained, probably regarded it as essential to the royal dignity.

The king did not affect an ostentation in his dress corresponding with that of his household. This seemed to be suited to the sober-colored livery of his own feelings, and was almost always of black velvet or satin, with shoes of the former material. He wore a cap, garnished with plumes after the Spanish fashion. He used few ornaments, scarce any but the rich jewel of the Golden Fleece, which hung from his neck. But in his attire he was scrupulously neat, says the Venetian diplomatist who tells these particulars; and he changed his dress for a new one every month, giving away his cast-off suits to his attendants.

It was a capital defect in Philip's administration that his love of power and his distrust of others made him desire to do everything himself—even those things which could be done much better by his ministers. As he was slow in making up his own opinions, and seldom acted without first ascertaining those of his council, we may well understand the mischievous consequences of such delay. Loud were the complaints of private suitors, who saw month after month pass away without an answer to their petitions. The state suffered no less, as the wheels of government seemed actually to stand still under the accumulated pressure of the public business. Even when a decision did come, it often came too late to be of service; for the circumstances which led to it had wholly changed. . . . The favorite saying of Philip, that "time and he were a match for any other two," was a sad mistake. The time he demanded was his ruin. It was in vain that Granvelle, who, at a later day, came to Castile to assume the direction of affairs, endeavored, in his courtly language, to convince the king of his error, telling him that no man could bear up under such a load of business, which sooner or later must destroy his health, perhaps his life.

A letter addressed to the king by his grand almoner, Don Luis Manrique, told the truth in plainer terms, such as had not often reached the royal ear. "Your majesty's subjects everywhere complain," he says, "of your manner of doing business— sitting all day long over your papers, from your desire, as they intimate, to seclude yourself from the world, and from a want of confidence in your ministers. Hence such interminable delays as fill the soul of every suitor with despair. Your subjects are discontented that you refuse to take your seat in the council of state. The Almighty," he adds, "did not send kings into the world to spend their days in reading or writing, or even in meditation and prayer"—in which Philip was understood to pass much of his time—"but to serve as public oracles, to which all may resort for answers. If any sovereign have received this grace, it is your majesty; and the greater the sin, therefore, if you do not give free access to all." One may be surprised to find that language such as this was addressed to a prince like Philip the Second, and that he should have borne it so patiently. But in this the king resembled his father. Churchmen and jesters— of which latter he had usually one or two in attendance—were privileged persons at his court. In point of fact, the homilies of the one had as little effect as the jests of the other.

The pomp of the royal establishment was imitated on a smaller scale by the great nobles living on their vast estates scattered over the country. Their revenues were very large, though often heavily burdened. Out of twenty-three dukes, in 1581, only three had an income so low as forty thousand ducats a year. That of most of the others ranged from fifty to a hundred thousand, and that of one, the duke of Medina Sidonia, was computed at a hundred and thirty-five thousand. Revenues like these would not easily have been matched in that day by the aristocracy of any other nation in Christendom.

The Spanish grandees preferred to live on their estates in the country. But in the winter they repaired to Madrid, and displayed their magnificence at the court of their sovereign. Here they dazzled the eye by the splendor of their equipages, the beauty of their horses, their rich liveries, and the throng of their retainers. But with all this the Castilian court was far from appearing in the eyes of foreigners a gay one—forming in this respect a contrast to the Flemish court of Margaret of Parma. It seemed to have imbibed much of the serious and indeed somber character of the monarch who presided over it. All was stately and ceremonious, with old-fashioned manners and usages. "There is nothing new to be seen there," write the Venetian envoys. "There is no pleasant gossip about the events of the day. If a man is acquainted with any news, he is too prudent to repeat it. The courtiers talk little, and for the most part are ignorant—in fact, without the least tincture of learning. The arrogance of the great lords is beyond belief; and when they meet a foreign ambassador, or even the nuncio of his holiness, they rarely condescend to salute him by raising their caps. They all affect that imperturbable composure, or apathy, which they term 'sosiego.' "

They gave no splendid banquets, like the Flemish nobles. Their chief amusement was gaming—the hereditary vice of the Spaniard. They played deep, often to the great detriment of their fortunes. This did not displease the king. It may seem strange that a society so cold and formal should be much addicted to intrigue. In this they followed the example of their master.

Thus passing their days in frivolous amusements and idle dalliance, the Spanish nobles, with the lofty titles and pretensions of their ancestors, were a degenerate race. With a few brilliant exceptions, they filled no important posts in the state or in the army. The places of most consideration to which they aspired were those connected with the royal household; and their greatest honor was to possess the empty privileges of the grandee, and to sit with their heads covered in the presence of the king.

From this life of splendid humiliation they were nothing loath to escape into the country, where they passed their days in their ancestral castles, surrounded by princely domains, which embraced towns and villages within their circuit, and a population sometimes reaching to thirty thousand families. Here the proud lords lived in truly regal pomp. Their households were formed on that of the sovereign. They had their major-domos, their gentlemen of the bedchamber, their grand equerries, and other officers of rank. Their halls were filled with hidalgos and cavaliers, and a throng of inferior retainers. They were attended by bodyguards of one or two hundred soldiers. Their dwellings were sumptuously furnished, and their sideboards loaded with plate from the silver quarries of the New World. Their chapels were magnificent. Their wives affected a royal state. They had their ladies of honor; and the page who served as cup-bearer knelt while his mistress drank. Even knights of ancient blood, whom she addressed from her seat, did not refuse to bend the knee to her.

Amidst all this splendor, the Spanish grandees had no real power to correspond with it. They could no longer, as in the days of their fathers, engage in feuds with one another; nor could they enjoy the privilege, so highly prized, of renouncing their allegiance and declaring war upon their sovereign. Their numerous vassals, instead of being gathered as of yore into a formidable military array, had sunk into the more humble rank of retainers, who served only to swell the idle pomp of their lord's establishment. They were no longer allowed to bear arms, except in the service of the crown; and after the Moriscoes had been reduced, the crown had no occasion for their services— unless in foreign war.

The measures by which Fedinand and Isabella had broken the power of the aristocracy had been enforced with still greater rigor by Charles the Fifth, and were now carried out even more effectually by Philip the Second. For Philip had the advantage of being always in Spain, while Charles passed most of his time in other parts of his dominions. Thus ever present, Philip was as prompt to enforce the law against the highest noble as against the humblest of his subjects.

Men of rank commanded the armies abroad, and were sent as viceroys to Naples, Sicily, Milan, and the provinces of the

New World. But at home they were rarely raised to civil or military office. They no longer formed a necessary part of the national legislature, and were seldom summoned to the meetings of the cortes; for the Castilian noble claimed exemption from the public burdens, and it was rarely that the cortes were assembled for any other purpose than to impose those burdens. Thus without political power of any kind, they resided like so many private gentlemen on their estates in the country. Their princely style of living gave no umbrage to the king, who was rather pleased to see them dissipate their vast revenues in a way that was attended with no worse evil than that of driving the proprietors to exactions which made them odious to their vassals. Such, we are assured by a Venetian envoy—who, with great powers of observation, was placed in the best situation for exerting them—was the policy of Philip. "Thus," he concludes, "did the king make himself feared by those who, if they had managed discreetly, might have made themselves feared by him."

While the aristocracy was thus depressed, the strong arm of Charles the Fifth had stripped the Castilian commons of their most precious rights. Philip, happily for himself, was spared the odium of having reduced them to this abject condition. But he was as careful as his father could have been that they should not rise from it. The legislative power of the commons, that most important of all their privileges, was nearly annihilated. The Castilian cortes were, it is true, frequently convoked under Philip—more frequently, on the whole, than in any preceding reign. For in them still resided the power of voting supplies for the crown. To have summoned them so often, therefore, was rather a proof of the necessities of the government than of respect for the rights of the commons.

The cortes, it is true, still enjoyed the privilege of laying their grievances before the king; but, as they were compelled to vote the supplies before they presented their grievances, they had lost the only lever by which they could effectually operate on the royal will. Yet when we review their petitions, and see the care with which they watched over the interests of the nation and the courage with which they maintained them, we cannot refuse our admiration. We must acknowledge that under every circumstance of discouragement and oppression the old Castilian spirit still lingered in the hearts of the people. In proof of this, it will not be amiss to cite a few of these petitions, which, whether successful or not, may serve at least to show the state of public opinion on the topics to which they relate.

One, of repeated recurrence, is a remonstrance to the king on the enormous expense of his household—"as great," says the cortes, "as would be required for the conquest of a kingdom." The Burgundian establishment, independently of its costliness, found little favor with the honest Castilian; and the cortes prayed his majesty to abandon it, and to return to the more simple and natural usage of his ancestors. They represented "the pernicious effects which this manner of living necessarily had on the great nobles and others of his subjects, prone to follow the example of their master." To one of these petitions Philip replied that "he would cause the matter to be inquired into, and such measures to be taken as were most for his service." No alteration took place during his reign; and the Burgundian establishment, which in 1562 involved an annual charge of a hundred and fifty-six millions of maravedis, was continued by his successor.

Another remonstrance of constant recurrence—a proof of its inefficacy—was that against the alienation of the crown lands and the sale of offices and the lesser titles of nobility. To this the king made answer in much the same equivocal language as before. Another petition besought him no longer to seek an increase of his revenue by imposing taxes without the sanction of the cortes required by the ancient law and usage of the realm. Philip's reply on this occasion was plain enough. It was, in truth, one worthy of an Eastern despot. "The necessities," he said, "which have compelled me to resort to these measures, far from having ceased, have increased, and are still increasing, allowing me no alternative but to pursue the course I have adopted." Philip's embarrassments were indeed great—far beyond the reach of any financial skill of his ministers to remove. His various expedients for relieving himself from the burden, which, as he truly said, was becoming heavier every day, form a curious chapter in the history of finance. But we have not yet reached the period at which they can be most effectively presented to the reader.

The commons strongly urged the king to complete the great work he had early undertaken, of embodying in one code the municipal law of Castile. They gave careful attention to the administration of justice, showed their desire for the reform of various abuses, especially for quickening the despatch of business, proverbially slow in Spain, and, in short, for relieving suitors as far as possible from the manifold vexations to which they were daily exposed in the tribunals. With a wise liberality, they recommended that, in order to secure the services of competent persons in judicial offices, their salaries—in many cases wholly inadequate—should be greatly increased.

The cortes watched with a truly parental care over the great interests of the state—its commerce, its husbandry, and its manufactures. They raised a loud, and, as it would seem, not an ineffectual, note of remonstrance against the tyrannical practice of the crown in seizing for its own use the bullion which, as elsewhere stated, had been imported from the New World on their own account by the merchants of Seville.

Some of the petitions of the cortes show what would be thought at the present day a strange ignorance of the true principles of legislation in respect to commerce. Thus, regarding gold and silver, independently of their value as a medium of exchange, as constituting in a peculiar manner the wealth of a country, they considered that the true policy was to keep the precious metals at home, and prayed that their exportation might be forbidden. Yet this was a common error in the sixteenth century with other nations besides the Spaniards. It may seem singular, however, that the experience of three-fourths of a century had not satisfied the Castilian of the futility of such attempts to obstruct the natural current of commercial circulation.

In the same spirit, they besought the king to prohibit the use of gold and silver in plating copper and other substances, as well as for wearing-apparel and articles of household luxury. It was a waste of the precious metals, which were needed for other purposes. This petition of the commons may be referred in part, no doubt, to their fondness for sumptuary laws, which in Castile formed a more ample code than could be easily found in any other country. The love of costly and ostentatious dress was a passion which they may have caught from their neighbors the Spanish Arabs, who delighted in this way of displaying their opulence. It furnished, accordingly, from an early period, a fruitful theme of declamation to the clergy, in their invectives against the pomp and vanities of the world.

Unfortunately, Philip, who was so frequently deaf to the wiser suggestions of the cortes, gave his sanction to this petition; and in a pragmatic devoted to the object he carried out the ideas of the legislature as heartily as the most austere reformer could have desired. As a state paper it has certainly a novel aspect, going at great length into such minute specifications of wearing-apparel, both male and female, that it would seem to have been devised by a committee of tailors and milliners rather than of grave legislators. The tailors, indeed, the authors of these seductive abominations, did not escape the direct animadversion of the cortes. In another petition they were denounced as unprofitable persons, occupied with needlework, like women, instead of tilling the ground or serving his majesty in the wars, like men.

In the same spirit of impertinent legislation, the cortes would have regulated the expenses of the table, which, they said, of late years had been excessive. They recommended that no one should be allowed to have more than four dishes of meat and four of fruit served at the same meal. They were further scandalized by the increasing use of coaches, a mode of conveyance which had been introduced into Spain only a few years before. They regarded them as tempting men to an effeminate indulgence which most of them could ill afford. They considered the practice, moreover, as detrimental to the good horsemanship for which their ancestors had been so renowned. They prayed, therefore, that, considering "the nation had done well for so many years without the use of coaches, it might henceforth be prohibited." Philip so far complied with their petition as to forbid anyone but the owner of four horses to keep a coach. Thus he imagined that, while encouraging the raising of horses, he should effectually discourage any but the more wealthy from affecting this costly luxury.

There was another petition, somewhat remarkable, and worth citing as it shows the attachment of the Castilians to a national institution which has often incurred the censure of foreigners. A petition of the cortes of 1573 prayed that some direct encouragement might be given to bull-fights, which of late had shown symptoms of decline. They advised that the principal towns should be required to erect additional circuses, and to provide lances for the combatants and music for the entertainments at the charge of the municipalities. They insisted on this as important for mending the breed of horses, as well as for furnishing a chivalrous exercise for the nobles and cavaliers. This may excite some surprise in a spectator of our day, accustomed to see only the most wretched hacks led to the slaughter and men of humble condition skirmishing in the arena. It was otherwise in those palmy days of chivalry, when the horses employed were of a generous breed, and the combatants were nobles, who entered the lists with as proud a feeling as that with which they would have gone to a tourney. Even so late as the sixteenth century it was the boast of Charles the Fifth that, when a young man, he had fought like a matador and killed his bull. Philip gave his assent to this petition with a promptness which showed that he understood the character of his countrymen.

It would be an error to regard the more exceptionable and frivolous petitions of the cortes, some of which have been above enumerated, as affording a true type of the predominant character of Castilian legislation. The laws, or, to speak correctly, the petitions, of that body, are strongly impressed with a wise and patriotic sentiment, showing a keen perception of the wants of the community and a tender anxiety to relieve them. Thus, we find the cortes recommending that guardians should be appointed to find employment for such young and destitute persons as, without friends to aid them, had no means of getting a livelihood for themselves. They propose to have visitors chosen, whose duty it should be to inspect the prisons every week and see that fitting arrangements were made for securing the health and cleanliness of the inmates. They desire that care should be taken to have suitable accommodations provided at the inns for travelers. With their usual fondness for domestic inquisition, they take notice of the behavior of servants to their masters, and, with a simplicity that may well excite a smile, they animadvert on the conduct of maidens who, "in the absence of their mothers, spend their idle hours in reading romances full of lies and vanities, which they receive as truths for the government of their own conduct in their intercourse with the world." The books thus stigmatized were doubtless the romances of chivalry, which at this period were at the height of their popularity in Castile.

Cervantes had not yet aimed at this pestilent literature those shafts of ridicule which did more than any legislation could have done towards driving it from the land.

The commons watched over the business of education as zealously as over any of the material interests of the state. They inspected the condition of the higher seminaries, and would have provision made for the foundation of new chairs in the universities. In accordance with their views, though not in conformity to any positive suggestion, Philip published a pragmatic in respect to these institutions. He complained of the practice, rapidly increasing among his subjects, of going abroad to get their education, when the most ample provision was made for it at home. The effect was eminently disastrous; for, while the Castilian universities languished for want of patronage, the student who went abroad was pretty sure to return with ideas not the best suited to his own country. The king, therefore, prohibited Spaniards from going to any university out of his dominions, and required all now abroad to return. This edict he accompanied with the severe penalty of forfeiture of the secular possessions for ecclesiastics, and of banishment and confiscation of property for laymen.

This kind of pragmatic, though made doubtless in accordance with the popular feeling, inferred a stretch of arbitrary power that cannot be charged on those which emanated directly from the suggestion of the legislature. In this respect, however, it fell far short of those ordinances which proceeded exclusively from the royal will, without reference to the wishes of the commons. Such ordinances—and they were probably more numerous than any other class of laws during this reign—are doubtless among the most arbitrary acts of which a monarch can be guilty; for they imply nothing less than as assumption of the law-making power into his own hands. Indeed, they met with a strong remonstrance in the year 1579, when Philip was besought by the commons not to make any laws but such as had first received the sanction of the cortes. Yet Philip might vindicate himself by the example of his predecessors—even of those who, like Ferdinand and Isabella, had most at heart the interests of the nation.

It must be further admitted that the more regular mode of proceeding, with the cooperation of the cortes, had in it much to warrant the idea that the real right of legislation was vested in the king. A petition, usually couched in the most humble terms, prayed his majesty to give his assent to the law proposed. This he did in a few words; or, what was much more common, he refused to give it, declaring that in the existing case "it was not expedient that any change should be made." It was observed that the number of cases in which Philip rejected the petitions of the commons was much greater than had been usual with former sovereigns.

A more frequent practice with Philip was one that better suited his hesitating nature and habit of procrastination. He replied, in ambiguous terms, that "he would take the matter into consideration," or "that he would lay it before his council and take such measures as would be best for his service." Thus the cortes adjourned in ignorance of the fate of their petitions. Even when he announced his assent, as it was left to him to prescribe the terms of the law, it might be more or less conformable to those of the petition. The cortes having been dismissed, there was no redress to be obtained if the law did not express their views, nor could any remonstrance be presented by that body until their next session, usually three years later. The practice established by Charles the Fifth, of postponing the presenting of petitions till the supplies had been voted, and the immediate adjournment of the legislature afterwards, secured an absolute authority to the princes of the house of Austria, that made a fearful change in the ancient constitution of Castile.

Yet the meetings of the cortes, shorn as that body was of its ancient privileges, were not without important benefits to the nation. None could be better acquainted than the deputies with the actual wants and wishes of their constituents. It was a manifest advantage for the king to receive this information. It enabled him to take the course best suited to the interests of the people, to which he would naturally be inclined when he did not regard them as conflicting with his own. Even when he did, the strenuous support of their own views by the commons might compel him to modify his measures. However absolute the monarch, he would naturally shrink from pursuing a policy so odious to the people that, if persevered in, it might convert remonstrance into downright resistance.

The freedom of discussion among the deputies is attested by

the independent tone with which in their petitions they denounce the manifold abuses in the state. It is honorable to Philip that he should not have attempted to stifle this freedom of debate; though perhaps this may be more correctly referred to his policy, which made him willing to leave this safety-valve open for the passions of the people. He may have been content to flatter them with the image of power, conscious that he alone retained the substance of it. However this may have been, the good effect of the exercise of these rights, imperfect as they were, by the third estate, must be highly estimated. The fact of being called together to consult on public affairs gave the people a consideration in their own eyes which raised them far above the abject condition of the subjects of an Eastern despotism. It cherished in them that love of independence which was their birthright, inherited from their ancestors, and thus maintained in their bosoms those lofty sentiments which were the characteristics of the humbler classes of the Spaniards beyond those of any other nation in Christendom.

One feature was wanting to complete the picture of absolute monarchy. This was a standing army—a thing hitherto unknown in Spain. There was, indeed, an immense force kept on foot in the time of Charles the Fifth, and many of the troops were Spaniards. But they were stationed abroad, and were intended solely for foreign enterprises. It is to Philip's time that we are to refer the first germs of a permanent military establishment, designed to maintain order and obedience at home.

The levies raised for this purpose amounted to twenty companies of men-at-arms, which, with the complement of four or five followers to each lance, made a force of some strength. It was further swelled by five thousand ginetes, or light cavalry. These corps were a heavy charge on the crown. They were called "the Guards of Castile." The men-at-arms, in particular, were an object of great care, and were under admirable discipline. Even Philip, who had little relish for military affairs, was in the habit of occasionally reviewing them in person. In addition to these troops there was a body of thirty thousand militia, whom the king could call into the field when necessary. A corps of some sixteen hundred horsemen patrolled the southern coasts of Andalusia, to guard the country from invasion by the African Moslems; and garrisons established in fortresses along the frontiers of Spain, both north and south, completed a permanent force for the defense of the kingdom against domestic insurrection, as well as foreign invasion.

The Escorial

1563–1584

There can be no place more proper to give an account of this extraordinary edifice than the part of the narrative in which I have been desirous to throw as much light as possible on the character and occupations of Philip. The Escorial engrossed the leisure of more than thirty years of his life; it reflects in a peculiar manner his tastes and the austere character of his mind; and, whatever criticism may be passed on it as a work of art, it cannot be denied that, if every other vestige of his reign were to be swept away, that wonderful structure would of itself suffice to show the grandeur of his plans and the extent of his resources.

The common tradition that Philip built the Escorial in pursuance of a vow which he made at the time of the great battle of St. Quentin, the tenth of August, 1557, has been rejected by modern critics, on the ground that contemporary writers, and among them the historians of the convent, make no mention of the fact. But a recently discovered document leaves little doubt that such a vow was actually made. However this may have been, it is certain that the king designed to commemorate the event by this structure, as is intimated by its dedication to St. Lawrence, the martyr on whose day the victory was gained. The name given to the place was El Sitio de San Lorenzo el Real. But the monastery was better known from the hamlet near which it stood—El Escurial, or El Escorial—which latter soon became the orthography generally adopted by the Castilians.

The motives which, after all, operated probably most powerfully on Philip, had no connection with the battle of St. Quentin.

His father the emperor had directed by his will that his bones should remain at Yuste until a more suitable place should be provided for them by his son. The building now to be erected was designed expressly as a mausoleum for Philip's parents, as well as for their descendants of the royal line of Austria. But the erection of a religious house on a magnificent scale, that would proclaim to the world his devotion to the faith, was the predominant idea in the mind of Philip. It was, moreover, a part of his scheme to combine in the plan a palace for himself; for, with a taste which he may be said to have inherited from his father, he loved to live in the sacred shadows of the cloister. These ideas, somewhat incongruous as they may seem, were fully carried out by the erection of an edifice dedicated at once to the threefold purpose of a palace, a monastery, and a tomb.

Soon after the king's return to Spain, he set about carrying his plan into execution. The site which, after careful examination, he selected for the building, was among the mountains of the Guadarrama, on the borders of New Castile, about eight leagues northwest of Madrid. The healthiness of the place and its convenient distance from the capital combined with the stern and solitary character of the region, so congenial to his taste, to give it the preference over other spots which might have found more favor with persons of a different nature. Encompassed by rude and rocky hills, which sometimes soar to the gigantic elevation of mountains, it seemed to be shut out completely from the world. The vegetation was of a thin and stunted growth, seldom spreading out into the luxuriant foliage of the lower regions; and the winds swept down from the neighboring sierra with the violence of a hurricane. Yet the air was salubrious, and the soil was nourished by springs of the purest water. To add to its recommendations, a quarry, close at hand, of excellent stone somewhat resembling granite in appearance, readily supplied the materials for building—a circumstance, considering the vastness of the work, of no little importance. . . .

On the twenty-third of April, 1563, the first stone of the monastery was laid. On the twentieth of August following, the cornerstone of the church was also laid, with still greater pomp and solemnity. The royal confessor, the bishop of Cuença, arrayed in his pontificals, presided over the ceremonies. The king was present, and laid the stone with his own hands. The principal nobles of the court were in attendance, and there was a great concourse of spectators, both ecclesiastics and laymen; the solemn services were concluded by the brotherhood, who joined in an anthem of thanksgiving and praise to the Almighty, to whom so glorious a monument was to be reared in this mountain wilderness.

The rude sierra now swarmed with life. The ground was covered with tents and huts. The busy hum of labor mingled with the songs of the laborers, which, from their various dialects, betrayed the different, and oftentimes distant, provinces from which they had come. In this motley host the greatest order and decorum prevailed; nor were the peaceful occupations of the day interrupted by any indecent brawls.

As the work advanced, Philip's visits to the Escorial were longer and more frequent. He had always shown his love for the retirement of the cloister, by passing some days of every year in it. Indeed, he was in the habit of keeping Holy Week not far from the scene of his present labors, at the convent of Guisando. In his present monastic retreat he had the additional interest afforded by the contemplation of the great work, which seemed to engage as much of his thoughts as any of the concerns of government.

Philip had given a degree of attention to the study of the fine arts seldom found in persons of his condition. He was a connoisseur in painting, and, above all, in architecture, making a careful study of its principles, and occasionally furnishing designs with his own hand. No prince of his time left behind him so many proofs of his taste and magnificence in building. The royal mint at Segovia, the hunting-seat of the Pardo, the pleasant residence of Aranjuez, the alcazar of Madrid, the "Armeria Real," and other noble works which adorned his infant capital, were either built or greatly embellished by him. The land was covered with structures, both civil and religious, which rose under the royal patronage. Churches and convents—the latter in lamentable profusion—constantly met the eye of the traveler. The general style of their execution was simple in the extreme. Some, like the great cathedral of Valladolid, of more pretension, but still showing the same austere character in their designs, furnished excellent models of architecture to counteract the meretricious tendencies of the age. Structures of a different kind from these were planted by Philip along the frontiers in the north and on the southern coasts of the kingdom; and the voyager in the Mediterranean beheld fortress after fortress crowning the heights above the shore, for its defense against the Barbary corsair. Nor was the king's passion for building confined to Spain. Wherever his armies penetrated in the semi-civilized regions of the New World, the march of the conqueror was sure to be traced by the ecclesiastical and military structures which rose in his rear.

Fortunately, similarity of taste led to the most perfect harmony between the monarch and his architect in their conferences on the great work which was to crown the architectural glories of Philip's reign. The king inspected the details, and watched over every step in the progress of the building, with as much care as Toledo himself. In order to judge of the effect from a distance, he was in the habit of climbing the mountains at a spot about half a league from the monastery, where a kind of natural chair was formed by the crags. Here, with his spy-glass in his hand, he would sit for hours and gaze on the complicated structure growing up below. The place is still known as the "king's seat."

It was certainly no slight proof of the deep interest which Philip took in the work that he was content to exchange his palace at Madrid for a place that afforded him no better accommodation than the poverty-stricken village of the Escorial. In 1571 he made an important change in these accommodations, by erecting a chapel which might afford the monks a more decent house of worship than their old weather-beaten hovel; and with this he combined a comfortable apartment for himself. In these new quarters he passed still more of his time in cloistered seclusion than he had done before. Far from confining his attention to a supervision of the Escorial, he brought his secretaries and his papers along with him, read here his despatches from abroad, and kept up a busy correspondence with all parts of his dominion. He did four times the amount of work here, says a Jeronymite, that he did in the same number of days in the capital. He used to boast that, thus hidden from the world, with a little bit of paper, he ruled over both hemispheres. That he did not always wisely rule is proved by more than one of his despatches relating to the affairs of Flanders, which issued from this consecrated place. Here he received accounts of the proceedings of his heretic subjects in the Netherlands, and of the Morisco insurgents in Granada. And as he pondered on their demolition of church and convent, and their desecration of the most holy symbols of the Catholic faith, he doubtless felt a proud satisfaction in proving his own piety to the world by the erection of the most sumptuous edifice ever dedicated to the cross.

In 1577 the Escorial was so far advanced towards completion as to afford accommodations not merely for Philip and his personal attendants, but for many of the court, who were in the habit of spending some time there with the king during the summer. On one of these occasions an accident occurred which had nearly been attended with most disastrous consequences to the building.

A violent thunderstorm was raging in the mountains, and the lightning struck one of the great towers of the monastery. In a short time the upper portion of the building was in a blaze. So much of it, fortunately, was of solid material that the fire made slow progress. But the difficulty of bringing water to bear on it was extreme. It was eleven o'clock at night when the fire broke out, and in the orderly household of Philip all had retired to rest. They were soon roused by the noise. The king took his station on the opposite tower, and watched with deep anxiety the progress of the flames. The duke of Alva was one among the guests. Though sorely afflicted with the gout at the time, he wrapped his dressing-gown about him and climbed to a spot which afforded a still nearer view of the conflagration. Here the "good duke" at once assumed the command, and gave his orders with as much promptness and decision as on the field of battle.

All the workmen, as well as the neighboring peasantry, were assembled there. The men showed the same spirit of subordination which they had shown throughout the erection of the building. The duke's orders were implicitly obeyed; and more than one instance is recorded of daring self-devotion among the workmen, who toiled as if conscious they were under the eye of their sovereign. The tower trembled under the fury of the flames; and the upper portion of it threatened every moment to fall in ruins. Great fears were entertained that it would crush the hospital, situated in that part of the monastery. Fortunately, it fell in an opposite direction, carrying with it a splendid chime of bells that was lodged in it, but doing no injury to the spectators. The loss which bore most heavily on the royal heart was that of sundry inestimable relics which perished in the flames. But Philip's sorrow was mitigated when he learned that a bit of the true cross, and the right arm of St. Lawrence, the martyred patron of the Escorial, were rescued from the flames. At length, by incredible efforts, the fire, which had lasted till six in the morning, was happily extinguished, and Philip withdrew to his chamber, where his first act, we are told, was to return thanks to the Almighty for the preservation of the building consecrated to his service.

The king was desirous that as many of the materials as possible for the structure should be collected from his own dominions. These were so vast, and so various in their productions, that they furnished nearly every article required for the construction of the edifice, as well as for its interior decoration. The gray stone of which its walls were formed was drawn from a neighboring quarry. It was called berroqueña—a stone bearing a resemblance to granite, though not so hard. The blocks hewn from the quarries, and dressed there, were of such magnitude as sometimes to require forty or fifty yoke of oxen to drag them. The jasper came from the neighborhood of Burgo de Osma. The more delicate marbles, of a great variety of colors, were furnished by the mountain ranges in the south of the peninsula. The costly and elegant fabrics were many of them supplied by native artisans. Such were the damasks and velvets of Granada. Other cities, as Madrid, Toledo, and Saragossa, showed the proficiency of native art in curious manufactures of bronze and iron, and occasionally of the more precious metals.

Yet Philip was largely indebted to his foreign possessions, especially those in Italy and the Low Countries, for the embellishment of the interior of the edifice, which, in its sumptuous style of decoration, presented a contrast to the stern simplicity of its exterior. Milan, so renowned at that period for its fine workmanship in steel, gold, and precious stones, contributed many exquisite specimens of art. The walls were clothed with gorgeous tapestries from the Flemish looms. Spanish convents vied with each other in furnishing embroideries for the altars. Even the rude colonies in the New World had their part in the great work, and the American forests supplied their cedar and ebony and richly tinted woods, which displayed all their magical brilliancy of color under the hands of the Castilian workman.

Though desirous as far as possible to employ the products of his own dominions and to encourage native art, in one particular he resorted almost exclusively to foreigners. The oil-paintings and frescoes which profusely decorated the walls and ceilings of the Escorial were executed by artists drawn chiefly from Italy, whose schools of design were still in their glory. But, of all living painters, Titian was the one whom Philip, like his father, most delighted to honor. To the king's generous patronage the world is indebted for some of that great master's noblest productions, which found a fitting place on the walls of the Escorial. . . .

Before this magnificent pile, in a manner the creation of his own taste, Philip's nature appeared to expand, and to discover some approach to those generous sympathies for humanity which elsewhere seem to have been denied him. He would linger for hours while he watched the labors of the artist, making occasional criticisms, and laying his hand familiarly on his shoulder. He seemed to put off the coldness and reserve which formed so essential a part of his character. On one occasion, it is said, a stranger, having come into the Escorial when the king was there, mistook him for one of the officials, and asked him some questions about the pictures. Philip, without undeceiving the man, humored his mistake, and good-naturedly undertook the part of cicerone, by answering his inquiries and showing him some of the objects most worth seeing. Similar anecdotes have been told of others. What is strange is that Philip should have acted the part of the good-natured man.

In 1584 the masonry of the Escorial was completed. Twenty-one years had elapsed since the first stone of the monastery was laid. This certainly must be regarded as a short period for the erection of so stupendous a pile. St. Peter's church, with which one naturally compares it as the building nearest in size and magnificence, occupied more than a century in its erection, which spread over the reigns of at least eighteen popes. But the Escorial, with the exception of the subterraneous chapel constructed by Philip the Fourth for the burial-place of the Spanish princes, was executed in the reign of one monarch. That monarch held in his hands the revenues of both the Old World and the New; and, as he gave in some sort a personal supervision to the work, we may be sure that no one was allowed to sleep on his post. . . .

It is impossible for language to convey any adequate idea of a work of art. Yet architecture has this advantage over the sister arts of design, that the mere statement of the dimensions helps us much in forming a conception of the work. A few of these dimensions will serve to give an idea of the magnitude of the edifice. They are reported to us by Los Santos, a Jeronymite monk, who has left one of the best accounts of the Escorial.

The main building, or monastery, he estimates at seven hundred and forty Castilian feet in length by five hundred and eighty in breadth. Its greatest height, measured to the central cross above the dome of the great church, is three hundred and fifteen feet. The whole circumference of the Escorial, including the palace, he reckons at two thousand nine hundred and eighty feet, or near three-fifths of a mile. The patient inquirer tells us there were no less than twelve thousand doors and windows in the building; that the weight of the keys alone amounted to fifty arrobas, or twelve hundred and fifty pounds; and, finally, that there were sixty-eight fountains playing in the halls and courts of this enormous pile. . . .

Probably no single edifice ever contained such an amount and variety of inestimable treasures as the Escorial—so many paintings and sculptures by the greatest masters—so many articles of exquisite workmanship, composed of the most precious materials. It would be a mistake to suppose that when the building was finished the labors of Philip were at an end. One might almost say they were but begun. The casket was completed; but the remainder of his days was to be passed in filling it with the rarest and richest gems. This was a labor never to be completed. It was to be bequeathed to his successors, who, with more or less taste, but with the revenues of the Indies at their disposal, continued to lavish them on the embellishment of the Escorial.

Philip the Second set the example. He omitted nothing which could give a value, real or imaginary, to his museum. He gathered at an immense cost several hundred cases of the bones of saints and martyrs, depositing them in rich silver shrines of elaborate workmanship. He collected four thousand volumes, in various languages, especially the Oriental, as the basis of the fine library of the Escorial.

The care of successive princes, who continued to spend there a part of every year, preserved the palace-monastery and its contents from the rude touch of Time. But what the hand of Time had spared the hand of violence destroyed. The French, who in the early part of the present century swept like a horde of Vandals over the peninsula, did not overlook the Escorial. For in it they saw the monument designed to commemorate their own humiliating defeat. A body of dragoons under La Houssaye burst into the monastery in the winter of 1808; and the ravages of a few days demolished what it had cost years and the highest efforts of art to construct. The apprehension of similar violence from the Carlists, in 1837, led to the removal of the finest paintings to Madrid. The Escorial ceased to be a royal residence. Tenantless and unprotected, it was left to the fury of the blasts which swept down the hills of the Guadarrama.

The traveler who now visits the place will find its condition very different from what it was in the beginning of the century. The bare and mildewed walls no longer glow with the magical tints of Raphael and Titian and the sober pomp of the Castilian school. The exquisite specimens of art with which the halls were filled have been wantonly demolished, or more frequently pilfered for the sake of the rich materials. The monks, so long the guardians of the place, have shared the fate of their brethren elsewhere since the suppression of religious houses, and their venerable forms have disappeared. Silence and solitude reign throughout the courts, undisturbed by any sound save that of the ceaseless winds, which seem to be ever chanting their melancholy dirge over the faded glories of the Escorial. There is little now to remind one of the palace or of the monastery. Of the three great objects to which the edifice was devoted, one alone survives —that of a mausoleum for the royal line of Castile. The spirit of the dead broods over the place—of the sceptered dead, who lie in the same dark chamber where they have lain for centuries, unconscious of the changes that have been going on all around them.

Bibliography

The Works of William Hickling Prescott, Montezuma Edition, edited by Wilfred H. Monroe. 22 vols., Philadelphia, 1904. (Last complete edition)

The Works of W. H. Prescott, edited by John Foster Kirk. 16 vols., Philadelphia, 1874. (Includes Prescott's revisions of *Mexico*, Ticknor's biography, and the complete Robertson's *Charles V*)

The Correspondence of William Hickling Prescott, 1833–1847, edited by Roger Wolcott. Boston, 1925. (Prepared from original drafts in the Massachusetts Historical Society by the historian's great-grandson)

Prescott: Unpublished Letters to Gayangos in the Library of the Hispanic Society of America, edited by Clara L. Penney. New York, 1927. (Contains added materials on Prescott's methods of scholarship)

The Literary Memoranda of William Hickling Prescott, edited with introduction by C. Harvey Gardiner. Norman, Oklahoma, 1961. (The historian's journals of literary work as well as his personal diary, ably edited)

William Hickling Prescott: Representative Selections, edited by William Charvet and Michael Kraus. New York, 1943. American Writers Series. (Contains excellent introductions and bibliography, though selections are poorly organized)

The Life of William Hickling Prescott, by George Ticknor. Boston, 1864. (Included in both editions of *Works*, it is still the standard biography. Ticknor knew the historian well. However, he failed to use much manuscript material, and a new, much needed biography is being written by C. Harvey Gardiner)

William Hickling Prescott, by Rollo Ogden. Boston, 1904. American Men of Letters Series. (A brief biography using materials of which Ticknor was ignorant or ignored)

William Hickling Prescott, by Harry Thurston Peck. New York, 1905. English Men of Letters Series. (A useful analysis of Prescott as a literary man)

"William Hickling Prescott" in *The Dictionary of American Biog-*

raphy, by Roger B. Merriman. New York, 1935. (The best short biography, written by Prescott's great successor in Spanish historiography)

William Hickling Prescott: A Memorial, edited by Howard F. Cline, C. Harvey Gardiner, and Charles Gibson. Durham, North Carolina, 1959. (*The Hispanic American Historical Review* centennial issue, containing articles, a check list of manuscripts, and a collection of original reviews)

Prescott and His Publishers, by C. Harvey Gardiner. Carbondale, Illinois, 1959. (Broader in concept than the title would indicate, this study contains excellent insights into both Prescott and the nineteenth-century business of writing)

History as Romantic Art: Bancroft, Prescott, Motley, Parkman, by David Levin. Stanford, California, 1959. (A brilliant critical analysis of the literary methods of these four New England historians and of *The Conquest of Mexico* as romantic epic)

William Hickling Prescott: An Annotated Bibliography of Published Works, by C. Harvey Gardiner. Washington, D.C., 1958. (A long-needed, careful listing of items)